ROTHMANS RUGBY LEAGU YEARBOOK 1993-94

**Raymond Fletcher
and David Howes**

ROTHMANS

HEADLINE

© Rothmans Publications Ltd 1993

First published in 1993
by HEADLINE BOOK PUBLISHING LTD

10 9 8 7 6 5 4 3 2 1

COVER PHOTOGRAPHS
Front Cover: Leeds stand off Garry Schofield, who captained Great Britain eight times and England once between June 1992 and May 1993.
Back Cover: Widnes centre Andy Currier, recalled by Great Britain in February 1993 after a four-year absence.

ACKNOWLEDGEMENTS
The compilers would like to acknowledge the assistance of the Rugby League Record Keepers' Club, club secretaries and individuals in providing material as a further source of reference for accuracy.

PHOTOGRAPHS
Modern day domestic photographs in this *Rothmans Rugby League Yearbook* are mainly from the files of the *Rugby Leaguer.* The compilers acknowledge the co-operation of Chief Photographer Gerald Webster and his staff.
The colour photographs on the front and back covers, plus a significant number of black-and-white contributions, are by freelance photographer Andrew Varley.

British Library Cataloguing in Publication Data
Rothmans Rugby League Yearbook — 1993-94
    1. Rugby football — Great Britain —
    Periodicals
    796.33.3.0941 GV945.9.G7

ISBN 0 7472 7890 3

Photoset by TTX LTD, London

Reproduced, printed and bound in Great Britain by
Clay Ltd, St. Ives plc

HEADLINE BOOK PUBLISHING LTD
A member of the Hodder Headline PLC Group
Headline House
79 Great Titchfield Street
London W1P 7FN

Rothmans Rugby League Yearbook 1993-94

CONTENTS

EDITORIAL PREFACE

A constant battle since the launch of a 384-page *Rothmans Rugby League Yearbook* in 1981 has been to cram in as much information as possible and the big increase to 448 pages this year has enabled us to expand more easily.

We have taken advantage of this to make three major additions and improvements.

For the first time we have included the date of birth, signing date and club signed from in the players' summary. This has been a mammoth and time-consuming task which would not have been possible without the assistance of Emma Rosewarne, who released a mass of details from the Rugby Football League's computer. We thank her and offer our congratulations on her becoming Administrative Executive and the League's first female senior officer.

Even with the computer's aid a few gaps in the registration details remained and we considered abandoning the task at one stage because of our aim to provide the highest possible standard of accuracy. But we felt that the overall result justified publication.

Another addition is an index for each of the game's three major Cup competitions, showing all the players who have appeared in the finals over the last 20 seasons.

Perhaps less noticeable, but hopefully just as useful, is the inclusion of players' first names instead of initials wherever possible and in particular in the Great Britain playing register.

In addition to the usual acknowledgments we would like to offer thanks and appreciation to our fellow members of the RL Record Keepers' Club. Their statistics have been particularly useful when dealing with career records from more than 50 years ago.

Once again, thanks to our wives for their unyielding support and understanding. Also to house editor Ian Marshall for combining expertise with all-important enthusiasm over more than eight months of preparation.

Finally, thanks to our media colleagues and all others who have taken the time to write encouragement and constructive criticism.

● Facts and figures in this *Rothmans Rugby League Yearbook* as at 1 June 1993.

RAYMOND FLETCHER, of the *Yorkshire Post.*

DAVID HOWES, Rugby League Public Affairs Executive.

COACHES SELECT XIII

Leeds full back Alan Tait and Castleford loose forward Tawera Nikau were the only outsiders to break a Wigan-St. Helens stranglehold on the 1992-93 Coaches Select XIII, an exclusive feature of the *Rothmans Rugby League Yearbook*.

For the fifth successive year, the coaches in the Stones Bitter Championship were invited to select their form team of the season, not including members of their own club sides, basing their choice on opposition performances during the 1992-93 campaign, while taking general form into account. It is based on individual form and does not necessarily represent their best team.

Four-trophy Wigan provided seven players for the form XIII, arch-rivals St. Helens contributing four. A total of 53 players were nominated, newly crowned Stones Bitter Man of Steel Andy Platt and clubmate Phil Clarke receiving 100 per cent support.

Great Britain and Wigan winger Martin Offiah becomes the only player to feature in all five Coaches Select XIIIs since introduction of this *Yearbook* feature, Leeds scrum half Andy Gregory failing to maintain his 100 per cent record.

Three overseas imports gained inclusion in the form line-up, the all-Kiwi trio being centre Dean Bell, stand off Tea Ropati and Nikau.

The largest category nomination was nine players for the centre berths. Five players were named in more than one position, Frano Botica at wing and stand off, Shaun Edwards at stand off and scrum half, plus Clarke, Ellery Hanley and Nikau in the second row and loose forward berths.

Of the 10 British players in the Coaches Select XIII, all played for Great Britain during the 1992-93 campaign, eight having served on the 1992 British Lions tour Down Under.

The pack showed only one change from the 1991-92 form side, New Zealander Gary Mercer being replaced by fellow-countryman Nikau. In the backs Graham Steadman, John Devereux, Gene Miles and Gregory were replaced by in-form Tait, Alan Hunte, Gary Connolly and Stones Bitter First Division Player of the Year Ropati.

Great Britain and Wigan back row forward Phil Clarke, who received 100 per cent backing from the 1992-93 coaches.

To comply with the wishes of some coaches who did not want their team published it was agreed to abandon this practice and replace it with a summary of nominations for each position.

The Coaches Select XIII poll produced the following nominees:

Full back

Alan Tait (Leeds) edged out last year's choice Graham Steadman, with votes being cast for Stuart Spruce (Widnes), Dave Watson (Bradford N.), David Lyon (St. Helens) and Garry Jack (Sheffield E.).

Wingers

Alan Hunte (St. Helens) and Martin Offiah (Wigan) shared top billing, one vote ahead of John Devereux (Widnes), the leading trio being well clear of fellow candidates Frano Botica (Wigan), Jason Robinson (Wigan) and Mark Preston (Halifax).

Centres

Dean Bell (Wigan) and Gary Connolly (St. Helens) were equal top, holding a convincing lead over Craig Innes (Leeds), Andy Currier (Widnes), Kevin Iro (Leeds), Allan Bateman (Warrington), Paul Newlove (Featherstone R.), Tea Ropati (St. Helens) and Paul Loughlin (St. Helens).

Stand off

New Zealander Tea Ropati was a clear winner ahead of Wigan's Shaun Edwards, with support for Daryl Powell (Sheffield E.) and Frano Botica (Wigan).

Scrum half

Despite being preferred by some coaches in the stand off role, Wigan's Shaun Edwards was still a clear winner in the scrum half ballot, votes also being cast for Mike Ford (Castleford), Dave Watson (Bradford N.), Bobby Goulding (Widnes), Deryck Fox (Bradford N.) and Andy Gregory (Leeds).

Props

Unanimous choice Andy Platt (Wigan) received twice as many votes as fellow front row man Kevin Ward (St. Helens), while in-form rating was also given to Kelvin Skerrett (Wigan), Lee Crooks (Castleford), Darren Fritz (Wakefield T.) and Harvey Howard (Widnes).

Coaches Select XIII debutant, St. Helens Test winger Alan Hunte.

Hooker

Wigan's Test hooker Martin Dermott polled 66 per cent of the votes, the remainder being cast for Duane Mann (Warrington), Lee Jackson (Hull) and Paul Hulme (Widnes).

Second row

Great Britain and Wigan back row man Phil Clarke's versatility was recognised in the coaches' ballot, his 100 per cent support being split between second row and loose forward. His second row partner is teammate Denis Betts, named for the fourth successive year. Other nominees were Richard Eyres (Widnes), Chris Joynt (St. Helens), Tawera Nikau (Castleford), Ellery Hanley (Leeds), Karl Fairbank (Bradford N.) and Andrew Farrell (Wigan).

Loose forward

Tawera Nikau topped the voting ahead of back row rivals Ellery Hanley (Leeds) and Phil Clarke (Wigan), already selected in the second row. The only other candidate was Dean Busby (Hull), who missed most of the season through injury.

7

COACHES SELECT XIII

1. **Alan Tait** (Leeds)
2. **Alan Hunte** (St. Helens)
3. **Dean Bell** (Wigan)
4. **Gary Connolly** (St. Helens)
5. **Martin Offiah** (Wigan)
6. **Tea Ropati** (St. Helens)
7. **Shaun Edwards** (Wigan)
8. **Kevin Ward** (St. Helens)
9. **Martin Dermott** (Wigan)
10. **Andy Platt** (Wigan)
11. **Denis Betts** (Wigan)
12. **Phil Clarke** (Wigan)
13. **Tawera Nikau** (Castleford)

Great Britain skipper Andy Platt, Stones Bitter Man of Steel 1993 and unanimous choice of the club coaches.

Castleford loose forward Tawera Nikau, one of only two selections from outside of Wigan and St. Helens.

Platt is a man of steel — official

MEMORIES

Three clubs face chop

Sevens farce

League trial blocks
Pilgrim's progress

Summer switch
on the agenda

Boss man
Maurice

Two divisions approved

MEMORIES

1992-93 HEADLINES

Behind the scoring feats and records of the 1992-93 season were a number of stories which made the headlines:

SCARBOROUGH PIRATES SINK

Scarborough Pirates folded after only one season when the club was placed in voluntary liquidation following a meeting of shareholders less than a month before the new campaign kicked off.

The club reported debts of £60,000 with a trading loss of £220,000 after paying out £235,000 in transfer fees and players' wages.

Chairman Geoffrey Richmond, who put more than £150,000 into the club, blamed lack of support rather than financial problems for the club's demise.

Scarborough's average attendance had been 777, with a top crowd of 1,427 for a Silk Cut Challenge Cup home tie against Bradford Northern.

Mr Richmond had predicted an average crowd of 2,000 when he persuaded clubs to elect Scarborough by the narrowest possible margin of an exact two-thirds majority 20 months earlier.

Scarborough's departure meant each Third Division club lost two fixtures for the forthcoming season and Nottingham City received a Yorkshire Cup bye after being drawn against them in the preliminary round.

RULE CHANGES

A controversial rule change during the season saw the offside distance at the play-the-ball doubled from five to 10 metres. It was introduced almost without notice on the weekend of 23 November. Although referees were told to enforce the change many clubs were not informed.

The League said the change was an experiment and an extension of an unofficial policy of many referees to allow a "generous" five metres.

While the rule was brought in to give the attacking side more room to move, its critics said it could encourage one-man forward drives. But a League survey revealed a vast majority of coaches were in favour and it was accepted by the International Board in June.

The experiment coincided with a League directive in November insisting that referees enforce the rule which forbids defenders holding down a tackled player. Both changes were aimed at speeding up the game.

Another rule change saw the outlawing of all tackles above the shoulder, introduced at the start of the season.

WORLD SEVENS ROW

Wigan and Wales were caught up in a World Sevens row that led to both being omitted from the Coca-Cola sponsored Sydney event within two weeks of the kick-off.

The invitation to Wigan, the Sevens trophy holders, was withdrawn after they named a 10-man squad of mainly reserve players and despite later offering to strengthen their team.

Wigan's defence was that they could not release more of their best players during the middle of a hectic Cup and League programme.

Wales were pulled out of the Sevens by the League following a legal threat from Warrington shortly after Widnes lost their appeal against having to supply four players to the Welsh squad.

Warrington served notice of legal action against the selection of Kevin Ellis for Wales. Like Wigan and Widnes, they objected to releasing players during the season.

The event was won by Eastern Suburbs, who beat fellow Australian side Manly 18-12 in the final of a tournament which attracted 65,000 spectators over three days on the weekend of 7 February.

PILGRIM'S PROGRESS HALTED

The Rugby Football Union attracted nationwide criticism when they banned Wasps RU full back Steve Pilgrim for a year after he played one trial match for Leeds reserves.

Even a parliamentary motion was tabled, deploring the suspension which was imposed because Pilgrim broke the following RFU law: "No person shall play in a trial or play with a non-amateur club or a non-amateur organisation involved in the playing of any other type of rugby football."

The 25-year-old former England 'B' player appeared as A.N. Other for Leeds reserves on 2 February 1993 when he scored a try and three goals in a 30-10 home victory over Wakefield Trinity.

Although it is normal practice for the media not to reveal the identity of Rugby Union trialists, Pilgrim's name was disclosed by a local newspaper the following day and the ban followed almost immediately. Pilgrim claimed he had not been paid for the trial match but the ban remained.

He played other matches for the reserves before making his one first team appearance for Leeds in a 19-8 Stones Bitter Championship defeat at Widnes on 17 March.

Leeds team manager Doug Laughton then decided not to sign Pilgrim and he had a brief spell at Halifax, making one first team appearance in a Stones Bitter Championship match at Castleford on 28 March when he was replaced after 29 minutes. He was not retained.

LINDSAY REPLACES OXLEY
Maurice Lindsay took over as the Rugby League Chief Executive on 1 November following the retirement of 55-year-old David Oxley, who had held the post — originally as RL Secretary — since 1974.

Lindsay, 51, relinquished his position as chairman and a director at Wigan, also stepping down as the Great Britain manager.

He also began to wind down his role in his own bookmaking and leisure business, but came under attack from some media quarters who claimed he was still active at horse racing meetings. Lindsay explained that it took time to transfer the running of his business, the handover date being 23 April.

Lindsay's first few months in office were full of incident as he was charged with fending off much of the criticism for the reversion to two divisions and in particular the demoting of three clubs to non-league status at short notice.

And, in severe financial cutbacks at League headquarters, nine of the 27 staff were made redundant, including Fred Lindop as Controller of Referees and Mike Turner as Marketing Executive.

He also instigated the mid-season rule-change which doubled the offside distance at the play-the-ball to 10 metres, later adopted worldwide by the International Board. The speeding up of the play-the-ball was also a personal project.

RETURN TO TWO DIVISIONS
After only two seasons of three divisions, the sudden decision to revert to two divisions caused much heated controversy. The new format also included the scrapping of the Lancashire and Yorkshire Cup competitions after 87 years. For full details see LEAGUE section.

LEAGUE — BARLA LATEST
The long-running dispute between the Rugby Football League and BARLA over youth rugby boiled over during the late summer of 1992. BARLA issued new edicts affecting the League's Under-18 Academy, the League retaliating by withdrawing invites for two amateur clubs to take part in the Regal Trophy and the Silk Cut Challenge Cup, plus hire of professional grounds. The youth row was staged against a backdrop of attempts to bring the amateur game back into the Rugby Football League fold on a policy of "unification". Early in 1993, new League Chief Executive Maurice Lindsay and BARLA President Peter Moran started head-to-head talks which resulted in peace being restored. BARLA were to be responsible up to Under-18 level and the Academy was upgraded to Under-19s, players having freedom of choice. There was also the introduction of more amateur clubs into the major knockout tournaments and the formation of a three-division National Conference League.

JUNE

Chorley Borough move to Horwich .... Great Britain gain a 14-10 success over Queensland Residents at Townsville .... Kiwi Joe Grima leaves Widnes for Third Division Keighley .... Whitehaven dismiss coach Jackie Davidson .... Wigan reserve full back Phil Ball joins Keighley .... Want-away Paul Topping listed at £95,000 by Leigh .... Unsettled prop Leo Casey put on offer by Featherstone Rovers .... Halifax price Brendan Hill at £30,000 and reduce £25,000 fee on Jason Ramshaw to £10,000 .... Wigan release Kiwi international Sam Panapa .... Hull K.R. list Welshman David Bishop at £80,000 .... Injury to scrum half Andy Gregory mars Great Britain's 24-12 victory over Canberra .... Kiwi David Watson, of Halifax, banned for three months after drug test reveals traces of cannabis .... Ryedale-York recruit David Close from Sheffield Eagles for £10,000 .... Leigh sack coach Kevin Ashcroft .... Spectacular touchline try by Graeme Hallas is highlight of 11-10 British win at Illawarra .... Wigan Test prop Andy Platt considers offer from Sydney club Parramatta .... Widnes utility packman Paul Hulme replaces injured British Lion Sonny Nickle .... Jim Crellin appointed coach of Leigh .... Australia win the first Test against Great Britain at Sydney, 22-6 .... Great Britain call up Halifax prop Karl Harrison for injured Wigan forward Ian Lucas .... More serious injuries for the British Lions in a 24-6 success over NSW Country at Parkes .... John Kear promoted to Rugby League Coaching and Academy Executive .... Scarborough Pirates threaten closure unless £113,000 debts are cleared .... Wigan's David Myers and Hull's Steve McNamara fly out to replace injured Lions duo Paul Loughlin and Les Holliday .... Swinton list Steve Garner at £35,000, plus Joe Graziano and Neil Clawson at £15,000 each .... Featherstone Rovers offer utility forward Trevor Clark at £35,000 .... Vintage Brett Kenny performance seals a 22-16 Parramatta victory over Great Britain .... Great Britain skipper Ellery Hanley lines up a

television commentator's role should injury rule him out of the tour .... Andy Gregory forced to return home from tour through injury .... Sheffield Eagles duo Mark Aston and Paul Broadbent, Sydney-bound for club experience, called into the British Lions camp .... Batley offer forward Steve Parrish at £65,000 .... Ellery Hanley makes his first appearance of the tour in the 10th game, lasting only nine minutes against Newcastle Knights .... Hanley ruled out of the tour and released to undertake television duties, Garry Schofield being promoted to captain .... Gordon Cottier appointed coach of Whitehaven .... Bramley list scrum half Steve Carroll at £25,000 .... Bradford Northern winger Richard Francis priced at £20,000 .... Warrington reject St. Helens exchange bid of David Cosgrove and Sean Devine for full back David Lyon .... Bramley list Ronnie Sharp at £20,000 .... Great Britain clinch epic 33-10 success over Australia in the second Test at Melbourne .... Halifax sack drug-ban Kiwi David Watson .... St. Helens recruit Wigan scrum half or hooker Gus O'Donnell in £80,000 deal .... St. Helens offer hooker Paul Groves at £50,000 and winger Les Quirk at £45,000.

JULY

Great Britain maintain their unbeaten midweek record by registering a 28-10 success over Gold Coast .... Sheffield Eagles sign former Australian Test full back Garry Jack from Balmain .... Record-breaking Mal Meninga inspires Australia to a 16-10 Ashes-winning Test victory over Great Britain in Brisbane .... Widnes list five players who reject new contracts, Tony Myler and David Hulme at £100,000, Kurt Sorensen at £60,000, Jason Critchley at £65,000 and Darren Whitfield at £10,000 .... Leeds Test back David Creasser forced to retire at 27 with a shoulder injury .... New Zealand, needing a 109-point victory margin to qualify for the World Cup final, beat Papua New Guinea 66-10, Great Britain thus going through to meet Australia .... Castleford prop Dean Sampson replaces Wigan's Neil

Cowie at the start of the New Zealand leg of the tour .... Contract row at Huddersfield results in the listing of winger Brimah Kebbie at £50,000, skipper Greg Shuttleworth at £25,000, Under-21 international Chris Parr at £70,000 and Stuart Cocker at £40,000 .... Great Britain clinch their first victory over Auckland for 13 years, 14-8 .... Wigan sign Warrington scrum half Martin Crompton .... Wigan ask £75,000 for scrum half Andy Gregory .... Great Britain dominate the first Kiwi Test for an hour, only to lose 15-14 .... Castleford line up St. George stand off Peter Coyne .... Wally Gibson seeks a move from Huddersfield .... Australia agree to play the World Cup final at Wembley in October .... British Lions overcome a six-hour airport delay to beat Canterbury 17-6 .... Leeds price Test threequarter Carl Gibson at £65,000 .... Oldham sign former Sheffield Eagles Kiwi Des Maea .... Hull ask £25,000 for Brian Blacker and £20,000 for skipper Greg Mackey .... Barrow part company with coach Paul Kavanagh .... Sheffield Eagles sign Australian packman Bruce McGuire for a second spell .... Wakefield Trinity offer tourist Gary Price for £160,000 .... Dewsbury get go-ahead to develop a new ground at Owl Lane, Shaw Cross .... Oldham put price tag of £50,000 on skipper Neil Flanagan .... Canberra half back Scott Gale joins Hull .... Great Britain level the Test series with New Zealand with a 19-16 victory in Auckland .... Highfield list Simon Chappell at £50,000 and Bob Tuavao at £30,000 .... Leeds suspend Bobby Goulding for two weeks for a breach of club discipline .... Packman Paul Fletcher listed at £120,000 by Hull K.R. .... Featherstone Rovers turn down a second transfer request from tourist scrum half Deryck Fox .... Swinton complete the signing of Widnes forward Darren Whitfield .... Hull K.R. offer tourist Graeme Hallas for a club record £180,000 .... Rochdale Hornets ask £40,000 for hooker Martin Hall.

AUGUST
League Tribunal fix the price of Martin Crompton's move from Warrington to Wigan at £65,000 plus a further £20,000 if capped for Great Britain .... As a club disciplinary measure, Leeds cancel Bobby Goulding's contract but retain his registration .... Australian television cancel Ellery Hanley's commentary contract, claiming that his Yorkshire accent could not be understood .... Widnes sign Salford's Welsh winger Adrian Hadley in exchange for Jason Critchley and Steve Wynne .... Oldham beat Salford for Bradford Northern winger Hugh Gumbs .... Swinton list Steve Snape at £20,000 for disciplinary reasons .... Scarborough Pirates fold with debts of £60,000 after only one season .... Leeds list Phil Ford at £30,000 .... Local council permission to sell Station Road heralds Swinton's move to Gigg Lane, home of Bury FC .... Wakefield Trinity offer centre Andy Mason at £70,000 .... Colin Hutton, of Hull K.R., elected President of the League .... St. Helens price half back Paul Bishop at £55,000 .... The League and BARLA launch battle of sanctions .... Swinton sign Rochdale Hornets' Ronnie Duane and sell Neil Clawson to Nottingham City .... Cash-conscious Wigan decide not to renew Gene Miles' contract .... Australian half back Greg Mackey joins Warrington for a second time .... Huddersfield value full back Wally Gibson at £125,000 .... Great Britain's tour Down Under returns a record profit of £233,645 .... Huddersfield to stage first team matches at Huddersfield Town FC's Leeds Road ground .... Barrow list New Zealander Aaron Conlon for £8,000 .... Warrington sign winger Rick Thackray for a second time .... Wigan reduce asking price for Andy Gregory from £75,000 to £50,000 .... Hunslet sign Australian trio Paul Beath, Paul Reece and John McKelvie .... Bradford Northern recruit New Zealander Trevor Clark from Featherstone Rovers .... Oldham swap winger Richard Blackman for London Crusaders forward Ben Olsen .... Leigh's £120,000-rated packman Mark Sheals moves to Oldham in exchange for Duncan Platt, Tim Street and Keith Newton

.... Castleford centre Ian Bragger joins Doncaster for £10,000 .... Huddersfield Under-21 forward Chris Parr moves to Swinton in exchange for Chris Pucill .... Widnes swap £230,000-rated Test full back Alan Tait for Leeds scrum half Bobby Goulding and cash .... Paul Bishop moves from St. Helens to Halifax for £55,000 .... Leigh suspend Andy Ruane and Phil Johnson for breach of club discipline .... Oldham swap Shaun Allen for Blackpool Gladiators' Mark Meadows .... Leeds duo Gary Divorty and John Bentley move to Halifax, who hand over £100,000 and hooker Seamus McCallion .... Batley complete the signing of Hull scrum half Mark Cass .... Stones Bitter pay £75,000 for title rights to the World Cup final at Wembley .... Oldham swap £50,000-rated scrum half Neil Flanagan and former tourist Des Foy for Huddersfield's Stuart Cocker .... Bradford Northern recruit Huddersfield winger Brimah Kebbie for £16,500 .... Leeds hand over £30,000 for Wigan scrum half Andy Gregory, plus a further £15,000 for a second season .... Halifax receive £25,000 from Bradford Northern for Kiwi Dave Watson .... Allan Agar resigns as coach of Featherstone Rovers for family reasons, Australian John Dorahy being appointed .... Wally Gibson returns to Huddersfield with the asking price being reduced to £55,000 .... Hull K.R.'s pay rebels accept a pay scale of £400 a win .... Leeds fail in a bid to sign Bradford Northern's Karl Fairbank .... League Tribunal orders Leigh to pay Bradford Northern £20,000 for loose forward John Pendlebury .... Huddersfield pay Hull £10,000 for centre Brian Blacker .... Carlisle recruit David Smith from Newcastle Knights .... St. Helens sign Oldham's Under-21 packman Chris Joynt in exchange for Sean Devine and Paul Jones .... St. Helens lift the CIS Insurance Charity Shield at Gateshead with a 17-0 victory over holders Wigan .... Wigan duo Martin Offiah and Kelvin Skerrett face a League inquiry after failing to collect their Charity Shield medals .... Hull and Bradford Northern chase scrum half Deryck Fox, who refuses to turn out for

St. Helens captain Shane Cooper lifts the CIS Insurance Charity Shield at Gateshead.

Featherstone Rovers and rejects a move to Halifax .... Halifax ask £40,000 for Australian loose forward Greg Pearce .... Leigh list hooker Andy Ruane at £25,000 .... Hull recruit St. George half back Ivan Henjak .... The League invite two top French clubs to enter the Regal Trophy .... Rochdale Hornets sign Leeds forward Cavill Heugh .... Wigan sign Australian centre Andrew Farrar from Western Suburbs .... Welshman Phil Ford leaves Leeds for Salford.

SEPTEMBER
Leeds sign Wigan forward Andy Goodway .... Welsh international Rob Ackerman moves from Carlisle to Salford .... Hooker Andy Ruane makes his peace at Leigh .... Hull and Bradford Northern appeal to fans to raise funds for the purchase of Featherstone Rovers scrum half Deryck Fox .... Workington Town recruit Junior Kiwi Wayne Kohlhase .... Leeds sign New Zealand Test centre Kevin Iro from Sydney club Manly .... Taking of unauthorised cough medicine costs Castleford full back Graham Steadman a £1,000 fine after failing a post-Test

drug test in New Zealand .... Wigan duo Martin Offiah, £250 fine, and Kelvin Skerrett, severe reprimand, punished by the League for not receiving their CIS Charity Shield runners-up medals .... Featherstone Rovers accept Hull bid for Deryck Fox, who refuses to move to the Boulevard .... St. Helens sign New Zealand Test centre Jarrod McCracken .... The League give Blackpool Gladiators permission to play at Blackpool Mechanics FC .... XIII Catalan qualify to join Carcassonne in the draw ceremony for the Regal Trophy .... Halifax chase Australian Test forward Bob Lindner after Leeds pull out of a deal .... Featherstone Rovers lose patience with new coach John Dorahy and cancel the appointment .... Bradford Northern pay club record £140,000 for Featherstone Rovers scrum half Deryck Fox .... Whitehaven sign Australian Steve Edwards .... Two-match ban imposed on Widnes scrum half Bobby Goulding after trial by video .... Garry Schofield accepts summer contract from Sydney club Manly .... Featherstone Rovers recruit scrum half Brett Daunt from Valleys club in Brisbane .... Former North Sydney coach Steve Martin takes over the reins at Featherstone Rovers .... Jim Crellin quits as coach of Leigh after only three matches .... Denis Ramsdale takes over as caretaker coach at Leigh .... Widnes list packman Chris Ashurst at £50,000 .... Hunslet and Whitehaven each fined £500 for brawling .... Workington complete the signing of Barrow's Paul Burns for £10,000 .... Castleford offer two players for Leigh full back Paul Topping .... Castleford put £50,000 price tag on hooker Graham Southernwood .... Bradford Northern offer winger Henderson Gill at £12,000 .... Blackpool Gladiators sign Chorley Borough scrum half Jeff Bimson .... Injured Laurie Daley and Andrew Ettingshausen pull out of Australia's World Cup final squad .... Former Bradford Northern forward David Croft walks out on Huddersfield only 24 hours after signing .... Featherstone Rovers pay £22,500 to Leeds for hooker Richard Gunn ....

Cumbria appoint Gordon Cottier as coach .... Huddersfield full back Wally Gibson joins Oldham .... Workington Town sign centre Tony Kay from Barrow .... Beverley RU stand off Neil Wardrobe joins Hull K.R. .... New Zealand Test half back Clayton Friend signs for Whitehaven .... Hunslet's James Lowes moves to Leeds.

OCTOBER

Blackpool Gladiators chairman Alan Sherratt puts the club up for sale at £50,000 .... Salford goalkicking utility back Steve Kerry joins Oldham in £30,000 deal .... Wigan accept Brisbane Broncos invitation to stage the World Club Challenge at the end of the month .... The League announce that African players do not count on the quota system .... Barrow offer Roy Haggerty at £10,000 .... Hunslet sign veteran scrum half Paul Harkin from Halifax .... Leigh recruit Balmain packman John Elias .... Widnes offer centre Darren Wright at £130,000 and utility back Paul Atcheson at £120,000 .... Andy Fisher priced at £80,000 by Featherstone Rovers, who offer Mark Gibbon at £7,500 .... Nottingham City sack coach Dave Sampson .... Halifax fail in bids to land Australian packmen Bob Lindner and Trevor Gillmeister .... Widnes Tongan forward Emosi Koloto joins Halifax on loan .... Maurice Lindsay appointed Rugby League Chief Executive .... Wigan swap David Myers for Paul Atcheson of Widnes .... Australia defeat Huddersfield in opening warm-up match .... Halifax halve the asking price for Warren Wilson to £25,000 .... The Sports Council offer to arbitrate on the RFL/BARLA dispute .... Garry Schofield named as Great Britain's World Cup final captain as Ellery Hanley is recalled to the squad .... Widnes list Test centre Andy Currier at £150,000 .... Hunslet sign Bradford Northern forward David Croft .... Huddersfield sign on-loan Roy Haggerty from Barrow .... Sheffield Eagles beaten 52-22 by Australia .... Kangaroo skipper Mal Meninga turns down Whitehaven offer of

£1,000 a match short-term contract .... Wigan beat arch rivals St. Helens 5-4 in Greenalls Lancashire Cup Final .... Wakefield Trinity lift John Smiths Yorkshire Cup, beating Sheffield Eagles 29-16 .... Cumbria go down to Australia, 44-0 .... Australia retain the World Cup with a 10-6 victory over Great Britain in front of a world record international crowd of 73,631 .... Halifax exchange Rob Hutchinson plus cash in £100,000 deal for Hull K.R. tourist threequarter Graeme Hallas .... Halifax recruit Kiwi Test prop Brent Stuart .... Wigan arrange trials for Great Britain sprinter Ade Mafe .... Hull K.R. offer Cumbrian prop Paul Vannett at £25,000.

NOVEMBER

St. Helens centre Gary Connolly lines up a summer stay with Australian club Canterbury-Bankstown .... Widnes cut short hooker Phil McKenzie's loan stay with Rochdale Hornets .... League Chairman Bob Ashby denies existence of a hit list of lower clubs .... Wigan list Test prop Ian Lucas at £150,000 .... Keighley offer scrum half Andy Eyres at £95,000 .... Sheffield Eagles pay Hunslet £10,000 for half back Tim Lumb after second loan spell .... Nottingham City sign Australian Kenny Isaacs, formerly with Halifax .... Widnes recruit

Brisbane Broncos' Julian O'Neill on short-term contract .... Carcassonne and XIII Catalan make French clubs' debut in Regal Trophy, losing to Wigan and Rochdale Hornets respectively .... Skipper Jonathan Davies pulls out of the Welsh side to meet England with a groin injury .... Leigh given High Court reprieve regarding threat of having to leave Hilton Park .... Salford pay Wigan £28,000 for reserve half back Steve Blakeley .... Leigh appoint South Sydney reserve grade coach Steve Simms as coach .... Wigan reject Wakefield Trinity exchange offer of Gary Price for Ian Lucas .... Former player Steve Crooks takes over as Rye-dale-York coach in place of Derek Foster .... Coach Tony Barrow takes a pay cut at Swinton to help ease financial burden .... Hull K.R. sign Australian prop Steve Pickett, released by Widnes .... Leeds stand off Francis Maloney joins Featherstone Rovers .... Salford prop David Young appointed skipper of Wales .... The League order a speeding up of the play-the-ball .... Doncaster sack coach Geoff Morris .... The League introduce experimental 10-metre offside line at play-the-ball .... Oldham sign England B, Lancashire and Orrell RU stand off Martin Strett .... Tony Fisher appointed coach of Doncaster .... England beat Wales 36-11 at Swansea.

Yorkshire Cup-winners Wakefield Trinity celebrate their first county cup haul for 28 years.

DECEMBER

The League's Board of Directors unveil proposals for two divisions of 16 with the current bottom three clubs being demoted to the Younger's Alliance League .... The Rugby League Council back the plans but insist that the County Cups should be compulsory and staged pre-season .... Salford sign Orrell RU full back Gary Tyrer .... A proposed swap deal between Featherstone Rovers prop Leo Casey and Rochdale Hornets centre Darren Abram falls through .... Featherstone Rovers Chairman Eric Gardner replaces David Oxley on the League's Board of Directors .... Bramley recruit Warrington's Des Drummond as a centre .... Doncaster pay Castleford £10,000 for prop Andy Clarke .... Hull K.R. sign Australian centre David Liddiard .... Halifax hooker Jason Ramshaw joins Keighley for £7,500 .... Kiwi Dean Clark rejoins Hull K.R. .... Leigh offer prop Tony Burke at £15,000 .... St. Helens coach Mike McClennan declares his intention to quit at the end of the season, skipper Shane Cooper putting in an early application .... Sheffield Eagles take on Dewsbury utility back Chris Vasey .... BBC TV wire up Regal Trophy referees for sound link to the commentators only .... Clubs to be fined £500 for pitch invasions by fans .... Widnes utility back David Hulme listed at £130,000 .... Workington Town stand off Stephen Wear offered at £60,000 .... Wales gain 19-18 victory over France at Perpignan .... Hull K.R. first team players refuse to turn out at Leigh in pay and bonus dispute, making peace after week-long talks .... Leigh reduce asking price for Paul Topping from £95,000 to £45,000 .... Garry Schofield takes legal advice after Leeds block his summer move to Manly .... Wigan coach John Monie agrees a three-year contract with newly approved Winfield Cup side Auckland Warriors .... Halifax list skipper John Fieldhouse at £55,000 .... The League announce that Regal Trophy semi-finals will revert to being played on the ground of the club drawn out first .... Wales accept invite to take part in the February Coca Cola World Sevens in Sydney .... Wigan given League permission to play Bradford Northern in the Stones Bitter Championship on the same weekend as the World Sevens .... Halifax sack coach Roger Millward .... Wakefield Trinity reveal that Leeds stand off Garry Schofield was offered in part exchange for Test forward Michael Jackson and teenage stand off Nigel Wright .... Widnes refuse permission for John Devereux to spend the summer with Manly .... Neil Holding rejoins St. Helens .... Widnes declare that they are open to offers for Jonathan Davies.

JANUARY

Doncaster recruit Huddersfield scrum half Greg Shuttleworth .... Hunslet fined £1,000 for refusing to play at frostbound Batley .... The Academy Challenge Cup final to be staged as a curtain-raiser to the Stones Bitter Premiership double-header .... Wakefield Trinity fail in sponsored bid to land Widnes utility back Jonathan Davies .... St. Helens packman Paul Forber joins Salford for £25,000 .... One third of Rugby League Headquarters staff of 27 made redundant in cost cutting exercise — they include Controller of Referees Fred Lindop and Marketing Executive Mike Turner .... Wakefield Trinity beat Silk Cut Challenge Cup deadline to sign South African threequarter Albertus Enslin .... Rochdale Hornets sack coach Stan Gittins .... Castleford exchange Neil Roebuck for Featherstone Rovers' Andy Fisher .... Wigan hand over £35,000 for Rochdale Hornets hooker Martin Hall .... Rochdale Hornets appoint former Parramatta prop Peter Regan as coach .... Carcassonne and French Test back row forward Daniel Divet joins Hull on a short-term contract .... Centre Craig McKeough quits Hull K.R. through injury .... Widnes receive transfer requests from Adrian Hadley, Les Holliday and Steve McCurrie .... Malcolm Reilly appointed coach of Halifax, retaining his Great Britain post part-time .... Veteran full back Keith Mumby returns to Bradford Northern from Sheffield Eagles .... Warrington refuse permission for half back Kevin Ellis to play for Wales in the World Sevens .... Hull winger Garry Clark forced to quit with a shoulder injury .... Australian promoters throw Wigan out of the World Sevens after submitting a 10-man squad featuring only one first team player .... Wigan add international trio Joe Lydon, Sam Panapa and Andrew Farrar, but still rejected .... Wigan lift the Regal Trophy by beating Bradford Northern 15-8 at Elland Road, Leeds .... Widnes lose appeal to have their four Welshmen released from the Wales squad for the World Sevens .... Wigan release South African Andre Stoop to return home .... St. Helens sign Kiwi prop Ricky Cowan to fill the overseas quota place vacated by the return home of centre Jarrod McCracken .... Swinton saved from liquidation by consortium headed by former chairman Malcolm White .... St. Helens give permission for Gus O'Donnell and John Harrison to play summer football in Queensland Country league .... The League introduce a Panel of Inspectors for referees .... The League withdraw Wales from the World Sevens under the threat of legal action by Warrington .... Australia retaliate by threatening to refuse to play Wigan, Warrington and Widnes on the 1994 tour of Britain.

FEBRUARY
Leigh fail in £300,000 bid to buy Hilton Park .... St. Helens utility back Tea Ropati is the halfway stage leader in the twin ballot for the title of Stones Bitter First Division Player of the Year .... The League suspend the CIS Insurance Charity Shield to stage two pre-season rounds of the County Cups .... Wakefield Trinity's request for a trial by video on Salford forward Paul Forber is turned down by the League .... The Rugby Football Union ban Wasps and England 'B' back Steve Pilgrim for a year for having trials as an amateur with Leeds .... Hull chairman Steve Watson appointed manager of Great Britain .... CIS Insurance criticise the League for not completing the remaining two years of their Charity

Shield contract .... Royce Simmons agrees a new one-year contract as coach of Hull .... MPs raise the Steve Pilgrim case in Parliament .... St. Helens coach Mike McClennan is persuaded to stay for another season .... Steve Pilgrim has further trials at Leeds .... Hull swap Paul Harrison for Hunslet's Alan Daniel .... Salford release Australian scrum half David Cruickshank .... England and Orrell RU winger Nigel Heslop joins Oldham .... Ross Strudwick resigns as manager and director of London Crusaders .... The League decide to take the first Test against New Zealand to Wembley, the other venues being Wigan and Leeds .... Wakefield Trinity sign Doncaster's goalkicking winger Mark Sims on loan .... The League release 14 of Great Britain's 19-man squad to play in midweek before the French Test to ease fixture congestion .... British Fuels and the Government fund a first-ever £80,000 Rugby League skills awards scheme for youngsters .... St. Helens fine several players for drinking in a nightclub after being barred .... Darryl Van de Velde to leave Castleford at the end of the season to be chief executive of newly formed Winfield Cup side Queensland Crushers .... New Zealand to open their autumn tour against Wales at Swansea .... London Crusaders appoint former New Zealand Test coach Tony Gordon as new manager.

MARCH
Leeds Chief Executive Alf Davies fined £500, suspended for 12 months, for comments likely to bring the game into disrepute .... Malcolm White heads a consortium to buy Swinton out of administration .... Swinton coach Tony Barrow given dual role of general manager .... Great Britain coach Malcolm Reilly blasts out after losing six players injured in midweek league matches only 36 hours before departing for a Test encounter in France .... The Rugby Union's decision to ban Rugby League trialist Steve Pilgrim is condemned in the House of Lords .... Skipper Garry Schofield scores a hat-trick of tries as Great Britain run up record

48-6 victory in France .... The League appoint a three-man study group to research the effects of a switch to summer rugby .... Hull coach Royce Simmons assaulted by a spectator while leaving the field after a defeat at Salford .... A special general meeting of clubs votes by 28-6 to return to two divisions in 1993-94, scrap the county cups and demote the bottom three clubs into the second division of the Younger's Alliance League .... Fire destroys the main stand at Doncaster's Tattersfield ground .... Wigan balance sheet shows a loss of nearly £300,000 from a turnover of around £3 million, which includes the £440,000 purchase of Martin Offiah and interest on the building of a new stand .... Widnes reach Wembley for the first time in nine years .... Public outcry as five clubs under the threat of demotion promise to fight the decision .... Bramley players back coach Maurice Bamford after section of the fans demand his resignation .... Emma Rosewarne appointed first-ever female senior executive at Rugby League Headquarters .... Banned RU back Steve Pilgrim given first team debut by Leeds at Widnes .... Four of the bottom five clubs in Division Three launch fighting fund .... Leigh turn down an Oldham bid to take Paul Topping on loan for the remainder of the season .... Leeds release Steve Pilgrim from trials .... League Chief Executive Maurice Lindsay clears the air over the winding down of his bookmaking activities .... Leeds suspend Garry Schofield for two weeks for missing training .... Halifax give trials to Steve Pilgrim, including a first team appearance .... Martin Offiah axed by Great Britain due to inconsistent form .... Wigan chairman Jack Robinson criticises the recall of Great Britain's senior players for the return Test with France, forcing their absence from midweek league matches .... Great Britain coach Malcolm Reilly describes his comments as "ludicrous" .... Wigan's Andy Platt appointed captain of Great Britain for the first time .... Brawl fines of £1,000 imposed on Rochdale Hornets and Huddersfield, and £500 on Featherstone Rovers and Oldham, half

suspended for a year .... Leigh coach Steve Simms applies for vacant posts at Wigan and Castleford .... Leeds sell forward Mick Worrall to Rochdale Hornets for £10,000 .... Wigan beat Bradford Northern at Elland Road, Leeds, to reach Wembley for the sixth consecutive season.

APRIL
Welshman Rob Ackerman announces his retirement as a player . . . Featherstone Rovers clinch the Stones Bitter Second Division title . . . Wigan lift the Younger's Alliance Challenge Cup with a 32-8 success over Leeds at Headingley . . . Ellery Hanley axed from the Great Britain side to entertain France after being absent from the team hotel without permission in the 24 hours before kick-off . . . Great Britain beat France by a world record score of 72-6 . . . Scrum halves Paul Bishop (Halifax) and Sean Devine (Oldham) each fined £200 for making obscene gestures to the crowd . . . Tongan Emosi Koloto ruled out of Wembley and ordered to quit the game with a neck injury . . . The League prepared to invest £250,000 over three years in the formation of a three-division Conference League involving the three demoted professional clubs and leading amateur outfits . . . Barrow and Highfield secure safety at the foot of the Third Division, condemning Nottingham City, Chorley Borough and Blackpool Gladiators to demotion . . . Castleford referee Russell Smith appointed for the Silk Cut Challenge Cup final . . . Australian Steve Simms signs a three-year contract at Leigh . . . Wigan make the surprise appointment of John Dorahy as coach, currently assistant at Sydney Premiership side Newcastle Knights and formerly in charge of Halifax . . . Sheffield Eagles chairman Gary Hetherington steps down as coach . . . Leigh consider sharing the purchase of their Hilton Park ground with part-time soccer neighbours Horwich RMI . . . Castleford appoint John Joyner and Allan Agar as new coaching team . . . The League reveal seven-point plan to aid three demoted clubs . . . Widnes fly in Brisbane Bronco utility back

Julian O'Neill for Wembley duty . . . Wigan attract a Stones Bitter Championship average attendance of 14,553, a record for two/three division football.

MAY

Widnes forward Richard Eyres becomes only the second player to be sent off at Wembley as Wigan register a 20-14 victory for a sixth successive Silk Cut Challenge Cup final triumph . . . League Chief Executive Maurice Lindsay proposes an administrative restructure including the introduction of a board director from outside of the game . . . Sheffield Eagles appoint Bill Gardner, assistant with Brisbane Broncos, as coach . . . Salford release Australian scrum half Craig Coleman for a return home . . . Prop Ged Stazicker listed at £75,000 by Salford . . . Widnes half back Chris Kelly named as Younger's Alliance Player of the Year . . . Llanelli RU scrum half Rupert Moon turns down an approach by Halifax . . . Keighley Cougars sign Australian centre Greg Austin on a free transfer from Halifax . . . Barrow appoint Denis Ramsdale as coach . . . Wigan crowned as Stones Bitter Team of the Year . . . Doncaster sign South African centre Jamie Bloem from Oldham . . . Ryedale-York utility back Nick Pinkney joins Keighley Cougars . . . St. Helens prop Kevin Ward reveals that he came close to losing his leg after breaking it in the Good Friday match with Wigan . . . Welsh winger Adrian Hadley, listed by Widnes at £60,000, threatens to quit if a move is not forthcoming . . . Wigan's Andy Platt named as Stones Bitter Man of Steel . . . Bradford Northern's Australian centre Tony Anderson moves to Huddersfield as Alliance coach . . . Wigan's bid for a first-ever Grand Slam of all five major trophies is halted by St. Helens' 10-4 success in the Stones Bitter Premiership

Trophy final . . . Second Division champions Featherstone Rovers complete a Stones Bitter double by beating Third Division Workington Town 20-16 in the Divisional Premiership final . . . Salford sign winger Jake Ogden from Northampton RU club . . . League announce plans to stage Great Britain Academy versus the Junior Kiwis as a curtain-raiser to the Anglo-Kiwi first Test at Wembley . . . Leeds assistant coach Gary Stephens joins Halifax in the same role . . . Rochdale Hornets re-appoint Australian coach Peter Regan . . . Wigan winger Martin Offiah contributes £11,000 towards the insurance cost of his £2,000-a-match summer stay with Sydney club Eastern Suburbs . . . Widnes scrum half Bobby Goulding fined £1,000, half suspended for a year, by the League for misconduct in Silk Cut Challenge Cup final at Wembley . . . Hull list want-away Test duo Steve McNamara and Lee Jackson at £500,000 and £400,000 respectively . . . Rugby League Council agree to meet only four times a year rather than monthly and recommend that the Board of Directors have the right to co-opt outside members . . . Australian Test forward Bob Lindner agrees a two-year contract with Oldham . . . Wigan offer Test full back Steve Hampson at £15,000 . . . The League and BARLA agree a peace plan to end the long-running dispute over youth rugby . . . Australian centre Andrew Farrar announces his retirement at Wigan . . . Halifax and Wigan lead the chase for Wakefield Trinity stand off Nigel Wright . . . Hull K.R. list winger Bright Sodje at £120,000, hooker Lee Richardson at £80,000, prop Wayne Jackson at £85,000 and utility man Sean Hoe at £50,000 . . . Castleford referee Russell Smith appointed for the three-match Test series between New Zealand and Australia . . . Widnes prop Kurt Sorensen appointed player-coach of Whitehaven.

Hunslet's goalkicking forward Andy Precious, scorer of 197 points in 28 appearances during 1992-93.

CLUBS

The following is a focus on last season's 35 professional Rugby League clubs, the section providing each club with a profile and an analysis of their 1992-93 campaign on a match-by-match basis with a summary for each first team player.

KEY

In the individual club profiles the following headings are featured:

First season refers to when the club gained senior league status. In some instances clubs have disbanded and re-formed, sometimes under different titles. For record purposes these changes are ignored except where there has been a break of more than one full season.

Honours. Until they were scrapped in 1970, the Yorkshire and Lancashire Leagues were among the honours in the professional game. Before 1903 they operated under the title of the Lancashire and Yorkshire Senior Competitions. Winners of these competitions are included under the Lancashire and Yorkshire League Champions. The pre-1903 Yorkshire Senior Competition should not be confused with the league operating for A-teams in Yorkshire which had the same title.

Regal Trophy is the current title for the John Player/Player's No. 6 Trophy competition.

Coaches. The clubs' individual coaching register is from the start of the 1974-75 season.

Attendances. Crowds in brackets are at neutral venues.

Appearances. Players' totals are based on official teamsheets submitted to the League after each first team match. + indicates playing substitute appearance.

Great Britain Register. The figure in brackets after a player's name is the number of Great Britain appearances he made while serving the club under whose entry he is listed, and the number after the + sign indicates playing substitute. This is followed by the time-span between his first and last British cap while at that club.

Signings Register. ★ Indicates where clubs have agreed to a player being signed 'on loan', a temporary transfer, the Rugby Football League prohibiting a subsequent transfer within 28 days. Where a player on loan has not been retained, his return to his original club is also marked ★.

Date of Birth: The dates are supplied in good faith by the Rugby Football League from their registration of players. This also applies to dates of signing and previous club.

In the match-by-match review for each club the following abbreviations are used:

YC	—	Yorkshire Cup	A	—	Away
LC	—	Lancashire Cup	W	—	Won
SBC	—	Stones Bitter Championship	L	—	Lost
SD	—	Second Division	D	—	Drawn
TD	—	Third Division	dg	—	Drop goal
RT	—	Regal Trophy	Fr	—	France
CC	—	Challenge Cup	Aus	—	Australia
PT	—	Premiership Trophy	NZ	—	New Zealand
DP	—	Divisional Premiership	PNG	—	Papua New Guinea
P	—	Preliminary Round	SA	—	South Africa
H	—	Home	Pr	—	Probationer

BARROW

Ground: Craven Park (0229-820273)
First Season: 1900-01
Nickname: Shipbuilders
Chairman: Steve Johnson
Honours: **Division Two** Champions, 1975-76, 1983-84
Challenge Cup Winners, 1954-55
Beaten finalists, 1937-38, 1950-51, 1956-57, 1966-67
Regal Trophy Beaten finalists, 1980-81
Lancashire Cup Winners, 1954-55, 1983-84
Beaten finalists, 1937-38

RECORDS

Match

Goals: 12 by Frank French v. Maryport, 19 Feb 1938
Willie Horne v. Cardiff, 8 Sep 1951
Steve Tickle v. Kent Invicta, 8 Apr 1984
Mike Kavanagh v. Blackpool G., 21 Mar 1993
Tries: 6 by Val Cumberbatch v. Batley, 21 Nov 1936
Jim Thornburrow v. Maryport, 19 Feb 1938
Frank Castle v. York, 29 Sep 1951
Steve Rowan at Nottingham C., 15 Nov 1992
Points: 28 by Keith Jarrett v. Doncaster, 25 Aug 1970
Steve Tickle v. Kent Invicta, 8 Apr 1984
Dean Marwood at Runcorn H., 16 Apr 1989
Mike Kavanagh v. Blackpool G., 21 Mar 1993

Season

Goals: 135 by Joe Ball, 1956-57
Tries: 50 by Jim Lewthwaite, 1956-57
Points: 305 by Ian Ball, 1979-80

Career

Goals: 741 by Willie Horne, 1943-58
Tries: 352 by Jim Lewthwaite, 1943-57
Points: 1,818 by Willie Horne, 1943-58
Appearances: 500 by Jim Lewthwaite, 1943-57
Highest score: 83-3 v. Maryport, 19 Feb 1938
Highest against: 90-0 at Leeds, 11 Feb 1990
Attendance: 21,651 v. Salford (League), 15 Apr 1938

COACHING REGISTER

● **Since 1974-75**

Frank Foster	May 73 - Apr 83
Tommy Dawes	May 83 - Feb 85
Tommy Bishop	Feb 85 - Apr 85
Ivor Kelland	May 85 - Feb 87
Dennis Jackson	Feb 87 - Nov 87
Rod Reddy	Nov 87 - Nov 89
Dennis Jackson	Nov 89 - Apr 90
Steve Norton	May 90 - Feb 91
Paul Kavanagh	Feb 91 - July 92
Geoff Worrall	July 92- Apr 93
Denis Ramsdale	May 93 -

GREAT BRITAIN REGISTER

(19 players)

Bill Burgess	(16)	1924-29
Bill Burgess	(13)	1962-68
David Cairns	(2)	1984
Chris Camilleri	(2)	1980
Charlie Carr	(7)	1924-26
Frank Castle	(4)	1952-54
Roy Francis	(1)	1947
Harry Gifford	(2)	1908
Dennis Goodwin	(5)	1957-58
Jack Grundy	(12)	1955-57
Phil Hogan	(4+1)	1977-78
Willie Horne	(8)	1946-52
Phil Jackson	(27)	1954-58
Joe Jones	(1)	1946
Bryn Knowelden	(1)	1946
Eddie Szymala	(1+1)	1981
Ted Toohey	(3)	1952
Alec Troup	(2)	1936
Jack Woods	(1)	1933

1992-93 SIGNINGS REGISTER

Signed	Player	Club From
10.8.92	Robinson, Roy	Millom ARL
30.8.92	Kolose, Chris	Muakow, NZ
30.8.92	Moules, Rob	Scarborough P.
30.8.92	Potts, Steve	Scarborough P.
18.9.92	*Kavanagh, Mike	Carlisle
20.9.92	Tagaloa, Lawrence	Te'atuta, NZ
4.12.92	Bullen, Terry	St. Esteve
18.12.92	Carey, Steve	Ponsonby, NZ
23.12.92	Duncan, Darryl	Askam ARL
25.12.92	*Rea, Steve	Carlisle
29.12.92	*Cameron, Graham	Whitehaven
29.12.92	*Solarie, Tony	Whitehaven
5.1.93	Casson, Neil	Dalton ARL
11.1.93	Eccles, Bob	Blackpool G.
25.2.93	Carter, Dane	Workington T.

BARROW 1992-93 PLAYERS' SUMMARY

	(Date of Birth)	App	T	G	D	Pts	Previous club	Signed
Archer, Darren	(3.3.71)	1+1	—	—	—	—	Marsh H. ARL	6.9.90
Bullen, Terry	(31.7.65)	3+1	—	—	—	—	France	4.12.90
Butler, Rob	(29.7.64)	1	—	—	—	—	ARL	3.8.92
Cameron, Graham	(15.9.62)	5+2	—	—	—	—	Whitehaven	29.12.92
Carey, Steve	(8.2.67)	6+4	5	—	—	20	New Zealand	18.12.92
Carter, Dane	(8.5.61)	2	—	—	—	—	Workington T.	25.2.93
Casson, Neil	(13.6.67)	10	—	—	—	—	Dalton ARL	5.1.93
Crarey, Paul	(4.1.66)	14	6	—	—	24	Dalton ARL	6.10.86
Eccles, Bob	(10.7.57)	10	2	3	—	14	Blackpool G.	11.1.93
Fletcher, Andy	(23.11.57)	10+2	2	—	—	8	Nottingham C.	1.9.92
Hadley, Derek	(6.6.54)	7+13	1	—	—	4	ARL	26.8.73
Honey, Chris	(25.1.68)	23+1	6	—	—	24	Thatto Heath ARL	26.9.91
Jackson, Wayne	(17.9.66)	11+4	5	4	—	28	Dalton ARL	6.9.90
Kavanagh, Mike	(5.2.71)	21	6	53	—	130	Carlisle	17.10.92
Kendall, Dave	(7.6.63)	1+1	—	—	—	—	Carlisle	1.10.91
Kendall, Gary	(21.9.64)	3	—	—	—	—	Holker P. ARL	14.1.85
Keresoma, Moses		3	—	—	—	—	New Zealand	30.8.92
Kolose, Chris	(30.7.70)	22	7	—	—	28	New Zealand	30.8.92
Middleton, Glen	(3.9.68)	2	—	—	—	—	Barrow I. ARL	2.9.88
Morrison, Steve	(31.12.66)	3+1	1	—	—	4	Holker P. ARL	25.4.86
Morrow, Shaun	(31.12.63)	19+2	3	—	—	12	Walney I. ARL	3.7.91
Moses, Alan	(9.9.65)	0+1	—	—	—	—	Marsh H. ARL	5.9.84
Moules, Rob	(18.10.66)	0+1	—	—	—	—	Scarborough P.	30.8.92
Pemberton, Keith	(16.11.69)	17+3	2	—	—	8	ARL	8.11.88
Petcher, Graeme	(24.3.72)	15+3	1	—	—	4	ARL	26.6.91
Potts, Steve	(10.2.67)	2	—	—	—	—	Scarborough P.	30.8.92
Rea, Steve	(16.7.65)	7+2	4	—	—	16	Carlisle	25.12.92
Rhodes, Stuart	(16.1.72)	25+1	1	—	—	4	Askam ARL	6.9.90
Robinson, Roy	(18.1.65)	22	10	—	—	40	Millom ARL	10.8.92
Rowan, Steve	(15.4.69)	15+1	10	—	—	40	Walney C. ARL	14.3.89
Shaw, Steve	(29.9.71)	7	1	—	—	4	Ulverston ARL	—
Solarie, Tony	(2.11.61)	5	—	—	—	—	Whitehaven	29.12.92
Srama, Paul	(20.10.66)	10	—	—	—	—	Australia	12.10.92
Tagaloa, Lawrence		7+1	1	—	—	4	New Zealand	20.9.92
Thompson, Phil	(5.2.67)	2+1	—	1	—	2	Holker P. ARL	4.4.89
Trainor, Pat	(8.4.64)	21+1	10	—	—	40	Walney C. ARL	20.10.87
Wild, John	(9.12.69)	18+2	8	8	—	48	Walney C. ARL	1.7.91
Wright, Carl	(23.7.72)	1+4	—	—	—	—	Australia	9.10.92
TOTALS								
38 players			92	69	—	506		

Representative appearances 1992-93 Crarey — Cumbria (+1)

BARROW 1992-93 MATCH ANALYSIS

Date	Com-petition	H/A	Opponent	Rlt	Score	Tries	Goals	Atten-dance	Referee
30.8.92	TD	A	Batley	L	2-20	—	Jackson	—	—
6.9.92	TD	H	Nottingham C.	L	12-19	Honey, Kolose	Jackson (2)	574	Ollerton
13.9.92	LC(1)	H	St. Helens	L	2-36	—	Jackson	2317	Nicholson
20.9.92	TD	A	Keighley C.	L	10-40	Wild, Morrow	Kavanagh	—	—
27.9.92	TD	H	Whitehaven	L	14-28	Fletcher, Pemberton, Crarey	Thompson	866	Kershaw
4.10.92	TD	A	Blackpool G.	W	46-25	Rowan (3), Robinson (2), Honey, Wild, Pemberton	Kavanagh (7)	—	—
11.10.92	TD	H	Chorley B.	W	50-4	Robinson (3), Kavanagh (2), Wild (2), Morrison, Kolose	Kavanagh (7)	573	Tidball
18.10.92	TD	A	Doncaster	L	18-30	Kolose, Robinson, Kavanagh	Kavanagh (3)	—	—
1.11.92	TD	H	Batley	L	10-18	Crarey (2)	Kavanagh	784	Redfearn
8.11.92	RT(1)	A	Bradford N.	L	10-70	Crarey, Trainor	Kavanagh	—	—
15.11.92	TD	A	Nottingham C.	W	64-8	Rowan (6), Rhodes, Crarey, Robinson, Fletcher, Wild, Morrow, Kavanagh	Kavanagh (6)	—	—
22.11.92	TD	H	Ryedale-York	L	4-22	Tagaloa	—	693	Nicholson
29.11.92	TD	A	Whitehaven	L	6-38	Petcher	Kavanagh	—	—
6.12.92	TD	A	Dewsbury	L	8-34	Trainor, Rowan	—	—	—
13.12.92	TD	H	Doncaster	L	18-28	Kavanagh, Wild, Crarey	Kavanagh (3)	535	Galtress
20.12.92	TD	A	Ryedale-York	L	0-60	—	—	—	—
5.1.93	TD	H	Workington T.	L	6-30	Kolose	Kavanagh	1297	Wood
17.1.93	TD	H	Dewsbury	L	14-29	Kolose, Trainor	Kavanagh (3)	859	Crashley
24.1.93	TD	H	Hunslet	L	0-20	—	—	722	R. Connolly
31.1.93	CC(1)	A	Leeds	L	18-54	Carey, Honey, Trainor	Kavanagh (3)	—	—
7.2.93	TD	A	Chorley B.	L	20-22	Rea (3)	Kavanagh (4)	—	—
10.2.93	TD	A	Workington T.	L	8-42	Trainor (2)	—	—	—
13.2.93	TD	A	Highfield	W	50-16	Jackson (3), Kolose, Eccles, Honey, Morrow, Shaw, Trainor	Wild (4), Eccles (3)	—	—
28.2.93	TD	H	Keighley C.	L	20-42	Honey, Carey, Robinson, Kolose	Wild (2)	962	Carter
7.3.93	TD	A	Hunslet	L	16-30	Carey, Honey, Trainor	Wild (2)	—	—
21.3.93	TD	H	Blackpool G.	W	72-6	Carey (2), Jackson (2), Wild (2), Eccles, Hadley, Kavanagh, Rea, Robinson, Trainor	Kavanagh (12)	772	Volante
9.4.93	TD	H	Highfield	L	8-14	Robinson, Trainor	—	800	Whitelam

BATLEY

Ground: Mount Pleasant (0924-472208)
First Season: 1895-96
Nickname: Gallant Youths
Chairman: Stephen Ball
Secretary: Richard Illingworth
Honours: **Championship** Winners, 1923-24
              Challenge Cup Winners, 1896-97,
              1897-98, 1900-01
              Yorkshire Cup Winners, 1912-13
              Beaten finalists, 1909-10, 1922-23,
              1924-25, 1952-53
              Yorkshire League Winners,
              1898-99, 1923-24

RECORDS
Match
Goals: 10 by Steve Parrish at Nottingham C.,
            10 Nov 1991
Tries: 5 by Joe Oakland v. Bramley,
            19 Dec 1908
          Tommy Brannan v. Swinton,
            17 Jan 1920
          Jim Wale v. Bramley, 4 Dec 1926
          Jim Wale v. Cottingham,
            12 Feb 1927
Points: 26 by Jack Perry v. Liverpool C.,
            16 Sep 1951

Season
Goals: 120 by Stan Thompson, 1958-59
Tries: 29 by Jack Tindall, 1912-13
Points: 281 by Jack Perry, 1950-51
Career
Goals: 463 by Wharton "Wattie" Davies,
             1897-1912
Tries: 123 by Wharton "Wattie" Davies,
             1897-1912
Points: 1,297 by Wharton "Wattie" Davies,
             1897-1912
Appearances: 421 by Wharton "Wattie" Davies,
             1897-1912
Highest score: 64-0 at Nottingham C.,
             10 Nov 1991
Highest against: 78-9 at Wakefield T.,
             26 Aug 1967
Attendance: 23,989 v. Leeds (RL Cup),
             14 Mar 1925

COACHING REGISTER
● **Since 1974-75**

Don Fox	Nov 72 - Oct 74
Alan Hepworth	Nov 74 - Apr 75
Dave Cox	May 75 - June 75
Trevor Walker	June 75 - June 77
Albert Fearnley	June 77 - Oct 77
Dave Stockwell	Oct 77 - June 79
*Tommy Smales	June 79 - Oct 81
Trevor Lowe	Oct 81 - May 82
Terry Crook	June 82 - Nov 84
George Pieniazek	Nov 84 - Nov 85
Brian Lockwood	Nov 85 - May 87
Paul Daley	July 87 - Apr 90
Keith Rayne	May 90 - Apr 91
David Ward	May 91 -

Ex-forward

GREAT BRITAIN REGISTER
(4 players)

Norman Field	(1)	1963
Frank Gallagher	(8)	1924-26
Carl Gibson	(+1)	1985
Joe Oliver	(4)	1928

1992-93 SIGNINGS REGISTER

Signed	Player	Club From
15.6.92	Smith, Steve	Halifax
22.6.92	*Walton, Tony	Doncaster
30.6.92	Mahmood, Rashid	Hemel Hempstead ARL
1.7.92	Eastwood, Jonathan	—
1.7.92	Roadnight, John	Leeds
1.7.92	Ellis, Steve	—
31.7.92	*Oldroyd, Tommy	Hunslet
14.8.92	George, Wilf	Halifax
8.9.92	Barnes, Scott	Port Macquarie, Aus
8.9.92	Cameron, Mick	Port Macquarie, Aus
2.10.92	Irvine, Jimmy	Halifax
11.12.92	*Moxon, Darren	Bradford N.
17.12.92	Walker, Steve	Dudley Hill ARL
12.3.93	Gibson, Chris	St. John Fisher ARL
14.3.93	Whittaker, Gary	Shaw Cross ARL

BATLEY 1992-93 PLAYERS' SUMMARY

	(Date of Birth)	App	T	G	D	Pts	Previous club	Signed
Bargate, Lee	(12.9.71)	12+1	7	—	—	28	Middleton ARL	27.6.90
Barnes, Scott	(31.12.71)	1	—	—	—	—	Australia	8.9.92
Beevers, Graham "Ben"	(14.6.61)	3+7	—	—	—	—	London C.	4.9.92
Booth, Michael	(20.3.60)	30	6	—	—	24	Australia	20.8.90
Bownass, Mark	(1.6.66)	2+2	—	—	—	—	ARL	2.8.90
Cameron, Mick	(19.12.67)	23	3	—	—	12	Australia	8.9.92
Cass, Mark	(17.11.71)	9+8	4	—	—	16	Hull	29.2.92
Child, Darren	(30.10.66)	6+5	1	—	—	4	Morley RU	13.9.90
Ellis, Steve	(10.1.71)	1	2	2	—	12	ARL	1.7.92
Fortis, Mark	(28.6.64)	0+2	—	—	—	—	Dewsbury M. ARL	11.11.87
George, Wilf	(24.1.60)	5	1	—	—	4	Halifax	14.8.92
Grayshon, Jeff	(4.3.49)	25+1	1	—	—	4	Featherstone R.	11.8.91
Hanlan, Lee	(6.10.71)	27	8	3	—	38	Hull	2.3.92
Hardcastle, Danny	(27.8.72)	0+1	—	—	—	—	Middleton ARL	27.6.90
Hartley, Neil	(5.4.67)	1+1	—	—	—	—	Oulton ARL	30.12.86
Heron, Wayne	(5.5.61)	23	2	—	—	8	Bradford N.	22.2.90
Holmes, Philip	(25.7.74)	1	—	1	—	2	East Leeds ARL	—
Irvine, Jimmy	(28.4.60)	19	6	—	—	24	Halifax	2.10.92
Kellett, Neil	(20.12.61)	6+14	4	—	—	16	Sheffield E.	11.8.91
Marshall, Paul	(17.4.65)	13+1	6	—	—	24	Shaws ARL	17.3.89
Moxon, Darren	(17.9.70)	5	2	—	—	8	Bradford N.	11.12.92
Oldroyd, Tommy	(30.12.69)	15+1	4	—	—	16	Hunslet	30.9.92
Parkinson, Andrew	(8.7.65)	26+1	1	—	—	4	Dewsbury	2.1.90
Redick, Paul	(22.1.67)	5	3	—	—	12	Shaws ARL	6.7.90
Roadnight, John	(3.1.73)	1	1	—	—	4	Leeds	1.7.92
Scott, Mark	(30.1.65)	14	6	—	—	24	Batley Boys ARL	9.5.84
Smith, Steve	(19.1.62)	4+1	2	—	—	8	Halifax	15.6.92
Spendler, Mark	(24.5.63)	5+4	1	—	—	4	Dewsbury M. ARL	25.11.86
Stainburn, John	(5.7.64)	1+2	—	—	—	—	Batley Boys ARL	15.8.83
Thornton, Gary	(9.3.63)	28+1	11	—	—	44	Wakefield T.	24.8.90
Tomlinson, Glen	(18.3.70)	27	17	—	—	68	Australia	29.8.91
Walker, Steve	(8.11.69)	5+1	1	1	—	6	Dudley Hill ARL	17.12.92
Walton, Tony	(20.12.63)	3+1	2	—	—	8	Doncaster	22.6.92
Whittaker, Gary	(29.7.69)	1+2	—	—	—	—	Shaw Cross ARL	14.3.93
Wilkinson, Shaun	(23.9.63)	13	2	—	—	8	—	—
Wilson, Simon	(22.10.67)	30	11	63	—	170	Batley Boys ARL	16.11.84
TOTALS								
36 players			115	70	—	600		

BATLEY 1992-93 MATCH ANALYSIS

Date	Competition	H/A	Opponent	Rlt	Score	Tries	Goals	Attendance	Referee
30.8.92	TD	H	Barrow	W	20-2	Thornton, Kellett, Wilson, Scott	Hanlan (2)	739	R. Connolly
6.9.92	TD	A	Ryedale-York	L	14-24	Redick, Thornton, Wilkinson	Hanlan	—	—
13.9.92	YC(1)	A	Huddersfield	L	8-16	Redick, George	—	—	—
20.9.92	TD	H	Doncaster	W	14-8	Wilson, Thornton, Smith	Wilson	1189	R. Connolly
27.9.92	TD	A	Blackpool G.	W	22-8	Redick, Oldroyd, Tomlinson, Hanlan	Wilson (3)	—	—
4.10.92	TD	H	Workington T.	W	20-8	Irvine (2), Thornton	Wilson (4)	819	Galtress
11.10.92	TD	A	Highfield	W	22-7	Tomlinson (2), Hanlan, Smith	Wilson (3)	—	—
18.10.92	TD	H	Ryedale-York	W	18-12	Oldroyd (2), Wilkinson	Wilson (3)	1238	Gilmour
1.11.92	TD	A	Barrow	W	18-10	Tomlinson, Wilson, Irvine	Wilson (3)	—	—
8.11.92	RT(1)	H	Hunslet	L	6-13	Tomlinson	Wilson	709	R. Connolly
15.11.92	TD	H	Blackpool G.	W	8-0	Thornton, Heron	—	428	Whitelam
22.11.92	TD	A	Hunslet	L	14-17	Bargate, Irvine	Wilson (3)	—	—
6.12.92	TD	A	Doncaster	L	12-14	Tomlinson, Thornton	Wilson (2)	—	—
13.12.92	TD	A	Chorley B.	W	30-16	Tomlinson (3), Booth, Hanlan, Spendler	Wilson (3)	—	—
28.12.92	TD	A	Dewsbury	L	0-8	—	—	—	—
13.1.93	TD	H[1]	Dewsbury	W	10-6	Bargate, Moxon	Wilson	1724	Morris
17.1.93	CC(P)	H	Blackpool G.	W	20-10	Bargate, Hanlan, Thornton, Wilson	Wilson (2)	628	Carter
24.1.93	TD	H	Chorley B.	W	52-7	Wilson (3), Bargate, Booth, Cameron, Cass, Irvine, Kellett, Moxon, Scott	Wilson (4)	501	Kershaw
31.1.93	CC(1)	A	Chorley B.	W	20-6	Cass, Heron, Tomlinson, Thornton	Wilson (2)	—	—
17.2.93	CC(2)	A	Halifax	L	20-50	Scott (2), Bargate, Hanlan	Walker, Wilson	—	—
21.2.93	TD	H	Whitehaven	L	16-20	Cameron, Irvine, Tomlinson	Wilson (2)	869	Asquith
26.2.93	TD	A	Nottingham C.	W	60-0	Bargate (2), Scott (2), Marshall (2), Kellett (2), Thornton, Tomlinson, Booth, Walker	Wilson (6)	—	—
28.2.93	TD	H	Nottingham C.	W	46-0	Walton (2), Cameron, Cass, Child, Marshall, Parkinson, Roadnight, Wilson	Wilson (4), Holmes	501	Nicholson
7.3.93	TD	A	Workington T.	L	12-20	Tomlinson (2)	Wilson (2)	—	—
14.3.93	TD	H	Highfield	W	24-5	Ellis (2), Hanlan, Oldroyd, Thornton	Ellis (2)	427	Carter
28.3.93	TD	A	Whitehaven	W	24-4	Booth, Cass, Hanlan, Tomlinson	Wilson (4)	—	—
4.4.93	TD	H	Hunslet	W	28-12	Booth, Marshall, Tomlinson, Thornton, Wilson	Wilson (4)	858	Cross
9.4.93	TD	A	Keighley C.	L	10-34	Hanlan, Wilson	Wilson	—	—
12.4.93	TD	H	Keighley C.	L	14-26	Booth, Marshall, Wilson	Wilson	1809	Kershaw
18.4.93	DP(1)	A	Dewsbury	L	18-22	Grayshon, Marshall, Tomlinson	Wilson (3)	—	—

[1] Leeds

BLACKPOOL GLADIATORS

Ground: Blackpool Mechanics FC
First Season: 1954-55 as Blackpool Borough;
             changing to Springfield Borough in
             1987-88; Chorley Borough in
             1988-89; Trafford Borough from
             1989-90; and Blackpool Gladiators
             from 1992-93. Demoted to the
             National Conference for 1993-94
Nickname: Gladiators
Chairman: Alan Sherratt
Secretary: Barry Pennington
Honours: **Regal Trophy** Beaten finalists,
             1976-77

RECORDS

Match

Goals: 11 by Norman Turley v. Carlisle,
        26 Apr 1984
Tries: 4 by Tony Wilkshire v. Bradford N.,
          14 Jan 1961
          John Stockley v. Doncaster,
          1 Apr 1984
          Tommy Frodsham v. Bridgend,
          14 Apr 1985
          Tommy Frodsham v. Mansfield M.,
          30 Nov 1986
Points: 27 by Norman Turley v. Carlisle,
        26 Apr 1984

Season

Goals: 98 by Mike Smith, 1987-88
Tries: 30 by Tommy Frodsham, 1985-86
Points: 201 by Peter Fearis, 1957-58

Career

Goals: 334 by Terry McCarrick, 1963-69
Tries: 82 by Jimmy Johnson, 1969-76
Points: 689 by Terry McCarrick, 1963-69
Appearances: 322+18 by Paul Gamble, 1973-88
Highest score: 56-2 v. Runcorn H., 1 Jan 1989
Highest against: 104-12 at St. Helens,
                  15 Sep 1991
Attendance: 21,000 v. Leigh (RL Cup),
              9 Mar 1957 — at Blackpool AFC

COACHING REGISTER

● **Since 1974-75**

Tommy Blakeley	Aug 74 - Apr 76
Jim Crellin	May 76 - Mar 77
Joe Egan Jnr	Mar 77 - Oct 77
Albert Fearnley (Mgr)	Nov 77 - Apr 79
Bakary Diabira	Nov 78 - June 79
Graham Rees	June 79 - Mar 80
Geoff Lyon	July 80 - Aug 81
Bob Irving	Aug 81 - Feb 82
John Mantle	Feb 82 - Mar 82
Tommy Dickens	Mar 82 - Nov 85
*Stan Gittins	Nov 85 - June 88
*Mike Peers	Aug 87 - May 91
Norman Turley	June 91 - Dec 91
Gary Ainsworth	Dec 91 - May 92
Jack Melling	July 92 - Nov 92
Bob Eccles	Nov 92 - Jan 93
Mike Peers	Jan 93 - Feb 93
Paul Gamble	Feb 93 -

Joint coaches Aug 87 - June 88

1992-93 SIGNINGS REGISTER

Signed	Player	Club From
23.7.92	Elseworth, Steve	Chadderton ARL
29.7.92	Fox, Phil	Rochdale H.
29.7.92	Viller, Mark	Rochdale H.
29.7.92	Viller, Paul	Rochdale H.
29.7.92	Eccles, Bob	Rochdale H.
6.8.92	Bent, Peers	Leigh Miners ARL
6.8.92	Flannery, Steve	Leigh Miners ARL
6.8.92	Hudson, Julian	Swinton
6.8.92	Pemberton, Tony	Fitton Hill ARL
14.8.92	Allen, Shaun	Oldham
23.8.92	Frodsham, Tommy	St. Helens
28.8.92	Marsh, Ian	Salford
28.8.92	Swann, Chris	St. Cuthberts ARL
19.9.92	Callan, Dave	Berry Shoalhaven, Aus
19.9.92	Hayburn, Adam	Berry Shoalhaven, Aus
24.9.92	*Bimson, Jeff	Chorley B.
10.1.93	Grainey, Gary	Leigh
10.1.93	Smith, Joe	Chorley B.
4.2.93	*Moore, Jonathan	Huddersfield
12.2.93	Stansfield, Ivan	Workington T.
14.2.93	Gavaghan, David	Blackpool Scorp. ARL
14.2.93	Padgett, Daniel	Blackpool Scorp. ARL
14.2.93	Shaw, Andy	Blackpool Stanley ARL
18.2.93	*Gaffney, Mike	Whitehaven

Signed	Player	Club From	Signed	Player	Club From
21.2.93	Basson, John	Eccles ARL	7.3.93	Sankey, Dave	Blackpool Stanley ARL
21.2.93	Pyne, Nick	Swinton Victoria ARL	7.3.93	Sankey, John	Blackpool Stanley ARL
21.2.93	Shaw, Robert	Eccles ARL	9.3.93	Jones, Graeme	Woolston R. ARL
28.2.93	McLellan, Neville	Eccles ARL	14.3.93	Runciman, Andy	Blackpool Stanley ARL
28.2.93	O'Hara, Mick	Blackpool Stanley ARL	20.3.93	Horrocks, Brian	Folly Lane ARL
7.3.93	Phelan, Andy	Blackpool Stanley ARL	20.3.93	Taylor, Glyn	Winwick ARL

BLACKPOOL GLADIATORS 1992-93 PLAYERS' SUMMARY

	(Date of Birth)	App	T	G	D	Pts	Previous club	Signed
Allen, Shaun	(23.9.65)	15	—	—	—	—	Oldham	14.8.92
Basson, John	(25.4.72)	6+1	—	—	1	1	Eccles ARL	21.2.93
Bimson, Jeff	(15.1.67)	3	—	—	—	—	Chorley B.	24.9.92
Bent, Peers	(28.12.70)	20+3	—	—	—	—	Leigh M. ARL	6.8.92
Brown, Dave	(17.2.65)	1+1	—	—	—	—	Whitehaven	8.1.92
Brydon, Jason	(10.11.66)	3	—	—	—	—	Huddersfield	28.3.93
Callan, Dave	(11.9.67)	1+1	1	—	—	4	Australia	19.9.92
Doherty, Paul	(30.3.67)	4	—	—	—	—	Hull	15.8.92
Eccles, Bob	(10.7.57)	14	6	28	3	83	Rochdale H.	29.7.92
Elseworth, Steve	(24.1.69)	5	—	—	—	—	Chadderton ARL	23.7.92
Erentz, Dave	(27.10.64)	3+1	—	—	—	—	—	—
Flannery, Steve	(3.2.71)	17	4	—	—	16	Leigh M. ARL	6.8.92
Fox, Phil	(9.11.57)	10	2	—	—	8	Rochdale H.	29.7.92
Frodsham, Tommy	(12.1.62)	1	1	—	—	4	St. Helens	23.8.92
Gaffney, Mike	(21.6.60)	3	—	—	—	—	Whitehaven	18.2.93
Gamble, Paul	(24.2.55)	5+5	—	—	—	—	—	—
Gavaghan, David	(7.1.59)	1	—	—	—	—	Blackpool S. ARL	14.2.93
Horrocks, Brian	(19.6.66)	1	—	—	—	—	Folly Lane ARL	20.3.93
Hudson, Julian	(14.6.67)	11	—	—	—	—	Swinton	6.8.92
Hughes, John	(21.2.64)	9	4	—	—	16	Salford Univ. ARL	20.1.93
Iddon, Tim	(2.9.68)	19+3	2	—	—	8	Crosfields ARL	21.2.89
Johnson, Chris	(29.5.60)	11+3	2	—	1	9	Swinton	4.1.92
Johnson, Phil	(24.12.63)	1	—	—	—	—	Rochdale H.	20.1.93
McLellan, Neville	(30.12.65)	4	—	—	—	—	Eccles ARL	28.2.93
Marsh, Ian	(15.4.66)	10+1	3	—	—	12	Salford	28.8.92
Moore, Jonathan	(8.7.74)	2	1	—	—	4	Huddersfield	4.2.93
O'Hara, Mick	(1.10.63)	7	1	—	—	4	Blackpool St. ARL	15.8.83
Pearson, Richard	(9.10.74)	1	1	—	—	4	Huddersfield	5.2.93
Pemberton, Tony	(26.5.64)	17	1	—	1	5	Fitton Hill ARL	6.8.92
Phelan, Andy	(2.5.64)	4	—	—	—	—	Blackpool St. ARL	7.3.93
Pyne, Nick	(27.2.64)	2+1	—	—	—	—	Swinton V. ARL	21.2.93
Reid, Terry	(9.9.67)	9+5	1	—	—	4	Crosfields ARL	28.9.90
Rippon, Andy	(10.2.65)	23+2	6	23	1	71	Swinton	29.8.89
Runciman, Andy	(8.8.62)	2+1	—	—	—	—	Blackpool St. ARL	14.3.93
Sankey, Dave	(3.6.63)	2+1	1	—	—	4	Blackpool St. ARL	7.3.93
Sankey, John	(4.9.65)	3+1	1	—	—	4	Blackpool St. ARL	7.3.93
Shaw, Andy	(15.1.69)	9	—	—	—	—	Blackpool St. ARL	14.2.93
Shaw, Robert	(15.8.71)	1+2	—	—	—	—	Eccles ARL	29.7.92
Smith, Graham	(2.4.67)	10+1	2	1	—	10	Woolston ARL	19.10.88
Smith, Dennis "Joe"	(16.8.64)	3+1	—	—	—	—	Chorley B.	10.1.93
Stansfield, Ivan	(7.12.67)	2	—	—	—	—	Workington T.	12.2.93

	(Date of Birth)	App	T	G	D	Pts	Previous club	Signed
Swann, Chris	(19.4.65)	1+5	—	—	—	—	St. Cuthberts ARL	28.8.92
Taylor, Glyn	(31.8.58)	2	—	—	—	—	Winwick ARL	20.3.93
Viller, Mark	(25.10.65)	16	6	—	—	24	Rochdale H.	29.7.92
Viller, Paul	(24.5.67)	16+1	3	—	—	12	Rochdale H.	29.7.92
Watts, Jason	(22.6.67)	10	2	—	—	8	Australia	17.1.93
Williams, Paul	(12.6.68)	8+2	—	—	—	—	Winwick ARL	1.12.91
Wood, David		23+2	3	—	1	13	Chorley B.	—
TOTALS								
48 players			54	52	8	328		

BLACKPOOL GLADIATORS 1992-93 MATCH ANALYSIS

Date	Com-petition	H/A	Opponent	Rlt	Score	Tries	Goals	Atten-dance	Referee
29.8.92	TD	A	Nottingham C.	W	32-12	Eccles (2), Frodsham, Marsh, P. Viller, Flannery	Eccles (4)	—	—
13.9.92	LC(1)	H	Workington T.	L	8-22	Eccles	Eccles (2)	736	Ollerton
20.9.92	TD	A	Chorley B.	W	28-16	M. Viller (2), Wood, Marsh, G. Smith	Eccles (4)	—	—
27.9.92	TD	H	Batley	L	8-22	Marsh, Callan	—	366	Atkin
4.10.92	TD	H	Barrow	L	25-46	Eccles, Flannery, Rippon, Fox	Eccles (4, 1dg)	342	Gilmour
11.10.92	TD	H	Whitehaven	L	12-32	Fox, Wood	Eccles, G. Smith	463	Wood
13.10.92	RT(P)	A	Warrington	L	8-32	Rippon	Eccles (2)	—	—
1.11.92	TD	H	Doncaster	W	22-18	C. Johnson, M. Viller, P. Viller	Eccles (4, 1dg), C. Johnson (dg)	514	Asquith
15.11.92	TD	A	Batley	L	0-8	—	—	—	—
29.11.92	TD	A	Doncaster	L	14-34	G. Smith, M. Viller	Eccles (3)	—	—
13.12.92	TD	A	Hunslet	L	10-22	Flannery	Eccles (3)	—	—
16.12.92	TD	H	Chorley B.	L	8-13	P. Viller	Eccles, Wood (dg), Pemberton (dg)	338	R. Connolly
27.12.92	TD	H	Nottingham C.	W	35-20	M. Viller (2), Pemberton, Iddon, Reid, Eccles	Rippon (5), Eccles (dg)	326	Tidball
10.1.93	TD	H	Ryedale-York	L	12-32	Eccles, Flannery	Rippon (2)	347	Wood
17.1.93	CC(P)	A	Batley	L	10-20	C. Johnson	Rippon (3)	—	—
20.1.93	TD	A	Keighley C.	L	4-36	Rippon	—	—	—
24.1.93	TD	A	Workington T.	L	6-56	Iddon	Rippon	—	—
7.2.93	TD	H	Highfield	L	23-24	Moore, Pearson, Rippon	Rippon (5,1dg)	260	Crashley
14.2.93	TD	A	Whitehaven	L	0-72	—	—	—	—
21.2.93	TD	A	Ryedale-York	L	6-56	Watts	Rippon	—	—
28.2.93	TD	H	Workington T.	L	12-78	Hughes (2), Rippon	—	646	Crashley
7.3.93	TD	H	Keighley C.	L	8-82	Hughes, O'Hara	—	1214	Nicholson
14.3.93	TD	H	Hunslet	L	14-42	Rippon, Wood	Rippon (3)	408	Crashley
21.3.93	TD	A	Barrow	L	6-72	J. Sankey	Rippon	—	—
28.3.93	TD	A	Highfield	L	12-19	Hughes, Watts	Rippon (2)	—	—
4.4.93	TD	H	Dewsbury	L	5-90	D. Sankey	Basson (dg)	486	Redfearn
11.4.93	TD	A	Dewsbury	L	0-56	—	—	—	—

BRADFORD NORTHERN

Ground: Odsal Stadium (0274-733899)
First Season: 1895-96 as "Bradford". Disbanded and became Bradford Northern in 1907-08. Disbanded during 1963-64 and re-formed for start of 1964-65
Nickname: Northern
Chairman: Chris Caisley
Secretary: Gary Tasker
Honours: **Championship** Beaten finalists, 1947-48, 1951-52
War Emergency League Championship winners, 1939-40, 1940-41, 1944-45
Beaten finalists, 1941-42
Division One Champions, 1903-04, 1979-80, 1980-81
Division Two Champions, 1973-74
Challenge Cup Winners, 1905-06, 1943-44, 1946-47, 1948-49
Beaten finalists, 1897-98, 1944-45, 1947-48, 1972-73
Regal Trophy Winners, 1974-75, 1979-80
Beaten finalists, 1990-91, 1992-93
Premiership Winners, 1977-78
Beaten finalists, 1978-79, 1979-80, 1989-90
Yorkshire Cup Winners, 1906-07, 1940-41, 1941-42, 1943-44, 1945-46, 1948-49, 1949-50, 1953-54, 1965-66, 1978-79, 1987-88, 1989-90
Beaten finalists, 1913-14, 1981-82, 1982-83, 1991-92
Yorkshire League Winners, 1899-1900, 1900-01, 1939-40, 1940-41, 1947-48

RECORDS

Match
Goals: 14 by Joe Phillips v. Batley, 6 Sep 1952
Tries: 7 by Joe Dechan v. Bramley, 13 Oct 1906
Points: 36 by John Woods v. Swinton, 13 Oct 1985

Season
Goals: 173 by Eddie Tees, 1971-72
Tries: 63 by Jack McLean, 1951-52
Points: 364 by Eddie Tees, 1971-72

Career
Goals: 779 by Keith Mumby, 1973-90 & 1992-93
Tries: 261 by Jack McLean, 1950-56
Points: 1,828 by Keith Mumby, 1973-90 & 1992-93
Appearances: 579+7 by Keith Mumby, 1973-90 & 1992-93
Highest score: 76-0 v. Leigh East, 17 Nov 1991
Highest against: 75-18 at Leeds, 14 Sep 1931
Attendance: 102,569 Warrington v. Halifax (RL Cup final replay), 5 May 1954
Home match: 69,429 v. Huddersfield (RL Cup), 14 Mar 1953

COACHING REGISTER
● **Since 1974-75**

Ian Brooke	Jan 73 - Sep 75
Roy Francis	Oct 75 - Apr 77
Peter Fox	Apr 77 - May 85
Barry Seabourne	May 85 - Sep 89
Ron Willey	Oct 89 - Mar 90
David Hobbs	Mar 90 - Oct 91
Peter Fox	Oct 91 -

Ian Brooke, Northern coach from January 1973 to September 1975

GREAT BRITAIN REGISTER
(32 players)

David Barends	(2)	1979
Eric Batten	(4)	1946-47
Ian Brooke	(5)	1966
Len Casey	(5)	1979
Gerald Cordle	(1)	1990
Willie Davies	(3)	1946-47
Karl Fairbank	(6+6)	1987-93
Tony Fisher	(8)	1970-78
Phil Ford	(7)	1987-88
Trevor Foster	(3)	1946-48
Deryck Fox	(1)	1992
Jeff Grayshon	(11)	1979-82
Ellery Hanley	(10+1)	1984-85
David Hobbs	(1+1)	1989
Dick Jasiewicz	(1)	1984
Jack Kitching	(1)	1946
Arthur Mann	(2)	1908
Keith Mumby	(11)	1982-84
Brian Noble	(11)	1982-84
Terry Price	(1)	1970
Johnny Rae	(1)	1965
Bill Ramsey	(+1)	1974
Alan Rathbone	(4+1)	1982-85
Alan Redfearn	(1)	1979
David Redfearn	(6+1)	1972-74
Kelvin Skerrett	(8)	1989-90
Tommy Smales	(3)	1965
Bert Smith	(2)	1926
Jimmy Thompson	(1)	1978
Ken Traill	(8)	1950-54
Ernest Ward	(20)	1946-52
Frank Whitcombe	(2)	1946

1992-93 SIGNINGS REGISTER

Signed	Player	Club From
30.6.92	Russell, Phil	Waterhead ARL
13.7.92	Smith, Gerrard	Waterhead ARL
27.7.92	Heron, David	Leeds
10.8.92	Roper, Lee	BP Chemicals ARL
13.8.92	Clark, Trevor	Featherstone R.
19.8.92	Kebbie, Brimah	Huddersfield
19.8.92	Watson, Dave	Halifax
28.8.92	*Raw, Andrew	Hunslet
9.9.92	Fox, Deryck	Featherstone R.
22.9.92	Boothroyd, Alan	Huddersfield
22.9.92	Darkes, Richard	Huddersfield
22.9.92	McDermott, Brian	Eastmoor ARL
5.11.92	Taylor, Mick	London C.
23.11.92	Austerfield, Shaun	Oulton ARL
11.12.92	*Mumby, Keith	Sheffield E.
18.12.92	*Bownass, Mark	Batley
8.1.92	*Hall, Dean	Dewsbury
11.1.92	*Armstrong, Mick	Doncaster
25.4.92	Moore, Craig	Bradford N. Academy

BRADFORD NORTHERN 1992-93 PLAYERS' SUMMARY

	(Date of Birth)	App	T	G	D	Pts	Previous club	Signed
Anderson, Tony	(23.7.61)	24+5	7	—	—	28	Oldham	4.9.91
Barraclough, Glenn	(24.4.66)	5+1	—	—	—	—	Bramley	11.1.88
Boothroyd, Alan	(19.6.66)	4+3	—	—	—	—	Huddersfield	22.9.92
Clark, Trevor	(28.5.62)	8+20	4	—	—	16	Featherstone R.	13.8.92
Cordle, Gerald	(29.9.60)	13	7	—	—	28	Cardiff RU	12.7.89
Darkes, Richard	(5.10.68)	5	1	—	—	4	Huddersfield	22.9.92
Fairbank, Karl	(1.6.63)	33+2	9	—	—	36	Elland ARL	24.7.86
Fox, Deryck	(17.9.64)	23+1	5	38	2	98	Featherstone R.	9.9.92
Grayshon, Paul	(11.7.67)	2+1	—	—	—	—	Bradford N. Colts	2.12.85
Greenwood, Adam	(26.5.67)	0+4	—	—	—	—	Calder V. ARL	27.1.92
Hamer, Jon	(23.2.62)	30+2	3	—	—	12	Elland ARL	29.8.84
Heron, David	(1.3.58)	34+4	1	—	—	4	Leeds	27.7.92
Hobbs, David	(13.9.58)	33+5	2	66	6	146	Oldham	1.4.87
Iti, Brett	(28.3.65)	0+1	—	—	—	—	New Zealand	18.7.90
Kebbie, Brimah	(21.9.65)	10	9	—	—	36	Huddersfield	19.8.92
McGowan, Steve	(25.2.64)	34+1	20	1	—	82	Leeds Colts	31.5.83
Marchant, Tony	(22.12.62)	29+3	19	14	—	104	Castleford	21.12.89
Medley, Paul	(21.9.66)	23+15	18	—	—	72	Halifax	31.8.89
Mumby, Keith	(21.2.57)	5+3	—	4	—	8	Sheffield E.	11.12.92

(Continued)

	(Date of Birth)	App	T	G	D	Pts	Previous club	Signed
Noble, Brian	(14.2.61)	27	3	—	—	12	Queensbury ARL	14.2.78
Powell, Daio	(9.3.73)	3+1	1	—	—	4	Middleton ARL	3.7.90
Powell, Roy	(30.4.65)	40	5	1	—	22	Leeds	28.2.92
Richards, Craig	(27.1.70)	0+1	—	—	—	—	Queensbury ARL	7.10.87
Shelford, Darrall	(29.7.62)	29	10	—	—	40	New Zealand	20.7.90
Simpson, Roger	(27.8.67)	34+3	6	—	—	24	Moldgreen ARL	17.1.85
Summers, Neil	(10.10.68)	36+1	10	2	—	44	Headingley RU	4.6.90
Taylor, Mick	(11.9.61)	7+1	1	—	—	4	London C.	5.11.92
Turpin, David	(21.1.73)	1	1	—	—	4	Dudley H. ARL	13.8.91
Watson, Dave	(24.5.66)	28+1	6	—	—	24	Halifax	19.8.92
TOTALS								
29 players			148	126	8	852		

Representative appearances 1992-93
Cordle — Wales (1)
Fairbank — Britain (+1)
Fox — Britain (1, 3g)

BRADFORD NORTHERN 1992-93 MATCH ANALYSIS

Date	Com-petition	H/A	Opponent	Rlt	Score	Tries	Goals	Atten-dance	Referee
23.8.92	YC(P)	A	Castleford	W	16-10	Kebbie (2), Medley	Hobbs (2)	—	—
30.8.92	SBC	A	Hull	L	14-24	Kebbie (2)	Hobbs (3)	—	—
6.9.92	SBC	H	Leigh	W	23-10	Kebbie (2), Cordle, Marchant	Hobbs (3, 1dg)	3247	Redfearn
13.9.92	YC(1)	H	Bramley	W	34-22	Kebbie (2), Marchant (2), Shelford, Clark	Hobbs (5)	3108	Kershaw
20.9.92	SBC	A	Widnes	W	24-12	Cordle, Medley, Simpson, Marchant	Fox (3), Hobbs	—	—
23.9.92	YC(2)	H	Sheffield E.	L	8-17	Cordle	Fox, Hobbs	3333	J. Smith
27.9.92	SBC	H	Leeds	W	36-6	Cordle, Marchant, McGowan, Fox, Noble, Medley, Hamer	Hobbs (3), Fox	8659	Whitfield
4.10.92	SBC	H	Salford	W	28-26	Marchant, Anderson, Hamer, R. Powell, Medley	Fox (2), Hobbs (2)	4017	Morris
9.10.92	SBC	A	Warrington	W	22-4	Cordle (2), Shelford, R. Powell	Fox (3)	—	—
18.10.92	SBC	H	Hull K.R.	W	44-0	R. Powell (2), Anderson, McGowan, Shelford, Clark, Fairbank, Medley	Fox (4), Summers (2)	4027	Steele
1.11.92	SBC	A	St. Helens	W	35-18	McGowan (3), Fox (2), Fairbank	Fox (5, 1dg)	—	—
8.11.92	RT(1)	H	Barrow	W	70-10	McGowan (6), Simpson, Marchant, Watson, Hamer, Medley, Clark	Fox (11)	3049	Campbell
15.11.92	SBC	H	Castleford	L	6-28	Cordle	Fox	7003	Gilmour
22.11.92	SBC	H	St. Helens	L	4-16	Marchant	—	7320	J. Connolly
29.11.92	SBC	A	Castleford	L	20-30	Shelford (2), Medley, McGowan	Marchant (2)	—	—
5.12.92	RT(2)	A	Warrington	D	12-12	Anderson, Shelford	Hobbs (2)	—	—
13.12.92	SBC	A	Wakefield T.	L	16-30	Shelford, Summers, McGowan	Marchant (2)	—	—
16.12.92	RT(2) Replay	H	Warrington	W	9-6	Fairbank	Marchant (2), Hobbs (dg)	3474	J. Smith
29.12.92	RT(3)	H[1]	Widnes	W	21-10	Fox, Shelford, Marchant	Fox (4, 1dg)	5346	Ollerton
9.1.93	RT(SF)	H[1]	Castleford	W	19-12	Summers, McGowan, Hobbs	Fox (3), Hobbs (dg)	5602	Ollerton
17.1.93	SBC	A	Leigh	W	18-14	R. Powell, Summers, Watson	Mumby (3)	—	—

Date	Competition	H/A	Opponent	Rlt	Score	Tries	Goals	Attendance	Referee
23.1.93	RT(F)	N[2]	Wigan	L	8-15	McGowan	Hobbs, Mumby	(13,221)	Holdsworth
31.1.93	CC(1)	H	Workington T.	W	28-18	Marchant, McGowan, Medley, Shelford, Simpson	Hobbs (4)	3323	Atkin
4.2.93	SBC	H	Hull	W	30-14	Anderson, Heron, Summers, Turpin, Watson	Hobbs (5)	3310	R. Smith
7.2.93	SBC	A	Wigan	L	16-34	McGowan, Simpson, Watson	Hobbs (2)	—	—
14.2.93	CC(2)	A	Wakefield T.	W	20-18	Marchant, McGowan, Summers	Hobbs (4)	—	—
19.2.93	SBC	A	Salford	L	4-38	Darkes	—	—	—
3.3.93	CC(3)	A	Oldham	W	42-4	Medley (2), Anderson, Fairbank, Marchant, McGowan, Noble, Simpson	Hobbs (3), Marchant (2)	—	—
5.3.93	SBC	H	Wakefield T.	W	31-10	Medley (4), Clark	Marchant (3), Hobbs (2, 1dg)	3583	Atkin
12.3.93	SBC	A	Sheffield E.	L	12-21	Marchant (2)	Hobbs, Marchant	—	—
17.3.93	SBC	H	Wigan	W	23-16	Fairbank (2), Marchant, Medley	Hobbs (3, 1dg)	7352	Whitfield
21.3.93	SBC	H	Warrington	L	8-21	Anderson	Hobbs (2)	4095	Holdsworth
27.3.93	CC(SF)	N[2]	Wigan	L	6-15	Simpson	Hobbs	(20,085)	Holdsworth
31.3.93	SBC	H	Widnes	W	28-0	Hobbs, Marchant, Medley, Noble, Summers	Hobbs (4)	3536	J. Connolly
4.4.93	SBC	H	Sheffield E.	W	50-8	Fairbank (2), Fox, McGowan, Medley, Shelford, Summers, Taylor, Watson	Hobbs (6), R. Powell	3269	Atkin
9.4.93	SBC	H	Halifax	W	10-8	Medley, Summers	Hobbs	6518	Steele
12.4.93	SBC	A	Halifax	W	33-14	Summers (2), Fairbank, Marchant, D. Powell, Watson	Hobbs (2, 1dg), Marchant (2)	—	—
14.4.93	SBC	A	Hull K.R.	L	6-12	Anderson	McGowan	—	—
18.4.93	SBC	A	Leeds	L	12-20	Marchant (2)	Hobbs (2)	—	—
25.4.93	PT(1)	H	Castleford	L	6-19	Kebbie	Hobbs	4680	Ollerton

[1] Bradford C. FC
[2] Elland Road, Leeds

Bradford Northern record by Deryck Fox, a tally of 98 points in 24 games.

Australian centre Tony Anderson, scorer of seven tries in his farewell season at Odsal.

BRAMLEY

Ground: McLaren Field (0532-564842)
First Season: 1896-97
Nickname: Villagers
Chairman: Jeff Wine
General
  Manager: Maurice Bamford
Honours: **BBC2 Floodlit Trophy** Winners,
              1973-74

RECORDS

Match
Goals: 11 by Bernard Ward v. Doncaster,
       1 Sep 1974
Tries: 7 by Joe Sedgewick v. Normanton,
       16 Apr 1906
Points: 28 by Bernard Ward v. Doncaster,
       1 Sep 1974

Season
Goals: 138 by Steve Carroll, 1991-92
Tries: 34 by Peter Lister, 1985-86
Points: 288 by Steve Carroll, 1991-92

Career
Goals: 926 by John Wilson, 1953-64
Tries: 140 by Peter Lister, 1982-91
Points: 1,903 by John Wilson, 1953-64
Appearances: 406+4 by John Wolford, 1962-76
Highest score: 62-14 v. Dewsbury, 30 Oct 1988
Highest against: 92-7 v. Australia, 9 Nov 1921
Attendance: 12,600 v. Leeds (League),
              7 May 1947 — at Barley Mow
              7,500 v. Bradford N. (RL Cup),
              17 Feb 1972 — at McLaren Field

COACHING REGISTER
● **Since 1974-75**

Arthur Keegan	May 73 - Sep 76
Peter Fox	Sep 76 - Apr 77
*Tommy Smales	May 77 - Dec 77
Les Pearce	Jan 78 - Oct 78
Don Robinson	Oct 78 - May 79
Dave Stockwell	June 79 - June 80
Keith Hepworth	June 80 - May 82
Maurice Bamford	May 82 - Oct 83
Peter Jarvis	Oct 83 - Apr 85
Ken Loxton	Apr 85 - Dec 85
Allan Agar	Dec 85 - Apr 87
Chris Forster	June 87 - Nov 87
Tony Fisher	Nov 87 - Feb 89
Barry Johnson	Mar 89 - Dec 90
John Kear	Dec 90 - Jan 91
Roy Dickinson	Jan 91 - Apr 92
Maurice Bamford	Apr 92 -

Ex-forward

1992-93 SIGNINGS REGISTER

Signed	Player	Club From
1.7.92	Brier, Simon	Milford ARL
17.7.92	Twigg, Mike	Canberra, Aus
23.7.92	Rayne, Kevin	Doncaster
27.7.92	Roche, Michael	Drighlington ARL
29.7.92	Riddlesden, Eddie	Halifax
29.7.92	Morse, Ian	Normanton ARL
29.7.92	Hunter, Richard	Leeds Academy
29.7.92	Hester, Terry	Fitton Hill ARL
29.7.92	Brooksbank, Jason	Birkenshaw ARL
29.7.92	Smith, Damien	Drighlington ARL
13.8.92	Toole, Tim	—
27.8.92	*Shuttleworth, Greg	Huddersfield
23.9.92	Costello, Dave	Waterhead ARL
24.9.92	*Rudd, Chris	Hull K.R.
24.9.92	*Wigglesworth, Iain	Ryedale-York
13.11.92	*Bugg, Dave	Featherstone R.
13.11.92	*Sharp, Tim	Featherstone R.
20.11.92	*Keebles, Mick	Keighley C.
9.12.92	*Drummond, Des	Warrington
11.12.92	Kelly, Richard	Dewsbury
15.12.92	Stead, Richard	Normanton ARL
15.12.92	Fisher, Julian	Normanton ARL
15.12.92	Hampshire, Richard	Normanton ARL
17.12.92	Collins, Dale	Nottingham C.
11.1.93	*Whiteley, Lee	Featherstone R.
11.2.93	Tichener, Lee	Acorn ARL
15.2.93	*Willis, Chris	Nottingham C.
25.2.93	*Labourn, Terry	Dewsbury
15.3.93	Stansfield, Ivan	Blackpool G.
24.3.93	Hema, Arnold	Brighouse R. ARL

BRAMLEY 1992-93 PLAYERS' SUMMARY

	(Date of Birth)	App	T	G	D	Pts	Previous club	Signed
Agar, Andy	(27.5.73)	0+1	—	—	—	—	Pudsey ARL	4.6.91
Ashton, Ray	(26.10.60)	7+1	1	1	2	8	Hull K.R.	—
Barnett, Gary	(25.3.71)	9+1	—	—	—	—	Stanningley ARL	8.12.89
Beevers, Graham "Ben"	(14.6.61)	0+2	—	—	—	—	Batley	—
Bell, Kevin	(13.10.64)	25	14	—	—	56	Wakefield R. ARL	2.7.91
Blankley, Dean	(28.10.68)	17	6	—	—	24	Castleford	2.11.90
Brentley, Gary	(9.2.60)	2	—	—	—	—	Bradford N.	9.2.88
Brier, Simon	(10.2.68)	1	—	—	—	—	Milford ARL	1.7.92
Bugg, Dave	(28.3.69)	6	2	—	—	8	Featherstone R.	13.11.92
Carroll, Steve	(9.11.60)	9	—	18	—	36	ARL	11.7.78
Carter, Darren	(2.3.71)	1	—	—	—	—	Workington T.	—
Coen, Darren	(28.9.60)	28+1	6	—	—	24	Dewsbury	9.8.91
Collins, Dale	(20.5.68)	0+1	—	—	—	—	Nottingham C.	17.12.92
Costello, Dave	(3.11.70)	1	—	—	—	—	Waterhead ARL	23.9.92
Creasser, Dean	(18.8.70)	16	3	25	—	62	Bison S. ARL	17.12.91
Drummond, Des	(17.6.58)	4	—	—	—	—	Warrington	9.12.92
Edmondson, Steve	(25.3.66)	12+6	—	—	—	—	ARL	18.1.86
Fisher, Julian	(4.10.70)	6+4	—	—	—	—	Normanton ARL	15.12.92
Francis, Norman	(2.10.64)	13	6	—	—	24	Oldham	11.10.91
Freeman, Glen	(9.4.72)	4+2	—	—	—	—	Pudsey ARL	4.6.91
Freeman, Wayne	(30.4.74)	14+4	2	—	—	8	Pudsey ARL	27.8.91
Gee, Mark	(22.2.65)	2+1	1	—	—	4	Australia	1.7.92
Hall, Gary	(11.1.68)	3+6	—	—	—	—	Featherstone R.	30.8.91
Hampshire, Richard	(18.4.70)	5+4	—	—	—	—	Normanton ARL	15.12.90
Harker, Keith	(27.9.72)	19	3	—	—	12	Ryedale-York	4.3.91
Harwood, Dean	(8.5.71)	0+1	—	—	—	—	Eastmoor ARL	5.4.90
Hema, Arnold	(19.12.59)	2+2	—	—	—	—	Brighouse R. ARL	24.3.93
Hester, Terry	(21.1.65)	0+3	—	—	—	—	Fitton Hill ARL	29.7.92
Keebles, Mick	(24.11.65)	1+1	—	—	—	—	Keighley C.	20.11.92
Labourn, Terry	(21.8.68)	2	—	—	—	—	Dewsbury	25.2.93
Lyons, Paddy	(23.1.63)	24+1	4	—	—	16	Hunslet	12.8.91
Marson, Andy	(19.5.65)	15+5	2	—	—	8	Hunslet	12.8.91
Morse, Ian	(19.4.69)	4	—	—	—	—	Normanton ARL	27.9.92
Nui, Dave	(6.8.67)	0+1	—	—	—	—	France	13.11.92
Rayne, Kevin	(23.5.56)	25+3	1	—	—	4	Doncaster	23.7.92
Riddlesden, Eddie	(26.9.67)	25	3	—	—	12	Halifax	29.7.92
Sharp, Ron	(6.10.64)	7+1	2	5	—	18	ARL	16.3.88
Sharp, Tim	(20.2.70)	2	—	—	—	—	Featherstone R.	13.11.92
Shuttleworth, Greg	(17.7.67)	5	1	—	—	4	Huddersfield	27.8.92
Stead, Richard	(22.3.70)	9+1	—	4	—	8	Normanton ARL	15.12.92
Timson, Andy	(13.4.61)	15+1	—	—	—	—	Doncaster	12.10.90
Twigg, Mike	(12.11.67)	24+1	1	—	2	6	Australia	17.7.92
Whakarau, Sonny	(13.11.66)	23	5	—	—	20	Batley	—
Whitehead, Craig	(3.2.63)	11+2	—	—	—	—	Dewsbury	24.12.91
Whiteley, Lee	(25.3.71)	5	—	—	—	—	Featherstone R.	11.1.93
TOTALS								
45 players			63	53	4	362		

BRAMLEY 1992-93 MATCH ANALYSIS

Date	Com-petition	H/A	Opponent	Rlt	Score	Tries	Goals	Atten-dance	Referee
30.8.92	SD	A	Carlisle	L	10-18	Coen, Francis	Creasser	—	—
6.9.92	SD	H	Huddersfield	W	34-10	Bell (2), Coen, Gee, Creasser	Creasser (7)	1138	R. Smith
13.9.92	YC(1)	A	Bradford N.	L	22-34	Blankley (2), Twigg	Creasser (5)	—	—
20.9.92	SD	A	Swinton	W	11-6	Coen, Shuttleworth	Creasser, Twigg (dg)	—	—
27.9.92	SD	H	Rochdale H.	L	12-20	Riddlesden, Lyons	Creasser (2)	1035	Campbell
4.10.92	SD	H	London C.	W	30-8	Blankley (2), Bell, Coen, Creasser	Creasser (5)	705	Asquith
11.10.92	SD	H	Featherstone R.	L	4-22	Bell	—	1727	R. Connolly
18.10.92	SD	H	Oldham	L	16-23	Bell (2)	Carroll (4)	1556	Tidball
1.11.92	SD	A	Rochdale H.	L	22-29	Marson, W. Freeman, Whakarau, Riddlesden	Carroll (3)	—	—
8.11.92	RT(1)	H	Carlisle	L	12-16	Francis, Whakarau	Carroll (2)	550	Atkin
15.11.92	SD	A	Huddersfield	L	12-18	Bell (2), Whakarau	—	—	—
22.11.92	SD	H	Carlisle	D	18-18	Marson, Blankley	Carroll (5)	472	Redfearn
29.11.92	SD	A	Rochdale H.	L	22-62	Bugg (2), Bell, Blankley	Sharp (3)	—	—
13.12.92	SD	H	London C.	W	16-8	Whakarau, Bell, Coen	Sharp (2)	515	Gilmour
27.12.92	SD	H	Swinton	W	22-16	Francis (2), Coen, Whakarau	Creasser (3)	925	Morris
6.1.93	SD	A	Oldham	L	0-36	—	—	—	—
10.1.93	SD	A	Oldham	L	2-40	—	Creasser	—	—
17.1.93	SD	A	London C.	L	0-20	—	—	—	—
20.1.93	SD	H	Carlisle	W	6-2	Creasser	Carroll	377	Whitelam
24.1.93	SD	A	Swinton	L	20-35	Bell (3), Lyons	Carroll (2)	—	—
31.1.93	CC(1)	A	Hull K.R.	L	0-30	—	—	—	—
7.2.93	SD	H	Huddersfield	L	10-27	Harker (2)	Carroll	1455	Galtress
21.2.93	SD	A	London C.	L	12-20	R. Sharp, Riddlesden	Stead, Ashton (2dg)	—	—
7.3.93	SD	A	Carlisle	W	11-8	W. Freeman, Harker	Stead, Twigg (dg)	—	—
10.3.93	SD	H	Swinton	L	4-14	R. Sharp	—	525	Cross
14.3.93	SD	H	Rochdale H.	L	14-30	Francis (2), Rayne	Ashton	746	Nicholson
21.3.93	SD	A	Featherstone R.	L	0-60	—	—	—	—
4.4.93	SD	H	Oldham	L	16-32	Lyons (2), Ashton	Stead (2)	1300	J. Smith
9.4.93	SD	A	Huddersfield	L	4-20	Bell	—	—	—
12.4.93	SD	H	Featherstone R.	L	0-52	—	—	1444	Cross
18.4.93	SD	A	Featherstone R.	L	0-78	—	—	—	—

CARLISLE

Ground: Gillford Park (0228-401212)
First Season: 1981-82. Carlisle City entered the League in 1928-29 but withdrew after 10 matches
Chairman: Alan Tucker

RECORDS

Match

Goals: 10 by Barry Vickers at Nottingham C., 11 Mar 1990
Tries: 4 by Gary Peacham v. Workington T., 25 Jan 1987
Kevin Pape v. Rochdale H., 11 Feb 1987
Points: 24 by Barry Vickers at Nottingham C., 11 Mar 1990

Season

Goals: 113 by Steve Ferres, 1981-82
Tries: 25 by Mick Morgan, 1981-82
Gary Peacham, 1984-85
Points: 242 by Steve Ferres, 1981-82

Career

Goals: 352 by Barry Vickers, 1988-92
Tries: 160 by Kevin Pape, 1984-
Points: 733 by Barry Vickers, 1988-92
Appearances: 281 by Kevin Pape, 1984-
Highest score: 60-0 v. Nottingham C., 11 Mar 1990
Highest against: 112-0 at St. Helens, 14 Sep 1986
Attendance: 5,903 v. Workington T. (League), 6 Sep 1981 — at Brunton Park
1,874 v. Widnes (Regal Trophy), 24 Nov 1991 — at Gillford Park

COACHING REGISTER
● **Since formation in 1981**

Allan Agar	May 81 - June 82
Mick Morgan	July 82 - Feb 83
John Atkinson	Feb 83 - Feb 86
Alan Kellett	Feb 86 - May 86
Roy Lester	June 86 - Nov 88
Tommy Dawes	Dec 88 - Jan 90
Cameron Bell	Feb 90 -

1992-93 SIGNINGS REGISTER

Signed	Player	Club From
27.8.92	Fox, Kevin	Salford
27.8.92	*Wassell, Colin	Barrow
18.9.92	*Archer, Darren	Barrow

28.9.92	Harris, Grant	Hawick RU
1.10.92	Clarke, Troy	Canterbury, Aus
11.12.92	*Richardson, Willie	Whitehaven
29.12.92	*Vannett, Paul	Hull K.R.
31.12.92	Bethwaite, Kevin	Aspatria RU
7.1.93	Hibberd, Craig	Swinton
7.1.93	Knox, Paul	Distington ARL
9.1.93	Riley, Steve	Carlisle ARL
9.1.93	Tait, Alan	Carlisle RU
9.1.93	Thomas, Phil	—
9.1.93	Wilkinson, Les	Aspatria H. ARL
4.2.93	Montford, Craig	Vale of Lune RU
13.2.93	Burns, William	Whitehaven
17.2.93	*Iti, Brett	Bradford N.
19.2.93	*Sanders, Kevin	Whitehaven
5.5.93	Roy, Jeff	Heysham ARL

CARLISLE 1992-93 PLAYERS' SUMMARY

	(Date of Birth)	App	T	G	D	Pts	Previous club	Signed
Archer, Darren	(3.3.71)	1	—	—	—	—	Barrow	18.9.92
Armstrong, Derek	(2.11.66)	10+2	—	—	—	—	Hawick RU	20.4.92
Armstrong, Ian	(13.3.70)	23+1	—	—	—	—	Cockermouth RU	8.1.90
Bethwaite, Kevin	(11.4.68)	13+2	4	25	—	66	Aspatria RU	31.12.92
Brierley, Steve	(30.3.61)	19+2	1	—	—	4	ARL	22.8.83
Burns, William	(4.10.71)	0+2	—	—	—	—	Whitehaven	13.2.93
Charlton, Gary	(5.3.67)	26	2	—	—	8	Whitehaven	27.11.90
Clarke, Troy	(19.4.67)	12	2	13	—	34	Australia	1.10.92
Doyle, Mark	(17.10.65)	1+1	1	—	—	4	Union ARL	9.4.84
Fox, Kevin	(16.2.69)	29	5	—	—	20	Salford	27.8.92
Friend, Clayton	(22.3.62)	2	—	—	—	—	Australia	23.8.90
Gaffney, Mike	(21.6.60)	0+1	—	—	—	—	Whitehaven	5.9.92
Georgallis, Steve	(17.6.68)	15	9	—	—	36	Australia	28.9.92
Graham, George	(19.1.66)	21	4	—	—	16	Stirling C. RU	22.10.91
Harris, Grant	(23.12.67)	15+3	—	—	—	—	Hawick RU	28.9.92
Hibberd, Craig	(20.2.67)	17+1	4	2	2	22	Swinton	7.1.93
Iti, Brett	(28.3.65)	5	3	—	—	12	Bradford N.	17.2.93
Kavanagh, Mike	(5.2.71)	1+1	1	—	—	4	Barrow	4.12.89
Knox, Simon	(14.10.72)	32	8	—	—	32	Hensingham ARL	1.12.91
Lunt, Peter	(28.10.63)	10+4	—	—	—	—	Aspatria H. ARL	6.8.90
Manning, Phil	(23.2.62)	7+5	4	7	—	30	Ayr RU	13.8.90
Montford, Craig	(18.11.70)	5+3	—	—	—	—	Vale of Lune RU	4.2.93
Murdock, Gary	(6.1.68)	21+1	4	—	—	16	ARL	15.6.87
Murdock, Paul	(16.4.65)	0+4	—	—	—	—	Ellenborough ARL	16.12.87
Pape, Kevin	(17.12.61)	29	19	—	—	76	Glasson R. ARL	29.7.84
Richardson, Willie	(6.10.60)	7+1	1	5	—	14	Whitehaven	11.12.92
Robinson, Paul	(19.1.69)	4+3	—	—	—	—	ARL	14.7.88
Rossen, Geoff		1	—	—	—	—	—	—
Roy, Jeff	(7.10.69)	2	1	—	—	4	Heysham ARL	5.5.93
Scott, Tony	(17.5.62)	22+3	—	—	—	—	Horse & Farrier ARL	9.4.84
Smith, David	(11.4.67)	7+1	4	17	—	50	Australia	2.10.92

(Continued)

39

	(Date of Birth)	App	T	G	D	Pts	Previous club	Signed
Southwell, Eddie..........(12.1.67)......		10+8	1	—	—	4	—	9.5.88
Spee, Milt Van Der		0+1	—	—	—	—	South Africa	—
Tait, Alan...................(20.9.67)......		0+1	—	—	—	—	Carlisle RU	9.1.93
Thomas, Phil..............(6.12.67)......		0+2	—	—	—	—	ARL	9.1.93
Thomason, Malcolm ....(24.9.64)......		31	2	—	—	8	Broughton ARL	30.9.85
Vannett, Paul ....(19.10.62).....		5	—	—	—	—	Hull K.R.	29.12.92
Wassell, Colin..............(29.9.70)......		7	—	—	—	—	Barrow	27.8.92
Wilkinson, Les ....(9.4.70)........		0+4	—	—	—	—	Aspatria H. ARL	9.1.93
Williams, Barry ....(15.5.71)......		6+5	7	3	—	34	Broughton ARL	6.9.89
TOTALS								
40 players			87	72	2	494		

Representative appearances 1992-93
Pape — Cumbria (1); G. Murdock — Cumbria (1); Williams — Cumbria (1)

CARLISLE 1992-93 MATCH ANALYSIS

Date	Com-petition	H/A	Opponent	Rlt	Score	Tries	Goals	Atten-dance	Referee
30.8.92	SD	H	Bramley	W	18-10	Kavanagh, Doyle, Pape	Manning (2), Williams	502	Redfearn
6.9.92	SD	A	Oldham	L	14-38	Williams (2), Pape	Manning	—	—
13.9.92	LC(1)	A	Widnes	L	8-52	Pape, Williams	—	—	—
20.9.92	SD	H	London C.	L	14-46	Manning, Williams	Manning (2), Williams	493	Asquith
27.9.92	SD	A	Featherstone R.	L	10-30	Pape, Georgallis	Williams	—	—
4.10.92	SD	H	Rochdale H.	W	24-12	Williams, Knox, Graham, Fox	Smith (3), Clarke	508	Cross
15.10.92	SD	A	Huddersfield	W	24-4	Georgallis (2), Knox, Smith	Smith (4)	—	—
1.11.92	SD	A	London C.	D	18-18	Charlton, Pape, Graham	Smith (3)	—	—
8.11.92	RT(1)	A	Bramley	W	16-12	Smith, Georgallis, Pape	Smith (2)	—	—
15.11.92	SD	H	Oldham	L	20-25	Pape, Georgallis, Fox, Smith	Smith, Clarke	983	Holdsworth
22.11.92	SD	A	Bramley	D	18-18	Smith, Thomason, Georgallis, Pape	Smith	—	—
29.11.92	SD	H	Featherstone R.	L	14-38	G. Murdock, Thomason	Smith (3)	1068	Steele
6.12.92	RT(2)	A	Castleford	L	0-54	—	—	—	—
13.12.92	SD	A	Rochdale H.	L	18-26	Knox (2), Georgallis	Clarke (3)	—	—
10.1.93	SD	H	Rochdale H.	W	16-12	Richardson, Bethwaite, Pape	Clarke (2)	508	Campbell
14.1.93	SD	A	Huddersfield	L	24-36	Clarke (2), Hibberd, Georgallis, Pape	Clarke (2)	—	—
17.1.93	SD	H	Oldham	L	21-32	Pape (2), Georgallis	Bethwaite (2), Manning (2), Hibberd (dg)	885	Morris
20.1.93	SD	A	Bramley	L	2-6		Hibberd	—	—
24.1.93	SD	H	Huddersfield	L	12-28	Graham, Hibberd	Clarke (2)	763	Volante
31.1.93	CC(1)	A	Halifax	L	16-66	Fox, Pape, Roy	Clarke (2)	—	—
7.2.93	SD	H	London C.	L	14-28	Graham, Knox	Bethwaite (3)	301	Cross
14.2.93	SD	H	Swinton	W	26-22	G. Murdock (3), Fox, Williams	Bethwaite (3)	340	Campbell
21.2.93	SD	A	Oldham	L	16-56	Iti (2)	Bethwaite (4)	—	—
28.2.93	SD	A	Featherstone R.	L	10-26	Bethwaite, Iti	Bethwaite	—	—
7.3.93	SD	H	Bramley	L	8-11	Knox	Richardson (2)	502	Crashley
14.3.93	SD	A	Swinton	W	19-18	Knox (2), Pape	Richardson (3), Hibberd (dg)	—	—
21.3.93	SD	H	Huddersfield	L	16-29	Brierley, Pape, Williams	Bethwaite (2)	640	Kershaw
28.3.93	SD	A	London C.	L	8-30	Pape	Bethwaite (2)	—	—
4.4.93	SD	H	Featherstone R.	D	30-30	Hibberd (2), Manning (2), Southwell	Bethwaite (4), Hibberd	913	Galtress
9.4.93	SD	A	Swinton	L	12-23	Bethwaite, Manning	Bethwaite (2)	—	—
12.4.93	SD	H	Swinton	L	16-19	Pape (2), Charlton, Fox	—	521	Asquith
18.4.93	SD	A	Rochdale H.	L	12-50	Bethwaite, Pape	Bethwaite (2)	—	—

CASTLEFORD

Ground: Wheldon Road (0977-552674)
First Season: 1926-27. There was also a
Castleford team from 1896-97 to
1905-06 inclusive
Nickname: Tigers
Chairman: Eddie Ashton
Secretary: Denise Cackett
Honours: **Championship** Beaten finalists,
1938-39, 1968-69
Challenge Cup Winners, 1934-35,
1968-69, 1969-70, 1985-86
Beaten finalists, 1991-92
Regal Trophy Winners, 1976-77
Premiership Beaten finalists,
1983-84
Yorkshire Cup Winners, 1977-78,
1981-82, 1986-87, 1990-91, 1991-92
Beaten finalists, 1948-49, 1950-51,
1968-69, 1971-72, 1983-84,
1985-86, 1987-88, 1988-89
Yorkshire League Winners,
1932-33, 1938-39, 1964-65
Eastern Division Championship
Beaten finalists, 1963-64
Charity Shield Beaten finalists,
1986-87
BBC2 Floodlit Trophy Winners,
1965-66, 1966-67, 1967-68, 1976-77

RECORDS

Match
Goals: 17 by Geoff "Sammy" Lloyd v. Millom,
16 Sep 1973
Tries: 5 by Derek Foster v. Hunslet,
10 Nov 1972
John Joyner v. Millom, 16 Sep 1973
Steve Fenton v. Dewsbury,
27 Jan 1978
Ian French v. Hunslet, 9 Feb 1986
St. John Ellis at Whitehaven,
10 Dec 1989
Points: 43 by Geoff "Sammy" Lloyd v. Millom,
16 Sep 1973

Season
Goals: 158 by Geoff "Sammy" Lloyd, 1976-77
Tries: 36 by Keith Howe, 1963-64
Points: 334 by Bob Beardmore, 1983-84

Career
Goals: 875 by Albert Lunn, 1951-63
Tries: 206 by Alan Hardisty, 1958-71
Points: 1,870 by Albert Lunn, 1951-63
Appearances: 585+28 by John Joyner, 1973-92
Highest score: 94-12 v. Huddersfield,
18 Sep 1988
Highest against: 62-12 at St. Helens,
16 Apr 1986
Attendance: 25,449 v. Hunslet (RL Cup),
9 Mar 1935

COACHING REGISTER
● **Since 1974-75**

Dave Cox	Apr 74 - Nov 74
*Malcolm Reilly	Dec 74 - May 87
Dave Sampson	May 87 - Apr 88
Darryl Van de Velde	July 88 - May 93
John Joyner	May 93 -

*Shortly after his appointment Reilly returned
to Australia to fulfil his contract before
resuming at Castleford early the next season.*

GREAT BRITAIN REGISTER
(28 players)

Arthur Atkinson	(11)	1929-36
Kevin Beardmore	(13+1)	1984-90
Bill Bryant	(4+1)	1964-67
Lee Crooks	(4)	1992
Jim Croston	(1)	1937
Bernard Cunniffe	(1)	1937
Billy Davies	(1)	1933
Derek Edwards	(3+2)	1968-71
St. John Ellis	(+2)	1991
Keith England	(6+5)	1987-91
Mike Ford	(+2)	1993
Alan Hardisty	(12)	1964-70
Dennis Hartley	(9)	1968-70
Keith Hepworth	(11)	1967-70
Shaun Irwin	(+4)	1990
John Joyner	(14+2)	1978-84
Brian Lockwood	(7)	1972-74
Tony Marchant	(3)	1986
Roger Millward	(1)	1966
Steve Norton	(2+1)	1974

David Plange	(1)	1988
Malcolm Reilly	(9)	1970
Peter Small	(1)	1962
Graham Steadman	(7+1)	1990-92
Gary Stephens	(5)	1979
Doug Walton	(1)	1965
Johnny Ward	(3)	1963-64
Kevin Ward	(14)	1984-89

1992-93 SIGNINGS REGISTER

Signed	Player	Club From
31.7.92	Williams, Dean	Ryedale-York
18.9.92	Darley, Paul	Kippax W. ARL
2.10.92	Coyne, Peter	St. George, Aus
22.10.92	Leake, Chance	Jubilee ARL
6.2.93	Bloem, Jamie	Cape Town C., SA
13.2.93	Tonks, Ian	Redhill ARL

CASTLEFORD 1992-93 PLAYERS' SUMMARY

	(Date of Birth)	App	T	G	D	Pts	Previous club	Signed
Anderson, Grant	(21.2.69)	17+12	4	—	—	16	Castleford Colts	23.2.87
Battye, Neil	(11.8.63)	1+1	—	—	—	—	Castleford Colts	3.2.82
Blackmore, Richard	(2.7.69)	21	11	—	—	44	New Zealand	17.7.91
Bloem, Jamie	(26.5.71)	0+1	1	—	—	4	South Africa	6.12.92
Boothroyd, Giles	(17.3.69)	4+3	2	—	—	8	Lock Lane ARL	8.4.87
Coyne, Peter	(28.10.64)	29	2	1	—	10	Australia	2.10.92
Crooks, Lee	(18.9.63)	34	2	112	—	232	Leeds	8.1.90
Ellis, St. John	(3.10.64)	36	11	—	—	44	York	15.9.89
England, Keith	(27.2.64)	10+9	1	—	—	4	Castleford Colts	22.6.81
Fisher, Andy	(17.11.67)	14+2	—	—	—	—	Featherstone R.	11.1.93
Fletcher, Paul	(26.1.62)	0+3	—	—	—	—	Hull	12.10.90
Ford, Mike	(18.11.65)	34	21	—	—	84	Oldham	24.6.91
Hay, Andy	(5.11.73)	0+7	1	—	—	4	Redhill ARL	12.11.90
Irwin, Shaun	(8.12.68)	7+1	1	—	—	4	Redhill ARL	13.2.86
Ketteridge, Martin	(2.10.64)	23+7	1	—	—	4	Moorends ARL	22.6.83
Leake, Chance	(21.5.70)	0+1	—	—	—	—	Jubilee ARL	22.10.92
Middleton, Simon	(2.2.66)	29	19	4	—	84	Knottingley RU	20.4.91
Morrison, Tony	(17.12.65)	34	6	—	—	24	Swinton	27.5.92
Nelson, David	(8.9.62)	9+2	1	—	—	4	Sheffield E.	27.8.91
Nikau, Tawera	(1.1.67)	36	2	—	—	8	Ryedale-York	19.8.91
Roebuck, Neil	(4.10.69)	6	1	—	—	4	Bradford N.	15.12.89
Sampson, Dean	(27.6.67)	21+13	2	—	—	8	Stanley R. ARL	1.9.86
Smith, Chris	(31.10.75)	2	—	—	—	—	Redhill ARL	28.1.92
Smith, Tony	(16.7.70)	36	24	—	—	96	Wheldale ARL	25.1.88
Southernwood, Graham	(5.11.71)	17	1	—	1	5	Redhill ARL	14.11.88
Steadman, Graham	(8.12.61)	24+1	9	13	1	63	Featherstone R.	23.8.89
Sykes, Nathan	(8.9.74)	0+5	—	—	—	—	Moldgreen ARL	14.9.91
Watson, Chris	(9.9.67)	13	1	—	—	4	Cutsyke ARL	15.11.91
Williams, Dean	(13.8.64)	0+1	—	—	—	—	Ryedale-York	31.7.92
Wray, Jon	(19.5.70)	11	1	—	—	4	Morley RU	24.10.90
TOTALS								
30 players			125	130	2	762		

Representative appearances 1992-93
Crooks — England (1, 1t, 4g)
Ford — Britain (+2, 2t); England (1)

CASTLEFORD 1992-93 MATCH ANALYSIS

Date	Competition	H/A	Opponent	Rlt	Score	Tries	Goals	Attendance	Referee
23.8.92	YC(P)	H	Bradford N.	L	10-16	Middleton, Ford	Crooks	4988	Volante
30.8.92	SBC	A	Widnes	L	6-16	Middleton	Crooks	–	–
6.9.92	SBC	H	Salford	L	20-24	T. Smith (2), Ford	Crooks (4)	4500	J. Connolly
20.9.92	SBC	A	Leigh	W	38-0	Ford (2), Steadman, Nikau, Ellis, England	Steadman (7)	–	–
27.9.92	SBC	H	Hull	W	34-6	Middleton, Irwin, T. Smith, Boothroyd, Ford	Crooks (7)	5473	J. Smith
4.10.92	SBC	A	Sheffield E.	L	16-20	Ellis, Middleton, Ford	Coyne, Middleton	–	–
11.10.92	SBC	H	Widnes	W	26-14	Middleton (2), Roebuck, Ellis	Crooks (5)	6036	Steele
16.10.92	SBC	A	Salford	L	18-21	Ellis (2), Ford	Crooks (3)	–	–
1.11.92	SBC	H	Leigh	W	46-12	Blackmore (2), Middleton (2), Coyne, Ellis, Ford, T. Smith, Anderson	Crooks (3), Middleton (2)	3913	Cross
8.11.92	RT(1)	A	Oldham	W	40-22	Blackmore (2), Middleton (2), Watson, Ford, Nelson	Crooks (6)	–	–
15.11.92	SBC	A	Bradford N.	W	28-6	T. Smith (2), Blackmore, Sampson, Morrison	Crooks (4)	–	–
22.11.92	SBC	A	Hull K.R.	W	8-2	T. Smith	Crooks (2)	–	–
29.11.92	SBC	H	Bradford N.	W	30-20	T. Smith (2), Ellis, Middleton	Crooks (6), Middleton	5866	Kershaw
6.12.92	RT(2)	H	Carlisle	W	54-0	Blackmore (3), T. Smith (2), Wray, Ellis, Ketteridge, Bloem	Crooks (9)	2539	Tidball
11.12.92	SBC	H	St. Helens	W	16-6	Middleton, T. Smith	Crooks (4)	5203	Ollerton
19.12.92	RT(3)	A	St. Helens	W	12-8	Ellis, T. Smith	Crooks (2)	–	–
26.12.92	SBC	A	Leeds	L	12-40	Ford, Sampson	Crooks (2)	–	–
1.1.93	SBC	H	Wakefield T.	D	22-22	Blackmore (2), T. Smith (2)	Crooks (3)	7864	J. Smith
9.1.93	RT(SF)	A[1]	Bradford N.	L	12-19	T. Smith, Middleton	Crooks (2)	–	–
15.1.93	SBC	H	Warrington	L	10-13	Blackmore	Crooks (3)	3639	Gilmour
24.1.93	SBC	A	Hull	W	14-2	Coyne, Middleton, Steadman	Crooks	–	–
30.1.93	CC(1)	A	Warrington	W	21-6	Ford, Middleton, Steadman	Crooks (4), Southernwood (dg)	–	–
7.2.93	SBC	H	Sheffield E.	W	14-8	Ford, Middleton, Steadman	Crooks	4670	Atkin
14.2.93	CC(2)	H	Hunslet	W	34-16	Morrison (2), T. Smith (2), Steadman (2)	Crooks (5)	3719	Cummings
21.2.93	SBC	A	Warrington	L	18-23	Anderson, Boothroyd, Ford	Crooks (3)	–	–
27.2.93	CC(3)	A	Leeds	L	8-12	Ford	Crooks (2)	–	–
3.3.93	SBC	A	St. Helens	L	20-24	Anderson, Ford, Middleton, Steadman	Steadman (2)	–	–
7.3.93	SBC	A	Halifax	L	16-28	T. Smith, Southernwood	Crooks (4)	–	–
21.3.93	SBC	H	Hull K.R.	W	36-18	Ellis, Ford, Morrison, Nikau, T. Smith, Steadman	Crooks (6)	3908	Campbell
28.3.93	SBC	H	Halifax	W	32-16	Ford (2), Middleton, Morrison, Ellis	Crooks (6)	6119	Cummings
4.4.93	SBC	H	Wigan	W	26-17	Anderson, Crooks, T. Smith, Steadman	Steadman (3), Crooks (2)	8803	Steele
9.4.93	SBC	A	Wakefield T.	W	14-8	Crooks, Hay	Crooks (3)	–	–
12.4.93	SBC	H	Leeds	L	6-10	Middleton	Crooks	7557	Ollerton
16.4.93	SBC	A	Wigan	L	18-25	Ford (2), Morrison	Crooks (3)	–	–
25.4.93	PT(1)	A	Bradford N.	W	19-6	T. Smith (2), Ford	Crooks (3), Steadman (dg)	–	–
7.5.93	PT(SF)	A	Wigan	L	8-25	T. Smith	Crooks, Steadman	–	–

A[1] Bradford C. FC

CHORLEY BOROUGH

Ground: Grundy Hill, Horwich
(0204-696908)
First Season: 1989-90 as Chorley. Officially
became Chorley Borough in
1991-92. Not to be confused
with the Chorley Borough
who succeeded Springfield/
Blackpool Borough in 1988-89.
Demoted to the National Conference
for 1993-94
Chairman: Lindsay Hoyle
Secretary: Brian Green

RECORDS

Match
Goals: 9 by Mike Smith v. Nottingham C.,
28 Mar 1993
Tries: No player has scored more than 3
Points: 17 by Mike Smith v. Nottingham C.,
28 Mar 1993

Season
Goals: 73 by Mike Smith, 1989-90
Tries: 10 by David Bacon, 1989-90
Joe Walsh, 1992-93
Points: 142 by Mike Smith, 1989-90

Career
Goals: 236 by Mike Smith, 1989-
Tries: No player has scored 20 or more
Points: 484 by Mike Smith, 1989-
Appearances: 109+2 by Mike Smith, 1989-

Highest score: 57-20 v. Nottingham C.,
28 Mar 1993
Highest against: 78-6 at Keighley C.,
21 Feb 1993
Attendance: 2,851 v. Oldham (League),
21 Jan 1990 — at Victory Park
5,026 v. Wigan (Lancs Cup),
15 Sep 1989 — at Leigh

COACHING REGISTER
● **Since formation in 1989**

Stan Gittins	June 89 - Apr 90
Bob Eccles	May 90 - Sep 91
John Taylor	Sep 91 - Jan 93
Carl Briscoe	Jan 93 -

1992-93 SIGNINGS REGISTER

Signed	Player	Club From
1.7.92	Painter, Trevor	Wigan St. Pat's ARL
16.8.92	Walsh, Joe	Salford
21.8.92	Robinson, Jeff	Leigh Miners ARL
21.8.92	Sedgewick, Peter	Huddersfield
21.8.92	Maskery, Mark	Huddersfield
26.8.92	Whiteside, Shaun	Wigan St. Pat's ARL
29.8.92	Duckworth, Simon	Adlington ARL
9.10.92	Benson, Karl	Northcote Tigers, NZ
9.10.92	Watene, Vaughan	Northcote Tigers, NZ
18.11.92	Taylor, John	Salford
27.11.92	Kohlhase, Wayne	Workington T.
25.12.92	Marsh, Ian	Blackpool G.
10.1.93	Tollitt, Andy	Rose Bridge ARL
26.3.93	*Burke, Tony	Leigh
26.3.93	*Dickinson, Andy	Dewsbury
26.3.93	*Garforth, David	Dewsbury

CHORLEY BOROUGH 1992-93 PLAYERS' SUMMARY

	(Date of Birth)	App	T	G	D	Pts	Previous club	Signed
Ashcroft, Steve	(29.12.69)	26	4	—	—	16	Leigh M. ARL	8.11.91
Benson, Karl	(4.7.71)	14+1	2	—	—	8	New Zealand	9.10.92
Bimson, Jeff	(15.1.67)	3	—	—	—	—	Wigan St. P. ARL	16.7.87
Briscoe, Carl	(22.2.62)	17+2	1	—	—	4	Blackpool	31.7.82
Carney, John	(7.11.68)	3	—	—	—	—	Wigan St. P. ARL	17.11.91
Clayton, Richard	(24.2.70)	20+1	7	—	—	28	Wigan St. J. ARL	3.10.91
Crook, Lee	(15.2.71)	11+4	3	—	—	12	Wigan St. P. ARL	12.9.91
Dickinson, Andy	(26.8.61)	2	—	—	—	—	Dewsbury	26.3.93
Duckworth, Simon	(7.11.67)	4	1	—	—	4	Adlington ARL	29.8.92
Edwards, Mark	(22.2.64)	22+2	—	—	—	—	Rose Bridge ARL	10.8.89
Ellis, John	(12.11.66)	2	—	—	—	—	Wigan St. P. ARL	16.8.87

	(Date of Birth)	App	T	G	D	Pts	Previous club	Signed
Evans, Andy	(19.4.70)	2+1	1	—	—	4	Adlington ARL	3.9.91
Fletcher, Darren	(25.10.73)	10+6	1	—	—	4	Wigan St. P. ARL	27.11.91
Garforth, David	(24.11.66)	0+2	—	—	—	—	Dewsbury	26.3.93
Hodson, Tony		5+2	1	—	—	4	Warrington	10.8.87
Knight, Mark	(10.10.65)	3+1	1	—	—	4	Warrington	22.8.89
Kohlhase, Wayne	(12.10.67)	13	3	—	—	12	Workington T.	27.11.92
McTigue, Mike	(13.12.59)	26	4	—	—	16	Huddersfield	5.1.92
Marsh, Ian	(15.4.66)	13	3	—	—	12	Blackpool G.	25.12.92
Marsh, Peter	(27.1.65)	3	—	—	—	—	Leigh M. ARL	11.3.92
Maskery, Mark	(4.10.66)	24	—	—	—	—	Huddersfield	21.8.92
Meadows, Kevin	(27.2.61)	8	1	—	—	4	Trafford B.	24.8.90
Painter, Trevor	(10.8.71)	14	7	—	—	28	Wigan St. P. ARL	1.7.92
Price, Billy	(6.1.61)	14+9	2	2	2	14	Blackpool	31.7.89
Robinson, Jeff	(9.9.71)	5+3	1	—	—	4	Leigh M. ARL	21.8.92
Sedgewick, Peter	(31.10.66)	14+2	3	—	—	12	Huddersfield	21.8.92
Smith, Mike	(24.11.67)	25	2	49	6	112	Springfield	31.7.89
Tollitt, Andy	(17.2.67)	1+4	—	—	—	—	Rose Bridge ARL	10.1.93
Walsh, Joe	(8.1.68)	24	10	—	—	40	Salford	16.8.92
Watene, Vaughan	(13.10.70)	4+7	—	—	—	—	New Zealand	9.10.92
Whiteside, Shaun	(25.9.70)	19+5	—	—	—	—	Wigan St. P. ARL	26.8.92
TOTALS								
31 players			58	51	8	342		

CHORLEY BOROUGH 1992-93 MATCH ANALYSIS

Date	Com-petition	H/A	Opponent	Rlt	Score	Tries	Goals	Atten-dance	Referee
30.8.92	TD	H	Ryedale-York	L	13-23	Knight, Painter	Smith (2), Price (dg)	483	Nicholson
6.9.92	TD	A	Workington T.	L	8-54	Painter	Smith (2)	—	—
13.9.92	LC(1)	A	Leigh	L	9-50	Evans	Smith (2, 1dg)	—	—
20.9.92	TD	H	Blackpool G.	L	16-28	Hodson, Robinson, Smith	Smith (2)	518	Cross
27.9.92	TD	A	Nottingham C.	W	18-15	Duckworth, Ashcroft, Clayton, McTigue	Smith	—	—
4.10.92	TD	H	Keighley C.	L	12-54	Clayton, Walsh	Smith (2)	534	Campbell
11.10.92	TD	A	Barrow	L	4-50	Walsh	—	—	—
18.10.92	TD	H	Dewsbury	L	8-18	Sedgewick, Ashcroft	—	522	Carter
27.10.92	RT(P)	H	Sheffield E.	L	10-38	Sedgewick, Briscoe	Smith	368	Galtress
1.11.92	TD	A	Ryedale-York	L	6-36	McTigue	Smith	—	—
15.11.92	TD	H	Hunslet	L	14-18	Walsh, Painter	Smith (3)	317	Atkin
29.11.92	TD	A	Workington T.	L	12-29	Ashcroft, Walsh	Smith (2)	405	Volante
13.12.92	TD	H	Batley	L	16-30	Walsh, Benson, Clayton	Smith (2)	385	Asquith
16.12.92	TD	A	Blackpool G.	W	13-8	Clayton, Ashcroft	Smith (2, 1dg)	—	—
26.12.92	TD	A	Hunslet	L	13-21	Sedgewick, Kohlhase	Price (2, 1dg)	—	—
6.1.93	TD	A	Whitehaven	L	12-42	Clayton, Kohlhase	Smith (2)	—	—
10.1.93	TD	A	Dewsbury	L	0-58	—	—	—	—
17.1.93	TD	H	Doncaster	L	14-34	Kohlhase, Price	Smith (3)	305	Whitelam
24.1.93	TD	A	Batley	L	7-52	Fletcher	Smith (1, 1dg)	—	—
31.1.93	CC(1)	H	Batley	L	6-20	I. Marsh	Smith	475	Asquith
7.2.93	TD	H	Barrow	W	22-20	I. Marsh (2), Benson, Walsh	Smith (3)	222	Redfearn
21.2.93	TD	A	Keighley C.	L	6-78	Crook	Smith	—	—
7.3.93	TD	A	Doncaster	L	12-31	Painter, Walsh	Smith (2)	—	—
14.3.93	TD	H	Whitehaven	L	8-36	Crook, Walsh	—	263	Morris
21.3.93	TD	A	Highfield	L	8-18	Painter	Smith (2)	—	—
28.3.93	TD	H	Nottingham C.	W	57-20	McTigue (2), Painter (2), Walsh (2), Clayton, Crook, Meadows, Price	Smith (8, 1dg)	485	Crashley
4.4.93	TD	H	Highfield	W	18-8	Clayton, Smith	Smith (4, 2dg)	767	Morris

DEWSBURY

Ground: Mount Pleasant, Batley (0924-472208)
First Season: 1901-02
Chairman: Rodney Hardcastle
Secretary: Ian Clough
Honours: **Championship** Winners, 1972-73
Beaten finalists, 1946-47
War Emergency League
Winners, 1941-42 (1942-43 won
final but championship declared
null and void because Dewsbury
played an ineligible player.)
Beaten finalists, 1943-44
Division Two Champions, 1904-05
Challenge Cup Winners, 1911-12,
1942-43
Beaten finalists, 1928-29
Yorkshire Cup Winners, 1925-26,
1927-28, 1942-43
Beaten finalists, 1918-19, 1921-22,
1940-41, 1972-73
Yorkshire League Winners, 1946-47
BBC2 Floodlit Trophy Beaten
finalists, 1975-76

Great Britain Academy threequarter Darren Rogers, scorer
of 19 tries in 27 appearances for Dewsbury in 1992-93.

Highest score: 90-5 at Blackpool G., 4 Apr 1993
Highest against: 82-0 at Widnes, 30 Nov 1986
Attendance: 26,584 v. Halifax (Yorks Cup),
30 Oct 1920 — at Crown Flatt

COACHING REGISTER
● **Since 1974-75**

Maurice Bamford	June 74 - Oct 74
Alan Hardisty	Oct 74 - June 75
Dave Cox	June 75 - July 77
Ron Hill	July 77 - Dec 77
Lewis Jones	Dec 77 - Apr 78
Jeff Grayshon	May 78 - Oct 78
Alan Lockwood	Oct 78 - Oct 80
Bernard Watson	Oct 80 - Oct 82
Ray Abbey	Nov 82 - Apr 83
*Tommy Smales	May 83 - Feb 84
Jack Addy	Feb 84 - Jan 87
Dave Busfield	Jan 87 - Apr 87
Terry Crook	Apr 87 - Dec 88
Maurice Bamford	Dec 88 - Dec 90
Jack Addy	Dec 90 -

Ex-forward

RECORDS

Match
Goals: 13 by Greg Pearce at Blackpool G.,
4 Apr 1993
Tries: 8 by Dai Thomas v. Liverpool C.,
13 Apr 1907
Points: 29 by Joe Lyman v. Hull,
22 Apr 1919

Season
Goals: 145 by Nigel Stephenson, 1972-73
Tries: 40 by Dai Thomas, 1906-07
Points: 368 by Nigel Stephenson, 1972-73

Career
Goals: 863 by Nigel Stephenson, 1967-78 &
1984-86
Tries: 144 by Joe Lyman, 1913-31
Points: 2,082 by Nigel Stephenson, 1967-78 &
1984-86
Appearances: 454 by Joe Lyman, 1913-31

GREAT BRITAIN REGISTER
(6 players)

Alan Bates	(2+2)	1974
Frank Gallagher	(4)	1920-21
Jim Ledgard	(2)	1947
Roy Pollard	(1)	1950
Mick Stephenson	(5+1)	1971-72
Harry Street	(4)	1950

1992-93 SIGNINGS REGISTER

Signed	Player	Club From
1.6.92	Cornforth, Phil	Bradford N.
1.6.92	Williams, Shane	Dewsbury C. ARL
19.8.92	Parker, Russ	Redhill ARL
2.10.92	★Pearce, Greg	Halifax
6.11.92	McRae, Ian	Wigan
6.12.92	Lee, David	Crofton ARL
1.3.93	Woodcock, Robert	Eastmoor ARL

DEWSBURY 1992-93 PLAYERS' SUMMARY

	(Date of Birth)	App	T	G	D	Pts	Previous club	Signed
Bailey, Dennis	(15.2.66)	30	18	—	—	72	Queensbury ARL	12.12.85
Bell, Glen	(23.6.65)	25+2	4	—	—	16	New Zealand	10.8.91
Charles, Marquis	(5.12.66)	8+1	3	—	—	12	Bramley	24.12.91
Cocks, Gary	(7.6.61)	24	5	—	—	20	Wakefield T.	7.9.87
Collins, Darren	(7.3.73)	5+1	3	—	—	12	Clayton ARL	26.5.92
Cooper, Andrew	(6.10.65)	0+2	—	—	—	—	Leeds Colts	10.4.85
Cornforth, Phil	(16.11.69)	10+1	4	—	—	16	Bradford N.	1.6.92
Coughlan, Glen	(3.2.63)	14+8	8	—	—	32	Dewsbury M. ARL	10.12.89
Delaney, Paul	(18.10.68)	29	13	—	—	52	Leeds	21.5.91
Fleary, Darren	(2.12.72)	4+8	1	—	—	4	Moldgreen ARL	19.9.91
Graham, Nathan	(23.11.71)	31	13	32	—	116	Dewsbury Colts	23.11.89
Haigh, Mark	(24.1.70)	30+1	2	—	—	8	Hanging Heaton ARL	26.7.89
Hughes, Paul	(25.6.63)	14+6	5	—	—	20	Featherstone R.	18.2.91
James, Sean	(15.4.72)	1	—	—	—	—	Moldgreen ARL	19.9.91
Kelly, Neil	(10.5.62)	28+1	4	—	—	16	Wakefield T.	31.10.88
Parker, Russ	(2.7.71)	0+2	—	—	—	—	Redhill ARL	19.8.92
Pearce, Greg	(2.9.67)	17+2	4	63	1	143	Halifax	2.10.92
Rogers, Darren	(6.5.74)	27	19	—	—	76	Stanley R. ARL	31.5.91
Rombo, Eddie	(19.3.67)	31	24	—	—	96	Leeds	28.11.91
Shuttleworth, Paul	(18.3.64)	26+2	5	—	11	31	Salford	14.6.85
Sidebottom, Gary	(16.4.66)	0+3	1	—	—	4	Nottingham C.	2.8.91
Spooner, Chris	(9.12.63)	0+3	—	—	—	—	Hanging Heaton ARL	5.10.88
Squires, Chris	(21.12.60)	16+5	12	—	—	48	Fox & Hounds ARL	2.9.81
Vasey, Chris	(28.2.63)	3	—	4	—	8	Leeds	3.12.90
Williams, Shane	(20.10.71)	3+9	1	—	—	4	Dewsbury C. ARL	1.6.92
Worthy, Paul	(14.5.68)	24+1	2	—	—	8	Leeds	21.5.91
TOTALS								
26 players			151	99	12	814		

DEWSBURY 1992-93 MATCH ANALYSIS

Date	Com-petition	H/A	Opponent	Rlt	Score	Tries	Goals	Atten-dance	Referee
30.8.92	TD	A	Highfield	W	22-12	Delaney (3), Bailey	Graham (3)	—	—
6.9.92	TD	H	Whitehaven	W	30-21	Rombo (2), Graham (2), Delaney, Hughes	Vasey (3)	844	Cross
13.9.92	YC(1)	A	Featherstone R.	L	8-40	Bailey, Hughes	—	—	—
27.9.92	TD	H	Keighley C.	W	24-13	Rombo (2), Delaney, Worthy	Graham (4)	1325	Tidball
4.10.92	TD	A	Hunslet	W	22-12	Cornforth (2), Rombo, Bailey	Graham (3)	—	—
11.10.92	TD	H	Nottingham C.	W	36-12	Rogers (2), Graham, Delaney, Hughes, Cornforth, Squires	Pearce (4)	845	Whitelam
18.10.92	TD	A	Chorley B.	W	18-8	Pearce, Delaney, Hughes	Pearce (3)	—	—
8.11.92	RT(1)	A	Hull	L	16-22	Collins, Rombo, Hughes	Pearce (2)	—	—
15.11.92	TD	A	Whitehaven	L	2-23	—	Pearce	—	—
29.11.92	TD	A	Nottingham C.	W	78-2	Graham (3), Bailey (3), Haigh (2), Rogers (2), Shuttleworth, Squires, Rombo, Worthy, Pearce	Pearce (9)	—	—
6.12.92	TD	H	Barrow	W	34-8	Squires (4), Rombo, Kelly, Bell	Pearce (3)	765	Cross
13.12.92	TD	H	Highfield	W	52-12	Graham (2), Rombo (2), Bailey (2), Rogers (2), Coughlan, Cocks	Graham (6)	658	Kershaw
28.12.92	TD	H	Batley	W	8-0	Coughlan	Pearce, Graham	2799	Carter
6.1.93	TD	A	Doncaster	W	24-0	Coughlan, Rogers, Squires, Graham, Kelly, Cocks	—	—	—
10.1.93	TD	H	Chorley B.	W	58-0	Rombo (2), Rogers (2), Graham, Delaney, Bailey, Shuttleworth, Kelly, Bell, Cocks	Graham (7)	854	Galtress
13.1.93	TD	A[1]	Batley	L	6-10	Squires	Graham	—	—
17.1.93	TD	A	Barrow	W	29-14	Rogers (2), Squires (2), Cocks, Rombo	Graham (2), Shuttleworth (dg)	—	—
24.1.93	TD	A	Ryedale-York	W	30-12	Squires (2), Delaney, Rogers, Rombo	Graham (4), Shuttleworth (2dg)	—	—
31.1.93	CC(1)	H	Wigan	L	4-20	Rogers	—	4156	Crashley
7.2.93	TD	H	Workington T.	L	2-15	—	Pearce	1554	Volante
21.2.93	TD	A	Workington T.	W	7-33	Delaney	Graham, Shuttleworth (dg)	—	—
28.2.93	TD	H	Hunslet	L	10-18	Cornforth, Rombo	Vasey	1044	R. Connolly
14.3.93	TD	A	Keighley C.	L	24-33	Bailey (2), Fleary, Shuttleworth	Pearce (3), Shuttleworth (2dg)	—	—
21.3.93	TD	H	Doncaster	W	39-16	Coughlan (2), Rogers (2), Delaney, Rombo, Shuttleworth	Pearce (5), Shuttleworth (dg)	986	Tidball
28.3.93	TD	H	Ryedale-York	W	17-12	Bailey, Charles, Rombo	Pearce (1, 1dg), Shuttleworth (2dg)	975	Gilmour
4.4.93	TD	A	Blackpool G.	W	90-5	Rombo (4), Bailey (3), Charles (2), Graham (2), Coughlan, Delaney, Rogers, Shuttleworth, Sidebottom	Pearce (13)	—	—
11.4.93	TD	H	Blackpool G.	W	56-0	Bailey (2), Collins (2), Bell, Coughlan, Pearce, Rogers, Rombo, Williams	Pearce (8)	654	Carter
18.4.93	DP(1)	H	Batley	W	22-18	Coughlan, Delaney, Graham, Rombo	Pearce (3)	1533	Crashley
25.4.93	DP(2)	A	Oldham	D	14-14	Bell, Rogers, Rombo	Pearce	—	—
28.4.93	DP(2) Replay	H	Oldham	W	20-18	Bailey, Pearce, Rogers	Pearce (3), Shuttleworth (2dg)	1490	Morris
9.5.93	DP(SF)	A	Featherstone R.	L	12-35	Cocks, Kelly	Pearce (2)	—	—

[1] at Leeds

DONCASTER

Ground: Tattersfield (0302-390150)
First Season: 1951-52
Nickname: Dons
Chairman: John Desmond
Secretary: Ray Green

RECORDS

Match

Goals: 12 by Tony Zelei v. Nottingham C.,
       1 Sep 1991
Tries: 4 by Vernon Grace v. Rochdale H.,
          4 Oct 1952
          Brian Tasker v. Leeds, 26 Oct 1963
          John Buckton v. Rochdale H.,
          30 Aug 1981
          Tony Kemp v. Carlisle,
          23 Nov 1986
          Neil Turner v. Keighley,
          22 Nov 1989
          Mark Roache v. Nottingham C.,
          1 Sep 1991
Points: 32 by Tony Zelei v. Nottingham C.,
          1 Sep 1991

Season

Goals: 118 by David Noble, 1985-86
Tries: 21 by Mark Roache, 1989-90
Points: 250 by David Noble, 1986-87

Career

Goals: 850 by David Noble, 1976-77, 1980-89
          & 1992
Tries: 90 by Mark Roache, 1985-
Points: 1,751 by David Noble, 1976-77, 1980-89
          & 1992
Appearances: 305+15 by David Noble, 1976-77,
          1980-89 & 1992
Highest score: 88-6 v. Nottingham C., 1 Sep 1991
Highest against: 75-3 v. Leigh, 28 Mar 1976
Attendance: 5,274 v. Wigan (RL Cup),
          29 Jan 1989 — at Tattersfield
          10,000 v. Bradford N. (RL Cup),
          16 Feb 1952 - at York Road Stadium

COACHING REGISTER

● Since 1974-75

Ted Strawbridge	Feb 73 - Apr 75
Derek Edwards	July 75 - Nov 76
Don Robson	Nov 76 - Sep 77
Trevor Lowe	Sep 77 - Apr 79
*Tommy Smales	Feb 78 - Apr 79
Billy Yates	Apr 79 - May 79
Don Vines	Sep 79 - Jan 80
Bill Kenny	June 80 - May 81
Alan Rhodes	Aug 81 - Mar 83
Clive Sullivan	Mar 83 - May 84
John Sheridan	June 84 - Nov 87
Graham Heptinstall	Nov 87 - Jan 88
John Sheridan	Jan 88 - Apr 89
Dave Sampson	May 89 - Jan 92
Geoff Morris	Jan 92 - Nov 92
Tony Fisher	Nov 92 -

Ex-forward, who shared the coaching post with Trevor Lowe for just over a year.

1992-93 SIGNINGS REGISTER

Signed	Player	Club From
13.8.92	Blockley, Jason	Normanton ARL
13.8.92	Jones, Kevin	Dewsbury
13.8.92	Lidbury, Steve	Scarborough P.
13.8.92	McGowan, Andy	Normanton ARL
13.8.92	Potter, Michael	Heworth ARL
13.8.92	Roockley, David	Scarborough P.
13.8.92	Thornton, Wayne	Castleford
13.8.92	Wilkinson, Darren	Featherstone R.
13.8.92	Wright, Chris	Scarborough P.
13.8.92	Young, Neil	—
14.8.92	Bragger, Ian	Castleford
4.9.92	Blackburn, John	Rochdale H.
4.9.92	Hayes, Brad	St. Mary's, Aus
15.9.92	Lingard, Glynn	Scarborough P.
18.9.92	*Reeves, Mark	Wakefield T.
4.10.92	*Gibbon, Mark	Featherstone R.
9.10.92	Edwards, Steve	Whitehaven
1.11.92	*Clarke, Andy	Castleford
6.12.92	*Carroll, Steve	Bramley
6.12.92	*Lister, Peter	Bramley
13.12.92	*Turner, Neil	Hull
17.12.92	Saul, Carl	Ryhill ARL
18.12.92	*Mallinder, Paul	Wakefield T.
4.1.93	Booker, Andrew	Scarborough P.
7.1.93	Mycock, Shaun	Bentley ARL
7.1.93	Hutchinson, Lee	Nottingham C.
10.1.93	*Green, Alex	Bradford N.
6.2.93	Subritzky, Peter	—
4.3.93	Davison, Simon	Askern W. ARL
30.3.93	*Marsden, Lee	Hull
8.4.93	*Gascoigne, Andy	Keighley C.

49

DONCASTER 1992-93 PLAYERS' SUMMARY

	(Date of Birth)	App	T	G	D	Pts	Previous club	Signed
Armstrong, Mick	(21.1.72)	6+4	—	—	—	—	ARL	18.12.91
Booker, Andy	(29.4.67)	0+3	—	—	—	—	Scarborough P.	4.1.93
Bragger, Ian	(11.8.60)	20	9	—	—	36	Castleford	14.8.92
Carr, Alan	(4.1.66)	14+5	3	—	—	12	Askern W. ARL	18.1.86
Carroll, Steve	(9.11.60)	3	—	3	—	6	Bramley	6.12.92
Clarke, Andy	(27.7.64)	21	—	—	—	—	Castleford	28.11.92
Collins, Dale	(20.5.68)	0+3	—	—	—	—	Bramley	5.2.93
Cooper, Paul	(24.6.65)	1	—	—	—	—	Nottingham C.	14.11.92
Davison, Simon	(28.12.67)	4	1	—	—	4	Askern W. ARL	4.3.93
Edwards, Steve	(9.4.69)	5+1	—	—	—	—	Whitehaven	9.10.92
Ellis, Mark	(23.5.67)	16+1	2	—	—	8	Walnut W. ARL	24.8.90
Evans, David	(17.6.69)	19+4	10	—	—	40	Staffs Poly ARL	3.1.92
Evans, John	(22.7.62)	5+5	2	—	—	8	Bentley ARL	25.8.87
Firth, Steve	(28.4.66)	0+1	—	—	—	—	Oulton ARL	19.12.88
Fletcher, Ian	(4.3.65)	5	3	—	—	12	York	28.3.89
Gibbon, Mark	(23.5.62)	2+1	—	—	—	—	Featherstone R.	4.10.92
Green, Alex	(9.2.71)	14	7	31	—	90	Bradford N.	10.2.93
Hayes, Brad	(22.4.67)	28	11	—	—	44	Australia	4.9.92
Heptinstall, Jason	(3.12.69)	2	—	—	—	—	Hull	3.1.92
Hudson, Justin	(3.12.72)	3+1	—	—	—	—	—	30.12.92
Iti, Clarry	(28.12.63)	0+1	—	—	—	—	Featherstone R.	15.10.92
Jones, Kevin	(25.2.64)	3	2	—	—	8	Dewsbury	17.1.92
Lidbury, Steve		12	6	—	—	24	Scarborough P.	13.8.92
Lingard, Glynn	(1.1.69)	2+3	—	—	—	—	Scarborough P.	15.9.92
Lister, Peter	(16.11.59)	1	—	—	—	—	Bramley	6.12.92
McGowan, Andy	(22.8.73)	0+1	—	—	—	—	Normanton ARL	13.8.92
Mallinder, Paul	(23.3.62)	11	1	—	—	4	Wakefield T.	18.12.92
Miller, Tony	(30.3.68)	28	5	—	—	20	Oldham	14.2.91
Pell, Richard	(17.10.66)	8+5	1	—	—	4	Cutsyke ARL	3.1.92
Pennant, Audley	(26.2.63)	21+5	4	—	—	16	Bradford N.	24.9.85
Reeves, Mark	(14.1.70)	2+1	—	—	—	—	Wakefield T.	18.9.92
Roache, Mark	(24.10.62)	11	7	—	—	28	Castleford	2.9.85
Roockley, David	(5.1.63)	15	1	2	—	8	Scarborough P.	13.8.92
Rothwell, Andy		3	1	—	—	4	Moorends ARL	9.1.93
Rowse, Martin	(8.3.69)	21+2	3	—	—	12	Leeds	3.1.92
Shuttleworth, Greg	(17.7.67)	15	6	—	3	27	Huddersfield	—
Sims, Mark	(18.11.65)	23	14	65	—	186	Nottingham RU	19.12.88
Subritzky, Peter	(3.3.63)	4	1	—	—	4	New Zealand	6.2.93
Thornton, Wayne	(31.8.66)	9+3	—	—	—	—	Castleford	13.8.92
Turner, Neil	(30.10.63)	2	1	—	—	4	Hull	13.12.92
Watkin, Darren	(20.5.71)	3+1	—	—	—	—	Middleton ARL	24.8.90
Wilkinson, Darren	(27.10.66)	2	—	—	—	—	Featherstone R.	13.8.92
Wright, Chris	(13.10.69)	0+2	—	—	—	—	Scarborough P.	13.8.92
TOTALS								
43 players			101	101	3	609		

DONCASTER 1992-93 MATCH ANALYSIS

Date	Competition	H/A	Opponent	Rlt	Score	Tries	Goals	Attendance	Referee
6.9.92	TD	H	Highfield	W	50-4	Bragger (2), Jones (2), Lidbury, Rowse, Hayes, Sims	Sims (9)	728	Crashley
13.9.92	YC(1)	A	Wakefield T.	L	14-54	Sims, Bragger	Sims (3)	—	—
20.9.92	TD	A	Batley	L	8-14	Hayes	Sims (2)	—	—
27.9.92	TD	H	Hunslet	W	28-4	Pennant, Sims, Hayes, Roockley	Sims (6)	1121	Wood
4.10.92	TD	A	Whitehaven	L	12-28	Pell, Hayes	Sims (2)	—	—
11.10.92	TD	A	Ryedale-York	L	22-42	Bragger (2), Lidbury, Hayes	Sims (3)	—	—
18.10.92	TD	H	Barrow	W	30-18	D. Evans, Ellis, Miller, Bragger, Hayes	Sims (5)	1013	Atkin
1.11.92	TD	A	Blackpool G.	L	18-22	D. Evans, Miller, Sims	Sims (3)	—	—
8.11.92	RT(1)	H	Workington T.	L	4-30	—	Sims (2)	893	Redfearn
15.11.92	TD	H	Workington T.	L	6-22	Lidbury	Roockley	1015	Carter
29.11.92	TD	H	Blackpool G.	W	34-14	Lidbury (3), Bragger, Carr, D. Evans	Sims (4), Roockley	853	Campbell
6.12.92	TD	H	Batley	W	14-12	Sims (3)	Carroll	1109	Nicholson
13.12.92	TD	A	Barrow	W	28-18	Sims (2), D. Evans, Turner, Miller, Pennant	Carroll (2)	—	—
6.1.93	TD	H	Dewsbury	L	0-24	—	—	1102	Volante
10.1.93	TD	H	Nottingham C.	W	42-4	Green (2), Roache (2), Hayes, Pennant, Bragger	Sims (7)	694	Asquith
13.1.93	TD	A	Keighley C.	L	10-31	D. Evans (2)	Sims	—	—
17.1.93	TD	A	Chorley B.	W	34-14	Roache (2), Bragger, Ellis, D. Evans, Pennant, Sims	Sims (3)	—	—
24.1.93	TD	H	Whitehaven	W	20-4	D. Evans (2), Sims	Sims (4)	806	Tidball
31.1.93	CC(1)	A	Rochdale H.	L	13-34	Roache, Sims	Sims (2), Shuttleworth (dg)	—	—
7.2.93	TD	A	Hunslet	W	26-10	Mallinder, Miller, Sims, Shuttleworth	Sims (5)	—	—
21.2.93	TD	A	Highfield	W	60-16	Green (2), Hayes (2), Carr, J. Evans, Miller, Roache, Rowse, Subritzky	Green (10)	—	—
28.2.93	TD	H	Ryedale-York	W	14-9	Roache, Shuttleworth	Green (3)	950	Volante
7.3.93	TD	H	Chorley B.	W	31-12	Shuttleworth (2), Davison, J. Evans, D. Evans	Green (5), Shuttleworth (dg)	824	Whitelam
14.3.93	TD	A	Nottingham C.	W	25-24	Fletcher, Green, Rowse, Shuttleworth	Green (4), Shuttleworth (dg)	—	—
21.3.93	TD	A	Dewsbury	L	16-39	Green (2)	Sims (4)	—	—
28.3.93	TD	A	Workington T.	L	6-52	Fletcher	Green	—	—
4.4.93	TD	H	Keighley C.	L	30-32	Carr, Hayes, Rothwell, Sims, Shuttleworth	Green (5)	1748	Crashley
18.4.93	DP(1)	A	Workington T.	L	14-44	Fletcher, Hayes	Green (3)	—	—

FEATHERSTONE ROVERS

Ground: Post Office Road (0977-702386)
First Season: 1921-22
Nickname: Colliers
Chairman: Eric Gardner
Secretary: Terry Jones
Honours: **Championship** Beaten finalists,
1927-28
Division One Champions, 1976-77
Division Two Champions, 1979-80,
1992-93
Challenge Cup Winners, 1966-67,
1972-73, 1982-83
Beaten finalists, 1951-52, 1973-74
**Second Division/Divisional
Premiership** Winners, 1992-93
Beaten finalists, 1987-88
Yorkshire Cup Winners, 1939-40,
1959-60
Beaten finalists, 1928-29, 1963-64,
1966-67, 1969-70, 1970-71,
1976-77, 1977-78, 1989-90
Captain Morgan Trophy Beaten
finalists, 1973-74

RECORDS

Match
Goals: 13 by Mark Knapper v. Keighley,
17 Sep 1989
Tries: 6 by Mike Smith v. Doncaster,
13 Apr 1968
Chris Bibb v. Keighley, 17 Sep 1989
Points: 30 by Mark Knapper v. Keighley,
17 Sep 1989

Season
Goals: 163 by Steve Quinn, 1979-80
Tries: 48 by Paul Newlove, 1992-93
Points: 391 by Martin Pearson, 1992-93

Career
Goals: 1,210 by Steve Quinn, 1975-88
Tries: 162 by Don Fox, 1953-66
Points: 2,654 by Steve Quinn, 1975-88
Appearances: 440 by Jim Denton, 1921-34

Highest score: 86-18 v. Keighley, 17 Sep 1989
Highest against: 70-2 at Halifax, 14 Apr 1941
Attendance: 17,531 v. St. Helens (RL Cup),
21 Mar 1959

COACHING REGISTER
● Since 1974-75

*Tommy Smales	July 74 - Sep 74
Keith Goulding	Sep 74 - Jan 76
†Tommy Smales	Feb 76 - May 76
Keith Cotton	June 76 - Dec 77
Keith Goulding	Dec 77 - May 78
Terry Clawson	July 78 - Nov 78
†Tommy Smales	Nov 78 - Apr 79
Paul Daley	May 79 - Jan 81
Vince Farrar	Feb 81 - Nov 82
Allan Agar	Dec 82 - Oct 85
George Pieniazek	Nov 85 - Nov 86
Paul Daley	Nov 86 - Apr 87
Peter Fox	May 87 - Oct 91
Allan Agar	Oct 91 - Aug 92
Steve Martin	Sep 92 -

*Ex-forward
†Ex-scrum half

GREAT BRITAIN REGISTER
(15 players)

Tommy Askin	(6)	1928
Chris Bibb	(1)	1990
John "Keith" Bridges	(3)	1974
Terry Clawson	(2)	1962
Malcolm Dixon	(2)	1962-64
Steve Evans	(5+3)	1979-80
Deryck Fox	(9+4)	1985-92
Don Fox	(1)	1963
David Hobbs	(7+1)	1984
Gary Jordan	(2)	1964-67
Arnold Morgan	(4)	1968
Steve Nash	(16)	1971-74
Paul Newlove	(7+3)	1989-93
Peter Smith	(1+5)	1977-84
Jimmy Thompson	(19+1)	1970-77

1992-93 SIGNINGS REGISTER

Signed	Player	Club From
24.6.92	Milner, Mark	Ossett T. ARL
1.7.92	Thompson, Alex	Travellers ARL
1.7.92	Child, Simon	Travellers ARL
1.7.92	Goodwin, Steve	Travellers ARL
1.8.92	Evans, Daniel	Travellers ARL
1.9.92	Morgan, Jonathan	Travellers ARL

23.9.92	Taekata, Wayne	Western Suburbs, Aus	12.11.92	*Kelly, Andy	Wakefield T.	
24.9.92	Gunn, Richard	Leeds	12.11.92	Maloney, Francis	Leeds	
24.9.92	Daunt, Brett	Brisbane Valleys, Aus	18.12.92	*Brentley, Gary	Bramley	
25.9.92	Palmer, Craig	Scarborough P.	7.1.93	Heptinstall, Andy	Travellers ARL	
1.10.92	Senior, Lee	Sharlston ARL	27.4.93	Grice, Darren	Hessle RU	
1.11.92	Richardson, Sean	Prince of Wales ARL	27.4.93	O'Brien, Richard	West Hull ARL	

FEATHERSTONE ROVERS 1992-93 PLAYERS' SUMMARY

	(Date of Birth)	App	T	G	D	Pts	Previous club	Signed
Appleby, Darren	(14.6.67)	1	—	—	—	—	Australia	3.7.92
Bibb, Chris	(3.6.68)	25	5	—	—	20	Lock Lane ARL	21.6.85
Bonson, Paul	(18.10.71)	0+1	—	—	—	—	Featherstone MW ARL	21.10.88
Booth, Craig	(28.10.70)	0+2	—	—	—	—	Travellers ARL	3.7.90
Burton, Chris	(5.10.56)	6+23	2	—	—	8	Hull K.R.	8.1.89
Butt, Ikram	(25.10.68)	37	17	—	—	68	Leeds	9.8.90
Casey, Leo	(17.9.65)	28+2	3	—	—	12	Oldham	26.7.90
Daunt, Brett	(8.10.65)	29	13	—	—	52	Australia	24.9.92
Fisher, Andy	(17.11.67)	17+1	4	—	—	16	Travellers ARL	19.1.89
Gibbon, Mark	(23.5.62)	2	—	—	—	—	Doncaster	27.2.90
Goulbourne, Alex	(20.7.74)	2	—	—	—	—	Northern Dairies ARL	1.7.91
Gunn, Richard	(25.2.67)	14+4	3	—	—	12	Leeds	24.9.92
Maloney, Francis	(26.5.73)	11+7	11	4	—	52	Leeds	12.11.92
Manning, Terry	(4.12.65)	37	10	—	—	40	Keighley	17.10.89
Minter, Steve	(17.3.73)	2	4	—	—	16	Travellers ARL	1.7.91
Newlove, Paul	(10.8.71)	35	48	—	—	192	Featherstone MW ARL	10.8.88
Pearson, Martin	(24.10.71)	33+2	28	139	1	391	Travellers ARL	16.11.88
Price, Gary	(9.3.61)	25+4	6	—	—	24	Leeds	4.8.89
Roebuck, Neil	(4.10.69)	2+5	1	—	—	4	Castleford	13.1.93
Rose, Gary	(25.7.65)	18+10	—	—	—	—	Keighley	2.1.90
Sharp, Tim	(20.2.70)	7+4	2	6	—	20	Travellers ARL	11.8.87
Simpson, Owen	(12.9.65)	33	34	—	—	136	Keighley	9.11.90
Smales, Ian	(26.9.68)	35	22	14	—	116	Lock Lane ARL	3.4.87
Taekata, Wayne	(19.6.67)	30+1	—	—	—	—	Australia	23.9.92
Tuuta, Brendon	(29.4.65)	28+1	6	—	—	24	Australia	14.9.90
Whiteley, Lee	(25.3.71)	3	—	—	—	—	Featherstone MW ARL	25.7.88
Wilson, Mark	(3.10.65)	21+7	2	—	—	8	Bradford N.	22.7.91
TOTALS								
27 players			221	163	1	1,211		

Representative appearances 1992-93

Newlove — Britain (1, 3t); England (1, 1t)
Pearson — GB Under-21 (1, 1t, 5g)

FEATHERSTONE ROVERS 1992-93 MATCH ANALYSIS

Date	Com-petition	H/A	Opponent	Rlt	Score	Tries	Goals	Atten-dance	Referee
30.8.92	SD	A	Huddersfield	W	34-15	Simpson (2), Manning (2), Butt, Newlove	Pearson (4), Smales	—	—
6.9.92	SD	H	Swinton	W	14-8	Manning, Tuuta	Smales (3)	2481	Carter
13.9.92	YC(1)	H	Dewsbury	W	40-8	Newlove (2), Price (2), Fisher, Sharp, Smales, Pearson	Pearson (4)	2468	Wood
20.9.92	SD	A	Rochdale H.	L	22-26	Butt, Smales, Manning, Simpson	Pearson (2), Sharp	—	—

(Continued)

FEATHERSTONE ROVERS 1992-93 MATCH ANALYSIS

Date	Competition	H/A	Opponent	Rlt	Score	Tries	Goals	Attendance	Referee
23.9.92	YC(2)	H	Huddersfield	W	18-8	Fisher, Simpson	Sharp (5)	2385	Galtress
27.9.92	SD	H	Carlisle	W	30-10	Smales (2), Bibb, Fisher, Newlove	Smales (5)	2285	Whitelam
2.10.92	SD	A	Oldham	W	24-4	Pearson, Tuuta, Newlove	Pearson (6)	—	—
7.10.92	YC(SF)	H	Wakefield T.	L	8-22	Smales	Pearson (2)	5544	Morris
11.10.92	SD	A	Bramley	W	22-4	Simpson (2), Butt, Daunt	Pearson (3)	—	—
18.10.92	SD	H	London C.	W	40-10	Newlove (3), Butt, Pearson, Manning, Simpson	Pearson (6)	2394	Galtress
1.11.92	SD	H	Huddersfield	L	18-25	Gunn, Newlove, Smales	Pearson (3)	2632	J. Connolly
8.11.92	RT(1)	A	Salford	W	18-14	Newlove, Gunn, Simpson	Pearson (3)	—	—
15.11.92	SD	A	Swinton	W	44-10	Simpson (2), Butt, Manning, Newlove, Price, Smales, Tuuta, Pearson	Pearson (4)	—	—
22.11.92	SD	H	Rochdale H.	W	18-6	Simpson (2), Daunt	Pearson (3)	2664	Carter
29.11.92	SD	A	Carlisle	W	38-14	Pearson (2), Smales (2), Simpson, Newlove, Gunn, Price	Pearson (3)	—	—
6.12.92	RT(2)	H	St. Helens	L	8-25	Smales	Pearson (2)	4473	Volante
13.12.92	SD	H	Oldham	W	24-20	Newlove (3), Pearson, Smales	Pearson, Smales	3298	Atkin
20.12.92	SD	A	London C.	W	30-8	Smales (2), Daunt, Bibb, Newlove, Fisher	Pearson (3)	—	—
5.1.93	SD	A	Huddersfield	W	24-20	Pearson (2), Manning, Butt	Pearson (4)	—	—
10.1.93	SD	H	Huddersfield	W	34-12	Newlove (2), Pearson, Daunt, Tuuta, Maloney	Pearson (5)	3304	Cummings
17.1.93	SD	H	Swinton	W	64-6	Simpson (3), Pearson (2), Daunt (2), Bibb, Burton, Casey, Newlove, Price	Pearson (8)	2396	Kershaw
24.1.93	SD	A	London C.	W	32-6	Simpson (2), Daunt, Newlove, Pearson, Smales	Pearson (4)	—	—
31.1.93	CC(1)	H	St. Helens	L	22-24	Simpson (2), Newlove, Pearson	Smales (2), Pearson	5854	Cummings
7.2.93	SD	H	Oldham	W	52-14	Newlove (2), Simpson (2), Bibb, Butt, Maloney, Manning, Smales, Tuuta	Maloney (4), Smales (2)	4332	Cummings
14.2.93	SD	H	London C.	W	58-12	Newlove (2), Simpson (2), Smales (2), Butt, Casey, Pearson, Tuuta, Wilson	Pearson (7)	2242	Nicholson
21.2.93	SD	A	Swinton	W	42-12	Simpson (3), Newlove (2), Bibb, Butt, Pearson, Smales	Pearson (3)	—	—
28.2.93	SD	H	Carlisle	W	26-10	Butt, Maloney, Manning, Pearson, Smales	Pearson (3)	1985	Galtress
7.3.93	SD	A	Rochdale H.	W	40-24	Simpson (2), Daunt, Newlove, Pearson, Price, Smales	Pearson (6)	—	—
14.3.93	SD	A	Oldham	L	22-24	Maloney, Newlove, Pearson, Simpson	Pearson (3)	—	—
21.3.93	SD	H	Bramley	W	60-0	Daunt (3), Newlove (3), Simpson (2), Casey, Manning, Pearson	Pearson (8)	2194	Morris
28.3.93	SD	H	Rochdale H.	W	24-22	Newlove (3), Maloney	Pearson (4)	2482	J. Smith
4.4.93	SD	A	Carlisle	D	30-30	Pearson (2), Burton, Butt, Newlove, Sharp	Pearson (3)	—	—
12.4.93	SD	A	Bramley	W	52-0	Newlove (3), Minter (3), Maloney (2), Butt, Daunt	Pearson (6)	—	—
18.4.93	SD	H	Bramley	W	78-0	Newlove (4), Butt (4), Maloney (3), Minter, Pearson, Roebuck, Wilson	Pearson (9)	2693	Morris
25.4.93	DP(2)	H	Ryedale-York	W	46-8	Pearson (3), Newlove (2), Butt, Smales, Simpson	Pearson (7)	2193	Wood
9.5.93	DP(SF)	H	Dewsbury	W	35-12	Pearson (2), Daunt, Newlove, Simpson, Smales	Pearson (5, 1dg)	3353	Atkin
16.5.93	DP(F)	N[1]	Workington T.	W	20-16	Newlove (2), Maloney	Pearson (4)	(—)	J. Connolly

[1] at Manchester U.FC

HALIFAX

Ground: Thrum Hall (0422-361026)
First Season: 1895-96
Nickname: Thrum Hallers
Chairman: Tony Gartland
Secretary: David Fleming
Honours: **Championship** Winners, 1906-07,
               1964-65
               Beaten finalists, 1952-53, 1953-54,
               1955-56, 1965-66
               War Emergency League Beaten
               finalists, 1942-43, 1944-45
               Division One Champions, 1902-03,
               1985-86
               Challenge Cup Winners, 1902-03,
               1903-04, 1930-31, 1938-39, 1986-87
               Beaten finalists, 1920-21, 1940-41,
               1941-42, 1948-49, 1953-54, 1955-56,
               1987-88
               Regal Trophy Winners, 1971-72
               Beaten finalists, 1989-90
               Premiership Trophy Beaten
               finalists, 1985-86
               Second Division Premiership
               Beaten finalists, 1990-91
               Yorkshire Cup Winners, 1908-09,
               1944-45, 1954-55, 1955-56, 1963-64
               Beaten finalists, 1905-06, 1907-08,
               1941-42, 1979-80
               Yorkshire League Winners,
               1908-09, 1920-21, 1952-53, 1953-54,
               1955-56, 1957-58
               Eastern Division Championship
               Winners, 1963-64
               Charity Shield Winners, 1986-87
               Beaten finalists, 1987-88

RECORDS

Match
Goals: 14 by Bruce Burton v. Hunslet,
        27 Aug 1972
Tries: 8 by Keith Williams v. Dewsbury,
        9 Nov 1957
Points: 31 by Bruce Burton v. Hunslet,
        27 Aug 1972

Season
Goals: 147 by Tysul Griffiths, 1955-56
Tries: 48 by Johnny Freeman, 1956-57
Points: 298 by Colin Whitfield, 1986-87

Career
Goals: 1,028 by Ron James, 1960-72
Tries: 290 by Johnny Freeman, 1954-67
Points: 2,191 by Ron James, 1960-72
Appearances: 481 by Stan Kielty, 1946-58
Highest score: 82-8 v. Runcorn H., 14 Oct 1990
Highest against: 64-0 at Wigan, 7 Mar 1923
Attendance: 29,153 v. Wigan (RL Cup),
               21 Mar 1959

COACHING REGISTER
● **Since 1974-75**

Derek Hallas	Aug 74 - Oct 74
Les Pearce	Oct 74 - Apr 76
Alan Kellett	May 76 - Apr 77
Jim Crellin	June 77 - Oct 77
Harry Fox	Oct 77 - Feb 78
Maurice Bamford	Feb 78 - May 80
Mick Blacker	June 80 - June 82
Ken Roberts	June 82 - Sep 82
Colin Dixon	Sep 82 - Nov 84
Chris Anderson	Nov 84 - May 88
Graham Eadie	May 88 - Aug 88
Ross Strudwick	Aug 88 - Feb 89
Alan Hardisty	Feb 89 - Apr 89
John Dorahy	June 89 - Aug 90
Peter Roe	Aug 90 - May 91
Roger Millward	May 91 - Dec 92
Malcolm Reilly	Jan 93 -

GREAT BRITAIN REGISTER
(30 players)

Alvin Ackerley	(2)	1952-58
Arthur Bassett	(2)	1946
Jack Beames	(2)	1921
Nat Bentham	(2)	1929
Harry Beverley	(2)	1937
Oliver Burgham	(1)	1911
Arthur Daniels	(3)	1952-55
Will Davies	(1)	1911
Colin Dixon	(1)	1968
Paul Dixon	(3+3)	1987-88
Percy Eccles	(1)	1907

Terry Fogerty	(+1)	1966
Tony Halmshaw	(1)	1971
Karl Harrison	(3+3)	1991-93
Neil James	(1)	1986
Robbie Lloyd	(1)	1920
Alf Milnes	(2)	1920
Stuart Prosser	(1)	1914
Dai Rees	(1)	1926
Charlie Renilson	(7+1)	1965-68
Joe Riley	(1)	1910
Ken Roberts	(10)	1963-66
Asa Robinson	(3)	1907-08
Derrick Schofield	(1)	1955
John Shaw	(5)	1960-62
Cyril Stacey	(1)	1920
John Thorley	(4)	1954
Jack Wilkinson	(6)	1954-55
Frank Williams	(2)	1914
David Willicombe	(1)	1974

1992-93 SIGNINGS REGISTER

Signed	Player	Club From
1.6.92	Lawless, John	Siddal ARL
20.8.92	Broadbent, Nigel	Eastmoor ARL
20.8.92	Grant, Carl	Wigan St. Pat's ARL
20.8.92	Hassan, Phil	Wigan St. Pat's ARL
20.8.92	Litherland, Roy	Pilkington ARL
21.8.92	Bentley, John	Leeds
21.8.92	Divorty, Gary	Leeds
10.9.92	Kerr, Ken	Workington T.
1.10.92	*Koloto, Emosi	Widnes
28.10.92	McLean, Mike	Gold Coast, Aus
29.10.92	Hallas, Graeme	Hull K.R.
4.11.92	Stuart, Brent	NZ
5.11.92	Stott, Lynton	Woolston R. ARL
5.2.93	*Wear, Steve	Workington T.
25.3.93	Pilgrim, Steve	Leeds

HALIFAX 1992-93 PLAYERS' SUMMARY

	(Date of Birth)	App	T	G	D	Pts	Previous club	Signed
Austin, Greg	(14.6.63)	26	27	—	—	108	Hull K.R.	19.9.90
Bailey, Mark	(5.5.68)	28+1	8	—	—	32	St. Helens	4.3.92
Bell, Peter	(29.6.62)	1+4	—	—	—	—	David Brown ARL	23.10.85
Bentley, John	(5.9.66)	29	20	1	—	82	Leeds	21.8.92
Bishop, Paul	(5.7.67)	33	8	116	2	266	St. Helens	—
Cooper, David	(29.3.64)	26+1	6	2	—	28	Bradford N.	28.2.92
Divorty, Gary	(28.1.66)	31+1	12	—	—	48	Leeds	21.8.92
Fieldhouse, John	(28.6.62)	19+2	4	—	—	16	Oldham	17.10.91
Fogerty, Adam	(6.3.69)	8+7	3	—	—	12	—	5.9.91
Hallas, Graeme	(27.2.71)	23	10	2	—	44	Hull K.R.	29.10.92
Hancock, Andy	(11.6.69)	0+3	—	—	—	—	—	17.5.88
Harrison, Karl	(20.2.64)	32+1	4	—	—	16	Hull	8.8.91
Hill, Brendan	(15.9.64)	0+9	1	—	—	4	Bradford N.	11.1.89
Hutchinson, Rob	(20.9.68)	1+3	—	—	—	—	Norland ARL	7.7.88
Irvine, Jimmy	(28.4.60)	1	1	—	—	4	Hull K.R.	23.11.90
Kerr, Ken	(18.10.69)	1+2	—	—	—	—	Workington T.	10.9.92
Koloto, Emosi	(23.1.65)	2	—	—	—	—	Widnes	1.10.92
Litherland, Roy	(1.11.70)	4	1	—	—	4	Pilkington ARL	20.8.92
Lord, Gary	(6.7.66)	25+3	4	—	—	16	Leeds	15.10.91
McLean, Mike	(11.3.64)	15+6	2	—	—	8	Australia	28.10.92
Milner, Richard	(2.5.65)	4+4	—	—	—	—	Milford ARL	6.1.89
Perrett, Mark	(18.7.73)	14+5	1	—	—	4	Ovenden ARL	18.9.91
Pickles, Damien	(2.12.70)	1	1	—	—	4	Siddal ARL	10.10.91
Pilgrim, Steve	(26.10.67)	1	—	—	—	—	Leeds	25.3.93
Preston, Mark	(3.4.67)	30	23	—	—	92	Wigan	11.6.91
Richardson, Gary	(23.5.66)	3	1	—	—	4	Calder V. ARL	6.9.90
Robinson, Chris	(2.9.70)	5+4	—	—	—	—	Dudley Hill ARL	27.11.90
Sharp, Henry	(17.9.66)	16+5	2	—	—	8	Dudley Hill ARL	18.2.91
Southernwood, Roy	(23.6.68)	31	3	—	—	12	Castleford	24.8.90

	(Date of Birth)	App	T	G	D	Pts	Previous club	Signed
Stuart, Brent ....(19.8.65)		14	2	—	—	8	New Zealand	4.11.92
Tiffany, Richard ....(25.5.73)		0+1	—	—	—	—	Dudley Hill ARL	25.3.92
Wilson, Warren ....(3.5.63)		5	—	—	—	—	Leeds	13.9.90
TOTALS								
32 players			144	121	2	820		

Representative appearances 1992-93 Harrison — Britain (1)

HALIFAX 1992-93 MATCH ANALYSIS

Date	Competition	H/A	Opponent	Rlt	Score	Tries	Goals	Attendance	Referee
30.8.92	SBC	A	Wakefield T.	W	30-10	Austin (2), Bishop, Irvine, Divorty, Preston	Cooper (2), Bishop	—	—
6.9.92	SBC	H	Leeds	W	26-8	Austin (2), Cooper, Bentley, Bailey	Bishop (3)	10,070	Holdsworth
11.9.92	YC(1)	A	Sheffield E.	L	14-34	Bentley (2), Divorty	Bishop	—	—
20.9.92	SBC	A	Salford	L	22-27	Austin (2), Preston, Fieldhouse	Bishop (3)	—	—
27.9.92	SBC	H	Leigh	W	34-18	Austin (3), Preston, Cooper, Fieldhouse	Bishop (5)	5590	Steele
4.10.92	SBC	A	Hull	L	8-26	Southernwood	Bishop (2)	—	—
11.10.92	SBC	H	Sheffield E.	W	18-13	Austin, Preston	Bishop (5)	6016	Morris
18.10.92	SBC	A	Widnes	L	6-20	Perrett	Bishop	—	—
1.11.92	SBC	H	Wakefield T.	L	16-24	Bishop, Preston, Divorty	Bishop (2)	7450	Holdsworth
8.11.92	RT(1)	H	Nottingham C.	W	76-6	Austin (5), Hallas (3), Preston (2), Harrison (2), Divorty, Fieldhouse, Cooper, McLean	Bishop (3), Hallas (2), Bentley	3547	Gilmour
15.11.92	SBC	A	Leigh	W	28-4	Bentley (2), Austin (2), Preston	Bishop (4)	—	—
22.11.92	SBC	H	Warrington	W	21-20	Southernwood, Preston, Cooper	Bishop (4, 1dg)	5458	Kershaw
6.12.92	RT(2)	A	Hull	L	14-28	McLean, Austin	Bishop (3)	—	—
11.12.92	SBC	H	Wigan	L	8-32	Preston	Bishop (2)	6560	Campbell
18.12.92	SBC	A	Leeds	L	14-42	Bailey, Divorty	Bishop (3)	—	—
6.1.93	SBC	A	Sheffield E.	W	26-10	Austin, Preston, Sharp, Bailey	Bishop (5)	—	—
10.1.93	SBC	H	Hull K.R.	W	20-12	Divorty, Bishop, Preston, Bentley	Bishop (2)	5477	Holdsworth
22.1.93	SBC	A	St. Helens	L	16-18	Bentley, Preston	Bishop (4)	—	—
31.1.93	CC(1)	H	Carlisle	W	66-16	Bentley (3), Austin (2), Preston (2), Bailey, Bishop, Cooper, Divorty, Stuart	Bishop (9)	4348	R. Connolly
7.2.93	SBC	H	Salford	W	36-14	Bailey (2), Preston (2), Harrison, Southernwood	Bishop (6)	5795	Gilmour
17.2.93	CC(2)	H	Batley	W	50-20	Bentley (3), Austin (2), Cooper, Fieldhouse, Hallas, Stuart	Bishop (7)	5243	Cross
21.2.93	SBC	A	Wigan	L	14-30	Bailey, Bentley, Bishop	Bishop	—	—
28.2.93	CC(3)	H	Wigan	L	18-19	Hallas (2), Austin	Bishop (3)	9841	Holdsworth
3.3.93	SBC	H	Hull	W	34-0	Preston (2), Bishop, Bailey, Divorty, Hallas	Bishop (5)	4566	Whitfield
7.3.93	SBC	H	Castleford	W	28-16	Divorty, Fogerty, Harrison, Preston	Bishop (6)	6786	Campbell
14.3.93	SBC	A	Warrington	L	24-56	Bentley (2), Bishop, Litherland	Bishop (4)	—	—
19.3.93	SBC	H	St. Helens	L	12-18	Preston (2)	Bishop (2)	5503	Ollerton
28.3.93	SBC	A	Castleford	L	16-32	Austin, Bentley, Lord	Bishop (2)	—	—
4.4.93	SBC	H	Widnes	W	40-6	Bishop (2), Austin, Divorty, Hallas, Lord, Preston	Bishop (6)	6011	Holdsworth
9.4.93	SBC	A	Bradford N.	L	8-10	Hallas	Bishop (2)	—	—
12.4.93	SBC	H	Bradford N.	L	14-33	Bentley, Fogerty, Hallas	Bishop	8590	Holdsworth
18.4.93	SBC	A	Hull K.R.	W	38-6	Lord (2), Bentley, Fogerty, Hill, Richardson, Sharp	Bishop (5)	—	—
23.4.93	PT(1)	A	St. Helens	L	25-34	Divorty (2), Bentley, Pickles	Bishop (4, 1dg)	—	—

HIGHFIELD

Ground: Hoghton Road (0744-812376)
First Season: 1922-23 as Wigan Highfield.
Became London Highfield in 1933-34. Became Liverpool Stanley in 1934-35 and changed to Liverpool City in 1951-52. Became Huyton in 1968-69 and changed to Runcorn Highfield in 1984-85. Became Highfield in 1991-92.
Chairman: Geoff Fletcher
Secretary: Phil Thomas
Honours: **Lancashire League** Winners, 1935-36

RECORDS
Match
Goals: 11 by Peter Wood v. Batley, 21 Oct 1984
Tries: 5 by John Maloney v. Bramley, 25 Apr 1931
Points: 30 by Norman Barrow v. Keighley, 31 Mar 1991
Season
Goals: 126 by Peter Wood, 1984-85
Tries: 28 by John Maloney, 1930-31
Points: 240 by Peter Wood, 1984-85
Career
Goals: 304 by Wilf Hunt, 1955-66
Tries: 204 by John Maloney, 1926-45
Points: 731 by Wilf Hunt, 1955-66
Appearances: 413 by John Maloney, 1926-45
Highest score: 59-11 v. Bramley, 4 May 1934
Highest against: 92-2 v. Wigan, 13 Nov 1988
92-0 v. Rochdale H., 5 Nov 1989
Attendance: 18,000 v. Wigan (League),
2 Sep 1922 — at Tunstall Lane, Pemberton
1,600 v. Halifax (League), 6 Jan 1991 — at Hoghton Road

COACHING REGISTER
● **Since 1974-75**

Terry Gorman	Aug 74 - May 77
Geoff Fletcher	Aug 77 - June 86
Frank Wilson	July 86 - Nov 86
Arthur Daley	Nov 86 - Apr 87
Paul Woods	

Bill Ashurst	Apr 87 - Jan 89
John Cogger	Jan 89 - Feb 89
Geoff Fletcher	Feb 89 - Apr 89
Dave Chisnall	June 89 - Oct 90
Alan Bishop	Oct 90 - Apr 91
Chris Arkwright	Apr 91 - Aug 91
Willie Johnson	Aug 91 - Apr 93
Mike Peers	Apr 93 -

GREAT BRITAIN REGISTER
(4 players)

Ray Ashby	(1)	1964
Billy Belshaw	(6)	1936-37
Nat Bentham	(6)	1928
Harry Woods	(5)	1936

Full back Ray Ashby, capped once in 1964.

1992-93 SIGNINGS REGISTER

Signed	Player	Club From
7.8.92	Ashcroft, John	Blackbrook ARL
11.8.92	Carr, Mike	Pilkington ARL
11.8.92	Durnin, Paul	Bramley

11.8.92	Partington, Adam	Leigh Victoria ARL
17.8.92	Faimalo, Joe	Swinton
20.8.92	Moffatt, Ian	Clock Face ARL
4.9.92	*Meadows, Kevin	Chorley B.
22.9.92	Denning, Mike	Pilkington ARL
22.9.92	Pojunas, David	Parkside ARL
2.10.92	Dobson, Mark	Salford
13.10.92	Lewis, Glyn	Nutgrove ARL
20.10.92	Hawry, Paul	RU
7.11.92	Barnes, Dave	Wigan St. Judes ARL
7.11.92	Rushton, Andrew	Wigan St. Judes ARL
10.11.92	Roscoe, Brian	Wigan St. Judes ARL
10.11.92	Keech, Philip	—
10.11.92	*Haggerty, Gary	Wakefield T.
13.11.92	*Bacon, Mike	Warrington
13.11.92	Potter, Ian	Bramley
17.11.92	Hunter, Paul	Burton ARL
24.11.92	Hall, Dave	Haydock ARL
11.12.92	Gregory, Ryan	Crown Springs ARL
24.12.92	Erentz, David	Chorley B.
7.1.93	*Carney, John	Chorley B.
7.1.93	*Evans, Andy	Chorley B.
9.2.93	Parnell, Paul	Pilkington ARL
25.2.93	Meadows, Dave	Bold Miners ARL
12.3.93	*Hester, Terry	Bramley
12.3.93	*Pemberton, Tony	Blackpool G.
12.3.93	*Viller, Mark	Blackpool G.
14.3.93	*Hudson, Julian	Blackpool G.
16.3.93	*Johnson, Chris	Blackpool G.
16.3.93	*Whitfield, Darren	Swinton
17.3.93	*Haggerty, Roy	Barrow
21.3.93	Stephenson, Colin	Crosfields ARL

HIGHFIELD 1992-93 PLAYERS' SUMMARY

	(Date of Birth)	App	T	G	D	Pts	Previous club	Signed
Ashcroft, John	(16.7.67)	13+2	2	—	—	8	Blackbrook ARL	7.8.92
Bacon, Mike	(26.1.67)	12	4	—	—	16	Warrington	13.11.92
Barnes, Dave	(21.10.73)	11+1	—	—	—	—	Wigan St. J. ARL	7.11.92
Barrow, Norman	(5.8.65)	8+2	2	2	1	13	Thatto Heath ARL	29.1.91
Barrow, Shaun	(8.11.67)	25	6	—	—	24	St. Helens	24.8.89
Beckett, Peter	(15.12.69)	3+9	—	—	—	—	Blackbrook ARL	24.8.89
Brown, Dave		0+1	—	—	—	—	—	—
Carney, John	(7.11.68)	5	—	—	—	—	Chorley B.	7.1.93
Carr, Mike	(14.11.64)	20	1	26	—	56	Pilkington ARL	11.8.92
Chappell, Simon	(19.5.66)	15	5	—	—	20	Halifax	3.2.91
Cooney, Paul	(9.1.66)	10+4	2	1	—	10	Clock Face ARL	1.1.91
Dean, Geoff	(31.5.62)	24	5	—	—	20	Wigan St. J. ARL	24.8.87
Denning, Mike	(11.1.65)	7	3	—	—	12	Pilkington ARL	22.9.92
Dobson, Mark	(26.6.67)	4	—	—	—	—	Salford	2.10.92
Dolan, Shaun	(1.1.70)	15+2	2	—	—	8	Blackbrook ARL	24.8.89
Dray, Henry	(19.10.72)	1	—	—	—	—	Crystal Palace ARL	26.11.92
Durnin, Paul	(5.11.60)	10	2	—	—	8	Bramley	11.8.92
Erentz, David	(27.10.64)	2+3	—	—	—	—	Chorley B.	24.12.92
Evans, Andy	(19.4.70)	12+1	3	—	—	12	Chorley B.	7.1.93
Faimalo, Joe	(28.7.70)	7	1	—	—	4	Swinton	17.8.92
Forber, Gary	(22.1.68)	2+2	—	—	—	—	Swinton	28.2.91
Goulding, Dean	(5.7.66)	0+2	—	—	—	—	Wigan St. J. ARL	1.11.90
Grady, Mick	(1.11.69)	6+1	—	—	—	—	—	8.1.90
Gregory, Ryan	(6.6.73)	0+2	—	—	—	—	Crown Springs ARL	11.12.92
Haggerty, Gary	(9.4.61)	6	—	—	—	—	Wakefield T.	14.3.92
Haggerty, Roy	(22.3.60)	3	—	—	1	1	Barrow	17.3.93
Hall, Dave	(17.9.71)	5	—	2	—	4	Haydock ARL	24.11.92
Hester, Terry	(21.1.65)	6	1	—	—	4	Bramley	12.3.93
Hine, David	(5.3.67)	9+2	2	—	—	8	Ruskin Park RU	1.9.89
Hudson, Julian	(14.6.67)	1	—	—	—	—	Blackpool G.	14.3.93
Hunter, Paul	(3.5.65)	3	—	—	—	—	Burton ARL	17.11.92

(Continued)

	(Date of Birth)	App	T	G	D	Pts	Previous club	Signed
Johnson, Chris	(29.5.60)	4	—	13	4	30	Blackpool G.	16.3.93
Johnson, Willie	(26.10.60)	19	5	—	1	21	Dewsbury	25.1.91
Jones, Gary		0+2	—	—	—	—	—	—
Kerapa, Jason	(16.7.70)	1	1	—	—	4	New Zealand	—
Lewis, Glyn	(29.3.63)	6+1	1	—	—	4	Nutgrove ARL	13.10.92
Littler, Paul	(25.8.66)	13+1	—	—	—	—	Thatto Heath ARL	3.2.91
Meadows, Dave	(17.5.71)	0+1	—	—	—	—	Bold Miners ARL	25.2.93
Meadows, Kevin	(27.2.61)	4	1	—	—	4	Chorley B.	4.9.92
Moffatt, Ian	(30.6.70)	4	—	—	—	—	Clock Face ARL	28.8.92
Parnell, Paul	(28.5.62)	2	—	—	—	—	Pilkington ARL	9.2.93
Partington, Adam	(19.12.70)	6+3	2	—	—	8	Leigh Victoria ARL	11.8.92
Pemberton, Tony	(26.5.64)	5	—	—	—	—	Blackpool G.	12.3.93
Potter, Ian	(6.8.58)	10	1	—	—	4	Bramley	13.11.92
Roscoe, Brian	(24.2.64)	2	—	—	—	—	Wigan St. J. ARL	10.11.92
Stephenson, Colin	(4.2.70)	3	1	—	—	4	Crosfields ARL	21.3.93
Tinsley, Eddie	(31.7.63)	12+5	3	—	—	12	Thatto Heath ARL	3.1.91
Twist, Bobby	(27.8.64)	7+2	1	—	—	4	Leigh Victoria ARL	1.12.91
Tyrell, Kenny	(9.6.63)	3+1	—	—	—	—	RU	22.9.92
Viller, Mark	(25.10.65)	5	—	4	1	9	Blackpool G.	12.3.93

TOTALS

			T	G	D	Pts		
50 players			57	48	8	332		

HIGHFIELD 1992-93 MATCH ANALYSIS

Date	Competition	H/A	Opponent	Rlt	Score	Tries	Goals	Attendance	Referee
30.8.92	TD	H	Dewsbury	L	12-22	Durnin, Chappell	Carr (2)	349	Atkin
6.9.92	TD	A	Doncaster	L	4-50	Twist	—	—	—
13.9.92	LC(1)	A	Swinton	L	10-40	Hine, Chappell	Carr	—	—
20.9.92	TD	H	Workington T.	L	6-48	Cooney	Cooney	283	Wood
27.9.92	TD	A	Ryedale-York	L	12-60	K. Meadows, Partington	Carr (2)	—	—
11.10.92	TD	H	Batley	L	7-22	Chappell	N. Barrow, W. Johnson (dg)	432	Carter
27.10.92	RT(P)	A	Wakefield T.	L	12-90	W. Johnson, Faimalo, S. Barrow	—	—	—
1.11.92	TD	A	Workington T.	L	0-78	—	—	—	—
15.11.92	TD	H	Ryedale-York	L	12-34	N. Barrow, W. Johnson	Carr (2)	338	Campbell
22.11.92	TD	A	Keighley C.	L	10-44	Chappell, Denning	Carr	—	—
29.11.92	TD	H	Hunslet	L	14-36	Chappell, Kerapa, Ashcroft	Carr	367	Galtress
13.12.92	TD	A	Dewsbury	L	12-52	Dean, S. Barrow	Carr (2)	—	—
10.1.93	TD	H	Whitehaven	L	18-40	Bacon (2), Dolan	Carr (3)	399	J. Connolly
17.1.93	TD	A	Hunslet	L	16-50	Denning (2), W. Johnson	Carr (2)	—	—
31.1.93	CC(1)	A	Keighley C.	L	0-86	—	—	—	—
7.2.93	TD	A	Blackpool G.	W	24-23	Bacon, Carr, Evans, Hine	Carr (4)	—	—
14.2.93	TD	H	Barrow	L	16-50	S. Barrow, Cooney, Tinsley	Carr (2)	330	Asquith
21.2.93	TD	H	Doncaster	L	16-60	Dean, Evans, Tinsley	Carr (2)	419	Nicholson
28.2.93	TD	A	Whitehaven	L	0-72	—	—	—	—
7.3.93	TD	H	Nottingham C.	W	20-18	N. Barrow, Evans, Dean, W. Johnson	Carr (2)	333	Volante
14.3.93	TD	A	Batley	L	5-24	S. Barrow	N. Barrow (dg)	—	—
16.3.93	TD	H	Keighley C.	L	8-80	Partington	Hall (2)	526	Redfearn
21.3.93	TD	H	Chorley B.	W	18-8	S. Barrow, Dean	C. Johnson (4, 2dg)	411	Redfearn
28.3.93	TD	H	Blackpool G.	W	19-12	Dean, Dolan, Lewis, Stephenson	N. Barrow, R. Haggerty (dg)	354	Nicholson
4.4.93	TD	A	Chorley B.	L	8-18	Bacon	C. Johnson (2)	—	—
9.4.93	TD	A	Barrow	W	14-8	Durnin	C. Johnson (4, 2dg)	—	—
11.4.93	TD	A	Nottingham C.	W	39-6	Ashcroft, S. Barrow, Hester, W. Johnson, Potter, Tinsley	Viller (4, 1dg), C. Johnson (3)	—	—

HUDDERSFIELD

Ground: Leeds Road (0484-530710)
First Season: 1895-96; added Barracudas to title
from 1984-85 to 1987-88 inclusive
Nickname: Fartowners
Chairman: Mick Murphy
General
Manager: Les Coulter
Honours: **Championship** Winners, 1911-12,
1912-13, 1914-15, 1928-29,
1929-30, 1948-49, 1961-62
Beaten finalists, 1913-14, 1919-20,
1922-23, 1931-32, 1945-46, 1949-50
Division Two Champions, 1974-75
Division Three Champions, 1991-92
Challenge Cup Winners, 1912-13,
1914-15, 1919-20, 1932-33, 1944-45,
1952-53
Beaten finalists, 1934-35, 1961-62
Yorkshire Cup Winners, 1909-10,
1911-12, 1913-14, 1914-15, 1918-19,
1919-20, 1926-27, 1931-32, 1938-39,
1950-51, 1952-53, 1957-58
Beaten finalists, 1910-11, 1923-24,
1925-26, 1930-31, 1937-38, 1942-43,
1949-50, 1960-61
Yorkshire League Winners,
1911-12, 1912-13, 1913-14, 1914-15,
1919-20, 1921-22, 1928-29, 1929-30,
1948-49, 1949-50, 1951-52
Eastern Division Beaten finalists,
1962-63

RECORDS

Match
Goals: 18 by Major Holland v. Swinton Park,
28 Feb 1914
Tries: 10 by Lionel Cooper v. Keighley,
17 Nov 1951
Points: 39 by Major Holland v. Swinton Park,
28 Feb 1914

Season
Goals: 147 by Ben Gronow, 1919-20
Tries: 80 by Albert Rosenfeld, 1913-14
Points: 332 by Pat Devery, 1952-53

Career
Goals: 958 by Frank Dyson, 1950-63
Tries: 420 by Lionel Cooper, 1947-55
Points: 2,072 by Frank Dyson, 1950-63
Appearances: 485 by Doug Clark, 1909-29
Highest score: 119-2 v. Swinton Park,
28 Feb 1914
Highest against: 94-12 at Castleford, 18 Sep 1988
Attendance: 35,136 Leeds v. Wakefield T.
(RL Cup SF), 19 Apr 1947
Home match: 32,912 v. Wigan
(League), 4 Mar 1950

COACHING REGISTER
● **Since 1974-75**

Brian Smith	Jan 73 - Mar 76
Keith Goulding	Mar 76 - Dec 76
Bob Tomlinson	Jan 77 - May 77
Neil Fox	June 77 - Feb 78
*Roy Francis	-
Keith Goulding	May 78 - July 79
Ian Brooke	July 79 - Mar 80
Maurice Bamford	May 80 - May 81
Les Sheard	June 81 - Nov 82
Dave Mortimer	Nov 82 - Aug 83
Mel Bedford	Aug 83 - Nov 83
Brian Lockwood	Nov 83 - Feb 85
Chris Forster	Feb 85 - Dec 86
Jack Addy	Jan 87 - Mar 88
Allen Jones Neil Whittaker	} Mar 88 - Nov 88
Nigel Stephenson	Nov 88 - Mar 90
Barry Seabourne	Mar 90 - Feb 91
Mick Blacker Francis Jarvis	} Feb 91 - Sep 91
Alex Murphy	Sep 91 -

*Although Roy Francis was appointed he was
unable to take over and Dave Heppleston
stood in until the next appointment.*

GREAT BRITAIN REGISTER
(**24 players**)

Jim Bowden	(3)	1954
Ken Bowman	(3)	1962-63
Brian Briggs	(1)	1954
Stan Brogden	(9)	1929-33
Jack Chilcott	(3)	1914
Doug Clark	(11)	1911-20
Don Close	(1)	1967
Dick Cracknell	(2)	1951
Jim Davies	(2)	1911

Frank Dyson	(1)	1959
Ben Gronow	(7)	1911-20
Fred Longstaff	(2)	1914
Ken Loxton	(1)	1971
Stan Moorhouse	(2)	1914
Bob Nicholson	(3)	1946-48
Johnny Rogers	(7)	1914-21
Ken Senior	(2)	1965-67
Tommy Smales	(5)	1962-64
Mick Sullivan	(16)	1954-57
Gwyn Thomas	(8)	1920-21
Dave Valentine	(15)	1948-54
Rob Valentine	(1)	1967
Harold Wagstaff	(12)	1911-21
Harold Young	(1)	1929

1992-93 SIGNINGS REGISTER

Signed	Player	Club From
8.8.92	Bryden, Jason	RU
8.8.92	Lee, Bryan	—
8.8.92	Riley, Mark	Deighton W. ARL
12.8.92	Armson, Alan	—
12.8.92	Slater, Lee	Ovenden ARL
15.8.92	Moore, Jonathan	Park ARL
20.8.92	Blacker, Brian	Hull
21.8.92	Flanagan, Neil	Oldham
21.8.92	Foy, Des	Oldham
21.8.92	Pucill, Andy	Swinton
3.9.92	Lister, Peter	Bramley
22.9.92	Barnett, Steve	Bradford N.
22.9.92	Hellewell, Phil	Bradford N.
18.10.92	*Haggerty, Roy	Barrow
30.10.92	Alderson, Dale	Elland ARL
30.10.92	Kerr, Ken	Halifax
26.11.92	McDermott, Paul	Nottingham C.
27.11.92	*Needham, David	Workington T.
18.12.92	*Knight, Mark	St. Helens
28.1.93	Rees, Robert	—
26.2.93	*Burns, Gary	Oldham
29.3.93	*Kelly, Andy	Wakefield T.
29.3.93	*Tong, Michael	Dewsbury

Huddersfield assistant coach Terry Flanagan, who stepped down at the end of 1992-93, having served for two years.

HUDDERSFIELD 1992-93 PLAYERS' SUMMARY

	(Date of Birth)	App	T	G	D	Pts	Previous club	Signed
Armson, Alan	(29.10.72)	0+2	—	—	—	—	ARL	12.8.92
Barnett, Steve	(8.10.68)	20+4	2	—	—	8	Bradford N.	22.9.92
Blacker, Brian	(20.3.63)	26+3	6	—	—	24	Hull	20.8.92
Boothroyd, Alan	(19.6.66)	3	—	—	—	—	David Brown ARL	24.1.86
Burns, Gary	(10.2.72)	1+1	—	—	—	—	Oldham	26.2.93
Chapman, Chris	(14.4.66)	31	13	—	—	52	Castleford	11.6.90
Coop, Chris	(25.1.69)	1	—	—	—	—	Milnrow ARL	3.11.92
Coulter, Gary	(12.7.69)	30	3	—	—	12	Doncaster	17.1.92
Darkes, Richard	(5.10.68)	2	—	—	—	—	Deighton ARL	25.6.91
Davis, Bradley	(13.3.68)	24+3	12	1	1	51	Nottingham C.	8.10.92
Derrick, Carl	(31.7.72)	1	—	—	—	—	ARL	2.10.92
Fairbank, Richard	(30.4.61)	7+7	2	—	—	8	Nottingham C.	30.10.92
Flanagan, Neil	(11.6.70)	32	6	1	8	34	Oldham	21.8.92
Fogerty, Jason	(4.10.67)	21+2	3	—	—	12	—	26.11.92
Foy, Des	(29.12.63)	4+1	—	—	—	—	Oldham	21.8.92
Gibson, Wally	(5.4.67)	2	—	—	—	—	Australia	1.9.89
Greenwood, Brandon	(28.4.72)	0+1	—	—	—	—	Ovenden ARL	21.10.92
Haggerty, Roy	(22.3.60)	3+1	1	—	—	4	Barrow	18.10.92
Hellewell, Phil	(23.4.67)	31	10	88	—	216	Bradford N.	22.9.92
Huck, Phil	(3.2.63)	9+1	2	—	—	8	Halifax	16.10.86
Kelly, Andy	(8.11.60)	2	—	—	—	—	Wakefield T.	29.3.93
Kenworthy, Simon	(11.12.63)	7	1	8	—	20	Underbank ARL	16.9.85
Kerr, Ken	(18.10.69)	23	6	—	—	24	Halifax	30.10.92
Laurence, Jason	(23.1.70)	28	13	1	—	54	Nottingham C.	8.10.92
Maders, Martin	(29.6.73)	7+9	1	—	—	4	Saddleworth ARL	30.1.92
Meillam, Paul	(30.8.70)	6+1	1	—	—	4	York All Blacks ARL	24.8.90
Metcalf, Richard	(21.2.71)	0+1	—	—	—	—	ARL	1.9.92
Mitchell, Tony	(10.6.60)	0+3	—	—	—	—	Australia	18.9.92
Naidole, Joe	(23.12.67)	32+1	7	—	—	28	Deighton W. ARL	8.1.90
Needham, David	(25.10.64)	2+6	2	—	—	8	Workington T.	27.11.92
Oates, David	(22.9.65)	4	—	9	—	18	Nottingham C.	—
Pearce, Rion	(30.4.67)	3+1	—	—	—	—	Australia	2.10.92
Pearson, Richard	(9.10.74)	0+4	1	—	—	4	Ovenden ARL	31.10.91
Pucill, Andy	(19.11.67)	32+1	5	—	—	20	Swinton	21.8.92
Royston, Paul	(20.10.66)	1+3	—	—	—	—	West Bowling ARL	24.8.90
Senior, Gary	(11.9.62)	17+4	6	—	1	25	Hunslet	21.8.89
Sewell, Andy	(5.4.69)	2+4	—	—	—	—	Moldgreen ARL	2.8.89
St. Hilaire, Lee	(15.2.67)	11+1	2	—	—	8	ARL	30.12.92
Simpson, Andy	(16.3.66)	8+7	2	—	—	8	ARL	4.8.92
Thomas, Ian	(6.11.64)	34	21	—	—	84	—	3.6.83
Yates, Warren	(1.10.65)	1+1	—	—	—	—	Australia	18.9.92

TOTALS

			T	G	D	Pts		
41 players			128	108	10	738		

HUDDERSFIELD 1992-93 MATCH ANALYSIS

Date	Competition	H/A	Opponent	Rlt	Score	Tries	Goals	Attendance	Referee
23.8.92	YC(P)	H[1]	Ryedale-York	W	36-12	Kenworthy, Senior, Huck, Thomas, Naidole, Flanagan	Oates (4), Kenworthy (2)	1619	Cross
30.8.92	SD	H	Featherstone R.	L	15-34	Senior, Blacker	Kenworthy (3), Flanagan (dg)	3008	Steele
6.9.92	SD	A	Bramley	L	10-34	Blacker	Kenworthy (2), Flanagan	—	—
13.9.92	YC(1)	H	Batley	W	16-8	Blacker, Thomas, Naidole	Oates (2)	1714	Asquith
20.9.92	SD	H	Oldham	L	24-28	Thomas, St. Hilaire, Meillam, Senior	Oates (3), Kenworthy	2891	Kershaw
23.9.92	YC(2)	A	Featherstone R.	L	8-18	Pucill	Hellewell (2)	—	—
27.9.92	SD	A	London C.	L	10-46	Thomas (2)	Hellewell	—	—
4.10.92	SD	H	Swinton	W	37-10	Hellewell, Flanagan, Coulter, Blacker, Pucill, Laurence	Hellewell (6), Senior (dg)	1502	Crashley
9.10.92	Tour	H	Australia	L	2-66	—	Hellewell	4716	Holdsworth
15.10.92	SD	H	Carlisle	L	4-24	Chapman	—	1160	Wood
18.10.92	SD	H	Rochdale H.	L	14-22	Davis (2), Naidole	Hellewell	1570	R. Connolly
27.10.92	RT(P)	A	St. Helens	L	18-44	Huck, Pearson, Haggerty	Hellewell (3)	—	—
1.11.92	SD	A	Featherstone R.	W	25-18	Blacker, Laurence, Flanagan, Hellewell	Hellewell (4), Flanagan (dg)	—	—
15.11.92	SD	H	Bramley	W	18-12	Fairbank, Kerr, Thomas	Hellewell (3)	1563	Crashley
22.11.92	SD	A	Oldham	W	17-6	Davis, Thomas, Kerr	Hellewell (2), Flanagan (dg)	—	—
29.11.92	SD	H	London C.	W	18-14	Thomas, Flanagan, Davis	Hellewell (3)	2032	Holdsworth
13.12.92	SD	H	Swinton	W	19-12	Naidole, Davis, Flanagan	Hellewell (3), Flanagan (dg)	1894	Wood
5.1.93	SD	H	Featherstone R.	L	20-24	Fairbank, Laurence, Senior	Hellewell (4)	2849	Cross
10.1.93	SD	A	Featherstone R.	L	12-34	Needham, Maders	Hellewell (2)	—	—
14.1.93	SD	H	Carlisle	W	36-24	Chapman (3), Thomas (2), Pucill, Hellewell	Hellewell (4)	1307	Asquith
24.1.93	SD	A	Carlisle	W	28-12	Chapman, Davis, Laurence, Simpson	Hellewell (6)	—	—
31.1.93	CC(1)	H	Nottingham C.	W	66-1	Hellewell (2), Laurence (2), Naidole (2), Thomas (2), Chapman, Coulter, Davis, Pucill, Senior	Hellewell (7)	1765	Nicholson
7.2.93	SD	A	Bramley	W	27-10	Laurence (2), Barnett, Hellewell, Naidole	Hellewell (3), Flanagan (dg)	—	—
14.2.93	CC(2)	A	Oldham	L	17-20	Davis, Laurence	Hellewell (4), Flanagan (dg)	—	—
21.2.93	SD	H	Rochdale H.	L	12-17	Chapman, Hellewell	Hellewell (2)	2182	Crashley
3.3.93	SD	A	Rochdale H.	L	14-24	Laurence (2), Fogerty	Hellewell	—	—
7.3.93	SD	H	Oldham	W	14-8	Laurence, Pucill, Simpson	Hellewell	2413	Galtress
14.3.93	SD	A	London C.	L	17-31	Hellewell (2), Coulter	Hellewell (2), Flanagan (dg)	—	—
21.3.93	SD	A	Carlisle	W	29-16	Davis, Flanagan, Kerr, St. Hilaire, Thomas	Hellewell (4), Flanagan (dg)	—	—
25.3.93	SD	H	London C.	W	17-2	Chapman (2), Kerr	Hellewell (2), Davis (dg)	1596	Wood
28.3.93	SD	A	Swinton	L	18-19	Fogerty, Kerr, Laurence	Hellewell (2), Davis	—	—
4.4.93	SD	A	Rochdale H.	W	38-27	Davis (2), Blacker, Chapman, Fogerty, Needham, Thomas	Hellewell (4), Laurence	—	—
9.4.93	SD	H	Bramley	W	20-4	Chapman (2), Thomas (2)	Hellewell (2)	1822	Galtress
12.4.93	SD	A	Oldham	L	24-28	Thomas (2), Chapman, Hellewell	Hellewell (4)	—	—
18.4.93	SD	A	Swinton	W	28-8	Thomas (2), Barnett, Kerr, Senior	Hellewell (4)	—	—
25.4.93	DP(2)	H	Workington T.	L	10-24	Davis, Thomas	Hellewell	3312	J. Smith

[1] at Fartown, Huddersfield

HULL

Ground: The Boulevard (0482-29040)
First Season: 1895-96
Nickname: Airlie Birds
Chairman: Steve Watson
Secretary: Brian Johnson
Honours: **Championship** Winners, 1919-20,
             1920-21, 1935-36, 1955-56, 1957-58
             Beaten finalists, 1956-57
             Division One Champions, 1982-83
             Division Two Champions, 1976-77,
             1978-79
             Challenge Cup Winners, 1913-14,
             1981-82
             Beaten finalists, 1907-08, 1908-09,
             1909-10, 1921-22, 1922-23, 1958-59,
             1959-60, 1979-80, 1982-83, 1984-85
             Regal Trophy Winners, 1981-82
             Beaten finalists, 1975-76, 1984-85
             Premiership Winners, 1990-91
             Beaten finalists, 1980-81, 1981-82,
             1982-83, 1988-89
             Yorkshire Cup Winners, 1923-24,
             1969-70, 1982-83, 1983-84, 1984-85
             Beaten finalists, 1912-13, 1914-15,
             1920-21, 1927-28, 1938-39, 1946-47,
             1953-54, 1954-55, 1955-56, 1959-60,
             1967-68, 1986-87
             Yorkshire League Winners,
             1918-19, 1922-23, 1926-27, 1935-36
             Charity Shield Beaten finalists,
             1991-92
             BBC2 Floodlit Trophy Winners,
             1979-80

RECORDS
Match
Goals: 14 by Jim Kennedy v. Rochdale H.,
        7 Apr 1921
        Geoff "Sammy" Lloyd v. Oldham,
        10 Sep 1978
Tries: 7 by Clive Sullivan at Doncaster,
        15 Apr 1968
Points: 36 by Jim Kennedy v. Keighley,
        29 Jan 1921

Season
Goals: 170 by Geoff "Sammy" Lloyd, 1978-79
Tries: 52 by Jack Harrison, 1914-15
Points: 369 by Geoff "Sammy" Lloyd, 1978-79

Career
Goals: 687 by Joe Oliver, 1928-37 & 1943-45
Tries: 250 by Clive Sullivan, 1961-74 &
        1981-85
Points: 1,842 by Joe Oliver, 1928-37 & 1943-45
Appearances: 501 by Edward Rogers, 1906-25
Highest score: 86-0 v. Elland, 1 Apr 1899
Highest against: 64-2 at St. Helens, 17 Feb 1988
Attendance: 28,798 v. Leeds (RL Cup),
        7 Mar 1936

COACHING REGISTER
● **Since 1974-75**

David Doyle-Davidson	May 74 - Dec 77
Arthur Bunting	Jan 78 - Dec 85
Kenny Foulkes	Dec 85 - May 86
Len Casey	June 86 - Mar 88
Tony Dean	Mar 88 - Apr 88
Keith Hepworth	
*Brian Smith	July 88 - Jan 91
*Noel Cleal	Sep 90 - Apr 92
Royce Simmons	May 92-

Joint coaches Sep 90 - Jan 91.

*Former Australian Test hooker Royce Simmons,
a debutant coach for Hull in 1992-93.*

GREAT BRITAIN REGISTER
(35 players)

Billy Batten	(1)	1921
Harold Bowman	(8)	1924-29
Frank Boylen	(1)	1908
Robin Coverdale	(4)	1954
Mick Crane	(1)	1982
Lee Crooks	(11+2)	1982-87
Andy Dannatt	(3)	1985-91
Gary Divorty	(2)	1985
Jim Drake	(1)	1960
Bill Drake	(1)	1962
Paul Eastwood	(13)	1990-92
Steve Evans	(2)	1982
Vince Farrar	(1)	1978
Dick Gemmell	(2)	1968-69
Emlyn Gwynne	(3)	1928-29
Tommy Harris	(25)	1954-60
Karl Harrison	(3)	1990
Mick Harrison	(7)	1967-73
Billy Holder	(1)	1907
Lee Jackson	(11)	1990-92
Mark Jones	(+1)	1992
Arthur Keegan	(9)	1966-69
Steve McNamara	(+2)	1992-93
Edgar Morgan	(2)	1921
Steve Norton	(9)	1978-82
Wayne Proctor	(+1)	1984
Paul Rose	(1)	1982
Garry Schofield	(15)	1984-87
Trevor Skerrett	(6)	1980-82
Billy Stone	(8)	1920-21
Clive Sullivan	(17)	1967-73
Harry Taylor	(3)	1907
Bob Taylor	(2)	1921-26
David Topliss	(1)	1982
Johnny Whiteley	(15)	1957-62

Hull forward Bill Drake, capped once in 1962.

1992-93 SIGNINGS REGISTER

Signed	Player	Club From
8.6.92	Duke, Gary	Hull Academy
1.7.92	Gray, Kevin	Minehead ARL
15.7.92	Gale, Scott	Canberra, Aus
27.7.92	Grant, James	Balmain, Aus
21.8.92	*Shaw, Neil	Barrow
12.9.92	Donkin, Matt	Beverley RU
23.9.92	*Dusher, Mark	Warrington
24.9.92	Clark, Garry	Scarborough P.
30.9.92	Henjak, Ivan	St. George, Aus
31.10.92	Cassidy, Jeremy	—
6.1.93	Divet, Daniel	Carcassonne, Fr
9.3.93	Hewitt, Mark	Hull Academy
9.3.93	Hodgson, Matthew	Hull Academy
9.3.93	Markham, Lee	Hull Academy
9.3.93	Murray, Matthew	Hull Academy
16.3.93	Greenwood, Brandon	Ovenden ARL
3.4.93	Sedman, Lance	Hull Boys Club ARL
20.4.93	Beet, Carl	Minehead ARL
22.4.93	Fraser, Lee	Hull Academy
23.4.93	Baird, Stewart	North Bransholme ARL

HULL 1992-93 PLAYERS' SUMMARY

	(Date of Birth)	App	T	G	D	Pts	Previous club	Signed
Busby, Dean	(1.12.73)	14+4	4	—	—	16	Bransholme YC ARL	1.2.90
Carlyle, Brendan	(25.12.68)	2	—	—	—	—	Featherstone R.	22.8.92
Clark, Garry	(4.1.65)	3	—	—	—	—	Scarborough P.	24.9.92
Danby, Rob	(30.8.74)	1	—	—	—	—	Hull Boys Club ARL	30.8.91
Dannatt, Andy	(20.11.65)	22+3	3	—	—	12	Villa YC ARL	7.6.82
Dearlove, Andrew	(19.9.72)	6+6	2	—	—	8	British Gas ARL	14.8.90
Divet, Daniel	(11.12.66)	2+2	—	—	—	—	France	6.9.93
Dixon, Mike	(6.4.71)	7+9	1	—	—	4	East Park ARL	29.8.89
Donkin, Matt	(23.11.71)	11	3	—	—	12	Beverley RU	12.9.92
Durham, Steve	(12.10.63)	1	—	—	—	—	Bramley	22.3.91
Eastwood, Paul	(3.12.65)	29+1	11	84	—	212	Hullensians RU	21.1.85
Gale, Scott	(10.2.65)	26	9	—	—	36	Australia	15.7.92
Gay, Richard	(9.3.69)	30	8	—	—	32	Hull Boys Club ARL	13.9.89
Grant, James	(22.5.64)	26	10	—	—	40	Australia	27.7.92
Harrison, Paul	(24.9.70)	7+3	4	—	—	16	Featherstone MW ARL	30.9.88
Henjak, Ivan	(9.3.63)	22	2	—	—	8	Australia	30.9.92
Hunter, Paul	(12.4.71)	0+1	—	—	—	—	Eureka ARL	21.9.88
Jackson, Anthony	(20.11.69)	11+10	3	—	—	12	Greatfield ARL	8.7.88
Jackson, Lee	(12.3.69)	28	6	—	—	24	Villa ARL	17.4.86
Jones, Mark	(22.6.65)	13+4	1	—	—	4	Neath RU	12.10.90
McNamara, Steve	(18.9.71)	25	5	—	—	20	Skirlaugh ARL	15.6.89
Marlow, Ian	(18.1.63)	21+3	—	—	—	—	Beverley RU	25.7.90
Mighty, Andrew	(25.10.67)	8	1	—	—	4	Fulham	27.3.89
Nolan, Gary	(31.5.66)	20+1	1	—	—	4	NDLB ARL	2.4.91
Nolan, Rob	(2.10.68)	30+3	4	—	—	16	Hull Colts	1.1.88
O'Donnell, Craig	(2.10.73)	1+3	1	—	—	4	Hull Boys Club ARL	23.7.91
Rushton, Nick	(10.12.71)	0+2	—	—	—	—	Barrow I. ARL	15.8.91
Sharp, Jon	(8.3.67)	31	1	—	—	4	Travellers ARL	12.3.84
Smirk, Terry	(5.8.66)	3	—	4	1	9	Hull Dockers ARL	23.10.91
Stevens, Ian	(18.2.67)	4+1	—	—	—	—	Swansea RU	11.12.91
Sullivan, Scott	(25.10.73)	2	—	—	—	—	Crown Malet ARL	23.7.91
Turner, Neil	(30.10.63)	7	3	—	—	12	Doncaster	14.12.89
Walker, Russ	(1.9.62)	25+8	—	—	—	—	Barrow	8.1.90
Wilson, Rob	(31.8.72)	4+3	—	—	—	—	West Hull ARL	13.8.91

TOTALS

			T	G	D	Pts		
34 players			83	88	1	509		

Representative appearances 1992-93

Busby — England (+1)
Jackson, Lee — England (1)
Jones — Wales (1, 1t)
McNamara — Britain (+1); GB Under-21 (1)

Marlow — Wales (2)
Stevens — Wales (+1)
Walker — Cumbria (1)

HULL 1992-93 MATCH ANALYSIS

Date	Com- petition	H/A	Opponent	Rlt	Score	Tries	Goals	Atten- dance	Referee
30.8.92	SBC	H	Bradford N.	W	24-14	Dannatt, Harrison, Sharp	Eastwood (6)	5312	Cummings
6.9.92	SBC	A	Wigan	W	14-13	G. Nolan, O'Donnell	Eastwood (3)	–	–
13.9.92	YC(1)	H	Hull K.R.	W	14-6	Gale, Harrison	Eastwood (3)	8825	Holdsworth
18.9.92	SBC	H	Warrington	L	14-29	Busby, Mighty	Eastwood (3)	4489	J. Connolly
23.9.92	YC(2)	H	Leeds	W	26-16	Eastwood, R. Nolan, Dixon, Busby	Eastwood (5)	6609	Redfearn
27.9.92	SBC	A	Castleford	L	6-34	Dearlove	Eastwood	–	–
4.10.92	SBC	H	Halifax	W	26-8	McNamara (3), Eastwood, L. Jackson	Eastwood (3)	6906	Holdsworth
6.10.92	YC(SF)	A	Sheffield E.	L	8-12	L. Jackson	Eastwood (2)	–	–
11.10.92	SBC	A	St. Helens	L	8-38	Grant, Harrison	–	–	–
18.10.92	SBC	A	Leigh	W	14-8	McNamara, Dearlove, Grant	Eastwood	–	–
1.11.92	SBC	A	Warrington	L	10-34	Harrison, Grant	Eastwood	–	–
8.11.92	RT(1)	H	Dewsbury	W	22-16	Eastwood, Grant, A. Jackson, Gay	Eastwood (3)	2984	Whitfield
15.11.92	SBC	H	Leeds	W	22-19	Gale, Gay, L. Jackson, Eastwood	Eastwood (3)	6033	J. Connolly
20.11.92	SBC	A	Wakefield T.	L	4-6	–	Eastwood (2)	–	–
29.11.92	SBC	H	Salford	W	42-10	Eastwood (2), Busby (2), Grant, L. Jackson, R. Nolan	Eastwood (7)	4047	J. Smith
6.12.92	RT(2)	H	Halifax	W	28-14	Dannatt, Gale, Grant, L. Jackson, Donkin	Eastwood (4)	5494	Gilmour
20.12.92	RT(3)	H	Leigh	W	24-14	Eastwood, R. Nolan, Henjak	Eastwood (6)	4835	Whitfield
26.12.92	SBC	H	Sheffield E.	W	24-10	Gay (2), Donkin, Gale	Eastwood (4)	4551	J. Smith
2.1.93	RT(SF)	A	Wigan	L	4-19	Donkin	–	–	–
6.1.93	SBC	H	Wakefield T.	L	16-20	Grant, Gale	Eastwood (4)	4213	Steele
10.1.93	SBC	H	Widnes	W	20-4	Gale (2), R. Nolan	Eastwood (4)	4347	Gilmour
17.1.93	CC(P)	A	Wigan	L	2-40	–	Eastwood	–	–
20.1.93	SBC	A	Hull K.R.	L	0-8	–	–	–	–
24.1.93	SBC	H	Castleford	L	2-14	–	Eastwood	4176	Ollerton
4.2.93	SBC	A	Bradford N.	L	14-30	Gale, Grant	Eastwood (3)	–	–
7.2.93	SBC	A	Widnes	L	4-22	A. Jackson	–	–	–
17.2.93	SBC	H	Wigan	L	0-42	–	–	5172	Whitfield
21.2.93	SBC	H	St. Helens	W	21-16	Dannatt, A. Jackson, Turner	Smirk (4, 1dg)	4291	R. Smith
3.3.93	SBC	A	Halifax	L	0-34	–	–	–	–
7.3.93	SBC	A	Salford	L	10-26	Grant, Henjak	Eastwood	–	–
14.3.93	SBC	H	Leigh	L	20-36	Gay, L. Jackson, Jones	Eastwood (4)	3363	Steele
28.3.93	SBC	A	Leeds	L	34-38	Gay (3), Eastwood, McNamara, Turner	Eastwood (5)	–	–
9.4.93	SBC	H	Hull K.R.	W	14-4	Eastwood, Gale	Eastwood (3)	6281	R. Smith
11.4.93	SBC	A	Sheffield E.	D	18-18	Eastwood (2), Grant, Turner	Eastwood	–	–

HULL KINGSTON ROVERS

Ground: Craven Park (0482-74648)
First Season: 1899-1900
Nickname: Robins
Chairman: Phil Lowe
Secretary: Ron Turner
Honours: **Championship** Winners, 1922-23, 1924-25
Beaten finalists, 1920-21, 1967-68
Division One Champions, 1978-79, 1983-84, 1984-85
Division Two Champions, 1989-90
Challenge Cup Winners, 1979-80
Beaten finalists, 1904-05, 1924-25, 1963-64, 1980-81, 1985-86
Regal Trophy Winners, 1984-85
Beaten finalists, 1981-82, 1985-86
Premiership Winners, 1980-81, 1983-84
Beaten finalists, 1984-85
Second Division Premiership Beaten finalists, 1989-90
Yorkshire Cup Winners, 1920-21, 1929-30, 1966-67, 1967-68, 1971-72, 1974-75, 1985-86
Beaten finalists, 1906-07, 1911-12, 1933-34, 1962-63, 1975-76, 1980-81, 1984-85
Yorkshire League Winners, 1924-25, 1925-26
Eastern Division Championship Winners, 1962-63
Charity Shield Beaten finalists, 1985-86
BBC2 Floodlit Trophy Winners, 1977-78
Beaten finalists, 1979-80

RECORDS

Match
Goals: 14 by Alf Carmichael v. Merthyr Tydfil, 8 Oct 1910
Mike Fletcher v. Whitehaven, 18 Mar 1990

Colin Armstrong v. Nottingham C. (at Doncaster), 19 Aug 1990
Tries: 11 by George West v. Brookland R., 4 Mar 1905
Points: 53 by George West v. Brookland R., 4 Mar 1905

Season
Goals: 199 by Mike Fletcher, 1989-90
Tries: 45 by Gary Prohm, 1984-85
Points: 450 by Mike Fletcher, 1989-90

Career
Goals: 1,192 by Cyril Kellett, 1956-67
Tries: 207 by Roger Millward, 1966-80
Points: 2,489 by Cyril Kellett, 1956-67
Appearances: 481+8 by Mike Smith, 1974-91
Highest score: 100-6 v. Nottingham C. (at Doncaster), 19 Aug 1990
Highest against: 76-8 at Halifax, 20 Oct 1991
Attendance: 27,670 v. Hull (League), 3 Apr 1953 — at Boothferry Park, Hull C. AFC
8,557 v. Hull (League), 1 Jan 1991 — at new Craven Park

COACHING REGISTER
● **Since 1974-75**

Arthur Bunting	Feb 72 - Nov 75
Harry Poole	Dec 75 - Mar 77
Roger Millward	Mar 77 - May 91
George Fairbairn	May 91 -

GREAT BRITAIN REGISTER
(26 players)

David Bishop	(+1)	1990
Chris Burton	(8+1)	1982-87
Alan Burwell	(7+1)	1967-69
Len Casey	(7+2)	1977-83
Garry Clark	(3)	1984-85
Alec Dockar	(1)	1947
George Fairbairn	(3)	1981-82
Jack Feetham	(1)	1929
Peter Flanagan	(14)	1962-70
Frank Foster	(1)	1967
David Hall	(2)	1984
Paul Harkin	(+1)	1985
Steve Hartley	(3)	1980-81
Phil Hogan	(2+2)	1979
Roy Holdstock	(2)	1980
Bill Holliday	(8+1)	1964-67
David Laws	(1)	1986

Brian Lockwood	(1+1)	1978-79
Phil Lowe	(12)	1970-78
Roger Millward	(27+1)	1967-78
Harry Poole	(1)	1964
Paul Rose	(1+3)	1974-78
Mike Smith	(10+1)	1979-84
Brian Tyson	(3)	1963-67
David Watkinson	(12+1)	1979-86
Chris Young	(5)	1967-68

1992-93 SIGNINGS REGISTER

Signed	Player	Club From
28.8.92	Windley, Phil	Scarborough P.
16.9.92	Brown, Gary	Embassy ARL
16.9.92	Sage, Tim	Eureka ARL
30.9.92	Wardrobe, Neil	Beverley RU
2.10.92	Goldman, Troy	Inverell Hawks, Aus
21.10.92	McKeough, Craig	Canterbury, Aus
27.10.92	Smith, Damien	Inverell Hawks, Aus
29.10.92	Hutchinson, Rob	Halifax
3.12.92	Liddiard, David	Manly, Aus
10.12.92	Clark, Dean	NZ
11.12.92	Hardy, Craig	Hull K.R. Academy
11.12.92	Lowe, Andrew	Hull K.R. Academy
8.2.93	Adams, Jonathan	Minehead ARL
4.3.93	Aston, Jon	Bransholme ARL
11.3.93	*Lazenby, Tracy	Wakefield T.
19.3.93	Hall, Carl	Newcastle Knights, Aus

HULL KINGSTON ROVERS 1992-93 PLAYERS' SUMMARY

	(Date of Birth)	App	T	G	D	Pts	Previous club	Signed
Barkworth, Julian	(10.4.69)	21+4	5	—	—	20	Ionians RU	11.9.91
Bibby, Mike	(23.10.70)	22	5	—	—	20	East Park ARL	21.6.89
Brown, Gary	(5.9.74)	5+2	1	—	—	4	Embassy ARL	16.9.92
Chamberlain, Richard	(1.4.73)	16	5	—	—	20	Greatfield ARL	1.6.91
Chatfield, Gary	(26.7.67)	18+3	2	12	1	33	Eureka ARL	24.8.90
Clark, Dean	(6.1.68)	13	8	—	—	32	New Zealand	10.12.92
Cook, Graham	(3.10.70)	9	2	—	—	8	Greatfield ARL	14.7.90
Crane, Mike	(11.2.71)	3+1	—	—	—	—	Greatfield ARL	14.7.90
Fletcher, Mike	(14.4.67)	29	—	71	—	142	Hull KR Colts	28.9.85
Fletcher, Paul	(17.3.70)	25+2	3	—	—	12	Eureka ARL	1.9.87
Goldman, Troy	(6.11.69)	2+3	2	—	—	8	Australia	2.10.92
Gotts, Andy	(26.10.69)	1+1	—	—	—	—	Skirlaugh ARL	21.6.89
Hall, Carl	(10.8.69)	3	2	—	—	8	Australia	19.3.93
Hardy, Craig	(24.8.73)	1	—	—	—	—	Hull KR Academy	11.12.92
Harrison, Chris	(28.9.67)	14+13	2	—	—	8	Eureka ARL	23.9.91
Harrison, Des	(10.10.64)	14+4	3	—	—	12	Hull KR Colts	16.4.85
Hoe, Sean	(3.12.70)	7+6	1	—	—	4	ARL	14.7.90
Hutchinson, Rob	(20.9.68)	19+2	5	—	—	20	Halifax	29.10.92
Jackson, Wayne	(19.9.67)	20+3	—	—	—	—	West Hull ARL	28.9.90
Lazenby, Tracy	(7.6.63)	0+2	1	—	—	4	Wakefield T.	11.3.93
Leighton, Jamie	(5.9.73)	1	—	—	—	—	Crown Malet ARL	22.7.91
Liddiard, David	(24.2.61)	17+1	8	—	—	32	Australia	3.12.92
Lowe, Andrew	(9.2.73)	1	—	—	—	—	Hull KR Academy	11.12.92
Lyman, Paul	(24.5.65)	10+2	4	—	—	16	Featherstone R.	8.1.89
McKeough, Craig	(28.5.69)	11	4	—	—	16	Australia	21.10.92
O'Brien, Craig	(4.4.69)	28+3	3	—	—	12	West Hull ARL	28.9.88
Parker, Wayne	(2.4.67)	25+5	4	—	1	17	ARL	8.9.86
Richardson, Lee	(29.10.68)	18	—	—	—	—	Hull BC	1.6.88
Richardson, Steve	(5.10.68)	1+5	—	—	—	—	Greatfield ARL	9.8.91
Robson, Steve	(13.3.70)	0+1	—	—	—	—	East Park ARL	2.8.89
Sims, Gary	(24.8.64)	3	—	—	—	—	ARL	28.1.85
Sodje, Bright	(21.4.66)	22	6	—	—	24	Blackheath RU	20.8.90
Speckman, Paul	(17.10.66)	29	—	—	2	2	ARL	21.1.85

	(Date of Birth)	App	T	G	D	Pts	Previous club	Signed
Thompson, Andy ....(29.6.68)......		28+1	2	—	—	8	Hull KR Colts	24.8.87
Vannett, Paul ....(19.10.62).....		2+2	—	—	—	—	Workington T.	7.9.89
Wardrobe, Neil...........(12.9.72)		1+1	—	—	—	—	Beverley RU	30.9.92
Windley, Phil ....(7.1.62)........		3	—	—	—	—	Scarborough P.	28.8.92
TOTALS								
37 players			78	83	4	482		

Representative appearances 1992-93

Chamberlain — GB Under-21s (+1); Vannett — Cumbria (1)

HULL KINGSTON ROVERS 1992-93 MATCH ANALYSIS

Date	Competition	H/A	Opponent	Rlt	Score	Tries	Goals	Attendance	Referee
30.8.92	SBC	A	Salford	W	14-10	Cook, O'Brien	M. Fletcher (3)	—	—
4.9.92	SBC	H	Widnes	L	2-16	—	M. Fletcher	3077	Steele
13.9.92	YC(1)	A	Hull	L	6-14	Sodje	M. Fletcher	—	—
20.9.92	SBC	A	Leeds	L	6-34	Sodje	M. Fletcher	—	—
27.9.92	SBC	H	Sheffield E.	L	6-19	O'Brien	M. Fletcher	2844	J. Connolly
4.10.92	SBC	A	Widnes	L	0-52	—	—	—	—
11.10.92	SBC	H	Leigh	W	30-1	Bibby, Sodje, Lyman, Hoe	M. Fletcher (7)	2514	Whitfield
18.10.92	SBC	A	Bradford N.	L	0-44	—	—	—	—
28.10.92	RT(P)	A	Swinton	W	32-12	Parker (2), Lyman, McKeough, D. Harrison, Barkworth	M. Fletcher (4)	—	—
1.11.92	SBC	H	Salford	L	10-16	McKeough	M. Fletcher (3)	3978	Cummings
8.11.92	RT(1)	H	Whitehaven	W	48-4	Lyman (2), Sodje, Parker, C. Harrison, D. Harrison, P. Fletcher, Goldman	M. Fletcher (8)	1627	Wood
15.11.92	SBC	A	Sheffield E.	L	12-28	Goldman	M. Fletcher (4)	—	—
22.11.92	SBC	H	Castleford	L	2-8	—	M. Fletcher	3172	J. Smith
29.11.92	SBC	A	Wigan	L	18-48	Sodje, Hutchinson, P. Fletcher	M. Fletcher (3)	—	—
6.12.92	RT(2)	H	Wigan	L	0-18	—	—	3779	R. Smith
13.12.92	SBC	A	Leigh	L	24-31	Clark (2), Liddiard, McKeough	Chatfield (4)	—	—
20.12.92	SBC	H	Warrington	W	13-11	O'Brien, McKeough	M. Fletcher (2), Speckman (dg)	2715	Campbell
28.12.92	SBC	A	Wakefield T.	W	17-10	Liddiard, Thompson, Chatfield	M. Fletcher (2), Speckman (dg)	—	—
10.1.93	SBC	A	Halifax	L	12-20	Liddiard, Chatfield	M. Fletcher (2)	—	—
17.1.93	SBC	H	St. Helens	L	11-22	Barkworth, Hutchinson	M. Fletcher, Chatfield (dg)	4077	J. Smith
20.1.93	SBC	H	Hull	W	8-0	Liddiard	M. Fletcher (2)	6580	Whitfield
24.1.93	SBC	A	Warrington	L	26-47	Parker, Chamberlain, Clark, Cook, C. Harrison	M. Fletcher (3)	—	—
31.1.93	CC(1)	H	Bramley	W	30-0	Hutchinson (2), Barkworth, Clark, Liddiard	M. Fletcher (5)	2017	Wood
7.2.93	SBC	H	Leeds	L	16-18	Chamberlain (2), Bibby	Chatfield (2)	5287	R. Smith
14.2.93	CC(2)	H	Keighley C.	W	30-28	Clark (3), Barkworth (2),	Chatfield (3)	3109	Galtress
28.2.93	CC(3)	H	Widnes	D	4-4	P. Fletcher	—	6286	Steele
3.3.93	CC(3) Replay	A	Widnes	L	11-16	Bibby, Clark	Chatfield, Parker (dg)	—	—
9.3.93	SBC	H	Wigan	L	12-26	Chamberlain, Bibby	M. Fletcher (2)	8660	J. Smith
12.3.93	SBC	A	St. Helens	L	14-34	Bibby, D. Harrison	Chatfield (2), M. Fletcher	—	—
21.3.93	SBC	A	Castleford	L	18-36	Hall (2), Liddiard	M. Fletcher (3)	—	—
4.4.93	SBC	H	Wakefield T.	W	28-10	Chamberlain, Hutchinson, Liddiard, Thompson	M. Fletcher (6)	3049	R. Connolly
9.4.93	SBC	A	Hull	L	4-14	—	M. Fletcher (2)	—	—
14.4.93	SBC	H	Bradford N.	W	12-6	Brown, Sodje	M. Fletcher (2)	2702	Cummings
18.4.93	SBC	H	Halifax	L	6-38	Lazenby	M. Fletcher	3260	Whitfield

HUNSLET

Ground: Elland Road (0532-711675)
First Season: 1895-96. Disbanded at end of 1972-73. Re-formed as New Hunslet in 1973-74. Retitled Hunslet from start of 1979-80
Chairman: Graham Liles
Secretary: Wendy Anderson
Honours: **Championship** Winners, 1907-08, 1937-38
Beaten finalists, 1958-59
Division Two Champions, 1962-63, 1986-87
Challenge Cup Winners, 1907-08, 1933-34
Beaten finalists, 1898-99, 1964-65
Second Division Premiership Beaten finalists, 1986-87
Yorkshire Cup Winners, 1905-06, 1907-08, 1962-63
Beaten finalists, 1908-09, 1929-30, 1931-32, 1944-45, 1956-57, 1965-66
Yorkshire League Winners, 1897-98, 1907-08, 1931-32

RECORDS

Match
Goals: 12 by Billy Langton v. Keighley, 18 Aug 1959
Tries: 7 by George Dennis v. Bradford N., 20 Jan 1934
Points: 28 by Tim Lumb v. Runcorn H., 7 Oct 1990

Season
Goals: 181 by Billy Langton, 1958-59
Tries: 34 by Alan Snowden, 1956-57
Points: 380 by Billy Langton, 1958-59

Career
Goals: 1,044 by Billy Langton, 1955-66
Tries: 154 by Fred Williamson, 1943-55
Points: 2,202 by Billy Langton, 1955-66
Appearances: 569+10 by Geoff Gunney, 1951-73
572 by Jack Walkington, 1927-48

Highest score: 76-4 at Nottingham C., 21 Feb 1993
Highest against: 76-8 v. Halifax, 27 Aug 1972
Attendance: 54,112 v. Leeds (Championship final), 30 Apr 1938
Home match: 14,004 v. Castleford (RL Cup), 13 Mar 1983

COACHING REGISTER
● **Since 1974-75**

Paul Daley	Apr 74 - Aug 78
Bill Ramsey	Aug 78 - Dec 79
Drew Broatch	Dec 79 - Apr 81
Paul Daley	Apr 81 - Nov 85
*Peter Jarvis	Nov 85 - Apr 88
*David Ward	July 86 - Apr 88
Nigel Stephenson	June 88 - Oct 88
Jack Austin	Oct 88 - Jan 89
John Wolford	
David Ward	Jan 89 - May 89
Graeme Jennings	Sep 89 - Apr 90
Paul Daley	May 90 -

Joint coaches from July 1986.

GREAT BRITAIN REGISTER
(23 players)

Billy Batten	(9)	1907-11
Harry Beverley	(4)	1936-37
Alf Burnell	(3)	1951-54
Hector Crowther	(1)	1929
Jack Evans	(4)	1951-52
Ken Eyre	(1)	1965
Brian Gabbitas	(1)	1959
Geoff Gunney	(11)	1954-65
Dennis Hartley	(2)	1964
John Higson	(2)	1908
Dai Jenkins	(1)	1929
Albert Jenkinson	(2)	1911
Bill Jukes	(6)	1908-10
Bernard Prior	(1)	1966
Bill Ramsey	(7)	1965-66
Brian Shaw	(5)	1956-60
Geoff Shelton	(7)	1964-66
Fred Smith	(9)	1910-14
Sam Smith	(4)	1954
Cecil Thompson	(2)	1951
Les White	(7)	1932-33
Dicky Williams	(3)	1954
Harry Wilson	(3)	1907

1992-93 SIGNINGS REGISTER

Signed	Player	Club From
14.7.92	Rose, Ian	Ossett Trinity ARL
30.7.92	Speight, Mark	Batley
31.7.92	*Speight, Darren	Batley
18.8.92	Francis, Richard	Bradford N.
20.8.92	Rees, Paul	Toronto Workers, Aus
2.9.92	Beath, Paul	Toronto Workers, Aus
3.9.92	*Gearey, Paul	Batley
16.9.92	Yeomans, Richard	Farnley Eagles ARL
30.9.92	Harkin, Paul	Halifax
14.10.92	Snee, Gavin	Bradford N.
16.10.92	Croft, David	Bradford N.
6.12.92	Bailey, Adam	Travellers ARL
6.12.92	Sampson, Lee	Nottingham C.
18.12.92	*McElhatton, Craig	Wakefield T.
11.2.93	*Harrison, Paul	Hull
21.2.93	*Ellis, Mark	Doncaster
25.2.93	*Johnson, Dean	Sheffield E.
12.3.93	*Lee, Darren	Bradford N.
17.3.93	*Booth, Craig	Featherstone R.

HUNSLET 1992-93 PLAYERS' SUMMARY

	(Date of Birth)	App	T	G	D	Pts	Previous club	Signed
Bartliff, Andrew	(10.7.64)	28	7	10	—	48	Queenswood ARL	9.10.91
Beath, Paul	(17.1.68)	28	11	—	—	44	Australia	2.9.92
Bell, Keith	(25.9.53)	0+9	—	—	—	—	Featherstone R.	23.11.90
Booth, Craig	(28.10.70)	4	—	—	—	—	Featherstone R.	17.3.93
Brook, David	(4.2.71)	28+2	20	—	—	80	Middleton ARL	4.6.90
Burrow, Paul	(8.5.64)	11+2	2	—	—	8	ARL	18.4.89
Campling, Steve	(18.3.68)	2+1	—	—	—	—	Travellers ARL	19.9.91
Cook, Mark	(7.3.66)	3	—	—	—	—	—	—
Coyle, Michael	(5.3.71)	17	6	—	—	24	Middleton ARL	18.7.90
Croft, David	(2.8.69)	2	—	—	—	—	Bradford N.	16.10.92
Currie, Eugene	(25.2.65)	2	—	—	—	—	—	16.9.92
Daniel, Alan	(1.2.69)	15+1	7	—	—	28	Queens ARL	6.1.91
Ellis, Mark	(23.5.67)	9+1	1	—	—	4	Doncaster	21.2.93
Francis, Richard	(10.9.64)	30	13	—	—	52	Bradford N.	18.8.92
Gearey, Paul	(5.12.61)	2+1	1	—	—	4	Batley	3.9.92
Harkin, Paul	(8.3.58)	25	1	—	3	7	Halifax	30.9.92
Harrison, Paul	(24.9.70)	5	2	—	—	8	Hull	22.3.93
Johnson, Dean	(10.10.71)	1	1	—	—	4	Sheffield E.	25.2.93
Langton, Steve	(24.3.64)	5+1	1	—	—	4	Batley	3.10.89
Lay, Steve	(28.3.68)	17+1	11	—	—	44	Dewsbury Moor ARL	9.3.87
Lee, Darren	(23.9.72)	2	—	—	—	—	Bradford N.	12.3.93
Liles, Richard	(5.12.69)	9+8	—	—	—	—	Oulton ARL	26.3.90
Lowes, James	(11.10.69)	5	2	—	—	8	Hunslet P. ARL	3.11.86
McElhatton, Craig	(24.2.70)	1+4	—	—	—	—	Wakefield T.	18.12.92
McKelvie, John	(19.8.67)	7+3	1	—	—	4	Australia	2.9.92
Mitchell, Keith	(5.6.64)	14+1	2	—	—	8	Glasshoughton ARL	30.9.82
Petch, Andrew	(3.9.66)	2+2	—	—	—	—	Middleton ARL	26.3.90
Precious, Andrew	(10.10.70)	28	6	83	7	197	York All Blacks ARL	27.9.90
Rees, Paul	(30.12.67)	4	—	—	—	—	Australia	20.8.92
Rose, Ian	(24.10.66)	18+1	2	—	—	8	Ossett T. ARL	14.7.92
Sampson, Lee	(11.4.66)	14+6	4	—	—	16	Nottingham C.	6.12.92
Sampson, Roy	(28.11.61)	27	7	—	—	28	Dewsbury	17.2.87
Snee, Gavin	(6.1.71)	18+1	4	—	—	16	Bradford N.	14.10.92
Sowerby, Gary	(5.5.69)	0+1	—	—	—	—	ARL	16.9.92

(Continued)

73

	(Date of Birth)	App	T	G	D	Pts	Previous club	Signed
Speight, Darren ....(8.1.67)........		2	—	—	—	—	Batley	31.7.92
Speight, Mark ....(28.6.64)......		1+6	1	—	—	4	Batley	30.7.92
Wood, Mark ....(29.11.65).....		1	—	—	—	—	Hunslet BC	30.1.83
Wright, Jason..............(14.3.73)......		3+1	—	—	—	—	ARL	6.12.90
TOTALS								
38 players			113	93	10	648		

HUNSLET 1992-93 MATCH ANALYSIS

Date	Com-petition	H/A	Opponent	Rlt	Score	Tries	Goals	Atten-dance	Referee
30.8.92	TD	A	Whitehaven	L	2-42	—	Precious	—	—
6.9.92	TD	H	Keighley C.	W	28-12	Beath (2), Lay (2), McKelvie	Precious (4)	964	Asquith
13.9.92	YC(1)	A	Leeds	L	20-28	Rose, Brook, Beath, Bartliff	Precious (2)	—	—
20.9.92	TD	H	Nottingham C.	W	40-6	Beath (2), Lowes (2), Lay (2), Brook	Precious (6)	507	Gilmour
27.9.92	TD	A	Doncaster	L	4-28	Bartliff	—	—	—
4.10.92	TD	H	Dewsbury	L	12-22	Daniel, Beath	Precious (2)	1224	Nicholson
11.10.92	TD	A	Workington T.	L	19-40	Geary, Brook, Daniel	Precious (3, 1dg)	—	—
1.11.92	TD	H	Whitehaven	W	20-14	Mitchell, Precious, R. Sampson	Precious (3, 2dg)	494	Atkin
8.11.92	RT(1)	A	Batley	W	13-6	Precious, Francis	Precious (1, 2dg), Harkin (dg)	—	—
15.11.92	TD	A	Chorley B.	W	18-14	Daniel (2), Brook	Precious (3)	—	—
22.11.92	TD	H	Batley	W	17-14	Brook	Precious (4), Bartliff (2), Harkin (dg)	1056	Tidball
29.11.92	TD	A	Highfield	W	36-14	Daniel, L. Sampson, R. Sampson, Lay, Beath, Francis, Brook	Bartliff (4)	—	—
6.12.92	RT(2)	H	Workington T.	L	12-34	Precious, Brook	Precious (2)	1225	Morris
13.12.92	TD	H	Blackpool G.	W	22-10	Brook (2), L. Sampson, R. Sampson	Precious (3)	449	Cummings
26.12.92	TD	H	Chorley B.	W	21-13	Lay (3), Francis	Bartliff (2), Harkin (dg)	597	Kershaw
17.1.93	TD	H	Highfield	W	50-16	Daniel (2), Lay (2), R. Sampson (2), Beath, Brook, Precious	Precious (7)	447	Nicholson
24.1.93	TD	A	Barrow	W	20-0	Bartliff, Coyle, Francis	Precious (4)	—	—
31.1.93	CC(1)	H	Ryedale-York	W	27-22	Beath, Coyle, Francis, Lay, Rose	Precious (3, 1dg)	864	Galtress
7.2.93	TD	H	Doncaster	L	10-26	Mitchell	Precious (3)	890	Asquith
14.2.93	CC(2)	A	Castleford	L	16-34	Brook, Burrow, Coyle	Precious (2)	—	—
21.2.93	TD	A	Nottingham C.	W	76-4	Francis (4), Snee (3), Bartliff (2), Beath (2), Coyle (2), Ellis, Harrison, L. Sampson	Precious (6)	—	—
28.2.93	TD	A	Dewsbury	W	18-10	Coyle, Francis, Harkin	Bartliff (2), Precious	—	—
7.3.93	TD	H	Barrow	W	30-16	Francis (2), Precious, R. Sampson, Snee	Precious (5)	528	Kershaw
14.3.93	TD	A	Blackpool G.	W	42-14	Brook (3), Bartliff, Francis, Harrison, Precious, L. Sampson	Precious (5)	—	—
21.3.93	TD	H	Workington T.	L	11-34	R. Sampson	Precious (3, 1dg)	848	Cross
28.3.93	TD	A	Keighley C.	L	8-49	Brook	Precious (2)	—	—
4.4.93	TD	A	Batley	L	12-28	Brook, Burrow	Precious (2)	—	—
9.4.93	TD	A	Ryedale-York	L	26-44	Brook (4), Johnson	Precious (3)	—	—
12.4.93	TD	H	Ryedale-York	L	12-28	Bartliff, M. Speight	Precious (2)	679	Gilmour
18.4.93	DP(1)	A	Keighley C.	L	6-34	Langton	Precious	—	—

KEIGHLEY COUGARS

Ground: Cougar Park (0535-602602), previously titled Lawkholme Park until the 1992-93 season.
First Season: 1901-02. Added Cougars to title at start of 1991-92.
Nickname: Cougars
Chairman: Ian Mahady
Secretary: John Bleazard
Honours: **Division Two** Champions, 1902-03
Division Three Champions, 1992-93
Challenge Cup Beaten finalists, 1936-37
Yorkshire Cup Beaten finalists, 1943-44, 1951-52

RECORDS

Match
Goals: 15 by John Wasyliw v. Nottingham C., 1 Nov 1992
Tries: 5 by Ike Jagger v. Castleford, 13 Jan 1906
Sam Stacey v. Liverpool C., 9 Mar 1907
Points: 34 by John Wasyliw v. Nottingham C., 1 Nov 1992

Season
Goals: 187 by John Wasyliw, 1992-93
Tries: 30 by Joe Sherburn, 1934-35
Points: 490 by John Wasyliw, 1992-93

Career
Goals: 967 by Brian Jefferson, 1965-77
Tries: 155 by Sam Stacey, 1904-20
Points: 2,116 by Brian Jefferson, 1965-77
Appearances: 372 by Hartley Tempest, 1902-15
David McGoun, 1925-38
Highest score: 86-0 v. Nottingham C., 1 Nov 1992
86-0 v. Highfield, 31 Jan 1993
Highest against: 92-2 at Leigh, 30 Apr 1986
Attendance: 14,500 v. Halifax (RL Cup), 3 Mar 1951

COACHING REGISTER
● **Since 1974-75**

Alan Kellett	Jan 73 - May 75
Roy Sabine	Aug 75 - Oct 77
Barry Seabourne	Nov 77 - Mar 79
Albert Fearnley (Mgr)	Apr 79 - Aug 79
Alan Kellett	Apr 79 - Apr 80
Albert Fearnley	May 80 - Feb 81
Bakary Diabira	Feb 81 - Sep 82
Lee Greenwood	Sep 82 - Oct 83
Geoff Peggs	Nov 83 - Sep 85
Peter Roe	Sep 85 - July 86
Colin Dixon	July 86 - June 89
Les Coulter	July 89 - Apr 90
Tony Fisher	June 90 - Sep 91
Peter Roe	Sep 91 -

GREAT BRITAIN REGISTER
(1 player)

Terry Hollindrake	(1)	1955

1992-93 SIGNINGS REGISTER

Signed	Player	Club From
5.6.92	Ball, Phil	Wigan
22.6.92	Grima, Joe	Widnes
27.7.92	Ramshaw, Jason	Halifax
18.8.92	Gateley, Ian	Canberra, Aus
20.8.92	Bailey, Mark	Ovenden ARL
20.8.92	Walsh, Peter	Underbank ARL
25.8.92	Kerr, Ken	Workington T.
12.9.92	Webb, Darren	Birkenshaw ARL
18.9.92	Appleby, Darren	Featherstone R.
21.9.92	*Pryce, Geoff	Ryedale-York
25.9.92	*Mumby, Keith	Sheffield E.
9.12.92	*McLean, Ian	Workington T.
17.12.92	Smith, David	Underbank ARL
8.1.93	Milner, Mark	Featherstone R.
18.2.93	*Godfrey, Heath	Bradford N.
20.2.93	*McAlister, Charlie	Whitehaven

KEIGHLEY COUGARS 1992-93 PLAYERS' SUMMARY

	(Date of Birth)	App	T	G	D	Pts	Previous club	Signed
Appleby, Darren	(14.6.67)	17+1	16	—	—	64	Featherstone R.	18.9.92
Ball, Phil	(20.6.69)	20	3	—	—	12	Wigan	5.6.92
Brooke-Cowden, Mark	(12.6.63)	22+6	3	—	—	12	Halifax	12.12.91
Dixon, Keith	(16.9.66)	21+1	11	—	3	47	Keighley Albion ARL	28.8.84
Eyres, Andy	(1.10.68)	23+2	13	—	1	53	Widnes	24.3.91
Farrell, Carlton	(23.6.66)	25+3	8	—	—	32	Deighton ARL	2.8.90
Gateley, Ian	(21.3.66)	31	6	—	—	24	Australia	18.8.92
Grima, Joe	(18.9.60)	26	6	—	—	24	Widnes	22.6.92
Hall, Steve	(7.9.67)	19+10	5	—	—	20	Dudley Hill ARL	13.7.91
Hiley, Greg	(11.6.64)	27	4	—	—	16	New Zealand	6.11.90
Hinchliffe, Andy	(26.10.69)	4+3	3	—	—	12	Leeds Poly ARL	21.11.91
Kerr, Ken	(18.10.69)	2	1	—	—	4	Workington T.	25.8.92
McAlister, Charlie	(17.3.63)	2+8	5	—	—	20	Whitehaven	20.2.93
McLean, Ian	(20.5.65)	2+1	—	—	—	—	Workington T.	9.12.92
Milner, Mark	(21.6.66)	11+1	12	—	—	48	Featherstone R.	8.1.93
Moses, Paul	(21.8.63)	13+9	7	—	—	28	Halifax	2.1.85
Mumby, Keith	(21.2.57)	1+2	—	—	—	—	Sheffield E.	25.9.92
Race, Wayne	(17.4.66)	28+1	9	—	—	36	Doncaster	13.8.91
Ramshaw, Jason	(23.7.69)	18+3	11	—	2	46	Halifax	27.7.92
Reeves, Bob	(16.5.70)	0+1	1	—	—	4	Mayfield ARL	6.2.92
Smith, Tony		1+1	1	—	—	4	Hull Poly ARL	21.12.92
Stephenson, Andy	(28.8.67)	17	8	—	—	32	Clayton ARL	19.3.91
Stephenson, Phil	(17.6.72)	2+6	—	—	—	—	Clayton ARL	19.3.91
Walker, John	(27.12.68)	12+1	4	—	—	16	Otley RU	29.10.91
Wasyliw, John	(23.10.67)	31	29	187	—	490	Halifax RU	5.3.91
Wood, Martin	(24.6.70)	28	27	—	1	109	Scarborough P.	17.1.92
TOTALS								
26 players			193	187	7	1,153		

Keighley Cougars, Stones Bitter Third Division Team of the Month in January and March 1993.

KEIGHLEY COUGARS 1992-93 MATCH ANALYSIS

Date	Com-petition	H/A	Opponent	Rlt	Score	Tries	Goals	Atten-dance	Referee
30.8.92	TD	H	Workington T.	W	18-2	Hinchliffe, Eyres	Wasyliw (5)	1351	Crashley
6.9.92	TD	A	Hunslet	L	12-28	Hinchliffe, Kerr	Wasyliw (2)	—	—
13.9.92	YC(1)	A	Nottingham C.	W	30-4	Walker, Race, Ramshaw, Wood	Wasyliw (7)	—	—
20.9.92	TD	H	Barrow	W	40-10	Appleby (2), Walker (2), Race, Wasyliw	Wasyliw (8)	1684	Whitelam
23.9.92	YC(2)	A	Wakefield T.	L	16-22	Appleby, Ramshaw, Eyres	Wasyliw (2)	—	—
27.9.92	TD	A	Dewsbury	L	13-24	Grima	Wasyliw (4), Wood (dg)	—	—
4.10.92	TD	A	Chorley B.	W	54-12	Wasyliw (2), Dixon (2), Wood (2), Appleby, Hinchliffe, Ball	Wasyliw (9)	—	—
22.10.92	TD	A	Whitehaven	W	18-8	Race, Wood, Wasyliw	Wasyliw (3)	—	—
1.11.92	TD	H	Nottingham C.	W	86-0	Wood (3), Eyres (2), Appleby (2), Moses (2), Farrell, Grima, Ball, Brooke-Cowden, Wasyliw	Wasyliw (15)	1269	Nicholson
8.11.92	RT(1)	A	Leigh	L	24-32	Wasyliw (2), Appleby (2)	Wasyliw (4)	—	—
22.11.92	TD	H	Highfield	W	44-10	Gateley (2), Appleby (2), Grima, Hiley, Moses, Wasyliw	Wasyliw (6)	1138	Atkin
29.11.92	TD	A	Ryedale-York	W	16-14	Wasyliw, Moses	Wasyliw (4)	—	—
13.12.92	TD	H	Whitehaven	L	8-21	A. Stephenson	Wasyliw (2)	1324	Carter
20.12.92	TD	A	Nottingham C.	W	42-2	Ramshaw (2), Appleby (2), Hall, Reeves	Wasyliw (9)	—	—
10.1.93	TD	A	Workington T.	W	21-0	Farrell, Wood, Hall, Wasyliw	Wasyliw (2), Ramshaw (dg)	—	—
13.1.93	TD	H	Doncaster	W	31-10	Wasyliw (2), Farrell, Moses, Ramshaw, Wood	Wasyliw (3), Dixon (dg)	1269	Nicholson
20.1.93	TD	H	Blackpool G.	W	36-4	Dixon (2), Wood (2), Appleby, Hall, Wasyliw	Wasyliw (4)	1265	Volante
31.1.93	CC(1)	H	Highfield	W	86-0	Appleby (3), Dixon (2), Milner (2), Ramshaw (2), Brooke-Cowden, Farrell, Race, Gateley, Wasyliw, Wood	Wasyliw (13)	1100	Whitelam
7.2.93	TD	H	Ryedale-York	W	22-15	Ball, Race, Wood	Wasyliw (5)	2100	Morris
14.2.93	CC(2)	A	Hull K.R.	L	28-30	Wasyliw (2), Moses, Wood	Wasyliw (6)	—	—
21.2.93	TD	H	Chorley B.	W	78-6	Milner (4), Dixon (3), Ramshaw (2), Wasyliw (2), Eyres, Grima, Hiley, A. Stephenson	Wasyliw (9)	1717	Tidball
28.2.93	TD	A	Barrow	W	42-20	Eyres (2), Wasyliw (2), Dixon, Farrell, Wood	Wasyliw (7)	—	—
7.3.93	TD	A	Blackpool G.	W	82-8	Wood (4), Eyres (2), A. Stephenson (2), Hiley, McAlister, Milner, Ramshaw, Smith, Wasyliw	Wasyliw (13)	—	—
14.3.93	TD	H	Dewsbury	W	33-24	Eyres, Grima, Hiley, Ramshaw, Wood	Wasyliw (6), Dixon (dg)	3432	Cross
16.3.93	TD	A	Highfield	W	80-8	Wasyliw (3), Milner (2), A. Stephenson (2), Wood (2), Eyres, Farrell, Gateley, Hall, McAlister, Moses	Wasyliw (10)	—	—
28.3.93	TD	H	Hunslet	W	49-8	Milner (2), Wasyliw (2), Wood (2), Eyres, Walker	Wasyliw (8), Eyres (dg)	2923	Morris
4.4.93	TD	A	Doncaster	W	32-30	Dixon, Farrell, Gateley, Milner, Race, Wood	Wasyliw (4)	—	—
9.4.93	TD	H	Batley	W	34-10	A. Stephenson (2), Eyres, Farrell, Gateley, Hall	Wasyliw (5)	5226	J. Smith
12.4.93	TD	A	Batley	W	26-14	McAlister (2), Race (2), Wasyliw	Wasyliw (3)	—	—
18.4.93	DP(1)	H	Hunslet	W	34-6	Wood (2), Brooke-Cowden, McAlister, Race, Wasyliw	Wasyliw (5)	2421	Galtress
25.4.93	DP(2)	A	Rochdale H.	L	18-26	Grima, Wasyliw	Wasyliw (4), Dixon (dg), Ramshaw (dg)	—	—

77

LEEDS

Ground: Headingley (0532-786181)
First Season: 1895-96
Nickname: Loiners
Chairman: Dennis Greenwood
Chief Exec: Alf Davies
Honours: **Championship** Winners, 1960-61,
              1968-69, 1971-72
              Beaten finalists, 1914-15, 1928-29,
              1929-30, 1930-31, 1937-38, 1969-70,
              1972-73
              League Leaders Trophy Winners,
              1966-67, 1967-68, 1968-69, 1969-70,
              1971-72
              Challenge Cup Winners, 1909-10,
              1922-23, 1931-32, 1935-36, 1940-41,
              1941-42, 1956-57, 1967-68, 1976-77,
              1977-78
              Beaten finalists, 1942-43, 1946-47,
              1970-71, 1971-72
              Regal Trophy Winners, 1972-73,
              1983-84
              Beaten finalists, 1982-83, 1987-88,
              1991-92
              Premiership Winners, 1974-75,
              1978-79
              Yorkshire Cup Winners, 1921-22,
              1928-29, 1930-31, 1932-33, 1934-35,
              1935-36, 1937-38, 1958-59, 1968-69,
              1970-71, 1972-73, 1973-74, 1975-76,
              1976-77, 1979-80, 1980-81, 1988-89
              Beaten finalists, 1919-20, 1947-48,
              1961-62, 1964-65
              Yorkshire League Winners,
              1901-02, 1927-28, 1930-31, 1933-34,
              1934-35, 1936-37, 1937-38, 1950-51,
              1954-55, 1956-57, 1960-61, 1966-67,
              1967-68, 1968-69, 1969-70
              BBC2 Floodlit Trophy Winners,
              1970-71

RECORDS

Match
Goals: 13 by Lewis Jones v. Blackpool B.,
       19 Aug 1957

Tries: 8 by Fred Webster v. Coventry,
        12 Apr 1913
        Eric Harris v. Bradford N.,
        14 Sep 1931
Points: 31 by Lewis Jones v. Bradford N.,
        22 Aug 1956

Season
Goals: 166 by Lewis Jones, 1956-57
Tries: 63 by Eric Harris, 1935-36
Points: 431 by Lewis Jones, 1956-57

Career
Goals: 1,244 by Lewis Jones, 1952-64
Tries: 391 by Eric Harris, 1930-39
Points: 2,920 by Lewis Jones, 1952-64
Appearances: 608+18 by John Holmes, 1968-89
Highest score: 102-0 v. Coventry, 12 Apr 1913
Highest against: 74-6 at Wigan, 10 May 1992
Attendance: 40,175 v. Bradford N. (League),
        21 May 1947

COACHING REGISTER
● **Since 1974-75**

Roy Francis	June 74 - May 75
Syd Hynes	June 75 - Apr 81
Robin Dewhurst	June 81 - Oct 83
Maurice Bamford	Nov 83 - Feb 85
Malcolm Clift	Feb 85 - May 85
Peter Fox	May 85 - Dec 86
Maurice Bamford	Dec 86 - Apr 88
Malcolm Reilly	Aug 88 - Sep 89
David Ward	Sep 89 - May 91
Doug Laughton	May 91 -

*New Zealand Test forward Gary Mercer, scorer of seven tries
in 27 games in his debut season for Leeds.*

GREAT BRITAIN REGISTER

(73 players)

Les Adams	(1)	1932
John Atkinson	(26)	1968-80
Jim Bacon	(11)	1920-26
Ray Batten	(3)	1969-73
John Bentley	(1)	1992
Jim Birch	(1)	1907
Stan Brogden	(7)	1936-37
Jim Brough	(5)	1928-36
Gordon Brown	(6)	1954-55
Mick Clark	(5)	1968
Terry Clawson	(3)	1972
David Creasser	(2+2)	1985-88
Lee Crooks	(1)	1989
Willie Davies	(2)	1914
Kevin Dick	(2)	1980
Roy Dickinson	(2)	1985
Paul Dixon	(8+1)	1990-92
Les Dyl	(11)	1974-82
Tony Fisher	(3)	1970-71
Phil Ford	(5)	1989
Dick Gemmell	(1)	1964
Carl Gibson	(10)	1990-91
Bobby Goulding	(1)	1992
Jeff Grayshon	(2)	1985
Bob Haigh	(3+1)	1970-71
Derek Hallas	(2)	1961
Ellery Hanley	(2)	1992-93
Fred Harrison	(3)	1911
David Heron	(1+1)	1982
John Holmes	(14+6)	1971-82
Syd Hynes	(12+1)	1970-73
Billy Jarman	(2)	1914
David Jeanes	(3)	1972
Dai Jenkins	(1)	1947
Lewis Jones	(15)	1954-57
Ken Jubb	(2)	1937
John Lowe	(1)	1932
Paul Medley	(3+1)	1987-88
Steve Molloy	(1)	1993
Ike Owens	(4)	1946
Steve Pitchford	(4)	1977
Harry Poole	(2)	1966
Roy Powell	(13+6)	1985-91
Dai Prosser	(1)	1937
Keith Rayne	(4)	1984
Kevin Rayne	(1)	1986
Bev Risman	(5)	1968
Don Robinson	(5)	1956-60

David Rose	(4)	1954
Garry Schofield	(25)	1988-93
Barry Seabourne	(1)	1970
Brian Shaw	(1)	1961
Mick Shoebottom	(10+2)	1968-71
Barry Simms	(1)	1962
Alan Smith	(10)	1970-73
Stanley Smith	(10)	1929-33
David Stephenson	(4+1)	1988
Jeff Stevenson	(15)	1955-58
Squire Stockwell	(3)	1920-21
Alan Tait	(1+1)	1992-93
Abe Terry	(1)	1962
Arthur "Ginger" Thomas	(4)	1926-29
Phil Thomas	(1)	1907
Joe Thompson	(12)	1924-32
Andrew Turnbull	(1)	1951
Hugh Waddell	(1)	1989
Billy Ward	(1)	1910
David Ward	(12)	1977-82
Fred Webster	(3)	1910
Dicky Williams	(9)	1948-51
Harry Woods	(1)	1937
Geoff Wriglesworth	(5)	1965-66
Frank Young	(1)	1908

1992-93 SIGNINGS REGISTER

Signed	Player	Club From
6.7.92	Fallon, Jim	Bath RU
5.8.92	Mercer, Gary	Warrington
9.8.92	Schultz, Matthew	—
14.8.92	Tait, Alan	Widnes
19.8.92	Gregory, Andy	Wigan
21.8.92	McCallion, Seamus	Halifax
27.8.92	Worrall, Mick	Salford
28.8.92	Goodway, Andy	Wigan
22.9.92	*Paver, Ian	Ryedale-York
24.9.92	Harland, Lee	Drighlington ARL
24.9.92	Holroyd, Graham	Siddal ARL
24.9.92	Summers, James	Middleton ARL
30.9.92	Lowes, James	Hunslet
29.10.92	Iro, Kevin	Manly, Aus
13.11.92	*Simpson, Anthony	Sheffield E.
1.12.92	Cook, Paul	Hull ARL
11.1.93	*Smirk, Terry	Hull
2.2.93	Handford, Steve	Magnet ARL
22.2.93	Pilgrim, Steve	Wasps RU
3.3.93	Shaw, Michael	Elland ARL
28.3.93	Scales, Jonathan	Gosforth RU

LEEDS 1992-93 PLAYERS' SUMMARY

	(Date of Birth)	App	T	G	D	Pts	Previous club	Signed
Anderson, Paul	(25.10.71)	2+15	—	—	—	—	Redhill ARL	9.8.91
Cook, Paul	(23.7.76)	2	3	—	—	12	Hull ARL	1.12.92
Dixon, Paul	(28.10.62)	30+5	12	—	—	48	Halifax	6.1.89
Edwards, Morvin	(8.5.68)	5	—	—	—	—	New Zealand	12.9.91
Fallon, Jim	(27.3.65)	33	15	—	—	60	Bath RU	6.7.92
Fawcett, Vince	(13.11.70)	10+3	5	—	—	20	Middleton ARL	13.11.87
Gallagher, John	(29.1.64)	7+1	2	18	1	45	New Zealand RU	11.6.90
Gibson, Carl	(23.4.63)	15+1	3	—	—	12	Batley	20.1.86
Goodway, Andy	(2.6.61)	17+7	1	—	—	4	Wigan	28.8.92
Gregory, Andy	(10.8.61)	25	2	1	—	10	Wigan	19.8.92
Grigg, Carl	(21.9.70)	1+1	—	—	—	—	Australia	16.10.92
Hanley, Ellery	(27.3.61)	31	31	—	—	124	Wigan	6.9.91
Harland, Lee	(4.9.73)	5+3	—	—	—	—	Drighlington ARL	24.9.92
Holroyd, Graham	(25.10.75)	3+7	4	—	—	16	Siddal ARL	24.9.92
Innes, Craig	(10.9.69)	34	9	—	—	36	New Zealand RU	4.1.92
Iro, Kevin	(25.5.68)	19	10	1	—	42	Australia	29.10.92
Irving, Simon	(22.3.67)	19+1	9	64	—	164	Headingley RU	30.1.90
Lowes, James	(11.10.69)	28+1	5	—	—	20	Hunslet	30.9.92
Maskill, Colin	(15.3.64)	10	—	10	—	20	Wakefield T.	21.1.85
Mercer, Gary	(22.6.66)	27	7	—	—	28	Warrington	5.8.92
Middleton, Graham	(2.11.70)	3	1	—	—	4	East Leeds ARL	20.9.89
Molloy, Steve	(11.3.69)	23+6	1	—	—	4	Warrington	23.9.90
O'Neill, Mike	(29.11.60)	18+6	3	—	—	12	Rochdale H.	21.8.91
Pilgrim, Steve	(26.10.67)	1	—	—	—	—	Wasps RU	22.2.93
Scales, Jonathan	(28.7.74)	1	—	—	—	—	Gosforth RU	28.8.93
Schofield, Garry	(1.7.65)	25	14	18	2	94	Hull	23.10.87
Stephens, Gareth	(15.4.74)	10	1	—	—	4	Lock Lane ARL	21.9.90
Tait, Alan	(2.11.64)	32	9	—	—	36	Widnes	14.8.92
Wane, Shaun	(14.9.64)	14+3	—	—	—	—	Wigan	19.9.90
Worrall, Mick	(22.3.62)	5+1	—	—	—	—	Salford	27.8.92

TOTALS

			T	G	D	Pts		
30 players			147	112	3	815		

Representative appearances 1992-93
Anderson — GB Under-21s (1)
Hanley — Britain (2, 2t); England (1, 1t)
Molloy — Britain (1); England (1)
Schofield — Britain (2, 3t); England (1, 1t)
Stephens — GB Under-21s (+1)
Tait — Britain (1+1, 2t)

LEEDS 1992-93 MATCH ANALYSIS

Date	Competition	H/A	Opponent	Rlt	Score	Tries	Goals	Attendance	Referee
30.8.92	SBC	H	St. Helens	L	14-27	Schofield, Hanley	Gallagher (3)	15,572	J. Smith
6.9.92	SBC	A	Halifax	L	8-26	Gibson, Fawcett	—	—	—
13.9.92	YC(1)	H	Hunslet	W	28-20	Hanley (2), Dixon, Fallon, Innes, Schofield	Schofield (2)	5952	Crashley
20.9.92	SBC	H	Hull K.R.	W	34-6	Dixon (2), Tait, Innes, Schofield, Fallon, Fawcett	Maskill (3)	9526	Morris
23.9.92	YC(2)	A	Hull	L	16-26	Schofield, Gibson	Maskill (4)	—	—
27.9.92	SBC	A	Bradford N.	L	6-36	Hanley	Maskill	—	—
2.10.92	SBC	H	Warrington	W	13-4	Schofield, Hanley	Maskill (2), Schofield (dg)	7016	Steele
11.10.92	SBC	A	Wigan	L	6-24	Schofield	Schofield	—	—
21.10.92	SBC	A	Wakefield T.	L	16-17	Fawcett, Mercer, Goodway	Gallagher (2)	—	—
1.11.92	SBC	H	Widnes	W	48-16	Iro (2), Hanley (2), Fallon, Dixon, Mercer, Tait	Schofield (8)	12,040	Ollerton
8.11.92	RT(1)	A	St. Helens	L	14-15	Mercer, Fallon	Gallagher (3)	—	—
15.11.92	SBC	A	Hull	L	19-22	Hanley (2), Dixon	Gallagher (3, 1dg)	—	—
22.11.92	SBC	A	Leigh	D	12-12	Dixon, Fallon, Gibson	—	—	—
13.12.92	SBC	A	Sheffield E.	L	14-31	Hanley (2), Mercer	Iro	—	—
18.12.92	SBC	H	Halifax	W	42-14	Hanley (3), Dixon (2), Iro (2), Innes	Schofield (5)	7847	Gilmour
26.12.92	SBC	H	Castleford	W	40-12	Lowes, Iro, Tait, Hanley, Innes, Fallon, Schofield	Irving (5), Schofield	20,258	Campbell
1.1.93	SBC	H	Salford	W	38-14	Fallon (2), Tait, Iro, Hanley, Mercer, Irving	Irving (5)	14,828	R. Smith
8.1.93	SBC	A	Warrington	W	31-24	Schofield (2), Innes, Hanley, Molloy	Irving (4), Schofield (1, 1dg)	—	—
17.1.93	SBC	A	Salford	W	46-15	Hanley (2), Gallagher (2), Innes, Iro, Mercer, O'Neill, Tait	Irving (5)	—	—
31.1.93	CC(1)	H	Barrow	W	54-18	Hanley (2), Gregory (2), Iro (2), Innes, Lowes, Schofield, Tait	Gallagher (7)	7492	Cross
7.2.93	SBC	A	Hull K.R.	W	18-16	Dixon, Iro, Stephens	Irving (2), Gregory	—	—
14.2.93	CC(2)	H	Rochdale H.	W	68-6	Hanley (4), Schofield (3), Cook (2), Fallon, Irving, Lowes, O'Neill	Irving (8)	8219	Morris
27.2.93	CC(3)	H	Castleford	W	12-8	Fallon (2)	Irving (2)	12,757	Ollerton
3.3.93	SBC	H	Wigan	L	6-31	Tait	Irving	20,057	R. Smith
7.3.93	SBC	H	Sheffield E.	W	46-10	Holroyd (2), Cook, Dixon, Lowes, Middleton, O'Neill, Tait	Irving (7)	8010	Whitfield
13.3.93	CC(SF)	N[1]	Widnes	L	4-39	—	Irving (2)	(13,823)	Ollerton
17.3.93	SBC	A	Widnes	L	8-19	Hanley	Irving (2)	—	—
21.3.93	SBC	H	Wakefield T.	D	26-26	Irving (2), Dixon, Fallon, Hanley	Irving (3)	8434	Cummings
28.3.93	SBC	H	Hull	W	38-34	Fawcett (2), Hanley (2), Holroyd, Irving, Mercer	Irving (5)	8074	Annesley (Aus)
4.4.93	SBC	A	St. Helens	L	8-42	Irving	Irving (2)	—	—
12.4.93	SBC	A	Castleford	W	10-6	Irving, Lowes	Irving	—	—
15.4.93	SBC	H	Leigh	W	28-26	Hanley (2), Innes, Fallon, Holroyd	Irving (4)	7039	Whitfield
18.4.93	SBC	H	Bradford N.	W	20-12	Fallon (2), Dixon, Tait	Irving (2)	11,157	J. Connolly
25.4.93	PT(1)	A	Widnes	W	22-10	Irving (2), Innes, Schofield	Irving (3)	—	—
9.5.93	PT(SF)	A	St. Helens	L	2-15	—	Irving	—	—

N[1] Wigan

LEIGH

Ground: Hilton Park (0942-674437)
First Season: 1895-96
Chairman: Mick Higgins
General
  Manager: John Stringer
Honours: **Championship** Winners, 1905-06
Division One Champions, 1981-82
Division Two Champions, 1977-78,
1985-86, 1988-89
Challenge Cup Winners, 1920-21,
1970-71
Lancashire Cup Winners, 1952-53,
1955-56, 1970-71, 1981-82
Beaten finalists, 1905-06, 1909-10,
1920-21, 1922-23, 1949-50, 1951-52,
1963-64, 1969-70
BBC2 Floodlit Trophy Winners,
1969-70, 1972-73
Beaten finalists, 1967-68, 1976-77

RECORDS

Match

Goals: 15 by Mick Stacey v. Doncaster,
28 Mar 1976
Tries: 6 by Jack Wood v. York, 4 Oct 1947
Points: 38 by John Woods v. Blackpool B.,
11 Sep 1977
John Woods v. Ryedale-York,
12 Jan 1992

Season

Goals: 173 by Chris Johnson, 1985-86
Tries: 49 by Steve Halliwell, 1985-86
Points: 400 by Chris Johnson, 1985-86

Career

Goals: 1,043 by Jim Ledgard, 1948-58
Tries: 189 by Mick Martyn, 1954-67
Points: 2,492 by John Woods, 1976-85 & 1990-
Appearances: 503 by Albert Worrall, 1921-35 &
1936-38
Highest score: 92-2 v. Keighley, 30 Apr 1986
Highest against: 64-9 at St. Helens, 6 Jan 1993
Attendance: 31,324 v. St. Helens (RL Cup),
14 Mar 1953

COACHING REGISTER

● **Since 1974-75**

Eddie Cheetham	May 74 - Mar 75
Kevin Ashcroft	June 75 - Jan 77
Bill Kindon	Jan 77 - Apr 77
John Mantle	Apr 77 - Nov 78
Tom Grainey	Nov 78 - Dec 80
*Alex Murphy	Nov 80 - June 82
*Colin Clarke	June 82 - Dec 82
Peter Smethurst	Dec 82 - Apr 83
Tommy Bishop	June 83 - June 84
John Woods	June 84 - May 85
Alex Murphy	Feb 85 - Nov 85
Tommy Dickens	Nov 85 - Dec 86
Billy Benyon	Dec 86 - Mar 90
Alex Murphy	Mar 90 - Aug 91
Kevin Ashcroft	Sep 91 - June 92
Jim Crellin	June 92 - Sep 92
Steve Simms	Nov 92 -

*From Dec 80 to June 82 Clarke was
officially appointed coach and Murphy
manager.*

GREAT BRITAIN REGISTER

(19 players)

Kevin Ashcroft	(5)	1968-70
Joe Cartwright	(7)	1920-21
Dave Chisnall	(2)	1970
Joe Darwell	(5)	1924
Steve Donlan	(+2)	1984
Des Drummond	(22)	1980-86
Peter Foster	(3)	1955
Chris Johnson	(1)	1985
Frank Kitchen	(2)	1954
Jim Ledgard	(9)	1948-54
Gordon Lewis	(1)	1965
Mick Martyn	(2)	1958-59
Walter Mooney	(2)	1924
Stan Owen	(1)	1958
Charlie Pawsey	(7)	1952-54
Bill Robinson	(2)	1963
Joe Walsh	(1)	1971
Billy Winstanley	(2)	1910
John Woods	(7+3)	1979-83

1992-93 SIGNINGS REGISTER

Signed	Player	Club From
1.7.92	Hansen, Lee	Orange Utd, NZ
18.7.92	Pendlebury, John	Bradford N.
10.8.92	Burke, Tony	Warrington

12.8.92	Moran, Mark	Salford	10.12.92	Robinshaw, Alan	Leigh East ARL
14.8.92	Newton, Keith	Oldham	10.1.93	Gunning, John	Leigh East ARL
14.8.92	Platt, Duncan	Oldham	1.2.93	Clarke, Troy	Carlisle
14.8.92	Street, Tim	Oldham	1.2.93	Hanger, Dean	Erina, Aus
1.9.92	Pugsley, Stuart	Whitehaven	26.3.93	*Broxton, Paul	Chorley B.
5.9.92	Pratt, Gareth	Mayfield ARL	26.3.93	*Fletcher, Darren	Chorley B.
17.9.92	Cassidy, James	Appleton Park ARL			

LEIGH 1992-93 PLAYERS' SUMMARY

	(Date of Birth)	App	T	G	D	Pts	Previous club	Signed
Baldwin, Simon	(31.3.75)	14+2	5	2	—	24	Leigh E. ARL	31.3.92
Blakeley, Mike	(22.11.70)	5+1	2	9	1	27	Leigh M. ARL	16.7.90
Booth, Simon	(9.12.71)	12+1	3	—	—	12	Leigh M. ARL	16.7.90
Bridge, Russ	(8.10.64)	12+1	1	—	—	4	Fulham	12.10.90
Burke, Tony	(25.8.61)	4	—	—	—	—	Warrington	10.8.92
Clarke, Troy	(19.4.67)	7+1	4	4	—	24	Carlisle	1.2.93
Collier, Andrew	(14.2.67)	0+6	—	—	—	—	Wigan	28.8.91
Collier, Andy	(3.6.68)	20+2	4	—	—	16	Leigh M. ARL	30.4.86
Costello, John	(10.3.70)	10+6	2	—	—	8	Leigh M. ARL	6.9.91
Dainty, Mark	(18.11.64)	1+2	—	—	—	—	Leigh E. ARL	13.10.91
Donohue, Jason	(18.4.72)	19+2	6	—	—	24	Golborne ARL	24.3.88
Dunn, Brian	(16.3.63)	5	2	—	—	8	Rochdale H.	8.6.87
Elias, John	(24.5.64)	11+4	2	—	—	8	Australia	2.10.92
Fanning, Sean	(16.6.62)	7+2	1	—	—	4	Hare & Hounds ARL	5.4.92
Gunning, John	(30.3.69)	10	3	—	—	12	Leigh E. ARL	10.1.93
Hanger, Dean	(24.2.70)	8	4	—	—	16	Australia	1.2.93
Hansen, Lee	(23.7.68)	25+1	1	—	—	4	New Zealand	1.7.92
Hill, David	(4.9.68)	21	5	—	—	20	Blackbrook ARL	5.10.88
Johnson, Kevin	(4.4.72)	0+1	—	—	—	—	Golborne ARL	13.10.91
Ledger, Barry	(19.6.62)	6	1	—	—	4	St. Helens	5.8.88
Mahon, Scott	(26.2.70)	18	3	—	—	12	Australia	10.9.92
Martin, Scott	(29.12.74)	10+7	1	—	—	4	—	29.12.91
Moran, Mark	(15.10.64)	4+1	—	—	—	—	Salford	12.8.92
Newton, Keith	(30.7.64)	7+4	—	—	—	—	Oldham	14.8.92
Pendlebury, Gary	(22.8.66)	0+1	—	—	—	—	Wigan	13.10.91
Pendlebury, John	(18.4.61)	29	5	—	1	21	Bradford N.	18.7.92
Platt, Duncan	(19.7.65)	17+2	6	27	—	78	Oldham	14.8.92
Pratt, Gareth	(23.8.69)	4	1	—	—	4	Mayfield ARL	5.9.92
Pugsley, Stuart	(14.11.67)	14+1	2	—	—	8	Whitehaven	1.9.92
Robinshaw, Alan	(8.3.74)	0+1	—	—	—	—	Leigh E. ARL	10.12.92
Rowley, Paul	(12.3.75)	3+5	2	—	—	8	Leigh M. ARL	29.3.92
Ruane, Andy	(6.9.62)	22+8	4	—	7	23	Oldham	28.8.91
Ruane, David	(24.9.63)	32	14	—	—	56	Oldham	29.8.91
Street, Tim	(29.6.68)	30	4	—	—	16	Oldham	14.8.92
Tanner, David	(29.9.65)	21+1	4	19	—	54	St. Helens	2.1.92
Woods, John	(14.9.56)	8+1	1	19	—	42	Rochdale H.	24.8.90
TOTALS								
36 players			93	80	9	541		

Representative appearances 1992-93
Donohue — GB Under-21s (+1)
Moran — Wales (+2)

LEIGH 1992-93 MATCH ANALYSIS

Date	Com-petition	H/A	Opponent	Rlt	Score	Tries	Goals	Atten-dance	Referee
30.8.92	SBC	H	Warrington	L	12-30	D. Ruane, J. Pendlebury	Woods (2)	4734	Holdsworth
6.9.92	SBC	A	Bradford N.	L	10-23	J. Pendlebury, Booth	Woods	—	—
13.9.92	LC(1)	H	Chorley B.	W	50-9	Platt (2), A. Ruane (2), D. Ruane (2), J. Pendlebury, Bridge, Street, Booth	Woods (5)	1332	Gilmour
20.9.92	SBC	H	Castleford	L	0-38	—	—	2844	Whitfield
23.9.92	LC(2)	H	Oldham	L	14-26	Costello (2)	Woods (3)	3395	Campbell
27.9.92	SBC	A	Halifax	L	18-34	Blakeley, Mahon, Hill	Blakeley (3)	—	—
4.10.92	SBC	H	Wigan	L	16-36	Blakeley, Hill, Pratt	Blakeley (2)	8618	Cummings
11.10.92	SBC	A	Hull K.R.	L	1-30	—	Blakeley (dg)	—	—
18.10.92	SBC	H	Hull	L	8-14	D. Ruane	Blakeley (2)	2396	Kershaw
1.11.92	SBC	A	Castleford	L	12-46	Hansen, Woods	Blakeley (2)	—	—
8.11.92	RT(1)	H	Keighley C.	W	32-24	Tanner (3), Andy Collier, Fanning, Elias	Woods (3), Tanner	2113	Asquith
11.11.92	SBC	H	St. Helens	W	11-6	Pugsley	Woods (3), A. Ruane (dg)	3739	R. Smith
15.11.92	SBC	H	Halifax	L	4-28	—	Woods (2)	4257	Cummings
22.11.92	SBC	H	Leeds	D	12-12	Pugsley, Baldwin	Tanner (2)	3673	Holdsworth
29.11.92	SBC	A	Warrington	D	7-7	Street	Tanner, Pendlebury (dg)	—	—
6.12.92	RT(2)	H	London C.	W	16-6	Hill, Ledger, Donohue	Tanner (2)	2181	Crashley
13.12.92	SBC	H	Hull K.R.	W	31-24	J. Pendlebury (2), D. Ruane, Street, Baldwin	Tanner (5), A. Ruane (dg)	2775	Steele
20.12.92	RT(3)	A	Hull	L	14-24	Donohue, Andy Collier	Baldwin (2), Tanner	—	—
6.1.93	SBC	A	St. Helens	L	9-64	Baldwin, Hill	A. Ruane (dg)	—	—
10.1.93	SBC	H	Sheffield E.	W	16-14	Mahon, Elias, Dunn	Tanner (2)	2253	R. Smith
13.1.93	SBC	A	Salford	L	16-24	Dunn, Mahon, Platt	Tanner (2)	—	—
17.1.93	SBC	H	Bradford N.	L	14-18	Platt, D. Ruane	Tanner (3)	3358	Atkin
24.1.93	SBC	A	Wakefield T.	W	41-8	Gunning (2), D. Ruane (2), Donohue, Hill, Tanner	Platt (6), A. Ruane (dg)	—	—
31.1.93	CC(1)	A	Sheffield E.	L	5-32	D. Ruane	A. Ruane (dg)	—	—
7.2.93	SBC	H	Wakefield T.	W	17-10	Donohue, Platt, D. Ruane	Platt (2), A. Ruane (dg)	3451	Steele
19.2.93	SBC	A	Sheffield E.	W	8-6	Donohue	Platt (2)	—	—
14.3.93	SBC	A	Hull	W	36-20	Baldwin (2), Martin, Rowley, D. Ruane, A. Ruane	Platt (6)	—	—
21.3.93	SBC	H	Widnes	L	11-14	Platt, D. Ruane	Platt, A. Ruane (dg)	5069	Annesley (Aus)
31.3.93	SBC	A	Wigan	L	0-50	—	—	—	—
12.4.93	SBC	H	Salford	W	46-20	Hanger (2), D. Ruane (2), Street, Clarke, Rowley, A. Ruane	Platt (7)	2253	J. Connolly
15.4.93	SBC	A	Leeds	L	26-28	Hanger (2), Gunning, Clarke, Andy Collier	Platt (3)	—	—
18.4.93	SBC	A	Widnes	W	28-26	Clarke (2), Booth, Andy Collier, Donohue	Clarke (4)	—	—

LONDON CRUSADERS

Ground: Crystal Palace National Sports Centre. Barnet Copthall from 1993-94 (081-203 4211)

First Season: 1980-81. Began as Fulham; became London Crusaders at start of 1991-92.

Chairman: Richard Bartram

General Manager: Graeme Pickering

Honours: **Division Two** Champions, 1982-83

RECORDS

Match

Goals: 11 by Steve Guyett v. Huddersfield, 23 Oct 1988
Greg Pearce v. Runcorn H., 26 Aug 1990

Tries: No player has scored more than 3

Points: 22 by Alan Platt v. Mansfield M., 10 May 1986
Greg Pearce v. Runcorn H., 26 Aug 1990

Season

Goals: 136 by Steve Diamond, 1982-83
Tries: 27 by John Crossley, 1982-83
Points: 308 by Steve Diamond, 1982-83

Career

Goals: 309 by Steve Diamond, 1981-84
Tries: 74 by Hussein M'Barki, 1981-84 & 1988-91
Points: 691 by Steve Diamond, 1981-84
Appearances: 148+14 by Hussein M'Barki, 1981-84 & 1988-91

Highest score: 61-22 v. Huddersfield, 23 Oct 1988
Highest against: 72-6 v. Whitehaven, 14 Sep 1986
Attendance: 2,324 v. Hull (John Player Trophy), 18 Nov 1984 — at Crystal Palace
15,013 v. Wakefield T. (RL Cup), 15 Feb 1981 — at Craven Cottage

COACHING REGISTER

● **Since formation in 1980**

Reg Bowden	July 80 - June 84
Roy Lester	June 84 - Apr 86
Bill Goodwin	Apr 86 - May 88
*Bev Risman	May 88 - Feb 89
Phil Sullivan	Feb 89 - Mar 89
Bill Goodwin	Mar 89 - Apr 89
Ross Strudwick	June 89 - Feb 93
Tony Gordon	Feb 93 -

Team manager

GREAT BRITAIN REGISTER

(1 player)

John Dalgreen	(1)	1982

1992-93 SIGNINGS REGISTER

Signed	Player	Club From
10.8.92	Fisher, Paul	Logan City, Aus
20.8.92	Berney, Gary	London ARL
20.8.92	Elder, Jay	Milford ARL
20.8.92	Gould, John	Fulham Travellers ARL
20.8.92	Mulkerin, Danny	Brothers, Aus
20.8.92	Shaw, Tony	Oxford Univ. ARL
20.8.92	Simpson, Ian	West London Inst. ARL
20.8.92	Winstanley, Chris	Aus
27.8.92	Bonsu, Andy	—
27.8.92	Corcoran, Colin	—
27.8.92	Dray, Matthew	Aus
27.8.92	Durham, Keith	Gravesend ARL
27.8.92	Gilbert, Bernie	Caloundra, NZ
27.8.92	Lemamn, Matthew	Hills Hawks, Aus
27.8.92	McCarron, Ian	Wath Brow Hornets ARL
27.8.92	Roskell, Scott	Runaway Bay, Aus
27.8.92	Shaw, Nicholas	Warrington
27.8.92	Whiteley, Chris	Salford
3.9.92	*Burrows, Alan	Highfield
3.9.92	King, David	Gold Coast, Aus
21.9.92	*Bishop, David	Hull K.R.
6.10.92	Riley, Mark	Peckham ARL
9.10.92	Duncan, Darryl	Norths, Aus
15.10.92	McKenzie, Grant	London Colonials ARL
29.10.92	Donohue, Warren	RU
3.12.92	Draper, Roger	Crystal Palace ARL
18.12.92	Graham, Mike	Cardiff RU
11.1.93	Pram, Jason	Ireland RU
9.2.93	Bolonkin, Sergey	Red Arrows, CIS
9.2.93	Sokolov, Andre	Red Arrows, CIS
9.2.93	Olar, Andre	Sportsmen, CIS
9.2.93	Piscunov, Mikhail	Sportsmen, CIS
12.2.93	Michalski, Darren	West Sydney, Aus
11.3.93	Ramsey, Neville	Te-atatu, NZ
22.3.93	Spencer, Adrian	Cambridge Univ. ARL

LONDON CRUSADERS 1992-93 PLAYERS' SUMMARY

(Date of Birth)	App	T	G	D	Pts	Previous club	Signed
Abderaman, Dazi ....(21.2.67)	2	1	—	—	4	France	28.9.90
Aiyede, Cola ....(21.8.63)	0+1	—	—	—	—	America	27.7.92
Atkinson, Colin..........(16.6.64)	14+2	1	—	—	4	Halifax	31.10.91
Berney, Gary...............(7.6.69)........	2+1	2	—	—	8	London ARL	20.8.92
Bishop, David.............(31.10.61).....	1	—	—	—	—	Hull K.R.	21.9.92
Blackman, Richard ......(29.3.70)	7	2	—	—	8	Oldham	14.8.92
Buckley, Shane............(23.3.68)	29	16	—	—	64	Australia	14.8.91
Burrows, Alan ....(16.1.68)	1	—	—	—	—	Highfield	3.9.92
Corcoran, Colin..........(25.2.67)	1+2	—	—	—	—	—	27.8.92
Draper, Roger.............(19.1.70)	0+1	—	—	—	—	Crystal Palace ARL	3.12.92
Dray, Matthew ....(2.4.69)........	13+4	4	—	—	16	Australia	27.8.92
Duncan, Darryl ....(3.12.62)	6	—	—	—	—	Australia	9.10.92
Durham, Keith ....(15.10.67).....	0+1	—	—	—	—	Gravesend ARL	27.8.92
Fisher, Paul................(15.7.70)	29	6	3	1	31	Australia	10.8.92
Gilbert, Bernie............(6.1.67)........	4+2	—	—	—	—	New Zealand	27.8.92
Gould, John ....(16.10.68).....	0+1	—	—	—	—	Fulham T. ARL	20.8.92
Graham, Mike ....(10.5.67)	1	—	—	—	—	Cardiff RU	18.12.92
Halafihi, Nick ....(23.12.67).....	29+2	5	—	—	20	Sheffield E.	6.12.91
Holderness, Kevin ....(6.11.72)	1+3	—	—	—	—	Essex S. ARL	11.10.90
Johnson, Mark............(28.2.69)	5	4	—	—	16	South Africa	18.3.93
Kerapa, Jason ....(16.7.70)	5+1	2	—	—	8	New Zealand	11.1.93
Kimaingatau, Alan......................	3	—	—	—	—	—	—
King, David ....(6.9.67)........	20+7	10	—	—	40	Australia	3.9.92
McCarron, Ian ....(10.2.66)	7+3	—	—	—	—	Wath Brow H. ARL	27.8.92
McKenzie, Grant ....(7.8.67)........	2	2	—	—	8	London Col. ARL	15.10.92
Mann, Warren ....(17.7.64)	6	2	—	—	8	New Zealand	11.1.93
Mulkerin, Danny.........(19.11.68).....	23+2	1	—	—	4	Australia	20.8.92
Peart, Barry ....(15.9.65)	0+1	—	—	—	—	—	20.8.90
Pitt, Darryl ....(31.5.67)	25+1	9	12	—	60	Australia	7.12.89
Pram, Jason ....(4.5.71)........	2+1	—	—	—	—	Ireland RU	11.1.93
Ramsey, Neville...........(7.4.63)........	6	—	—	—	—	New Zealand	11.3.93
Riley, Mark ....(16.6.67)	22	12	—	1	49	Peckham ARL	6.10.92
Roskell, Scott..............(25.4.69)	24+1	10	—	—	40	Australia	27.8.92
Rosolen, Steve ....(16.11.68).....	30	4	—	—	16	Australia	2.1.92
Rotheram, Dave..........(16.8.68)	23+6	1	—	—	4	W. London Inst. ARL	28.8.90
Simpson, Ian ....(21.11.70).....	10+1	1	—	—	4	W. London Inst. ARL	20.8.92
Smith, Kris.................(8.8.66)........	24+5	2	61	—	130	Twickenham RU	30.8.91
Sokolov, Andre............(8.4.65)........	1+1	—	—	—	—	Russia	9.2.93
Spencer, Adrian...........(3.3.73)........	3	1	7	—	18	Cambridge Uni. ARL	22.3.93
Whiteley, Chris ....(31.1.67)	3+3	—	—	—	—	Salford	27.8.92
Why, Adrian...............(14.6.67)	0+1	—	—	—	—	Fulham ARL	—
Wilby, Tim ....(18.3.59)	0+2	1	—	—	4	Sheffield E.	6.12.91
Winbourn, Doug..........(10.4.68)	0+2	—	—	—	—	—	28.8.90
Winstanley, Chris ....(29.6.66)	5	2	—	—	8	Australia	20.8.92
Workman, Glen ....(29.9.62)	14	1	—	—	4	Australia	31.8.91
TOTALS							
45 players		102	83	2	576		

Representative appearances 1992-93
Bishop — Wales (2)

LONDON CRUSADERS 1992-93 MATCH ANALYSIS

Date	Com-petition	H/A	Opponent	Rlt	Score	Tries	Goals	Atten-dance	Referee
30.8.92	SD	A	Oldham	L	12-27	Halafihi, Atkinson	Smith, Pitt	—	—
6.9.92	SD	H	Rochdale H.	W	30-10	Roskell (2), Fisher, Pitt, Buckley	Smith (5)	499	Atkin
20.9.92	SD	A	Carlisle	W	46-14	Roskell (3), Winstanley, Buckley, Fisher, Dray, Berney	Smith (6), Fisher	—	—
27.9.92	SD	H	Huddersfield	W	46-10	Dray (2), King, Winstanley, Rosolen, Berney, Buckley, Blackman	Smith (7)	850	Carter
4.10.92	SD	A	Bramley	L	8-30	Blackman	Smith, Fisher	—	—
11.10.92	SD	A	Swinton	L	6-16	Buckley	Smith	—	—
18.10.92	SD	A	Featherstone R.	L	10-40	McKenzie (2)	Smith	—	—
25.10.92	SD	H	Rochdale H.	L	12-24	Halafihi, Fisher	Smith (2)	800	Whitfield
1.11.92	SD	H	Carlisle	D	18-18	Fisher, King, Buckley	Smith (3)	500	Crashley
8.11.92	RT(1)	H	Wakefield T.	W	30-0	Pitt (2), King, Roskell, Buckley	Smith (5)	860	J. Connolly
15.11.92	SD	A	Rochdale H.	L	16-25	Riley, Workman	Smith (4)	—	—
22.11.92	SD	H	Swinton	W	20-6	Buckley, King, Riley	Smith (3), Pitt	500	Galtress
29.11.92	SD	A	Huddersfield	L	14-18	Pitt (2), King	Pitt	—	—
6.12.92	RT(2)	A	Leigh	L	6-16	Riley	Pitt	—	—
13.12.92	SD	A	Bramley	L	8-16	Pitt, Wilby	—	—	—
20.12.92	SD	H	Featherstone R.	L	8-30	Rosolen	Smith (2)	600	R. Connolly
10.1.93	SD	H	Swinton	W	12-6	Buckley, King	Pitt (2)	350	Cross
17.1.93	SD	H	Bramley	W	20-0	Buckley, King, Mann, Rotheram	Pitt (2)	460	Cummings
24.1.93	SD	H	Featherstone R.	L	6-32	King	Smith	750	Atkin
31.1.93	CC(1)	A	Oldham	L	6-34	Mann	Smith	—	—
7.2.93	SD	A	Carlisle	W	28-14	Riley (3), Buckley, Dray	Smith (4)	—	—
14.2.93	SD	A	Featherstone R.	L	12-58	Kerapa (2), Riley	—	—	—
21.2.93	SD	H	Bramley	W	20-12	Abderaman, Simpson, Riley	Smith (4)	451	Wood
24.2.93	SD	A	Rochdale H.	L	18-30	King, Pitt, Smith, Riley	Smith	—	—
7.3.93	SD	A	Swinton	L	24-26	Pitt (2), Buckley, Riley, Rosolen	Smith (2)	—	—
14.3.93	SD	H	Huddersfield	W	31-17	Buckley, Fisher, Mulkerin, Riley, Roskell	Smith (5), Riley (dg)	555	J. Smith
21.3.93	SD	A	Oldham	W	27-20	Buckley, Halafihi, King, Riley, Roskell	Smith (2), Fisher (1, 1dg)	—	—
25.3.93	SD	A	Huddersfield	L	2-17	—	Spencer	—	—
28.3.93	SD	H	Carlisle	W	30-8	Johnson (2), Fisher, Halafihi, Roskell, Rosolen	Spencer (3)	450	Cross
31.3.93	SD	H	Oldham	D	20-20	Buckley (2), Halafihi	Pitt (4)	350	Kershaw
18.4.93	SD	H	Oldham	W	30-18	Johnson (2), Buckley, Roskell, Smith, Spencer	Spencer (3)	638	Nicholson

NOTTINGHAM CITY

Ground: Harvey Hadden Stadium
            (0602-691666)
First Season: 1984-85 as Mansfield Marksman.
            Moved and became Nottingham
            City at start of 1989-90. Demoted to
            the National Conference for 1993-94.
Nickname: Outlaws
Chairman: Paul Tomlinson
Secretary: Joan Tomlinson

RECORDS

Match
Goals: 7 by Barry Holden v. Keighley,
        10 Mar 1985
        Wayne Sanchez v. Hunslet,
        2 Oct 1988
Tries: 4 by Keith Whiteman v. Doncaster,
        4 Nov 1984
Points: 18 by Barry Holden v. Keighley,
        10 Mar 1985
        Mick Howarth v. Dewsbury,
        17 Jan 1988

Season
Goals: 63 by Carl Sanderson, 1984-85
Tries: 13 by Steve Nicholson, 1984-85
        Keith Whiteman, 1984-85
Points: 136 by Carl Sanderson, 1984-85

Career
Goals: 79 by Carl Sanderson, 1984-86
Tries: 26 by Chris Willis, 1984-91
Points: 195 by David Oates, 1986-91
Appearances: 103+12 by Chris Willis, 1984-91
Highest score: 54-10 v. Doncaster, 4 Nov 1984
Highest against: 100-6 v. Hull K.R.
            (at Doncaster), 19 Aug 1990
Attendance: 2,545 v. Halifax (Div. 2), 1 Oct 1989

COACHING REGISTER
● **Since formation in 1984**

Mick Blacker	May 84 - Oct 85
Bill Kirkbride	Nov 85 - Mar 86
Steve Dennison	Apr 86 - Dec 86
Jim Crellin	Dec 86 - June 88
Billy Platt	July 88 - Dec 88
Steve Nash	Dec 88 - Feb 89
Lee Greenwood	Feb 89 - Mar 90
Mel Wibberley	Mar 90 - Feb 91
Arnold Hema	Feb 91 - June 91
Mark Burgess	June 91 - Apr 92
Dave Sampson	May 92 - Oct 92
Mark Burgess	Nov 92 -

1992-93 SIGNINGS REGISTER

Signed	Player	Club From
13.8.92	Binns, Stephen	Lock Lane ARL
13.8.92	Greenwood, Ian	—
13.8.92	Hennigan, Mark	Stanningley ARL
13.8.92	Marsh, Darren	Chesterfield RU
13.8.92	McDermott, Paul	—
13.8.92	Turton, Stuart	Eastmoor ARL
14.8.92	Woods, Graham	Sainte Livrade, Aus
14.8.92	*Roache, Mark	Doncaster
14.8.92	Okiwe, Anderson	Sheffield E.
14.8.92	Nicholson, John	Eastmoor ARL
14.8.92	Mills, Mick	Ossett ARL
14.8.92	*McElhatton, Craig	Wakefield T.
14.8.92	Hare, Tyrone	—
15.8.92	*James, Tony	Keighley C.
29.8.92	*Dickinson, Andy	Dewsbury
4.9.92	*Clawson, Neil	Swinton
4.9.92	*Green, Mark	Sheffield E.
4.9.92	*Holmes, David	Doncaster
11.9.92	Cole, Paul	Eastmoor ARL
8.10.92	Harp, Duane	Canning, Aus
14.10.92	*Jones, Kevin	Dewsbury
28.10.92	*Dyer, Peter	Sheffield E.
6.11.92	Bryden, Jason	Huddersfield ARL
6.11.92	Isaacs, Kenny	Brisbane Souths, Aus
12.11.92	Williams, John	Ryedale Supporters ARL
12.11.92	Hough, Phil	Hoyland Vikings ARL
19.11.92	*Drummond, Barry	Dewsbury
20.11.92	*Tong, Michael	Dewsbury
17.12.92	Spink, David	Clowne ARL
17.12.92	Waller, Rob	Clowne ARL
7.1.93	Middleton, Roger	Hanging Heaton ARL
7.1.93	Hudson, Shaun	Normanton ARL
23.2.93	Thompson, Simon	Clowne ARL
24.2.93	*Wright, Chris	Doncaster

NOTTINGHAM CITY 1992-93 PLAYERS' SUMMARY

	(Date of Birth)	App	T	G	D	Pts	Previous club	Signed
Afao, Malua	(2.4.66)	1	—	—	—	—	—	—
Bentley, Valu	(8.6.65)	1	—	—	—	—	—	—
Bond, Richard	(19.9.70)	0+1	—	—	—	—	South Africa RU	27.11.92
Bryden, Jason	(10.11.66)	4	—	—	—	—	Huddersfield ARL	6.11.92
Burgess, Mark	(3.10.61)	3+2	—	—	—	—	Dewsbury	3.3.91
Butler, Lee	(8.3.63)	4+4	—	—	—	—	Clowne ARL	20.2.91
Chappell, Tony	(9.10.64)	26	5	26	7	79	Doncaster	20.8.90
Clawson, Neil	(5.5.60)	2	—	—	—	—	Swinton	4.9.92
Cole, Paul	(30.6.71)	2	—	—	—	—	Eastmoor ARL	11.9.92
Collins, Paul	(20.5.68)	1	—	—	—	—	Australia	26.11.92
Cooper, Paul	(24.6.65)	4+3	—	—	—	—	Dewsbury	28.8.91
Davis, Bradley	(13.3.68)	2	—	—	—	—	Australia	17.9.92
Dickinson, Andy	(26.8.61)	2	—	—	—	—	Dewsbury	29.8.92
Drummond, Barry	(18.1.68)	2	—	—	—	—	Dewsbury	19.11.92
Dyer, Peter	(4.8.67)	4+1	—	—	—	—	Sheffield E.	28.10.92
Eyre, Tyrone	(30.3.65)	5	—	—	—	—	Dewsbury	21.1.91
Fairbank, Dick	(30.4.61)	6	1	—	—	4	Scarborough P.	13.8.92
Foy, Anthony	(7.1.71)	3	—	—	—	—	Australia	10.9.92
Green, Mark	(13.3.72)	3	—	—	—	—	Sheffield E.	4.9.92
Greenwood, Ian	(25.5.61)	10+1	1	—	—	4	—	10.1.91
Harp, Duane	(16.5.67)	16	4	—	—	16	Australia	8.10.92
Hennigan, Mark	(2.7.72)	4	—	—	—	—	Stanningley ARL	13.8.92
Holmes, David	(3.3.61)	3+1	—	—	—	—	Doncaster	4.9.92
Hough, Phil	(21.6.72)	9+1	—	—	—	—	Hoyland V. ARL	12.11.92
Hoyle, Bob	(2.11.67)	2	—	—	—	—	Dewsbury	27.2.90
Hudson, Shaun	(19.10.65)	3	—	—	—	—	Normanton ARL	7.1.93
Idle, Graham	(10.3.50)	18+1	1	—	—	4	Doncaster	12.2.92
Isaacs, Kenny	(4.4.65)	1+1	—	—	—	—	Australia	6.11.92
Jackson, Darryl	(6.2.71)	23+4	2	—	—	8	Clowne ARL	20.8.90
Jackson, Dean	(6.2.71)	15	—	2	—	4	Clowne ARL	20.8.90
James, Tony	(12.12.62)	2	1	—	—	4	Keighley C.	15.8.92
Jones, Kevin	(25.2.64)	1	—	—	—	—	Dewsbury	14.10.92
Kibe, Eric	(23.3.71)	16+2	3	—	—	12	Dewsbury	13.10.92
Laurence, Jason	(23.1.70)	2	—	—	—	—	Australia	17.9.92
McDermott, Paul	(30.12.56)	9	2	—	—	8	—	13.8.92
McElhatton, Craig	(24.2.70)	5	1	—	—	4	Wakefield T.	14.8.92
McKie, Andy	(27.6.68)	4+1	—	—	—	—	ARL	18.1.93
McKie, Phil	(9.10.64)	3	—	—	—	—	ARL	18.1.93
Maitland, Justin	(6.2.71)	3	—	—	—	—	De la Salle ARL	27.11.92
Middleton, Roger	(18.12.70)	3+4	—	—	—	—	Hanging Heaton ARL	7.1.93
Mills, Mick	(20.4.65)	1	—	—	—	—	Ossett ARL	14.8.92
Moore, Gary	(12.2.63)	18	3	—	—	12	Dewsbury	29.9.91
Nicholson, John	(8.10.72)	18+4	—	—	—	—	Eastmoor ARL	14.8.92
Okiwe, Anderson	(4.5.64)	12+2	2	—	—	8	Sheffield E.	14.8.92
Rudd, Neil	(8.6.62)	9+1	—	—	—	—	Hunslet	9.9.88

(Continued)

89

NOTTINGHAM CITY 1992-93 PLAYERS' SUMMARY

(Date of Birth)	App	T	G	D	Pts	Previous club	Signed
Sampson, Lee...........(11.4.66)......	5	—	—	—	—	Doncaster	19.9.92
Sankey, Paul..............(4.5.64)........	23+1	2	—	—	8	Burton RU	13.8.92
Spink, David.............(24.11.67).....	3+4	—	—	—	—	Clowne ARL	17.12.92
Taylor, Adrian............(20.9.67)......	0+1	—	—	—	—	Clowne ARL	10.3.91
Thompson, Simon.......(10.1.68)......	7	1	—	—	4	Clowne ARL	23.2.93
Tong, Michael.............(3.6.71)........	2	—	—	—	—	Dewsbury	20.11.92
Turton, Stuart.............(12.1.73)......	1+3	—	—	—	—	Eastmoor ARL	13.8.92
Tyers, Andy................(10.8.62)......	3	—	—	—	—	Keighley C.	1.4.92
Waller, Rob...............(30.9.70)......	9+1	—	—	1	1	Clowne ARL	17.12.92
Watkin, Darren ....(20.5.71)......	1	—	—	—	—	Middleton M. ARL	—
Williams, John ....(14.9.73)......	1	—	—	—	—	Ryedale S. ARL	12.11.92
Wood, Richard ....(10.4.71)......	0+2	—	—	—	—	Clowne ARL	20.8.90
Woods, Graham ....(11.8.68)......	4+1	2	—	—	8	Australia	14.8.92
Wright, Chris.............(13.10.69).....	7	1	—	—	4	Doncaster	24.2.93
TOTALS							
59 players		32	28	8	192		

NOTTINGHAM CITY 1992-93 MATCH ANALYSIS

Date	Com-petition	H/A	Opponent	Rlt	Score	Tries	Goals	Atten-dance	Referee
29.8.92	TD	H	Blackpool G.	L	12-32	Woods (2)	Chappell (2)	205	Kershaw
6.9.92	TD	A	Barrow	W	19-12	Okiwe, James, McDermott	Chappell (3, 1dg)	—	—
13.9.92	YC(1)	H	Keighley C.	L	4-30	McDermott	—	327	Tidball
20.9.92	TD	A	Hunslet	L	6-40	Chappell	Chappell	—	—
27.9.92	TD	H	Chorley B.	L	15-18	McElhatton, Okiwe	Chappell (3, 1dg)	156	Crashley
4.10.92	TD	H	Ryedale-York	L	0-84	—	—	239	Atkin
11.10.92	TD	A	Dewsbury	L	12-36	Fairbank, Greenwood	Dean Jackson (2)	—	—
16.10.92	TD	H	Workington T.	L	1-24	—	Chappell (dg)	109	Asquith
1.11.92	TD	A	Keighley C.	L	0-86	—	—	—	—
8.11.92	RT(1)	A	Halifax	L	6-76	Moore	Chappell	—	—
15.11.92	TD	H	Barrow	L	8-64	Chappell	Chappell (2)	101	Morris
22.11.92	TD	A	Workington T.	L	0-68	—	—	—	—
29.11.92	TD	H	Dewsbury	L	2-78	—	Chappell	318	Wood
20.12.92	TD	H	Keighley C.	L	2-42	—	Chappell	208	Whitelam
27.12.92	TD	A	Blackpool G.	L	20-35	Harp (2), Sankey, Darryl Jackson	Chappell (2)	—	—
10.1.93	TD	A	Doncaster	L	4-42	Kibe	—	—	—
17.1.93	TD	A	Ryedale-York	L	0-52	—	—	—	—
31.1.92	CC(1)	A	Huddersfield	L	1-66	—	Chappell (dg)	—	—
7.2.93	TD	A	Whitehaven	L	1-56	—	Waller (dg)	—	—
21.2.93	TD	H	Hunslet	L	4-76	Darryl Jackson	—	213	Redfearn
26.2.93	TD	H	Batley	L	0-60	—	—	170	Tidball
28.2.93	TD	A	Batley	L	0-46	—	—	—	—
7.3.93	TD	A	Highfield	L	18-20	Harp (2), Chappell	Chappell (2, 2dg)	—	—
14.3.93	TD	H	Doncaster	L	24-25	Chappell, Kibe, Moore, Sankey	Chappell (4)	463	Kershaw
21.3.93	TD	H	Whitehaven	L	7-40	Idle	Chappell (1, 1dg)	203	Wood
28.3.93	TD	A	Chorley B.	L	20-57	Kibe, Moore, Thompson, Wright	Chappell (2)	—	—
11.4.93	TD	H	Highfield	L	6-39	Chappell	Chappell	851	J. Smith

OLDHAM

Ground: Watersheddings (061-624-4865)
First Season: 1895-96
Nickname: Roughyeds
Chairman: Jim Quinn
Secretary: Fred Howarth
Honours: **Championship** Winners, 1909-10, 1910-11, 1956-57
Beaten finalists, 1906-07, 1907-08, 1908-09, 1921-22, 1954-55
Division One Champions, 1904-05
Division Two Champions, 1963-64, 1981-82, 1987-88
Challenge Cup Winners, 1898-99, 1924-25, 1926-27
Beaten finalists, 1906-07, 1911-12, 1923-24, 1925-26
Second Division/Divisional Premiership Winners, 1987-88, 1989-90
Beaten finalists, 1991-92
Lancashire Cup Winners, 1907-08, 1910-11, 1913-14, 1919-20, 1924-25, 1933-34, 1956-57, 1957-58, 1958-59
Beaten finalists, 1908-09, 1911-12, 1918-19, 1921-22, 1954-55, 1966-67, 1968-69, 1986-87, 1989-90
Lancashire League Winners, 1897-98, 1900-01, 1907-08, 1909-10, 1921-22, 1956-57, 1957-58

RECORDS

Match

Goals: 14 by Bernard Ganley v. Liverpool C., 4 Apr 1959
Tries: 7 by James Miller v. Barry, 31 Oct 1908
Points: 30 by Abe Johnson v. Widnes, 9 Apr 1928

Season

Goals: 200 by Bernard Ganley, 1957-58
Tries: 49 by R. Farrar, 1921-22
Points: 412 by Bernard Ganley, 1957-58

Career

Goals: 1,365 by Bernard Ganley, 1951-61
Tries: 173 by Alan Davies, 1950-61
Points: 2,775 by Bernard Ganley, 1951-61
Appearances: 626 by Joe Ferguson, 1899-1923

Highest score: 67-6 v. Liverpool C., 4 Apr 1959
Highest against: 67-11 at Hull K.R., 24 Sep 1978
Attendance: 28,000 v. Huddersfield (League), 24 Feb 1912

COACHING REGISTER

● **Since 1974-75**

Jim Challinor	Aug 74 - Dec 76
Terry Ramshaw	Jan 77 - Feb 77
Dave Cox	July 77 - Dec 78
Graham Starkey (Mgr)	Jan 79 - May 81
Bill Francis	June 79 - Dec 80
Frank Myler	May 81 - Apr 83
Peter Smethurst	Apr 83 - Feb 84
Frank Barrow	Feb 84 - Feb 84
Brian Gartland	Mar 84 - June 84
Frank Myler	June 84 - Apr 87
*Eric Fitzsimons	June 87 - Nov 88
*Mal Graham	June 87 - Apr 88
Tony Barrow	Nov 88 - Jan 91
John Fieldhouse	Jan 91 - Apr 91
Peter Tunks	Apr 91 -

Joint coaches June 87 - Apr 88

1992-93 SIGNINGS REGISTER

Signed	Player	Club From
3.8.92	Gumbs, Hugh	Bradford N.
14.8.92	Meadows, Mark	Blackpool G.
14.8.92	Olsen, Ben	London C.
14.8.92	Sheals, Mark	Leigh
21.8.92	Cocker, Stuart	Huddersfield
26.8.92	Badby, Richard	St. Annes ARL
26.8.92	Bradbury, Phil	Saddleworth ARL
26.8.92	Halkyard, Martin	Saddleworth ARL
28.8.92	Devine, Sean	St. Helens
2.9.92	Jones, Paul	St. Helens
23.9.92	*Stansfield, Ivan	Workington T.
25.9.92	Pye, David	Parkside ARL
25.9.92	Norman, Paul	Parkside ARL
25.9.92	Heaton, Steve	Parkside ARL
25.9.92	Gibson, Wally	Huddersfield
5.11.92	*Wooton, Tony	Rochdale H.
2.10.92	Kerry, Steve	Salford
26.11.92	Strett, Martin	Orrell RU
2.12.92	*Graziano, Joe	Swinton
11.12.92	Higgins, John	South Perth, Aus
18.12.92	Bloem, Jamie	Castleford
18.2.93	Heslop, Nigel	Orrell RU
19.2.93	Abram, Darren	Rochdale H.
10.3.93	*Phillips, Rowland	Warrington
28.3.93	*Stewart, Mike	Rochdale H.

GREAT BRITAIN REGISTER
(40 players)

Albert Avery	(4)	1910-11
Charlie Bott	(1)	1966
Albert Brough	(2)	1924
Terry Clawson	(9)	1973-74
Alan Davies	(20)	1955-60
Evan Davies	(3)	1920
Terry Flanagan	(4)	1983-84
Des Foy	(3)	1984-85
Bernard Ganley	(3)	1957-58
Andy Goodway	(11)	1983-85
Billy Hall	(4)	1914
Herman Hilton	(7)	1920-21
David Hobbs	(2)	1987
Dave Holland	(4)	1914
Bob Irving	(8+3)	1967-72
Ken Jackson	(2)	1957
Ernest Knapman	(1)	1924
Syd Little	(10)	1956-58
Tom Llewellyn	(2)	1907
Jim Lomas	(2)	1911
Bill Longworth	(3)	1908
Les McIntyre	(1)	1963
Terry O'Grady	(5)	1954
Jack Oster	(1)	1929
Dave Parker	(2)	1964
Doug Phillips	(3)	1946
Frank Pitchford	(2)	1958-62
Tom Rees	(1)	1929
Sid Rix	(9)	1924-26
Bob Sloman	(5)	1928
Arthur Smith	(6)	1907-08
Ike Southward	(7)	1959-62
Les Thomas	(1)	1947
Derek Turner	(11)	1956-58
George Tyson	(4)	1907-08
Hugh Waddell	(4)	1988
Tommy White	(1)	1907
Charlie Winslade	(1)	1959
Alf Wood	(4)	1911-14
Mick Worrall	(3)	1984

Andy Goodway, 11 Test caps between 1983 and 1985.

*Hugh Waddell, won four of his five caps for
Great Britain while at Oldham.*

OLDHAM 1992-93 PLAYERS' SUMMARY

	(Date of Birth)	App	T	G	D	Pts	Previous club	Signed
Abram, Darren	(27.9.67)	11	3	—	—	12	Rochdale H.	19.2.93
Bates, Ian	(2.3.68)	5	—	—	—	—	Gate Inn ARL	10.9.87
Bloem, Jamie	(26.5.71)	11+1	2	—	—	8	Castleford	18.12.92
Bradbury, David	(16.3.72)	20+5	4	—	—	16	Leigh M. ARL	15.8.91
Byrne, Ged	(14.6.62)	1+1	—	—	—	—	Wakefield T.	16.10.91
Christie, Gary	(23.1.72)	14+1	12	—	—	48	Widnes Tigers ARL	15.8.91
Cocker, Stuart	(8.5.66)	14	8	—	—	32	Huddersfield	21.8.92
Devine, Sean	(25.1.70)	10	6	6	1	37	St. Helens	28.8.92
Gibson, Wally	(5.4.67)	32	15	—	—	60	Huddersfield	25.9.92
Graziano, Joe	(6.5.68)	3+5	1	—	—	4	Swinton	2.12.92
Gumbs, Hugh	(4.9.69)	15	6	—	—	24	Bradford N.	3.8.92
Heslop, Nigel	(4.12.63)	3	2	—	—	8	Orrell RU	18.2.93
Higgins, John	(28.12.65)	1	—	—	—	—	Australia	11.12.92
Jones, Paul	(26.5.68)	3+4	—	—	—	—	St. Helens	2.9.92
Kerry, Steve	(10.3.66)	24	7	82	3	195	Salford	2.10.92
McDermott, Barrie	(22.7.72)	10+5	2	—	—	8	Waterhead ARL	15.8.91
Martyn, Tommy	(4.6.71)	22+1	8	39	4	114	Leigh M. ARL	14.2.89
Maxwell, John	(14.9.69)	4+1	1	—	—	4	Leigh M. ARL	14.12.89
Meadows, Mark	(9.5.65)	9+5	2	—	—	8	Blackpool G.	14.8.92
Olsen, Ben	(17.3.65)	22+6	4	—	—	16	London C.	14.8.92
Pachniuk, Richard	(24.3.71)	10+3	5	—	—	20	Dewsbury Moor ARL	19.6.89
Phillips, Abraham	(22.1.72)	1	—	—	—	—	Moldgreen ARL	2.8.91
Phillips, Rowland	(28.7.65)	6+3	1	—	—	4	Warrington	10.3.93
Ranson, Scott	(20.9.67)	24	12	—	—	48	Swinton	6.2.92
Ropati, Iva	(18.7.68)	27+1	22	—	—	88	Sheffield E.	30.3.92
Russell, Richard	(24.11.69)	28+1	6	—	—	24	Wigan	19.7.89
Sheals, Mark	(26.11.63)	32	5	—	—	20	Leigh	14.8.92
Sherratt, Ian	(9.8.65)	18+6	2	—	—	8	Salford	8.11.91
Solomona, Se'e	(9.3.65)	24+7	5	—	—	20	Widnes	31.3.92
Stephenson, David	(6.10.72)	11+5	2	—	—	8	Queens Park ARL	3.2.92
Stewart, Mike	(16.1.66)	2	1	—	—	4	Rochdale H.	28.3.93
Strett, Martin	(4.4.68)	4+3	—	11	—	22	Orrell RU	26.11.92
Tupaea, Shane	(24.12.63)	26+3	1	—	—	4	Swinton	13.9.91
Tyrer, Sean	(2.3.70)	25+4	8	10	—	52	Wigan	6.12.91
Warburton, Steve	(6.2.69)	9+3	4	—	—	16	Woolston ARL	9.4.91
TOTALS								
35 players			157	148	8	932		

Representative appearances 1992-93
Christie — GB Under-21s (1, 1t)

OLDHAM 1992-93 MATCH ANALYSIS

Date	Competition	H/A	Opponent	Rlt	Score	Tries	Goals	Attendance	Referee
30.8.92	SD	H	London C.	W	27-12	Cocker (2), Meadows, Devine	Martyn (5, 1dg)	2438	Volante
5.9.92	SD	H	Carlisle	W	38-14	Cocker (2), Devine (2), Meadows, Tyrer, Ranson	Martyn (5)	2292	Galtress
13.9.92	LC(1)	H	Warrington	W	33-20	Ropati (3), Ranson, Solomona, Tyrer	Martyn (4), Devine (dg)	4041	Whitfield

(Continued)

93

OLDHAM 1992-93 MATCH ANALYSIS (continued)

Date	Com- petition	H/A	Opponent	Rlt	Score	Tries	Goals	Atten- dance	Referee
20.9.92	SD	A	Huddersfield	W	28-24	Gumbs (2), Martyn, McDermott, Ranson	Devine (3), Martyn	—	—
23.9.92	LC(2)	A	Leigh	W	26-14	Ranson (2), Pachniuk, Tyrer	Martyn (4, 2dg)	—	—
27.9.92	SD	H	Swinton	W	16-8	Cocker, Devine	Martyn (4)	3246	R. Connolly
2.10.92	SD	H	Featherstone R.	L	4-24	—	Kerry (2)	3353	Tidball
6.10.92	LC(SF)	A	Wigan	L	8-48	McDermott, Russell	—	—	—
11.10.92	SD	A	Rochdale H.	W	21-20	Gibson (2), Cocker	Kerry (4, 1dg)	—	—
18.10.92	SD	A	Bramley	W	23-16	Sherratt, Tyrer, Gumbs	Kerry (5, 1dg)	—	—
1.11.92	SD	H	Swinton	W	56-6	Gibson (3), Cocker (2), Kerry, Sheals, Ropati, Olsen, Bradbury	Kerry (8)	2721	R. Smith
8.11.92	RT(1)	H	Castleford	L	22-40	Olsen, Gumbs, Ropati	Kerry (5)	4393	Ollerton
15.11.92	SD	A	Carlisle	W	25-20	Russell, Ropati, Gibson	Kerry (3, 1dg), Tyrer (3)	—	—
22.11.92	SD	H	Huddersfield	L	6-17	Tyrer	Kerry	3220	Steele
29.11.92	SD	A	Swinton	W	18-12	Tyrer, Kerry, Bradbury	Kerry (3)	—	—
13.12.92	SD	A	Featherstone R.	L	20-24	Ropati (2), Graziano, Russell	Kerry, Martyn	—	—
6.1.93	SD	H	Bramley	W	36-0	Pachniuk (2), Sheals, Christie, Ropati, Warburton	Kerry (5), Martyn	2209	Nicholson
10.1.93	SD	H	Bramley	W	40-2	Martyn (2), Christie (2), Ranson, Bloem, Ropati, Warburton	Kerry (2), Martyn (2)	2295	R. Connolly
13.1.93	SD	H	Rochdale H.	W	47-22	Gumbs (2), Russell, Gibson, Christie, Kerry, Martyn, Ropati	Kerry (6), Martyn (1, 1dg)	2653	Wood
17.1.93	SD	A	Carlisle	W	32-21	Solomona (2), Christie, Kerry, Ranson	Kerry (6)	—	—
24.1.93	SD	H	Rochdale H.	W	28-12	Gibson, Kerry, Martyn, Pachniuk, Ranson, Warburton	Kerry (2)	2991	Cross
27.1.93	SD	A	Swinton	W	36-10	Ranson (2), Ropati (2), Maxwell, Pachniuk, Tyrer	Kerry (4)	—	—
31.1.93	CC(1)	H	London C.	W	34-6	Christie (2), Gibson, Kerry, Olsen, Ranson	Kerry (4), Martyn	2653	Steele
7.2.93	SD	A	Featherstone R.	L	14-52	Solomona, Warburton	Kerry (3)	—	—
14.2.93	CC(2)	H	Huddersfield	W	20-17	Christie (2), Bloem, Gibson	Kerry (2)	4583	R. Connolly
21.2.93	SD	H	Carlisle	W	56-16	Christie (2), Heslop (2), Abram, Bradbury, Devine, Ropati, Sheals, Solomona	Martyn (5), Strett (3)	2808	Volante
3.3.93	CC(3)	H	Bradford N.	L	4-42	Martyn	—	5405	Campbell
7.3.93	SD	A	Huddersfield	L	8-14	Tyrer	Strett (2)	—	—
14.3.93	SD	H	Featherstone R.	W	24-22	Ropati (2), Tupaea	Strett (6)	3685	Gilmour
21.3.93	SD	H	London C.	L	20-27	Abram, Christie, Gibson, Ranson	Devine (2)	2269	Asquith
31.3.93	SD	A	London C.	D	20-20	Gibson, Kerry, Sheals	Kerry (4)	—	—
4.4.93	SD	A	Bramley	W	32-16	Ropati (2), Abram, Stephenson, Stewart	Kerry (3), Martyn (3)	—	—
9.4.93	SD	A	Rochdale H.	W	32-18	Ropati (2), Gibson, Martyn, Olsen	Kerry (6)	—	—
12.4.93	SD	H	Huddersfield	W	28-24	Gibson, Ranson, Ropati, Stephenson	Kerry (3), Tyrer (3)	3142	Wood
18.4.93	SD	A	London C.	L	18-30	Bradbury, Russell, Sheals, Sherratt	Tyrer	—	—
25.4.93	DP(2)	H	Dewsbury	D	14-14	Devine, Gibson	Martyn (2), Devine	2556	Morris
28.4.93	DP(2) Replay	A	Dewsbury	L	18-20	Martyn, R. Phillips, Ropati	Tyrer (3)	—	—

ROCHDALE HORNETS

Ground: Spotland (0706-48004)
First Season: 1895-96
Nickname: Hornets
Chairman: John Nicholson
Secretary: Ian McMahon
Honours: **Challenge Cup** Winners, 1921-22
Regal Trophy Beaten finalists, 1973-74
Lancashire Cup Winners, 1911-12, 1914-15, 1918-19
Beaten finalists, 1912-13, 1919-20, 1965-66, 1991-92
Lancashire League Winners, 1918-19
BBC2 Floodlit Trophy Beaten finalists, 1971-72

RECORDS

Match

Goals: 14 by Steve Turner v. Runcorn H., 5 Nov 1989
Tries: 5 by Jack Corsi v. Barrow, 31 Dec 1921
Jack Corsi v. Broughton Moor, 25 Feb 1922
Jack Williams v. St. Helens, 4 Apr 1933
Norman Brelsford v. Whitehaven, 3 Sep 1972
Points: 32 by Steve Turner v. Runcorn H., 5 Nov 1989

Season

Goals: 115 by Kevin Harcombe, 1985-86
Tries: 30 by Jack Williams, 1934-35
Points: 276 by Steve Gartland, 1992-93

Career

Goals: 741 by Walter Gowers, 1922-46
Tries: 103 by Jack Williams, 1931-37
Points: 1,497 by Walter Gowers, 1922-46
Appearances: 456 by Walter Gowers, 1922-46
Highest score: 92-0 v. Runcorn H., 5 Nov 1989
Highest against: 79-2 at Hull, 7 Apr 1921
Attendance: 8,150 v. Oldham (Div. 2), 26 Dec 1989 — at Spotland
26,664 v. Oldham (RL Cup), 25 Mar 1922 — at Athletic Grounds

Welsh international Kel Coslett, coach of Rochdale Hornets from November 1976 to August 1979.

COACHING REGISTER

● Since 1974-75

Frank Myler	May 71 - Oct 74
Graham Starkey	Oct 74 - Nov 75
Henry Delooze	Nov 75 - Nov 76
Kel Coslett	Nov 76 - Aug 79
Paul Longstaff	Sep 79 - May 81
Terry Fogerty	May 81 - Jan 82
Dick Bonser	Jan 82 - May 82
Bill Kirkbride	June 82 - Sep 84
Charlie Birdsall	Sep 84 - Apr 86
Eric Fitzsimons	June 86 - June 87
Eric Hughes	June 87 - June 88
Jim Crellin	June 88 - June 89
Allan Agar	July 89 - Jan 91
Neil Holding	Jan 91 - Apr 91
Stan Gittins	Apr 91 - Jan 93
Peter Regan	Jan 93 -

GREAT BRITAIN REGISTER

(**8 players**)

Johnie Baxter	(1)	1907
Jack Bennett	(6)	1924
Joe Bowers	(1)	1920
Terry Fogerty	(1)	1974
Ernest Jones	(4)	1920
Malcolm Price	(2)	1967
Jack Robinson	(2)	1914
Tommy Woods	(2)	1911

1992-93 SIGNINGS REGISTER

Signed	Player	Club From
11.6.92	Brown, Colin	Skirlaugh ARL
11.6.92	Gotts, Richard	Skirlaugh ARL
29.7.92	Reynolds, Paul	Blackpool G.
29.7.92	Stewart, Mike	Blackpool G.
10.9.92	Bannon, John	Crosfields ARL
10.9.92	Finney, Ian	St. Helens
23.9.92	Green, Jason	Wigan St. Patricks ARL
9.10.92	*McKenzie, Phil	Widnes
19.10.92	*Phillips, Rowland	Warrington
9.11.92	Johnson, Phil	Leigh
7.12.92	*O'Brien, Darren	St. Helens
19.2.93	Pachniuk, Richard	Oldham
19.3.93	Warburton, Steve	Oldham
23.3.93	*Hourigan, Paul	Oldham
25.3.93	*Allen, John	Swinton
25.3.93	*Partington, Carl	Swinton
26.3.93	Worrall, Mick	Leeds

ROCHDALE HORNETS 1992-93 PLAYERS' SUMMARY

	(Date of Birth)	App	T	G	D	Pts	Previous club	Signed
Abram, Darren	(27.9.67)	12+3	4	2	—	20	Trafford B.	9.11.90
Bamber, Simon	(3.2.63)	9+10	2	—	—	8	Trafford B.	8.12.88
Belle, Adrian	(23.11.70)	17	3	—	—	12	Oldham St. A. ARL	20.8.90
Brown, Colin	(17.6.71)	6+1	—	—	—	—	Skirlaugh ARL	11.6.92
Calland, Matt	(20.8.71)	32	18	—	—	72	Oldham St. A. ARL	20.8.90
Chrimes, David	(16.12.69)	7+1	1	—	—	4	Mayfield ARL	10.3.93
Clark, Brett	(1.11.61)	22+3	6	—	—	24	Oldham	16.8.91
Eccles, Cliff	(4.9.67)	33+1	4	—	—	16	Trafford B.	19.9.91
Gartland, Steve	(3.10.70)	35	17	103	2	276	Oldham St. A. ARL	17.8.90
Green, Jason	(19.1.72)	17	9	—	—	36	Wigan St. P. ARL	23.9.92
Hall, Martin	(5.12.68)	18	5	—	—	20	Oldham	1.8.89
Hall, Robert	(13.5.71)	7+7	—	—	—	—	Oldham St. A. ARL	8.1.90
Heugh, Cavill	(31.8.62)	31	5	—	—	20	Leeds	25.8.92
Hourigan, Paul	(15.10.71)	4	4	7	—	30	Oldham	23.3.93
Humphries, Tony	(3.9.63)	7+8	—	—	—	—	Warrington	29.8.89
Kay, Martin	(16.2.71)	14	1	—	—	4	Oldham St. A. ARL	20.8.90
Kuiti, Mike	(18.3.63)	12+2	1	—	—	4	Leeds	2.9.91
McKenzie, Phil	(13.6.63)	3+1	—	—	—	—	Widnes	9.11.92
Marriott, Karl	(21.11.69)	15+8	7	—	—	28	Mayfield ARL	17.8.89
Marsden, Bob	(28.2.66)	34	8	—	—	32	Oldham	29.8.89
O'Brien, Darren	(28.9.70)	1	—	—	—	—	St. Helens	7.12.92
O'Keefe, Paul	(28.6.71)	9+3	3	—	—	12	—	15.12.91
Pachniuk, Richard	(24.3.71)	12	8	—	1	33	Oldham	19.2.93
Phillips, Rowland	(28.7.65)	3+1	3	—	—	12	Warrington	19.10.92
Reddican, Mal	(21.11.68)	1+2	—	—	—	—	Langworthy ARL	26.12.91
Reynolds, Paul	(1.4.68)	18+1	6	—	1	25	Blackpool G.	29.7.92
Stewart, Mike	(16.1.66)	12+1	—	—	—	—	Blackpool G.	29.7.92
Turner, Steve	(5.12.61)	3+2	—	—	—	—	Swinton	22.2.88
Warburton, Steve	(6.2.69)	11	7	—	—	28	Oldham	19.3.93
Webster, David	(20.10.68)	24+4	2	—	—	8	Widnes St. M. ARL	20.4.91
Whitfield, Colin	(20.9.60)	24	3	3	—	18	Halifax	17.8.90
Williams, Mike	(21.10.70)	1+1	—	—	—	—	Golborne ARL	17.9.90
Worrall, Mick	(22.3.62)	1+5	1	—	—	4	Leeds	26.3.93
TOTALS								
33 players			128	115	4	746		

ROCHDALE HORNETS 1992-93 MATCH ANALYSIS

Date	Competition	H/A	Opponent	Rlt	Score	Tries	Goals	Attendance	Referee
30.8.92	SD	A	Swinton	W	14-10	Abram, Calland, Gartland	Abram	—	—
6.9.92	SD	A	London C.	L	10-30	Bamber	Gartland (3)	—	—
11.9.92	LC(1)	H	Wigan	L	8-36	Kuiti	Gartland (2)	2936	Campbell
20.9.92	SD	H	Featherstone R.	W	26-22	Gartland, Reynolds, Calland, Abram	Gartland (5)	1695	J. Smith
27.9.92	SD	A	Bramley	W	20-12	Gartland (2), Abram, Calland	Gartland, Abram	—	—
4.10.92	SD	A	Carlisle	L	12-24	Gartland, Webster	Gartland (2)	—	—
11.10.92	SD	H	Oldham	L	20-21	Calland, Reynolds, Gartland	Gartland (4)	2772	Crashley
18.10.92	SD	A	Huddersfield	W	22-14	Gartland (2), Reynolds, Clark	Gartland (3)	—	—
25.10.92	SD	A	London C.	W	24-12	Calland (2), Whitfield, Reynolds	Gartland (4)	—	—
1.11.92	SD	H	Bramley	W	29-22	Phillips, Marsden, Reynolds, M. Hall, Gartland	Gartland (4), Reynolds (dg)	1116	Morris
8.11.92	RT(1)	H	XIII Catalan	W	32-16	Bamber, Phillips, Marsden, Webster	Gartland (8)	1507	Cummings
15.11.92	SD	H	London C.	W	25-16	Phillips, Clark, Eccles, M. Hall	Gartland (4, 1dg)	1222	Wood
22.11.92	SD	A	Featherstone R.	L	6-18	Heugh	Gartland	—	—
29.11.92	SD	H	Bramley	W	62-22	Green (2), Gartland (2), M. Hall (2), Calland (2), Marriott (2), Heugh	Gartland (7), Whitfield (2)	1065	Asquith
6.12.92	RT(2)	A	Widnes	L	2-30	—	Whitfield	—	—
13.12.92	SD	H	Carlisle	W	26-18	Abram, Heugh, Gartland, M. Hall	Gartland (5)	873	R. Smith
6.1.93	SD	A	Swinton	L	12-14	Marsden, Marriott	Gartland (2)	—	—
10.1.93	SD	A	Carlisle	L	12-16	Marriott (2)	Gartland (2)	—	—
13.1.93	SD	A	Oldham	L	22-47	Calland, Kay, Marriott, Whitfield	Gartland (3)	—	—
24.1.93	SD	A	Oldham	L	12-28	Clark, O'Keefe	Gartland (2)	—	—
31.1.93	CC(1)	H	Doncaster	W	34-13	Calland (3), Gartland, Heugh, Marsden	Gartland (5)	1072	Kershaw
7.2.93	SD	H	Swinton	L	12-32	Marsden, Reynolds	Gartland (2)	1037	Wood
14.2.93	CC(2)	A	Leeds	L	6-68	Whitfield	Gartland	—	—
21.2.93	SD	A	Huddersfield	W	17-12	Eccles (2)	Gartland (4, 1dg)	—	—
24.2.93	SD	H	London C.	W	30-18	Clark, Gartland, Heugh, Marriott, Pachniuk	Gartland (5)	726	Morris
3.3.93	SD	H	Huddersfield	W	24-14	Green, O'Keefe, Pachniuk, Warburton	Gartland (4)	1003	Cummings
7.3.93	SD	H	Featherstone R.	L	24-40	Marsden (2), Belle, Pachniuk	Gartland (4)	1646	Asquith
14.3.93	SD	A	Bramley	W	30-14	Gartland (2), Belle, Clark, Warburton	Gartland (5)	—	—
21.3.93	SD	H	Swinton	L	14-25	Pachniuk (2), Calland	Gartland	1039	Gilmour
28.3.93	SD	A	Featherstone R.	L	22-24	Warburton (2), Belle, Clark, Pachniuk	Gartland	—	—
4.4.93	SD	H	Huddersfield	L	27-38	Green (2), Calland, Hourigan, Warburton	Gartland (3), Pachniuk (dg)	1415	Asquith
9.4.93	SD	H	Oldham	L	18-32	Green (2), Hourigan, Worrall	Gartland	1929	Morris
18.4.93	SD	H	Carlisle	W	50-12	Calland (2), Warburton (2), Chrimes, Eccles, Gartland, Green, Marsden, O'Keefe	Gartland (5)	781	Wood
25.4.93	DP(2)	H	Keighley C.	W	26-18	Pachniuk (2), Calland, Green	Hourigan (5)	2457	Gilmour
9.5.93	DP(SF)	H	Workington T.	L	16-30	Hourigan (2), Calland	Hourigan (2)	4024	Ollerton

RYEDALE-YORK

Ground: Ryedale Stadium (0904-634636)
First Season: 1901-02 as York. Moved and became Ryedale-York at start of 1989-90
Nickname: Wasps
Chairman: John Stabler
Secretary: Roland Davis
Honours: **Division Two** Champions, 1980-81
Challenge Cup Beaten finalists, 1930-31
Yorkshire Cup Winners, 1922-23, 1933-34, 1936-37
Beaten finalists, 1935-36, 1957-58, 1978-79

RECORDS

Match
Goals: 12 by Gary Pearce at Nottingham C., 4 Oct 1992
Tries: 6 by Roy Hardgrave v. Bramley, 5 Jan 1935
David Kettlestring at Keighley, 11 Mar 1990
Points: 28 by Gary Pearce at Nottingham C., 4 Oct 1992

Season
Goals: 146 by Vic Yorke, 1957-58
Tries: 35 by John Crossley, 1980-81
Points: 318 by Graham Steadman, 1984-85

Career
Goals: 1,060 by Vic Yorke, 1954-67
Tries: 167 by Peter Foster, 1955-67
Points: 2,159 by Vic Yorke, 1954-67
Appearances: 449 by Willie Hargreaves, 1952-65
Highest score: 84-0 at Nottingham C., 4 Oct 1992
Highest against: 75-3 at Warrington, 23 Sep 1950
Attendance: 14,689 v. Swinton (RL Cup), 10 Feb 1934 — at Clarence Street
4,977 v. Halifax (Div. 2), 5 Jan 1990 — at Ryedale Stadium

COACHING REGISTER
● Since 1974-75

Keith Goulding	Nov 73 - Sep 74
Gary Cooper	Dec 74 - Sep 76
Mal Dixon	Sep 76 - Dec 78
Paul Daley	Jan 79 - May 79
David Doyle-Davidson	July 79 - July 80
Bill Kirkbride	Aug 80 - Apr 82
Alan Hardisty	May 82 - Jan 83
Phil Lowe	Mar 83 - Mar 87
Danny Sheehan	Mar 87 - Apr 88
Gary Stephens	Apr 88 - June 91
Derek Foster	July 91 - Nov 92
Steve Crooks	Nov 92 -

GREAT BRITAIN REGISTER
(7 players)

Edgar Dawson	(1)	1956
Harry Field	(3)	1936
Geoff Smith	(3)	1963-64
Jeff Stevenson	(4)	1959-60
Mick Sullivan	(1)	1963
Basil Watts	(5)	1954-55
Les White	(4)	1946

1992-93 SIGNINGS REGISTER

Signed	Player	Club From
20.6.92	Close, David	Sheffield E.
28.7.92	Connell, Phil	Bramley
30.7.92	Lydiat, John	Hull K.R.
31.7.92	Atkins, Gary	Castleford
13.8.92	Adie, Charlie	Heworth ARL
20.8.92	Stead, Ray	Scarborough P.
11.9.92	Judge, Chris	Heworth ARL
21.9.92	*Keebles, Mick	Keighley C.
24.9.92	Dunne, Terry	Toukley, Aus
24.9.92	Fitzgerald, Peter	Cootamundra, Aus
2.10.92	McVean, Sean	St. George, Aus
18.2.93	Galbraith, Jamie	Rooty Hill, Aus

RYEDALE-YORK 1992-93 PLAYERS' SUMMARY

	(Date of Birth)	App	T	G	D	Pts	Previous club	Signed
Adie, Charlie	(8.3.73)	3+2	—	—	—	—	Heworth ARL	13.8.92
Atkins, Gary	(12.10.66)	18	13	—	—	52	Castleford	31.7.92
Close, David	(7.5.66)	23+1	3	9	3	33	Sheffield E.	20.6.92
Connell, Phil	(14.11.69)	6+2	3	—	—	12	Bramley	26.3.92
Craven, Steve	(9.4.72)	20+6	8	—	—	32	York All Blacks ARL	28.2.90
Dobson, Steve	(27.4.63)	6+2	1	6	2	18	Sheffield E.	23.7.90
Dunne, Terry	(22.10.69)	15+7	3	—	—	12	Australia	24.9.92
Fitzgerald, Peter	(22.10.69)	6+1	13	5	—	62	Australia	24.9.92
Hammerton, Chris	(21.11.63)	10+1	2	—	—	8	Heworth ARL	28.8.87
Hayes, Richard	(21.2.70)	24+2	2	—	—	8	York All Blacks ARL	13.1.89
Holt, Richard	(24.10.71)	2	2	—	—	8	Heworth ARL	31.5.91
Hopcutt, Chris	(6.12.69)	1	—	—	—	—	Scarborough P.	12.11.91
Horton, Stuart	(10.9.63)	26+1	3	—	—	12	Castleford	27.8.87
Hutchinson, Paul	(13.1.71)	21+1	8	—	—	32	Redhill ARL	19.5.89
Kettlestring, David	(18.11.67)	10	9	—	—	36	York All Blacks ARL	8.1.90
Laws, Mark	(26.4.71)	0+2	—	—	—	—	Newland ARL	27.3.90
Lockwood, Peter	(15.1.64)	1	—	—	—	—	Acorn ARL	14.1.92
Lydiat, John	(10.1.60)	15	7	—	—	28	Hull K.R.	30.7.92
McVean, Sean	(13.10.69)	12+1	1	—	—	4	Australia	2.10.92
Morris, Stuart	(17.11.86)	10+2	12	—	—	48	Dewsbury	25.5.89
Pallister, Alan	(4.12.70)	3	—	—	—	—	York All Blacks ARL	1.11.90
Parsons, Matthew	(18.6.73)	3+4	—	—	—	—	Australia	8.2.93
Paver, Ian	(8.3.63)	10	—	—	—	—	Heworth ARL	2.11.90
Pearce, Gary	(11.11.60)	16+1	2	76	1	161	Scarborough P.	9.6.92
Pinkney, Nick	(6.12.70)	28	25	—	—	100	Greatfield ARL	23.7.90
Pryce, Steve	(12.5.69)	12+8	1	—	—	4	West Bowling ARL	23.7.90
Ramsden, Mick	(13.11.71)	3+3	3	—	—	12	York Civil S. ARL	1.6.91
Smith, Adrian	(24.11.63)	10+6	2	—	—	8	Heworth ARL	20.12.87
Stead, Ray	(28.6.62)	13+1	6	—	—	24	Scarborough P.	20.8.92
Sullivan, Graham	(27.1.67)	14+2	3	27	—	66	Punch Bowl ARL	27.7.87
Thomas, Dean	(10.5.66)	3	—	—	—	—	RU	15.8.92
Warters, Nick	(20.1.69)	3+2	1	—	—	4	Acorn ARL	24.8.88
White, Paul	(5.11.64)	24	9	—	—	36	—	6.11.86
Wigglesworth, Iain	(25.4.67)	6	1	—	—	4	Leeds Colts	14.7.86

TOTALS

34 players 143 123 6 824

Representative appearances 1992-93

Pearce — Wales (1+1, 3g, 1dg)

RYEDALE-YORK 1992-93 MATCH ANALYSIS

Date	Competition	H/A	Opponent	Rlt	Score	Tries	Goals	Attendance	Referee
23.8.92	YC(P)	A	Huddersfield	L	12-36	Pinkney, Ramsden	Close (2)	—	—
30.8.92	TD	A	Chorley B.	W	23-13	Pryce, Smith, Pinkney, Stead	Close (3, 1dg)	—	—
6.9.92	TD	H	Batley	W	24-14	Pearce, Hutchinson, White, Craven	Pearce (4)	1876	Whitelam
20.9.92	TD	A	Whitehaven	W	26-13	Lydiat, Connell, White, Pinkney, Horton	Pearce (3)	—	—
27.9.92	TD	H	Highfield	W	60-12	Connell (2), Morris (2), Close, Hutchinson, Pinkney, Horton, Lydiat, Stead	Pearce (9), Fitzgerald	1777	Ollerton
4.10.92	TD	A	Nottingham C.	W	84-0	White (3), Morris (3), Hutchinson (2), Pinkney (2), Lydiat, Hayes, Smith, Pearce, Craven	Pearce (12)	—	—
11.10.92	TD	H	Doncaster	W	42-22	Morris (2), Dunne, Close, Lydiat, McVean, Stead	Pearce (6, 1dg), Close (dg)	2522	Campbell
18.10.92	TD	A	Batley	L	12-18	Lydiat, Pinkney	Pearce (2)	—	—
1.11.92	TD	H	Chorley B.	W	36-6	Pinkney (2), Stead (2), Craven (2), Atkins	Close (4)	1542	Steele
8.11.92	RT(1)	A	Widnes	L	4-46	—	Pearce (2)	—	—
15.11.92	TD	A	Highfield	W	34-12	Hammerton (2), Hayes, Craven, Atkins, White	Pearce (5)	—	—
22.11.92	TD	A	Barrow	W	22-4	Atkins (3)	Pearce (5)	—	—
29.11.92	TD	H	Keighley C.	L	14-16	Pinkney (2), Hutchinson	Pearce	2346	R. Connolly
13.12.92	TD	A	Workington T.	L	10-42	Stead, Horton	Fitzgerald	—	—
20.12.92	TD	H	Barrow	W*	60-0	Fitzgerald (3), Morris (3), Hutchinson, Pinkney, Atkins, Wigglesworth	Pearce (10)	1132	Tidball
10.1.93	TD	A	Blackpool G.	W	32-12	Fitzgerald (3), Pinkney (2), Close	Pearce (4)	—	—
17.1.93	TD	H	Nottingham C.	W	52-0	Fitzgerald (4), Pinkney (3), Atkins, Morris, Sullivan	Pearce (6)	1329	Volante
24.1.93	TD	H	Dewsbury	L	12-30	Fitzgerald, Morris	Pearce (2)	2558	Cummings
31.1.93	CC(1)	A	Hunslet	L	22-27	Fitzgerald (2), Pinkney, Sullivan	Fitzgerald (3)	—	—
7.2.93	TD	A	Keighley C.	L	15-22	Craven, Pinkney, White	Sullivan, Dobson (dg)	—	—
21.2.93	TD	H	Blackpool G.	W	56-6	Holt (2), Kettlestring (2), Pinkney (2), White (2), Dobson, Hutchinson	Pearce (5), Sullivan (3)	1185	Whitelam
28.2.93	TD	A	Doncaster	L	9-14	Dunne	Dobson (2, 1dg)	—	—
14.3.93	TD	H	Workington T.	W	16-12	Pinkney (2), Kettlestring	Dobson (2)	1833	Galtress
28.3.93	TD	A	Dewsbury	L	12-17	Atkins (2)	Dobson (2)	—	—
4.4.93	TD	H	Whitehaven	W	24-12	Atkins, Kettlestring, Lydiat	Sullivan (6)	1144	Volante
9.4.93	TD	H	Hunslet	W	44-26	Craven (2), Kettlestring (2), Atkins, Ramsden, Sullivan, Warters	Sullivan (6)	1166	Wood
12.4.93	TD	A	Hunslet	W	28-12	Kettlestring (2), Lydiat, Pinkney, Ramsden	Sullivan (4)	—	—
18.4.93	DP(1)	H	Whitehaven	W	31-6	Atkins, Dunne, Hutchinson, Kettlestring, Pinkney	Sullivan (5), Close (dg)	729	J. Smith
25.4.93	DP(2)	A	Featherstone R.	L	8-46	Atkins	Sullivan (2)	—	—

*Abandoned after 68 minutes. Result stands.

ST. HELENS

Centre Paul Loughlin, a double match record-holder.

Ground: Knowsley Road (0744-23697)
First Season: 1895-96
Nickname: Saints
Chairman: Eric Latham
Secretary: Geoff Sutcliffe
Honours: **Championship** Winners, 1931-32, 1952-53, 1958-59, 1965-66, 1969-70, 1970-71
Beaten finalists, 1964-65, 1966-67, 1971-72
League Leaders Trophy Winners, 1964-65, 1965-66
Club Championship (Merit Table) Beaten finalists, 1973-74
Division One Champions, 1974-75
Challenge Cup Winners, 1955-56, 1960-61, 1965-66, 1971-72, 1975-76
Beaten finalists, 1896-97, 1914-15, 1929-30, 1952-53, 1977-78, 1986-87, 1988-89, 1990-91
Regal Trophy Winners, 1987-88
Premiership Winners, 1975-76, 1976-77, 1984-85, 1992-93
Beaten finalists, 1974-75, 1987-88, 1991-92
Lancashire Cup Winners, 1926-27, 1953-54, 1960-61, 1961-62, 1962-63, 1963-64, 1964-65, 1967-68, 1968-69, 1984-85, 1991-92
Beaten finalists, 1932-33, 1952-53, 1956-57, 1958-59, 1959-60, 1970-71, 1982-83, 1992-93
Lancashire League Winners, 1929-30, 1931-32, 1952-53, 1959-60, 1964-65, 1965-66, 1966-67, 1968-69
Western Division Championship Winners, 1963-64
Charity Shield Winners, 1992-93
BBC2 Floodlit Trophy Winners, 1971-72, 1975-76
Beaten finalists, 1965-66, 1968-69, 1970-71, 1977-78, 1978-79

RECORDS

Match
Goals: 16 by Paul Loughlin v. Carlisle, 14 Sep 1986
Tries: 6 by Alf Ellaby v. Barrow, 5 Mar 1932
Steve Llewellyn v. Castleford, 3 Mar 1956
Steve Llewellyn v. Liverpool C., 20 Aug 1956
Tom Van Vollenhoven v. Wakefield T., 21 Dec 1957
Tom Van Vollenhoven v. Blackpool B., 23 Apr 1962
Frank Myler v. Maryport, 1 Sep 1969
Shane Cooper v. Hull, 17 Feb 1988
Points: 40 by Paul Loughlin v. Carlisle, 14 Sep 1986

Season
Goals: 214 by Kel Coslett, 1971-72
Tries: 62 by Tom Van Vollenhoven, 1958-59
Points: 452 by Kel Coslett, 1971-72

Career
Goals: 1,639 by Kel Coslett, 1961-76
Tries: 392 by Tom Van Vollenhoven, 1957-68
Points: 3,413 by Kel Coslett, 1961-76
Appearances: 519+12 by Kel Coslett, 1961-76
Highest score: 112-0 v. Carlisle, 14 Sep 1986
Highest against: 78-3 at Warrington, 12 Apr 1909
Attendance: 35,695 v. Wigan (League), 26 Dec 1949

COACHING REGISTER
● **Since 1974-75**

Eric Ashton	May 74 - May 80
Kel Coslett	June 80 - May 82
Billy Benyon	May 82 - Nov 85
Alex Murphy	Nov 85 - Jan 90
Mike McClennan	Feb 90 -

GREAT BRITAIN REGISTER
(53 players)

Chris Arkwright	(+2)	1985
Len Aston	(3)	1947
Billy Benyon	(5+1)	1971-72
Tommy Bishop	(15)	1966-69
Frank Carlton	(1)	1958
Eric Chisnall	(4)	1974
Gary Connolly	(7+3)	1991-93
Eddie Cunningham	(1)	1978
Rob Dagnall	(4)	1961-65
David Eckersley	(2+2)	1973-74
Alf Ellaby	(13)	1928-33
Les Fairclough	(6)	1926-29
John Fieldhouse	(1)	1986
Alec Fildes	(4)	1932
Alf Frodsham	(3)	1928-29
Peter Gorley	(2+1)	1980-81
Doug Greenall	(6)	1951-54
Jonathan Griffiths	(1)	1992
Paul Groves	(1)	1987
Roy Haggerty	(2)	1987
Mervyn Hicks	(1)	1965
Neil Holding	(4)	1984
Dick Huddart	(12)	1959-63
Alan Hunte	(4)	1992-93
Les Jones	(1)	1971
Chris Joynt	(+1)	1993
Tony Karalius	(4+1)	1971-72
Vince Karalius	(10)	1958-61
Ken Kelly	(2)	1972
Barry Ledger	(2)	1985-86
Paul Loughlin	(14+1)	1988-92
Stan McCormick	(1)	1948
Tom McKinney	(1)	1957
John Mantle	(13)	1966-73
Roy Mathias	(1)	1979
Glyn Moses	(9)	1955-57
Alex Murphy	(26)	1958-66
Frank Myler	(9)	1970
George Nicholls	(22)	1973-79

Sonny Nickle	(+2)	1992-93
Harry Pinner	(5+1)	1980-86
Andy Platt	(4+3)	1985-88
Alan Prescott	(28)	1951-58
Austin Rhodes	(4)	1957-61
Jim Stott	(1)	1947
Anthony Sullivan	(1)	1991
Mick Sullivan	(10)	1961-62
Jim Tembey	(2)	1963-64
Abe Terry	(10)	1958-61
John Walsh	(4+1)	1972
Kevin Ward	(1+2)	1990-92
John Warlow	(3+1)	1964-68
Cliff Watson	(29+1)	1963-71

1992-93 SIGNINGS REGISTER

Signed	Player	Club From
1.7.92	O'Donnell, Gus	Wigan
1.7.92	Eastwood, Jon	Saddleworth ARL
7.7.92	O'Loughlin, Jason	Salford
2.9.92	Cunningham, Gareth	Blackpool Royals ARL
2.9.92	Joynt, Chris	Oldham
3.9.92	McCracken, Jarrod	Canterbury-B., Aus
4.9.92	Holding, Neil	Rochdale H.
23.9.92	Lyon, David	Warrington
9.10.92	McAtee, John	Eccles ARL
3.11.92	Prescott, Steve	Nutgrove ARL
20.11.92	*Knight, Mark	Chorley B.
8.12.92	Sheil, Richard	Blackbrook ARL
5.2.93	Cowan, Ricky	Wellington, NZ

*Second row forward Sonny Nickle,
holder of two Great Britain Test caps.*

ST. HELENS 1992-93 PLAYERS' SUMMARY

	(Date of Birth)	App	T	G	D	Pts	Previous club	Signed
Casey, Sean	(9.12.71)	1	—	—	—	—	Blackbrook ARL	16.12.91
Connolly, Gary	(22.6.71)	35	16	—	—	64	Blackbrook ARL	15.12.88
Connor, Ian	(21.3.70)	0+1	—	—	—	—	Swinton	15.12.89
Cooper, Shane	(26.5.60)	39	7	—	1	29	New Zealand	13.10.87
Cowan, Ricky	(28.12.63)	1+3	—	—	—	—	New Zealand	5.2.93
Dwyer, Bernard	(20.4.67)	35+2	4	26	—	68	Hare & Hounds ARL	22.5.84
Forber, Paul	(29.4.64)	4+8	1	1	—	6	St. Helens Colts	5.5.81
Griffiths, Jonathan	(23.8.64)	27+6	9	—	—	36	Llanelli RU	22.5.89
Groves, Paul	(27.5.65)	1+3	—	—	—	—	Salford	19.10.87
Harrison, John	(10.3.65)	25+3	2	—	—	8	Parkside ARL	30.12.87
Hunte, Alan	(11.7.70)	34	28	—	—	112	Wakefield T.	3.3.89
Joynt, Chris	(7.12.71)	33+2	10	—	—	40	Oldham	2.9.92
Loughlin, Paul	(28.7.66)	19+1	5	65	—	150	St. Helens Colts	8.8.83
Lyon, David	(3.9.65)	25	9	17	1	71	Warrington	23.9.92
McAtee, John	(11.11.75)	0+1	—	—	—	—	Eccles ARL	9.10.92
McCracken, Jarrod	(27.3.70)	21	5	—	—	20	New Zealand	3.9.92
Mann, George	(31.7.65)	28+1	—	—	—	—	New Zealand	31.7.89
Neill, Jonathan	(19.12.68)	26	1	—	—	4	Kells ARL	27.7.87
Nickle, Sonny	(4.5.69)	31+3	15	—	—	60	Sheffield E.	3.7.91
O'Donnell, Gus	(11.12.70)	12+16	1	—	9	13	Wigan	1.7.92
Quirk, Les	(6.3.65)	17+3	8	—	—	32	Barrow	5.10.87
Riley, Mike	(20.11.70)	9+2	—	—	—	—	Widnes Tigers ARL	5.1.90
Ropati, Tea	(7.9.65)	40	21	24	2	134	New Zealand	25.8.90
Sullivan, Anthony	(23.11.68)	24+3	8	—	—	32	Hull K.R.	29.4.91
Veivers, Phil	(25.5.64)	12+9	1	—	—	4	Australia	18.9.84
Ward, Kevin	(5.8.57)	21+3	3	—	—	12	Castleford	6.7.90
TOTALS								
26 players			154	133	13	895		

Representative appearances 1992-93
Connolly — Britain (3); England (1)
Griffiths — Wales (1, 1t)
Hunte — Britain (3, 2t); England (1)
Joynt — Britain (+1); England (+1); GB Under-21s (1)
Nickle — Britain (+1)
Sullivan — Wales (2)
Ward — Britain (1)

ST. HELENS 1992-93 MATCH ANALYSIS

Date	Com-petition	H/A	Opponent	Rlt	Score	Tries	Goals	Atten-dance	Referee
23.8.92	CS	N[1]	Wigan	W	17-0	Ropati, Cooper, Sullivan	Ropati (2), O'Donnell (dg)	(7364)	Cummings
30.8.92	SBC	A	Leeds	W	27-14	Ropati, Connolly, Hunte, Sullivan, Griffiths	Ropati (3), O'Donnell (dg)	—	—
6.9.92	SBC	H	Wakefield T.	W	24-12	Ward, Nickle, Hunte	Ropati (6)	9507	Cummings
13.9.92	LC(1)	A	Barrow	W	36-2	Hunte (3), Connolly (2), Nickle, McCracken	Ropati (4)	—	—
20.9.92	SBC	A	Sheffield E.	W	18-10	Quirk, Nickle, Hunte	Ropati (2), Dwyer	—	—
27.9.92	SBC	H	Salford	W	48-8	Sullivan (2), Hunte (2), McCracken (2), Ropati (2), Dwyer	Dwyer (6)	9159	R. Smith
30.9.92	LC(2)	H	Widnes	W	10-8	Connolly, Ropati	Dwyer	12,573	J. Connolly
4.10.92	SBC	A	Wakefield T.	W	18-5	Cooper, Hunte, Dwyer	Dwyer (3)	—	—
7.10.92	LC(SF)	H	Salford	W	18-5	Hunte (2), Connolly	Dwyer (3)	9289	J. Connolly
11.10.92	SBC	H	Hull	W	38-8	Veivers, Griffiths, Connolly, Cooper, Nickle, Ropati, Hunte	Dwyer (5)	8595	R. Smith
18.10.92	LC(F)	H	Wigan	L	4-5	—	Dwyer (2)	(20,534)	Cummings
27.10.92	RT(P)	H	Huddersfield	W	44-18	Ropati (3), Forber, Joynt, Quirk, Nickle, Harrison, McCracken	Ropati (3), Dwyer	4423	Kershaw
1.11.92	SBC	H	Bradford N.	L	18-35	Quirk (2), Hunte	Dwyer (3)	9967	Whitfield
8.11.92	RT(1)	H	Leeds	W	15-14	Hunte (2), Connolly	Forber, Ropati (dg)	11,052	J. Smith
11.11.92	SBC	A	Leigh	L	6-11	Griffiths	Dwyer	—	—
15.11.92	SBC	A	Salford	W	15-12	Cooper, Ropati	Lyon (3), Cooper (dg)	—	—
22.11.92	SBC	A	Bradford N.	W	16-4	Sullivan, Connolly, Ropati	Lyon (2)	—	—
29.11.92	SBC	H	Sheffield E.	W	30-20	Ropati (2), Nickle, Connolly, Griffiths	Ropati (3), Lyon (2)	7002	Cummings
6.12.92	RT(2)	A	Featherstone R.	W	25-8	Lyon, McCracken, Sullivan, Joynt	Lyon (4), O'Donnell (dg)	—	—
11.12.92	SBC	A	Castleford	L	6-16	Lyon	Lyon	—	—
19.12.92	RT(3)	H	Castleford	L	8-12	Quirk	Lyon (2)	4785	Steele
27.12.92	SBC	H	Wigan	W	41-6	Hunte (2), Nickle (2), Joynt, Lyon, Ropati	Loughlin (6), O'Donnell (dg)	17,495	Whitfield
6.1.93	SBC	H	Leigh	W	64-9	Hunte (4), Joynt (2), Quirk (2), Nickle (2), Ropati, Lyon	Loughlin (8)	7743	Gilmour
17.1.93	SBC	A	Hull K.R.	W	22-11	Connolly, Griffiths, Joynt, Lyon	Loughlin (3)	—	—
22.1.93	SBC	H	Halifax	W	18-16	Nickle (2), Ward	Lyon (3)	7219	Whitfield
31.1.93	CC(1)	A	Featherstone R.	W	24-22	Lyon (2), Connolly, Dwyer	Loughlin (4)	—	—
5.2.93	SBC	H	Warrington	W	12-4	Joynt, Loughlin	Loughlin, O'Donnell (2dg)	7660	Ollerton
13.2.93	CC(2)	A	Wigan	L	3-23	—	Loughlin, Lyon (dg)	—	—
17.2.93	SBC	A	Widnes	L	8-26	Ropati	Loughlin (2)	—	—
21.2.93	SBC	A	Hull	L	16-21	Joynt, Nickle, Ropati	Loughlin (2)	—	—
3.3.93	SBC	H	Castleford	W	24-20	Griffiths, Joynt, Nickle, Ropati	Loughlin (4)	5647	Steele
12.3.93	SBC	H	Hull K.R.	W	34-14	Hunte (2), Griffiths, Harrison, Lyon, Ropati	Loughlin (4), Ropati	4627	Annesley (Aus)
19.3.93	SBC	A	Halifax	W	18-12	Cooper, Loughlin, Ropati	Loughlin (3)	—	—
28.3.93	SBC	A	Warrington	W	32-17	Connolly, Cooper, Hunte, Ropati, Ward	Loughlin (6)	—	—
4.4.93	SBC	H	Leeds	W	42-8	Connolly (2), Hunte (2), Griffiths, Joynt, Nickle, Sullivan	Loughlin (5)	9208	J. Connolly
9.4.93	SBC	A	Wigan	D	8-8	Connolly, Hunte	—	—	—
12.4.93	SBC	H	Widnes	W	29-18	Dwyer, Loughlin, Quirk, Sullivan	Loughlin (6), Ropati (dg)	11,974	R. Smith
23.4.93	PT(1)	H	Halifax	W	34-25	Griffiths, Lyon, Loughlin, Neill, O'Donnell	Loughlin (7)	5871	Cummings
9.5.93	PT(SF)	H	Leeds	W	15-2	Cooper, Hunte	Loughlin (3), O'Donnell (dg)	11,178	J. Connolly
16.5.93	PT(F)	N[2]	Wigan	W	10-4	Connolly, Loughlin	O'Donnell (2dg)	(36,598)	Holdsworth

N[1] Gateshead   N[2] Manchester U.FC

SALFORD

Ground: The Willows (061-737-6363)
First Season: 1896-97
Nickname: Red Devils
Chairman: John Wilkinson
Secretary: Graham McCarty
Honours: **Championship** Winners, 1913-14, 1932-33, 1936-37, 1938-39
Beaten finalists, 1933-34
Division One Champions, 1973-74, 1975-76
Division Two Champions, 1990-91
Challenge Cup Winners, 1937-38
Beaten finalists, 1899-1900, 1901-02, 1902-03, 1905-06, 1938-39, 1968-69
Regal Trophy Beaten finalists, 1972-73
Premiership Beaten finalists, 1975-76
Second Division Premiership Winners, 1990-91
Lancashire Cup Winners, 1931-32, 1934-35, 1935-36, 1936-37, 1972-73
Beaten finalists, 1929-30, 1938-39, 1973-74, 1974-75, 1975-76, 1988-89, 1990-91
Lancashire League Winners, 1932-33, 1933-34, 1934-35, 1936-37, 1938-39
BBC2 Floodlit Trophy Winners, 1974-75

RECORDS

Match
Goals: 13 by Gus Risman v. Bramley, 5 Apr 1933
Gus Risman v. Broughton R., 18 May 1940
David Watkins v. Keighley, 7 Jan 1972
Steve Rule v. Doncaster, 4 Sep 1981
Tries: 6 by Frank Miles v. Leeds, 5 Mar 1898
Ernest Bone v. Goole, 29 Mar 1902
Jack Hilton v. Leigh, 7 Oct 1939
Points: 39 by Jim Lomas v. Liverpool C., 2 Feb 1907

Season
Goals: 221 by David Watkins, 1972-73
Tries: 46 by Keith Fielding, 1973-74
Points: 493 by David Watkins, 1972-73

Career
Goals: 1,241 by David Watkins, 1967-79
Tries: 297 by Maurice Richards, 1969-83
Points: 2,907 by David Watkins, 1967-79
Appearances: 496+2 by Maurice Richards, 1969-83
Highest score: 78-0 v. Liverpool C., 2 Feb 1907
Highest against: 70-6 at Wigan, 14 Mar 1993
Attendance: 26,470 v. Warrington (RL Cup), 13 Feb 1937

COACHING REGISTER
● **Since 1974-75**

Les Bettinson	Dec 73 - Mar 77
Colin Dixon	Mar 77 - Jan 78
Stan McCormick	Feb 78 - Mar 78
Alex Murphy	May 78 - Nov 80
Kevin Ashcroft	Nov 80 - Mar 82
Alan McInnes	Mar 82 - May 82
Malcolm Aspey	May 82 - Oct 83
Mike Coulman	Oct 83 - May 84
Kevin Ashcroft	May 84 - Oct 89
Kevin Tamati	Oct 89 -

GREAT BRITAIN REGISTER
(28 players)

Bill Burgess	(1)	1969
Paul Charlton	(17+1)	1970-74
Mike Coulman	(2+1)	1971
George Curran	(6)	1946-48
Eddie Curzon	(1)	1910
Tom Danby	(3)	1950
Colin Dixon	(11+2)	1969-74
Alan Edwards	(7)	1936-37
Jack Feetham	(7)	1932-33
Keith Fielding	(3)	1974-77
Ken Gill	(5+2)	1974-77
Jack Gore	(1)	1926
Chris Hesketh	(21+2)	1970-74
Barney Hudson	(8)	1932-37
Emlyn Jenkins	(9)	1933-37
Jim Lomas	(5)	1908-10
Tom McKinney	(7)	1951-54
Alf Middleton	(1)	1929
Steve Nash	(8)	1977-82
Maurice Richards	(2)	1974

Gus Risman	(17)	1932-46		7.7.92	Fairclough, Andy	St. Helens
Jack Spencer	(1)	1907		4.8.92	Critchley, Jason	Widnes
Johnny Ward	(1)	1970		4.8.92	Wynne, Steve	Widnes
Silas Warwick	(2)	1907		11.8.92	Griffin, Adam	Salford Academy
Billy Watkins	(7)	1933-37		27.8.92	Ackerman, Rob	Carlisle
David Watkins	(2+4)	1971-74		28.8.92	Ford, Phil	Leeds
Billy Williams	(2)	1929-32		10.9.92	Coleman, Craig	South Sydney, Aus
Peter Williams	(1+1)	1989		19.11.92	Blakeley, Steve	Wigan
				1.12.92	Tyrer, Gary	Orrell RU

1992-93 SIGNINGS REGISTER

Signed	Player	Club From
11.6.92	Brookfield, Keri	Wigan St. Patricks ARL

11.1.93	Forber, Paul	St. Helens
3.2.93	Laurie, Mark	Parramatta, Aus
22.4.93	Southern, Paul	Salford Academy

SALFORD 1992-93 PLAYERS' SUMMARY

	(Date of Birth)	App	T	G	D	Pts	Previous club	Signed
Ackerman, Rob	(2.3.61)	6+7	—	—	—	—	Carlisle	27.8.92
Birkett, Martin	(16.9.65)	19+3	4	39	—	94	Frizington ARL	7.12.89
Blakeley, Steve	(17.10.72)	14	4	34	—	84	Wigan	19.11.92
Blease, Ian	(1.1.65)	19+3	9	—	—	36	Folly Lane ARL	13.3.85
Bradshaw, Arthur	(1.11.63)	15+8	2	—	—	8	Thatto Heath ARL	22.6.89
Brookfield, Keri	(17.3.73)	1	—	—	—	—	Wigan St. P. ARL	11.6.92
Brown, Shaun	(19.10.69)	5+1	1	9	1	23	Leigh East ARL	3.8.89
Burgess, Andy	(1.4.70)	22+3	5	—	—	20	Irlam ARL	1.4.87
Coleman, Craig	(31.1.63)	28	7	—	—	28	Australia	10.9.92
Coussons, Phil	(2.8.73)	3	1	—	—	4	Salford Academy	11.2.92
Critchley, Jason	(7.12.70)	29+1	17	—	—	68	Widnes	4.8.92
Cruickshank, David	(4.7.65)	10+1	1	—	—	4	London C.	15.8.91
Donegan, Austin	(27.1.68)	1+5	—	—	—	—	Oldham	8.11.91
Evans, Tex	(25.1.64)	24+1	13	—	—	52	Swinton	17.8.88
Fairclough, Andy	(18.9.71)	0+1	—	—	—	—	St. Helens	7.7.92
Fell, David	(25.4.66)	0+1	—	—	—	—	Orrell RU	13.10.89
Forber, Paul	(29.4.64)	12	3	—	—	12	St. Helens	11.1.93
Ford, Phil	(16.3.61)	27	21	—	—	84	Leeds	28.8.92
Gibson, Steve	(23.11.62)	11+4	2	—	—	8	Australia	11.9.87
Gilfillan, John	(11.3.65)	13+2	2	—	—	8	Wigan	13.9.90
Hansen, Shane	(5.12.60)	8	—	—	—	—	New Zealand	20.9.90
Howard, Tony	(9.11.68)	7	2	—	—	8	Army RU	18.1.90
Laurie, Mark	(23.7.62)	8+1	1	—	—	4	Australia	3.2.93
Lee, Mark	(27.3.68)	29	6	—	4	28	St. Helens	8.1.90
O'Connor, Terry	(13.10.71)	2+3	—	—	—	—	Widnes Tigers ARL	5.8.91
Quigley, Jonathan	(6.6.73)	1+1	—	—	—	—	Leigh M. ARL	25.10.90
Randall, Craig	(22.9.72)	1	—	—	—	—	Leigh M. ARL	21.5.91
Reid, Wayne	(15.12.69)	14+11	4	—	—	16	Wigan	28.8.91
Stazicker, Ged	(2.1.68)	29+2	2	—	—	8	Wigan	8.7.91
Williams, Peter	(14.12.60)	16+2	2	—	—	8	Orrell RU	22.3.88
Young, David	(26.7.67)	29	3	7	—	26	Leeds	25.4.91

TOTALS

31 players		112	89	5	631

Representative appearances 1992-93
Ackerman — Wales (2, 1t); Birkett — Cumbria (1); Critchley — England (+1); Ford — Wales (2); Williams — Wales (+1); Young — Wales (2)

SALFORD 1992-93 MATCH ANALYSIS

Date	Com-petition	H/A	Opponent	Rlt	Score	Tries	Goals	Atten-dance	Referee
30.8.92	SBC	H	Hull K.R.	L	10-14	Cruickshank	Birkett (3)	3178	R. Smith
6.9.92	SBC	A	Castleford	W	24-20	Gilfillan, Ford, Critchley, Blease	Birkett (4)	—	—
13.9.92	LC(1)	H	Whitehaven	W	60-8	Ford (5), Coleman (2), Critchley (2), Reid, Blease, Williams	Birkett (6)	1985	Carter
20.9.92	SBC	H	Halifax	W	27-22	Coleman (2), Birkett, Critchley	Birkett (5), Lee (dg)	5515	Redfearn
23.9.92	LC(2)	H	Workington T.	W	42-20	Ford (2), Birkett, Gibson, Brown, Burgess, Evans	Birkett (7)	2143	Steele
27.9.92	SBC	A	St. Helens	L	8-48	Coleman	Birkett (2)	—	—
4.10.92	SBC	A	Bradford N.	L	26-28	Lee (2), Williams, Ford, Critchley	Birkett (3)	—	—
7.10.92	LC(SF)	A	St. Helens	L	5-18	—	Brown (2, 1dg)	—	—
11.10.92	SBC	H	Wakefield T.	W	14-8	Critchley, Ford	Brown (3)	3734	Cummings
16.10.92	SBC	H	Castleford	W	21-18	Ford (2), Critchley, Young	Brown (2), Lee (dg)	2945	J. Smith
1.11.92	SBC	A	Hull K.R.	W	16-10	Ford, Evans, Stazicker	Brown (2)	—	—
8.11.92	RT(1)	H	Featherstone R.	L	14-18	Ford, Lee	Birkett (3)	3088	Holdsworth
15.11.92	SBC	H	St. Helens	L	12-15	Burgess, Ford	Young (2)	6013	Kershaw
22.11.92	SBC	H	Wigan	L	18-26	Blease, Bradshaw, Gilfillan	Blakeley (3)	7681	R. Smith
29.11.92	SBC	A	Hull	L	10-42	Evans	Blakeley (3)	—	—
1.1.93	SBC	A	Leeds	L	14-38	Lee, Blakeley	Blakeley (3)	—	—
6.1.93	SBC	H	Widnes	L	12-48	Evans, Gibson	Blakeley (2)	3586	J. Smith
10.1.93	SBC	A	Wakefield T.	L	14-34	Blakeley, Evans, Ford	Blakeley	—	—
13.1.93	SBC	H	Leigh	W	24-16	Bradshaw, Coleman, Evans, Ford	Blakeley (4)	3389	Gilmour
17.1.93	SBC	H	Leeds	L	15-46	Evans (2), Blease	Blakeley, Lee (dg)	5244	Ollerton
24.1.93	SBC	A	Sheffield E.	L	16-30	Coleman, Critchley, Ford	Blakeley (2)	—	—
31.1.93	CC(1)	H	Wakefield T.	L	12-20	Birkett, Critchley	Birkett (2)	3732	Campbell
7.2.93	SBC	A	Halifax	L	14-36	Burgess, Evans, Lee	Birkett	—	—
19.2.93	SBC	H	Bradford N.	W	38-4	Ford (2), Burgess, Critchley, Evans, Forber, Young, Howard	Blakeley (3)	2842	Steele
7.3.93	SBC	H	Hull	W	26-10	Critchley, Evans, Forber, Ford, Howard	Blakeley (3)	3043	Steele
14.3.93	SBC	A	Wigan	L	6-70	Blakeley	Blakeley	—	—
21.3.93	SBC	H	Sheffield E.	W	48-12	Blease (3), Critchley (2), Birkett, Burgess, Reid, Stazicker	Blakeley (6)	3105	Steele
26.3.93	SBC	A	Widnes	L	22-38	Reid, Lee, Critchley, Laurie	Birkett (3)	—	—
4.4.93	SBC	H	Warrington	L	23-24	Critchley (3), Blease, Evans	Young, Lee (dg)	3693	R. Smith
12.4.93	SBC	A	Leigh	L	20-46	Blakeley, Evans, Forber, Young	Blakeley (2)	—	—
18.4.93	SBC	A	Warrington	L	20-22	Blease, Coussons, Reid	Young (4)	—	—

SHEFFIELD EAGLES

Honours: **Division Two** Champions, 1991-92
Second Division/Divisional Premiership Winners, 1988-89, 1991-92
Yorkshire Cup Beaten finalists, 1992-93

Ground: Don Valley Stadium (0742-610326)
First Season: 1984-85
Nickname: Eagles
Chairman: Gary Hetherington
Secretary: Julie Bush

RECORDS
Match
Goals: 12 by Roy Rafferty at Fulham, 21 Sep 1986

Mark Aston v. Keighley C.,
25 Apr 1992
Tries: 5 by Daryl Powell at Mansfield M.,
         2 Jan 1989
Points: 32 by Roy Rafferty at Fulham,
         21 Sep 1986

Season
Goals: 148 by Mark Aston, 1988-89
Tries: 30 by Iva Ropati, 1991-92
Points: 307 by Mark Aston, 1988-89

Career
Goals: 499 by Mark Aston, 1986-
Tries: 98 by Daryl Powell, 1984-
Points: 1,073 by Mark Aston, 1986-
Appearances: 263+3 by Daryl Powell, 1984-
Highest score: 80-8 v. Wigan St. Patricks,
         13 Nov 1988
Highest against: 62-11 at Warrington, 9 Feb 1986
Attendance: 8,000 v. Wakefield T. (Div. 1),
         26 Sep 1990 — at Don Valley
         8,636 v. Widnes (Div. 1), 8 Oct 1989
         — at Bramall Lane, Sheffield U. FC

COACHING REGISTER
● **Since formation in 1984**

Alan Rhodes	Apr 84 - May 86
Gary Hetherington	July 86 - Apr 93
Bill Gardner	May 93 -

GREAT BRITAIN REGISTER
(2 players)

Mark Aston	(+1)	1991
Daryl Powell	(17+4)	1990-93

1992-93 SIGNINGS REGISTER

Signed	Player	Club From
1.7.92	Carr, Paul	Hunslet
5.7.92	Boyer, Alan	—
14.7.92	Symonds, Andy	—
20.8.92	Mann, David	Dodworth ARL
20.8.92	Randall, Carl	Dodworth ARL
26.8.92	Cunningham, Mark	—
26.8.92	James, Neil	Leeds
1.9.92	Jack, Garry	Balmain, Aus
1.9.92	McGuire, Bruce	Aus
19.10.92	Lumb, Tim	Hunslet
11.12.92	*Vasey, Chris	Dewsbury
19.12.92	Stott, Lynton	Halifax

SHEFFIELD EAGLES 1992-93 PLAYERS' SUMMARY

	(Date of Birth)	App	T	G	D	Pts	Previous club	Signed
Aston, Mark	(27.9.67)	30+1	4	59	3	137	Selby ARL	25.11.86
Broadbent, Paul	(24.5.68)	30+2	3	—	—	12	Lock Lane ARL	26.10.87
Carr, Paul	(13.5.67)	25+3	14	—	—	56	Hunslet	1.7.92
Cook, Michael	(1.8.61)	29+1	—	—	—	—	Hunslet J. ARL	28.2.87
Crowther, Matt	(6.5.74)	2	—	—	—	—	Kippax ARL	11.9.91
Farrell, Anthony	(17.1.69)	28	8	—	—	32	Huddersfield	1.11.89
Gamson, Mark	(17.8.65)	35	6	—	—	24	Crigglestone ARL	27.7.84
Hughes, Ian	(13.3.72)	19+13	5	—	—	20	East Leeds ARL	1.7.91
Jack, Garry	(14.3.61)	33	8	1	—	34	Australia	1.9.92
James, Neil	(14.2.62)	13+8	—	—	—	—	Leeds	26.8.92
Laughton, Dale	(10.10.70)	25+5	2	—	—	8	Dodworth ARL	3.9.89
Lumb, Tim	(19.2.70)	10+15	3	—	3	15	Hunslet	2.3.92
McAlister, Charlie	(17.3.63)	1	—	—	—	—	Oldham	30.3.92
McGuire, Bruce	(31.1.62)	30	5	—	—	20	Australia	1.9.92
Mycoe, David	(1.5.72)	25	8	38	—	108	Crigglestone ARL	31.7.89
Plange, David	(24.7.65)	32	18	—	—	72	Castleford	27.8.91
Powell, Daryl	(21.7.65)	25	3	—	—	12	Redhill ARL	27.7.84
Price, Richard	(26.6.70)	35	5	—	—	20	Hull	19.3.91
Reilly, Glen	(26.1.74)	0+1	—	—	—	—	—	13.12.91
Robertson, Craig	(19.6.68)	0+2	—	—	—	—	Paddock ARL	17.7.91
Sheridan, Ryan	(24.5.75)	10+1	4	—	—	16	Dewsbury M. ARL	10.7.91
Simpson, Anthony	(12.3.69)	2	1	—	—	4	Paddock ARL	20.9.91

(Date of Birth)	App	T	G	D	Pts	Previous club	Signed
Stott, Lynton...............(9.5.71)........	5	1	—	—	4	Halifax	19.12.92
Thompson, Alex ....(29.7.74)......	0+5	—	—	—	—	Crown Malet ARL	1.7.91
Turner, Darren ....(13.10.73).....	2	—	—	—	—	Leeds Academy	1.1.92
Vasey, Chris................(28.2.63)......	1+2	1	—	—	4	Dewsbury	11.12.92
Waddell, Hugh ....(1.9.59)........	5+8	—	—	—	—	Leeds	12.3.90
Young, Andy ....(4.8.66)........	3+5	—	—	—	—	Eastmoor ARL	18.11.87
TOTALS							
28 players		99	98	6	598		

Representative appearances 1992-93

Hughes — GB Under-21s (1, 1t); Powell — Britain (+1, 1t); England (+1)

SHEFFIELD EAGLES 1992-93 MATCH ANALYSIS

Date	Com-petition	H/A	Opponent	Rlt	Score	Tries	Goals	Atten-dance	Referee
28.8.92	SBC	H	Wigan	L	6-46	Farrell	Aston	5950	Whitfield
6.9.92	SBC	A	Warrington	W	12-10	Powell, Price	Aston (2)	—	—
11.9.92	YC(1)	H	Halifax	W	34-14	Plange (3), Jack, Mycoe, Hughes	Aston (5)	3596	R. Smith
20.9.92	SBC	H	St. Helens	L	10-18	Plange (2)	Aston	4286	Cummings
23.9.92	YC(2)	A	Bradford N.	W	17-8	Plange (2), Farrell	Aston (1, 1dg), Mycoe	—	—
27.9.92	SBC	A	Hull K.R.	W	19-6	Plange, Gamson, Farrell	Aston (3, 1dg)	—	—
4.10.92	SBC	H	Castleford	W	20-16	Farrell, Carr, Mycoe	Aston (4)	3896	J. Connolly
6.10.92	YC(SF)	H	Hull	W	12-8	McGuire	Aston (4)	3017	J. Smith
11.10.92	SBC	A	Halifax	L	13-18	McGuire, Mycoe	Mycoe (2), Lumb (dg)	—	—
14.10.92	Tour	H	Australia	L	22-52	Plange, Broadbent, Jack, Simpson	Mycoe (3)	5500	Whitfield
18.10.92	YC(F)	N[1]	Wakefield T.	L	16-29	McGuire (2), Gamson	Mycoe (2)	(7918)	R. Smith
22.10.92	SBC	H	Warrington	W	15-10	Mycoe (2), Aston	Mycoe, Lumb (dg)	1662	Holdsworth
27.10.92	RT(P)	A	Chorley B.	W	38-10	Mycoe (2), Sheridan, Plange, Hughes, Laughton, Lumb	Mycoe (5)	—	—
2.11.92	SBC	A	Wigan	L	10-44	Plange, Mycoe	Mycoe	—	—
8.11.92	RT(1)	A	Warrington	L	16-31	Carr, Gamson	Mycoe (2), Aston (2)	—	—
15.11.92	SBC	H	Hull K.R.	W	28-12	Carr (2), Broadbent, Price	Aston (6)	1712	Ollerton
22.11.92	SBC	H	Widnes	W	32-30	Carr (2), Laughton, Broadbent, Plange	Aston (6)	2158	Gilmour
29.11.92	SBC	A	St. Helens	L	20-30	Farrell (2), Carr, Jack	Aston (2)	—	—
13.12.92	SBC	H	Leeds	W	31-14	Plange (2), Price (2), Jack	Aston (5, 1dg)	4777	J. Connolly
26.12.92	SBC	A	Hull	L	10-24	Plange, Farrell	Aston	—	—
6.1.93	SBC	H	Halifax	L	10-26	Powell	Mycoe (3)	2404	Atkin
10.1.93	SBC	A	Leigh	L	14-16	Carr, Powell	Mycoe (3)	—	—
17.1.93	SBC	A	Widnes	L	10-56	Plange, Vasey	Mycoe	—	—
24.1.93	SBC	H	Salford	W	30-16	Hughes (2), Lumb (2), McGuire	Mycoe (5)	2278	R. Smith
31.1.93	CC(1)	H	Leigh	W	32-5	Sheridan (2), Carr, Gamson, Jack	Mycoe (6)	2408	J. Smith
7.2.93	SBC	A	Castleford	L	8-14	Jack	Mycoe (2)	—	—
14.2.93	CC(2)	H	Widnes	L	6-52	Gamson	Mycoe	3407	J. Connolly
19.2.93	SBC	H	Leigh	L	6-8	Aston	Aston	1982	Holdsworth
7.3.93	SBC	A	Leeds	L	10-46	Aston, Jack	Aston	—	—
12.3.93	SBC	H	Bradford N.	W	21-12	Carr (2), Gamson	Aston (4), Lumb (dg)	2842	R. Connolly
21.3.93	SBC	A	Salford	L	12-48	Farrell, Hughes	Aston, Jack	—	—
28.3.93	SBC	H	Wakefield T.	W	26-19	Carr (2), Plange, Sheridan	Aston (5)	3245	R. Smith
4.4.93	SBC	A	Bradford N.	L	8-50	Plange, Price	—	—	—
11.4.93	SBC	H	Hull	D	18-18	Carr, Jack, Stott	Aston (3)	2706	Cummings
18.4.93	SBC	A	Wakefield T.	L	6-20	Aston	Aston	—	—

N[1] Elland Road, Leeds

SWINTON

Ground: Gigg Lane, Bury (061-761-2328)
First Season: 1896-97
Nickname: Lions
Chairman: Malcolm White
General
  Manager: Tony Barrow
Honours: **Championship** Winners, 1926-27,
1927-28, 1930-31, 1934-35
Beaten finalists, 1924-25, 1932-33
War Emergency League Beaten
finalists, 1939-40
Division One Champions, 1962-63,
1963-64
Division Two Champions, 1984-85
Challenge Cup Winners,
1899-1900, 1925-26, 1927-28
Beaten finalists, 1926-27, 1931-32
Second Division Premiership
Winners, 1986-87
Beaten finalists, 1988-89
Lancashire Cup Winners, 1925-26,
1927-28, 1939-40, 1969-70
Beaten finalists, 1910-11, 1923-24,
1931-32, 1960-61, 1961-62, 1962-63,
1964-65, 1972-73
Lancashire League Winners,
1924-25, 1927-28, 1928-29, 1930-31,
1960-61
Lancashire War League Winners,
1939-40
Western Division Championship
Beaten finalists, 1963-64
BBC2 Floodlit Trophy
Beaten finalists, 1966-67

RECORDS

Match
Goals: 12 by Ken Gowers v. Liverpool C.,
3 Oct 1959
Tries: 5 by Morgan Bevan v. Morecambe,
10 Sep 1898
Billy Wallwork v. Widnes,
15 Dec 1900
Jack Evans v. Bradford N.,
30 Sep 1922
Hector Halsall v. St. Helens,
24 Jan 1925
Dick Cracknell v. Whitehaven Rec.,
11 Feb 1928
Randall Lewis v. Keighley,
12 Jan 1946
John Stopford v. Bramley,
22 Dec 1962
Alan Buckley v. Salford, 8 Apr 1964
Joe Ropati v. Nottingham C.,
21 Jan 1990
Points: 29 by Bernard McMahon v. Dewsbury,
15 Aug 1959

Season
Goals: 128 by Albert Blan, 1960-61
Tries: 42 by John Stopford, 1963-64
Points: 283 by Albert Blan, 1960-61

Career
Goals: 970 by Ken Gowers, 1954-73
Tries: 197 by Frank Evans, 1921-31
Points: 2,105 by Ken Gowers, 1954-73
Appearances: 593+8 by Ken Gowers, 1954-73
Highest score: 76-4 v. Pontefract, 8 Sep 1906
Highest against: 78-0 v. Wigan, 29 Sep 1992
Attendance: 44,621 Wigan v. Warrington
(RL Cup SF), 7 Apr 1951
Home match: 26,891 v. Wigan
(RL Cup), 12 Feb 1964

COACHING REGISTER
● **Since 1974-75**

Austin Rhodes	June 74 - Nov 75
Bob Fleet	Nov 75 - Nov 76
John Stopford	Nov 76 - Apr 77
Terry Gorman	June 77 - Nov 78
Ken Halliwell	Nov 78 - Dec 79
Frank Myler	Jan 80 - May 81
Tom Grainey	May 81 - Oct 83
Jim Crellin	Nov 83 - May 86
Bill Holliday Mike Peers	} June 86 - Oct 87
Frank Barrow	Oct 87 - June 89
Jim Crellin	July 89 - July 91
Chris O'Sullivan	July 91 - Dec 91
Tony Barrow	Jan 92 -

GREAT BRITAIN REGISTER
(15 players)

Tom Armitt	(8)	1933-37
Alan Buckley	(7)	1963-66
Fred Butters	(2)	1929
Billy Davies	(1)	1968

Bryn Evans	(10)	1926-33
Frank Evans	(4)	1924
Jack Evans	(3)	1926
Ken Gowers	(14)	1962-66
Hector Halsall	(1)	1929
Martin Hodgson	(16)	1929-37
Ron Morgan	(2)	1963
Billo Rees	(11)	1926-29
Dave Robinson	(12)	1965-67
John Stopford	(12)	1961-66
Joe Wright	(1)	1932

1992-93 SIGNINGS REGISTER

Signed	Player	Club From
3.6.92	Ashcroft, Simon	Highfield
5.6.92	Welsby, Mark	Wigan
6.8.92	Duane, Ronnie	Rochdale H.

21.8.92	Parr, Chris	Huddersfield
25.8.92	Whitfield, Darren	Widnes
8.9.92	Errington, Craig	Folly Lane ARL
29.9.92	Hibberd, Craig	Lakes Utd, Aus
7.10.92	Machon, John	Keighley C.
7.10.92	Stansfield, Lucas	Lakes Utd, Aus
30.10.92	*Barratt, Dave	Leigh
3.11.92	Earner, Adrian	Leigh
3.11.92	Entwhistle, Steve	Bramley
4.1.93	*Conroy, Tony	Oldham
4.1.93	*Rogers, Darrell	Oldham
6.1.93	Massey, Neil	Warrington
24.2.93	*Waddell, Hugh	Sheffield E.
25.2.93	Welsby, Gary	Thatto Heath ARL
25.2.93	Crehan, Andy	Thatto Heath ARL
5.3.93	*Ledger, Barry	Leigh
25.3.93	*Humphries, Tony	Rochdale H.

SWINTON 1992-93 PLAYERS' SUMMARY

	(Date of Birth)	App	T	G	D	Pts	Previous club	Signed
Allan, John	(5.6.64)	4+2	—	—	—	—	Simms Cross ARL	10.8.84
Ashcroft, Simon	(27.6.70)	29	15	—	—	60	Highfield	3.6.92
Barker, Darren	(7.9.66)	1	—	—	—	—	—	30.10.92
Barratt, Dave	(20.11.63)	1	—	—	—	—	Leigh	30.11.92
Barrow, Tony	(19.10.71)	26	3	—	—	12	Oldham	6.2.92
Best, Brian	(26.9.69)	23	8	—	—	32	Oldham St. Annes ARL	14.1.91
Crehan, Andy	(27.11.67)	1+2	—	—	—	—	Thatto Heath ARL	25.2.93
Daintith, Ian	(23.11.67)	3+1	—	1	—	2	Farnworth ARL	20.2.91
Duane, Ronnie	(31.5.63)	17	2	—	—	8	Rochdale H.	6.8.92
Earner, Adrian	(19.11.66)	18+1	1	—	—	4	Leigh	3.11.92
Errington, Craig	(17.8.72)	26+2	10	51	4	146	Folly Lane ARL	8.9.92
Garner, Steve	(7.6.61)	6	4	—	—	16	Trafford B.	15.8.91
Graziano, Joe	(6.5.68)	1+1	1	—	—	4	Mayfield ARL	7.9.89
Hibberd, Craig	(20.2.67)	8	1	—	—	4	Australia	29.9.92
Humphries, Tony	(3.9.63)	4	2	—	—	8	Rochdale H.	25.3.93
Irving, Richard	(18.11.67)	1	—	—	—	—	Oldham	6.2.92
Kay, Paul	(30.11.68)	24+3	1	—	—	4	Batley	28.2.92
Kennett, Paul	(7.1.71)	27+1	5	—	—	20	Tondu RU	22.10.90
Ledger, Barry	(19.6.62)	1+4	—	—	1	1	Leigh	25.4.93
Leyland, Martin	(4.6.68)	6+1	3	—	—	12	Thatto Heath ARL	1.4.91
Longstaff, Simon	(2.1.70)	6+1	1	—	—	4	Oldham	6.2.92
Machon, John	(12.10.67)	2+1	—	—	—	—	Keighley C.	7.10.92
Massey, Neil	(29.9.70)	3+1	—	—	—	—	Warrington	6.1.93
Melling, Alex	(12.8.64)	21+1	2	—	—	8	Leigh	10.4.88
Parr, Chris	(31.5.71)	12+7	1	—	—	4	Huddersfield	21.8.92
Peters, Barry	(25.3.65)	1+1	—	—	—	—	Warrington	11.1.90
Pickavance, Ian	(20.9.68)	27	7	—	—	28	St. Helens	6.3.89
Prince, Glen	(8.4.67)	17+2	2	—	—	8	Langworthy ARL	9.5.91
Ratu, Emon	(30.10.65)	23+4	4	1	—	18	Smallbridge ARL	26.9.90
Rogers, Darrell	(11.7.72)	0+2	—	—	—	—	Oldham	4.1.93

	(Date of Birth)	App	T	G	D	Pts	Previous club	Signed
Skeech, Ian	(4.2.67)	6+9	1	—	—	4	Newton-le-Willows RU	24.11.87
Smith, Ian	(17.2.71)	5+6	—	—	—	—	Oldham St. Annes ARL	19.10.90
Snape, Steve	(17.9.63)	2	1	—	—	4	Folly Lane ARL	18.11.83
Waddell, Hugh	(1.9.59)	7+1	—	—	—	—	Sheffield E.	24.2.93
Welsby, Gary	(17.9.71)	1	—	—	—	—	Thatto Heath ARL	25.2.93
Welsby, Mark	(7.7.70)	27	7	1	—	30	Wigan	5.6.92
Whitfield, Darren	(15.9.65)	8+2	—	—	—	—	Widnes	1.4.92
Whittle, Danny	(18.7.70)	11+3	1	—	—	4	Nutgrove ARL	12.3.92
Wilkinson, Chris	(2.3.65)	10+1	—	15	—	30	Dewsbury	7.3.91
TOTALS								
39 players			83	69	5	475		

Representative appearances 1992-93
Kennett — Wales (+1)

SWINTON 1992-93 MATCH ANALYSIS

Date	Competition	H/A	Opponent	Rlt	Score	Tries	Goals	Attendance	Referee
30.8.92	SD	H	Rochdale H.	L	10-14	Melling, Leyland	Wilkinson	1803	Gilmour
6.9.92	SD	A	Featherstone R.	L	8-14	Ashcroft, Parr	—	—	—
13.9.92	LC(1)	H	Highfield	W	40-10	Garner (3), Longstaff, Leyland, Ashcroft, Pickavance	Wilkinson (5), Daintith	616	Steele
20.9.92	SD	H	Bramley	L	6-11	Leyland	Wilkinson	758	Nicholson
27.9.92	SD	A	Oldham	L	8-16	Garner	Wilkinson (2)	—	—
29.9.92	LC(2)	H	Wigan	L	0-78	—	—	3501	Cummings
4.10.92	SD	A	Huddersfield	L	10-37	Snape, Ratu	Wilkinson	—	—
11.10.92	SD	H	London C.	W	16-6	Kennett, Ratu, Pickavance	Wilkinson (2)	1009	Ollerton
28.10.92	RT(P)	H	Hull K.R.	L	12-32	Errington, Duane	Wilkinson (2)	582	Carter
1.11.92	SD	A	Oldham	L	6-56	Graziano	Wilkinson	—	—
15.11.92	SD	H	Featherstone R.	L	10-44	Ashcroft, Barrow	Errington	1370	Redfearn
22.11.92	SD	A	London C.	L	6-20	Kennett	Errington	—	—
29.11.92	SD	H	Oldham	L	12-18	Hibberd	Errington (4)	1560	Whitelam
13.12.92	SD	A	Huddersfield	L	12-19	Duane, Pickavance	Errington (2)	—	—
27.12.92	SD	A	Bramley	L	16-22	Best, Ashcroft, M. Welsby	Errington (2)	—	—
6.1.93	SD	H	Rochdale H.	W	14-12	Errington, Pickavance	Errington (3)	858	Cummings
10.1.93	SD	A	London C.	L	6-12	Best	Errington	—	—
13.1.93	CC(P)	A	Widnes	L	14-62	Ashcroft (2)	Errington (3)	—	—
17.1.93	SD	A	Featherstone R.	L	6-64	Prince	M. Welsby	—	—
24.1.93	SD	H	Bramley	W	35-20	Best (2), Errington, Kay, Pickavance, Whittle	Errington (5, 1dg)	750	Galtress
27.1.93	SD	H	Oldham	L	10-36	Errington (2)	Errington	1173	Crashley
7.2.93	SD	A	Rochdale H.	W	32-12	Ashcroft, Best, Errington, Melling, Pickavance	Errington (6)	—	—
14.2.93	SD	A	Carlisle	L	22-26	M. Welsby (2), Ashcroft, Best, Kennett	Errington	—	—
21.2.93	SD	H	Featherstone R.	L	12-42	Ashcroft, Earner	Errington, Ratu	1216	R. Connolly
7.3.93	SD	H	London C.	W	26-24	Ashcroft, Barrow, Best, Kennett, M. Welsby	Errington (3)	548	Morris
10.3.93	SD	A	Bramley	W	14-4	Ashcroft, Barrow	Errington (3)	—	—
14.3.93	SD	H	Carlisle	L	18-19	Ashcroft, Errington, Skeech, M. Welsby	Errington	594	Wood
21.3.93	SD	A	Rochdale H.	W	25-14	Errington (2), Best, M. Welsby	Errington (4, 1dg)	—	—
28.3.93	SD	H	Huddersfield	W	19-18	Ashcroft, Errington, Pickavance	Errington (3, 1dg)	1236	Kershaw
9.4.93	SD	H	Carlisle	W	23-12	Humphries (2), M. Welsby	Errington (5, 1dg)	631	Crashley
12.4.93	SD	A	Carlisle	W	19-16	Ratu (2), Ashcroft, Prince	Errington, Ledger (dg)	—	—
18.4.93	SD	H	Huddersfield	L	8-28	Ashcroft, Kennett	—	1214	Gilmour

WAKEFIELD TRINITY

Ground: Belle Vue (0924-372445)
First Season: 1895-96
Nickname: Dreadnoughts
Chairman: Rodney Walker
Honours: **Championship** Winners, 1966-67, 1967-68
Beaten finalists, 1959-60, 1961-62
Division Two Champions, 1903-04
Challenge Cup Winners, 1908-09, 1945-46, 1959-60, 1961-62, 1962-63
Beaten finalists, 1913-14, 1967-68, 1978-79
Regal Trophy Beaten finalists, 1971-72
Yorkshire Cup Winners, 1910-11, 1924-25, 1946-47, 1947-48, 1951-52, 1956-57, 1960-61, 1961-62, 1964-65, 1992-93
Beaten finalists, 1926-27, 1932-33, 1934-35, 1936-37, 1939-40, 1945-46, 1958-59, 1973-74, 1974-75, 1990-91
Yorkshire League Winners, 1909-10, 1910-11, 1945-46, 1958-59, 1959-60, 1961-62, 1965-66

RECORDS

Match

Goals: 13 by Mark Conway v. Highfield, 27 Oct 1992
Tries: 7 by Fred Smith v. Keighley, 25 Apr 1959
Keith Slater v. Hunslet, 6 Feb 1971
Points: 34 by Mark Conway v. Highfield, 27 Oct 1992

Season

Goals: 163 by Neil Fox, 1961-62
Tries: 38 by Fred Smith, 1959-60
David Smith, 1973-74
Points: 407 by Neil Fox, 1961-62

Career

Goals: 1,836 by Neil Fox, 1956-69 & 1970-74
Tries: 272 by Neil Fox, 1956-69 & 1970-74
Points: 4,488 by Neil Fox, 1956-69 & 1970-74
Appearances: 605 by Harry Wilkinson, 1930-49

Highest score: 90-12 v. Highfield, 27 Oct 1992
Highest against: 72-6 v. Wigan, 29 Mar 1987
Attendance: 37,906 Leeds v. Huddersfield (RL Cup SF), 21 Mar 1936
Home match: 30,676 v. Huddersfield (RL Cup), 26 Feb 1921

COACHING REGISTER

● **Since 1974-75**

Peter Fox	June 74 - May 76
Geoff Gunney	June 76 - Nov 76
Brian Lockwood	Nov 76 - Jan 78
Ian Brooke	Jan 78 - Jan 79
Bill Kirkbride	Jan 79 - Apr 80
Ray Batten	Apr 80 - May 81
Bill Ashurst	June 81 - Apr 82
Ray Batten	May 82 - July 83
Derek Turner	July 83 - Feb 84
Bob Haigh	Feb 84 - May 84
Geoff Wraith	May 84 - Oct 84
David Lamming	Oct 84 - Apr 85
Len Casey	Apr 85 - June 86
Tony Dean	June 86 - Dec 86
Trevor Bailey	Dec 86 - Apr 87
David Topliss	May 87 -

GREAT BRITAIN REGISTER

(24 players)

Ian Brooke	(8)	1967-68
Neil Fox	(29)	1959-69
Bob Haigh	(2)	1968-70
Bill Horton	(14)	1928-33
Michael Jackson	(2+2)	1991-92
David Jeanes	(5)	1971-72
Berwyn Jones	(3)	1964-66
Herbert Kershaw	(2)	1910
Frank Mortimer	(2)	1956
Harry Murphy	(1)	1950
Tommy Newbould	(1)	1910
Jonty Parkin	(17)	1920-29
Charlie Pollard	(1)	1924
Ernest Pollard	(2)	1932
Harold Poynton	(3)	1962
Gary Price	(+1)	1991
Don Robinson	(5)	1954-55
Gerry Round	(8)	1959-62
Trevor Skerrett	(4)	1979
Stanley Smith	(1)	1929
David Topliss	(3)	1973-79
Derek Turner	(13)	1959-62
Don Vines	(3)	1959
Jack Wilkinson	(7)	1959-62

1992-93 SIGNINGS REGISTER

Signed	Player	Club From
18.8.92	Benson, Peter	Gold Coast, Aus
3.9.92	Fritz, Darren	Canberra, Aus
21.11.92	Allen, Kieran	ARL
18.12.92	*Raw, Andy	Hunslet
11.1.93	Enslin, Albertus	Cape Town, SA

WAKEFIELD TRINITY 1992-93 PLAYERS' SUMMARY

	(Date of Birth)	App	T	G	D	Pts	Previous club	Signed
Allen, Kieran	(21.11.75)	0+1	—	—	—	—	ARL	21.11.92
Bagnall, Geoff	(4.11.65)	30+1	8	—	—	32	Australia	3.8.92
Bell, Nigel	(4.11.62)	31+3	7	—	—	28	Eastmoor ARL	1.9.83
Benson, Peter	(24.1.67)	30	9	37	—	110	Australia	18.8.92
Conway, Billy	(31.1.67)	18+11	3	3	—	18	Wakefield Colts	30.8.84
Conway, Mark	(31.1.64)	11	6	31	—	86	Leeds	3.8.87
Eden, Phil	(13.12.63)	13+5	1	—	—	4	ARL	21.10.82
Flynn, Adrian	(9.9.74)	4+4	1	—	—	4	Dewsbury M. ARL	4.1.92
Fritz, Darren	(15.7.69)	21	9	—	—	36	Australia	3.9.92
Glancy, John	(14.4.62)	27+2	—	—	—	—	Sheffield E.	9.8.88
Goddard, Richard	(28.4.74)	12+8	2	—	—	8	Stanley R. ARL	31.12.90
Hirst, John	(18.12.70)	0+1	—	—	—	—	Stanley R. ARL	15.8.89
Jackson, Michael	(11.10.69)	7+1	1	—	—	4	Hunslet	30.9.91
Jones, David	(7.12.67)	26+2	5	—	—	20	Wigan St. P. ARL	14.9.90
Kelly, Andy	(8.11.60)	2+1	1	—	—	4	Hull K.R.	11.1.88
Lazenby, Tracy	(7.6.63)	3+7		2	—	4	Hull K.R.	4.11.85
Lord, Paul	(22.12.67)	2+1	—	—	—	—	Oldham	17.10.91
Mason, Andy	(10.11.62)	29+1	22	—	—	88	Leeds	3.8.87
Mosley, James	(30.9.74)	11+2	5	—	—	20	Moldgreen ARL	24.1.92
Myers, David	(20.7.72)	1+2	—	—	—	—	Middleton ARL	14.11.91
Price, Gary	(28.10.69)	19+2	6	—	—	24	Sharlston ARL	29.10.86
Raw, Andy	(15.9.67)	0+1	—	—	—	—	Hunslet	18.12.92
Round, Paul	(24.9.63)	14+4	5	—	—	20	Oldham	17.10.91
Sims, Mark	(18.11.65)	2	—	4	—	8	Doncaster	17.2.93
Slater, Richard	(29.8.70)	23+3	2	—	—	8	Normanton ARL	4.8.88
Spencer, Gary	(16.9.66)	32	7	—	—	28	Leeds	16.1.91
Thompson, John	(3.5.59)	6	—	—	—	—	Eastmoor ARL	1.7.78
Timmins, Jason	(2.12.69)	0+2	—	—	—	—	Normanton ARL	4.8.88
Webster, Mark	(23.6.70)	24	1	—	—	4	St. Helens	23.8.90
Wilson, Andy	(5.10.63)	18	12	—	—	48	Queens Park ARL	8.11.88
Wright, Nigel	(8.11.73)	26+2	6	12	6	54	Stanley R. ARL	31.12.90
TOTALS								
31 players			119	89	6	660		

Representative appearances 1992-93
Mosley — GB Under-21s (1)
Wright — GB Under-21s (1)

WAKEFIELD TRINITY 1992-93 MATCH ANALYSIS

Date	Com- petition	H/A	Opponent	Rlt	Score	Tries	Goals	Atten- dance	Referee
30.8.92	SBC	H	Halifax	L	10-30	Kelly, Wilson	Benson	6820	J. Connolly
6.9.92	SBC	A	St. Helens	L	12-24	Bell, Jones	Benson (2)	—	—
13.9.92	YC(1)	H	Doncaster	W	54-14	Bell (2), Wilson (2), Spencer (2), Mason (2), Fritz, Benson	M. Conway (4), Lazenby (2), Benson	3229	Atkin
20.9.92	SBC	H	Wigan	L	14-19	Mason, Jones	Benson (3)	7240	R. Smith
23.9.92	YC(2)	H	Keighley C.	W	22-16	Benson (2), M. Conway, Spencer	M. Conway (3)	2508	Holdsworth
27.9.92	SBC	A	Warrington	L	6-22	Spencer	M. Conway	—	—
4.10.92	SBC	H	St. Helens	L	5-18	Benson	Wright (dg)	5546	Whitfield
7.10.92	YC(SF)	A	Featherstone R.	W	22-8	B. Conway, Mason, Benson	Benson (5)	—	—
11.10.92	SBC	A	Salford	L	8-14	Wright, Goddard	—	—	—
18.10.92	YC(F)	N[1]	Sheffield E.	W	29-16	Slater, Bagnall, Spencer, Mason, Price	Benson (3), Wright (1, 1dg)	(7918)	R. Smith
21.10.92	SBC	H	Leeds	W	17-16	Wright, Fritz	Benson (4), Wright (dg)	4470	Morris
27.10.92	RT(P)	H	Highfield	W	90-12	Wilson (5), Fritz (4), Mason (3), M. Conway (2), Price, Webster	M. Conway (13)	1650	Whitelam
1.11.92	SBC	A	Halifax	W	24-16	Mason (2), Wilson, Price, Fritz	Benson (2)	—	—
8.11.92	RT(1)	A	London C.	L	0-30	—	—	—	—
15.11.92	SBC	H	Warrington	W	34-8	Bagnall (2), Mason (2), Wright, Eden, Wilson	Benson (3)	3810	Whitfield
20.11.92	SBC	H	Hull	W	6-4	Mason	Benson	3058	Cummings
1.12.92	SBC	A	Widnes	L	10-16	Bagnall (2)	Benson	—	—
13.12.92	SBC	H	Bradford N.	W	30-16	Mason (2), Wilson, Bagnall, Jones	Benson (5)	4956	Cummings
28.12.92	SBC	H	Hull K.R.	L	10-17	Jones, Round	Benson	4058	Gilmour
1.1.93	SBC	A	Castleford	D	22-22	Wilson, Spencer, Jackson, Wright	Benson (2), B. Conway	—	—
6.1.93	SBC	A	Hull	W	20-16	Mosley (2), Fritz, Jones	M. Conway (2)	—	—
10.1.93	SBC	H	Salford	W	34-14	Bell (2), Mason, Mosley, B. Conway, Round	M. Conway (5)	3750	Whitfield
24.1.93	SBC	H	Leigh	L	8-41	Mason, Wright	—	3712	Campbell
31.1.93	CC(1)	A	Salford	W	20-12	Bell, B. Conway, Fritz, Spencer	Benson, B. Conway	—	—
4.2.93	SBC	A	Wigan	L	14-38	M. Conway, Goddard, Mason	M. Conway	—	—
7.2.93	SBC	A	Leigh	L	10-17	M. Conway, Round	M. Conway	—	—
14.2.93	CC(2)	H	Bradford N.	L	18-20	Bagnall, Bell, Benson	Benson (2), Wright (2dg)	6107	Whitfield
21.2.93	SBC	H	Widnes	L	18-36	Benson, Price, Wright	Sims (3)	4330	J. Smith
5.3.93	SBC	A	Bradford N.	L	10-31	Benson, Mosley	Sims	—	—
21.3.93	SBC	A	Leeds	D	26-26	Price (2), Bagnall, Mason, Mosley	Wright (3)	—	—
28.3.93	SBC	A	Sheffield E.	L	19-26	Flynn, Mason, Slater	Wright (3, 1dg)	—	—
4.4.93	SBC	A	Hull K.R.	L	10-28	Benson, M. Conway	Wright	—	—
9.4.93	SBC	H	Castleford	L	8-14	Round	B. Conway, M. Conway	4332	Atkin
18.4.93	SBC	H	Sheffield E.	W	20-6	Mason (2), Round	Wright (4)	2403	Ollerton

N[1] Elland Road, Leeds

WARRINGTON

Ground: Wilderspool (0925-35338)
First Season: 1895-96
Nickname: Wire
Chairman: Peter Higham
General
  Manager: Ron Close
Honours: **Championship** Winners, 1947-48, 1953-54, 1954-55
Beaten finalists, 1925-26, 1934-35, 1936-37, 1948-49, 1950-51, 1960-61
League Leaders Trophy Winners, 1972-73
Club Championship (Merit Table) Winners, 1973-74
Challenge Cup Winners, 1904-05, 1906-07, 1949-50, 1953-54, 1973-74
Beaten finalists, 1900-01, 1903-04, 1912-13, 1927-28, 1932-33, 1935-36, 1974-75, 1989-90
Regal Trophy Winners, 1973-74, 1977-78, 1980-81, 1990-91
Beaten finalists, 1978-79, 1986-87
Premiership Trophy Winners, 1985-86
Beaten finalists, 1976-77, 1986-87
Lancashire Cup Winners, 1921-22, 1929-30, 1932-33, 1937-38, 1959-60, 1965-66, 1980-81, 1982-83, 1989-90
Beaten finalists, 1906-07, 1948-49, 1950-51, 1967-68, 1985-86, 1987-88
Lancashire League Winners, 1937-38, 1947-48, 1948-49, 1950-51, 1953-54, 1954-55, 1955-56, 1967-68
BBC2 Floodlit Trophy Beaten finalists, 1974-75
Captain Morgan Trophy Winners, 1973-74

RECORDS

Match
Goals: 14 by Harold Palin v. Liverpool C., 13 Sep 1950
Tries: 7 by Brian Bevan v. Leigh, 29 Mar 1948
Brian Bevan v. Bramley, 22 Apr 1953
Points: 33 by George Thomas v. St. Helens, 12 Apr 1909

Season
Goals: 170 by Steve Hesford, 1978-79
Tries: 66 by Brian Bevan, 1952-53
Points: 363 by Harry Bath, 1952-53

Career
Goals: 1,159 by Steve Hesford, 1975-85
Tries: 740 by Brian Bevan, 1945-62
Points: 2,416 by Steve Hesford, 1975-85
Appearances: 620 by Brian Bevan, 1945-62
Highest score: 78-3 v. St. Helens, 12 Apr 1909
Highest against: 68-14 at Hunslet, 10 Apr 1928
Attendance: 34,304 v. Wigan (League), 22 Jan 1949

COACHING REGISTER
● **Since 1974-75**

Alex Murphy	May 71 - May 78
Billy Benyon	June 78 - Mar 82
Kevin Ashcroft	Mar 82 - May 84
Reg Bowden	June 84 - Mar 86
Tony Barrow	Mar 86 - Nov 88
Brian Johnson	Nov 88 -

GREAT BRITAIN REGISTER
(45 players)

Jack Arkwright	(6)	1936-37
Kevin Ashcroft	(+1)	1974
Willie Aspinall	(1)	1966
Allan Bateman	(1+1)	1992-93
Billy Belshaw	(2)	1937
Nat Bentham	(2)	1929
John Bevan	(6)	1974-78
Tom Blinkhorn	(1)	1929
Ernie Brooks	(3)	1908
Jim Challinor	(3)	1958-60
Neil Courtney	(+1)	1982
Billy Cunliffe	(11)	1920-26
George Dickenson	(1)	1908
Billy Dingsdale	(3)	1929-33
Des Drummond	(2)	1987-88
Ronnie Duane	(3)	1983-84
Bob Eccles	(1)	1982
Kevin Ellis	(+1)	1991
Jim Featherstone	(6)	1948-52
Mark Forster	(2)	1987
Eric Fraser	(16)	1958-61
Laurie Gilfedder	(5)	1962-63
Bobby Greenough	(1)	1960
Andy Gregory	(1)	1986
Mike Gregory	(19+1)	1987-90

Gerry Helme	(12)	1948-54		Ron Ryder	(1)	1952
Keith Holden	(1)	1963		Frank Shugars	(1)	1910
Albert Johnson	(6)	1946-47		George Skelhorne	(7)	1920-21
Ken Kelly	(2)	1980-82		George Thomas	(1)	1907
Tom McKinney	(3)	1955		Derek Whitehead	(3)	1971
Joe Miller	(6)	1933-36		John Woods	(+1)	1987
Alex Murphy	(1)	1971				
Albert Naughton	(2)	1954				
Terry O'Grady	(1)	1961				
Harold Palin	(2)	1947				
Ken Parr	(1)	1968				
Albert Pimblett	(3)	1948				
Ray Price	(9)	1954-57				
Bob Ryan	(5)	1950-52				

1992-93 SIGNINGS REGISTER

Signed	Player	Club From
1.7.92	Westwood, Lee	Warrington Academy
5.8.92	Griffiths, Steve	—
5.8.92	Thackray, Rick	Widnes
13.8.92	Hilton, Mark	Warrington Academy
18.8.92	Mackey, Greg	Hull

WARRINGTON 1992-93 PLAYERS' SUMMARY

	(Date of Birth)	App	T	G	D	Pts	Previous club	Signed
Bateman, Allan	(6.3.65)	30+1	11	—	—	44	Neath RU	28.9.90
Bennett, Andrew	(23.7.73)	1+4	—	—	—	—	Woolston R. ARL	10.8.90
Chambers, Gary	(5.1.70)	18+6	1	—	—	4	Kells ARL	1.8.89
Cullen, Paul	(4.3.63)	30	6	—	—	24	Crosfields ARL	25.11.80
Darbyshire, Paul	(3.12.69)	3+13	1	—	—	4	Wigan St. P. ARL	1.6.89
Ellis, Kevin	(29.5.65)	20+5	7	—	3	31	Bridgend RU	18.6.90
Forster, Mark	(25.11.64)	24+4	6	—	—	24	Woolston R. ARL	27.11.81
Harmon, Neil	(9.1.69)	27+4	2	—	—	8	Blackbrook ARL	15.1.86
Jackson, Bob	(13.8.60)	16+1	3	—	—	12	Australia	15.8.89
Kenyon, Neil	(26.10.67)	22	13	—	—	52	Bold ARL	9.12.88
Mackey, Greg	(20.10.61)	33	4	4	5	29	Hull	18.8.92
Mann, Duane	(28.6.65)	33	10	—	2	42	New Zealand	12.11.89
Myler, Robert	(4.3.70)	12	4	1	—	18	Widnes St. M. ARL	2.10.89
Penny, Lee	(24.9.74)	21	6	—	—	24	Orrell St. J. ARL	15.10.91
Phillips, Rowland	(28.7.65)	1+2	1	—	—	4	Neath RU	28.9.90
Richards, Basil	(9.7.65)	3+10	1	—	—	4	Queensbury ARL	11.7.88
Rudd, Chris	(17.12.69)	20	6	46	—	116	Kells ARL	15.2.88
Sanderson, Gary	(21.2.67)	32	4	—	—	16	Thatto Heath ARL	30.12.85
Shelford, Kelly	(4.5.66)	28	3	1	3	17	New Zealand	5.10.91
Sumner, Phil	(14.6.71)	5+2	2	—	—	8	Wigan St. P. ARL	14.6.88
Tees, Gary	(25.7.61)	13+9	1	—	—	4	Barrow	5.12.90
Thackray, Rick	(29.9.61)	6+1	—	—	—	—	Widnes	5.8.92
Thorniley, Tony	(10.10.66)	23+1	10	26	—	92	Woolston ARL	1.4.86
Turner, Robert	(14.3.69)	4+1	—	5	—	10	Blackbrook ARL	8.9.86
Williamson, Paul	(27.11.69)	4+1	3	—	—	12	Woolston ARL	9.11.87
TOTALS								
25 players			105	83	13	599		

Representative appearances 1992-93
Bateman — Britain (+1); Wales (2, 1t)
Ellis — Wales (2, 1dg)
Penny — GB Under-21s (1, 1t)
Phillips — Wales (1+1)

WARRINGTON 1992-93 MATCH ANALYSIS

Date	Competition	H/A	Opponent	Rlt	Score	Tries	Goals	Attendance	Referee
30.8.92	SBC	A	Leigh	W	30-12	Kenyon, Myler, Sanderson, Thorniley, Phillips	Rudd (4), Myler	—	—
6.9.92	SBC	H	Sheffield E.	L	10-12	Thorniley	Turner (3)	4089	J. Smith
13.9.92	LC(1)	A	Oldham	L	20-33	Ellis (2), Shelford, Myler	Turner (2)	—	—
18.9.92	SBC	A	Hull	W	29-14	Myler, Bateman, Mann, Kenyon, Sumner	Rudd (4), Mackey (dg)	—	—
27.9.92	SBC	H	Wakefield T.	W	22-6	Kenyon, Ellis, Mackey, Cullen	Rudd (3)	4418	Redfearn
2.10.92	SBC	A	Leeds	L	4-13	Mackey	—	—	—
9.10.92	SBC	H	Bradford N.	L	4-22	Kenyon	—	3625	R. Smith
13.10.92	RT(P)	H	Blackpool G.	W	32-8	Cullen, Forster, Penny, Harmon, Bateman, Kenyon	Rudd (4)	1412	Steele
22.10.92	SBC	A	Sheffield E.	L	10-15	Rudd, Mann	Rudd	—	—
1.11.92	SBC	H	Hull	W	34-10	Kenyon (3), Mann, Thorniley	Rudd (7)	3756	Gilmour
8.11.92	RT(1)	H	Sheffield E.	W	31-16	Thorniley (2), Chambers, Kenyon, Penny	Thorniley (5), Mann (dg)	3112	Cross
15.11.92	SBC	A	Wakefield T.	L	8-34	Sumner, Bateman	—	—	—
22.11.92	SBC	A	Halifax	L	20-21	Mann, Bateman, Sanderson, Tees	Thorniley (2)	—	—
29.11.92	SBC	H	Leigh	D	7-7	—	Thorniley (3), Mann (dg)	4025	Ollerton
5.12.92	RT(2)	H	Bradford N.	D	12-12	Bateman, Sanderson	Thorniley (2)	2145	J. Smith
16.12.92	RT (2) Replay	A	Bradford N.	L	6-9	Kenyon	Thorniley	—	—
20.12.92	SBC	A	Hull K.R.	L	11-13	Thorniley, Harmon	Thorniley, Mackey (dg)	—	—
5.1.93	SBC	A	Wigan	W	11-4	Thorniley, Myler	Thorniley, Shelford (dg)	—	—
8.1.93	SBC	H	Leeds	L	24-31	Rudd, Jackson, Bateman, Cullen, Mann	Rudd (2)	4008	Atkin
15.1.93	SBC	A	Castleford	W	13-10	Penny, Rudd	Thorniley (2), Ellis (dg)	—	—
20.1.93	SBC	H	Widnes	L	8-10	Bateman	Thorniley (2)	5832	R. Smith
24.1.93	SBC	H	Hull K.R.	W	47-26	Ellis (2), Forster (2), Jackson, Mann, Penny, Shelford, Thorniley	Thorniley (5), Ellis (dg)	3341	Steele
30.1.93	CC(1)	H	Castleford	L	6-21	Thorniley	Thorniley	2795	J. Connolly
5.2.93	SBC	A	St. Helens	L	4-12	—	Shelford, Thorniley	—	—
21.2.93	SBC	H	Castleford	W	23-18	Bateman, Ellis, Jackson, Kenyon	Rudd (3), Ellis (dg)	3790	Gilmour
14.3.93	SBC	H	Halifax	W	56-24	Mackey (2), Rudd (2), Bateman, Cullen, Ellis, Forster, Mann, Penny, Richards	Rudd (6)	4723	Atkin
21.3.93	SBC	A	Bradford N.	W	21-8	Kenyon, Mann, Rudd	Rudd (3), Shelford (2dg), Mackey (dg)	—	—
28.3.93	SBC	H	St. Helens	L	17-32	Bateman, Forster, Thorniley	Rudd (2), Mackey (dg)	6795	Steele
4.4.93	SBC	A	Salford	W	24-23	Bateman, Kenyon, Mann, Sanderson	Rudd (4)	—	—
9.4.93	SBC	A	Widnes	L	14-26	Shelford, Williamson	Rudd (3)	—	—
12.4.93	SBC	H	Wigan	L	14-27	Cullen, Mann, Williamson	Mackey	7949	Campbell
18.4.93	SBC	H	Salford	W	22-20	Cullen, Forster, Penny, Williamson	Mackey (3)	2809	Holdsworth
25.4.93	PT(1)	A	Wigan	L	5-40	Darbyshire	Mackey (dg)	—	—

WHITEHAVEN

Ground: Recreation Ground (0946-692915)
First Season: 1948-49
Nickname: Haven
Chairman: Derek Mossop
Secretary: Bill Madine

RECORDS

Match
Goals: 12 by Steve Maguire v. Nottingham C.,
       12 Apr 1992
Tries: 6 by Vince Gribbin v. Doncaster,
       18 Nov 1984
Points: 28 by Steve Maguire v. Highfield,
       28 Feb 1993

Season
Goals: 141 by John McKeown, 1956-57
Tries: 31 by Vince Gribbin, 1991-92
Points: 291 by John McKeown, 1956-57

Career
Goals: 1,050 by John McKeown, 1948-61
Tries: 148 by Bill Smith, 1950-62
Points: 2,133 by John McKeown, 1948-61
Appearances: 417 by John McKeown, 1948-61
Highest score: 80-6 v. Nottingham C.,
       12 Apr 1992
Highest against: 92-10 at Hull K.R., 18 Mar 1990
Attendance: 18,500 v. Wakefield T. (RL Cup),
       19 Mar 1960

COACHING REGISTER
● Since 1974-75

Jeff Bawden	May 72 - May 75
Ike Southward	Aug 75 - June 76
Bill Smith	Aug 76 - Oct 78
Ray Dutton	Oct 78 - Oct 79
Phil Kitchin	Oct 79 - Jan 82
Arnold Walker	Jan 82 - May 82
Tommy Dawes	June 82 - May 83
Frank Foster	June 83 - June 85
Phil Kitchin	June 85 - Oct 87
John McFarlane	Oct 87 - May 88
Barry Smith	July 88 - Sep 89

Eric Fitzsimons	Oct 89 - Mar 90
Norman Turley	June 90 - Apr 91
Jackie Davidson	May 91 - June 92
Gordon Cottier	June 92 - May 93
Kurt Sorensen	May 93 -

GREAT BRITAIN REGISTER
(5 players)

Vince Gribbin	(1)	1985
Bill Holliday	(1)	1964
Dick Huddart	(4)	1958
Phil Kitchin	(1)	1965
Arnold Walker	(1)	1980

1992-93 SIGNINGS REGISTER

Signed	Player	Club From
28.8.92	Dunn, Reg	Barrow
11.9.92	Edwards, Steve	Wentworth, Aus
2.10.92	Kendall, Dave	Barrow
2.10.92	McAlister, Charlie	Sheffield E.
6.11.92	Charlton, Jason	Canterbury, Aus
5.2.93	*Crarey, Paul	Barrow

*Former New Zealand Test packman Kurt Sorensen,
Whitehaven's new coach.*

WHITEHAVEN 1992-93 PLAYERS' SUMMARY

	(Date of Birth)	App	T	G	D	Pts	Previous club	Signed
Beckwith, Mark	(7.8.64)	28	14	—	—	56	Barrow	11.1.91
Blaney, Ged	(17.6.65)	4	3	—	—	12	Mirehouse ARL	8.1.89
Branthwaite, Steve	(25.12.61)	9+3	—	—	—	—	Gosforth RU	28.3.88
Brown, Dave	(17.2.65)	2	—	—	—	—	Trafford B.	9.11.90
Cameron, Graham	(15.9.62)	3+1	—	—	—	—	Barrow	23.3.83
Charlton, Jason	(29.1.71)	7+8	3	—	—	12	Australia	6.11.92
Crarey, Paul	(4.1.66)	5+3	2	—	—	8	Barrow	5.2.93
Davidson, Alan	(9.12.64)	13+6	4	—	1	17	Kells ARL	12.8.88
Dawson, Peter		2	—	—	—	—	—	—
Dover, Peter	(9.12.65)	11+1	5	—	—	20	Flimby ARL	1.7.89
Dunn, Reg	(23.5.68)	25+1	2	—	—	8	Barrow	28.1.92
Edwards, Steve	(9.4.69)	2+2	1	—	—	4	Australia	11.9.92
Fisher, Billy	(27.10.62)	24	6	—	—	24	St. Benedicts RU	20.7.81
Friend, Clayton	(22.3.62)	23+1	15	—	—	60	Carlisle	24.9.92
Gaffney, Mike	(21.6.60)	0+1	—	—	—	—	—	—
Gribbin, Vince	(15.3.65)	20+2	22	—	—	88	Hensingham ARL	23.7.82
Hetherington, Gary	(5.7.65)	22	2	—	—	8	Kells ARL	26.7.85
Howland, Kevin	(24.2.65)	4	1	—	—	4	Wath Brow H. ARL	29.3.88
Howse, Steve	(7.3.64)	2+3	—	—	—	—	Barrow	23.2.92
Kendall, Dave	(7.6.63)	22	4	—	—	16	Barrow	2.10.92
Lightfoot, David	(24.6.63)	15	4	—	—	16	Hull K.R.	28.2.92
Lofthouse, Norman	(30.1.63)	18	4	—	—	16	Mirehouse ARL	13.8.86
McAlister, Charlie	(17.3.63)	10+2	3	—	—	12	Sheffield E.	2.10.92
Maguire, Steve	(12.8.63)	27	4	95	—	206	Barrow	11.1.91
Mounsey, Gary	(21.8.61)	10	—	—	—	—	Glasson ARL	30.6.87
Rae, Neil	(6.9.68)	1	—	—	—	—	Whitehaven RU	24.8.90
Richardson, Willie	(6.10.60)	8+1	4	1	—	18	Egremont ARL	13.8.86
Routledge, John	(7.2.65)	28	19	—	—	76	Egremont RU	24.8.90
Ryan, Mark	(31.7.64)	7+13	3	3	3	21	Mirehouse ARL	10.11.87
Sanders, Kevin	(21.3.62)	4	2	—	—	8	Hensingham ARL	29.8.91
Solarie, Tony	(2.11.61)	4	3	—	—	12	Wath Brow H. ARL	20.12.84
Suafoa, George	(17.3.66)	1+2	—	—	—	—	—	28.8.92
Telford, Robert	(28.1.68)	3+1	—	—	—	—	Mirehouse ARL	2.2.87

TOTALS
33 players 130 99 4 722

Representative appearances 1992-93
Beckwith — Cumbria (1)
Lightfoot — Cumbria (1)
Routledge — Cumbria (1)
Kendall — Cumbria (1)

WHITEHAVEN 1992-93 MATCH ANALYSIS

Date	Com-petition	H/A	Opponent	Rlt	Score	Tries	Goals	Atten-dance	Referee
30.8.92	TD	H	Hunslet	W	42-2	Beckwith (2), Hetherington, Routledge, Solarie, Blaney	Maguire (8), Richardson	1173	Wood
6.9.92	TD	A	Dewsbury	L	21-30	Blaney (2), Howland	Maguire (4), Ryan (dg)	—	—
13.9.92	LC(1)	A	Salford	L	8-60	Routledge	Maguire (2)	—	—
20.9.92	TD	H	Ryedale-York	L	13-26	Routledge, Sanders	Ryan (2, 1dg)	1132	Galtress
27.9.92	TD	A	Barrow	W	28-14	Solarie (2), Friend (2), Edwards	Maguire (4)	—	—
4.10.92	TD	H	Doncaster	W	28-12	Richardson (2), McAlister, Friend, Beckwith	Maguire (4)	1502	Whitelam
11.10.92	TD	A	Blackpool G.	W	32-12	Richardson, Routledge, McAlister, Ryan, Maguire, Gribbin	Maguire (4)	—	—
22.10.92	TD	H	Keighley C.	L	8-18	Richardson	Maguire (2)	1526	Campbell
1.11.92	TD	A	Hunslet	L	14-20	Lofthouse (2), Sanders	Maguire	—	—
8.11.92	RT(1)	A	Hull K.R.	L	4-48	Gribbin	—	—	—
15.11.92	TD	H	Dewsbury	W	23-2	Beckwith (2), Gribbin, Davidson	Maguire (3), Davidson (dg)	1316	Galtress
29.11.92	TD	H	Barrow	W	38-6	Davidson (2), Routledge, Gribbin, Dunn, Fisher, Kendall	Maguire (5)	1303	Atkin
13.12.92	TD	A	Keighley C.	W	21-8	Lightfoot (2), Kendall, Charlton	Maguire (2), Ryan (dg)	—	—
26.12.92	TD	A	Workington T.	W	20-12	Friend (2), McAlister	Maguire (4)	—	—
6.1.93	TD	H	Chorley B.	W	42-12	Beckwith (2), Fisher (2), Friend, Gribbin, Ryan, Routledge	Maguire (5)	1433	Morris
10.1.93	TD	A	Highfield	W	40-18	Friend (3), Routledge (2), Dover, Gribbin	Maguire (6)	—	—
24.1.93	TD	A	Doncaster	L	4-20	Gribbin	—	—	—
31.1.93	CC(1)	H	Widnes	L	8-20	Gribbin	Maguire (2)	3791	Morris
7.2.93	TD	H	Nottingham C.	W	56-1	Routledge (3), Beckwith (2), Charlton (2), Dunn, Fisher, Gribbin	Maguire (7), Ryan	1083	Carter
14.2.93	TD	H	Blackpool G.	W	72-0	Gribbin (5), Routledge (3), Dover (2), Beckwith, Fisher, Kendall, Maguire	Maguire (8)	1065	Volante
21.2.93	TD	A	Batley	W	20-16	Crarey (2), Gribbin (2)	Maguire (2)	—	—
28.2.93	TD	H	Highfield	W	72-0	Gribbin (4), Lightfoot (2), Maguire (2), Beckwith, Davidson, Friend, Kendall, Routledge	Maguire (10)	1063	Redfearn
14.3.93	TD	A	Chorley B.	W	36-8	Lofthouse (2), Routledge (2), Friend, Gribbin, Hetherington	Maguire (4)	—	—
21.3.93	TD	A	Nottingham C.	W	40-7	Beckwith (3), Fisher, Friend, Gribbin, Routledge, Ryan	Maguire (4)	—	—
28.3.93	TD	H	Batley	L	4-24	Dover	—	1127	Galtress
4.4.93	TD	A	Ryedale-York	L	12-24	Friend, Routledge	Maguire (2)	—	—
9.4.93	TD	H	Workington T.	L	10-36	Dover, Friend	Maguire	3820	Cross
18.4.93	DP(1)	A	Ryedale-York	L	6-31	Friend	Maguire	—	—

WIDNES

Ground: Naughton Park (051-495-2250)
First Season: 1895-96
Nickname: Chemics
Chairman: Jim Mills
General
  Manager: Frank Myler
Honours: **Championship** Beaten finalists,
            1935-36
            Division One Champions, 1977-78,
            1987-88, 1988-89
            Challenge Cup Winners, 1929-30,
            1936-37, 1963-64, 1974-75, 1978-79,
            1980-81, 1983-84
            Beaten finalists, 1933-34, 1949-50,
            1975-76, 1976-77, 1981-82, 1992-93
            Regal Trophy Winners, 1975-76,
            1978-79, 1991-92
            Beaten finalists, 1974-75, 1977-78,
            1979-80, 1983-84, 1988-89
            Premiership Winners, 1979-80,
            1981-82, 1982-83, 1987-88, 1988-89,
            1989-90
            Beaten finalists, 1977-78, 1990-91
            Lancashire Cup Winners, 1945-46,
            1974-75, 1975-76, 1976-77, 1978-79,
            1979-80, 1990-91
            Beaten finalists, 1928-29, 1939-40,
            1955-56, 1971-72, 1981-82, 1983-84
            Lancashire League Winners,
            1919-20
            Western Division Championship
            Beaten finalists, 1962-63
            Charity Shield Winners, 1988-89,
            1989-90, 1990-91
            World Club Challenge Winners,
            1989-90
            BBC2 Floodlit Trophy Winners,
            1978-79
            Beaten finalists, 1972-73, 1973-74

RECORDS

Match
Goals: 11 by Robin Whitfield v. Oldham,
        28 Oct 1965
Tries: 5 by Eddie Cunningham v. Doncaster,
        15 Feb 1981
        John Basnett at Hunslet,
        17 Oct 1981
        John Basnett v. Hull K.R.,
        2 Nov 1986
        David Hulme v. Dewsbury,
        30 Nov 1986
        Andy Currier v. Featherstone R.,
        25 Sep 1988
        Martin Offiah v. Warrington,
        15 Mar 1989
Points: 34 by Andy Currier v. Featherstone R.,
        25 Sep 1988
        Jonathan Davies v. Whitehaven,
        26 Aug 1990

Season
Goals: 140 by Mick Burke, 1978-79
Tries: 58 by Martin Offiah, 1988-89
Points: 342 by Jonathan Davies, 1990-91

Career
Goals: 1,083 by Ray Dutton, 1966-78
Tries: 234 by Mal Aspey, 1964-80
Points: 2,195 by Ray Dutton, 1966-78
Appearances: 587+4 by Keith Elwell, 1970-86
Highest score: 82-0 v. Dewsbury, 30 Nov 1986
Highest against: 60-5 at Oldham, 9 Apr 1928
Attendance: 24,205 v. St. Helens (RL Cup),
        16 Feb 1961

COACHING REGISTER
● **Since 1974-75**

Vince Karalius	Jan 72 - May 75
Frank Myler	May 75 - May 78
Doug Laughton	May 78 - Mar 83
Harry Dawson Colin Tyrer	} Mar 83 - May 83
*Vince Karalius Harry Dawson	} May 83 - May 84
Eric Hughes	June 84 - Jan 86
Doug Laughton	Jan 86 - May 91
Frank Myler	June 91 - May 92
Phil Larder	May 92 -

*Dawson quit as coach in Mar 1984 with
Karalius continuing as team manager.*

GREAT BRITAIN REGISTER
(46 players)

Mick Adams	(11+2)	1979-84
John Basnett	(2)	1984-86
Keith Bentley	(1)	1980
Mick Burke	(14+1)	1980-86
Frank Collier	(1)	1964
Andy Currier	(2)	1989-93
Jonathan Davies	(8+1)	1990-93
John Devereux	(3+2)	1992-93
Ray Dutton	(6)	1970
Keith Elwell	(3)	1977-80
Richard Eyres	(3+4)	1989-93
John Fieldhouse	(6)	1985-86
Ray French	(4)	1968
Les Gorley	(4+1)	1980-82
Andy Gregory	(8+1)	1981-84
Ian Hare	(1)	1967
Fred Higgins	(6)	1950-51
Harold Higgins	(2)	1937
Les Holliday	(3)	1991-92
Eric Hughes	(8)	1978-82
David Hulme	(7+1)	1988-89
Paul Hulme	(3+5)	1988-92
Albert Johnson	(4)	1914-20
Vince Karalius	(2)	1963
George Kemel	(2)	1965
Doug Laughton	(4)	1973-79
Joe Lydon	(9+1)	1983-85
Tommy McCue	(6)	1936-46
Steve McCurrie	(1)	1993
Jim Measures	(2)	1963
Jim Mills	(6)	1974-79
Paul Moriarty	(1)	1991
Frank Myler	(14+1)	1960-67
Tony Myler	(14)	1983-86
George Nicholls	(7)	1971-72
Martin Offiah	(20)	1988-91
Dennis O'Neill	(2+1)	1971-72
Mike O'Neill	(3)	1982-83
Harry Pinner	(1)	1986
Glyn Shaw	(1)	1980
Nat Silcock	(12)	1932-37
Stuart Spruce	(1)	1993
Alan Tait	(9)	1989-92
John Warlow	(3)	1971
Darren Wright	(+1)	1988
Stuart Wright	(7)	1977-78

1992-93 SIGNINGS REGISTER

Signed	Player	Club From
4.8.92	Hadley, Adrian	Salford
13.8.92	Harris, Paul	St. Marie's ARL
14.8.92	Goulding, Bobby	Leeds
8.10.92	Myers, David	Wigan
9.10.92	*Byrne, Ged	Oldham
14.10.92	O'Neill, Julian	Brisbane B., Aus
1.2.93	Blackwood, Mark	Kells ARL

Widnes centre Andy Currier, scorer of six goals on his return to the Great Britain side in February 1993, his second Test cap.

WIDNES 1992-93 PLAYERS' SUMMARY

	(Date of Birth)	App	T	G	D	Pts	Previous club	Signed
Ashurst, Chris	(24.7.65)	2+1	—	—	—	—	Golborne ARL	5.6.87
Currier, Andy	(8.4.66)	27	16	4	—	72	Halton H. ARL	15.7.83
Davidson, Paul	(1.8.69)	1+5	—	—	—	—	Hensingham ARL	29.11.90
Davies, Jonathan	(24.10.62)	29+1	14	106	—	268	Llanelli RU	9.1.89
Devereux, John	(30.3.66)	33	21	—	—	84	Bridgend RU	10.10.89
Dowd, Barry	(17.5.65)	0+1	—	—	—	—	Halton H. ARL	19.10.82
Eyres, Richard	(7.12.64)	35	13	—	—	52	Widnes T. ARL	29.8.84
Faimalo, Esene	(11.10.66)	25+5	2	—	—	8	New Zealand	17.10.90
Goulding, Bobby	(4.2.72)	31+2	3	14	2	42	Leeds	14.8.92
Hadley, Adrian	(1.3.63)	15+5	4	—	—	16	Salford	4.8.92
Hammond, Karl	(25.4.74)	1+2	—	—	—	—	—	23.7.90
Holliday, Les	(8.8.62)	19+6	4	—	—	16	Halifax	23.3.90
Howard, Harvey	(29.8.68)	27+7	5	—	—	20	Waterloo RU	23.3.90
Hulme, David	(6.2.64)	32+3	7	—	—	28	Halton H. ARL	4.8.80
Hulme, Paul	(19.4.66)	33	6	—	—	24	Halton H. ARL	5.7.83
Ireland, Andy	(6.12.71)	1+1	—	—	—	—	Golborne ARL	24.7.91
Kelly, Chris	(29.8.73)	1	—	—	—	—	—	23.7.90
Koloto, Emosi	(23.1.65)	13+4	6	—	—	24	New Zealand RU	21.10.88
McCurrie, Steve	(1.6.73)	13+17	11	—	—	44	Hensingham ARL	23.7.90
Marsh, David	(8.10.68)	1+2	1	—	—	4	Blackbrook ARL	31.12.87
Moriarty, Paul	(16.7.64)	29	7	—	—	28	Swansea RU	3.4.89
Myers, David	(31.7.71)	26+1	13	—	—	52	Wigan	8.10.92
Myler, Tony	(26.9.60)	6	1	—	—	4	—	26.12.78
O'Neill, Julian	(14.10.72)	11+1	4	—	—	16	Australia	1.11.92
Pickett, Steve		0+1	—	—	—	—	Australia	16.10.92
Sarsfield, Mark	(22.3.71)	3+1	1	—	—	4	Leigh M. ARL	14.12.89
Smith, David	(15.3.68)	0+2	—	—	—	—	—	5.6.87
Sorensen, Kurt	(8.11.56)	26+3	3	—	—	12	Australia	18.12.85
Spruce, Stuart	(3.1.71)	35	14	—	—	56	Widnes T. ARL	8.1.90
Tyrer, Christian	(19.12.73)	3+4	—	5	—	10	Leigh R. ARL	23.7.90
Wright, Darren	(17.1.68)	29+2	7	—	—	28	Leigh M. ARL	23.3.85
TOTALS								
31 players			163	129	2	912		

Representative appearances 1992-93
Currier — Britain (1, 6g)
Davies — Britain (1, 10g)
Devereux — Britain (2+1, 2t); Wales (2, 1t, 1g)
Eyres — Britain (2+1, 1t); England (1)
Hadley — Wales (1+1)
McCurrie — Britain (1); GB Under-21s (1, 1t); Cumbria (1)
Moriarty — Wales (2)
Spruce — Britain (1); England (1, 1t)

WIDNES 1992-93 MATCH ANALYSIS

Date	Competition	H/A	Opponent	Rlt	Score	Tries	Goals	Attendance	Referee
30.8.92	SBC	H	Castleford	W	16-6	Eyres, Goulding, D. Hulme	Davies (2)	6257	Morris
4.9.92	SBC	A	Hull K.R.	W	16-2	Eyres (2), McCurrie	Davies (2)	—	—

Date	Com- petition	H/A	Opponent	Rlt	Score	Tries	Goals	Atten- dance	Referee
13.9.92	LC(1)	H	Carlisle	W	52-8	Spruce (2), P. Hulme (2), Davies, Howard, Hadley, McCurrie, Currier	Davies (8)	3733	R. Connolly
20.9.92	SBC	H	Bradford N.	L	12-24	Eyres, D. Hulme	Davies (2)	5751	Holdsworth
25.9.92	SBC	A	Wigan	L	2-14	—	Davies	—	—
30.9.92	LC(2)	A	St. Helens	L	8-10	McCurrie	Davies (2)	—	—
4.10.92	SBC	H	Hull K.R.	W	52-0	Devereux (4), Spruce (2), Davies, McCurrie, Hadley	Davies (8)	4699	J. Smith
11.10.92	SBC	A	Castleford	L	14-26	Holliday, Myers	Davies (3)	—	—
18.10.92	SBC	H	Halifax	W	20-6	Devereux, Myler, P. Hulme	Goulding (4)	3835	J. Connolly
1.11.92	SBC	A	Leeds	L	16-48	McCurrie, Hadley, Eyres	Davies (2)	—	—
8.11.92	RT(1)	H	Ryedale-York	W	46-4	Holliday (2), Moriarty (2), O'Neill (2), Wright, Myers	Davies (7)	3475	Nicholson
13.11.92	SBC	H	Wigan	L	6-18	D. Hulme	Goulding	6326	R. Smith
22.11.92	SBC	A	Sheffield E.	L	30-32	Currier (3), Goulding, Eyres, Spruce	Currier (2), Goulding	—	—
1.12.92	SBC	H	Wakefield T.	W	16-10	Devereux (2), O'Neill	Goulding (2)	3960	J. Connolly
6.12.92	RT(2)	H	Rochdale H.	W	30-2	Myers (2), Moriarty, P. Hulme, Koloto, Currier	Goulding (3)	3591	Ollerton
29.12.92	RT(3)	A[1]	Bradford N.	L	10-21	Koloto, Devereux	Currier	—	—
6.1.93	SBC	A	Salford	W	48-12	Devereux (2), Eyres, O'Neill, Spruce, Currier, Sorensen, P. Hulme, Hadley	Davies (6)	—	—
10.1.93	SBC	A	Hull	L	4-20	Eyres	—	—	—
13.1.93	CC(P)	H	Swinton	W	62-14	Koloto (3), Davies (2), Howard (2), Spruce (2), Currier, D. Hulme, Sorensen	Davies (7)	2154	Redfearn
17.1.93	SBC	H	Sheffield E.	W	56-10	Davies (3), Wright (2), Eyres, Currier, Koloto, Moriarty	Davies (10)	4220	Holdsworth
20.1.93	SBC	A	Warrington	W	10-8	Currier, Wright	Davies	—	—
31.1.93	CC(1)	A	Whitehaven	W	20-8	Devereux (2), Currier, Myers	Davies (2)	—	—
7.2.93	SBC	H	Hull	W	22-4	Currier, Davies, Faimalo, Sarsfield	Davies (3)	4592	Holdsworth
14.2.93	CC(2)	A	Sheffield E.	W	52-6	Currier (2), Davies (2), Devereux (2), Spruce (2), Wright (2)	Davies (3), Goulding (3)	—	—
17.2.93	SBC	H	St. Helens	W	26-8	Currier, Marsh, Moriarty, Wright	Davies (5)	8966	Ollerton
21.2.93	SBC	A	Wakefield T.	W	36-18	Moriarty (2), Davies, Devereux, Howard, McCurrie, Spruce	Davies (4)	—	—
28.2.93	CC(3)	A	Hull K.R.	D	4-4	Spruce	—	—	—
3.3.93	CC(3) Replay	H	Hull K.R.	W	16-11	Eyres, Howard	Davies (4)	7486	Holdsworth
13.3.93	CC(SF)	N[2]	Leeds	W	39-4	Davies (2), Myers (2), Currier, Devereux, Spruce	Davies (5), Goulding (dg)	(13,823)	Ollerton
17.3.93	SBC	H	Leeds	W	19-8	Devereux, McCurrie, Myers	Davies (3), Goulding (dg)	6192	R. Smith
21.3.93	SBC	A	Leigh	W	14-11	Devereux, P. Hulme	Tyrer (3)	—	—
26.3.93	SBC	H	Salford	W	38-22	Devereux (2), D. Hulme (2), Goulding, Eyres, Myers	Davies (5)	4139	R. Connolly
31.3.93	SBC	A	Bradford N.	L	0-28	—	—	—	—
4.4.93	SBC	A	Halifax	L	6-40	Eyres	Davies	—	—
9.4.93	SBC	H	Warrington	W	26-14	McCurrie (3), D. Hulme, Myers	Davies (3)	6190	J. Connolly
12.4.93	SBC	A	St. Helens	L	18-29	Holliday, Myers, Spruce	Davies (3)	—	—
18.4.93	SBC	H	Leigh	L	26-28	Myers (2), Currier, Faimalo, McCurrie	Tyrer (2), Currier	4989	Steele
25.4.93	PT(1)	H	Leeds	L	10-22	Davies, Devereux	Davies	6554	J. Connolly
1.5.93	CC(F)	N[3]	Wigan	L	14-20	Eyres, Sorensen	Davies (3)	(77,684)	R. Smith

A[1] Bradford C. FC; N[2] Wigan; N[3] Wembley

WIGAN

Ground: Central Park (0942-31321)
First Season: 1895-96
Nickname: Riversiders
Chairman: Jack Robinson
Secretary: Mary Charnock
Honours: **Championship** Winners, 1908-09, 1921-22, 1925-26, 1933-34, 1945-46, 1946-47, 1949-50, 1951-52, 1959-60
Beaten finalists, 1909-10, 1910-11, 1911-12, 1912-13, 1923-24, 1970-71
War Emergency League Winners, 1943-44
Beaten finalists, 1940-41
League Leaders Trophy Winners, 1970-71
Division One Champions, 1986-87, 1989-90, 1990-91, 1991-92, 1992-93
Challenge Cup Winners, 1923-24, 1928-29, 1947-48, 1950-51, 1957-58, 1958-59, 1964-65, 1984-85, 1987-88, 1988-89, 1989-90, 1990-91, 1991-92, 1992-93
Beaten finalists, 1910-11, 1919-20, 1943-44, 1945-46, 1960-61, 1962-63, 1965-66, 1969-70, 1983-84
Regal Trophy Winners, 1982-83, 1985-86, 1986-87, 1988-89, 1989-90, 1992-93
Premiership Winners, 1986-87, 1991-92
Beaten finalists, 1992-93
Lancashire Cup Winners, 1905-06, 1908-09, 1909-10, 1912-13, 1922-23, 1928-29, 1938-39, 1946-47, 1947-48, 1948-49, 1949-50, 1950-51, 1951-52, 1966-67, 1971-72, 1973-74, 1985-86, 1986-87, 1987-88, 1988-89, 1992-93
Beaten finalists, 1913-14, 1914-15, 1925-26, 1927-28, 1930-31, 1934-35, 1935-36, 1936-37, 1945-46, 1953-54, 1957-58, 1977-78, 1980-81, 1984-85
Lancashire League Winners, 1901-02, 1908-09, 1910-11, 1911-12, 1912-13, 1913-14, 1914-15, 1920-21, 1922-23, 1923-24, 1925-26, 1945-46, 1946-47, 1949-50, 1951-52, 1958-59, 1961-62, 1969-70

Lancashire War League Winners, 1940-41
Charity Shield Winners, 1985-86, 1987-88, 1991-92
Beaten finalists, 1988-89, 1989-90, 1990-91, 1992-93
World Club Challenge Winners, 1987-88, 1991-92
Beaten finalists, 1992-93
BBC2 Floodlit Trophy Winners, 1968-69
Beaten finalists, 1969-70

RECORDS
Match
Goals: 22 by Jim Sullivan v. Flimby & Fothergill, 14 Feb 1925
Tries: 10 by Martin Offiah v. Leeds, 10 May 1992
Shaun Edwards at Swinton, 29 Sep 1992
Points: 44 by Jim Sullivan v. Flimby & Fothergill, 14 Feb 1925

Season
Goals: 184 by Frano Botica, 1992-93
Tries: 62 by Johnny Ring, 1925-26
Points: 423 by Frano Botica, 1992-93

Career
Goals: 2,317 by Jim Sullivan, 1921-46
Tries: 478 by Billy Boston, 1953-68
Points: 4,883 by Jim Sullivan, 1921-46
Appearances: 774 by Jim Sullivan, 1921-46
Highest score: 116-0 v. Flimby & Fothergill, 14 Feb 1925
Highest against: 58-3 at Leeds, 14 Oct 1972
Attendance: 47,747 v. St. Helens (League), 27 Mar 1959

COACHING REGISTER
● **Since 1974-75**

Ted Toohey	May 74 - Jan 75
Joe Coan	Jan 75 - Sep 76
Vince Karalius	Sep 76 - Sep 79
Kel Coslett	Oct 79 - Apr 80
George Fairbairn	Apr 80 - May 81
Maurice Bamford	May 81 - May 82
Alex Murphy	June 82 - Aug 84
Colin Clarke	
Alan McInnes	Aug 84 - May 86
Graham Lowe	Aug 86 - June 89
John Monie	Sep 89 - May 93
John Dorahy	June 93 -

GREAT BRITAIN REGISTER
(82 players)

Ray Ashby	(1)	1965
Ernest Ashcroft	(11)	1947-54
Eric Ashton	(26)	1957-63
Bill Ashurst	(3)	1971-72
Frank Barton	(1)	1951
John Barton	(2)	1960-61
Jack Bennett	(1)	1926
Denis Betts	(20+1)	1990-93
Dai Bevan	(1)	1952
Billy Blan	(3)	1951
Dave Bolton	(23)	1957-63
Billy Boston	(31)	1954-63
Tommy Bradshaw	(6)	1947-50
Frank Carlton	(1)	1962
Brian Case	(6+1)	1984-88
Norman Cherrington	(1)	1960
Colin Clarke	(7)	1965-73
Phil Clarke	(9+1)	1990-93
Percy Coldrick	(4)	1914
Frank Collier	(1)	1963
Neil Cowie	(1)	1993
Jack Cunliffe	(4)	1950-54
Martin Dermott	(10)	1990-93
Shaun Edwards	(26+4)	1985-93
Joe Egan	(14)	1946-50
Roy Evans	(4)	1961-62
George Fairbairn	(14)	1977-80
Terry Fogerty	(1)	1967
Phil Ford	(1)	1985
Bill Francis	(4)	1967-77
Danny Gardiner	(1)	1965
Ken Gee	(17)	1946-51
Henderson Gill	(14+1)	1981-88
Andy Goodway	(12)	1985-90
Bobby Goulding	(5)	1990
John Gray	(5+3)	1974
Andy Gregory	(16)	1987-92
Steve Hampson	(11+1)	1987-92
Ellery Hanley	(23)	1985-91
Cliff Hill	(1)	1966
David Hill	(1)	1971
Jack Hilton	(4)	1950
Tommy Howley	(6)	1924
Bill Hudson	(1)	1948
Danny Hurcombe	(8)	1920-24
Bert Jenkins	(12)	1907-14
Ken Jones	(2)	1970

Roy Kinnear	(1)	1929
Nicky Kiss	(1)	1985
Doug Laughton	(11)	1970-71
Johnny Lawrenson	(3)	1948
Jim Leytham	(5)	1907-10
Ian Lucas	(1+1)	1991-92
Joe Lydon	(14+6)	1986-92
Billy McGinty	(4)	1992
Brian McTigue	(25)	1958-63
Joe Miller	(1)	1911
Jack Morley	(2)	1936-37
Martin Offiah	(7)	1992
Andy Platt	(17+1)	1989-93
Ian Potter	(7+1)	1985-86
Jack Price	(4)	1924
Dick Ramsdale	(8)	1910-14
Gordon Ratcliffe	(3)	1947-50
Johnny Ring	(2)	1924-26
Dave Robinson	(1)	1970
Martin Ryan	(4)	1947-50
Bill Sayer	(7)	1961-63
Jim Sharrock	(4)	1910-11
Nat Silcock	(3)	1954
Dick Silcock	(1)	1908
Kelvin Skerrett	(5+2)	1992
David Stephenson	(5)	1982-87
Jim Sullivan	(25)	1924-33
Mick Sullivan	(19)	1957-60
Gwyn Thomas	(1)	1914
Johnny Thomas	(8)	1907-11
Shaun Wane	(2)	1985-86
Edward Ward	(3)	1946-47
Les White	(2)	1947
David Willicombe	(2)	1974
Billy Winstanley	(3)	1911

1992-93 SIGNINGS REGISTER

Signed	Player	Club From
27.7.92	Crompton, Martin	Warrington
15.9.92	Farrar, Andrew	Western Suburbs, Aus
22.9.92	Johnson, Andrew	Wigan St. Patricks ARL
3.10.92	Knowles, Matthew	Blackbrook ARL
8.10.92	Atcheson, Paul	Widnes
19.10.92	Farrell, Andrew	Orrell St. James ARL
20.10.92	Hatton, Anthony	—
10.11.92	Haughton, Simon	Wigan St. Patricks ARL
29.12.92	Smith, Simon	Bamber Bridge ARL

WIGAN 1992-93 PLAYERS' SUMMARY

	(Date of Birth)	App	T	G	D	Pts	Previous club	Signed
Atcheson, Paul	(17.5.73)	4+3	1	—	—	4	Widnes	8.10.92
Bell, Dean	(29.4.62)	39	15	—	—	60	Australia	24.10.86
Betts, Denis	(14.9.69)	36	14	—	—	56	Leigh R. ARL	6.10.86
Blakeley, Steve	(17.10.72)	0+1	—	—	—	—	Leigh R. ARL	15.8.89
Botica, Frano	(3.8.63)	40	15	179	5	423	New Zealand RU	—
Cassidy, Mike	(3.7.73)	7+9	1	—	—	4	Wigan St. J. ARL	24.5.90
Clarke, Phil	(16.5.71)	34+1	4	—	—	16	Wigan St. P. ARL	26.10.87
Cowie, Neil	(16.1.67)	24+9	6	—	—	24	Rochdale H.	3.9.91
Crompton, Martin	(29.9.69)	15+4	4	—	—	16	Warrington	27.7.92
Dermott, Martin	(25.9.67)	31+1	2	—	2	10	Wigan St. P. ARL	7.11.84
Edwards, Shaun	(17.10.66)	44	43	—	1	173	Wigan St. P. ARL	18.10.83
Farrar, Andrew	(17.5.62)	38	13	—	—	52	Australia	15.9.92
Farrell, Andrew	(30.5.75)	5+7	2	6	—	20	Orrell St. J. ARL	3.1.92
Forshaw, Mike	(5.1.70)	5+5	3	—	—	12	Wigan St. P. ARL	12.1.87
Gildart, Ian	(14.10.69)	5+8	—	—	—	—	Wigan Colts	24.10.86
Goodway, Andy	(2.6.61)	0+1	—	—	—	—	Oldham	30.8.85
Hall, Martin	(5.12.68)	4+2	1	—	—	4	Rochdale H.	—
Hampson, Steve	(14.8.61)	30	2	10	2	30	Vulcan RU	3.11.83
Lucas, Ian	(5.11.67)	9+3	2	—	—	8	Wigan Colts	5.11.84
Lydon, Joe	(26.11.63)	29+4	7	11	3	53	Widnes	20.1.86
McGinty, Billy	(6.12.64)	26+1	2	—	—	8	Warrington	29.8.91
Mather, Barrie-Jon	(15.1.73)	2+9	3	—	—	12	—	—
Myers, David	(31.7.71)	1+1	—	—	—	—	Warrington	30.5.90
Naylor, Scott	(2.2.72)	0+1	—	—	—	—	—	9.6.88
Offiah, Martin	(29.12.66)	38	30	1	2	124	Widnes	3.1.92
Panapa, Sam	(14.5.62)	30+12	13	—	—	52	Sheffield E.	30.8.91
Platt, Andy	(9.10.63)	30+1	5	—	—	20	St. Helens	7.9.88
Robinson, Jason	(30.7.74)	35+6	13	—	—	52	Hunslet P. ARL	31.7.91
Skerrett, Kelvin	(22.5.66)	29+1	4	—	—	16	Bradford N.	13.8.90
Stoop, Andre	(8.10.66)	7+2	1	—	—	4	South Africa	24.9.91
Turner, Stuart	(13.11.69)	1	—	—	—	—	Widnes	6.9.91
TOTALS								
31 players			206	207	15	1,253		

Representative appearances 1992-93 Atcheson — GB Under-21s (1, 2t); Betts — Britain (2, 1t); Cassidy — GB Under-21s (+1); Clarke — Britain (3); England (1); Cowie — Britain (1); Dermott — Britain (2); Edwards — Britain (3, 3t); Lydon — Britain (1); Mather — GB Under-21s (1, 2t); Offiah — Britain (1); England — (1, 2t); Platt — Britain (2); Robinson — GB Under-21s (1); Skerrett — Britain (+1)

WIGAN 1992-93 MATCH ANALYSIS

Date	Competition	H/A	Opponent	Rlt	Score	Tries	Goals	Attendance	Referee
23.8.92	CS	N[1]	St. Helens	L	0-17	—	—	(7364)	Cummings
28.8.92	SBC	A	Sheffield E.	W	46-6	Edwards (3), Betts (2), Offiah, Skerrett, Platt	Lydon (7)	—	—
6.9.92	SBC	H	Hull	L	13-14	Robinson, Hampson	Lydon (2), Offiah (dg)	13,104	Morris
11.9.92	LC(1)	A	Rochdale H.	W	36-8	Edwards (2), Panapa, McGinty, Crompton, Stoop	Hampson (4), Lydon (2)	—	—
20.9.92	SBC	A	Wakefield T.	W	19-14	Crompton, Skerrett, Platt	Hampson (3, 1dg)	—	—
25.9.92	SBC	H	Widnes	W	14-2	Botica, Offiah	Botica (3)	13,032	Morris
29.9.92	LC(2)	A	Swinton	W	78-0	Edwards (10), Offiah, Panapa, Robinson, Bell	Botica (11)	—	—

Date	Competition	H/A	Opponent	Rlt	Score	Tries	Goals	Attendance	Referee
4.10.92	SBC	A	Leigh	W	36-16	Farrar (2), Edwards (2), Crompton, Robinson, Platt	Botica (4)	—	—
6.10.92	LC(SF)	H	Oldham	W	48-8	Robinson (2), Lydon (2), Edwards, Botica, Betts, Mather	Botica (8)	8954	Whitfield
11.10.92	SBC	H	Leeds	W	24-6	Farrar (2), Bell, Edwards	Botica (4)	19,011	Holdsworth
18.10.92	LC(F)	A	St. Helens	W	5-4	—	Botica (2, 1dg)	(20,534)	Cummings
30.10.92	WCC	H	Brisbane B.	L	8-22	Edwards	Botica (2)	(17,746)	Hale (NZ)
2.11.92	SBC	H	Sheffield E.	W	44-10	Betts (2), Edwards (2), Offiah (2), Crompton	Botica (8)	8081	J. Smith
7.11.92	RT(1)	H	Carcassonne	W	52-0	Botica (2), Panapa (2), Farrar, Betts, Offiah, Lydon, McGinty	Botica (8)	4306	R. Smith
13.11.92	SBC	A	Widnes	W	18-6	Edwards, Clarke, Betts	Botica (3)	—	—
22.11.92	SBC	A	Salford	W	26-18	Bell, Lucas, Panapa, Betts	Botica (5)	—	—
29.11.92	SBC	H	Hull K.R.	W	48-18	Panapa (2), Lucas, Farrar, Cowie, Offiah, Edwards, Bell	Botica (8)	10,990	Whitfield
6.12.92	RT(2)	A	Hull K.R.	W	18-0	Edwards, Farrar, Bell	Botica (3)	—	—
11.12.92	SBC	A	Halifax	W	32-8	Botica (2), Edwards, Bell, Skerrett, Offiah	Botica (4)	—	—
20.12.92	RT(3)	A	Workington T.	W	24-12	Botica, Panapa, Betts, Clarke	Botica (4)	—	—
27.12.92	SBC	A	St. Helens	L	6-41	Botica	Botica	—	—
2.1.93	RT(SF)	H	Hull	W	19-4	Cowie (2), Mather	Botica (3, 1dg)	8020	Whitfield
5.1.93	SBC	H	Warrington	L	4-11	—	Botica (2)	12,084	Holdsworth
17.1.93	CC(P)	H	Hull	W	40-2	Betts (2), Offiah (2), Botica, Edwards	Botica (8)	12,420	R. Smith
23.1.93	RT(F)	N[2]	Bradford N.	W	15-8	Edwards, Robinson	Botica (3), Hampson (dg)	(13,221)	Holdsworth
31.1.93	CC(1)	A	Dewsbury	W	20-4	Lydon (2), Botica	Botica (4)	—	—
4.2.93	SBC	H	Wakefield T.	W	38-14	Offiah (3), Botica, Edwards, Panapa, Robinson	Botica (5)	10,298	Steele
7.2.93	SBC	H	Bradford N.	W	34-16	Robinson (2), Betts, Edwards, Lydon, Panapa	Botica (5)	12,663	J. Smith
13.2.93	CC(2)	H	St. Helens	W	23-3	Bell, Clarke, Edwards	Botica (4), Lydon (2dg), Offiah (dg)	21,191	R. Smith
17.2.93	SBC	A	Hull	W	42-0	Bell (2), Botica (2), Dermott, Edwards, Farrar	Botica (7)	—	—
21.2.93	SBC	H	Halifax	W	30-14	Edwards (2), Offiah (2), Farrar	Botica (5)	15,368	Campbell
28.2.93	CC(3)	A	Halifax	W	19-18	Bell, Lydon, Panapa	Botica (3), Lydon (dg)	—	—
3.3.93	SBC	A	Leeds	W	31-6	Dermott, Edwards, Farrar, Offiah, Robinson	Botica (5), Dermott (dg)	—	—
9.3.93	SBC	A	Hull K.R.	W	26-12	Platt, Betts, Panapa, Edwards, Cassidy	Botica (3)	—	—
14.3.93	SBC	H	Salford	W	70-6	Offiah (5), Edwards (4), Farrar (2), Platt	Botica (7), Hampson (3), Offiah	12,420	Whitfield
17.3.93	SBC	A	Bradford N.	L	16-23	Cowie, Mather, Robinson	Farrell (2)	—	—
27.3.93	CC(SF)	N[2]	Bradford N.	W	15-6	Farrar, Hampson	Botica (3), Edwards (dg)	(20,085)	Holdsworth
31.3.93	SBC	H	Leigh	W	50-0	Offiah (2), Atcheson, Botica, Cowie, Forshaw, Hall, Robinson	Botica (9)	12,726	Atkin
4.4.93	SBC	A	Castleford	L	17-26	Cowie, Edwards	Botica (4), Dermott (dg)	—	—
9.4.93	SBC	H	St. Helens	D	8-8	Offiah	Botica (2)	29,839	Holdsworth
12.4.93	SBC	A	Warrington	W	27-14	Bell (2), Edwards, Farrell	Botica (5, 1dg)	—	—
16.4.93	SBC	H	Castleford	W	25-18	Botica, Clarke, Robinson	Botica (6, 1dg)	19,579	Cummings
25.4.93	PT(1)	H	Warrington	W	40-5	Offiah (5), Bell (2), Betts	Farrell (4)	11,976	Atkin
1.5.93	CC(F)	N[3]	Widnes	W	20-14	Skerrett, Bell, Panapa	Botica (4)	(77,684)	R. Smith
7.5.93	PT(SF)	H	Castleford	W	25-8	Edwards, Farrell, Forshaw, Offiah	Botica (4, 1dg)	12,675	Cummings
16.5.93	PT(F)	N[4]	St. Helens	L	4-10	Forshaw	—	(36,598)	Holdsworth

N[1] Gateshead; N[2] Elland Road, Leeds; N[3] Wembley; N[4] Manchester U.FC

WORKINGTON TOWN

Ground: Derwent Park (0900-603609)
First Season: 1945-46
Nickname: Town
Chairman: Kevan Gorge
Secretary: John Bell
Honours: **Championship** Winners, 1950-51
Beaten finalists, 1957-58
Challenge Cup Winners, 1951-52
Beaten finalists, 1954-55, 1957-58
Divisional Premiership Beaten
finalists, 1992-93
Lancashire Cup Winners, 1977-78
Beaten finalists, 1976-77, 1978-79,
1979-80
Western Division Championship
Winners, 1962-63

RECORDS

Match
Goals: 13 by Dean Marwood v. Highfield,
1 Nov 1992
Tries: 7 by Ike Southward v. Blackpool B.,
17 Sep 1955
Points: 42 by Dean Marwood v. Highfield,
1 Nov 1992

Season
Goals: 186 by Lynn Hopkins, 1981-82
Tries: 49 by Johnny Lawrenson, 1951-52
Points: 438 by Lynn Hopkins, 1981-82

Career
Goals: 809 by Iain MacCorquodale, 1972-80
Tries: 274 by Ike Southward, 1952-59 &
1960-68
Points: 1,800 by Iain MacCorquodale, 1972-80
Appearances: 415+4 Paul Charlton, 1961-69 &
1975-80
Highest score: 78-0 v. Highfield, 1 Nov 1992
78-12 at Blackpool G., 28 Feb 1993
Highest against: 68-0 at Wigan, 18 Jan 1987
68-6 at Leigh, 8 Mar 1992
Attendance: 17,741 v. Wigan (RL Cup),
3 Mar 1965 — at Derwent Park
20,403 v. St. Helens (RL Cup),
8 Mar 1952 — at Borough Park

COACHING REGISTER
● Since 1974-75

Ike Southward	Aug 73 - June 75
Paul Charlton	June 75 - June 76
Ike Southward	June 76 - Feb 78
Sol Roper	Feb 78 - Apr 80
Keith Irving	Aug 80 - Oct 80
Tommy Bishop	Nov 80 - June 82
Paul Charlton	July 82 - Dec 82
Dave Cox	Mar 83 - Mar 83
Harry Archer/Bill Smith	May 83 - June 84
Bill Smith	June 84 - Apr 85
Jackie Davidson	Apr 85 - Jan 86
Keith Davies	Feb 86 - Mar 87
Norman Turley	Mar 87 - Apr 88
Maurice Bamford	July 88 - Dec 88
Phil Kitchin	Dec 88 - May 90
Ray Ashton	June 90 - Dec 91
Dean Williams	Dec 91 - Apr 92
Peter Walsh	May 92 -

GREAT BRITAIN REGISTER
(9 players)

Eddie Bowman	(4)	1977
Paul Charlton	(1)	1965
Brian Edgar	(11)	1958-66
Norman Herbert	(6)	1961-62
Vince McKeating	(2)	1951
Billy Martin	(1)	1962
Albert Pepperell	(2)	1950-51
Ike Southward	(4)	1958
George Wilson	(3)	1951

1992-93 SIGNINGS REGISTER

Signed	Player	Club From
30.7.92	Bond, Terry	Seaton ARL
30.7.92	Morgan, John	Glasson Rangers ARL
31.7.92	Carter, Darren	Millom ARL
16.8.92	*Burns, Paul	Barrow
17.9.92	Mulligan, Mark	Lakes Utd, Aus
2.10.92	*Kay, Tony	Barrow
5.11.92	Pickering, James	Richmond Rovers, NZ
4.2.93	*McKenzie, Phil	Widnes
12.2.93	Byrne, Ged	Oldham
19.3.93	*Drummond, Des	Warrington

WORKINGTON TOWN 1992-93 PLAYERS' SUMMARY

	(Date of Birth)	App	T	G	D	Pts	Previous club	Signed
Armstrong, Colin	(26.1.63)	33+1	12	—	—	48	Hull K.R.	3.10.90
Beattie, John	(14.10.58)	0+1	—	—	—	—	Salford	1.3.82
Bond, Paul	(13.7.65)	13	9	—	—	36	—	27.8.92
Buglass, Barry	(9.2.72)	5+1	—	—	—	—	Cockermouth ARL	19.8.91
Burgess, Glen	(28.12.63)	0+1	—	—	—	—	Clifton ARL	5.11.85
Burns, Paul	(9.2.67)	18+1	9	—	—	36	Barrow	16.8.92
Byrne, Ged	(14.6.62)	14	3	—	—	12	Oldham	12.2.93
Carter, Darren	(8.1.72)	11	5	—	1	21	Millom ARL	31.10.92
Drummond, Des	(17.6.58)	7	7	—	—	28	Warrington	19.3.93
Graham, John	(15.10.59)	1	—	—	—	—	Carlisle	29.8.90
Hepi, Brad	(11.2.68)	29+1	15	—	—	60	Carlisle	1.5.92
Kay, Tony	(16.4.64)	26	18	—	—	72	Barrow	2.10.92
Kitchin, Wayne	(26.11.70)	16+3	8	—	—	32	Kells ARL	26.9.89
Kohlhase, Wayne	(12.10.67)	1+2	—	—	—	—	—	—
Lowden, David	(19.4.65)	23+2	18	—	—	72	Glasson ARL	22.1.86
McGuirk, Gary	(26.9.71)	9	1	—	—	4	British Steel ARL	18.6.90
McKenzie, Phil	(13.6.63)	13	5	—	—	20	Widnes	4.2.93
Marwood, Dean	(22.2.70)	34	15	179	—	418	Barrow	23.12.91
Morgan, John	(2.4.64)	5+1	2	—	—	8	Glasson ARL	30.7.92
Mulligan, Mark	(6.3.70)	27+2	16	—	2	66	Australia	17.9.92
Oglanby, Martin	(22.7.64)	20+9	4	—	—	16	Glasson ARL	24.7.90
Penman, Danny	(21.4.64)	6	1	—	—	4	Broughton ARL	12.1.90
Penrice, Paul	(27.2.66)	13	10	—	—	40	Gt. Clifton ARL	30.7.87
Pickering, Brendan	(13.7.62)	0+5	—	—	—	—	Westfield ARL	17.2.88
Pickering, James	(11.12.66)	20+1	1	—	—	4	New Zealand	5.11.92
Riley, Peter	(1.3.68)	23+7	4	—	—	16	Gt. Clifton ARL	30.7.87
Rooney, Neil	(15.6.65)	6+4	5	—	—	20	Netherall RU	28.8.86
Roskell, Mark	(5.3.66)	12	2	—	—	8	Warrington	4.11.90
Schubert, Gary	(18.9.66)	14+11	1	—	—	4	Carlisle	9.8.91
Scott, Ian	(20.4.69)	25+6	4	—	—	16	Carlisle	22.8.90
Smith, Garry	(2.10.62)	15+5	4	—	—	16	Egremont ARL	3.9.84
Wear, Steve	(13.12.70)	3	2	—	—	8	Kells ARL	26.9.89
TOTALS								
32 players			181	179	3	1,085		

Representative appearances 1992-93
Armstrong — Cumbria (1)
Burns — Cumbria (1)
Kitchin — Cumbria (+1)
Marwood — Cumbria (+1)
Riley — Cumbria (+1)

WORKINGTON TOWN 1992-93 MATCH ANALYSIS

Date	Com- petition	H/A	Opponent	Rlt	Score	Tries	Goals	Atten- dance	Referee
30.8.92	TD	A	Keighley C.	L	2-18	—	Marwood	—	—
6.9.92	TD	H	Chorley B.	W	54-8	Lowden (2), Rooney (2), Marwood (2), Morgan, Armstrong, Burns, Hepi	Marwood (7)	1449	Campbell
13.9.92	LC(1)	A	Blackpool G.	W	22-8	Penman, Armstrong	Marwood (7)	—	—

WORKINGTON TOWN 1992-93 MATCH ANALYSIS

Date	Competition	H/A	Opponent	Rlt	Score	Tries	Goals	Attendance	Referee
20.9.92	TD	A	Highfield	W	48-6	McGuirk, Burns, Morgan, Kitchin, Armstrong, Lowden, Mulligan, Marwood	Marwood (8)	—	—
23.9.92	LC(2)	A	Salford	L	20-42	Lowden (2), Burns, Kitchin	Marwood (2)	—	—
4.10.92	TD	A	Batley	L	8-20	Lowden, Hepi	—	—	—
11.10.92	TD	H	Hunslet	W	40-19	Burns (4), Hepi, Bond, Lowden	Marwood (6)	1526	Kershaw
16.10.92	TD	A	Nottingham C.	W	24-1	Armstrong (2), Hepi	Marwood (6)	—	—
1.11.92	TD	H	Highfield	W	78-0	Marwood (4), Lowden (2), Bond (2), Wear (2), Armstrong, Roskell, Hepi	Marwood (13)	1182	Tidball
8.11.92	RT(1)	A	Doncaster	W	30-4	Bond (2), Oglanby, Kay, Scott	Marwood (5)	—	—
15.11.92	TD	A	Doncaster	W	22-6	Hepi (2), Mulligan	Marwood (5)	—	—
22.11.92	TD	H	Nottingham C.	W	68-0	Mulligan (3), Bond (2), Carter (2), Hepi, Marwood, Scott, Riley, Rooney	Marwood (10)	1311	Cross
29.11.92	TD	A	Chorley B.	W	29-12	Carter (2), Armstrong, Hepi	Marwood (6), Carter (dg)	—	—
6.12.92	RT(2)	A	Hunslet	W	34-12	Kay (4), Lowden	Marwood (7)	—	—
13.12.92	TD	H	Ryedale-York	W	42-10	Marwood (2), Armstrong, Carter, Bond, Burns, Penrice	Marwood (7)	2124	Redfearn
20.12.92	RT(3)	H	Wigan	L	12-24	Mulligan, Penrice	Marwood (2)	7682	Holdsworth
26.12.92	TD	H	Whitehaven	L	12-20	Penrice, J. Pickering	Marwood (2)	4044	Galtress
5.1.93	TD	A	Barrow	W	30-6	Mulligan (2), Scott, Bond, Rooney	Marwood (5)	—	—
10.1.93	TD	H	Keighley C.	L	0-21	—	—	2035	Kershaw
24.1.93	TD	H	Blackpool G.	W	56-6	Kay (2), Mulligan (2), Penrice (2), Burns, Byrne, Rooney, Roskell	Marwood (8)	1565	Asquith
31.1.93	CC(1)	A	Bradford N.	L	18-28	Kay, Lowden, Oglanby	Marwood (3)	—	—
7.2.93	TD	A	Dewsbury	W	15-2	Lowden, McKenzie	Marwood (3), Mulligan (dg)	—	—
10.2.93	TD	H	Barrow	W	42-8	Hepi (3), Kay (3), Penrice, Smith	Marwood (5)	2024	Tidball
21.2.93	TD	H	Dewsbury	W	33-7	Marwood (2), Lowden, Oglanby, Penrice, Riley	Marwood (4), Mulligan (dg)	2922	Morris
28.2.93	TD	A	Blackpool G.	W	78-12	Penrice (3), Kay (3), Mulligan (2), Hepi, Kitchin, McKenzie, Riley, Smith, Marwood	Marwood (11)	—	—
7.3.93	TD	H	Batley	W	20-12	Kitchin, Riley, Smith	Marwood (4)	2361	Cummings
14.3.93	TD	A	Ryedale-York	L	12-16	Armstrong, McKenzie	Marwood (2)	—	—
21.3.93	TD	A	Hunslet	W	34-11	Lowden (4), Kay, Kitchin	Marwood (5)	—	—
28.3.93	TD	H	Doncaster	W	52-6	Hepi (2), Kitchin (2), Armstrong, Byrne, Drummond, Kay, Lowden	Marwood (8)	1944	Asquith
11.4.93	TD	A	Whitehaven	W	36-10	Armstrong, Marwood, McKenzie, Mulligan, Smith	Marwood (8)	—	—
18.4.93	DP(1)	H	Doncaster	W	44-14	Drummond (3), Mulligan (3), Kay, Scott	Marwood (6)	1705	Kershaw
25.4.93	DP(2)	A	Huddersfield	W	24-10	Armstrong, Drummond, Marwood, Kitchin	Marwood (4)	—	—
9.5.93	DP(SF)	A	Rochdale H.	W	30-16	Drummond (2), Byrne, Kay, Schubert	Marwood (5)	—	—
16.5.93	DP(F)	N[1]	Featherstone R.	L	16-20	McKenzie, Oglanby	Marwood (4)	—	J. Connolly

N[1] Manchester U.FC

Keighley Cougars wingman John Wasyliw, the League's top goal and points-scorer and breaker of a host of records in 1992-93.

RECORDS

LEADING SCORERS FOR 1992-93

TOP TEN TRIES

1. Paul Newlove (Featherstone R.)...................... 52
2. Shaun Edwards (Wigan).............................. 46
3. Ellery Hanley (Leeds) 34
   Owen Simpson (Featherstone R.).................... 34
5. Martin Offiah (Wigan) 32
6. Alan Hunte (St. Helens)............................. 30
7. John Wasyliw (Keighley C.) 29
   Martin Pearson (Featherstone R.) 29
9. Greg Austin (Halifax) 27
   Martin Wood (Keighley C.).......................... 27
● Others with 20 or more: Nick Pinkney (Ryedale-York) 25; John Devereux (Widnes), Eddie Rombo (Dewsbury), Tony Smith (Castleford) 24; Mike Ford (Castleford), Mark Preston (Halifax) 23; Vince Gribbin (Whitehaven), Andy Mason (Wakefield T.), Iva Ropati (Oldham), Ian Smales (Featherstone R.) 22; Phil Ford (Salford), Tea Ropati (St. Helens), Ian Thomas (Huddersfield) 21; John Bentley (Halifax), David Brook (Hunslet), Steve McGowan (Bradford N.) 20.

TOP TEN GOALS
(Including drop goals)

1. John Wasyliw (Keighley C.) 187
2. Frano Botica (Wigan) 184
3. Dean Marwood (Workington T.) 179
4. Martin Pearson (Featherstone R.) 145
5. Paul Bishop (Halifax)............................... 118
6. Lee Crooks (Castleford) 116
   Jonathan Davies (Widnes) 116
8. Steve Gartland (Rochdale H.) 105
9. Steve Maguire (Whitehaven) 95
10. Andy Precious (Hunslet) 90

TOP FIVE DROP GOALS

1. Paul Shuttleworth (Dewsbury) 11
2. Gus O'Donnell (St. Helens) 9
3. Neil Flanagan (Huddersfield) 8
4. Tony Chappell (Nottingham C.) 7
   Andy Precious (Hunslet) 7
   Andy Ruane (Leigh)................................. 7

TOP TEN POINTS

	T	G	DG	Pts
1. John Wasyliw (Keighley C.)	29	187	0	490
2. Frano Botica (Wigan)	15	179	5	423
3. Dean Marwood (Workington T.)...............	15	179	0	418
4. Martin Pearson (Featherstone R.)	29	144	1	405
5. Jonathan Davies (Widnes)..	14	116	0	288
6. Steve Gartland (Rochdale H.)	17	103	2	276
7. Paul Bishop (Halifax)	8	116	2	266
8. Lee Crooks (Castleford)	3	116	0	244
9. Phil Hellewell (Huddersfield)	10	88	0	216
10. Paul Eastwood (Hull)	11	84	0	212

Key:
SBC .... Stones Bitter Championship
SD .... Second Division
TD .... Third Division
PT .... Premiership Trophy
DP............. Divisional Premiership
LC .... Lancashire Cup
YC .... Yorkshire Cup
RT .... Regal Trophy
CC .... Challenge Cup
CS .... Charity Shield
WCC .... World Club Challenge
NA .... Non-appearance

OUTSTANDING SCORING FEATS IN 1992-93
INDIVIDUAL

Most tries in a match:
10 by Shaun Edwards (Wigan) at Swinton	LC
6 by Steve McGowan (Bradford N.) v. Barrow	RT
Steve Rowan (Barrow) at Nottingham C.	TD
5 by Martin Offiah (Wigan) v. Salford	SBC
Martin Offiah (Wigan) v. Warrington	PT
Phil Ford (Salford) v. Whitehaven	LC
Andy Wilson (Wakefield T.) v. Highfield	RT
Greg Austin (Halifax) v Nottingham C.	RT
Vince Gribbin (Whitehaven) v. Blackpool G.	TD

Most goals in a match:
15 by John Wasyliw (Keighley C.) v. Nottingham C.	TD
13 by John Wasyliw (Keighley C.) v. Highfield	CC
John Wasyliw (Keighley C.) at Blackpool G.	TD
Mark Conway (Wakefield T.) v. Highfield ...	RT
Dean Marwood (Workington T.) v Highfield	TD
Greg Pearce (Dewsbury) at Blackpool G.	TD
12 by Gary Pearce (Ryedale-York) at Nottingham C.	TD
Mike Kavanagh (Barrow) v. Blackpool G. ...	TD
11 by Frano Botica (Wigan) at Swinton	LC
Deryck Fox (Bradford N.) v. Barrow	RT
Dean Marwood (Workington T.) at Blackpool G.	TD
10 by John Wasyliw (Keighley C.) at Highfield	TD
Dean Marwood (Workington T.) v. Nottingham C.	TD
Gary Pearce (Ryedale-York) v. Barrow	TD
Jonathan Davies (Britain) v. France	Test
Jonathan Davies (Widnes) v. Sheffield E.	SBC
Alex Green (Doncaster) at Highfield	TD
Steve Maguire (Whitehaven) v. Highfield	TD

Most points in a match:
42 by Dean Marwood (Workington T.) v. Highfield	TD
40 by Shaun Edwards (Wigan) at Swinton	LC
34 by Mark Conway (Wakefield T.) v. Highfield ...	RT
John Wasyliw (Keighley C.) v. Nottingham C.	TD

32 by Jonathan Davies (Widnes) v. Sheffield E.	SBC
John Wasyliw (Keighley C.) at Highfield	TD
30 by John Wasyliw (Keighley C.) v. Highfield	CC
John Wasyliw (Keighley C.) at Blackpool G.	TD

TEAM

Highest score:

Wakefield T. 90 v. Highfield 12	RT
Blackpool G. 5 v. Dewsbury 90	TD

● There was a total of 73 matches in which a team scored 50 points or more, a record number in the 10 seasons since the try was increased from three to four points.

In the first season of the four-point try in 1983-84 there were 31 scores of 50 or more, dropping to a record low 26 in 1985-86. There has, of course, been a varying number of matches played each season. The other 60-plus scores in 1992-93 were:

Home:

Keighley C. 86 v. Nottingham C. 0	TD
Keighley C. 86 v. Highfield 0	CC
Keighley C. 78 v. Chorley B. 6	TD
Featherstone R. 78 v. Bramley 0	SD
Workington T. 78 v. Highfield 0	TD
Halifax 76 v. Nottingham C. 6	RT
Whitehaven 72 v. Blackpool G. 0	TD
Whitehaven 72 v. Highfield 0	TD
Barrow 72 v. Blackpool G. 6	TD
Great Britain 72 v. France 6	Test
Bradford N. 70 v. Barrow 10	RT
Wigan 70 v. Salford 6	SBC
Workington T. 68 v. Nottingham C. 0	TD
Leeds 68 v. Rochdale H. 6	CC
Halifax 66 v. Carlisle 16	CC
Huddersfield 66 v. Nottingham C. 1	CC
St. Helens 64 v. Leigh 9	SBC
Featherstone R. 64 v. Swinton 6	SD
Rochdale H. 62 v. Bramley 22	SD
Widnes 62 v. Swinton 14	CC
Salford 60 v. Whitehaven 8	LC
Ryedale-York 60 v. Highfield 12	TD
Ryedale-York 60 v. Barrow 0	TD
Featherstone R. 60 v. Bramley 0	SD

Away:

Nottingham C. 0 v. Ryedale-York 84	TD
Blackpool G. 8 v. Keighley C. 82	TD
Highfield 8 v. Keighley C. 80	TD
Nottingham C. 2 v. Dewsbury 78	TD
Swinton 0 v. Wigan 78	LC
Blackpool G. 12 v. Workington T. 78	TD
Nottingham C. 4 v. Hunslet 76	TD
Huddersfield 2 v. Australia 66	Tour
Nottingham C. 8 v. Barrow 64	TD
Nottingham C. 0 v. Batley 60	TD
Highfield 16 v. Doncaster 60	TD

Highest score by a losing team:

Leeds 38 v. Hull 34	SBC

● There was a total of 64 matches in which a team scored 20 points or more and lost, equalling the record number of 1988-89 since the try was increased from three to four points 10 seasons ago.

In the first season of the four-point try there were 62 such scores, dropping to a record low of 47 the following year.

High-scoring draws:

Carlisle 30 v. Featherstone R. 30	SD
Leeds 26 v. Wakefield T. 26	SBC
Castleford 22 v. Wakefield T. 22	SBC
London C. 20 v. Oldham 20	SD

● The record total of 20-20 plus draws in the 10 seasons of four-point tries is eight in 1985-86.

● From the start of the 1983-84 season, the value of a try was raised from three points to four. It was decided officially that records for most points in a match, season or career would subsequently include the four-point try and that no attempt would be made to adjust existing records featuring the three-point try.
● Substitute appearances do not count towards players' full appearance records.
● Points and appearances in abandoned matches are included in records, except in League matches which are replayed. Although the abandoned League match points and appearances are included in players' overall totals they do not count towards League records.

RECORD-BREAKING FEATS 1992-93

AT A GLANCE

JOHN WASYLIW of Keighley Cougars achieved the following club records: 187 goals and 490 points in a season; 15 goals and 34 points in a match. The 15 goals also equalled the British record for a League match. Wasyliw also equalled the fastest century of goals, in 18 matches, and scored in every match.

FRANO BOTICA of Wigan achieved club records of 184 goals and 423 points in a season, and raced to the fastest British career 1,000 points in 93 matches.

MARTIN PEARSON of Featherstone Rovers scored a club record 391 points in a season.

PAUL NEWLOVE of Featherstone Rovers scored a club record 48 tries in a season and added four in representative matches to become the first centre to score 50 or more in a season.

STEVE GARTLAND of Rochdale Hornets scored a club record 276 points in a season.

PAUL BISHOP of Halifax achieved the rare feat of scoring in each of his club's matches throughout a season.

DEAN MARWOOD of Workington Town scored a club and League match record of 42 points, including a club record 13 goals.

MARK CONWAY of Wakefield Trinity broke club match records with 13 goals and 34 points.

MIKE KAVANAGH of Barrow equalled two club records with 12 goals and 28 points in a match.

GARY PEARCE of Ryedale-York scored club records of 12 goals and 28 points in a match.

MIKE SMITH of Chorley Borough scored club match records of nine goals and 17 points.

STEVE MAGUIRE of Whitehaven broke the club match record with 28 points.

JONATHAN DAVIES equalled the Great Britain record of 10 goals in a match.

GREG PEARCE of Dewsbury kicked a club record 13 goals in a match.

SHAUN EDWARDS of Wigan scored a club record-equalling and a Lancashire Cup-tie record of 10 tries in a match.

STEVE ROWAN of Barrow scored a club record-equalling six tries in a match.

STEVE McGOWAN of Bradford Northern equalled the Regal Trophy match record of six tries.

GREAT BRITAIN ran up a world record Test score with their 72-6 defeat of France.

WAKEFIELD TRINITY scored a club record 90-12 win against Highfield.

WORKINGTON TOWN twice had club record victories of 78-0 against Highfield and 78-12 at Blackpool Gladiators.

DEWSBURY twice broke the club's highest score record with a 78-2 win at Nottingham City followed by a 90-5 victory at Blackpool Gladiators which was also a League record away win by any club.

RYEDALE-YORK ran up a club record 84-0 win at Nottingham City.

KEIGHLEY COUGARS twice scored club record victories of 86-0, against Nottingham City and Highfield.

HUNSLET gained a club record 76-4 win at Nottingham City.

CHORLEY BOROUGH ran up their highest score with a 57-20 defeat of Nottingham City, but suffered a club record 78-6 defeat at Keighley Cougars.

SALFORD conceded a club record score in a 70-6 defeat at Wigan.

LEIGH went down to a club record 64-9 defeat at St. Helens.

SWINTON suffered a club record 78-0 defeat at home to Wigan.

NEW RECORDS IN DETAIL . . .

JOHN WASYLIW of Keighley Cougars broke and equalled several records during the season. The winger set club records with 187 goals and 490 points in a season; 15 goals and 34 points in a match, with the goals total also equalling the British League record; equalled the fastest century of goals in a season in his 18th match and scored in every game throughout the campaign.

Wasyliw's 15 goals and 34 points, including a try, in a club record 86-0 Division Three home defeat of Nottingham City on 1 November beat Keighley records he already held.

His 15 goals beat the Keighley record of 11 which he shared with Robert Walker, who set the target 86 years earlier, and Bert Cook.

Walker's 11 goals were in a 67-0 home League win over the old Castleford side on 13 January 1906 and Cook's feat came in a 49-10 home League defeat of Hull K.R. on 31 October 1953.

Wasyliw equalled the old record with 11 in a Keighley's 70-0 home defeat of Nottingham on 23 February 1992.

The former Halifax RU winger achieved the Keighley points record for a third time inside a year. He held the previous record with 26 on two Division Three occasions.

He scored nine goals and two tries in a 54-12 win at Chorley Borough on 4 October 1992 and seven goals plus three tries in a 42-14 home defeat of Highfield on 10 November 1991.

Mick Stacey of Leigh set the British League goals record with 15 in a 75-3 Division Two home defeat of Doncaster on 28 March 1976.

Wasyliw equalled the fastest century of goals in a season with 13 in an 86-0 Silk Cut Challenge Cup first round home defeat of Highfield which took his total to 102 in 18 matches on 31 January.

The record is shared with Bernard Ganley (Oldham, 16 November 1957), David Watkins (Salford, 17 November 1972) and Steve Quinn (Featherstone R., 16 December 1979).

Wasyliw went on to beat Brian Jefferson's club record of 155 goals in 1973-74, passing his total with 10 in the 80-8 Division Three win at Highfield on 16 March.

He had already passed Jefferson's 1973-74 points record of 331, including seven tries, when scoring 22 points in a 42-20 League win at Barrow on 28 February.

Full back Jefferson played in 34 of Keighley's 39 matches in his record-breaking season. Wasyliw scored in every one of the club's 31 matches last term as follows:

		T	G	Pts
Workington T. .... (H)		0	5	10
Hunslet .... (A)		0	2	4
Nottingham C. (YC) .... (A)		0	7	14
Barrow .... (H)		1	8	20
Wakefield T. (YC) .... (A)		0	2	4
Dewsbury .... (A)		0	4	8
Chorley B. .... (A)		2	9	26
Whitehaven .... (A)		1	3	10
Nottingham C. .... (H)		1	15	34
Leigh (RT) .... (A)		2	4	16

Highfield	(H)	1	6	16
Ryedale-York	(A)	1	4	12
Whitehaven	(H)	0	2	4
Nottingham C.	(A)	0	9	18
Workington T.	(A)	1	2	8
Doncaster	(H)	2	3	14
Blackpool G.	(H)	1	4	12
Highfield (CC)	(H)	1	13	30
Ryedale-York	(H)	0	5	10
Hull K.R. (CC)	(A)	2	6	20
Chorley B.	(H)	2	9	26
Barrow	(A)	2	7	22
Blackpool G.	(A)	1	13	30
Dewsbury	(H)	0	6	12
Highfield	(A)	3	10	32
Hunslet	(H)	2	8	24
Doncaster	(A)	0	4	8
Batley	(H)	0	5	10
Batley	(A)	1	3	10
Hunslet (DP)	(H)	1	5	14
Rochdale H. (DP)	(A)	1	4	12
Totals				
31 appearances		**29**	**187**	**490**

FRANO BOTICA of Wigan scored club records of 184 goals, including five drop goals, and 423 points in a season.

He also raced to the fastest British career 1,000 points in 93 matches and less than three years. The New Zealander's club record points total of 423 included 15 tries and was totted up in 40 of Wigan's 46 matches, mainly at half back.

South African full back Fred Griffiths held the previous club records with 176 goals and 394 points, including 14 tries, in 1958-59 when he played in 39 of Wigan's 46 matches.

Botica broke the points record with 17 in the Stones Bitter Championship title-clinching 25-18 home defeat of Castleford on 16 April, taking his total to 406. The goals record was achieved with the second of four at Wembley in the 20-14 Silk Cut Challenge Cup final defeat of Widnes on 1 May. Botica's season went as follows:

		T	G	Pts
St. Helens (CS)	(N[1])	0	0	0
Sheffield E.	(A)	NA		
Hull	(H)	NA		
Rochdale H. (LC)	(A[1])	NA		
Wakefield T.	(A)	NA		
Widnes	(H)	1	3	10
Swinton (LC)	(A)	0	11	22
Leigh	(A)	0	4	8
Oldham (LC)	(H)	1	8	20
Leeds	(H)	0	4	8
St. Helens (LC)	(A)	0	3(1)	5
Brisbane B. (WCC)	(H)	0	2	4
Sheffield E.	(H)	0	8	16
Carcassonne (RT)	(H)	2	8	24
Widnes	(A)	0	3	6
Salford	(A)	0	5	10
Hull K.R.	(H)	0	8	16
Hull K.R. (RT)	(A)	0	3	6

Halifax	(A)	2	4	16
Workington T. (RT)	(A)	1	4	12
St. Helens	(A)	1	1	6
Hull (RT)	(H)	0	4(1)	7
Warrington	(H)	0	2	4
Hull (CC)	(H)	1	8	20
Bradford N. (RT)	(N[2])	0	3	6
Dewsbury (CC)	(A)	1	4	12
Wakefield T.	(H)	1	5	14
Bradford N.	(H)	0	5	10
St. Helens (CC)	(H)	0	4	8
Hull	(A)	2	7	22
Halifax	(H)	0	5	10
Halifax (CC)	(A)	0	3	6
Leeds	(A)	0	5	10
Hull K.R.	(A)	0	3	6
Salford	(H)	0	7	14
Bradford N.	(A)	NA		
Bradford N. (CC)	(N[2])	0	3	6
Leigh	(H)	1	9	22
Castleford	(A)	0	4	8
St. Helens	(H)	0	2	4
Warrington	(A)	0	6(1)	11
Castleford	(H)	1	7(1)	17
Warrington (PT)	(H)	NA		
Widnes (CC)	(N[3])	0	4	8
Castleford (PT)	(H)	0	5(1)	9
St. Helens (PT)	(N[4])	0	0	0
Totals				
40 appearances		**15**	**184(5)**	**423**

A[1] at Salford, N[1] at Gateshead, N[2] at Elland Road, Leeds, N[3] at Wembley, N[4] at Manchester U. FC
( ) Drop goals included in total.

A former New Zealand RU international, Botica registered his 1,000th point with 10 in Wigan's 31-6 Stones Bitter Championship win at Leeds on 3 March, just over two years six months after his debut.

Lewis Jones of Leeds held the previous record for scoring 1,000 points in the fewest number of matches by reaching the target in his 104th club and representative match. The former Welsh RU international achieved the feat just over three years after making his debut for Leeds in November 1952. Jonathan Davies of Widnes held the record for scoring 1,000 points in the shortest time span. Another former Welsh RU international, Davies reached the milestone two years 11 months after making his debut for Widnes on 15 January 1989. It was his 109th club and representative match and, like Jones, included a Great Britain tour Down Under.

Botica, signed from Northcote RU, made his debut for Wigan in the CIS Insurance Charity Shield at Swansea on 19 August 1990. His 1,000 points were rattled up as follows:

	App	Tries	Goals	Dr	Pts
1990-91	30	18	126	0	324
1991-92	34	11	159	2	364
1992-93	29	13	132	2	318
Totals	**93**	**42**	**417**	**4**	**1,006**

For British record purposes, Botica's figures do not include his representative appearances in New Zealand.

MARTIN PEARSON of Featherstone Rovers finished the season with a club record 391 points from 28 tries and 140 goals, including one drop goal.

The stand off or full back played in 35 of Featherstone's 37 matches, including two as a substitute.

Steve Quinn held the previous record, with the centre or stand off scoring 375 points in 1979-80 from 17 tries and 163 goals, including two drop goals, still a club record.

Quinn scored in all 31 matches for Featherstone when, like last season, they were a Division Two club.

Pearson also scored five goals and a try for Great Britain Under-21s to put him fourth in the points-scoring chart with 405.

His match-by-match figures for Featherstone were:

		T	G	Pts
Huddersfield	(A)	0	4	8
Swinton	(H)	NA		
Dewsbury (YC)	(H)	1	4	12
Rochdale H.	(A)	0	2	4
Huddersfield (YC)	(H)	0	0	0
Carlisle	(H)	0	0	0
Oldham	(A)	1	6	16
Wakefield T. (YC)	(H)	0	2	4
Bramley	(A)	0	3	6
London C.	(H)	1	6	16
Huddersfield	(H)	0	3	6
Salford (RT)	(A)	0	3	6
Swinton	(A)	1	4	12
Rochdale H.	(H)	0	3	6
Carlisle	(A)	2	3	14
St. Helens (RT)	(H)	0	2	4
Oldham	(H)	1	1	6
London C.	(A)	0	3	6
Huddersfield	(A)	2	4	16
Huddersfield	(H)	1	5	14
Swinton	(H)	2	8	24
London C.	(A)	1	4	12
St. Helens (CC)	(H)	1	1	6
Oldham	(H)	NA		
London C.	(H)	1	7	18
Swinton	(A)	1	3	10
Carlisle	(H)	1	3	10
Rochdale H.	(A)	1	6	16
Oldham	(A)	1	3	10
Bramley	(H)	1	8	20
Rochdale H.	(H)	0	4	8
Carlisle	(A)	2	3	14
Bramley	(A)	0	6	12
Bramley	(H)	1	9	22
Ryedale-York (DP)	(H)	3	7	26
Dewsbury (DP)	(H)	2	6(1)	19
Workington T. (DP)	(N[1])	0	4	8

Totals

35 appearances		28	140(1)	391

N[1] at Manchester U. FC

( ) Drop goals included in total.

PAUL NEWLOVE of Featherstone Rovers scored a club record 48 tries in a season and added four in representative matches to become the first centre to score 50 or more in one term. The previous club record was held by winger Cyril Woolford, who scored 31 playing in 38 of Featherstone's matches in 1958-59. Newlove's 48 tries were scored playing in all but two of Featherstone's 37 matches.

In fact, Newlove's winger partner OWEN SIMPSON was the first to pass Woolford's record with two tries in the 60-0 Division Two home defeat of Bramley on 21 March taking his total to 32. But Newlove scored the last three tries of the match to equal Simpson's record and break it with another hat-trick a week later in a 24-22 Division Two home defeat of Rochdale Hornets. Simpson finished the season with 34 tries in 33 matches.

Newlove became the first centre to score 50 tries in a season with one in the 35-12 Divisional Premiership semifinal home defeat of Dewsbury on 9 May.

The record was held by Steve Halliwell, who scored 48 in 36 matches as a centre for Leigh in 1985-86. Halliwell also touched down once as a stand off.

Newlove's total of 52 included one try for England and a hat-trick for Great Britain.

His record-breaking season also took him past a career century of tries (as detailed in MILESTONES). His match-by-match scoring for Featherstone went as follows:

Huddersfield	(A)	1
Swinton	(H)	0
Dewsbury (YC)	(H)	2
Rochdale H.	(A)	0
Huddersfield (YC)	(H)	NA
Carlisle	(H)	1
Oldham	(A)	1
Wakefield T. (YC)	(H)	0
Bramley	(A)	0
London C.	(H)	3
Huddersfield	(H)	1
Salford (RT)	(A)	1
Swinton	(A)	1
Rochdale H.	(H)	0
Carlisle	(A)	1
St. Helens (RT)	(H)	0
Oldham	(H)	3
London C.	(A)	1
Huddersfield	(A)	0
Huddersfield	(H)	2
Swinton	(H)	1
London C.	(A)	1
St. Helens (CC)	(H)	1
Oldham	(H)	2
London C.	(H)	2
Swinton	(A)	2
Carlisle	(H)	NA
Rochdale H.	(A)	1
Oldham	(A)	1
Bramley	(H)	3
Rochdale H.	(H)	3
Carlisle	(A)	1

Bramley .... (A)	3	
Bramley .... (H)	4	
Ryedale-York (DP) .... (H)	2	
Dewsbury (DP) .... (H)	1	
Workington T. (DP) ...... (N[1])	2	

Totals

35 appearances **48**

N[1] at Manchester U. FC

STEVE GARTLAND of Rochdale Hornets scored a club record 276 points in a season from 17 tries and 105 goals, including two drop goals. The half back played in all 35 of the Division Two club's matches.

Steve Turner set the record in 1988-89 with 243 points from 104 goals, including a drop goal, and nine tries. Usually a stand off, but also playing at wing, centre and loose forward, Turner played in 31 of Rochdale's 33 Division Two and Cup matches, including three as a substitute. Gartland broke the record with 18 points in a 30-14 League win at Bramley on 14 March. His match-by-match figures were as follows:

	T	G	Pts
Swinton .... (A)	1	0	4
London C. .... (A)	0	3	6
Wigan (LC) .... (H[1])	0	2	4
Featherstone R. .... (H)	1	5	14
Bramley .... (A)	2	1	10
Carlisle .... (A)	1	2	8
Oldham .... (H)	1	4	12
Huddersfield .... (A)	2	3	14
London C. .... (A)	0	4	8
Bramley .... (H)	1	4	12
XIII Catalan (RT) .... (H)	0	8	16
London C. .... (H)	0	5(1)	9
Featherstone R. .... (A)	0	1	2
Bramley .... (H)	2	7	22
Widnes (RT) .... (A)	0	0	0
Carlisle .... (H)	1	5	14
Swinton .... (A)	0	2	4
Carlisle .... (A)	0	2	4
Oldham .... (A)	0	3	6
Oldham .... (A)	0	2	4
Doncaster (CC) .... (H)	1	5	14
Swinton .... (H)	0	2	4
Leeds (CC) .... (A)	0	1	2
Huddersfield .... (A)	0	5(1)	9
London C. .... (H)	1	5	14
Huddersfield .... (H)	0	4	8
Featherstone R. .... (H)	0	4	8
Bramley .... (A)	2	5	18
Swinton .... (H)	0	1	2
Featherstone R. .... (A)	0	1	2
Huddersfield .... (H)	0	3	6
Oldham .... (H)	0	1	2
Carlisle .... (H)	1	5	14
Keighley C. (DP) .... (H)	0	0	0
Workington T. (DP) .... (H)	0	0	0

Totals

35 appearances .... **17 105(2) 276**

[1] at Salford

( ) Drop goals included in total.

PAUL BISHOP of Halifax scored in every one of his club's 33 matches throughout the season, totalling 266 points from eight tries and 118 goals, including two drop goals.

The scrum half and occasional stand off's match-by-match figures were as follows:

	T	G	Pts
Wakefield T. .... (A)	1	1	6
Leeds .... (H)	0	3	6
Sheffield E. (YC) .... (A)	0	1	2
Salford .... (A)	0	3	6
Leigh .... (H)	0	5	10
Hull .... (A)	0	2	4
Sheffield E. .... (H)	0	5	10
Widnes .... (A)	0	1	2
Wakefield T. .... (H)	1	2	8
Nottingham C. (RT) ..... (H)	0	3	6
Leigh .... (A)	0	4	8
Warrington .... (H)	0	5(1)	9
Hull (RT) .... (A)	0	3	6
Wigan .... (H)	0	2	4
Leeds .... (A)	0	3	6
Sheffield E. .... (A)	0	5	10
Hull K.R. .... (H)	1	2	8
St. Helens .... (A)	0	4	8
Carlisle (CC) .... (H)	1	9	22
Salford .... (H)	0	6	12
Batley (CC) .... (H)	0	7	14
Wigan .... (A)	1	1	6
Wigan (CC) .... (H)	0	3	6
Hull .... (H)	0	5	10
Castleford .... (H)	0	6	12
Warrington .... (A)	1	4	12
St. Helens .... (H)	0	2	4
Castleford .... (A)	0	2	4
Widnes .... (H)	2	6	20
Bradford N. .... (A)	0	2	4
Bradford N. .... (H)	0	1	2
Hull K.R. .... (A)	0	5	10
St. Helens (PT) .... (A)	0	5(1)	9

Totals

33 appearances .... **8 118(2) 266**

( ) Drop goals included in total.

DEAN MARWOOD of Workington Town scored a club and League match record 42 points, including a club best 13 goals, in their record 78-0 Division Three home defeat of Highfield on 1 November. The scrum half also scored four tries.

The League match record had lasted since 2 February 1907 when one of the game's legendary centres, Jim Lomas, scored 39 points from five tries and 12 goals in Salford's

78-0 home defeat of Liverpool City.

Marwood's total also beat the best individual tally against a professional side of 40 points shared by Paul Loughlin (St. Helens) v. Carlisle on 14 September 1986; Martin Offiah (Wigan) v. Leeds on 10 May 1992, and Shaun Edwards (Wigan) v. Swinton on 29 September 1992, all Cup ties.

The points record for any competitive match remains George West's 53 for Hull K.R. in a Challenge Cup tie against Brookland Rovers amateurs in 1905.

The previous Workington points record was 33 by winger Ike Southward with seven tries and six goals in a 42-10 home League defeat of Blackpool Borough on 17 September 1955.

Marwood's 13 goals beat the Town record of 11 by Iain MacCorquodale in a 55-13 home League victory over Blackpool on 6 January 1973.

MARK CONWAY of Wakefield Trinity broke two club match records, with the scrum half scoring 13 goals and 34 points, including two tries, in his side's biggest win of 90-12 at home to Highfield in the Regal Trophy preliminary round on 27 October.

Centre Neil Fox set the previous records with 12 goals and 33 points, including three tries, in a 78-9 Yorkshire Cup first round home defeat of Batley on 26 August 1967. Fox also kicked 12 goals in the 42-6 home League defeat of Workington Town on 19 December 1970.

Bernard Ward was another to kick 12 goals for Trinity, in the 72-8 home League defeat of Hunslet on 6 February 1971.

MIKE KAVANAGH of Barrow equalled two club records with 12 goals and 28 points, including a try, in the 72-6 Division Three home defeat of Blackpool Gladiators on 21 March.

The scrum half shares the goals record with Frank French v. Maryport amateurs, 19 February 1938; Willie Horne v. Cardiff, 8 September 1951; and Steve Tickle v. Kent Invicta, 8 April 1984.

Tickle also scored a try to give him a share of the points record with Keith Jarrett (11 goals, two tries) v. Doncaster, 25 August 1970, and Dean Marwood (10 goals, two tries) v. Runcorn Highfield, 16 April 1989.

GARY PEARCE set two club records of 12 goals and 28 points as Ryedale-York ran up their highest-ever score with an 84-0 Division Three win at Nottingham City on 4 October.

Pearce's 12 goals beat the 11 by Vic Yorke in York's 37-24 home League defeat of Whitehaven on 6 September 1958 and Chris Gibson in a 52-8 home League win over Dewsbury on 28 September 1980.

Pearce added a try for the Welsh stand off to claim a club record 28 points.

The previous record of 26 from nine goals and two tries was shared by stand off Graham Steadman in a 54-4 Division Two home defeat of Batley on 25 November 1984, and second row Graham Sullivan in a 70-8 Division Two win in Keighley on 11 March 1990.

MIKE SMITH beat two club records as Chorley Borough ran up their highest score with a 57-20 Division Three home defeat of Nottingham City on 28 March.

The full back set the individual records with 17 points from nine goals, including a drop goal. Since the club was formed in 1989 no player had scored more than six goals or 12 points in a match.

STEVE MAGUIRE of Whitehaven broke a club record with 28 points in the 72-0 Division Three home defeat of Highfield on 28 February.

He scored 10 goals and two tries, while Bill Holliday's old record of 25 points was made up of 11 goals and a try in a 61-0 home League defeat of Hunslet on 31 March 1962.

Maguire also holds the club goals record with 12 against Nottingham City on 12 April 1992.

JONATHAN DAVIES of Widnes equalled the Great Britain record of 10 goals in a match in their world record 72-6 British Coal Test defeat of France at Headingley, Leeds, on 2 April.

Others who have kicked 10 goals in a match for Britain are: Lewis Jones (Leeds) v. Australia at Brisbane, second Test, 3 July 1954; Bernard Ganley (Oldham) v. France at Wigan, Test, 23 November 1957; John Holmes (Leeds) v. New Zealand at Pau, France, World Cup, 4 November 1972.

GREG PEARCE of Dewsbury kicked a club record 13 goals in their biggest-ever win of 90-5 at Blackpool Gladiators in a Division Three match on 4 April.

The previous record of 10 goals was shared by: Jim Ledgard v. Yorkshire Amateurs, 13 September 1947; Nigel Stephenson v. Blackpool Borough, 28 August 1972; Chris Wilkinson v. Huddersfield, 27 March 1989.

SHAUN EDWARDS of Wigan scored a club record-equalling 10 tries and the most by any player in a Lancashire Cup tie in the 78-0 second round win at Swinton on 29 September.

He equalled the Wigan record set by winger Martin Offiah in the 74-6 Premiership semi-final home defeat of Leeds on 10 May 1992. It beat the Lancashire Cup record of seven by Wigan winger Green Vigo in a 37-5 first round home win over St. Helens on 21 August 1976.

Scrum half Edwards' 10 tries were also the most tries by a non-winger in any match.

The previous best of eight was shared by Dewsbury centre Dai Thomas in a 60-0 defeat of Liverpool City on 13 April 1907, and Leeds prop Fred Webster in the 102-0 defeat of Coventry on 12 April 1913.

STEVE ROWAN of Barrow scored a club record-equalling six tries in the 64-8 Division Three win at Nottingham City on 15 November.

The centre shares the record with three wingers who scored their six tries in home matches as follows: Val Cumberbatch in a 60-0 League defeat of Batley on 21 November 1936; Jim Thornburrow in a club record 83-3 defeat of Maryport amateurs in the Challenge Cup first round on 19 February 1938; and Frank Castle in a 61-3 League defeat of York on 29 September 1951.

STEVE McGOWAN, the Bradford Northern centre, equalled the Regal Trophy match record of six tries in the 70-10 first round home defeat of Barrow on 8 November.

Whitehaven centre Vince Gribbin set the record with six tries in a 64-0 first round home defeat of Doncaster on 18 November 1984.

GREAT BRITAIN ran up a world record Test score with their 72-6 defeat of France in the Test at Headingley on 2 April.

The previous highest score in a Test or World Cup match was Australia's 70-8 defeat of Papua New Guinea at Wagga on 20 July 1988. Australia scored 14 tries compared with Britain's 13.

Britain's previous highest score came in the 60-4 defeat of France at Headingley on 16 February 1991 when they scored 11 tries.

WAKEFIELD TRINITY's 90-12 home defeat of Highfield in the Regal Trophy preliminary round on 27 October produced their highest score.

Trinity's 16-try spree beat their 78-9 home defeat of Batley in the Yorkshire Cup first round on 26 August 1967 when they scored 18 tries.

WORKINGTON TOWN twice ran up club record scores of 78 points to beat their previous best 62-15 defeat of Hunslet in a Division One home match on 20 April 1964 when they scored 16 tries.

The old record was broken with a 13-try 78-0 Division Three home defeat of Highfield on 1 November.

Town then won 78-12 with a 14-try Division Three romp at Blackpool Gladiators on 28 February.

DEWSBURY twice broke the club's highest score record and also ran up a British record for an away League win.

They first broke the club record with a 78-2 Division Three win at Nottingham City on 29 November when the 15-try rout beat the 72-0 Division Two home defeat of Doncaster on 25 November 1984 when they scored 13 tries.

Dewsbury then won 90-5 at Blackpool Gladiators on 4 April, scoring 16 tries in the Division Three match for a League record away score by any club.

The previous highest away score was Leigh's 17-try Division Two 88-2 win at Runcorn Highfield on 15 January 1989.

The only higher away score is Hull K.R.'s 100-6 Yorkshire Cup preliminary round defeat of Nottingham City, which was played at Doncaster in 1990.

RYEDALE-YORK ran up their highest score with an 84-0 Division Three win at Nottingham City on 4 October when they scored 15 tries.

The previous best was a 12-try 70-8 Division Two win at Keighley on 11 March 1990.

KEIGHLEY COUGARS ran up their highest-ever score with an 86-0 Division Three 14-try home defeat of Nottingham City on 1 November.

The Cougars equalled their new record with an 86-0 home defeat of Highfield in the Challenge Cup first round on 31 January when they scored 15 tries.

Before last season, Keighley's biggest victory was a 70-0 12-try Division Three home defeat of Nottingham on 23 February 1992.

HUNSLET broke a club record that had stood for 96 years with their 76-4 Division Three win at Nottingham City on 21 February when they scored 16 tries.

The old record of 75-5 produced 21 tries at home to non-League Broughton Recreation in the first-ever round of the Challenge Cup on 20 March 1897.

CHORLEY BOROUGH gained a club record victory but also suffered their biggest defeat.

They ran up their highest score with a 57-20 Division Three home defeat of Nottingham City on 28 March. The 10-try victory beat the 46-12 Division Two home win over Runcorn Highfield on 1 January 1990 when they scored eight tries.

Borough's record defeat came with a 78-6 Division Three loss at Keighley Cougars on 21 February when they conceded 15 tries. Their previous biggest defeat was 66-16 in a Division Two match on 18 February 1990 at Oldham, who scored 12 tries.

SALFORD conceded a club record score when they lost 70-6 at Wigan, who scored 12 tries in the Division One match on 14 March.

The previous record was Castleford's 10-try 65-0 Division One home victory on 1 April 1990.

LEIGH suffered a club record defeat with their 64-9 Division One loss at St. Helens on 6 January 1993.

The previous highest score against Leigh was when they lost 60-8 at Salford in a Summer League competition on 25 May 1940.

Leigh conceded 12 tries against St. Helens compared with the 14 at Salford.

SWINTON suffered a club record 78-0 defeat at home to Wigan in the Lancashire Cup second round on 29 September.

The 14-try thrashing beat the 76-3, 18-try League defeat at Huddersfield on 20 April 1946 and the 76-16, 14-try reversal at Castleford on 6 March 1988.

MILESTONES . . .

SHAUN EDWARDS of Wigan scored the 200th try of his career during the season, including a double century for the club.

At the end of the season, Edwards's total was 232 made up of 211 for Wigan and 21 in representative matches, including 14 Test touchdowns for Great Britain.

The half back swept past his overall double century with a record 10 in Wigan's 78-0 Lancashire Cup second round win away to Swinton on 29 September.

It equalled the Wigan match record, was also a County Cup record and, playing at scrum half, the most by a non-winger in any match.

Edwards scored his 200th try for Wigan in the 42-0 Division One win at Hull on 17 February.

In addition to his 10-try feat, Edwards has thrice scored four tries in a match for Wigan and five other hat-tricks.

He was the game's top tryscorer in 1991-92 with 40, second last season with 46 and has finished in the top 10 on three other occasions.

The former schoolboy international signed for Wigan on his 17th birthday, 17 October 1983, and made his debut at stand off in a 30-13 John Player Trophy first round home defeat of York on 6 November 1983.

Edwards's season-by-season totals are as follows:

	App	Tries
Wigan		
1983-84	24	6
1984-85	34	11
1985-86	33+3	14 + GB Under-21s 1t
1986-87	41	24 + Britain 2t
1987-88	32+2	17 + GB 2t, Lancs 2t
1988-89	31+1	15 + Britain 3t*
1989-90	32+1	25 + Britain 1t
1990-91	33+1	16 + Britain 3t
1991-92	37	40
1992-93	44	43 + Britain 3t
Totals		
Wigan	341+8	211
Britain	*27+4	15*
Britain U-21s........	4	1
Lancashire	3+1	2
Chairman's XIII.....	1	0
1992 tour..............	4	3 (Not inc 1t in 5+1 Tests)

GRAND TOTALS 380+13 232

● 1988 tour: Played in only one match, the Test against Papua New Guinea, which is included in his Great Britain total.

*Includes one try and an appearance against a World XIII which was not a Test match.

GREG AUSTIN scored his 100th career try for Halifax in a 40-6 Stones Bitter Championship home defeat of Widnes on 4 April.

His total remained at 100 until the end of the season when he moved to Keighley Cougars after 89 appearances for Halifax, including one as a substitute.

Halifax signed Austin from Hull K.R. and the Australian made a tryscoring debut as a substitute at Bramley in a 56-8 Division Two win on 23 September 1990.

He was in the centre a week later for his full debut in a 26-18 home League win over Ryedale-York.

He equalled the Division Two match record with six for Halifax in a 66-26 home defeat of Trafford Borough on 7 April 1991.

Austin twice scored five tries in a match for Halifax, four on another occasion plus five hat-tricks.

He has finished in the top 10 tries list for the last four seasons and totalled 81 tries with other British clubs.

Formerly with North Sydney, he began his British career at Rochdale Hornets in September 1985 and scored 11 tries for them before moving to Salford a year later.

He totalled 25 tries in two seasons at Salford, joined Australian club Manly for a year and then signed for Hull K.R. in September 1989.

The Australian scored 38 tries in his one full season for Rovers and another seven before joining Halifax. Rovers had released Austin from their overseas quota to make way for New Zealand international forward James Goulding.

Austin's season-by-season totals for Halifax were as follows:

	App	Tries
1990-91	29+1	40
1991-92	33	33
1992-93	26	27
Totals	**88+1**	**100**

DEAN BELL of Wigan scored his 100th try in British club Rugby League during the season.

The New Zealander's total at the end of the season was 111 made up of 96 for Wigan, four Leeds and 11 Carlisle.

They have come in a total of 282 matches, including six substitute appearances, since he first arrived in England over 10 years ago.

Bell notched up his century with a try in Wigan's 48-18 Division One home defeat of Hull K.R. on 29 November.

A former Manukau player, Bell made his English debut in the centre for Carlisle at home to Wigan in a Division One match on 22 August 1982 when they lost 7-10.

He played 23 matches for Carlisle before joining Leeds the following season, making a tryscoring debut at centre in a 12-6 John Player Special second round home defeat of Hull K.R. on 20 November 1983.

Bell played 22 matches in his one season at Leeds and then had two years with Australian club Eastern Suburbs in the Sydney League.

Wigan brought him back to England two years later and he scored a try playing on the wing in a 35-0 Division One win at Leigh on 7 September 1986.

Bell's most prolific tryscoring season was his first for Wigan when he scored 22 tries. He has scored two hat-tricks for Wigan and one for Carlisle.

He took over the captaincy of Wigan early in 1991-92.

His season-by-season totals are as follows:

	App	Tries
Carlisle		
1982-83	23	11
Leeds		
1983-84	22	4
Wigan		
1986-87	42	22
1987-88	18+2	10
1988-89	31+2	15
1989-90	33	10
1990-91	36+1	11
1991-92	32+1	13
1992-93	39	15
Totals		
Carlisle................	23	11
Leeds.................	22	4
Wigan	231+6	96
GRAND TOTALS	**276+6**	**111**

ANDY CURRIER of Widnes reached a century of tries for the club with a hat-trick in the 32-30 Division One defeat at Sheffield Eagles on 22 November.

The centre's club total at the end of the season was 112 in 240 appearances, including 12 as substitute.

He holds the joint Widnes match record of five tries against Featherstone Rovers on 25 September 1988. Playing in the centre, he also kicked seven goals for a joint club record 34 points.

Formerly with Halton Hornets amateurs, Currier made a tryscoring debut for Widnes as a substitute in a 28-4 Division One home defeat of Salford on 18 September 1983.

He made his full debut on the wing when Widnes lost 21-4 in a Division One match at Featherstone Rovers on 4 December 1983.

In addition to his record five-try feat, Currier has scored four tries in a match once and two other hat-tricks.

His most prolific season was 1990-91 when 23 tries put him 10th in the try chart, the only time he has finished in the top 10.

Currier's season-by-season try totals for Widnes are as follows:

	App	Tries
1983-84	2+5	2
1984-85	33+1	17
1985-86	9+3	2
1986-87	4+1	1
1987-88	16+1	11
1988-89	41	18
1989-90	27	13
1990-91	40+1	23
1991-92	29	9
1992-93	27	16
Totals	**228+12**	**112**

PAUL EASTWOOD of Hull scored his 100th try for the club with one in the 26-16 John Smiths Yorkshire Cup second round home defeat of Leeds on 23 September.

The Great Britain Test winger's club total at the end of the season was 110 tries in 265 appearances, including eight as a substitute.

A former Hullensians RU player, Eastwood made his debut for Hull as a substitute in a 22-10 Division One win at Oldham on 3 February 1985.

His full debut followed on 29 March 1985 when Hull won 17-14 at home to Wigan in a Division One match.

Eastwood's only hat-trick for Hull was in a 48-0 Division One home defeat of Barrow in 1989-90 when he also kicked eight goals for a 28-point haul.

His best season's total was 22 tries in 1989-90 and he has yet to finish in the top 10.

Eastwood has also scored 19 tries in representative matches, including seven Test touchdowns for a career total of 129.

His season-by-season totals for Hull are as follows:

	App	Tries
1984-85	8+3	2
1985-86	24+3	11
1986-87	39	19
1987-88	33	13
1988-89	28	7
1989-90	31+1	22
1990-91	33	11
1991-92	32	14
1992-93	29+1	11
Totals	**257+8**	**110**

VINCE GRIBBIN of Whitehaven scored his 100th try for the club with the only one in an 8-20 Silk Cut Challenge Cup home defeat by Widnes on 31 January.

He had reached his century in representative and other club matches with a try in the 23-2 Division Three home defeat of Dewsbury on 15 November.

The centre or winger finished the season with a career total of 119, including 114 for Whitehaven.

Gribbin holds the Whitehaven records for most tries in a match and in a season.

Playing in the centre, he set the match figure with six in a 64-0 Regal Trophy first round home defeat of Doncaster on 18 November 1984, which is also still a joint record for the competition.

Gribbin broke Whitehaven's season record in the last match of 1991-92. Needing three tries to beat the old figure, he raced in for five on the wing to finish with a total of 31.

It gave him his highest placing of fifth in the try chart, Gribbin's only other top 10 finish being sixth with 27 in 1984-85.

He has achieved one other five-try feat plus three hat-tricks.

A former Hensingham amateur, Gribbin scored two tries and five goals on his left wing debut in a 25-16 Division Two win at Hunslet on 10 October 1982.

He had a four-match spell on loan to Salford in 1985-86, scoring three tries before fading out of the game for three seasons.

Gribbin's season-by-season try totals are as follows:

	App	Tries	
Whitehaven			
1982-83	25+1	11	
1983-84	29	8	
1984-85	22	25	+ Britain 1t, GB Under-21s 1t
1985-86	4	1	
1989-90	6+4	2	
1990-91	18	14	
1991-92	27	31	
1992-93	20+2	22	
Salford			
1985-86	4	3	
Totals			
Whitehaven	151+7	114	
Salford	4	3	
Britain	1	1	
GB Under-21s	1+1	1	
Cumbria	0+1	0	
GRAND TOTALS	**157+9**	**119**	

ALAN HUNTE of St. Helens passed a career century of tries during the season. The winger's total at the end of the season was 114, made up of 103 for St. Helens, one for Wakefield Trinity and 10 in representative matches, including three Test touchdowns for Great Britain.

Hunte reached his 100th club and representative try with the first two in the 41-6 Division One home defeat of Wigan on 27 December.

His St. Helens century came with the first of two tries in the 42-8 Division One home defeat of Leeds on 4 April.

Hunte's most prolific season was last term when he scored 30 tries to finish in the top 10 for a second time.

A former Eastmoor (Wakefield) junior, Hunte made his senior debut at centre for Wakefield Trinity in a 38-14 Division One defeat at Castleford on 22 January 1989.

He scored a try in one other match as a substitute for Trinity before signing for St. Helens in a then record deal for a junior player of more than £50,000.

The fee was held in trust to enable him to be vice-captain of the Great Britain Youth squad to tour Australia that year.

Hunte scored two tries on his debut for St. Helens, playing right wing in a 58-12 Division One home defeat of Oldham on 1 March 1989.

His eight hat-tricks, all for St. Helens, include two four-try feats.

Hunte's season-by-season totals are as follows:

	App	Tries
Wakefield T.		
1988-89	1+1	1

	App	Tries	
St. Helens			
1988-89	8	4	
1989-90	35	21	+ GB Under-21s 1t
1990-91	32	26	
1991-92	31	24	+ Britain 1t
1992-93	34	28	+ Britain 2t
Totals			
Wakefield T.	1+1	1	
St. Helens	140	103	
Great Britain	4	3	
England...............	1	0	
GB Under-21s.......	2	1	
1992 tour	8+1	6	
GRAND TOTALS	**156+2**	**114**	

PAUL MEDLEY of Bradford Northern scored the 100th try of his career when he touched down in a 28-26 Stones Bitter Championship home defeat of Salford on 4 October.

The Test second row forward's total at the end of the season was 114 made up of 63 for Bradford, 44 Leeds, one Halifax and six in representative including two in Tests.

He has made 255 appearances, including 59 as substitute.

Medley's most prolific season was last term when he scored 18 for Bradford.

His best match feat is four tries for Bradford, also scoring a hat-trick each for Northern and Leeds.

A former Leeds Colt, Medley signed for Leeds as a 17-year-old in July 1984 and made a tryscoring debut in a 38-0 Division One home defeat of Workington Town on 13 January 1985.

He moved to Halifax with half back John Lyons four years later in an exchange deal that took Test forward Paul Dixon to Leeds.

Medley made his Halifax debut at Wigan on 15 January 1989 when they lost 26-12 in a Division One match.

Injuries restricted his appearances to only seven matches, including one as substitute, before he was transferred to Bradford.

He scored two tries on his Bradford debut in a 30-12 Division One home defeat of Hull on 3 September 1989.

His season-by-season totals are as follows:

	App	Tries	
Leeds			
1984-85	4+2	3	
1985-86	16+7	8	
1986-87	22+4	11	+ GB Under-21s 1t
1987-88	23+4	12	+ Britain 1t
1988-89	6+14	10	
Halifax			
1988-89	6+1	1	
Bradford N.			
1989-90	21+6	13	+ Yorks 1t
1990-91	35+2	17	
1991-92	31+1	15	
1992-93	23+15	18	

Totals

Leeds..................	71+31	44
Halifax.................	6+1	1
Bradford N.	110+24	63
Britain (Tests)	3+1	2
1988 tour	4	2 (Not inc. 1t in 1 Test app.)
GB Under-21s.......	2	1
Yorkshire	0+2	1

GRAND TOTALS 196+59 114

STEVE McGOWAN of Bradford Northern reached a century of club tries with his last touchdown of the season in a 50-8 Stones Bitter Championship home defeat of Sheffield Eagles on 4 April.

The centre's 100 tries have been scored in a total of 233 appearances, including seven as substitute.

His best match feat was a Regal Trophy record-equalling six tries in a 70-10 first round home defeat of Barrow on 8 November 1992. He has scored three other hat-tricks.

His highest season's total was 21 in 1988-89, but he has yet to finish in the top 10.

A former Leeds Colt, McGowan made his Bradford debut as a substitute in a 32-23 Division One defeat at Widnes on 4 April 1984. Four days later he was in the centre when Bradford lost 10-8 in a League match at Featherstone Rovers.

His season-by-season tryscoring record for Bradford — he has also kicked six goals — is as follows:

	App	Tries
1983-84	5+1	1
1984-85	32+2	14
1985-86	8+2	0
1986-87	0	0
1987-88	34	14
1988-89	34	21
1989-90	38	14
1990-91	20	5
1991-92	21+1	11
1992-93	34+1	20
Totals	**226+7**	**100**

PAUL NEWLOVE of Featherstone Rovers passed the 100-try career mark during the season, including a century for the club.

The centre's total at the end of the season was 136 made up of 122 for Rovers and 14 in representative matches, including five Test touchdowns for Great Britain.

Newlove scored his 100th career try with the last of three in Featherstone's 24-20 Division Two home defeat of Oldham on 13 December.

He reached his century for Featherstone with the first of two in a 42-12 League win at Swinton on 21 February.

Newlove became the first centre to total a half-century of tries in a season when he finished as top tryscorer last term with 52, including a club record 48.

Signed from local amateur club Travellers, Newlove made his Featherstone debut on the wing seven weeks after his 17th birthday in an 18-0 Yorkshire Cup tie defeat at Hull on 27 September 1988.

Newlove's best match feat is four tries and he has scored eight other hat-tricks, including one for Great Britain.

His season-by-season try and appearance totals are as follows:

	App	Tries	
Featherstone R.			
1988-89	30	18	+ GB Under-21s 1t
1989-90	30	18	+ GB Under-21s 1t, Yorks 2t
1990-91	23	13	
1991-92	32	25	+ GB 1t, GB Under-21s 2t
1992-93	35	48	+ GB 3t, England 1t
Totals			
Featherstone R.	150	122	
Britain	7+3	5	
England...............	1	1	
1992 tour	6+1	2	(Not inc 1t in 3+2 Tests)
Yorkshire	1	2	
GB Under-21s.......	8	4	

GRAND TOTALS 173+4 136

DARYL POWELL of Sheffield Eagles scored the 100th try of his career with one in the 16-14 Division One defeat at Leigh on 10 January.

His total of 101 at the end of the season was made up of a club record 98 tries plus three for Great Britain.

The former Redhill (Castleford) Under-19 amateur was the first player to sign for Sheffield when they were formed in 1984-85.

He made his professional debut at centre in their first match when they beat Rochdale Hornets 29-10 on 2 September 1984.

Powell has remained a regular first team player at centre, stand off and loose forward with a club record 266 appearances, including three as substitute.

He also holds the club record of most tries in a match with five against Mansfield Marksman on 2 January 1989.

He has scored three other hat-tricks, including one in the 1992 Divisional Premiership final defeat of Oldham, which earned him the Man of the Match award.

Powell's best season's tally for Sheffield is 28 in 1988-89 which was a club record until broken by Iva Ropati's 30 in 1991-92. It also earned him his only final top 10 tryscorers' position of fifth. His season-by-season totals are as follows:

	App	Tries	
Sheffield E.			
1984-85	29	5	
1985-86	31	9	
1986-87	28+1	8	
1987-88	32	9	
1988-89	30	28	
1989-90	33	16	
1990-91	29+1	7	
1991-92	26+1	13	+ Britain 1t
1992-93	25	3	+ Britain 1t
Totals			
Sheffield E.	263+3	98	
Britain	17+4	3	
1990 tour	5+1	0	(Not inc 1t in 4+1 Tests)
1992 tour	3	0	(Not inc 6 Tests)
Yorkshire	1	0	
GRAND TOTALS	289+8	101	

MARK PRESTON of Halifax scored the 100th try of his career with two in the 66-16 Silk Cut Challenge Cup first round home defeat of Carlisle on 31 January.

The winger's total at the end of the season was 108, with 50 for Halifax, 57 for Wigan and one for Lancashire.

A former Fylde RU club player who gained Lancashire and England 'B' honours, Preston signed for Wigan in 1988.

He made his debut in a 10-9 Division One win at St. Helens on 1 April 1988 and totalled eight tries in six appearances that season.

Halifax signed Preston for £60,000 in June 1991 and he made a tryscoring debut on 1 September that year in a 12-40 Division One home defeat by Featherstone Rovers.

Preston's most prolific tryscoring season was 1989-90 when he finished fourth in the try chart with 33. His only other top 10 finish was 1991-92 when he was 10th with 27.

He achieved two five-try feats and scored one other hat-trick at Wigan. His only hat-trick for Halifax came with four tries against Hull K.R.

Preston's season-by-season figures are as follows:

	App	Tries	
Wigan			
1987-88	6	8	
1988-89	24+2	15	
1989-90	41	32	+ Lancs 1t
1990-91	7+1	2	
Halifax			
1991-92	32	27	
1992-93	30	23	
Totals			
Wigan	78+3	57	
Halifax	62	50	
Lancashire	2	1	
GRAND TOTALS	142+3	108	

GARRY SCHOFIELD of Leeds scored his 100th career try for the club with one in the 13-4 Division One home defeat of Warrington on 2 October. His century was clocked up after 149 matches, including one as substitute.

At the end of the season, Schofield's try total was 109 in 174 matches, including one as substitute.

The former Hunslet Parkside junior began his professional career at Hull in 1983 before being transferred to Leeds for a then record £155,000 in October 1987.

Playing at centre, he scored two tries on his Leeds debut in a 29-25 home defeat against the touring Auckland side on 25 October 1987.

Schofield played mostly at centre in his first two seasons with Leeds before moving more permanently to stand off in the latter half of 1989-90.

He has achieved three four-try feats for Leeds plus another hat-trick.

Schofield's season-by-season figures for Leeds are as follows:

	App	Tries
1987-88	27	22
1988-89	30	20
1989-90	29	20
1990-91	30	20
1991-92	32+1	13
1992-93	25	14
Totals	173+1	109

OWEN SIMPSON of Featherstone Rovers scored the 100th try of his career with one in the 46-8 Stones Bitter Divisional Premiership home defeat of Ryedale-York on 25 April.

The winger's total at the end of the season was 101 made up of 69 in 92 matches for Rovers plus 32 in 38 matches, including one substitute appearance, for Keighley.

Simpson briefly held the Featherstone tries in a season record last term when two tries in the 60-0 Division Two home defeat of Bramley on 21 March took his total to 32. That beat Cyril Woolford's 31 but Simpson's centre partner, Paul Newlove, also reached 32 in the match and went on to finish with 48.

Simpson's 34 tries made him last season's third top tryscorer, the winger's second top 10 placing after finishing 10th with 24 in his first season.

A former Army RU player, Simpson made his senior Rugby League debut for Keighley as a substitute in a 29-6 Division Two defeat at Dewsbury on 10 September 1989.

Simpson was on the right wing three days later when he scored a try in Keighley's 31-24 League win at home to Whitehaven.

Featherstone signed Simpson 14 months later for £50,000 and he scored their only try on his debut in a 22-6 Division One home defeat by Castleford on 11 November 1990.

Simpson has scored three hat-tricks for both Keighley and Featherstone. His season-by-season totals are as follows:

	App	Tries
Keighley		
1989-90	30+1	24
1990-91	7	8
Featherstone R.		
1990-91	23	12
1991-92	36	23
1992-93	33	34
Totals		
Keighley	37+1	32
Featherstone R.	92	69
GRAND TOTALS	**129+1**	**101**

IAN THOMAS of Huddersfield scored his 100th career try for the club with one in the 18-12 Division Two home defeat of Bramley on 14 November.

The winger's total at the end of the season was 115 tries in 215 matches, including 11 as a substitute.

A former Great Britain Colts international, Thomas signed for his home town club from Huddersfield Supporters.

He made his first team debut on the wing in a 40-8 Division Two defeat at Barrow on 21 August 1983.

Thomas was in the centre when he achieved his best match feat of four tries in a 52-18 Division Two home defeat of Whitehaven on 23 December 1990. He has not scored any other hat-tricks.

Last season was his most prolific, with 21 tries, playing mostly on the wing.

His season-by-season totals are as follows:

	App	Tries
Huddersfield		
1983-84	11	4
1984-85	22	10
1985-86	21	10
1986-87	15+5	8
1987-88	18+1	8
1988-89	22	13
1989-90	17+1	7
1990-91	20+2	16
1991-92	24+2	18
1992-93	34	21
Totals	**204+11**	**115**

NEIL TURNER of Hull scored the 100th try of his career when he returned on loan to Doncaster and touched down in the 28-18 Division Three win at Barrow on 13 December.

He finished the season back at Hull with a career total of 103 tries made up of 30 for the Airlie Birds and 73 for Doncaster.

A former Wheatley Hills RU club player, Turner made his original debut for Doncaster as an unnamed trialist winger in an 11-14 home defeat against Fulham on 8 September 1985.

He was signed soon after and became an immediate success,

breaking the club record with 20 in his first season and equalling it in 1988-89 before Mark Roache went one better the following year.

Roache also overtook Turner's Doncaster career record, which stood at 72 when he left for Hull in December 1989.

But Turner still has a share in the Doncaster match record with four against Keighley on 22 October 1989.

He scored three other hat-tricks for Doncaster and has achieved the feat once with Hull, for whom he made a two-try debut in a 28-24 home defeat of Leigh on 17 December 1989.

Turner's season-by-season totals are as follows:

	App	Tries
Doncaster		
1985-86	35	20
1986-87	32	12
1987-88	32+1	11
1988-89	30	20
1989-90	16	9
1992-93	2	1
Hull		
1989-90	17	12
1990-91	17+2	7
1991-92	22	8
1992-93	7	3
Totals		
Doncaster	147+1	73
Hull	63+2	30
GRAND TOTALS	**210+3**	**103**

MARK ASTON of Sheffield Eagles became the first player to score a career total of 1,000 points for the club with the last of six goals in a 28-12 Stones Bitter Championship home defeat of Hull K.R. on 15 November.

Aston's total at the end of the season was 1,073 from 26 tries and a club record 499 goals, including 29 drop goals, in 197 appearances, including four as substitute.

The half back and occasional loose forward holds a number of other Sheffield records, most of them set in 1988-89 when he became one of the few players to score in every match in a season.

He finished that term with club records of 148 goals and 307 points, including six tries and 13 drop goals.

Aston shares with Roy Rafferty the Eagles' goals in a match record with 12 in a 72-14 Divisional Premiership second round home defeat of Keighley Cougars on 25 April 1992.

Signed from Selby pub team The Gaffers, Aston made his Sheffield debut at scrum half in a 36-6 Division Two home defeat of Huddersfield Barracudas on 30 March 1986.

He had a two-match on-loan spell with Bramley in 1987-88, without scoring, and has since been a regular in Sheffield's team.

His season-by-season record for Sheffield is as follows:

RECORDS

	App	T	G	DG	Pts
1985-86	7	0	0	0	0
1986-87	22	7	26	0	80
1987-88	16+2	0	0	0	0
1988-89	36	6	135	13	307
1989-90	29	1	94	5	197
1990-91	22	6	58	2	142
1991-92	31+1	2	98	6	210
1992-93	30+1	4	59	3	137
Totals	**193+4**	**26**	**470**	**29**	**1,073**

STEVE CARROLL of Bramley scored his 1,000th career point for the club with the first of five goals in the 18-18 Division Two home draw against Carlisle on 22 November.

The half back's total at the end of the season was 1,016 from 54 tries and 430 goals, including 54 drop goals, in 330 matches, including 17 as substitute.

A former Batley Boys player, Carroll made his debut for Bramley as an 18-year-old, kicking a goal in an 8-17 Division Two home defeat by Blackpool on 11 March 1979.

His best points-scoring season was 1991-92 when he broke the Bramley goals and points record, while becoming one of the few players to score in every match throughout a season.

Carroll set the Bramley records with 288 points from five tries and 138 goals, including eight drop goals, in 33 appearances at stand off and scrum half.

Surprisingly, Carroll has never scored more than 18 points in a match with a best goals tally of eight and has scored only one hat-trick of tries.

His season-by-season totals for Bramley are as follows:

	App	T	G	DG	Pts
1978-79	1	0	1	0	2
1979-80	1	0	0	0	0
1980-81	0	0	0	0	0
1981-82	8+6	1	0	0	3
1982-83	35+1	5	4	5	28
1983-84	33+2	4	0	0	25
1984-85	22+2	5	0	11	31
1985-86	34+3	6	0	0	24
1986-87	24+2	6	0	0	24
1987-88	31	4	12	4	44
1988-89	25+1	8	77	1	187
1989-90	29	7	68	11	175
1990-91	28	3	66	5	149
1991-92	33	5	130	8	288
1992-93	9	0	18	0	36
Totals	**313+17**	**54**	**376**	**54**	**1,016**

JONATHAN DAVIES passed the 1,000 points mark for Widnes with seven goals in the 46-4 Regal Trophy first round home defeat of Ryedale-York on 8 November.

At the end of his fifth season the former Wales RU international stand off's club total was 1,192 from 80 tries and 442 goals, including four drop goals, in 134 matches, including eight as a substitute. The utility back holds the Widnes record for points in a season with 342 from 30 tries and 112 goals, including two drop goals, in 1990-91.

He shares the match record of 34 points with Andy Currier, scoring four tries and nine goals in the 70-6 Lancashire Cup first round win at Whitehaven on 26 August 1990.

The former Llanelli RU player signed for Widnes on 5 January 1989 on a four-year contract worth £150,000, making his debut as a substitute in a 50-8 Division One home defeat of Salford 10 days later.

Davies made one other substitute appearance before making his full debut at stand off, when he scored a try and five goals in a 38-14 home League defeat of Oldham on 5 February 1989. His totals for Widnes are as follows:

	App	T	G	Pts
1988-89	12+4	7	48(1)	123
1989-90	29+1	16	98	260
1990-91	32+2	30	112(2)	342
1991-92	24	13	74(1)	199
1992-93	29+1	14	106	268
Totals	**126+8**	**80**	**438(4)**	**1,192**

() denotes drop goal included in total.

MIKE FLETCHER of Hull K.R. passed the 500 goals mark in club and representative matches during the season.

He scored his 500th goal in all matches with one in a 6-19 Division One home defeat by Sheffield Eagles on 27 September. The total included four for Great Britain Under-21s, plus one for a Humberside XIII against Papua New Guinea. His 500th goal for Rovers came with the fifth of seven in a 30-1 home League defeat of Leigh on 11 October.

Fletcher's total at the end of the season was 564, including 559 for Rovers.

The centre or full back holds two club records for a season with 199 goals and 450 points, including 13 tries, in 1989-90 when he headed the two scoring lists.

During that season he also equalled a club match record with 14 goals against Whitehaven and has kicked 10 goals on two other occasions.

The former Rovers Colt made his first team debut at full back on 23 April 1985 when they lost 0-32 at home to Widnes. His season-by-season totals are as follows:

	App	Goals	
Hull K.R.			
1984-85	1	0	
1985-86	3+7	4	
1986-87	5+5	2	
1987-88	28	90	+ GB Under-21s 4g
1988-89	20+1	63	
1989-90	35	199	
1990-91	23+5	59	
1991-92	30	71	+ Humberside 1g
1992-93	29	71	
Totals			
Hull K.R.	174+18	559	
GB Under-21s	2	4	
Humberside	1	1	
GRAND TOTALS	**177+18**	**564**	

148

LEADING SCORERS 1895-1975

	TRIES	GOALS	POINTS
1895-96	Hurst (Oldham) 28	Lorimer (Manningham).....35	Cooper (Bradford).......... 106
			Lorimer (Manningham)... 106
1896-97	Hannah (Hunslet)............19	Goldthorpe (Hunslet)........26	Rigg (Halifax)............... 112
		Sharpe (Liversedge)..........26	
1897-98	Hoskins (Salford)..............30	Goldthorpe (Hunslet)........66	Goldthorpe (Hunslet)...... 135
1898-99	Williams (Oldham) 39	Goldthorpe (Hunslet)........67	Jaques (Hull)................ 169
1899-00	Williams (Oldham) 36	Cooper (Bradford)............39	Williams (Oldham) 108
1900-01	Williams (Oldham) 47	Goldthorpe (Hunslet)........44	Williams (Oldham) 141
1901-02	Wilson (Broughton R.) 38	James (Broughton R.).......75	Lomas (Salford) 172
1902-03	Evans (Leeds).................27	Goldthorpe (Hunslet)........48	Davies (Batley) 136
1903-04	Hogg (Broughton R.) 34	Lomas (Salford) 66	Lomas (Salford) 222
1904-05	Dechan (Bradford)...........31	Ferguson (Oldham)...........50	Lomas (Salford) 146
1905-06	Leytham (Wigan) 40	Ferguson (Oldham)...........49	Leytham (Wigan) 160
1906-07	Eccles (Halifax)...............41	Lomas (Salford) 86	Lomas (Salford) 280
1907-08	Leytham (Wigan) 44	Goldthorpe (Hunslet)...... 101	Goldthorpe (Hunslet)...... 217
1908-09	Miller (Wigan) 49	Lomas (Salford) 88	Lomas (Salford) 272
	Williams (Halifax) 49		
1909-10	Leytham (Wigan) 48	Carmichael (Hull K.R.) 78	Leytham (Wigan) 232
1910-11	Kitchen (Huddersfield) 40	Carmichael (Hull K.R.) .. 129	Carmichael (Hull K.R.) .. 261
	Rosenfeld (Huddersfield) 40		
	Miller (Wigan) 40		
1911-12	Rosenfeld (Huddersfield) 78	Carmichael (Hull K.R.) .. 127	Carmichael (Hull K.R.) .. 254
1912-13	Rosenfeld (Huddersfield) 56	Carmichael (Hull K.R.) 93	Thomas (Wigan)............ 198
1913-14	Rosenfeld (Huddersfield) 80	Holland (Huddersfield) ... 131	Holland (Huddersfield) ... 268
1914-15	Rosenfeld (Huddersfield) 56	Gronow (Huddersfield) 136	Gronow (Huddersfield) 284
● Competitive matches suspended during war years			
1918-19	Francis (Hull)...................25	Kennedy (Hull) 54	Kennedy (Hull) 135
1919-20	Moorhouse (Huddersfield)....39	Gronow (Huddersfield) 148	Gronow (Huddersfield) 332
1920-21	Stone (Hull) 41	Kennedy (Hull) 108	Kennedy (Hull) 264
1921-22	Farrar (Oldham)...............49	Sullivan (Wigan)............ 100	Farrar (Oldham)............ 213
1922-23	Ring (Wigan) 41	Sullivan (Wigan) 161	Sullivan (Wigan)............ 349
1923-24	Ring (Wigan) 49	Sullivan (Wigan) 158	Sullivan (Wigan)............ 319
1924-25	Ring (Wigan) 54	Sullivan (Wigan) 138	Sullivan (Wigan)............ 282
1925-26	Ring (Wigan) 63	Sullivan (Wigan) 131	Sullivan (Wigan)............ 274
1926-27	Ellaby (St. Helens)..........55	Sullivan (Wigan) 149	Sullivan (Wigan)............ 322
1927-28	Ellaby (St. Helens)..........37	Thompson (Leeds)......... 106	Thompson (Leeds)......... 233
1928-29	Brown (Wigan) 44	Sullivan (Wigan) 107	Sullivan (Wigan)............ 226
	Mills (Huddersfield) 44		
1929-30	Ellaby (St. Helens)..........39	Thompson (Leeds)......... 111	Thompson (Leeds)......... 243
1930-31	Harris, E. (Leeds) 58	Sullivan (Wigan) 133	Sullivan (Wigan)............ 278
1931-32	Mills (Huddersfield)........50	Sullivan (Wigan) 117	Sullivan (Wigan)............ 249
1932-33	Harris, E. (Leeds) 57	Sullivan (Wigan) 146	Sullivan (Wigan)............ 307
1933-34	Brown (Salford) 45	Sullivan (Wigan) 193	Sullivan (Wigan)............ 404
1934-35	Morley (Wigan) 49	Sullivan (Wigan) 165	Sullivan (Wigan)............ 348
1935-36	Harris, E. (Leeds) 63	Sullivan (Wigan) 117	Sullivan (Wigan)............ 246
1936-37	Harris, E. (Leeds) 40	Sullivan (Wigan) 120	Sullivan (Wigan)............ 258
1937-38	Harris, E. (Leeds) 45	Sullivan (Wigan) 135	Sullivan (Wigan)............ 285

	TRIES	GOALS	POINTS
1938-39	Markham (Huddersfield) 39	Sullivan (Wigan)............ 124	Risman (Salford) 267

● For the next six seasons emergency war-time competitions resulted in a reduction of matches and players were allowed to 'guest' for other clubs

	TRIES	GOALS	POINTS
1939-40	Batten (Hunslet)..............38	Hodgson (Swinton) 98	Hodgson (Swinton) 208
1940-41	Walters (Bradford N.)........32	Lockwood (Halifax) 70	Belshaw (Warrington)...... 174
1941-42	Francis (Barrow) 30	Lockwood (Halifax) 91	Lockwood (Halifax) 185
1942-43	Batten (Hunslet)..............24	Lockwood (Halifax) 65	Lockwood (Halifax) 136
1943-44	Lawrenson (Wigan)...........21	Horne (Barrow)...............57	Horne (Barrow)............. 144
1944-45	Batten (Bradford N.)........41	Stott (Wakefield T.)..........51	Stott (Wakefield T.) 129

● Normal peace-time rugby resumed

	TRIES	GOALS	POINTS
1945-46	Batten (Bradford N.)........35	Ledgard (Dewsbury).........89	Bawden (Huddersfield) 239
1946-47	Bevan (Warrington)...........48	Miller (Hull)................. 103	Bawden (Huddersfield) 243
1947-48	Bevan (Warrington)..........57	Ward (Wigan)............... 141	Ward (Wigan)................ 312
1948-49	Cooper (Huddersfield) 60	Ward (Wigan)............... 155	Ward (Wigan)................ 361
1949-50	Nordgren (Wigan)............57	Gee (Wigan) 133	Palin (Warrington) 290
		Palin (Warrington) 133	
1950-51	Bevan (Warrington)...........68	Cook (Leeds)................ 155	Cook (Leeds)................ 332
1951-52	Cooper (Huddersfield) 71	Ledgard (Leigh)............. 142	Horne (Barrow)............. 313
1952-53	Bevan (Warrington)...........72	Bath (Warrington) 170	Bath (Warrington) 379
1953-54	Bevan (Warrington)..........67	Metcalfe (St. Helens)...... 153	Metcalfe (St. Helens)...... 369
		Bath (Warrington) 153	
1954-55	Cooper (Huddersfield) 66	Ledgard (Leigh)............. 178	Ledgard (Leigh)............. 374
1955-56	McLean (Bradford N.)......61	Ledgard (Leigh)............. 155	Bath (Warrington) 344
1956-57	Boston (Wigan) 60	Jones (Leeds)................ 194	Jones (Leeds)................ 496
1957-58	Sullivan (Wigan)..............50	Ganley (Oldham)............ 219	Ganley (Oldham)............ 453
1958-59	Vollenhoven (St. Helens) 62	Ganley (Oldham)............ 190	Griffiths (Wigan) 394
1959-60	Vollenhoven (St. Helens) 54	Rhodes (St. Helens) 171	Fox (Wakefield T.).......... 453
		Fox (Wakefield T.).......... 171	
1960-61	Vollenhoven (St. Helens) 59	Rhodes (St. Helens) 145	Rhodes (St. Helens) 338
1961-62	Boston (Wigan) 51	Fox (Wakefield T.).......... 183	Fox (Wakefield T.).......... 456
1962-63	Glastonbury (Work'ton T.) ...41	Coslett (St. Helens)........ 156	Coslett (St. Helens) 321
1963-64	Stopford (Swinton)...........45	Coslett (St. Helens)........ 138	Fox (Wakefield T.).......... 313
1964-65	Lake (Wigan)..................40	Kellett (Hull K.R.)......... 150	Killeen (St. Helens) 360
1965-66	Killeen (St. Helens) 32	Killeen (St. Helens) 120	Killeen (St. Helens) 336
	Lake (Wigan)..................32		
1966-67	Young (Hull K.R.) 34	Risman (Leeds)............. 163	Killeen (St. Helens) 353
	Howe (Castleford).............34		
1967-68	Millward (Hull K.R.)........38	Risman (Leeds)............. 154	Risman (Leeds)............. 332
1968-69	Francis (Wigan)...............40	Risman (Leeds)............. 165	Risman (Leeds)............. 345
1969-70	Atkinson (Leeds)..............38	Tyrer (Wigan) 167	Tyrer (Wigan) 385
1970-71	Haigh (Leeds).................40	Coslett (St. Helens)........ 183	Coslett (St. Helens)........ 375
1971-72	Atkinson (Leeds).............36	Coslett (St. Helens)........ 214	Watkins (Salford) 473
	Lamb (Bradford N.).........36		
1972-73	Atkinson (Leeds)..............39	Watkins (Salford) 221	Watkins (Salford) 493
1973-74	Fielding (Salford) 49	Watkins (Salford) 183	Watkins (Salford) 438
1974-75	Dunn (Hull K.R.) 42	Fox (Hull K.R.)............. 146	Fox (Hull K.R.)............. 333
1975-76	Richards (Salford)............37	Watkins (Salford) 175	Watkins (Salford) 385

LEADING SCORERS 1976-92

TRIES

1976-77
Stuart Wright (Widnes) 31
Bruce Burton (Castleford).....................................29
David Smith (Leeds)..28
Keith Fielding (Salford).......................................27
Ged Dunn (Hull K.R.)..26
Eddie Cunningham (St. Helens).............................26
David Topliss (Wakefield T.)..................................24
Maurice Richards (Salford) 23
Roy Mathias (St. Helens) 23
David Barends (York) 22

1977-78
Stuart Wright (Widnes) 33
Keith Fielding (Salford).......................................31
Eddie Cunningham (St. Helens)..............................30
John Bevan (Warrington) 30
Steve Fenton (Castleford) 30
Green Vigo (Wigan)...29
Peter Glynn (St. Helens).......................................28
David Smith (Leeds)..28
Terry Morgan (York) 27
Bruce Burton (Castleford).....................................27

1978-79
Steve Hartley (Hull K.R.) 35
Stuart Wright (Widnes) 28
David Barends (Bradford N.)..................................25
Phil Lowe (Hull K.R.) 25
Paul Prendiville (Hull)..25
Keith Fielding (Salford).......................................24
David Redfearn (Bradford N.).................................23
Roy Mathias (St. Helens) 22
Graham Bray (Hull)..21
Keiron O'Loughlin (Wigan)...................................21
Clive Sullivan (Hull K.R.)....................................21

1979-80
Keith Fielding (Salford).......................................30
Steve Hubbard (Hull K.R.) 30
Geoff Munro (Oldham)...29
Ian Ball (Barrow) 27
Keith Bentley (Widnes)..27
Peter Glynn (St. Helens).......................................27
Roy Mathias (St. Helens) 27
John Bevan (Warrington) 26
David Redfearn (Bradford N.).................................26
David Smith (Leeds)..24

1980-81
John Crossley (York)...35
Terry Richardson (Castleford)................................28
Steve Hubbard (Hull K.R.) 25
Steve Hartley (Hull K.R.) 23
Paul McDermott (York)..23

Ian Slater (Huddersfield)......................................23
Des Drummond (Leigh) 20
Ian Ball (Barrow) 19
John Bevan (Warrington) 19
Peter Cramp (Huddersfield)...................................19
Gary Hyde (Castleford)..19
Denis Ramsdale (Wigan)......................................19

1981-82
John Jones (Workington T.) 31
Des Drummond (Leigh) 26
John Basnett (Widnes)...26
Ray Ashton (Oldham) 26
Mick Morgan (Carlisle)..25
Steve Hartley (Hull K.R.) 23
Lynn Hopkins (Workington T.) 23
Terry Day (Hull) 23
Steve Evans (Hull) 22
David Hobbs (Featherstone R.) 21
David Moll (Keighley)...21

1982-83
Bob Eccles (Warrington) 37
Steve Evans (Hull) 28
John Crossley (Fulham) 27
Tommy David (Cardiff C.) 26
David Topliss (Hull)...24
Hussein M'Barki (Fulham) 23
Gary Hyde (Castleford)..22
Paul McDermott (York)..22
James Leuluai (Hull)...21
Phil Ford (Warrington)..20
Garry Clark (Hull K.R.) 20

1983-84
Garry Schofield (Hull)...38
Joe Lydon (Widnes)..28
Graham King (Hunslet) 28
John Woods (Leigh) 27
John Basnett (Widnes)...26
Carl Gibson (Batley)...26
Steve Herbert (Barrow)..25
Graham Steadman (York) 25
Gary Prohm (Hull K.R.)..25
Garry Clark (Hull K.R.) 24

1984-85
Ellery Hanley (Bradford N.) 55
Gary Prohm (Hull K.R.)..45
Henderson Gill (Wigan)..34
Barry Ledger (St. Helens) 30
Mal Meninga (St. Helens) 28
Vince Gribbin (Whitehaven) 27
Carl Gibson (Batley)...26
Garry Peacham (Carlisle)......................................25
Ged Byrne (Salford)..25
Steve Evans (Hull) 24
John Ferguson (Wigan) 24

1985-86

Steve Halliwell (Leigh) 49
Ellery Hanley (Wigan).......................................38
Peter Lister (Bramley).......................................34
John Henderson (Leigh) 31
Tommy Frodsham (Blackpool B.).................30
Phil Fox (Leigh) 29
Stewart Williams (Barrow)..............................27
Brian Garrity (Runcorn H.) 24
Carl Gibson (Leeds)...23
David Beck (Workington T.)............................23

1986-87

Ellery Hanley (Wigan).......................................63
Garry Schofield (Hull).....................................37
Henderson Gill (Wigan)..................................32
Derek Bate (Swinton).......................................31
Phil Ford (Bradford N.)....................................30
John Henderson (Leigh) 27
Shaun Edwards (Wigan) 26
Brian Johnson (Warrington) 25
Joe Lydon (Wigan)...24
Brian Dunn (Rochdale H.) 23
Barry Ledger (St. Helens) 23
Kevin McCormack (St. Helens) 23

1987-88

Martin Offiah (Widnes) 44
Ellery Hanley (Wigan).......................................36
Garry Schofield (Leeds) 25
Carl Gibson (Leeds)...24
Andy Goodway (Wigan) 23
Kevin Pape (Carlisle) 23
Shaun Edwards (Wigan) 21
Des Foy (Oldham) 21
Peter Smith (Featherstone R.) 21
Chris Bibb (Featherstone R.)...........................20
Mark Conway (Wakefield T.) 20
Mark Elia (St. Helens) 20
Les Quirk (St. Helens) 20

1988-89

Martin Offiah (Widnes) 60
Barry Ledger (Leigh)..34
Derek Bate (Swinton).......................................32
Ellery Hanley (Wigan).......................................29
Peter Lister (Bramley).......................................28
Daryl Powell (Sheffield E.) 28
Peter Lewis (Bramley)......................................26
Les Quirk (St. Helens) 24
Grant Anderson (Castleford) 24
Paul Burns (Barrow) 24

1989-90

Martin Offiah (Widnes) 45
Greg Austin (Hull K.R.)...................................38
Anthony Sullivan (Hull K.R.) 35
Mark Preston (Wigan)......................................33
Gerald Cordle (Bradford N.) 32
Steve Larder (Castleford) 29
Paul Lord (Oldham) 29
Shaun Edwards (Wigan) 26
Andy Goodway (Wigan)...................................26
John Cogger (Oldham) 24
St. John Ellis (Castleford) 24
Wilf George (Halifax).......................................24
Mark Lord (Rochdale H.) 24
Owen Simpson (Keighley) 24

1990-91

Martin Offiah (Widnes) 49
Greg Austin (Halifax).......................................47
Martin Wood (Halifax) 31
Adrian Hadley (Salford)...................................31
Jonathan Davies (Widnes) 30
Ellery Hanley (Wigan).......................................29
Les Quirk (St. Helens) 26
Alan Hunte (St. Helens) 26
Garry Schofield (Leeds) 25
Graham Steadman (Castleford)........................23
Andy Currier (Widnes).....................................23
John Devereux (Widnes)...................................23

1991-92

Shaun Edwards (Wigan) 40
John Devereux (Widnes)...................................35
Iva Ropati (Oldham) 33
Greg Austin (Halifax).......................................33
Vince Gribbin (Whitehaven) 31
Graham Steadman (Castleford)........................31
Martin Offiah (Wigan)......................................30
David Myers (Wigan)..29
Paul Newlove (Featherstone R.) 28
Mark Preston (Halifax).....................................27

GOALS
(including drop goals)

1976-77

Geoff "Sammy" Lloyd (Castleford) 163
Steve Quinn (Featherstone R.)............................ 152
Geoff Pimblett (St. Helens)................................. 152
Steve Hesford (Warrington) 132
Iain MacCorquodale (Workington T.) 128
David Watkins (Salford)..................................... 125
Nigel Stephenson (Dewsbury) 106
George Fairbairn (Wigan).................................. 105
Ray Dutton (Widnes)... 97
John Woods (Leigh) 90

1977-78

Geoff Pimblett (St. Helens) 178
Steve Hesford (Warrington) 158
John Woods (Leigh) 149
Iain MacCorquodale (Workington T.) 138
Paul Woods (Widnes) 122
David Watkins (Salford) 110
Keith Mumby (Bradford N.) 107
Geoff "Sammy" Lloyd (Castleford) 104
Neil Fox (Bradford N.) 95
Willie Oulton (Leeds) 80

1978-79

Geoff "Sammy" Lloyd (Hull) 172
Steve Hesford (Warrington) 170
Mick Burke (Widnes) 140
Iain MacCorquodale (Workington T.) 114
Geoff Pimblett (St. Helens) 105
Graham Beale (Keighley) 96
John Woods (Leigh) 96
Jimmy Birts (Halifax) 86
George Fairbairn (Wigan) 86
Paul Norton (Castleford) 82

1979-80

Steve Quinn (Featherstone R.) 163
Steve Hubbard (Hull K.R.) 138
Steve Rule (Salford) 134
Steve Hesford (Warrington) 128
Mick Burke (Widnes) 127
Ian Ball (Barrow) 119
Steve Diamond (Wakefield T.) 116
Eric Fitzsimons (Oldham) 108
Mick Parrish (Hunslet) 98
Jimmy Birts (Halifax) 97

1980-81

Steve Hesford (Warrington) 147
Steve Quinn (Featherstone R.) 123
Steve Diamond (Wakefield T.) 112
Mick Burke (Widnes) 110
Steve Hubbard (Hull K.R.) 109
Ian Ball (Barrow) 104
Jimmy Birts (Halifax) 100
Graham Beale (Keighley) 97
Mick Parrish (Oldham) 95
George Fairbairn (Wigan) 94

1981-82

Lynn Hopkins (Workington T.) 190
George Fairbairn (Hull K.R.) 168
Mick Parrish (Oldham) 164
John Woods (Leigh) 158
Steve Rule (Salford) 130
Kevin Dick (Leeds) 125
Steve Quinn (Featherstone R.) 120
Malcolm Agar (Halifax) 119
Lee Crooks (Hull) 118
Steve Hesford (Warrington) 116

1982-83

Steve Diamond (Fulham) 136
Eric Fitzsimons (Hunslet) 121
Lee Crooks (Hull) 120
Bob Beardmore (Castleford) 117
Steve Hesford (Warrington) 113
Steve Fenwick (Cardiff C.) 111
Ken Jones (Swinton) 110
Colin Whitfield (Wigan) 104
Shaun Kilner (Bramley) 104
Steve Quinn (Featherstone R.) 98

1983-84

Steve Hesford (Warrington) 142
Bob Beardmore (Castleford) 142
Lyn Hallett (Cardiff C.) 140
Eric Fitzsimons (Hunslet) 131
John Woods (Leigh) 124
Colin Whitfield (Wigan) 122
Ian Ball (Barrow) 104
Mick Parrish (Oldham) 101
Malcolm Agar (Halifax) 94
Steve Tickle (Barrow) 91

1984-85

Sean Day (St. Helens) 157
George Fairbairn (Hull K.R.) 141
Peter Wood (Runcorn H.) 126
Graham Steadman (York) 122
Clive Griffiths (Salford) 118
Mick Parrish (Oldham) 117
Garry Schofield (Hull) 105
David Creasser (Leeds) 102
Malcolm Agar (Halifax) 87
Ken Jones (Swinton) 87

1985-86

Chris Johnson (Leigh) 173
David Stephenson (Wigan) 128
David Noble (Doncaster) 118
Kevin Harcombe (Rochdale H.) 115
Shaun Kilner (Bramley) 110
John Dorahy (Hull K.R.) 101
John Woods (Bradford N.) 98
David Creasser (Leeds) 84
Dean Carroll (Carlisle) 83
Gary Smith (Workington T.) 83

1986-87

Paul Loughlin (St. Helens) 190
Paul Bishop (Warrington) 117
David Noble (Doncaster) 114
Colin Whitfield (Halifax) 109
Alan Platt (Hunslet) 102
Paul Topping (Swinton) 100
Chris Johnson (Leigh) 86
Martin Ketteridge (Castleford) 80
David Wood (Rochdale H.) 80
Steve Quinn (Featherstone R.) 77

1987-88

John Woods (Warrington)	152
Steve Quinn (Featherstone R.)	128
Kevin Harcombe (Wakefield T.)	116
Paul Loughlin (St. Helens)	114
Gary Pearce (Hull)	111
Mike Smith (Springfield B.)	98
David Stephenson (Leeds)	95
Mike Fletcher (Hull K.R.)	94
David Hobbs (Bradford N.)	83
Ken Jones (Salford)	79

1988-89

Mark Aston (Sheffield E.)	148
Martin Ketteridge (Castleford)	129
David Hobbs (Bradford N.)	118
Chris Johnson (Leigh)	117
Dean Marwood (Barrow)	115
Paul Loughlin (St. Helens)	113
David Noble (Doncaster)	110
John Woods (Warrington)	107
Andy Currier (Widnes)	107
Steve Turner (Rochdale H.)	104

1989-90

Mike Fletcher (Hull K.R.)	199
Paul Loughlin (St. Helens)	145
Duncan Platt (Oldham)	126
Colin Maskill (Leeds)	114
Mark Conway (Wakefield T.)	107
David Hobbs (Bradford N.)	104
Paul Eastwood (Hull)	101
Mark Aston (Sheffield E.)	99
Jonathan Davies (Widnes)	98
Steve Turner (Rochdale H.)	98

1990-91

Steve Kerry (Salford)	177
Frano Botica (Wigan)	126
Paul Eastwood (Hull)	119
Jonathan Davies (Widnes)	112
Simon Irving (Leeds)	99
Graham Sullivan (Ryedale-York)	94
Paul Loughlin (St. Helens)	94
Alan Platt (Halifax)	91
Barry Vickers (Carlisle)	88
Tim Lumb (Hunslet)	85

1991-92

Frano Botica (Wigan)	161
Steve Carroll (Bramley)	138
Deryck Fox (Featherstone R.)	115
Lee Crooks (Castleford)	113
David Hobbs (Bradford N.)	110
Chris Vasey (Dewsbury)	109
Paul Eastwood (Hull)	108
Steve Parrish (Batley)	106
Mark Aston (Sheffield E.)	104
Jonathan Davies (Widnes)	99

St. Helens centre Paul Loughlin, the League's top points-scorer in 1986-87.

DROP GOALS

1976-77	Nigel Stephenson (Dewsbury)	16
1977-78	Jim Fiddler (Bramley, Leigh)	10
1978-79	Norman Turley (Blackpool B.)	18
1979-80	Tony Dean (Hunslet)	18
1980-81	Arnold Walker (Whitehaven)	22
1981-82	Malcolm Agar (Halifax)	17
	Steve Donlan (Leigh)	17
1982-83	Harry Pinner (St. Helens)	13
1983-84	Lyn Hallett (Cardiff C.)	29
1984-85	Peter Wood (Runcorn H.)	28
1985-86	Paul Bishop (Warrington)	13
1986-87	Billy Platt (Mansfield M.)	18
1987-88	Wayne Parker (Hull K.R.)	15
1988-89	Gary Pearce (Hull)	16
1989-90	Paul Harkin (Bradford N.)	12
1990-91	Ray Ashton (Workington T.)	13
	Dean Carroll (Doncaster)	13
1991-92	Andy Ruane (Leigh)	17

POINTS

1976-77	Geoff "Sammy" Lloyd (Castleford)	341
1977-78	Geoff Pimblett (St. Helens)	381
1978-79	Geoff "Sammy" Lloyd (Hull)	373
1979-80	Steve Quinn (Featherstone R.)	375
1980-81	Steve Hesford (Warrington)	310
1981-82	Lynn Hopkins (Workington T.)	446
1982-83	Steve Diamond (Fulham)	308
1983-84	John Woods (Leigh)	355
1984-85	Sean Day (St. Helens)	362
1985-86	Chris Johnson (Leigh)	400
1986-87	Paul Loughlin (St. Helens)	424
1987-88	John Woods (Warrington)	351
1988-89	Mark Aston (Sheffield E.)	307
1989-90	Mike Fletcher (Hull K.R.)	450
1990-91	Steve Kerry (Salford)	427
1991-92	Frano Botica (Wigan)	364

ALL-TIME RECORDS

Most goals in a match:
22 by Jim Sullivan (Wigan) v. Flimby & Fothergill (Challenge Cup), 14 February 1925

Most goals in a season:
DAVID WATKINS holds the record for most goals in a season with 221 — all for Salford — in 1972-73. Watkins played and scored a goal in every match that season as follows:

1972
Aug.	19	Leeds	(H)	5
	23	Featherstone R.	(A)	3
	26	Whitehaven	(A)	4
	28	Swinton	(H)	1
Sep.	1	Oldham	(LC) (H)	10
	9	Leeds	(A)	2
	15	Rochdale H.	(LC) (H)	11
	17	Leigh	(A)	6
	24	Barrow	(JP) (A)	4
	29	Huyton	(H)	10
Oct.	3	Oldham	(FT) (A)	4
	6	Wigan	(LC) (A)	4
	8	Blackpool B.	(A)	5
	13	Blackpool B.	(H)	8
	21	Swinton	(LCF)	5
Nov.	5	Huyton	(A)	8
	10	Rochdale H.	(H)	6
	17	Warrington	(A)	4
	19	New Zealand	(H)	10
	24	Dewsbury	(JP) (H)	4
	26	Workington T.	(H)	6
Dec.	1	Barrow	(H)	9
	10	Bradford N.	(JP) (H)	9
	13	Oldham	(A)	4
	15	Leigh	(H)	3
	24	Bradford N.	(A)	5
	26	Workington T.	(A)	3
	30	Hull K.R.	(JP) (A)	5
1973				
Jan.	3	Bradford N.	(H)	6
	7	Rochdale H.	(A)	2
	12	Featherstone R.	(H)	4
	28	Featherstone R.	(RL Cup) (A)	4
Feb.	2	Whitehaven	(H)	4
	11	Barrow	(A)	5
	23	St. Helens	(H)	3
Mar.	7	Widnes	(A)	3
	9	Dewsbury	(H)	3
	16	St. Helens	(A)	2
	24	Leeds	(JP Final)	2
	30	Warrington	(H)	1
Apr.	6	Widnes	(H)	4
	13	Oldham	(H)	3
	15	Dewsbury	(A)	2
	17	Wigan	(A)	3
	20	Swinton	(A)	7
	23	Wigan	(H)	3
	29	Rochdale H.	(top 16) (H)	2

	App	Goals
League	34	147
Lancs Cup	4	30
John Player	5	24
Tour match	1	10
RL Cup	1	4
Floodlit Cup	1	4
Top 16	1	2
Totals	**47**	**221**

Fastest goals century:
Four players share the record of scoring the fastest 100 goals from the start of a season in terms of number of matches played. They are Bernard Ganley, David Watkins, Steve Quinn and John Wasyliw, who achieved the century in 18 matches.

Ganley reached 100 goals on 16 November 1957, after playing 17 matches for Oldham and one for Great Britain.

Watkins scored his 100th goal on 17 November 1972, all for Salford.

Quinn scored his 100th goal on 16 December 1979, all for Featherstone Rovers.

Wasyliw equalled the record with his 100th goal for Keighley Cougars on 31 January 1993.

Most goals in a career:
JIM SULLIVAN holds the record for most goals in a career with 2,867 between 1921-22 and 1945-46. He scored a century of goals in every season after leaving Welsh Rugby Union for Wigan until the war interrupted the 1939-40 campaign. The Test full back played all of his club rugby for Wigan apart from war-time appearances with Bradford Northern, Dewsbury and Keighley.

Sullivan's total includes 441 in representative matches, including three tours of Australasia. These figures are accepted by the Record Keepers' Club following research by James Carter and Malcolm Bentley.

Most one-point drop goals in a match:
5 by Danny Wilson (Swinton) v. Hunslet (John Player Special), 6 November 1983
  Peter Wood (Runcorn H.) v.Batley, 21 October 1984
  Paul Bishop (Warrington) at Wigan (Premiership semi-final), 11 May 1986

Most one-point drop goals in a season:
29 by Lyn Hallett (Cardiff C.) 1983-84

Most one-point drop goals in a career:
97 by Norman Turley (Warrington, Runcorn H.,
  Swinton, Blackpool B., Rochdale H., Barrow,
  Workington T., Trafford B.,
  Whitehaven) 1974-91

155

Most tries in a match:
11 by George West (Hull K.R.) v Brookland Rovers
(Challenge Cup), 4 March 1905

Most tries in a career:
BRIAN BEVAN holds the record for most tries in a career
with 796 between 1946 and 1964. His season-by-season
record is:

1946-47	48
1947-48	57
1948-49	56
1949-50	33
1950-51	68
1951-52	51
1952-53	72
1953-54	67
1954-55	63
1955-56	57
1956-57	17
1957-58	46
1958-59	54
1959-60	40
1960-61	35
1961-62	15
1962-63	10
1963-64	7

Totals

Warrington	740
Blackpool Borough	17
Other Nationalities	26
Other representative matches	13
Grand Total	**796**

The Australian winger played his first game for
Warrington on 17 November 1945 and his last on 23 April
1962 before having two seasons at Blackpool Borough. His
last match for Borough was on 22 February 1964.

Most tries in a season:
ALBERT ROSENFELD holds the record for most tries
in a season with 80 — all for Huddersfield — in 1913-14.

Rosenfeld's match-by-match record:
1913

Sep.	6	York ....(A)	4
	8	Warrington .... (H)	2
	13	Leeds.................................. (H)	5
	20	Halifax .... (A)	1
	27	Batley..................................(A)	0
Oct.	4	Oldham .... (H)	2
	11	Rochdale H. ....(A)	0
	18	Bramley......................... (YC) (H)	2
	25	Dewsbury...........................(A)	4
Nov.	1	Halifax ....(YC) (A)	2
	8	Wigan ....(A)	1
	15	Dewsbury....................... (YC) (H)	3

	19	Bradford N. ....(H)	3
	22	Leeds...................................(A)	3
	29	Bradford N. ....(Halifax, YCF)	1
Dec.	3	Halifax ....(H)	3
	6	Hunslet ....(A)	2
	13	Rochdale H. ....(H)	3
	20	Hull K.R. ....(A)	2
	25	Hull.....................................(A)	1
	26	Wakefield T. ....(H)	3
	27	Hunslet ....(H)	0
1914			
Jan.	1	St. Helens .... (A)	0
	3	Warrington ....(A)	0
	10	York ....(H)	3
	17	Keighley ....(A)	2
	24	Dewsbury..............................(H)	1
	31	Batley..................................(H)	0
Feb.	7	Oldham .... (A)	0
	14	Bramley ....(H)	5
	21	Wigan ....(H)	3
	28	Swinton Park R. ....(RL Cup) (H)	7
Mar.	7	Wakefield T. ....(A)	2
	14	Hull K.R. ....(RL Cup) (A)	2
	18	Bramley ....(A)	3
	21	Widnes ....(RL Cup) (H)	0
	25	Keighley ....(H)	3
	28	Hull K.R. ....(H)	1
	30	Bradford N. ....(A)	1
Apr.	4	Hull...............(Leeds, RL Cup SF)	0
	11	Hull.................... (H) did not play	
	13	St. Helens .... (A)	0
	20	Hull.........(Play-off) (H) did not play	
	25	Salford ......(Leeds, Championship final)	0

	App	Tries
League	33	63
Yorks Cup	4	8
RL Cup	4	9
Play-off	1	0
Totals	**42**	**80**

Most points in a season:
LEWIS JONES holds the record for most points in a
season with 496 from 194 goals and 36 tries for Leeds and
representative teams in 1956-57.

Jones's match-by-match record:

For Leeds
1956

			G	T	Pts
Aug.	17	Halifax.....................(H)	3	0	6
	22	Bradford N. ....(A)	11	3	31
	25	Wigan.......................(A)	4	0	8
	27	Featherstone R. ....(H)	4	1	11
Sep.	1	Wakefield T. ....(YC) (A)	3	1	9
	8	Dewsbury ....(A)	6	0	12
	15	Warrington..................(H)	7	0	14
	22	Huddersfield ....(A)	3	0	6

	29	York...........................(H)	6	0	12
Oct.	6	Batley.........................(A)	4	2	14
	13	Australia ....(H)	Did not play		
	20	Hull K.R. .... (A)	Did not play		
	27	Wigan.......................(H)	2	0	4
Nov.	3	Hunslet......................(A)	1	0	2
	10	Barrow......................(H)	3	2	12
	17	Halifax......................(A)	4	0	8
	24	Keighley....................(H)	3	3	15
Dec.	1	Barrow.......................(A)	4	0	8
	8	Bramley.....................(A)	5	0	10
	15	Doncaster...................(H)	1	2	8
	22	Bradford N. ...(abandoned) (H)	1	1	5
	25	Batley........................(H)	8	1	19
	29	Keighley.....................(A)	3	0	6
1957					
Jan.	5	Hull ....(H)	5	2	16
	12	Warrington..................(A)	0	3	9
	19	St. Helens ....(H)	5	1	13
	26	Doncaster .... (A)	Did not play		
Feb.	2	Huddersfield ....(H)	6	0	12
	9	Wigan...........(RL Cup) (H)	2	1	7
	16	York.........................(A)	7	1	17
	23	Warrington.....(RL Cup) (A)	5	1	13
	27	Castleford...................(H)	4	1	11
Mar.	9	Halifax..........(RL Cup) (A)	5	0	10
	16	Wakefield T. ....(H)	5	1	13
	20	Bradford N. ....(H)	5	1	13
	23	Hull ....(A)	2	0	4
	30	Whitehaven ....(Odsal, RL Cup SF)	1	0	2
Apr.	3	Wakefield T. ....(A)	3	0	6
	6	St. Helens ....(A)	0	0	0
	12	Hull K.R. ....(H)	Did not play		
	13	Dewsbury....................(H)	6	2	18
	19	Hunslet.......................(H)	5	2	16
	20	Featherstone R. ....(A)	2	0	4
	22	Castleford .... (A)	2	0	4
	23	Bramley ....(H)	7	1	17
May	4	Oldham..........(Play-off) (A)	3	0	6
	11	Barrow .....(Wembley, RL Cup final)	0	0	0

Representative matches
For Great Britain:

Jan.	26	France ....(at Leeds)	9	1	21
Mar.	3	France ....(at Toulouse)	5	1	13
Apr.	10	France ....(at St. Helens)	7	1	17

For The Rest:

Oct.	3	Britain XIII .... (at Bradford)	4	0	8

For RL XIII:

Oct.	29	Australia ....(Leigh)	3	0	6

	App	G	T	Pts
League	36	147	30	384
RL Cup	5	13	2	32
Yorks Cup	1	3	1	9
Play-off	1	3	0	6
Representative.......................	5	28	3	65
Totals................................	**48**	**194**	**36**	**496**

Most points in a match:
53 (11t,10g) by George West (Hull K.R.) v. Brookland Rovers (RL Cup), 4 March 1905

Most points in a career:
NEIL FOX holds the record for most points in a career with 6,220 between 1956 and 1979. This total does not include points scored during a spell of club rugby in New Zealand.

Fox was a month short of his 17th birthday when he made his debut for Wakefield Trinity on 10 April 1956. Apart from a brief time at Bradford Northern, Fox had 19 seasons at Wakefield before moving to a succession of clubs in later years.

After a long career as an international centre Fox moved into the forwards and played his last professional match for Bradford in their opening fixture of the 1979-80 season, on 19 August. That match enabled him to join the elite few who have played first team rugby at 40 years of age.

Fox's season-by-season tally is as follows:

	G	T	Pts
1955-56...............................	6	0	12
1956-57...............................	54	10	138
1957-58...............................	124	32	344
1958-59...............................	148	28	380
1959-60...............................	171	37	453
1960-61...............................	94	20	248
1961-62...............................	183	30	456
1962 Tour			
Australasia..............................	85	19	227
South Africa...........................	19	4	50
1962-63...............................	125	14	292
1963-64...............................	125	21	313
1964-65...............................	121	13	281
1965-66...............................	98	11	229
1966-67...............................	144	16	336
1967-68...............................	98	18	250
1968-69...............................	95	9	217
1969-70...............................	17	5	49
1970-71...............................	110	12	256
1971-72...............................	84	6	186
1972-73...............................	138	8	300
1973-74...............................	62	8	148
1974-75...............................	146(1)	14	333
1975-76...............................	102(1)	4	215
1976-77...............................	79(1)	6	175
1977-78...............................	95(1)	9	216
1978-79...............................	50	4	112
1979-80...............................	2	0	4

A breakdown of Fox's club and representative totals is as follows:

157

	App	G	T	Pts
Wakefield T.	574	1,836	272	4,488
Bradford N.	70	85(1)	12	205
Hull K.R.	59	212(2)	16	470
York	13	42	2	90
Bramley.....................	23	73	6	164
Huddersfield..............	21	73(1)	5	160
Club Totals................	**760**	**2,321(4)**	**313**	**5,577**
Yorkshire	17	60	9	147
Britain v. Australia	8	26	3	61
New Zealand	4	11	1	25
France	17	56	10	142
Other representative				
games including tour	22	101	22	268
Representative Totals....	**68**	**254**	**45**	**643**
Grand Totals	**828**	**2,575(4)**	**358**	**6,220**

( ) Figures in brackets are one-point drop goals included in total.

Score-a-match:

The following players have appeared and scored in all of their club's matches in one season:

Jim Hoey (Widnes) 1932-33
Billy Langton (Hunslet) 1958-59
Stuart Ferguson (Leigh)............................... 1970-71
David Watkins (Salford)............................... 1972-73
David Watkins (Salford)............................... 1973-74
John Woods (Leigh) 1977-78
Steve Quinn (Featherstone R.)....................... 1979-80
Mick Parrish (Hunslet)................................ 1979-80
John Gorton (Swinton) 1980-81
Mick Parrish (Oldham)................................ 1981-82
Peter Wood (Runcorn H.) 1984-85
David Noble (Doncaster) 1986-87
Mark Aston (Sheffield E.) 1988-89
Mike Fletcher (Hull K.R.) 1989-90
Steve Carroll (Bramley)................................ 1991-92
Paul Bishop (Halifax)................................... 1992-93
John Wasyliw (Keighley C.)............................ 1992-93

Longest scoring run:

DAVID WATKINS holds the record for the longest scoring run, playing and scoring in 92 consecutive matches for Salford from 19 August 1972 to 25 April 1974. He totalled 403 goals, 41 tries and 929 points.

Longest run of appearances:

KEITH ELWELL holds the record for the longest run of appearances with one club with a total of 239 for Widnes. The consecutive run started at Wembley in the 1977 Challenge Cup final against Leeds on 7 May, and ended after he played in a Lancashire Cup tie at home to St. Helens on 5 September 1982. He was dropped for the match at Featherstone Rovers a week later. Although he went on as a substitute the record refers to full appearances only. Elwell played as a substitute in the next match and then made a full appearance before his run of all appearances ended at 242.

TEAM

Highest score:

Huddersfield 119 v. Swinton Park 2 (RL Cup)
.... 28 February 1914

Highest score away:

Nottingham C. 6 v. Hull K.R. 100 (Yorks. Cup played at Doncaster) 19 Aug 1990

Most points in all matches in a season:

1,436 by Leigh from 43 matches in 1985-86 as follows:
34 Division Two matches 1,156
 2 Lancashire Cup 54
 4 John Player Special Trophy 161
 3 RL Challenge Cup...................................... 65

Most League points in a season:

1,156 by Leigh from 34 Division Two matches in 1985-86.

Longest winning run:

29 by Wigan from February to October 1987, as follows: 20 Division One, 3 Premiership, 4 Lancashire Cup, 1 Charity Shield and 1 World Club Challenge.

Longest unbeaten run:

43 Cup and League matches, including two draws, by Huddersfield in 1914-19.

They were unbeaten in the last 38 matches of 1914-15 and after the interruption of the First World War won their next five competitive matches — four Yorkshire Cup ties in 1918-19 and the first League match of 1919-20.

Longest winning run in the League:

31 matches by Wigan. Last 8 matches of 1969-70 and first 23 of 1970-71.

● In 1978-79 Hull won all of their 26 Division Two matches, the only time a club has won all its League matches in one season.

Longest losing run:

61 Cup and League matches by Runcorn Highfield from January 1989 to February 1991. Made up of 55 Division Two, 2 Challenge Cup, 2 Regal Trophy and 2 Lancs Cup.

Longest run without a win:

75 Cup and League matches by Runcorn Highfield from October 1988 to March 1991. Made up of 67 Division Two, 3 Challenge Cup, 3 Regal Trophy and 2 Lancs Cup.

Longest League losing run and run without a win:

Included in the above.

● Only three teams have lost all their matches in a season: Liverpool City (1906-07)*, Runcorn Highfield (1989-90) and Nottingham City (1991-92).

*Liverpool drew a League match against Bramley but this was expunged from the records as the return fixture was cancelled.

Lance Todd Trophy winner Dean Bell lifts the Silk Cut Challenge Cup, Wigan's sixth successive Wembley victory.

CUPS

RUGBY LEAGUE CHALLENGE CUP

1993 Final

Wigan extended their record Wembley winning run to six consecutive Silk Cut Challenge Cup finals as Widnes back row forward Richard Eyres became only the second player to be sent off at the stadium.

Widnes made a mockery of the 1-5 odds on Wigan romping to another Wembley win, twice taking a six-point first-half lead before going down to a 20-14 defeat.

Ill discipline in the second period played a part in the Chemics' downfall, resulting in the 65th-minute dismissal of Great Britain forward Eyres for a late elbow to the head of former teammate Martin Offiah, Wigan's world record £440,000 recruit from Naughton Park.

Castleford referee Russell Smith, believed to be the youngest whistler in a Challenge Cup final, and in only his second season as a senior official, heeded the advice of his touch judges and issued the red card. Smith became only the second referee to dismiss a player in a Wembley final, emulating Huddersfield official Billy Thompson, who sent off Leeds centre Syd Hynes in the 1971 meeting with Leigh.

Many thought Widnes scrum half Bobby Goulding should also have been sent off for a high tackle on Wigan's teenage winger Jason Robinson, but he escaped with a warning. Goulding was later charged by the League's Board of Directors for misconduct and fined £1,000, half suspended for 12 months.

Although Widnes later decried claims of indiscipline, they committed seven of the eight penalties awarded for foul play.

Ironically, it was Eyres and Goulding who combined after seven minutes to open the scoring. Former Wigan half back Goulding prised open the defence to send Eyres storming through three tacklers for a surprise lead, Jonathan Davies adding a superb goal from near touch.

The outsiders' superiority lasted only four minutes as Great Britain prop Kelvin Skerrett powered his way through two tackles to touch down, despite the last-ditch effort of Widnes full back Stuart Spruce. Frano Botica's goal took his season's tally to 176 to equal the 34-year club record set by Fred Griffiths, and he went on to add another three successful shots.

Veteran Widnes prop Kurt Sorensen, at nearly 37 one of the oldest ever performers at Wembley, celebrated his first appearance in the Silk Cut Challenge Cup final by putting the Chemics ahead again with a 25-yard powerhouse charge through the attempted tackles of Botica and full back Steve Hampson. Davies again added the goal to re-establish a six-point lead.

Wigan trailed for only six minutes before Great Britain winger John Devereux showed a second attack of Wembley nerves, after earlier misfielding a high kick. In the 23rd minute of an exciting first half, the Welshman casually retrieved a Wigan kick through and decided to try to power his way past opposite number Offiah, only to lose the ball in the tackle.

Offiah, the continual target of Widnes boo-boys, scooped up the ball to feed skipper Dean Bell with a basketball pass for an open run to the line, allowing Botica to level the scores at 12-12.

As the half-time hooter went, referee Smith awarded Wigan a penalty, Botica hitting the target to give Wigan a fortunate interval lead.

Wigan made their customary powerful start to the second half, 30th-minute substitute Sam Panapa diving over for a try only two minutes after the restart, Bell providing the vital pass as part of his claim for the Lance Todd Trophy honour, only the second Kiwi to receive the individual award.

Wembley became a suffocating cauldron as the energy-sapping heat took its toll, Sorensen being replaced at half-time while Wigan brought on 17-year-old forward Andrew Farrell as a 55th-minute substitute, the Great Britain Academy skipper going on to become the youngest-ever winner at Wembley, not being 18 until 30 May.

Wales skipper Davies kicked a 49th-minute penalty goal to close the gap to six points, but Wigan survived the remaining half hour of tension and Widnes's ill discipline to extend their Silk Cut Challenge Cup winning run to 31 ties.

Bell, with his touchdown, try creation, powerful thrusts and general leadership, topped the voting for the Lance Todd Trophy. The New Zealander was challenged by clubmates Denis Betts and Phil Clarke, the trio forming an effective back row, although Bell reverted to centre in place of Joe Lydon after 30 minutes.

Having been the youngest finalist at 17½ in 1984, scrum half Shaun Edwards equalled two Challenge Cup records by making an eighth final appearance and collecting his seventh winners' medal. The British Lion used his experience to organise Wigan's midfield in impressive style.

The 77,684 capacity crowd — paying a record £1.98m — basked in the sunshine and warmed to the competitiveness of Widnes's challenge after their week-long fitness battle to put out their strongest side, flying over Brisbane Bronco full back Julien O'Neill on the Tuesday of Wembley week to fill the substitute back role.

Wigan heard the final whistle with more relief than in recent years as Australian John Monie became the first to coach four teams to Wembley success. As the celebrations of a fourth successive League-Cup double began, Wigan set their sights on the Stones Bitter Premiership and a first-ever Grand Slam of the five major trophies in the same season.

SILK CUT CHALLENGE CUP FINAL

1 May		Wembley
WIGAN 20		**WIDNES 14**
Steve Hampson	1.	Stuart Spruce
Jason Robinson	2.	John Devereux
Joe Lydon	3.	Andy Currier
Andrew Farrar	4.	Darren Wright
Martin Offiah	5.	David Myers
Frano Botica	6.	Jonathan Davies
Shaun Edwards	7.	Bobby Goulding
Kelvin Skerrett	8.	Kurt Sorensen
Martin Dermott	9.	Paul Hulme, Capt.
Andy Platt	10.	Harvey Howard
Denis Betts	11.	Richard Eyres
Phil Clarke	12.	Esene Faimalo
Dean Bell, Capt.	13.	David Hulme
Sam Panapa	14.	Julien O'Neill
Andrew Farrell	15.	Steve McCurrie

T: Skerrett, Bell, Panapa
G: Botica (4)
Substitutions:
Panapa for Lydon (30 min.)
Farrell for Skerrett (55 min.)
Half-time: 14-12
Referee: Russell Smith (Castleford)

T: Eyres, Sorensen
G: Davies (3)
Substitutions:
O'Neill for Faimalo (28 min.)
McCurrie for Currier (55 min.)
Attendance: 77,684
Receipts: £1,981,591

1993 Round by Round

In a three-tie preliminary round, Wigan started their bid for a sixth successive Wembley final by disposing of Hull 40-2 at Central Park, Test winger Martin Offiah returning from a five-day stay at a London clinic to score two tries, Frano Botica contributing 20 points with a try and eight goals. Widnes entertained Second Division Swinton and won 62-14 with a hat-trick of tries from Emosi Koloto and a 22-point haul from Jonathan Davies from two tries and seven goals. After visitors Blackpool Gladiators had built a shock 10-4 lead, Australian scrum half Glen Tomlinson inspired a spell of three tries in 12 minutes to give Batley a 20-10 success.

In the first round, Castleford visited Warrington in the televised tie, Challenge Cup deadline signing Andy Fisher receiving the Silk Cut Award for inspiring a 21-6 success, topping the tackle count and creating two tries. St. Helens powered back at Featherstone to score 20 match-winning points in the last half hour after trailing 16-4. The Colliers were awarded a last-minute penalty, but elected to take a tap rather than go for an equalising goal and lost 22-24. Only a try by Joe Lydon, from a dropped pass, separated Dewsbury and visitors Wigan, who led 6-0 at the break. Despite the Third Division side's valiant efforts, Wigan continued to pull away to win 20-4, the home side's late consolation being a Darren Rogers try. Welshman John Devereux scored two tries as Widnes overcame the mud at Whitehaven to register a 20-8 success.

Third Division pacesetters Workington Town refused to lie down at Bradford Northern, trailing only 16-14 at half-time before Northern finished 28-18 winners. Scrum half Tomlinson was outstanding as Batley won 20-6 at Chorley Borough, taking their tally of points in three meetings during the season to 102. Halifax winger John Bentley scored a hat-trick of tries in the runaway 66-16 victory over visitors Carlisle, with two tries each for Greg Austin and Mark Preston, including his 100th career

touchdown. First Division strugglers Hull K.R. took 30 minutes to break the Bramley defence before Dean Clark crashed over for the first of five tries in a 30-0 victory.

Nottingham City took a third-minute lead through a Tony Chappell drop goal, home side Huddersfield replying within two minutes en route to a 66-1 victory featuring 13 tries. Ryedale-York, going down 27-22 at Hunslet, rued a last-second touchdown by Graham Sullivan which was disallowed for offside. Rampant Keighley Cougars ran up a club record 86-0 win against lowly Highfield, Carlton Farrell opening the scoring after eight minutes. Leeds struggled to build a 16-6 half-time lead after Third Division visitors Barrow took a shock eighth-minute lead, the Loiners getting into their stride with a 22-point burst inside 15 minutes to pave the way for a 54-18 success.

Oldham scored three tries in each half as they disposed of London Crusaders 34-6 at the Watersheddings, Under-21 centre Gary Christie scoring twice. Doncaster's pack laid the foundations for a 13-6 half-time lead at Rochdale before the Red Rose side pulled clear with a Matt Calland hat-trick of tries to secure a 34-13 victory. Packman Darren Fritz, in his last match before a return to Australia, scored the try which put visitors Wakefield Trinity in front at Salford, a lead they never lost on the way to a 20-12 success. A potent mixture of sheer hard graft and inspired rugby took Sheffield Eagles to a 32-5 home triumph over Leigh, Australian Paul Carr taking the Silk Cut Award.

In the second round, Wigan entertained St. Helens in the televised tie, the Riversiders dominating the derby with tries from Dean Bell, Phil Clarke and Shaun Edwards in a 23-3 victory. Controversy surrounded Bradford Northern's 20-18 success at Wakefield, video recordings proving that Neil Summers' try was grounded short, plus Australian centre Peter Benson missing a series of easy kicks at goal. Sheffield Eagles slumped to their highest home defeat of the season with a 52-6 thrashing from Widnes, who ran in 10 tries, the contest being over after the first quarter with the Chemics leading 16-2. Third Division title contenders Keighley came close to a giant-killing act at Hull K.R. before going down 30-28. Only a dramatic last-second try from New Zealander Clark denied them a quarter-final place.

Castleford scrum half Mike Ford set up three of their six tries, scored by Graham Steadman, Tony Smith and Tony Morrison, as visitors Hunslet were beaten 34-16. Wingman Bentley notched a hat-trick of tries as Halifax disposed of Batley 50-20 in a Thrum Hall tie delayed by frost. Batley's former Halifax centre Jimmy Irvine was sent off. Silk Cut Award-winner Ellery Hanley scored four of Leeds' 13 tries in a 68-6 demolition of visitors Rochdale Hornets, Garry Schofield adding a hat-trick and teenage winger Paul Cook scoring two on his debut. Huddersfield ran in nine points while Oldham's centre Christie was in the sin bin, the Roughyeds rallying to lead 10-9 at the break before disposing of the visitors with a second-half burst to win 20-17.

The quarter-finals were hit by heavy snow. On a quagmire of a Hull K.R. pitch, Widnes led 4-0 at the interval, Stuart Spruce sliding over in the last minute. Never-say-die Rovers, inspired by prop Wayne Jackson, battled back and secured a replay with a try from makeshift winger Paul Fletcher. At Naughton Park, Rovers again belied their lowly position to go down only 16-11, after leading 5-2 at the break. Wigan stayed on the Wembley trail with a last-second drop goal from Joe Lydon, the first time they had been in the lead at snow-bound Halifax, the home side leading 14-6 with half an hour to go, before letting Wigan back into the game for a 19-18 success. Former Bath RU winger Jim Fallon took the Silk Cut Award with a two-try display which clinched a 12-8 Leeds victory in the home televised tie with Castleford. Oldham's hopes of a third Silk Cut semi-final in four years were dashed by a 42-4 home defeat by Bradford Northern in a postponed tie, the home side's only consolation being a Tommy Martyn try.

In the semi-finals, cash crisis club Widnes secured a money-spinning Wembley appearance by hammering Leeds 39-4 at Wigan. The Chemics reached Wembley for the first time in nine years led by half backs Jonathan Davies, scorer of 18 points, and Silk Cut Award-winner Bobby Goulding, who tormented the club he left under a cloud at the start of the season. At Elland Road, Leeds, Wigan took their unbeaten Silk Cut Challenge Cup run to 30 ties, reaching Wembley for the sixth successive season. A crowd of more than 20,000 saw the Riversiders beat Bradford Northern 15-6, with tries from Andrew Farrar and Silk Cut Award-winner Steve Hampson.

Wigan's Phil Clarke, an impressive second row pairing with Denis Betts.

1993 RESULTS

Preliminary Round

Batley	20	Blackpool G.	10
Widnes	62	Swinton	14
Wigan	40	Hull	2

First Round

Bradford N.	28	Workington T.	18
Chorley B.	6	Batley	20
Dewsbury	4	Wigan	20
Featherstone R.	22	St. Helens	24
Halifax	66	Carlisle	16
Huddersfield	66	Nottingham C.	1
Hull K.R.	30	Bramley	0
Hunslet	27	Ryedale-York	22
Keighley C.	86	Highfield	0
Leeds	54	Barrow	18
Oldham	34	London C.	6
Rochdale H.	34	Doncaster	13
Salford	12	Wakefield T.	20
Sheffield E.	32	Leigh	5
Warrington	6	Castleford	21
Whitehaven	8	Widnes	20

Second Round

Castleford	34	Hunslet	16
Halifax	50	Batley	20
Hull K.R.	30	Keighley C.	28
Leeds	68	Rochdale H.	6
Oldham	20	Huddersfield	17
Sheffield E.	6	Widnes	52
Wakefield T.	18	Bradford N.	20
Wigan	23	St. Helens	3

Third Round

Halifax	18	Wigan	19
Hull K.R.	4	Widnes	4
Leeds	12	Castleford	8
Oldham	4	Bradford N.	42

Replay

Widnes	16	Hull K.R.	11

Semi-Finals

Widnes	39	Leeds	4
(at Wigan)			
Wigan	15	Bradford N.	6
(at Elland Rd, Leeds)			

Final

Wigan	20	Widnes	14
(at Wembley)			

1993 Prizes

Preliminary Round ...	£2,650 each club
First Round	£2,650 to losers
Second Round	£3,950 to losers
Third Round	£6,275 to losers
Semi-Finals.............	£10,000 to losers
Runners-up.............	£19,000
Winners	£36,000
Total Prize Money	£190,000
Capital Development Fund	£150,000
Grand Total	£340,000

Wigan celebrate six Silk Cut Challenge Cup triumphs on the trot.

CHALLENGE CUP ROLL OF HONOUR

Year	Winners		Runners-up		Venue	Attendance	Receipts
1897	Batley	10	St. Helens	3	Leeds	13,492	£624.17.7
1898	Batley	7	Bradford	0	Leeds	27,941	£1,586.3.0
1899	Oldham	19	Hunslet	9	Manchester	15,763	£946.16.0
1900	Swinton	16	Salford	8	Manchester	17,864	£1,100.0.0
1901	Batley	6	Warrington	0	Leeds	29,563	£1,644.16.0
1902	Broughton R.	25	Salford	0	Rochdale	15,006	£846.11.0
1903	Halifax	7	Salford	0	Leeds	32,507	£1,834.8.6
1904	Halifax	8	Warrington	3	Salford	17,041	£936.5.6
1905	Warrington	6	Hull K.R.	0	Leeds	19,638	£1,271.18.0
1906	Bradford	5	Salford	0	Leeds	15,834	£920.0.0
1907	Warrington	17	Oldham	3	Broughton	18,500	£1,010.0.0
1908	Hunslet	14	Hull	0	Huddersfield	18,000	£903.0.0
1909	Wakefield T.	17	Hull	0	Leeds	23,587	£1,490.0.0
1910	Leeds	7	Hull	7	Huddersfield	19,413	£1,102.0.0
Replay	Leeds	26	Hull	12	Huddersfield	11,608	£657.0.0
1911	Broughton R.	4	Wigan	0	Salford	8,000	£376.0.0
1912	Dewsbury	8	Oldham	5	Leeds	15,271	£853.0.0
1913	Huddersfield	9	Warrington	5	Leeds	22,754	£1,446.9.6
1914	Hull	6	Wakefield T.	0	Halifax	19,000	£1,035.5.0
1915	Huddersfield	37	St. Helens	3	Oldham	8,000	£472.0.0
1920	Huddersfield	21	Wigan	10	Leeds	14,000	£1,936.0.0
1921	Leigh	13	Halifax	0	Broughton	25,000	£2,700.0.0
1922	Rochdale H.	10	Hull	9	Leeds	32,596	£2,964.0.0
1923	Leeds	28	Hull	3	Wakefield	29,335	£2,390.0.0
1924	Wigan	21	Oldham	4	Rochdale	41,831	£3,712.0.0
1925	Oldham	16	Hull K.R.	3	Leeds	28,335	£2,879.0.0
1926	Swinton	9	Oldham	3	Rochdale	27,000	£2,551.0.0
1927	Oldham	26	Swinton	7	Wigan	33,448	£3,170.0.0
1928	Swinton	5	Warrington	3	Wigan	33,909	£3,158.1.11
1929	Wigan	13	Dewsbury	2	Wembley	41,500	£5,614.0.0
1930	Widnes	10	St. Helens	3	Wembley	36,544	£3,102.0.0
1931	Halifax	22	York	8	Wembley	40,368	£3,908.0.0
1932	Leeds	11	Swinton	8	Wigan	29,000	£2,479.0.0
1933	Huddersfield	21	Warrington	17	Wembley	41,874	£6,465.0.0
1934	Hunslet	11	Widnes	5	Wembley	41,280	£6,686.0.0
1935	Castleford	11	Huddersfield	8	Wembley	39,000	£5,533.0.0
1936	Leeds	18	Warrington	2	Wembley	51,250	£7,070.0.0
1937	Widnes	18	Keighley	5	Wembley	47,699	£6,704.0.0
1938	Salford	7	Barrow	4	Wembley	51,243	£7,174.0.0
1939	Halifax	20	Salford	3	Wembley	55,453	£7,681.0.0
1940	*No competition*						
1941	Leeds	19	Halifax	2	Bradford	28,500	£1,703.0.0
1942	Leeds	15	Halifax	10	Bradford	15,250	£1,276.0.0
1943	Dewsbury	16	Leeds	9	Dewsbury	10,470	£823.0.0
	Dewsbury	0	Leeds	6	Leeds	16,000	£1,521.0.0
	Dewsbury won on aggregate 16-15						
1944	Bradford	0	Wigan	3	Wigan	22,000	£1,640.0.0
	Bradford	8	Wigan	0	Bradford	30,000	£2,200.0.0
	Bradford won on aggregate 8-3						
1945	Huddersfield	7	Bradford N.	4	Huddersfield	9,041	£1,184.3.7
	Huddersfield	6	Bradford N.	5	Bradford	17,500	£2,050.0.0
	Huddersfield won on aggregate 13-9						

Year	Winners		Runners-up		Venue	Attendance	Receipts
1946	Wakefield T.	13	Wigan	12	Wembley	54,730	£12,013.13.6
1947	Bradford N.	8	Leeds	4	Wembley	77,605	£17,434.5.0
1948	Wigan	8	Bradford N.	3	Wembley	91,465	£21,121.9.9
1949	Bradford N.	12	Halifax	0	Wembley	★95,050	£21,930.5.0
1950	Warrington	19	Widnes	0	Wembley	94,249	£24,782.13.0
1951	Wigan	10	Barrow	0	Wembley	94,262	£24,797.19.0
1952	Workington T.	18	Featherstone R.	10	Wembley	72,093	£22,374.2.0
1953	Huddersfield	15	St. Helens	10	Wembley	89,588	£30,865.12.3
1954	Warrington	4	Halifax	4	Wembley	81,841	£29,706.7.3
Replay	Warrington	8	Halifax	4	Bradford	102,569	£18,623.7.0
1955	Barrow	21	Workington T.	12	Wembley	66,513	£27,453.16.0
1956	St. Helens	13	Halifax	2	Wembley	79,341	£29,424.7.6
1957	Leeds	9	Barrow	7	Wembley	76,318	£32,671.14.3
1958	Wigan	13	Workington T.	9	Wembley	66,109	£33,175.17.6
1959	Wigan	30	Hull	13	Wembley	79,811	£35,718.19.9
1960	Wakefield T.	38	Hull	5	Wembley	79,773	£35,754.16.0
1961	St. Helens	12	Wigan	6	Wembley	94,672	£38,479.11.9
1962	Wakefield T.	12	Huddersfield	6	Wembley	81,263	£33,390.18.4
1963	Wakefield T.	25	Wigan	10	Wembley	84,492	£44,521.17.0
1964	Widnes	13	Hull K.R.	5	Wembley	84,488	£44,840.19.0
1965	Wigan	20	Hunslet	16	Wembley	89,016	£48,080.4.0
1966	St. Helens	21	Wigan	2	Wembley	★98,536	£50,409.0.0
1967	Featherstone R.	17	Barrow	12	Wembley	76,290	£53,465.14.0
1968	Leeds	11	Wakefield T.	10	Wembley	87,100	£56,171.16.6
1969	Castleford	11	Salford	6	Wembley	★97,939	£58,848.1.0
1970	Castleford	7	Wigan	2	Wembley	95,255	£89,262.2.0
1971	Leigh	24	Leeds	7	Wembley	85,514	£84,452.15
1972	St. Helens	16	Leeds	13	Wembley	89,495	£86,414.30
1973	Featherstone R.	33	Bradford N.	14	Wembley	72,395	£125,826.40
1974	Warrington	24	Featherstone R.	9	Wembley	77,400	£132,021.05
1975	Widnes	14	Warrington	7	Wembley	85,098	£140,684.45
1976	St. Helens	20	Widnes	5	Wembley	89,982	£190,129.40
1977	Leeds	16	Widnes	7	Wembley	80,871	£241,488.00
1978	Leeds	14	St. Helens	12	Wembley	★96,000	£330,575.00
1979	Widnes	12	Wakefield T.	3	Wembley	94,218	£383,157.00
1980	Hull K.R.	10	Hull	5	Wembley	★95,000	£448,202.90
1981	Widnes	18	Hull K.R.	9	Wembley	92,496	£591,117.00
1982	Hull	14	Widnes	14	Wembley	92,147	£684,500.00
Replay	Hull	18	Widnes	9	Elland Rd., L'ds	41,171	£180,525.00
1983	Featherstone R.	14	Hull	12	Wembley	84,969	£655,510.00
1984	Widnes	19	Wigan	6	Wembley	80,116	£686,171.00
1985	Wigan	28	Hull	24	Wembley	★97,801	£760,322.00
1986	Castleford	15	Hull K.R.	14	Wembley	82,134	£806,676.00
1987	Halifax	19	St. Helens	18	Wembley	91,267	£1,009,206.00
1988	Wigan	32	Halifax	12	Wembley	★94,273	£1,102,247.00
1989	Wigan	27	St. Helens	0	Wembley	★78,000	£1,121,293.00
1990	Wigan	36	Warrington	14	Wembley	★77,729	£1,360,000.00
1991	Wigan	13	St. Helens	8	Wembley	75,532	£1,610,447.00
1992	Wigan	28	Castleford	12	Wembley	77,286	£1,877,564.00
1993	Wigan	20	Widnes	14	Wembley	★77,684	£1,981,591.00

★Indicates a capacity attendance, the limit being fixed annually taking into account variable factors.

RUGBY LEAGUE CHALLENGE CUP ....
A 20-YEAR REVIEW
Initials are included where more than one player
shared a surname in a team in the same era.
1972-73
Featherstone R. 33 C. Kellett (8g); Coventry,
M. Smith (1t) (Hartley 1t), Newlove (2t),
K. Kellett; Mason, Nash (1g); Tonks, Bridges,
Farrar (1t), Rhodes (Hollis), Thompson, Stone
Bradford N. 14 Tees (4g); Lamb, Stockwell,
Watson, D. Redfearn (1t); Blacker (Treasure),
Seabourne; Hogan, Dunn, Earl (Long), Joyce,
W. Pattinson, Fearnley (1t)
Referee: M.J. Naughton (Widnes)
1973-74
Warrington 24 Whitehead (7g); M. Philbin,
Noonan, Whittle, Bevan; Murphy (2g) (Pickup),
Gordon; D. Chisnall, Ashcroft (1t), Brady
(Wanbon), Wright, Nicholas (1t), B. Philbin
Featherstone R. 9 Box (3g); Dyas, M. Smith,
Hartley, Bray; Newlove (1t), Nash; Tonks,
Bridges, Harris, Rhodes (Busfield), Thompson
(Stone), Bell
Referee: S. Shepherd (Oldham)
1974-75
Widnes 14 Dutton (5g, 1dg); A. Prescott, George,
Aspey, Anderson; Hughes, Bowden; Mills (1t),
Elwell, Sheridan, Foran, Adams, Laughton
Warrington 7 Whitehead (2g); M. Philbin,
Noonan, Reynolds (W. Briggs), Bevan (1t);
Whittle, Gordon; D. Chisnall, Ashcroft, Wanbon,
Conroy, Martyn (Nicholas), B. Philbin
Referee: P. Geraghty (York)
1975-76
St. Helens 20 G. Pimblett (3g, 2dg); L. Jones,
Cunningham (1t), Noonan, Mathias; Benyon
(Glynn 2t), Heaton (1t); Mantle (James),
A. Karalius, Coslett, Nicholls, E. Chisnall, Hull
Widnes 5 Dutton (2g); A. Prescott (D. O'Neill),
Hughes, George, Jenkins; Eckersley, Bowden;
Nelson, Elwell (1dg), Wood, Foran (Sheridan),
Adams, Laughton
Referee: R. Moore (Wakefield)
1976-77
Leeds 16 Murrell; Alan Smith (D. Smith),
Hague, Dyl (1t), Atkinson (1t); Holmes,
Dick (1t, 3g, 1dg); Harrison, Ward, Pitchford,
Eccles, Cookson, Fearnley (Dickinson)
Widnes 7 Dutton (2g); S. Wright (George),
Aspey (1t), Eckersley, D. O'Neill; Hughes,
Bowden; Ramsey, Elwell, Mills, Dearden
(Foran), Adams, Laughton
Referee: V. Moss (Manchester)

1977-78
Leeds 14 Oulton (1g); D. Smith (1t), Hague, Dyl,
Atkinson (1t); Holmes (1dg), J. Sanderson (Dick);
Harrison (Dickinson), Ward (2dg), Pitchford,
Cookson (1t), Eccles, Crane
St. Helens 12 G. Pimblett (3g); L. Jones,
Noonan, Glynn, Mathias; Francis (1t),
K. Gwilliam; D. Chisnall, Liptrot (1t), James,
Nicholls, Cunningham, Pinner
Referee: W.H. Thompson (Huddersfield)
1978-79
Widnes 12 Eckersley (1dg); S. Wright (1t),
Aspey, George (Hull), Burke (2g); Hughes (1t),
Bowden; Mills, Elwell (1dg), Shaw, Adams,
Dearden (M. O'Neill), Laughton
Wakefield T. 3 Sheard; Fletcher (1t), K. Smith,
Diamond, Juliff; Topliss, Lampkowski; Burke,
McCurrie, Skerrett, Ashurst, Keith Rayne, Idle
Referee: J.E. Jackson (Pudsey)
1979-80
Hull K.R. 10 Hall; Hubbard (1t, 3g) (Hogan),
M. Smith, Hartley, Sullivan; Millward (1dg),
Agar; Holdstock, Watkinson, Lockwood, Lowe,
Rose (Millington), Casey
Hull 5 Woods; Bray, Walters, Wilby (1t),
Prendiville; Newlove (Hancock), Pickerill;
Tindall, Wileman, Stone (Farrar), Birdsall,
Lloyd (1g), Norton
Referee: G.F. Lindop (Wakefield)
1980-81
Widnes 18 Burke (1t, 4g); S. Wright, George (1t),
Cunningham (J. Myler), Bentley; Hughes,
Gregory (1t); M. O'Neill (Shaw), Elwell,
Lockwood, L. Gorley, E. Prescott, Adams (1dg)
Hull K.R. 9 Hall; Hubbard (3g), M. Smith,
Hogan, Muscroft; Hartley, Harkin; Holdstock
(Millington), Watkinson, Crooks (Proctor), Lowe,
Burton (1t), Casey
Referee: D.G. Kershaw (Easingwold)
1981-82
Hull 14 Kemble; O'Hara (1t), Day, S. Evans,
Prendiville; Topliss, Harkin; Skerrett, Wileman,
Stone, Crane (Crooks), Lloyd (4g), Norton (1t)
Widnes 14 Burke (1g) (A. Myler); S. Wright (1t),
Keiron O'Loughlin, Cunningham (2t), Basnett;
Hughes, Gregory (1g); M. O'Neill, Elwell (1dg),
Lockwood (S. O'Neill), L. Gorley, E. Prescott,
Adams
Referee: G.F. Lindop (Wakefield)
Replay
Hull 18 Kemble (1t); Sullivan, Leuluai, S. Evans,
Prendiville; Topliss (2t), Dean; Tindall, Duke,
Stone, Skerrett, Crooks (1t, 3g), Norton (Crane)

Widnes 9 Burke (3g); S. Wright (1t), Keiron O'Loughlin, Cunningham, Basnett; Hughes, Gregory; M. O'Neill, Elwell, Lockwood, L. Gorley, E. Prescott, Adams
Referee: G.F. Lindop (Wakefield)
1982-83
Featherstone R. 14 N. Barker; Marsden, Quinn (4g), Gilbert (Lyman), K. Kellett; A. Banks, Hudson; Gibbins, Handscombe, Hankins, D. Hobbs (2t), Slatter (Siddall), Smith
Hull 12 Kemble; O'Hara, S. Evans, Leuluai (1t), Prendiville; Topliss, Harkin (Day) (Crane); Skerrett, Bridges, Stone, Rose, Crooks (1t, 3g), Norton
Referee: M.R. Whitfield (Widnes)
1983-84
Widnes 19 Burke (3g); S. Wright, Hughes (D. Hulme), Lydon (2t), Basnett; Keiron O'Loughlin (1t), Gregory; S. O'Neill (1dg), Elwell, K. Tamati, L. Gorley, M. O'Neill (Whitfield), Adams
Wigan 6 Edwards; Ramsdale, Stephenson, Whitfield (1g) (Elvin), Gill; Cannon, Stephens; Hemsley (1t), H. Tamati, Case (Juliff), West, Scott, Pendlebury
Referee: W.H. Thompson (Huddersfield)
1984-85
Wigan 28 Edwards (1t); Ferguson (2t), Stephenson (1g), Donlan, Gill (1t, 3g); Kenny (1t), M. Ford; Courtney, Kiss, Case (Campbell), West, Dunn, Potter
Hull 24 Kemble; James (1t), S. Evans (1t), Leuluai (2t), O'Hara (Schofield); Ah Kuoi, Sterling; Crooks (2g), Patrick, Puckering (Divorty 1t), Muggleton, Rose, Norton
Referee: R. Campbell (Widnes)
1985-86
Castleford 15 Lord (Roockley); Plange, Marchant (1t), Hyde, Sandy (1t); Joyner, R. Beardmore (1t, 1dg); Ward, K. Beardmore (Horton), Johnson, England, Ketteridge (1g), French
Hull K.R. 14 Fairbairn; Clark, M. Smith, Prohm (2t), Laws; Dorahy (1g), Harkin; P. Johnston, Watkinson, Ema, Kelly (G. Smith), Des Harrison (Lydiat 1t), Miller
Referee: R. Whitfield (Widnes)
1986-87
Halifax 19 Eadie (1t); Wilson, Whitfield (3g), Rix, George (1t); C. Anderson (Juliff), Stephens; Beevers (James), McCallion (1t), Neller, Dixon, Scott, Pendlebury (1dg)

St. Helens 18 Veivers; Ledger, Loughlin (1t, 3g), Elia (1t), McCormack; Clark, Holding; Burke, Liptrot, Fieldhouse, Platt, Haggerty (Round 1t), Arkwright
Referee: J. Holdsworth (Kippax)
1987-88
Wigan 32 Lydon (1t, 1g); T. Iro (1t), K. Iro (2t), Bell (1t), Gill (1t); Edwards (Byrne), Gregory (1g); Case, Kiss, Shelford, Goodway, Potter (Wane), Hanley (1t)
Halifax 12 Eadie; Meredith, T. Anderson (1t), Wilkinson, Whitfield (2g); Grogan, Robinson (Fairbank); James (1t), McCallion, Neller, Holliday (Scott), Dixon, Pendlebury
Referee: G.F. Lindop (Wakefield)
1988-89
Wigan 27 Hampson (1t); T. Iro, K. Iro (2t), Bell, Lydon (3g); Edwards, Gregory (1t, 1dg); Lucas, Kiss (Betts), Shelford, Platt, Potter (Goodway), Hanley (1t)
St. Helens 0 Connolly; O'Connor, Veivers, Loughlin (Bloor), Quirk; Cooper, Holding; Burke, Groves, Forber, Dwyer (Evans), Haggerty, Vautin
Referee: R. Tennant (Castleford)
1989-90
Wigan 36 Hampson; Lydon (6g), K. Iro (2t), Bell, Preston (2t) (Gildart); Edwards, Gregory; Shelford, Dermott (Goulding), Platt, Betts (1t), Goodway, Hanley (1t)
Warrington 14 Lyon (1t); Drummond, Mercer, Darbyshire (1g), Forster; Crompton, Bishop (2g) (McGinty); Burke, D. Mann, Harmon, Jackson (Thomas), Sanderson, Gregory (1t)
Referee: J. Holdsworth (Kippax)
1990-91
Wigan 13 Hampson; Myers (1t), K. Iro, Bell, Botica (1t, 2g); Edwards, Gregory (1dg); Lucas, Dermott (Goulding), Platt, Betts, Clarke (Goodway), Hanley
St. Helens 8 Veivers (Connolly); Hunte (1t), T. Ropati, Loughlin, Quirk; Griffiths, Bishop (2g); Neill (Groves), Dwyer, Ward, Harrison, G. Mann, Cooper
Referee: J. Smith (Halifax)
1991-92
Wigan 28 Lydon (2dg); Botica (5g), Bell, Miles, Offiah (2t); Edwards (1t), Gregory; Skerrett, Dermott, Platt, Betts, McGinty (Hampson 1t) (Cowie), Clarke
Castleford 12 Steadman; Wray, Ellis, Blackmore (1t), Nelson; Anderson (Smith), Ford; Crooks (Sampson), Southernwood, England (1t), Bradley, Ketteridge (2g), Nikau
Referee: R. Whitfield (Widnes)

RUGBY LEAGUE CHALLENGE CUP FINAL PLAYERS' REGISTER
The following is an index of players who have appeared in the Rugby League Challenge Cup final over the last 20 seasons. It also includes the pre-1973-74 record of any listed player. W — winners, L — losers, D — draw. Substitute appearances in lower case letters. The year denotes the second half of the season. ★ denotes replay.

ADAMS, Mick: Widnes 75W, 76L, 77L, 79W, 81W, 82DL★, 84W
AGAR, Allan: Hull K.R. 80W
AH KUOI, Fred: Hull 85L
ANDERSON, Chris: Widnes 75W; Halifax 87W
ANDERSON, Grant: Castleford 92L
ANDERSON, Tony: Halifax 88L
ARKWRIGHT, Chris: St. Helens 87L
ASHCROFT, Kevin: Leigh 71W; Warrington 74W, 75L
ASHURST, Bill: Wigan 70L; Wakefield T. 79L
ASPEY, Malcolm: Widnes 75W, 77L, 79W
ATKINSON, John: Leeds 68W, 71L, 72L, 77W, 78W

BANKS, Alan: Featherstone R. 83W
BARKER, Nigel: Featherstone R. 83W
BASNETT, John: Widnes 82DL★, 84W
BEARDMORE, Kevin: Castleford 86W
BEARDMORE, Bob: Castleford 86W
BEEVERS, Graham: Halifax 87W
BELL, Dean: Wigan 88W, 89W, 90W, 91W, 92W, 93W
BELL, Keith: Featherstone R. 74L
BENTLEY, Keith: Widnes 81W
BENYON, Billy: St. Helens 66W, 72W, 76W
BETTS, Denis: Wigan 89w, 90W, 91W, 92W, 93W
BEVAN, John: Warrington 74W, 75L
BIRDSALL, Charlie: Hull 80L
BISHOP, Paul: Warrington 90L; St. Helens 91L
BLACKMORE, Richard: Castleford 92L
BLOOR, Darren: St. Helens 89l
BOTICA, Frano: Wigan 91W, 92W, 93W
BOWDEN, Reg: Widnes 75W, 76L, 77L, 79W
BOX, Harold: Featherstone R. 74L
BRADLEY, Graeme: Castleford 92L
BRADY, Brian: Warrington 74W
BRAY, Graham: Featherstone R. 74L; Hull 80L
BRIDGES, John "Keith": Featherstone R. 73W, 74L; Hull 83L
BRIGGS, Wilf: Warrington 75l
BURKE, John: Leeds 71L; Wakefield T. 79L
BURKE, Mick: Widnes 79W, 81W, 82DL★, 84W
BURKE, Tony: St. Helens 87L, 89L; Warrington 90L
BURTON, Chris: Hull K.R. 81L
BUSFIELD, Dave: Featherstone R. 74l
BYRNE, Ged: Wigan 88w

CAMPBELL, Danny: Wigan 85w
CANNON, Mark: Wigan 84L
CASE, Brian: Wigan 84L, 85W, 88W
CASEY, Len: Hull K.R. 80W, 81L
CHISNALL, Dave: Warrington 74W, 75L; St. Helens 78L
CHISNALL, Eric: St. Helens 72W, 76W
CLARK, Brett: St. Helens 87L
CLARK, Garry: Hull K.R. 86L
CLARKE, Phil: Wigan 91W, 92W, 93W
CONNOLLY, Gary: St. Helens 89L, 91l
CONROY, Tom: Warrington 75L
COOKSON, Phil: Leeds 72L, 77W, 78W
COOPER, Shane: St. Helens 89L, 91L
COSLETT, Kel: St. Helens 72W, 76W

COURTNEY, Neil: Wigan 85W
COWIE, Neil: Wigan 92w
CRANE, Mick: Leeds 78W; Hull 82Dw★, 83l
CROMPTON, Martin: Warrington 90L
CROOKS, Lee: Hull 82dW★, 83L, 85L; Castleford 92L
CROOKS, Steve: Hull K.R. 81L
CUNNINGHAM, Eddie: St. Helens 76W, 78L; Widnes 81W, 82DL★
CURRIER, Andy: Widnes 93L

DARBYSHIRE, Paul: Warrington 90L
DAVIES, Jonathan: Widnes 93L
DAY, Terry: Hull 82D, 83l
DEAN, Tony: Hull 82W★
DEARDEN, Alan: Widnes 77L, 79W
DERMOTT, Martin: Wigan 90W, 91W, 92W, 93W
DEVEREUX, John: Widnes 93L
DIAMOND, Steve: Wakefield T. 79L
DICK, Kevin: Leeds 77W, 78w
DICKINSON, Roy: Leeds 77w, 78w
DIVORTY, Gary: Hull 85l
DIXON, Paul: Halifax 87W, 88L
DONLAN, Steve: Wigan 85W
DORAHY, John: Hull K.R. 86L
DRUMMOND, Des: Warrington 90L
DUKE, Tony: Hull 82W★
DUNN, Brian: Wigan 85W
DUTTON, Ray: Widnes 75W, 76L, 77L
DWYER, Bernard: St. Helens 89L, 91L
DYAS, David: Featherstone R. 74L
DYL, Les: Leeds 71l, 72L, 77W, 78W

EADIE, Graham: Halifax 87W, 88L
ECCLES, Graham: Leeds 77W, 78W
ECKERSLEY, David: Leigh 71W; Widnes 76L, 77L, 79W
EDWARDS, Shaun: Wigan 84L, 85W, 88W, 89W, 90W, 91W, 92W, 93W
ELIA, Mark: St. Helens 87L
ELLIS, St. John: Castleford 92L
ELVIN, Wayne: Wigan 84l
ELWELL, Keith: Widnes 75W, 76L, 77L, 79W, 81W, 82DL★, 84W
EMA, Asuquo: Hull K.R. 86L
ENGLAND, Keith: Castleford 86W, 92L
EVANS, Steve: Hull 82DW★, 83L, 85L
EVANS, Stuart: St. Helens 89l
EYRES, Richard: Widnes 93L

FAIMALO, Esene: Widnes 93L
FAIRBAIRN, George: Hull K.R. 86L
FAIRBANK, Dick: Halifax 88l
FARRAR, Andrew: Wigan 93W
FARRAR, Vince: Featherstone R. 73W; Hull 80l
FARRELL, Andrew: Wigan 93w
FEARNLEY, Stan: Bradford N. 73L; Leeds 77W
FERGUSON, John: Wigan 85W
FIELDHOUSE, John: St. Helens 87L
FLETCHER, Andrew: Wakefield T. 79L
FORAN, John: Widnes 75W, 76L, 77l
FORBER, Paul: St. Helens 89L

FORD, Mike: Wigan 85W; Castleford 92L
FORSTER, Mark: Warrington 90L
FRANCIS, Bill: Wigan 70L; St. Helens 78L
FRENCH, Ian: Castleford 86W

GEORGE, Derek "Mick": Widnes 75W, 76L, 77l, 79W, 81W
GEORGE, Wilf: Halifax 87W
GIBBINS, Mick: Featherstone R. 83W
GILBERT, John: Featherstone R. 83W
GILDART, Ian: Wigan 90w
GILL, Henderson: Wigan 84L, 85W, 88W
GLYNN, Peter: St. Helens 76w, 78L
GOODWAY, Andy: Wigan 88W, 89w, 90W, 91w
GORDON, Parry: Warrington 74W, 75L
GORLEY, Les: Widnes 81W, 82DL*, 84W
GOULDING, Bobby: Wigan 90w, 91w; Widnes 93L
GREGORY, Andy: Widnes 81W, 82DL*, 84W; Wigan 88W, 89W, 90W, 91W, 92W
GREGORY, Mike: Warrington 90L
GRIFFITHS, Jonathan: St. Helens 91L
GROGAN, Bob: Halifax 88L
GROVES, Paul: St. Helens 89L, 91l
GWILLIAM, Ken: Salford 69L; St. Helens 78L

HAGGERTY, Roy: St. Helens 87L, 89L
HAGUE, Neil: Leeds 77W, 78W
HALL, David: Hull K.R. 80W, 81L
HAMPSON, Steve: Wigan 89W, 90W, 91W, 92w, 93W
HANCOCK, Brian: Hull 80l
HANDSCOMBE, Ray: Featherstone R. 83W
HANKINS, Steve: Featherstone R. 83W
HANLEY, Ellery: Wigan 88W, 89W, 90W, 91W
HARKIN, Kevin: Hull 82D, 83L
HARKIN, Paul: Hull K.R. 81L, 86L
HARMON, Neil: Warrington 90L
HARRIS, Billy: Featherstone R. 74L
HARRISON, Des: Hull K.R. 86L
HARRISON, John: St. Helens 91L
HARRISON, Mick: Leeds 77W, 78W
HARTLEY, David: Featherstone R. 73w, 74L
HARTLEY, Steve: Hull K.R. 80W, 81L
HEATON, Jeff: St. Helens 72W, 76W
HEMSLEY, Kerry: Wigan 84L
HOBBS, David: Featherstone R. 83W
HOGAN, Phil: Hull K.R. 80w, 81L
HOLDING, Neil: St. Helens 87L, 89L
HOLDSTOCK, Roy: Hull K.R. 80W, 81L
HOLLIDAY, Les: Halifax 88L
HOLMES, John: Leeds 71L, 72L, 77W, 78W
HORTON, Stuart: Castleford 86w
HOWARD, Harvey: Widnes 93L
HUBBARD, Steve: Hull K.R. 80W, 81L
HUDSON, Terry: Featherstone R. 83W
HUGHES, Eric: Widnes 75W, 76L, 77L, 79W, 81W, 82DL*, 84W
HULL, David: St. Helens 76W; Widnes 79w
HULME, David: Widnes 84w, 93L
HULME, Paul: Widnes 93L
HUNTE, Alan: St. Helens 91L
HYDE, Gary: Castleford 86W

IDLE, Graham: Wakefield T. 79L
IRO, Kevin: Wigan 88W, 89W, 90W, 91W
IRO, Tony: Wigan 88W, 89W

JACKSON, Bob: Warrington 90L
JAMES, Kevin: Hull 85L
JAMES, Mel: St. Helens 76w, 78L
JAMES, Neil: Halifax 87w, 88L
JENKINS, David: Widnes 76L
JOHNSON, Barry: Castleford 86W
JOHNSTON, Peter: Hull K.R. 86L
JONES, Les: St. Helens 72W, 76W, 78L
JOYNER, John: Castleford 86W
JULIFF, Brian: Wakefield T. 79L; Wigan 84l; Halifax 87w

KARALIUS, Tony: St. Helens 76W
KELLETT, Ken: Featherstone R. 73W, 83W
KELLY, Andy: Hull K.R. 86L
KEMBLE, Gary: Hull 82DW*, 83L, 85L
KENNY, Brett: Wigan 85W
KETTERIDGE, Martin: Castleford 86W, 92L
KISS, Nicky: Wigan 85W, 88W, 89W

LAMPKOWSKI, Mike: Wakefield T. 79L
LAUGHTON, Doug: Wigan 70L; Widnes 75W, 76L, 77L, 79W
LAWS, David: Hull K.R. 86L
LEDGER, Barry: St. Helens 87L
LEULUAI, James: Hull 82W*, 83L, 85L
LIPTROT, Graham: St. Helens 78L, 87L
LLOYD, Geoff "Sammy": Hull 80L, 82D
LOCKWOOD, Brian: Castleford 69W, 70W; Hull K.R. 80W; Widnes 81W, 82DL*
LORD, Gary: Castleford 86W
LOUGHLIN, Paul: St. Helens 87L, 89L, 91L
LOWE, Phil: Hull K.R. 80W, 81L
LUCAS, Ian: Wigan 89W, 91W
LYDIAT, John: Hull K.R. 86l
LYDON, Joe: Widnes 84W; Wigan 88W, 89W, 90W, 92W, 93W
LYMAN, Paul: Featherstone R. 83w
LYON, David: Warrington 90L

McCALLION, Seamus: Halifax 87W, 88L
McCORMACK, Kevin: St. Helens 87L
McCURRIE, Alan: Wakefield T. 79L
McCURRIE, Steve: Widnes 93l
McGINTY, Billy: Warrington 90l; Wigan 92W
MANN, Duane: Warrington 90L
MANN, George: St. Helens 91L
MANTLE, John: St. Helens 66W, 72W, 76W
MARCHANT, Tony: Castleford 86W
MARSDEN, John: Featherstone R. 83W
MARTYN, Tommy: Warrington 75L
MATHIAS, Roy: St. Helens 76W, 78L
MERCER, Gary: Warrington 90L
MEREDITH, Martin: Halifax 88L
MILES, Gene: Wigan 92W
MILLER, Gavin: Hull K.R. 86L
MILLINGTON, John: Hull K.R. 80w, 81l
MILLS, Jim: Widnes 75W, 77L, 79W
MILLWARD, Roger: Hull K.R. 80W
MUGGLETON, John: Hull 85L
MURPHY, Alex: St. Helens 61L, 66W; Leigh 71W; Warrington 74W
MURRELL, Brian: Leeds 77W
MUSCROFT, Peter: Hull K.R. 81L
MYERS, David: Wigan 91W; Widnes 93L

MYLER, John: Widnes 81w
MYLER, Tony: Widnes 82d

NASH, Steve: Featherstone R. 73W, 74L
NEILL, Jonathan: St. Helens 91L
NELLER, Keith: Halifax 87W, 88L
NELSON, David: Castleford 92L
NELSON, Nick: Widnes 76L
NEWLOVE, John: Featherstone R. 73W, 74L; Hull 80L
NICHOLAS, Mike: Warrington 74W, 75l
NICHOLLS, George: St. Helens 76W, 78L
NIKAU, Tawera: Castleford 92L
NOONAN, Derek: Warrington 74W, 75L; St. Helens 76W, 78L
NORTON, Steve: Hull 80L, 82DW*, 83L, 85L

O'CONNOR, Michael: St. Helens 89L
OFFIAH, Martin: Wigan 92W, 93W
O'HARA, Dane: Hull 82D, 83L, 85L
O'LOUGHLIN, Keiron: Widnes 82DL*, 84W
O'NEILL, Dennis: Widnes 76l, 77L
O'NEILL, Julien: Widnes 93l
O'NEILL, Mike: Widnes 79w, 81W, 82DL*, 84W
O'NEILL, Steve: Widnes 82d, 84W
OULTON, Willie: Leeds 78W

PANAPA, Sam: Wigan 93w
PATRICK, Shaun: Hull 85L
PENDLEBURY, John: Wigan 84L; Halifax 87W, 88L
PHILBIN, Barry: Warrington 74W, 75L
PHILBIN, Mike: Warrington 74W, 75L
PICKERILL, Clive: Hull 80L
PICKUP, Bill: Warrington 74w
PIMBLETT, Geoff: St. Helens 72W, 76W, 78L
PINNER, Harry: St. Helens 78L
PITCHFORD, Steve: Leeds 77W, 78W
PLANGE, David: Castleford 86W
PLATT, Andy: St. Helens 87L; Wigan 89W, 90W, 91W, 92W, 93W
POTTER, Ian: Wigan 85W, 88W, 89W
PRENDIVILLE, Paul: Hull 80L, 82DW*, 83L
PRESCOTT, Alan: Widnes 75W, 76L
PRESCOTT, Eric: Widnes 81W, 82DL*
PRESTON, Mark: Wigan 90W
PROCTOR, Paul: Hull K.R. 81l
PROHM, Gary: Hull K.R. 86L
PUCKERING, Neil: Hull 85L

QUINN, Steve: Featherstone R. 83W
QUIRK, Les: St. Helens 89L, 91L

RAMSDALE, Denis: Wigan 84L
RAMSEY, Bill: Hunslet 65L; Leeds 68W, 71L, 72L; Widnes 77L
RAYNE, Keith: Wakefield T. 79L
REYNOLDS, Frank: Warrington 75L
RHODES, Alan: Featherstone R. 73W, 74L
RIX, Grant: Halifax 87W
ROBINSON, Jason: Wigan 93W
ROBINSON, Steve: Halifax 88L
ROOCKLEY, David: Castleford 86w
ROPATI, Tea: St. Helens 91L
ROSE, Paul: Hull K.R. 80W; Hull 83L, 85L
ROUND, Paul: St. Helens 87l

SAMPSON, Dean: Castleford 92l
SANDERSON, Gary: Warrington 90L
SANDERSON, John "Sammy": Leeds 78W
SANDY, Jamie: Castleford 86W
SCHOFIELD, Garry: Hull 85l
SCOTT, Mick: Wigan 84L; Halifax 87W, 88l
SHAW, Glyn: Widnes 79W, 81w
SHEARD, Les: Wakefield T. 79L
SHELFORD, Adrian: Wigan 88W, 89W, 90W
SHERIDAN, Barry: Widnes 75W, 76l
SIDDALL, Gary: Featherstone R. 83w
SKERRETT, Kelvin: Wigan 92W, 93W
SKERRETT, Trevor: Wakefield T. 79L; Hull 82DW*, 83L
SLATTER, Tim: Featherstone R. 83W
SMITH, Alan: Leeds 68W, 72L, 77W
SMITH, David: Leeds 77w, 78W
SMITH, Gordon: Hull K.R. 86l
SMITH, Keith: Wakefield T. 79L
SMITH, Mike: Hull K.R. 80W, 81L, 86L
SMITH, Mike: Featherstone R. 67W, 73W, 74L
SMITH, Peter: Featherstone R. 83W
SMITH, Tony: Castleford 92l
SORENSEN, Kurt: Widnes 93L
SOUTHERNWOOD, Graham: Castleford 92L
SPRUCE, Stuart: Widnes 93L
STEADMAN, Graham: Castleford 92L
STEPHENS, Gary: Wigan 84L; Halifax 87W
STEPHENSON, David: Wigan 84L, 85W
STERLING, Peter: Hull 85L
STONE, Richard "Charlie": Featherstone R. 73W, 74l; Hull 80L, 82DW*, 83L
SULLIVAN, Clive: Hull K.R. 80W; Hull 82W*

TAMATI, Howie: Wigan 84L
TAMATI, Kevin: Widnes 84W
THOMAS, Mark: Warrington 90l
THOMPSON, Jimmy: Featherstone R. 67W, 73W, 74L
TINDALL, Keith: Hull 80L, 82W*
TONKS, Les: Featherstone R. 73W, 74L
TOPLISS, David: Wakefield T. 79L; Hull 82DW*, 83L

VAUTIN, Paul: St. Helens 89L
VEIVERS, Phil: St. Helens 87L, 89L, 91L

WALTERS, Graham: Hull 80L
WANBON, Bobby: Warrington 74w, 75L
WANE, Shaun: Wigan 88w
WARD, David: Leeds 77W, 78W
WARD, Kevin: Castleford 86W; St. Helens 91L
WATKINSON, David: Hull K.R. 80W, 81L, 86L
WEST, Graeme: Wigan 84L, 85W
WHITEHEAD, Derek: Warrington 74W, 75L
WHITFIELD, Colin: Wigan 84L; Halifax 87W, 88L
WHITFIELD, Fred: Widnes 84w
WHITTLE, Alan: Warrington 74W, 75L
WILBY, Tim: Hull 80L
WILEMAN, Ron: Hull 80L, 82D
WILKINSON, Ian: Halifax 88L
WILSON, Scott: Halifax 87W
WOOD, John: Widnes 76L
WOODS, Paul: Hull 80L
WRAY, Jon: Castleford 92L
WRIGHT, Darren: Widnes 93L
WRIGHT, David: Warrington 74W
WRIGHT, Stuart: Widnes 77L, 79W, 81W, 82DL*, 84W

171

THE LANCE TODD TROPHY

The Lance Todd Trophy is presented to the Man of the Match in the Rugby League Challenge Cup Final, the decision being reached by a ballot of members of the Rugby League Writers' Association present at the game.

Lance Todd made his name in Britain as a player with Wigan and as manager of Salford. His untimely death in a road accident on the return journey from a game at Oldham was commemorated by the introduction of the Lance Todd Trophy.

The award was instituted by Australian-born Harry Sunderland, Warrington director Bob Anderton and Yorkshire journalist John Bapty.

Around 1950, the Red Devils' Association at Salford, comprising players and officials who had worked with Todd, raised sufficient funds to provide a trophy and replica for each winner.

Hull's Tommy Harris is the only hooker to earn the title; and Ray Ashby and Brian Gabbitas the only players to share the honour.

Following the 1954 replay, it was decided by the Red Devils that in the future the trophy would be awarded for the Wembley game. In 1954, Gerry Helme had received the trophy for his performance in the Odsal replay. In the 1982 replay at Elland Road, Leeds, the Man of the Match award went to Hull skipper David Topliss, the Lance Todd Trophy having been awarded to Eddie Cunningham, of Widnes, in the drawn Wembley tie.

In 1990 Andy Gregory, of Wigan, became the first player to win the trophy twice at Wembley, having also won it two years earlier.

The Lance Todd Trophy Roll of Honour

Year	Winner	Team	Position
1946	Billy Stott	Wakefield Trinity (v Wigan)	Centre
1947	Willie Davies	Bradford Northern (v Leeds)	Stand off
1948	Frank Whitcombe	Bradford Northern (v Wigan)	Prop
1949	Ernest Ward	Bradford Northern (v Halifax)	Centre
1950	Gerry Helme	Warrington (v Widnes)	Scrum half
1951	Cec Mountford	Wigan (v Barrow)	Stand off
1952	Billy Ivison	Workington T. (v Featherstone R.)	Loose forward
1953	Peter Ramsden	Huddersfield (v St. Helens)	Stand off
1954	Gerry Helme	Warrington (v Halifax)	Scrum half
1955	Jack Grundy	Barrow (v Workington Town)	Second row
1956	Alan Prescott	St. Helens (v Halifax)	Prop
1957	Jeff Stevenson	Leeds (v Barrow)	Scrum half
1958	Rees Thomas	Wigan (v Workington Town)	Scrum half
1959	Brian McTigue	Wigan (v Hull)	Second row
1960	Tommy Harris	Hull (v Wakefield Trinity)	Hooker
1961	Dick Huddart	St. Helens (v Wigan)	Second row
1962	Neil Fox	Wakefield Trinity (v Huddersfield)	Centre
1963	Harold Poynton	Wakefield Trinity (v Wigan)	Stand off
1964	Frank Collier	Widnes (v Hull K.R.)	Prop
1965	Ray Ashby	Wigan	Full back
	Brian Gabbitas	Hunslet	Stand off

1966	Len Killeen	St. Helens (v Wigan)	Winger
1967	Carl Dooler	Featherstone Rovers (v Barrow)	Scrum half
1968	Don Fox	Wakefield Trinity (v Leeds)	Prop
1969	Malcolm Reilly	Castleford (v Salford)	Loose forward
1970	Bill Kirkbride	Castleford (v Wigan)	Second row
1971	Alex Murphy	Leigh (v Leeds)	Scrum half
1972	Kel Coslett	St. Helens (v Leeds)	Loose forward
1973	Steve Nash	Featherstone R. (v Bradford N.)	Scrum half
1974	Derek Whitehead	Warrington (v Featherstone Rovers)	Full back
1975	Ray Dutton	Widnes (v Warrington)	Full back
1976	Geoff Pimblett	St. Helens (v Widnes)	Full back
1977	Steve Pitchford	Leeds (v Widnes)	Prop
1978	George Nicholls	St. Helens (v Leeds)	Second row
1979	David Topliss	Wakefield Trinity (v Widnes)	Stand off
1980	Brian Lockwood	Hull K.R. (v Hull)	Prop
1981	Mick Burke	Widnes (v Hull K.R.)	Full back
1982	Eddie Cunningham	Widnes (v Hull)	Centre
1983	David Hobbs	Featherstone Rovers (v Hull)	Second row
1984	Joe Lydon	Widnes (v Wigan)	Centre
1985	Brett Kenny	Wigan (v Hull)	Stand off
1986	Bob Beardmore	Castleford (v Hull K.R.)	Scrum half
1987	Graham Eadie	Halifax (v St. Helens)	Full back
1988	Andy Gregory	Wigan (v Halifax)	Scrum half
1989	Ellery Hanley	Wigan (v St. Helens)	Loose forward
1990	Andy Gregory	Wigan (v Warrington)	Scrum half
1991	Denis Betts	Wigan (v St. Helens)	Second row
1992	Martin Offiah	Wigan (v Castleford)	Winger
1993	Dean Bell	Wigan (v Widnes)	Loose forward

1993 Lance Todd Trophy winner Dean Bell, only the second Kiwi to receive the coveted award.

CHALLENGE CUP RECORDS

ALL ROUNDS

TEAM

Highest score:
Huddersfield 119 v. *Swinton Park 2 1914

INDIVIDUAL

Most goals in a match:
22 by Jim Sullivan (Wigan) v. *Flimby and Fothergill
. . . . 1925

Most tries in a match:
11 by George West (Hull K.R.) v. *Brookland Rovers
. . . . 1905

Most points in a match:
53 (11t,10g) by George West (Hull K.R.) as above.

*Amateur teams

FINAL RECORDS

TEAM

Most wins: 14 by Wigan

Most finals: 23 by Wigan

Highest score:
Wakefield T. 38 v. Hull 5 1960

Widest margin:
Huddersfield 37 v. St. Helens 3 1915

Biggest attendance:
102,569 Warrington v. Halifax (Replay) at Bradford
. . . . 1954

INDIVIDUAL

Most goals:
8 by Cyril Kellett (Featherstone R.) v. Bradford N.
. . . . 1973

Most tries:
3 by Bob Wilson (Broughton R.) v. Salford 1902
Stan Moorhouse (Huddersfield) v. Warrington . 1913
Tom Holliday (Oldham) v. Swinton 1927

Most points:
20 (7g,2t) by Neil Fox (Wakefield T.) v. Hull . . . 1960

WEMBLEY FACTS

WIGAN have made a record 19 appearances at Wembley and won there a record 13 times, including a record six successive appearances from 1988.

A RECORD 10 overseas players trod the Wembley turf in 1985. Hull fielded six — a record for one club. The Airlie Birds sextet were Australians Peter Sterling and John Muggleton, plus New Zealanders Gary Kemble, James Leuluai, Dane O'Hara and Fred Ah Kuoi. Wigan added Australians John Ferguson and Brett Kenny together with New Zealanders Graeme West and Danny Campbell, who went on as substitute. South African Nick Du Toit was substitute back but did not play.

THE 1985 aggregates of 10 tries and 52 points were both record totals for a Challenge Cup final with Hull's 24 points the most by a losing side. There were also 10 tries in the 1915 final when Huddersfield beat St. Helens 37-3, which is the widest margin. Wakefield Trinity ran up the highest Cup final score when they beat Hull 38-5 in 1960.

WORLD RECORD receipts of £1,981,591 were taken at the 1993 final between Wigan and Widnes from a capacity crowd of 77,684.

ANDY GREGORY and Shaun Edwards hold the record for most Cup-winning appearances at Wembley with seven. Gregory has never been on a losing side in a record eight finals at the stadium, having also been in the Widnes side that drew with Hull in 1982 before losing the replay at Elland Road, Leeds.

Gregory's winning appearances were with Widnes (1981, 1984) and Wigan (1988, 1989, 1990, 1991, 1992).

Edwards made his debut in Wigan's losing side of 1984, earning winners' medals in 1985 and from 1988-93 inclusive.

ERIC ASHTON captained a record six teams at Wembley — Wigan in 1958, 1959, 1961, 1963, 1965 and 1966. His record of three wins (in 1958, 1959, 1965) is shared with Derek Turner (Wakefield Trinity 1960, 1962, 1963), Alex Murphy (St. Helens 1966, Leigh 1971 and Warrington 1974) and Ellery Hanley (Wigan 1989, 1990, 1991), this being the only three successive wins.

THE YOUNGEST player to appear in a Wembley Cup final was Shaun Edwards who was 17 years, 6 months and 19 days when he played full back for Wigan against Widnes in 1984. He was also the youngest captain at Wembley, leading Wigan to success in the 1988 final against Halifax at the age of 21 years, 6 months and 14 days. The youngest winner at Wembley was Wigan's Andrew Farrell, a substitute in the 1993 final against Widnes at 17 years, 11 months.

ALEX MURPHY has been a record six times to Wembley as a coach. He has a winner as player-coach with Leigh (1971) and Warrington (1974), but losing each time when confined to the bench with Warrington (1975), Wigan (1984) and St. Helens (1987 and 1989). Murphy also went twice solely as a player, with St. Helens in 1961 and 1966.

MOST WINS as a coach at Wembley is four, by John Monie (Wigan 1990, 1991, 1992 and 1993).

THE OLDEST player at Wembley was Gus Risman, who at 41 years, 29 days led Workington Town to victory over Featherstone Rovers in 1952. He played full back.

THE TALLEST player at Wembley was St. Helens second row man John Harrison who appeared in the 1991 final against Wigan. He measured 6ft. 7in.

SCHOOLBOYS who have appeared in an Under-11 curtain-raiser at Wembley and gone on to play in the major final at the stadium are Joe Lydon, David Hulme, Mike Ford, Neil Puckering, David Plange, Denis Betts, Bobby Goulding and Phil Clarke. Lydon became the first to achieve the feat with Widnes in the 1984 final against Wigan, followed by teammate Hulme who went on as a 72nd-minute substitute. Both had played in the first schoolboys' curtain-raiser in 1975 — Lydon for Wigan, and Hulme for Widnes.

CYRIL KELLETT holds the record for most goals in a Challenge Cup final with his eight for Featherstone Rovers in 1973.

In the most remarkable exhibition of kicking seen at Wembley, the veteran full back was successful with every one of his attempts as Bradford Northern crashed 33-14.

Nine years earlier he scored only one for Hull Kingston Rovers in the 13-5 defeat by Widnes.

NEIL FOX — the record aggregate points scorer of all time — piled up the most points in a Challenge Cup final in 1960. His 20 points helped Wakefield Trinity to a 38-5 defeat of Hull. Fox's points came from two tries and seven goals.

His three drop goals for Trinity in the 12-6 victory over Huddersfield two years later was another extraordinary feat in the days when the drop goal was a rarity.

NO player has scored a hat-trick of tries at Wembley, the feat being achieved only three times in the preceding era.

The last to do it was Oldham winger Tom Holliday in the 26-7 defeat of Swinton in 1927.

Bob Wilson, the Broughton Rangers centre and captain, was the first to score three tries, in the 25-0 victory over Salford in 1902.

In between, Stan Moorhouse's three-try feat accounted for all of Huddersfield's points when they beat Warrington 9-5 in 1913.

MANY great players have gone through an entire career without achieving their ambition of playing at Wembley. Hull's Mike Smith achieved it in his first senior game.

Smith made one of the most remarkable debuts in sporting history when he played in the second row of an injury-hit Boulevard side against Wakefield Trinity in 1960.

In contrast, Freddie Miller signed for Hull in 1932 and did not play at Wembley until 1952...two years after joining Featherstone Rovers.

The legendary Neil Fox, holder of the record for most points in a Challenge Cup final.

A NOTABLE Wembley captain was Gus Risman who led two clubs to victory...14 years apart.

He was captain of Salford when they beat Barrow in 1938. At 41, he led Workington Town to their triumph over Featherstone Rovers in 1952.

PROBABLY the unluckiest Challenge Cup finalist was Dai Davies who appeared in four finals and was on the losing side each time. Three of those occasions were at Wembley with different clubs. He was a loser with Warrington (1933), Huddersfield (1935) and Keighley (1937). Before the Wembley era he was also in Warrington's beaten team of 1928.

Steve Norton and Lee Crooks played at Wembley four times and were never on the winning side. Norton was in the beaten Hull teams of 1980, 1983 and 1985 in addition to playing in the 1982 drawn final. In 1970 he was a non-playing substitute for Castleford, who won the Cup.

Crooks was in the beaten Hull sides of 1983 and 1985 plus the drawn final of 1982. He was then in Castleford's beaten 1992 team.

Norton and Crooks both won winners' medals in the 1982 replay.

Bill Ramsey was on the losing side in four Wembley finals but gained a winners' medal with Leeds in 1968. He picked up losers' medals with Hunslet (1965), Leeds (1971 and 1972) and Widnes (1977).

FOURTEEN of last season's clubs have never appeared at Wembley. They are: Batley, Blackpool Gladiators, Bramley, Carlisle, Chorley Borough, Doncaster, Highfield, London Crusaders, Nottingham City, Oldham, Rochdale Hornets, Sheffield Eagles, Swinton and Whitehaven.

Fate seems to be against Swinton and Oldham. In the five years preceding the move to Wembley, one or the other appeared in the final, twice meeting each other. Oldham played in four successive finals in that period. Swinton's run of three finals ended when the first Wembley took place in 1929. They got through to the final three years later ...only for it to be played at Wigan!

WEMBLEY ERA SEMI-FINALS

It is generally felt that it is better to have played at Wembley and lost than never to have played there at all. This makes the semi-final stage of the RL Challenge Cup almost as important as the final, with no consolation for the losers.

Of the 14 current clubs who have never appeared at Wembley, four have been beaten semi-finalists. They are Oldham (six times), Rochdale Hornets (twice), Swinton and Whitehaven.

Probably the unluckiest are Oldham. They have reached the penultimate stage six times without being able to realise their ambition. Oldham almost made it in 1964. After drawing 5-5 with Hull K.R., they were winning 17-14 in extra time of the replay when bad light stopped play and they were beaten in the third game.

Swinton did win a semi-final in 1932 but the final that year was switched from Wembley to Wigan!

There have been three occasions when Yorkshire has provided all four semi-finalists in one year — in 1962, 1973 and 1983. Four times have all four semi-finalists come from west of the Pennines — in 1930, 1989, 1990 and 1991.

Until 1962 the two semi-finals were always played on the same Saturday, but with four Yorkshire clubs competing for the first time it was decided to play one midweek. Both matches were played at Odsal Stadium, Bradford. The first was on a Wednesday evening — without floodlights — when 43,625 saw Wakefield Trinity beat Featherstone Rovers and on the following Saturday there were 31,423 to see Huddersfield beat Hull K.R.

The following year both semi-finals were again played on the same Saturday, but since then they have been staged on different Saturdays.

Some semi-final facts during the Wembley era are:

Biggest attendance: 69,898 Warrington v. Leeds at Bradford in 1950

Biggest aggregate: 104,453 in 1939 (Only other six-figure aggregate was 102,080 in 1951)

Record receipts: £177,161 St. Helens v. Wigan at Old Trafford, Manchester in 1990

Lowest attendance: 7,971 Featherstone R. v. Leigh at Leeds in 1974

Highest score and widest margin: Wigan 71 v. Bradford N. 10 in 1992

CHALLENGE CUP SEMI-FINALS

Year	Winners		Runners-up		Venue	Attendance	Receipts
1929	Dewsbury	9	Castleford	3	Huddersfield	25,000	£1,562
	Wigan	7	St. Helens Recs.	7	Swinton	31,000	£2,209
Replay	Wigan	13	St. Helens Recs.	12	Leigh	21,940	£1,437
1930	Widnes	10	Barrow	3	Warrington	25,500	£1,630
	St. Helens	5	Wigan	5	Swinton	37,169	£2,666
Replay	St. Helens	22	Wigan	10	Leigh	24,000	£1,657
1931	Halifax	11	St. Helens	2	Rochdale	21,674	£1,498
	York	15	Warrington	5	Leeds	32,419	£2,329
1932★	Leeds	2	Halifax	2	Huddersfield	31,818	£2,456
Replay	Leeds	9	Halifax	2	Wakefield	21,000	£1,417
	Swinton	7	Wakefield T.	4	Rochdale	21,273	£1,369
★	*Final was played at Wigan, not Wembley*						
1933	Huddersfield	30	Leeds	8	Wakefield	36,359	£2,299
	Warrington	11	St. Helens	5	Swinton	30,373	£2,055
1934	Hunslet	12	Huddersfield	7	Wakefield	27,450	£1,797
	Widnes	7	Oldham	4	Swinton	17,577	£1,050

Year	Winners		Runners-up		Venue	Attendance	Receipts
1935	Castleford	11	Barrow	5	Swinton	24,469	£1,534
	Huddersfield	21	Hull	5	Leeds	37,111	£2,753
1936	Leeds	10	Huddersfield	5	Wakefield	37,906	£2,456
	Warrington	7	Salford	2	Wigan	41,538	£2,796
1937	Keighley	0	Wakefield T.	0	Leeds	39,998	£2,793
Replay	Keighley	5	Wakefield T.	3	Huddersfield	14,400	£1,052
	Widnes	13	Wigan	9	Warrington	29,260	£1,972
1938	Barrow	4	Halifax	2	Huddersfield	31,384	£2,431
	Salford	6	Swinton	0	Belle Vue, Manchester	31,664	£2,396
1939	Halifax	10	Leeds	4	Bradford	64,453	£3,645
	Salford	11	Wigan	2	Rochdale	40,000	£2,154

● *During the war the semi-finals were two-legged and the finals were not played at Wembley*

Year	Winners		Runners-up		Venue	Attendance	Receipts
1946	Wakefield T.	7	Hunslet	3	Leeds	33,000	£4,991
	Wigan	12	Widnes	5	Swinton	36,976	£4,746
1947	Bradford N.	11	Warrington	7	Swinton	33,474	£4,946
	Leeds	21	Wakefield T.	0	Huddersfield	35,136	£6,339
1948	Bradford N.	14	Hunslet	7	Leeds	38,125	£7,437
	Wigan	11	Rochdale H.	0	Swinton	26,004	£4,206
1949	Bradford N.	10	Barrow	0	Swinton	26,572	£4,646
	Halifax	11	Huddersfield	10	Bradford	61,875	£8,638
1950	Warrington	16	Leeds	4	Bradford	69,898	£9,861
	Widnes	8	Bradford N.	0	Wigan	25,390	£3,936
1951	Barrow	14	Leeds	14	Bradford	57,459	£8,248
Replay	Barrow	28	Leeds	13	Huddersfield	31,078	£5,098
	Wigan	3	Warrington	2	Swinton	44,621	£7,358
1952	Featherstone R.	6	Leigh	2	Leeds	35,621	£6,494
	Workington T.	5	Barrow	2	Wigan	31,206	£4,782
1953	Huddersfield	7	Wigan	0	Bradford	58,722	£10,519
	St. Helens	9	Warrington	3	Swinton	38,059	£7,768
1954	Halifax	18	Hunslet	3	Bradford	46,961	£8,243
	Warrington	8	Leeds	4	Swinton	36,993	£7,596
1955	Barrow	9	Hunslet	6	Wigan	25,493	£4,671
	Workington T.	13	Featherstone R.	2	Leeds	33,499	£7,305
1956	Halifax	11	Wigan	10	Bradford	51,889	£9,054
	St. Helens	5	Barrow	5	Swinton	38,897	£7,793
Replay	St. Helens	10	Barrow	5	Wigan	44,731	£7,750
1957	Barrow	2	Leigh	2	Wigan	34,628	£6,340
Replay	Barrow	15	Leigh	10	Swinton	28,081	£5,695
	Leeds	10	Whitehaven	9	Bradford	49,094	£8,987
1958	Wigan	5	Rochdale H.	3	Swinton	28,597	£6,354
	Workington T.	8	Featherstone R.	2	Bradford	31,517	£6,325
1959	Wigan	5	Leigh	0	Swinton	27,906	£6,068
	Hull	15	Featherstone R.	5	Bradford	52,131	£9,776
1960	Wakefield T.	11	Featherstone R.	2	Bradford	55,935	£10,390
	Hull	12	Oldham	9	Swinton	27,545	£6,093
1961	St. Helens	26	Hull	9	Bradford	42,935	£9,231
	Wigan	19	Halifax	10	Swinton	35,118	£7,557
1962	Wakefield T.	9	Featherstone R.	0	Bradford	43,625	£8,496
	Huddersfield	6	Hull K.R.	0	Bradford	31,423	£6,685

Year	Winners		Runners-up		Venue	Attendance	Receipts
1963	Wakefield T.	5	Warrington	2	Swinton	15,565	£3,530
	Wigan	18	Hull K.R.	4	Leeds	21,420	£6,029
1964	Widnes	7	Castleford	7	Swinton	25,603	£5,541
Replay	Widnes	7	Castleford	5	Wakefield	28,739	£5,313
	Hull K.R.	5	Oldham	5	Leeds	28,823	£7,411
Replay	Hull K.R.	14	Oldham	17	Swinton	27,209	£5,929

● *Score after 80 minutes was 14-14, then bad light caused match to be abandoned after 12 minutes of extra time with Oldham winning 17-14*

Year	Winners		Runners-up		Venue	Attendance	Receipts
Second Replay	Hull K.R.	12	Oldham	2	Huddersfield	28,732	£6,183
1965	Wigan	25	Swinton	10	St. Helens	26,658	£6,384
	Hunslet	8	Wakefield T.	0	Leeds	21,262	£6,090
1966	St. Helens	12	Dewsbury	5	Swinton	13,046	£3,102
	Wigan	7	Leeds	2	Huddersfield	22,758	£5,971
1967	Featherstone R.	16	Leeds	8	Huddersfield	20,052	£6,276
	Barrow	14	Dewsbury	9	Swinton	13,744	£4,560
1968	Leeds	25	Wigan	4	Swinton	30,058	£9,845
	Wakefield T.	0	Huddersfield	0	Bradford	21,569	£6,196
Replay	Wakefield T.	15	Huddersfield	10	Leeds	20,983	£6,425
1969	Castleford	16	Wakefield T.	10	Leeds	21,497	£8,477
	Salford	15	Warrington	8	Wigan	20,600	£7,738
1970	Castleford	6	St. Helens	3	Swinton	18,913	£7,171
	Wigan	19	Hull K.R.	8	Leeds	18,495	£7,862
1971	Leeds	19	Castleford	8	Bradford	24,464	£9,120
	Leigh	10	Huddersfield	4	Wigan	14,875	£5,670
1972	St. Helens	10	Warrington	10	Wigan	19,300	£8,250
Replay	St. Helens	10	Warrington	6	Wigan	32,380	£12,604
	Leeds	16	Halifax	3	Bradford	16,680	£6,851
1973	Featherstone R.	17	Castleford	3	Leeds	15,369	£9,454
	Bradford N.	23	Dewsbury	7	Leeds	14,028	£9,221
1974	Warrington	17	Dewsbury	7	Wigan	11,789	£6,821
	Featherstone R.	21	Leigh	14	Leeds	7,971	£4,461
1975	Widnes	13	Wakefield T.	7	Bradford	9,155	£5,856
	Warrington	11	Leeds	4	Wigan	13,168	£9,581
1976	Widnes	15	Featherstone R.	9	Swinton	13,019	£9,078
	St. Helens	5	Keighley	4	Huddersfield	9,829	£6,113
1977	Leeds	7	St. Helens	2	Wigan	12,974	£11,379
	Widnes	14	Hull K.R.	5	Leeds	17,053	£16,068
1978	Leeds	14	Featherstone R.	9	Bradford	12,824	£11,322
	St. Helens	12	Warrington	8	Wigan	16,167	£13,960
1979	Widnes	14	Bradford N.	11	Swinton	14,324	£16,363
	Wakefield T.	9	St. Helens	7	Leeds	12,393	£14,195
1980	Hull K.R.	20	Halifax	7	Leeds	17,910	£31,650
	Hull	10	Widnes	5	Swinton	18,347	£29,415
1981	Widnes	17	Warrington	9	Wigan	12,624	£20,673
	Hull K.R.	22	St. Helens	5	Leeds	17,073	£30,616
1982	Hull	15	Castleford	11	Leeds	21,207	£41,867
	Widnes	11	Leeds	8	Swinton	13,075	£25,796
1983	Featherstone R.	11	Bradford N.	6	Leeds	10,784	£22,579
	Hull	14	Castleford	7	Elland Rd., L'ds	26,031	£65,498
1984	Wigan	14	York	8	Elland Rd., L'ds	17,156	£52,888
	Widnes	15	Leeds	4	Swinton	14,046	£37,183

178

Year	Winners		Runners-up		Venue	Attendance	Receipts
1985	Wigan	18	Hull K.R.	11	Elland Rd., L'ds	19,275	£70,192
	Hull	10	Castleford	10	Leeds	20,982	£64,163
Replay	Hull	22	Castleford	16	Leeds	20,968	£65,005
1986	Castleford	18	Oldham	7	Wigan	12,430	£38,296
	Hull K.R.	24	Leeds	24	Elland Rd., L'ds	23,866	£83,757
Replay	Hull K.R.	17	Leeds	0	Elland Rd., L'ds	32,485	£113,345
1987	St. Helens	14	Leigh	8	Wigan	13,105	£48,627
	Halifax	12	Widnes	8	Leeds	16,064	£61,260
1988	Wigan	34	Salford	4	Bolton W. FC	20,783	£95,876
	Halifax	0	Hull	0	Leeds	20,534	£82,026
Replay	Halifax	4	Hull	3	Elland Rd., L'ds	25,117	£113,679
1989	St. Helens	16	Widnes	14	Wigan	17,119	£70,411
	Wigan	13	Warrington	6	Man. C. FC	26,529	£144,056
1990	Wigan	20	St. Helens	14	Man. U. FC	26,489	£177,161
	Warrington	10	Oldham	6	Wigan	15,631	£80,500
1991	Wigan	30	Oldham	16	Bolton W. FC	19,057	£116,937
	St. Helens	19	Widnes	2	Wigan	16,109	£81,342
1992	Castleford	8	Hull	4	Leeds	14,636	£91,225
	Wigan	71	Bradford N.	10	Bolton W. FC	18,027	£131,124
1993	Widnes	39	Leeds	4	Wigan	13,823	£83,914
	Wigan	15	Bradford N.	6	Elland Rd., L'ds	20,085	£150,167

NON-LEAGUE CLUBS IN THE CHALLENGE CUP

AMATEUR clubs were invited to compete in the 1986 Rugby League Challenge Cup after a five-year break. The League asked for two of the three county cup competition winners to enter the preliminary round.

The League later decided that from 1987 the Silk Cut Challenge Cup campaign would feature 38 teams, amateur clubs joining the professionals for a preliminary round of six ties. But amateur clubs were not invited to enter the 1993 tournament due to a prolonged dispute between the League and BARLA.

In the early years of the Northern Union Challenge Cup — as it was then called — the line between professional and amateur was less clearly defined.

A variety of Leagues also make it difficult to set non-League clubs apart. Fifty-six clubs appeared in the inaugurating first round of 1897 and four others received byes. The complications continued until 1904 when the League format settled down and non-League clubs had to qualify for the first round.

Between 1904 and 1907 there was a preliminary round of up to 14 ties involving mostly non-League clubs. In 1906-07 SAVILLE GREEN beat Bramley 10-0, and NEWINGTON ROVERS drew 3-3 and 13-13 with York before losing 14-5.

Not since 1909 when BEVERLEY beat Ebbw Vale 7-2 has a senior team been knocked out by a non-League club although amateur teams twice had victories in the two-leg era of 1946-54.

NON-LEAGUE CLUB VICTORIES OVER SENIOR CLUBS SINCE 1904

(Excluding preliminary rounds before 1908)
Non-League Clubs in Capitals

1905-06
*FEATHERSTONE ROVERS 23 v. Widnes 2
(second round)

1907-08
WHITEHAVEN RECREATION 13 v. St. Helens 8
(Lost 33-5 at Merthyr Tydfil in second round)

1908-09
BEVERLEY 7 v. Ebbw Vale 2
(Lost 53-2 at Halifax in second round)

1945-46
SHARLSTON 12 v. Workington Town 7
(1st leg) (Workington Town won 2nd leg 16-2)

1947-48
RISEHOW AND GILLHEAD 10 v. Keighley 2 (2nd leg)
(Keighley won 1st leg 11-0)

*FEATHERSTONE ROVERS are the only non-League club to appear in the third round when they lost 3-0 at Keighley. In the first round they beat BROOKLAND ROVERS 16-5.

There have been seven drawn clashes, with the professional club winning through each time. The last draw was in 1986-87 when KELLS drew 4-4 with Fulham at Whitehaven. Fulham won the replay 22-14 at Chiswick.

There have been several other instances of non-League clubs meeting in the first round. The last occasion was in 1960 when WALNEY CENTRAL beat LOCK LANE 10-5 before losing at Oldham 55-4 in the second round.

In 1964 THAMES BOARD MILLS received a bye when Bradford Northern disbanded, but lost 48-8 at Blackpool Borough in the second round.

CHALLENGE CUP PROGRESS CHART

A 20-year review . . . .

Key: W — Winners. F — Beaten finalists. SF — Semi-final. P — Preliminary round.

	1992-93	1991-92	1990-91	1989-90	1988-89	1987-88	1986-87	1985-86	1984-85	1983-84	1982-83	1981-82	1980-81	1979-80	1978-79	1977-78	1976-77	1975-76	1974-75	1973-74
BARROW	1	2	2	1	2	1	2	2	P	1	2	2	1	2	3	1	2	1	1	1
BATLEY	2	1	1	1	1	1	1	1	1	1	1	2	1	1	1	1	1	1	1	1
BLACKPOOL G.	P	1	1	2	2	2	1	2	1	1	1	1	1	1	1	1	1	1	1	1
BRADFORD N.	SF	SF	3	3	2	1	2	3	3	3	SF	3	1	3	SF	3	3	2	3	3
BRAMLEY	1	P	1	1	P	P	1	2	3	1	1	1	1	1	2	1	1	1	1	2
CARLISLE	1	P	P	1	2	1	2	1	1	P	1	1								
CASTLEFORD	3	F	1	P	2	1	1	W	SF	3	SF	SF	2	2	3	3	3	1	1	1
CHORLEY B.	1	P	1	1																
DEWSBURY	1	2	1	2	1	1	1	1	1	1	1	2	1	2	1	3	1	1		SF
DONCASTER	1	2	1	P	1	3	1	2	P	2	1	1	1	1	1	1	1	2	1	1
FEATHERSTONE R.	1	3	1	1	3	2	1	1	P	1	W	P	3	1	1	SF	2	SF	1	F
HALIFAX	3	3	3	1	1	F	W	1	2	1	2	3	2	SF	1	1	1	1	1	1
HIGHFIELD	1	1	1	1	1	1	1	1	2	1	2	1	1	1	1	1	1	1	1	2
HUDDERSFIELD	2	P	P	P	1	P	1	1	1	1	1	1	1	2	3	3	1	1	1	1
HULL	P	SF	P	2	1	SF	3	1	F	2	F	W	2	F	3	2	2	1	2	1
HULL K.R.	3	1	1	1	3	3	3	F	SF	3	1	2	F	W	2	1	SF	2	3	2
HUNSLET	2	2	1	1	P	1	2	1	3	2	3	1	1	1	2	1	2	3	1	
KEIGHLEY C.	2	1	2	2	2	2	2	1	1	1	1	2	1	2	1	1	SF	1	1	
LEEDS	SF	2	2	P	3	2	3	SF	1	SF	2	SF	1	2	1	W	W	3	SF	3
LEIGH	1	1	1	1	1	1	SF	3	2	1	1	3	2	1	2	1	1	3	2	SF
LONDON C.	1	2	1	2	1	1	1	1	1	2	2	2	1							
NOTTINGHAM C.	1	P	1	1	1	2	2	P	1											
OLDHAM	3	1	SF	SF	3	1	2	SF	1	2	1	2	3	2	2	2	1	3	3	1
ROCHDALE H.	2	1	2	2	1	2	1	2	2	1	1	2	1	2	2	1	2	1	2	2
RYEDALE-YORK	1	1	1	1	1	1	P	2	1	SF	1	1	2	2	1	1	1	2	2	1
ST. HELENS	2	3	F	SF	F	3	F	2	1	3	3	1	SF	2	SF	F	SF	W	2	3
SALFORD	1	1	3	2	1	SF	1	1	2	1	2	1	3	3	1	2	2	2	2	2
SHEFFIELD E.	2	2	2	2	2	2	1	1	1											
SWINTON	P	1	1	1	1	1	P	P	1	P	2	1	1	1	1	2	2	1	1	2
WAKEFIELD T.	2	1	2	3	2	1	2	1	2	2	2	3	3	3	F	2	2	1	SF	1
WARRINGTON	1	2	3	F	SF	2	1	2	2	2	3	1	SF	3	1	SF	1	3	F	W
WHITEHAVEN	1	1	2	3	1	P	3	1	1	1	1	1	1	1	1	1	1	1	1	1
WIDNES	F	1	SF	3	SF	3	SF	3	3	W	1	F	W	SF	W	3	F	F	W	2
WIGAN	W	W	W	W	W	W	1	3	W	F	1	2	1	1	2	2	2	2	2	3
WORKINGTON T.	1	3	2	1	P	1	P	1	2	2	3	2	2	1	1	2	3	2	2	2

REGAL TROPHY

1992-93 Final

Wigan won their 18th consecutive victory in all finals, but only after a mighty scare from battling Bradford Northern. The Riversiders celebrated a 15-8 success at Elland Road, Leeds, Northern having restored their pride after a humiliating 71-10 hammering at the hands of Wigan in the Silk Cut Challenge Cup semi-final less than a year earlier.

At half-time in that rout at Burnden Park, Bolton, coach John Monie had supped tea, his only priority in mid-romp. Ten months on, the usually cool and collected Monie muttered a few home truths during the break. For Northern had fiercely contested the first half. Whereas in the semi-final victory over Castleford, Bradford had turned opportunities into points, this time their enterprise left them empty handed.

Kiwi full back Dave Watson was outstanding in attack as Northern raided Wigan's territory from long range, stand off Neil Summers emulating his probing style.

Ironically, it was Watson who made vital errors either side of the interval to cost Northern the tie and himself the Man of the Match rating.

Wigan scrum half Shaun Edwards boosted his own claim to the individual award by kicking through to the Northern in-goal area three minutes before the interval. Watson hastily booted the ball back into play for Frano Botica to feed the roaming Martin Offiah who passed on to teenager Jason Robinson to nip inside for the first score of the match. Botica added the goal.

Northern skipper David Hobbs cut the margin to 6-2 with a penalty one minute before the half-time whistle, leaving the Yorkshiremen to rue what might have been.

Three minutes after the restart, Watson blundered again, with Edwards taking the ultimate advantage. While still shining on

attack, Watson again faltered under pressure in defence when he just managed to scramble over his own line to touch down the ball as Offiah chased another speculative kick. Within six tackles of the resultant drop out, Edwards rushed in at close range off Martin Dermott's pass from a play-the-ball.

Summers combined with centre Tony Anderson, an 11th-hour replacement for flu victim Darrall Shelford, to get Steve McGowan over for a 78th-minute consolation try, veteran Keith Mumby marking his return to the Bradford ranks with the goal.

Edwards complemented his 22nd winners' medal at the age of 26 with the Regal Man of the Match award. Wigan celebrated the historic landmark of being the first club to hold all five major trophies at the same time, the Regal Trophy joining the early season capture of the Greenalls Lancashire Cup, plus the previous campaign's Silk Cut Challenge Cup, Stones Bitter Championship and Premiership Trophies.

Northern's gamble on playing chief organiser Deryck Fox after painkilling injections for a serious groin injury failed. The inspirational scrum half struggled through to the 68th minute before retiring, but his eagerly awaited duel with Test rival Edwards was a no-contest.

Wigan's victory was workmanlike rather than adventurous, adopting Australian one-man rugby tactics and proving that the doubling of the play-the-ball zone does not always encourage open play.

On the rare occasions Wigan did move the ball wide, Bradford's cover was superb, most notably when second row man Paul Medley cut across in classic second row style to bring down Botica and then Sam Panapa.

But, having weathered the early Northern storm, Wigan succeeded in their now traditional pattern of steamrollering the opposition into submission. Not even the off-the-field problems associated with their planned participation in the World Sevens could distract them, despite hearing on the morning of the final that they had been expelled from the Sydney competition.

REGAL TROPHY FINAL

23 January   Elland Road, Leeds

WIGAN 15   **BRADFORD NORTHERN 8**

Steve Hampson	1.	Dave Watson
Jason Robinson	2.	Tony Marchant
Dean Bell, Capt.	3.	Steve McGowan
Andrew Farrar	4.	Tony Anderson
Martin Offiah	5.	Roger Simpson
Frano Botica	6.	Neil Summers
Shaun Edwards	7.	Deryck Fox
Neil Cowie	8.	David Hobbs, Capt.
Martin Dermott	9.	Brian Noble
Andy Platt	10.	Roy Powell
Denis Betts	11.	Paul Medley
Billy McGinty	12.	Karl Fairbank
Phil Clarke	13.	David Heron
Joe Lydon	14.	Keith Mumby
Sam Panapa	15.	Trevor Clark

T: Robinson, Edwards   T: McGowan
G: Botica (3), Hampson (dg)   G: Hobbs, Mumby
Substitutions: Substitutions:
Panapa for Clarke (9 min.)   Mumby for Anderson (44 min.)
Lydon for Offiah (59 min.)   Clark for Noble (44 min.)
Half-time: 6-2   Referee: John Holdsworth (Kippax)
Attendance: 13,221

Dressing-room joy for Man of the Match Shaun Edwards with the Regal Trophy.

Wigan's Australian centre Andrew Farrar receives the attentions of Bradford Northern trio, from the left, Brian Noble, Neil Summers and Paul Medley.

Cover from Bradford Northern winger Roger Simpson forces opposite number Jason Robinson to kick ahead.

1992-93 Round by Round

The 1992-93 Regal Trophy was marked by the introduction of two French teams into the tournament, designed to boost the prestige of Gallic Rugby League on the Continent. The Rugby Football League's dispute with BARLA included a League edict that the amateurs should be excluded from the Regal Trophy and the Silk Cut Challenge Cup. But this was a separate issue to the inclusion of French clubs in the Regal Trophy.

Alex Murphy returned to former club St. Helens for his Huddersfield charges to go down 44-18. World Cup final selections Gary Connolly, Alan Hunte and Kevin Ward showed their international class as St. Helens eased through to the next round. Wakefield Trinity disposed of lowly Third Division outfit Highfield with a club record 90-12 at Belle Vue. Mark Conway broke two Trinity records with 13 goals and 34 points, including two tries. Warrington beat Blackpool Gladiators 32-8 at home, full back Lee Penny scoring a debut try after only 10 minutes. The Wire were leading 28-0 at the break before Blackpool rallied to win the second half. Chorley Borough entertained Sheffield Eagles and went down 10-38, David Mycoe taking the Man of the Match award with an 18-point haul. Australian import Craig McKeough capped his debut for Hull K.R. with a try after a 60-yard move as the Robins beat Swinton 32-12 at Bury. The Man of the Match award went to Wayne Parker despite his being on the field for less than an hour.

In the first round, Tea Ropati dropped a goal four minutes from time to give St. Helens a 15-14 victory at home to a battling Leeds, whose John Gallagher had kicked a penalty goal five minutes earlier and looked to have earned a well deserved replay. In the televised tie, Wigan entertained Carcassonne in a battle of the champions, the Riversiders storming to a 52-0 success with Frano Botica claiming two tries and eight goals. In the second French encounter, Catalan XIII visited Rochdale Hornets, who

registered a 32-16 victory, David Webster sealing success after the French rallied with three touchdowns. The shock of the round was Wakefield Trinity's 30-0 defeat at London Crusaders, who ran in five tries to reach the second round for only the second time in their 13-year history.

Second Division Featherstone Rovers also pulled off a major surprise by winning 18-14 at First Division Salford. Rovers trailed 14-8 at half time, but rallied through Richard Gunn and Owen Simpson tries to secure victory. At Bramley, visitors Carlisle made an ideal start to open a 10-0 lead in as many minutes. Bramley fought back through tries from Norman Francis and Sonny Whakarau before going down 16-12. Workington Town overcame the first-half dismissal of Kiwi Brad Hepi to win 30-4 at Doncaster. Australian capture Julian O'Neill marked his debut for Widnes by scoring two tries and creating another in the 46-4 home success over Ryedale-York. Widnes international John Devereux was sent off.

Props Lee Crooks and Martin Ketteridge were too powerful for Oldham as visitors Castleford won 40-22, the strength of Kiwi international Richard Blackmore bringing him two tries. Centre Tony Thorniley collected 18 points from two tries and five goals in Warrington's 31-16 home win over Sheffield Eagles, the visitors making the score respectable with two late tries. Hull led visitors Dewsbury 22-6 after 52 minutes before the unbeaten Third Division leaders pulled back to 22-16. Across the city, Hull K.R. were flattered to lead 14-4 at half-time against a Clayton Friend-inspired Whitehaven. But the Robins ran in six tries after the break, including two for Paul Lyman, in a 48-4 victory.

Bradford Northern centre Steve McGowan scored a hat-trick in each half to equal the competition record of six tries in the 70-10 home defeat of Barrow. His unselfish pass to Roger Simpson prevented McGowan claiming a share of the club record of seven touchdowns. Great Britain Under-21 packman Andy Precious was Hunslet's hero in the 13-6 success at Batley, the youngster contributing a try, a goal and two drop goals. Batley's sole touchdown came from Glen Tomlinson. Australian centre Greg Austin grabbed five touchdowns in a 16-try home rout as Halifax beat lowly Nottingham City 76-6. There was also a hat-trick of tries for Graeme Hallas, though Halifax could only manage six goals from 16 attempts. Visitors Keighley went behind 14-2 at Leigh, with three tries being scored while prop Joe Grima was in the sin bin. Winger John Wasyliw kept the Cougars in the picture with two tries and four goals before Leigh's Dave Tanner sealed a 32-24 victory by completing his hat-trick of tries.

In the second round, Warrington entertained Bradford Northern in the televised tie, which ended level at 12-all, Northern having pulled back from 12-2 with 10 minutes left. In the Odsal replay, Northern relied on the slick handling of loose forward David Heron and some rugged defence to earn a 9-6 passage into the quarter-finals. Holders Widnes took nearly half an hour to prise open Second Division Rochdale Hornets, leading only 10-2 at the break, after which a Bobby Goulding-inspired home side coasted to a 30-2 victory. Second Division pacesetters Featherstone Rovers were trailing by only one point midway through the second half before tries from Anthony Sullivan, David Lyon and Chris Joynt provided visitors St. Helens with a flattering 25-8 scoreline. Wigan spluttered into a 6-0 half-time lead at Hull K.R. before Test loose forward Phil Clarke inspired a second-half improvement for an 18-0 win.

Hunslet's five-match winning run ended at home to Workington Town as centre Tony Kay grabbed four touchdowns in the 34-12 win. Town became the first Third Division side to reach the last eight of the Regal Trophy. London Crusaders let themselves down at Leigh with bad handling in the atrocious conditions, Leigh leading 10-6 at the break and adding a Jason Donohue try in the last four

minutes. Castleford gave a debut to South African trialist Jamie Bloem, scorer of one of their nine tries. Kiwi centre Richard Blackmore notched a hat-trick in a 54-0 romp over visitors Carlisle. Halifax were trailing only 16-14 on the hour when Hull forward Jon Sharp charged down a Paul Bishop kick for hooker Lee Jackson to touch down and steer the home side to a 28-14 success.

In the quarter-finals, Castleford secured a 12-8 victory at St. Helens, who had Test prop Kevin Ward dismissed for a trip after only five minutes. Saints led 8-6 at the break and were well served by Man of the Match Joynt, but soon after the interval, Castleford's Tawera Nikau put centre Tony Smith through for what proved to be the winning try. Widnes lost their grip on the Regal Trophy with a 21-10 defeat at Bradford City's Valley Parade soccer ground, where Bradford Northern welcomed back scrum half Deryck Fox after losing four consecutive matches in his absence. Fox contributed 13 points in an outstanding Man of the Match performance. Nearly 8,000 fans packed Derwent Park for Workington Town's tie with Wigan, who raced into an 18-0 lead after 25 minutes before the Cumbrians staged a second-half rally to pull back to 18-12 before a Clarke try sealed a 24-12 victory seven minutes from time. Test winger Paul Eastwood was the key figure of Hull's 24-14 home victory over Leigh, scoring a try and six goals.

After 13 seasons of being staged at neutral venues, the semi-finals reverted to home advantage. Injury-hit Wigan and Hull met at Central Park, the Riversiders' young replacements starring in a 19-4 success. Among 10 enforced changes, youngsters Paul Atcheson and Mick Cassidy took centre stage, well supported by the experienced Shaun Edwards, Clarke and Frano Botica. Bradford Northern again hired Valley Parade for their tie with Castleford. Northern provided nine minutes of inspiration and 71 of perspiration for a 19-12 victory, leaving Castleford to rue lost chances after Northern had opened an 18-0 lead.

1992-93 RESULTS

Preliminary Round

Chorley B.	10	Sheffield E.	38
St. Helens	44	Huddersfield	18
Swinton	12	Hull K.R.	32
Wakefield T.	90	Highfield	12
Warrington	32	Blackpool G.	8

First Round

Batley	6	Hunslet	13
Bradford N.	70	Barrow	10
Bramley	12	Carlisle	16
Doncaster	4	Workington T.	30
Halifax	76	Nottingham C.	6
Hull	22	Dewsbury	16
Hull K.R.	48	Whitehaven	4
Leigh	32	Keighley C.	24
London C.	30	Wakefield T.	0
Oldham	22	Castleford	40
Rochdale H.	32	Catalan XIII	16
St. Helens	15	Leeds	14
Salford	14	Featherstone R.	18
Warrington	31	Sheffield E.	16
Widnes	46	Ryedale-York	4
Wigan	52	Carcassonne	0

Second Round

Castleford	54	Carlisle	0
Featherstone R.	8	St. Helens	25
Hull	28	Halifax	14
Hull K.R.	0	Wigan	18
Hunslet	12	Workington T.	34
Leigh	16	London C.	6
Warrington	12	Bradford N.	12
Widnes	30	Rochdale H.	2

Replay

Bradford N.	9	Warrington	6

Third Round

Bradford N.	21	Widnes	10
(at Bradford C. FC)			
Hull	24	Leigh	14
St. Helens	8	Castleford	12
Workington T.	12	Wigan	24

Semi-finals

Bradford N.	19	Castleford	12
(at Bradford C. FC)			
Wigan	19	Hull	4

Final

Wigan	15	Bradford N.	8
(at Elland Road, Leeds)			

1992-93 PRIZES

Preliminary Round	£2,600 each club
First Round	£2,600 to losers
Second Round	£3,775 to losers
Third Round	£6,000 to losers
Semi-finals	£9,500 to losers
Runners-up	£18,000
Winners	£34,000

Total Prize Money	**£198,000**
Capital Development Fund	**£132,000**
Grand Total	**£330,000**

Bradford Northern's Paul Medley, top-class cover tackler in the 1992-93 Regal final.

REGAL TROPHY ROLL OF HONOUR

Season	Winners		Runners-up		Venue	Attendance	Receipts
1971-72	Halifax	22	Wakefield T.	11	Bradford	7,975	£2,545
1972-73	Leeds	12	Salford	7	Huddersfield	10,102	£4,563
1973-74	Warrington	27	Rochdale H.	16	Wigan	9,347	£4,380
1974-75	Bradford N.	3	Widnes	2	Warrington	5,935	£3,305
1975-76	Widnes	19	Hull	13	Leeds	9,035	£6,275
1976-77	Castleford	25	Blackpool B.	15	Salford	4,512	£2,919
1977-78	Warrington	9	Widnes	4	St. Helens	10,258	£8,429
1978-79	Widnes	16	Warrington	4	St. Helens	10,743	£11,709
1979-80	Bradford N.	6	Widnes	0	Leeds	9,909	£11,560
1980-81	Warrington	12	Barrow	5	Wigan	12,820	£21,020
1981-82	Hull	12	Hull K.R.	4	Leeds	25,245	£42,987
1982-83	Wigan	15	Leeds	4	Elland Rd, Leeds	19,553	£49,027
1983-84	Leeds	18	Widnes	10	Wigan	9,510	£19,824
1984-85	Hull K.R.	12	Hull	0	Hull City FC	25,326	£69,555
1985-86	Wigan	11	Hull K.R.	8	Elland Rd, Leeds	17,573	£66,714
1986-87	Wigan	18	Warrington	4	Bolton W. FC	21,144	£86,041
1987-88	St. Helens	15	Leeds	14	Wigan	16,669	£62,232
1988-89	Wigan	12	Widnes	6	Bolton W. FC	20,709	£94,874
1989-90	Wigan	24	Halifax	12	Leeds	17,810	£73,688
1990-91	Warrington	12	Bradford N.	2	Leeds	11,154	£57,652
1991-92	Widnes	24	Leeds	0	Wigan	15,070	£90,453
1992-93	Wigan	15	Bradford N.	8	Elland Rd, Leeds	13,221	£90,204

REGAL TROPHY FINAL ....
A REVIEW
1971-72
Halifax 22 Hepworth; Rayner, Davies (1t),
Willicombe (1t), Kelly (1t); Burton (5g), Baker
(Sanderson); Dewhirst, Hawksley, Callon (1t),
(Reeves), Fogerty, J. Martin, Halmshaw
Wakefield T. 11 Wraith (Ward); Slater (1t),
Marston, Hegarty, Major; Topliss (1t), Harkin;
Jeanes, Morgan, Lyons, Harrison (Spencer),
Valentine (1t), N. Fox (1g)
Referee: S. Shepherd (Oldham)
1972-73
Leeds 12 Holmes (1g); Alan Smith, Hynes,
Dyl, Atkinson (2t); Hardisty, Hepworth;
Clawson (2g) (Ward), Fisher (Pickup), Jeanes,
Haigh, Cookson, Eccles
Salford 7 Charlton; Colloby, Watkins (2g),
Hesketh, Richards; Gill (P. Ward), Banner;
Ramshaw, J. Ward, Mackay, Grice (Davies),
Kirkbride, Dixon (1t)
Referee: W.H. Thompson (Huddersfield)

1973-74
Warrington 27 Whitehead (1t, 6g); M. Philbin,
Noonan (2t), Reynolds (Pickup), Bevan (1t);
Whittle, Gordon; D. Chisnall (Nicholas 1t),
Ashcroft, Brady, Wright, Wanbon, B. Philbin
Rochdale H. 16 Crellin; Brelsford (2t), Brophy
(1t), Taylor (1t), Aspinall; Butler (Wood),
Gartland; Holliday (2g), Harris, Whitehead,
Fogerty, Sheffield, Halmshaw
Referee: D.G. Kershaw (York)
1974-75
Bradford N. 3 Carlton (1t); Francis, Ward,
Gant, D. Redfearn; Blacker, Seabourne; Earl,
Jarvis, Jackson, Joyce, Trotter, Fearnley
Widnes 2 Dutton (1g); A. Prescott, D.O'Neill,
Aspey, Anderson; Hughes, Bowden; Mills,
Elwell, Sheridan, Adams, Blackwood,
Laughton
Referee: G.F. Lindop (Wakefield)

1975-76
Widnes 19 Dutton (3g); A. Prescott, George, Aspey, Jenkins (2t); Hughes, Bowden (1t, 1dg); Mills, Elwell, Wood, Foran, Sheridan, Adams (1t)
Hull 13 Stephenson; A. Macklin, Clark, Portz, Hunter (1t); Hancock, Foulkes (Davidson); Ramsey, Flanagan, Wardell, Boxall (2g), Walker, Crane (2t)
Referee: J.V. Moss (Manchester)
1976-77
Castleford 25 Wraith (1t); Fenton, Joyner (1t), P. Johnson (1t), Briggs; Burton (1t), Stephens (1t); Kahn, Spurr, A. Dickinson, Reilly, Lloyd (5g), S. Norton
Blackpool B. 15 Reynolds; Robinson, Heritage, Machen (1t), Pitman (Lamb); Marsh, Newall; Hamilton, Allen (1t), Egan (1t, 3g), Gamble, Groves (Hurst), M. Pattinson
Referee: M.J. Naughton (Widnes)
1977-78
Warrington 9 Finnigan; Hesford (3g), Benyon, Wilson, Bevan (1t); K. Kelly, Gordon; Lester, Dalgreen, Nicholas, Martyn, B. Philbin, Potter
Widnes 4 Eckersley; Wright, Aspey, George, Woods (2g); Hughes, Bowden; Ramsey, Elwell, Shaw (Dearden), Adams, Hull, Laughton
Referee: W.H. Thompson (Huddersfield)
1978-79
Widnes 16 Eckersley; Wright (1t), Aspey, Hughes, Burke (3g); Moran, Bowden; Mills, Elwell (2dg), Shaw, Dearden, Hull (1t), Adams (2dg)
Warrington 4 Finnigan; M. Kelly, Hesford (2g), Benyon, Sutton; K. Kelly (Hunter), Gordon; Lester, Waller, Nicholas, Case, Martyn, A. Gwilliam
Referee: G.F. Lindop (Wakefield)
1979-80
Bradford N. 6 Mumby (1g); Barends, D. Redfearn, D. Parker (1t), Gant; Stephenson (1dg), A. Redfearn; Thompson, Bridges, Forsyth (I. Van Bellen), Grayshon, G. Van Bellen (Ferres), Casey
Widnes 0 Eckersley; Wright, Aspey, George, Burke; Hughes, Bowden; Hogan (Mills), Elwell, Shaw, L. Gorley, Hull, Adams
Referee: W.H. Thompson (Huddersfield)
1980-81
Warrington 12 Hesford (2g, 2dg); Thackray, I. Duane, Bevan (2t), M. Kelly; K. Kelly, A. Gwilliam; Courtney, Waller, Case, Martyn, Potter, Hunter (Eccles)
Barrow 5 Elliott; McConnell, French, Ball (1g), Wainwright; Mason (1t), Cairns; D. Chisnall, Allen (Szymala), Flynn, K. James, Kirkby, Hadley
Referee: W.H. Thompson (Huddersfield)

1981-82
Hull 12 Banks; O'Hara, Harrison, Leuluai, Prendiville; Day, Dean (1dg) (K. Harkin); Skerrett, Wileman (1t), Stone, Crane, L. Crooks (4g), Norton
Hull K.R. 4 Fairbairn (2g); Hubbard, M. Smith, Hogan, Muscroft; Hartley, P. Harkin (Burton); Holdstock (Millington), Watkinson, S. Crooks, Lowe, Casey, Hall
Referee: G.F. Lindop (Wakefield)
1982-83
Wigan 15 Williams; Ramsdale, Stephenson, Whitfield (4g, 1dg), Gill (1t) (Juliff 1t); M. Foy, Fairhurst; Shaw, Kiss, Campbell, West (Case), Scott, Pendlebury
Leeds 4 Hague; Campbell, Wilkinson, Dyl, Andy Smith; Holmes, Dick (2g); Dickinson, Ward, Burke, Sykes, W. Heron, D. Heron
Referee: R. Campbell (Widnes)
1983-84
Leeds 18 Wilkinson; Prendiville, Creasser (5g), D. Bell, Andy Smith; Holmes (1t), Dick (1t); Keith Rayne, Ward (Squire), Kevin Rayne, Moorby, Laurie, Webb
Widnes 10 Burke (1g); Wright, Keiron O'Loughlin, Lydon (1t), Linton (1t); Hughes, Gregory; S. O'Neill, Elwell, K. Tamati, L. Gorley, Whitfield, Adams
Referee: W.H. Thompson (Huddersfield)
1984-85
Hull K.R. 12 Fairbairn; Clark (1t), Robinson, Prohm (1t), Laws; M. Smith, Harkin; Broadhurst, Watkinson, Ema, Burton, Hogan (1t), Miller
Hull 0 Kemble (Schofield); S. Evans, Ah Kuoi, Leuluai, O'Hara; Topliss; Sterling; Edmonds (Dannatt), Patrick, Rose, L. Crooks, Proctor, Divorty
Referee: S. Wall (Leigh)
1985-86
Wigan 11 Hampson; Mordt, Stephenson (1g), Hanley, Gill (Edwards); Ella, M. Ford (1t); Dowling (1dg), Kiss, Wane (1t), West, Goodway, Potter (Du Toit)
Hull K.R. 8 Lydiat (1t); Clark, M. Smith, Dorahy, Laws (1t); G. Smith, Harkin; P. Johnston (Robinson), Watkinson, Ema, Burton, Kelly, Miller
Referee: J. Holdsworth (Kippax)
1986-87
Wigan 18 Hampson; Stephenson, Lydon, Bell (1t), Gill (2t, 1g); Hanley, Edwards; West, Dermott, Case, Roberts, Potter, Goodway (1t)
Warrington 4 Johnson; Meadows, Cullen, Ropati, Forster (1t); K. Kelly, Peters (Duane); Boyd, K. Tamati (Rathbone), Jackson, Sanderson, Roberts, M. Gregory
Referee: J. Holdsworth (Kippax)

1987-88
St. Helens 15 Veivers; Tanner, Loughlin
(2t, 3g), Elia, Quirk; Cooper, Holding (1dg);
Burke, Groves, Souto (Evans), Forber,
Haggerty, Platt
Leeds 14 Gurr; Morris, Schofield, Jackson (1t),
Basnett (Gibson); Creasser (1t, 3g), Ashton;
Tunks, Maskill, Kevin Rayne (Fairbank),
Powell, Medley, D. Heron
Referee: G.F. Lindop (Wakefield)
1988-89
Wigan 12 Hampson; Bell, K. Iro (1t), Lydon
(2g) (Gregory), T. Iro; Byrne, Edwards;
Shelford (Goodway), Dermott, Wane, Betts,
Potter, Hanley (1t)
Widnes 6 Tait; Thackray, Currier (1g), Wright
(1t), Offiah; T. Myler, D. Hulme; Sorensen,
McKenzie, Grima, M. O'Neill, Koloto
(P. Hulme), Eyres
Referee: J. Holdsworth (Kippax)
1989-90
Wigan 24 Lydon (2g); Marshall, K. Iro, Bell,
Preston; Edwards (1t), A. Gregory; Lucas
(Wane), Dermott, Platt, Betts, Gildart
(Goodway 1t), Hanley (3t)

Halifax 12 Whitfield (Smith) (Scott);
Riddlesden, T. Anderson, Hetherington, George;
Dorahy, Lyons; Hill (1t), McCallion, Johnston,
Bell, Milner, Holliday (4g)
Referee: D.G. Kershaw (Easingwold)
1990-91
Warrington 12 Lyon (4g); Drummond,
Bateman, Thorniley, Forster; O'Sullivan, Ellis;
Harmon (Phillips), D. Mann, Chambers
(Thomas 1t), Mercer, McGinty, Cullen
Bradford N. 2 Wilkinson; Cordle, Shelford,
Simpson, Marchant (Hellewell); Summers, Iti;
Hobbs (1g), Noble, Hamer, Medley, Croft,
Pendlebury
Referee: J. Smith (Halifax)
1991-92
Widnes 24 Tait (1t); Devereux, Currier, Wright,
Sarsfield (Atcheson); Davies (1t, 3g, 1dg), Dowd;
Sorensen (1t), P. Hulme, Smith, Howard, Eyres,
Holliday (1t, 1dg) (Grima)
Leeds 0 Edwards; Ford, Creasser, Irving (Gibson),
Bentley; Schofield, Goulding; Wane (Molloy),
Gunn, O'Neill, Powell, Dixon, Divorty
Referee: B. Galtress (Bradford)

REGAL TROPHY MAN OF THE MATCH

Season	Winner	Team	Position
1971-72	Bruce Burton	Halifax (v. Wakefield T.)	Stand off
1972-73	Keith Hepworth	Leeds (v. Salford)	Scrum half
1973-74	Kevin Ashcroft	Warrington (v. Rochdale H.)	Hooker
1974-75	Barry Seabourne	Bradford N. (v. Widnes)	Scrum half
1975-76	Reg Bowden	Widnes (v. Hull)	Scrum half
1976-77	Gary Stephens	Castleford	Scrum half
	Howard Allen	Blackpool B.	Hooker
1977-78	Steve Hesford	Warrington (v. Widnes)	Winger
1978-79	David Eckersley	Widnes (v. Warrington)	Full back
1979-80	Len Casey	Bradford N. (v. Widnes)	Loose forward
1980-81	Tommy Martyn	Warrington (v. Barrow)	Second row
1981-82	Trevor Skerrett	Hull (v. Hull K.R.)	Prop
1982-83	Martin Foy	Wigan (v. Leeds)	Stand off
1983-84	Mark Laurie	Leeds (v. Widnes)	Second row
1984-85	Paul Harkin	Hull K.R. (v. Hull)	Scrum half
1985-86	Paul Harkin	Hull K.R. (v. Wigan)	Scrum half
1986-87	Andy Goodway	Wigan (v. Warrington)	Loose forward
1987-88	Paul Loughlin	St. Helens (v. Leeds)	Centre
1988-89	Ellery Hanley	Wigan (v. Widnes)	Loose forward
1989-90	Ellery Hanley	Wigan (v. Halifax)	Loose forward
1990-91	Billy McGinty	Warrington (v. Bradford N.)	Second row
1991-92	Les Holliday	Widnes (v. Leeds)	Loose forward
1992-93	Shaun Edwards	Wigan (v. Bradford N.)	Scrum half

REGAL TROPHY FINAL PLAYERS' REGISTER

The following is an index of players who have appeared in the Regal Trophy final since its inauguration as the Player's No. 6 Trophy in 1971-72.
W — winners, L — losers. Substitute appearances in lower case letters. The year denotes the second half of the season.

ADAMS, Mick: Widnes 75L, 76W, 78L, 79W, 80L, 84L
AH KUOI, Fred: Hull 85L
ALLEN, Howard: Blackpool B. 77L; Barrow 81L
ANDERSON, Chris: Widnes 75L
ANDERSON, Tony: Halifax 90L; Bradford N. 93L
ASHCROFT, Kevin: Warrington 74W
ASHTON, Ray: Leeds 88L
ASPEY, Mal: Widnes 75L, 76W, 78L, 79W, 80L
ASPINALL, Willie: Rochdale H. 74L
ATCHESON, Paul: Widnes 92w
ATKINSON, John: Leeds 73W

BAKER, Gordon: Halifax 72W
BALL, Ian: Barrow 81L
BANKS, Barry: Hull 82W
BANNER, Peter: Salford 73L
BARENDS, David: Bradford N. 80W
BASNETT, John: Leeds 88L
BATEMAN, Allan: Warrington 91W
BELL, Dean: Leeds 84W; Wigan 87W, 89W, 90W, 93W
BELL, Peter: Halifax 90L
BENTLEY, John: Leeds 92L
BENYON, Billy: Warrington 78W, 79L
BETTS, Denis: Wigan 89W, 90W, 93W
BEVAN, John: Warrington 74W, 78W, 81W
BLACKER, Mick: Bradford N. 75W
BLACKWOOD, Bob: Widnes 75L
BOTICA, Frano: Wigan 93W
BOWDEN, Reg: Widnes 75L, 76W, 78L, 79W, 80L
BOXALL, Keith: Hull 76L
BOYD, Les: Warrington 87L
BRADY, Brian: Warrington 74W
BRELSFORD, Norman: Rochdale H. 74L
BRIDGES, John "Keith": Bradford N. 80W
BRIGGS, Trevor: Castleford 77W
BROADHURST, Mark: Hull K.R. 85W
BROPHY, Tom: Rochdale H. 74L
BURKE, Mick: Widnes 79W, 80L, 84L
BURKE, Tony: Leeds 83L; St. Helens 88W
BURTON, Bruce: Halifax 72W; Castleford 77W
BURTON, Chris: Hull K.R. 82l, 85W, 86L
BUTLER, John: Rochdale H. 74L
BYRNE, Ged: Wigan 89W

CAIRNS, David: Barrow 81L
CALLON, David: Halifax 72W
CAMPBELL, Danny: Wigan 83W
CAMPBELL, Mark: Leeds 83l

CARLTON, Stuart: Bradford N. 75W
CASE, Brian: Warrington 79L, 81W; Wigan 83w, 87W
CASEY, Len: Bradford N. 80W; Hull K.R. 82L
CHAMBERS, Gary: Warrington 91W
CHARLTON, Paul: Salford 73L
CHISNALL, Dave: Warrington 74W; Barrow 81L
CLARK, Garry: Hull K.R. 85W, 86L
CLARK, George: Hull 76L
CLARK, Trevor: Bradford N. 93l
CLARKE, Phil: Wigan 93W
CLAWSON, Terry: Leeds 73W
COLLOBY, Tony: Salford 73L
COOKSON, Phil: Leeds 73W
COOPER, Shane: St. Helens 88W
CORDLE, Gerald: Bradford N. 91L
COURTNEY, Neil: Warrington 81W
COWIE, Neil: Wigan 93W
CRANE, Mick: Hull 76L, 82W
CREASSER, David: Leeds 84W, 88L, 92L
CRELLIN, Jim: Rochdale H. 74L
CROFT, David: Bradford N. 91L
CROOKS, Lee: Hull 82W, 85L
CROOKS, Steve: Hull K.R. 82L
CULLEN, Paul: Warrington 87L, 91W
CURRIER, Andy: Widnes 89L, 92W

DALGREEN, John: Warrington 78W
DANNATT, Andy: Hull 85l
DAVIDSON, Chris: Hull 76l
DAVIES, Doug: Salford 73l
DAVIES, Jonathan: Widnes 92W
DAVIES, Phil: Halifax 72W
DAY, Terry: Hull 82W
DEAN, Tony: Hull 82W
DEARDEN, Alan: Widnes 78l, 79W
DERMOTT, Martin: Wigan 87W, 89W, 90W, 93W
DEVEREUX, John: Widnes 92W
DEWHIRST, Terry: Halifax 72W
DICK, Kevin: Leeds 83L, 84W
DICKINSON, Alan: Castleford 77W
DICKINSON, Roy: Leeds 83L
DIVORTY, Gary: Hull 85L; Leeds 92L
DIXON, Colin: Salford 73L
DIXON, Paul: Leeds 92L
DORAHY, John: Hull K.R. 86L; Halifax 90L
DOWD, Barry: Widnes 92W
DOWLING, Greg: Wigan 86W
DRUMMOND, Des: Warrington 91W
DUANE, Ian: Warrington 81W
DUANE, Ronnie: Warrington 87l

DU TOIT, Nick: Wigan 86w
DUTTON, Ray: Widnes 75L, 76W
DYL, Les: Leeds 73W, 83L

EARL, Kelvin: Bradford N. 75W
ECCLES, Bob: Warrington 81w
ECCLES, Graham: Leeds 73W
ECKERSLEY, David: Widnes 78L 79W, 80L
EDMONDS, Phil: Hull 85L
EDWARDS, Morvin: Leeds 92L
EDWARDS, Shaun: Wigan 86w, 87W, 89W, 90W, 93W
EGAN, Joe: Blackpool B. 77L
ELIA, Mark: St. Helens 88W
ELLA, Steve: Wigan 86W
ELLIOTT, David: Barrow 81L
ELLIS, Kevin: Warrington 91W
ELWELL, Keith: Widnes 75L, 76W, 78L, 79W, 80L, 84L
EMA, Asuquo: Hull K.R. 85W, 86L
EVANS, Steve: Hull 85L
EVANS, Stuart: St. Helens 88w
EYRES, Richard: Widnes 89L, 92W

FAIRBAIRN, George: Hull K.R. 82L, 85W
FAIRBANK, John: Leeds 88l
FAIRBANK, Karl: Bradford N. 93L
FAIRHURST, Jimmy: Wigan 83W
FARRAR, Andrew: Wigan 93W
FEARNLEY, Stan: Bradford N. 75W
FENTON, Steve: Castleford 77W
FERRES, Steve: Bradford N. 80w
FINNIGAN, Derek: Warrington 78W, 79L
FISHER, Tony: Leeds 73W
FLANAGAN, Peter: Hull 76L
FLYNN, Malcolm: Barrow 81L
FOGERTY, Terry: Halifax 72W; Rochdale H. 74L
FORAN, John: Widnes 76W
FORBER, Paul: St. Helens 88W
FORD, Mike: Wigan 86W
FORD, Phil: Leeds 92L
FORSTER, Mark: Warrington 87L, 91W
FORSYTH, Colin: Bradford N. 80W
FOULKES, Kenny: Hull 76L
FOX, Deryck: Bradford N. 93L
FOX, Neil: Wakefield T. 72L
FOY, Martin: Wigan 83W
FRANCIS, Rudi: Bradford N. 75W
FRENCH, Nigel: Barrow 81L

GAMBLE, Paul: Blackpool B. 77L
GANT, Les: Bradford N. 75W, 80W
GARTLAND, Peter: Rochdale H. 74L
GEORGE, Derek "Mick": Widnes 76W, 78L, 80L
GEORGE, Wilf: Halifax 90L
GIBSON, Carl: Leeds 88l, 92l
GILDART, Ian: Wigan 90W

GILL, Henderson: Wigan 83W, 86W, 87W
GILL, Ken: Salford 73L
GOODWAY, Andy: Wigan 86W, 87W, 89w, 90w
GORDON, Parry: Warrington 74W, 78W, 79L
GORLEY, Les: Widnes 80L, 84L
GOULDING, Bobby: Leeds 92L
GRAYSHON, Jeff: Bradford N. 80W
GREGORY, Andy: Widnes 84L; Wigan 89w, 90W
GREGORY, Mike: Warrington 87L
GRICE, Alan: Salford 73L
GRIMA, Joe: Widnes 89L, 92w
GROVES, Ken: Blackpool B. 77L
GROVES, Paul: St. Helens 88W
GUNN, Richard: Leeds 92L
GURR, Marty: Leeds 88L
GWILLIAM, Alan: Warrington 79L, 81W

HADLEY, Derek: Barrow 81L
HAGGERTY, Roy: St. Helens 88W
HAGUE, Neil: Leeds 83l
HAIGH, Bob: Leeds 73W
HALL, David: Hull K.R. 82L
HALMSHAW, Tony: Halifax 72W; Rochdale H. 74L
HAMER, Jon: Bradford N. 91L
HAMILTON, Jim: Blackpool B. 77L
HAMPSON, Steve: Wigan 86W, 87W, 89W, 93W
HANCOCK, Brian: Hull 76L
HANLEY, Ellery: Wigan 86W, 87W, 89W, 90W
HARDISTY, Alan: Leeds 73W
HARKIN, Kevin: Wakefield T. 72L; Hull 82w
HARKIN, Paul: Hull K.R. 82L, 85W, 86L
HARMON, Neil: Warrington 91W
HARRIS, Ray: Rochdale H. 74L
HARRISON, Chris: Hull 82W
HARRISON, Peter: Wakefield T. 72L
HARTLEY, Steve: Hull K.R. 82L
HAWKSLEY, Roy: Halifax 72W
HEGARTY, John: Wakefield T. 72L
HELLEWELL, Phil: Bradford N. 911
HEPWORTH, Keith: Leeds 73W
HEPWORTH, Tony: Halifax 72W
HERITAGE, John: Blackpool B. 77L
HERON, David: Leeds 83L, 88L; Bradford N. 93L
HERON, Wayne: Leeds 83L
HESFORD, Steve: Warrington 78W, 79L, 81W
HESKETH, Chris: Salford 73L
HETHERINGTON, Brian: Halifax 90L
HILL, Brendan: Halifax 90L
HOBBS, David: Bradford N. 91L, 93L
HOGAN, Brian: Widnes 80L
HOGAN, Phil: Hull K.R. 82L, 85W
HOLDING, Neil: St. Helens 88W
HOLDSTOCK, Roy: Hull K.R. 82L
HOLLIDAY, Bill: Rochdale H. 74L
HOLLIDAY, Les: Halifax 90L; Widnes 92W
HOLMES, John: Leeds 73W, 83L, 84W

HOWARD, Harvey: Widnes 92W
HUBBARD, Steve: Hull K.R. 82L
HUGHES, Eric: Widnes 75L, 76W, 78L, 79W, 80L, 84L
HULL, David: Widnes 78L, 79W, 80L
HULME, David: Widnes 89L
HULME, Paul: Widnes 89l, 92W
HUNTER, Eddie: Warrington 79l, 81W
HUNTER, Paul: Hull 76L
HURST, Phil: Blackpool B. 77l
HYNES, Syd: Leeds 73W

IRO, Kevin: Wigan 89W, 90W
IRO, Tony: Wigan 89W
IRVING, Simon: Leeds 92L
ITI, Brett: Bradford N. 91L

JACKSON, Bob: Warrington 87L
JACKSON, Peter: Leeds 88L
JACKSON, Phil: Bradford N. 75W
JAMES, Kevin: Barrow 81L
JARVIS, Francis: Bradford N. 75W
JEANES, David: Wakefield T. 72L; Leeds 73W
JENKINS, David: Widnes 76W
JOHNSON, Brian: Warrington 87L
JOHNSON, Phil: Castleford 77W
JOHNSTON, Lindsay: Halifax 90L
JOHNSTON, Peter: Hull K.R. 86L
JOYCE, Graham: Bradford N. 75W
JOYNER, John: Castleford 77W
JULIFF, Brian: Wigan 83w

KAHN, Paul: Castleford 77W
KELLY, Andy: Hull K.R. 86L
KELLY, Ken: Warrington 78W, 79L, 81W, 87L
KELLY, Mike: Halifax 72W
KELLY, Mike: Warrington 79L, 81W
KEMBLE, Gary: Hull 85L
KIRKBRIDE, Bill: Salford 73L
KIRKBY, Steve: Barrow 81L
KISS, Nicky: Wigan 83W, 86W
KOLOTO, Emosi: Widnes 89L

LAMB, Cliff: Blackpool B. 77l
LAUGHTON, Doug: Widnes 75L, 78L
LAURIE, Mark: Leeds 84W
LAWS, David: Hull K.R. 85W, 86L
LESTER, Roy: Warrington 78W, 79L
LEULUAI, James: Hull 82W, 85L
LINTON, Ralph: Widnes 84L
LLOYD, Geoff "Sammy": Castleford 77W
LOUGHLIN, Paul: St. Helens 88W
LOWE, Phil: Hull K.R. 82L
LUCAS, Ian: Wigan 90W
LYDIAT, John: Hull K.R. 86L
LYDON, Joe: Widnes 84L; Wigan 87W, 89W, 90W, 93w

LYON, David: Warrington 91W
LYONS, John: Halifax 90L
LYONS, Steve: Wakefield T. 72L

McCALLION, Seamus: Halifax 90L
McCONNELL, Ralph: Barrow 81L
McGINTY, Billy: Warrington 91W; Wigan 93W
McGOWAN, Steve: Bradford N. 93L
MACKAY, Graham: Salford 73L
McKENZIE, Phil: Widnes 89L
MACHEN, Paul: Blackpool B. 77L
MACKLIN, Alf: Hull 76L
MAJOR, Mick: Wakefield T. 72L
MANN, Duane: Warrington 91W
MARCHANT, Tony: Bradford N. 91L, 93L
MARSH, Ged: Blackpool B. 77L
MARSHALL, David: Wigan 90W
MARSTON, Jack: Wakefield T. 72L
MARTIN, John: Halifax 72W
MARTYN, Tommy: Warrington 78W, 79L, 81W
MASKILL, Colin: Leeds 88L
MASON, Mel: Barrow 81L
MEADOWS, Kevin: Warrington 87L
MEDLEY, Paul: Leeds 88L; Bradford N. 91L, 93L
MERCER, Gary: Warrington 91W
MILLER, Gavin: Hull K.R. 85W, 86L
MILLINGTON, John: Hull K.R. 82l
MILLS, Jim: Widnes 75L, 76W, 79W, 80l
MILNER, Richard: Halifax 90L
MOLLOY, Steve: Leeds 92l
MOORBY, Gary: Leeds 84W
MORAN, Dave: Widnes 79W
MORDT, Ray: Wigan 86W
MORGAN, Mick: Wakefield T. 72L
MORRIS, Steve: Leeds 88L
MUMBY, Keith: Bradford N. 80W, 93l
MUSCROFT, Peter: Hull K.R. 82L
MYLER, Tony: Widnes 89L

NEWALL, Jackie: Blackpool B. 77L
NICHOLAS, Mike: Warrington 74w, 78W, 79L
NOBLE, Brian: Bradford N. 91L, 93L
NOONAN, Derek: Warrington 74W
NORTON, Steve: Castleford 77W; Hull 82W

OFFIAH, Martin: Widnes 89L; Wigan 93W
O'HARA, Dane: Hull 82W, 85L
O'LOUGHLIN, Keiron: Widnes 84L
O'NEILL, Dennis: Widnes 75L
O'NEILL, Mike: Widnes 89L; Leeds 92L
O'NEILL, Steve: Widnes 84L
O'SULLIVAN, Chris: Warrington 91W

PANAPA, Sam: Wigan 93w
PARKER, Derek: Bradford N. 80W
PATRICK, Shaun: Hull 85L
PATTINSON, Malcolm: Blackpool B. 77L

PENDLEBURY, John: Wigan 83W;
   Bradford N. 91L
PETERS, Steve: Warrington 87L
PHILBIN, Barry: Warrington 74W, 78W
PHILBIN, Mike: Warrington 74W
PHILLIPS, Rowland: Warrington 91w
PICKUP, Bill: Warrington 74w
PICKUP, Fred: Leeds 73w
PITMAN, Phil: Blackpool B. 77L
PLATT, Andy: St. Helens 88W; Wigan 90W, 93W
PORTZ, Steve: Hull 76L
POTTER, Ian: Warrington 78W, 81W;
   Wigan 86W, 87W, 89W
POWELL, Roy: Leeds 88L, 92L; Bradford N.
   93L
PRENDIVILLE, Paul: Hull 82W; Leeds 84W
PRESCOTT, Alan: Widnes 75L, 76W
PRESTON, Mark: Wigan 90W
PROCTOR, Wayne: Hull 85L
PROHM, Gary: Hull K.R. 85W

QUIRK, Les: St. Helens 88W

RAMSDALE, Denis: Wigan 83W
RAMSEY, Bill: Hull 76L; Widnes 78L
RAMSHAW, Terry: Salford 73L
RATHBONE, Alan: Warrington 87l
RAYNE, Keith: Leeds 84W
RAYNE, Kevin: Leeds 84W, 88L
RAYNER, David: Halifax 72W
REDFEARN, Alan: Bradford N. 80W
REDFEARN, David: Bradford N. 75W, 80W
REEVES, Derek: Halifax 72w
REILLY, Malcolm: Castleford 77W
REYNOLDS, Doug: Blackpool B. 77L
REYNOLDS, Frank: Warrington 74W
RICHARDS, Maurice: Salford 73L
RIDDLESDEN, Eddie: Halifax 90L
ROBERTS, Ian: Wigan 87W
ROBERTS, Mark: Warrington 87L
ROBINSON, Doug: Blackpool B. 77L
ROBINSON, Ian: Hull K.R. 85W, 86l
ROBINSON, Jason: Wigan 93W
ROPATI, Joe: Warrington 87L
ROSE, Paul: Hull 85L

SANDERSON, Gary: Warrington 87L
SANDERSON, John "Sammy": Halifax 72w
SARSFIELD, Mark: Widnes 92W
SCHOFIELD, Garry: Hull 85l; Leeds 88L, 92L
SCOTT, Mick: Wigan 83W; Halifax 90l
SEABOURNE, Barry: Bradford N. 75W
SHAW, Glyn: Widnes 78L, 79W, 80L; Wigan 83W
SHEFFIELD, Bill: Rochdale H. 74L
SHELFORD, Adrian: Wigan 89W
SHELFORD, Darrall: Bradford N. 91L
SHERIDAN, Barry: Widnes 75L, 76W
SIMPSON, Roger: Bradford N. 91L, 93L

SKERRETT, Trevor: Hull 82W
SLATER, Keith: Wakefield T. 72L
SMITH, Alan: Leeds 73W
SMITH, Andy: Leeds 83L, 84W
SMITH, David: Widnes 92W
SMITH, Gordon: Hull K.R. 86L
SMITH, Mike: Hull K.R. 82L, 85W, 86L
SMITH, Steve: Halifax 90l
SORENSEN, Kurt: Widnes 89L, 92W
SOUTO, Peter: St. Helens 88W
SPENCER, Ray: Wakefield T. 72l
SPURR, Bob: Castleford 77W
SQUIRE, Kevin: Leeds 84w
STEPHENS, Gary: Castleford 77W
STEPHENSON, David: Wigan 83W, 86W, 87W
STEPHENSON, Mike: Hull 76L
STEPHENSON, Nigel: Bradford N. 80W
STERLING, Peter: Hull 85L
STONE, Richard "Charlie": Hull 82W
SUMMERS, Neil: Bradford N. 91L, 93L
SUTTON, Dave: Warrington 79L
SYKES, Andy: Leeds 83L
SZYMALA, Eddie: Barrow 81l

TAIT, Alan: Widnes 89L, 92W
TAMATI, Kevin: Widnes 84L; Warrington 87L
TANNER, David: St. Helens 88W
TAYLOR, David: Rochdale H. 74L
THACKRAY, Rick: Warrington 81W; Widnes 89L
THOMAS, Mark: Warrington 91w
THOMPSON, Jimmy: Bradford N. 80W
THORNILEY, Tony: Warrington 91W
TOPLISS, David: Wakefield T. 72L; Hull 85L
TROTTER, Dennis: Bradford N. 75W
TUNKS, Peter: Leeds 88L

VALENTINE, Rob: Wakefield T. 72L
VAN BELLEN, Gary: Bradford N. 80W
VAN BELLEN, Ian: Bradford N. 80w
VEIVERS, Phil: St. Helens 88W

WAINWRIGHT, Tony: Barrow 81L
WALKER, Malcolm: Hull 76L
WALLER, Tony: Warrington 79L, 81W
WANBON, Bobby: Warrington 74W
WANE, Shaun: Wigan 86W, 89W, 90w; Leeds 92L
WARD, Bernard: Wakefield T. 72l
WARD, David: Leeds 73w, 83L, 84W
WARD, Johnny: Salford 73L
WARD, Phil: Salford 73l; Bradford N. 75W
WARDELL, Alan: Hull 76L
WATKINS, David: Salford 73L
WATKINSON, David: Hull K.R. 82L, 85W, 86L
WATSON, David: Bradford N. 93L
WEBB, Terry: Leeds 84W
WEST, Graeme: Wigan 83W, 86W, 87W
WHITEHEAD, Derek: Warrington 74W
WHITEHEAD, Stuart: Rochdale H. 74L

193

WHITFIELD, Colin: Wigan 83W; Halifax 90L
WHITFIELD, Fred: Widnes 84L
WHITTLE, Alan: Warrington 74W
WILEMAN, Ron: Hull 82W
WILKINSON, Ian: Leeds 83L, 84W;
 Bradford N. 91L
WILLIAMS, Barry: Wigan 83W
WILLICOMBE, David: Halifax 72W
WILSON, Frank: Warrington 78W
WOOD, Harry: Rochdale H. 74l
WOOD, John: Widnes 76W
WOODS, Paul: Widnes 78L
WRAITH, Geoff: Wakefield T. 72L;
 Castleford 77W
WRIGHT, Darren: Widnes 89L, 92W
WRIGHT, Dave: Warrington 74W
WRIGHT, Stuart: Widnes 78L, 79W, 80L, 84L

REGAL TROPHY RECORDS

ALL ROUNDS

TEAM
Highest score: Wigan 92 v. Runcorn H. 2 (1988-89)
Biggest attendance: 25,326 Hull v. Hull K.R.
 (at Hull C. FC) ....Final 1984-85

INDIVIDUAL
Most tries: 6 by Vince Gribbin (Whitehaven) v. Doncaster
 1984-85
 6 by Steve McGowan (Bradford N.) v. Barrow
 1992-93
*Most goals: 17 by Sammy Lloyd (Castleford)
*Most points: 43 (3t, 17g) by Sammy Lloyd (Castleford)
*The above records were achieved in the Castleford v.
Millom first round tie in 1973-74.

REGAL TROPHY FINAL RECORDS

Most final appearances: 8 by Widnes
Most wins: 6 by Wigan
Most tries: 3 by Ellery Hanley (Wigan) v. Halifax
1989-90
Most goals: 6 by Derek Whitehead (Warrington) v.
 Rochdale H. 1973-74
Most points: 15 (1t,6g) by Derek Whitehead (Warrington)
 v. Rochdale H. 1973-74
Highest score: Warrington 27 v. Rochdale H. 16..1973-74
Widest margin win: Widnes 24 v. Leeds 0 1991-92
Biggest attendance: 25,326 Hull v. Hull K.R.
 (at Hull C. FC) 1984-85
Biggest receipts: £94,874 Widnes v. Wigan
 (at Bolton W. FC).................1988-89

Wigan captain Dean Bell shows off the 1992-93 Regal Trophy.

● *BEFORE 1977-78 the competition was known as the Player's No.6 Trophy, then the John Player Trophy. In 1983-84 it became the John Player Special Trophy, renamed the Regal Trophy in 1989-90. It was not until 1979-80 that semi-finals were played at neutral venues, reverting to home advantage in 1992-93.*

FRENCH CLUBS IN REGAL TROPHY
French clubs were admitted into the Regal tournament for the first time in 1992-93. The inaugural entrants were champions Carcassonne and XIII Catalan who qualified through a play-off.

NON-LEAGUE CLUBS IN THE REGAL TROPHY
Amateur clubs have entered the Regal tournament in every season apart from a period between 1981 and 1984, plus 1992-93 when the League and BARLA were in dispute. Two figured in the first round up to 1979-80 and one the following season. They were then left out from 1981-82 because the number of professional clubs had grown beyond the mathematically suitable 32.

But the amateurs returned in 1984-85 with two clubs joining the professionals in a small preliminary round, the number being increased to three in 1989-90.

The fate of the amateurs has varied from the record 88-5 hammering Millom received at Castleford to victories by Cawoods over Halifax, Myson over Batley and Leigh East over Chorley.

The full list of amateur clubs' results — all first round matches except where stated (P) Preliminary (2) Second Round — is:

Season							Attendance
1971-72		Wigan	33	v	Ace Amateurs (Hull)	9	2,678
		Thames Board Mill (Warr.)	7	v	Huddersfield	27	1,175
1972-73		Bramley	26	v	Pilkington Recs. (St. Helens)	5	616
		Dewsbury	22	v	Dewsbury Celtic	4	1,897
1973-74		Whitehaven	26	v	Dewsbury Celtic	3	1,276
		Castleford	88	v	Millom (Cumbria)	5	1,031
1974-75		Whitehaven	32	v	Lock Lane (Castleford)	6	537
		Doncaster	15	v	Kippax White Swan	6	453
1975-76		Salford	57	v	Mayfield (Rochdale)	3	3,449
		Barrow	16	v	Pilkington Recs. (St. Helens)	9	612
1976-77		Halifax	24	v	Ovenden (Halifax)	4	3,680
		Salford	39	v	Ace Amateurs (Hull)	15	3,037
1977-78		N.D.L.B. (Hull)	4	v	New Hunslet	18	3,845
		Halifax	8	v	Cawoods (Hull)	9	1,168
	(2)	Wakefield T.	31	v	Cawoods (Hull)	7	3,380
1978-79		Leigh Miners Welfare	9	v	Halifax	21	1,621
		Milford (Leeds)	5	v	Dewsbury	38	3,129
1979-80		Pilkington Recs. (St. Helens)	9	v	Wigan	18	6,707
		Blackpool B.	6	v	West Hull	3	555
1980-81		Castleford	30	v	Pilkington Recs. (St. Helens)	17	2,823
1984-85	(P)	Myson (Hull)	2	v	Dewsbury	8	1,572
	(P)	Keighley	24	v	Dudley Hill (Bradford)	10	1,570
1985-86	(P)	Keighley	24	v	Jubilee (Featherstone)	6	1,007
	(P)	West Hull	10	v	Castleford	24	2,500
1986-87	(P)	Batley	2	v	Myson (Hull)	8	687
	(P)	Millom (Cumbria)	4	v	Wakefield T.	18	2,000
		Myson (Hull)	11	v	Swinton	18	1,648
1987-88	(P)	Featherstone R.	34	v	Thatto Heath (St. Helens)	16	1,045
	(P)	Heworth (York)	5	v	Swinton	32	1,063
1988-89	(P)	Wigan St. Patricks	36	v	Elland (Halifax)	2	2,510
		Sheffield E.	80	v	Wigan St. Patricks	8	621
1989-90	(P)	Batley	28	v	West Hull	14	844
	(P)	Crosfields (Warrington)	14	v	Workington T.	19	942
	(P)	Kells (Whitehaven)	2	v	Doncaster	28	2,127
1990-91	(P)	Dudley Hill (Bradford)	18	v	Dewsbury	24	970
	(P)	Saddleworth R. (Oldham)	35	v	Egremont (Cumbria)	18	900
		Rochdale H.	30	v	Saddleworth R. (Oldham)	10	2,434
1991-92	(P)	Saddleworth R. (Oldham)	0	v	Workington T.	30	1,650
	(P)	Leigh East	20	v	Chorley	10	1,393
		Bradford N.	76	v	Leigh East	0	1,613

REGAL TROPHY PROGRESS CHART

Key: W — Winners. F — Beaten finalists. SF — Semi-final. P — Preliminary round.

	1992-93	1991-92	1990-91	1989-90	1988-89	1987-88	1986-87	1985-86	1984-85	1983-84	1982-83	1981-82	1980-81	1979-80	1978-79	1977-78	1976-77	1975-76	1974-75	1973-74	1972-73	1971-72
BARROW	1	1	1	1	1	1	3	2	1	2	3	3	F	1	1	1	1	2	1	1	1	3
BATLEY	1	1	3	1	1	2	P	1	1	P	1	1	1	1	1	1	1	2	1	1	2	1
BLACKPOOL G.	P	1	1	1	2	3	2	1	1	1	2	P	2	2	1	1	F	1	1	1	1	3
BRADFORD N.	F	3	F	2	SF	1	3	2	2	1	3	2	1	W	SF	SF	2	1	W	1	3	1
BRAMLEY	1	1	2	1	2	P	1	1	3	*	1	1	1	2	1	1	2	1	2	SF	2	2
CARLISLE	2	2	P	1	1	1	2	P	P	2	2	2										
CASTLEFORD	SF	3	3	SF	2	2	2	1	2	1	1	2	SF	3	3	2	W	SF	1	2	1	2
CHORLEY B.	P	P	1	1																		
DEWSBURY	1	P	1	2	1	2	1	1	3	1	1	1	1	1	2	1	1	1	1	3	2	1
DONCASTER	1	2	2	1	2	1	2	2	1	1	1	1	1	1	1	1	1	1	2	1	1	1
FEATHERSTONE R.	2	3	2	3	1	1	2	P	2	3	1	2	2	2	2	3	2	1	1	1	2	1
HALIFAX	2	2	P	F	2	2	2	1	SF	1	1	1	3	1	2	1	2	1	1	2	1	W
HIGHFIELD	P	1	1	1	1	1	1	1	2	2	P	1	1	1	1	1	1	2	1	1	1	
HUDDERSFIELD	P	1	1	2	1	1	P	1	1	1	2	2	2	1	3	1	3	1	1	2	2	
HULL	SF	2	1	1	2	3	SF	3	F	2	2	W	SF	1	2	1	3	F	1	1	3	3
HULL K.R.	2	1	1	1	3	2	1	F	W	2	3	F	2	1	SF	1	1	3	SF	1	SF	2
HUNSLET	2	1	1	2	P	1	1	2	P	1	1	1	2	1	1	2	1	2	1	1	1	1
KEIGHLEY C.	1	2	2	1	1	1	1	2	1	2	1	2	1	2	3	2	1	1	2	3	1	2
LEEDS	1	F	2	3	1	F	1	1	SF	W	F	3	1	2	1	1	3	2	3	3	W	SF
LEIGH	3	P	2	1	3	2	3	SF	1	SF	2	1	3	3	3	3	SF	2	1	2	2	1
LONDON C.	2	1	1	P	P	1	1	1	1	1	1	2										
NOTTINGHAM C.	1	1	1	1	1	2	1	1	1													
OLDHAM	1	2	2	3	1	SF	1	2	2	1	1	SF	1	1	1	2	2	2	2	1	1	1
ROCHDALE H.	2	P	SF	1	2	1	1	1	2	1	2	1	1	1	1	1	1	1	1	F	1	2
RYEDALE-YORK	1	1	P	P	1	1	P	3	1	1	2	1	2	2	1	3	1	2	2	2	2	
ST. HELENS	3	SF	3	SF	SF	W	3	SF	3	SF	2	1	1	2	2	2	2	3	1	SF	SF	SF
SALFORD	1	SF	1	2	1	3	1	2	1	2	3	3	2	SF	2	2	2	SF	3	2	F	1
SCARBOROUGH P.		P																				
SHEFFIELD E.	1	2	P	3	2	1	2	1	1													
SWINTON	P	1	1	2	1	1	2	1	1	3	1	SF	1	1	1	1	1	1	3	1	3	1
WAKEFIELD T.	1	2	2	P	3	2	2	2	P	1	1	1	1	SF	3	SF	1	2	2	3	2	F
WARRINGTON	2	1	W	P	3	3	F	3	1	2	SF	2	W	3	F	W	1	1	3	W	1	1
WHITEHAVEN	1	1	1	2	1	1	1	2	P	1	1	3	1	1	1	1	1	SF	2	1	2	
WIDNES	3	W	SF	2	F	1	SF	3	3	F	SF	3	3	F	W	F	SF	W	F	1	3	1
WIGAN	W	3	3	W	W	SF	W	W	2	3	W	1	1	2	2	3	2	2	2	2	1	3
WORKINGTON T.	3	1	1	1	P	1	1	1	1	1	1	2	1	3	2	2	3	3	1	2	1	1

*Bramley withdrew from the Trophy while in liquidation, opponents Hull K.R. receiving a bye.

PREMIERSHIP TROPHY

1993 Final

Wigan's valiant bid for a history-making Grand Slam of all five major trophies failed in the final 20 minutes of a long, gruelling campaign.

Arch rivals St. Helens fully deserved their 10-4 victory after being pipped by Wigan for the Stones Bitter Championship on points difference and the Lancashire Cup, by just one point.

This Old Trafford encounter again showed how well matched the two Lancashire giants were, with the scores level at 4-4 on the hour.

A scoreless first half was on the cards until the Saints got the lucky touch needed to break the deadlock. Captain Shane Cooper chanced a speculative kick to the Wigan line and when it deflected off a defender, centre Gary Connolly was on hand to accept the touchdown. Paul Loughlin failed to add the goal.

The lead lasted until the 60th minute when sustained Wigan pressure paid off with stand off Frano Botica putting in Mike Forshaw at the right-hand corner. Botica hit the post with his conversion attempt and St. Helens became more determined not to repeat the collapse that led to Wigan piling up a record 48-16 victory in the previous year's final.

Two snappy drop goals in the 63rd and 68th minutes by former Wigan reserve scrum half Gus O'Donnell edged the Saints back in front, sealing success with a well-worked try five minutes from the end.

Wigan, lacking injured internationals Andy Platt, Steve Hampson, Joe Lydon, skipper Dean Bell and Denis Betts, as well as long-term casualties Billy McGinty and Ian Lucas, had their tired defence exposed by the swift movement of the ball for Loughlin to stride over to open up a six-point victory margin.

Wigan rallied to try to end coach John Monie's four-year reign with a unique triumph, but Saints held on to receive the Premiership Trophy for the fourth time, adding to the CIS Insurance Charity Shield gained by defeating Wigan at Gateshead on the first day of the season.

The defeat was Wigan's first in 19 finals since they lost to St. Helens in the 1984 Lancashire Cup and ended a run of 25 consecutive victories in knockout competitions over the previous 18 months.

St. Helens received the trophy and an £18,000 Stones Bitter prize cheque, taking their 1992-93 result tally against Wigan to three victories, a draw and two defeats.

It was the Saints' youngsters who took the individual honours, with 21-year-old second row man Chris Joynt making up for the disappointment of being a runner-up for the title of Stones Bitter Young Player of the Year by being voted Man of the Match, receiving the Harry Sunderland Trophy.

Wigan's ace marksman Botica finished with a rare goalkicking blank to leave Keighley Cougars winger John Wasyliw three ahead of him as the season's top kicker, collecting a Stones Bitter prize of £1,870.

A crowd of 36,598 paid a Premiership record £454,013 to watch Rugby League's first triple-header, the two Stones Bitter finals being preceded by the Academy Challenge Cup final between Warrington and Hull, the young Wire winning 19-12.

Andrew Farrell, a first appearance in a final at only 17 years of age.

STONES BITTER PREMIERSHIP FINAL

16 May   **Old Trafford, Manchester**

ST. HELENS   10   **WIGAN   4**

David Lyon	1.	Paul Atcheson
Mike Riley	2.	Jason Robinson
Gary Connolly	3.	Sam Panapa
Paul Loughlin	4.	Andrew Farrar
Alan Hunte	5.	Martin Offiah
Tea Ropati	6.	Frano Botica
Gus O'Donnell	7.	Shaun Edwards, Capt.
Jonathan Neill	8.	Neil Cowie
Bernard Dwyer	9.	Martin Dermott
George Mann	10.	Kelvin Skerrett
Chris Joynt	11.	Mick Cassidy
Sonny Nickle	12.	Andrew Farrell
Shane Cooper, Capt.	13.	Phil Clarke
Jonathan Griffiths	14.	Mike Forshaw
Phil Veivers	15.	Ian Gildart

T: Connolly, Loughlin

G: O'Donnell (2dg)

Substitutions:

Griffiths for Mann (47 min.)

Half-time: 4-0

Attendance: 36,598

T: Forshaw

Substitutions:

Forshaw for Cassidy (25 min.)

Gildart for Skerrett (71 min.)

Referee: John Holdsworth (Kippax)

Receipts: £454,013

1993 Round by Round

Silk Cut Challenge Cup finalists Widnes registered the fifth defeat in their last six outings as trophy-starved Leeds won 22-10 at Naughton Park, Simon Irving collecting 14 points. Widnes also suffered the loss of Test forward Paul Moriarty with a broken arm. In contrast, Wembley opponents Wigan demolished Warrington 40-5 at home, Great Britain winger Martin Offiah returning to form with a five-try haul. Third-placed Bradford Northern went down 19-6 at home to Castleford, Northern's display being as dismal as the weather as Test prop Lee Crooks inspired the visitors with three goals and the creation of two tries. Great Britain centre Paul Loughlin scored a try and seven goals as St. Helens disposed of visitors Halifax 34-25, Saints having held an 8-7 half-time lead before being well

led by Under-21 forward Chris Joynt.

In the semi-finals, Wigan beat Castleford 25-8 at home with Man of the Match rating being awarded to Andrew Farrell, who at 17 and starting a first team match for only the fourth time, killed the Tigers' hopes by creating a try for Shaun Edwards in the 18th minute and scoring one himself five minutes later. Leeds went down 15-2 at St. Helens but were not disgraced in a tremendous contest which was scoreless for 58 minutes. St. Helens' Gus O'Donnell broke the deadlock with a drop goal before Shane Cooper and Alan Hunte scored tries in a 10-minute period.

1993 Prizes

Winners: £18,000

Runners-up: £7,250

1993 Results

First Round

Bradford N.	6	Castleford	19
St. Helens	34	Halifax	25
Widnes	10	Leeds	22
Wigan	40	Warrington	5

Semi-Finals

| St. Helens | 15 | Leeds | 2 |
| Wigan | 25 | Castleford | 8 |

Final

| St. Helens | 10 | Wigan | 4 |

(at Old Trafford, Manchester)

History

With the reintroduction of two divisions in 1973-74 there was no longer a need for a play-off to decide the championship.

However, it was decided to continue the tradition of an end-of-season play-off, the winners to receive the newly instituted Premiership Trophy.

In the first season of the Premiership, 1974-75, the top 12 Division One clubs and the top four from Division Two went into a first round draw, the luck of the draw operating through to the final, played at a neutral venue.

The following season the play-off was reduced to the top eight clubs in the First Division, the ties being decided on a merit basis i.e. 1st v. 8th, 2nd v. 7th etc. At the semi-final stage the highest placed clubs had the option of when to play at home in the two-legged tie.

In 1978-79 the two-leg system was suspended because of fixture congestion, and the higher placed clubs had home advantage right through to the neutrally staged final. Two legs returned the following season, but were finally abolished from 1980-81.

A Second Division Premiership tournament was introduced for the first time in 1986-87, Manchester United's Old Trafford being selected as a new fixed venue for a double-header final. With the introduction of a Third Division in 1991-92, the top eight Division Three clubs played off to visit the top four Second Division clubs, the second tier event being renamed the Divisional Premiership.

Gary Connolly, St. Helens tryscorer in the 1993 final.

PREMIERSHIP ROLL OF HONOUR

Year	Winners	Runners-up	Venue	Attendance	Receipts
1975	Leeds (3)............26	St. Helens (1) 11	Wigan 14,531		£7,795
1976	St. Helens (4) 15	Salford (1) 2	Swinton 18,082		£13,138
1977	St. Helens (2) 32	Warrington (5).....20	Swinton 11,178		£11,626
1978	Bradford N. (2)....17	Widnes (1)......... 8	Swinton 16,813		£18,677
1979	Leeds (4)............24	Bradford N. (8).... 2	Huddersfield 19,486		£21,291
1980	Widnes (2)..........19	Bradford N. (1).... 5	Swinton 10,215		£13,665
1981	Hull K.R. (3) 11	Hull (7).............. 7	Leeds 29,448		£47,529
1982	Widnes (3)..........23	Hull (2)............. 8	Leeds 12,100		£23,749
1983	Widnes (5)..........22	Hull (1)..............10	Leeds 17,813		£34,145
1984	Hull K.R. (1) 18	Castleford (4).......10	Leeds 12,515		£31,769
1985	St. Helens (2) 36	Hull K.R. (1) 16	Elland Rd, Leeds 15,518		£46,950
1986	Warrington (4) 38	Halifax (1) 10	Elland Rd, Leeds 13,683		£50,879
1987	Wigan (1) 8	Warrington (3)..... 0	Old Trafford, Man'r 38,756		£165,166
1988	Widnes (1)..........38	St. Helens (2) 14	Old Trafford, Man'r 35,252		£202,616
1989	Widnes (1)..........18	Hull (4).............10	Old Trafford, Man'r 40,194		£264,242
1990	Widnes (3)..........28	Bradford N. (4).... 6	Old Trafford, Man'r 40,796		£273,877
1991	Hull (3)..............14	Widnes (2).......... 4	Old Trafford, Man'r 42,043		£384,300
1992	Wigan (1) 48	St. Helens (2) 16	Old Trafford, Man'r 33,157		£389,988
1993	St. Helens (2) 10	Wigan (1) 4	Old Trafford, Man'r 36,598		£454,013

() denotes final league position

PREMIERSHIP FINAL . . . . A REVIEW

Initials are included where more than one player shared a surname in the club in the same era.

1974-75
Leeds 26 Holmes (2g) (Marshall 3g); Alan Smith (1t), Hynes (1t, 1dg) (Eccles), Dyl, Atkinson (2t); Mason (1t), Hepworth; Dickinson, Ward, Pitchford, Cookson, Batten, Haigh
St. Helens 11 G. Pimblett; L. Jones (1t), Wilson, Hull, Mathias (1t); Walsh, Heaton (1t); Warlow (Cunningham), A. Karalius, Mantle (K. Gwilliam), E. Chisnall, Nicholls, Coslett (1g)
Referee: W.H. Thompson (Huddersfield)
1975-76
St. Helens 15 G. Pimblett (3g); L. Jones, Glynn (1t), Noonan, Mathias; Benyon, Heaton (K. Gwilliam); Mantle, A. Karalius (1t), James, Nicholls, E. Chisnall (1t), Coslett
Salford 2 Watkins (2dg); Fielding, Richards, Hesketh, Graham; Butler, Nash; Coulman, Raistrick, Sheffield, Knighton (Turnbull), Dixon, E. Prescott
Referee: M.J. Naughton (Widnes)
1976-77
St. Helens 32 G. Pimblett (1t, 7g); L. Jones, Benyon (1t), Cunningham (1t), Mathias (1t); Glynn (Ashton), K. Gwilliam (1t); D. Chisnall, Liptrot, James (1t), Nicholls (A. Karalius), E. Chisnall, Pinner
Warrington 20 Finnegan; Curling, Bevan (Cunliffe), Hesford (4g), Kelly; A. Gwilliam (1t), Gordon (1t); Weavill (1t), Price, Case, Martyn (Peers), Lester, B. Philbin (1t)
Referee: G.F. Lindop (Wakefield)
1977-78
Bradford N. 17 Mumby (2g); Barends (1t), Roe (1t), Austin, D. Redfearn (1t); Wolford (1dg), A. Redfearn; I. Van Bellen (Fox), Raistrick, Thompson, Joyce (Forsyth), Trotter, Haigh (1t)
Widnes 8 Eckersley; Wright, Hughes, Aspey (2t), Woods (1g); Gill, Bowden; Mills, Elwell, Shaw (Ramsey) (George), Adams, Hull, Laughton
Referee: J.E. Jackson (Pudsey)
1978-79
Leeds 24 Hague; Alan Smith (1t), D. Smith (1t), Dyl (Fletcher), Atkinson; Dick (7g, 1dg), J. Sanderson; Harrison, Ward (1t), Pitchford, Joyce, Eccles (Adams), Cookson
Bradford N. 2 Mumby; D. Parker, Okulicz, Gant, Spencer; Ferres (1g), A. Redfearn; Thompson, Bridges, Forsyth (I. Van Bellen), Trotter (Mordue), Grayshon, Casey
Referee: W.H. Thompson (Huddersfield)

1979-80
Widnes 19 Burke (1g); Wright (1t), George, Aspey (1t), Bentley (1t); Eckersley (1dg), Bowden; Shaw, Elwell (1t, 1dg), M. O'Neill, L. Gorley (1t), Hull (Hogan), Adams
Bradford N. 5 Mumby (1g); MacLean (Ferres), D. Redfearn (1t), D. Parker, Gant; Stephenson, A. Redfearn; Thompson, Bridges, Forsyth, Clarkson (G. Van Bellen), Grayshon, Hale
Referee: W.H. Thompson (Huddersfield)
1980-81
Hull K.R. 11 Proctor; Hubbard (1g), M. Smith (1t), Hogan (1t), Muscroft; Hartley (1t), Harkin; Holdstock, Watkinson, Millington, Lowe, Casey, Hall (Burton)
Hull 7 Woods (2g); Peacham, Elliott, Wilby, Prendiville; Banks, Dean; Tindall, Wileman, Stone, Skerrett (Madley), Crane (1t), Norton
Referee: J. Holdsworth (Kippax)
1981-82
Widnes 23 Burke (1t, 4g); Wright (1t), Kieron O'Loughlin, Cunningham (A. Myler), Basnett (1t); Hughes (1t), Gregory; M. O'Neill, Elwell, Lockwood (Whitfield), L. Gorley, Prescott, Adams (1t)
Hull 8 Kemble; O'Hara (Day), Leuluai, S. Evans, Prendiville; Topliss, Harkin; Tindall, Wileman (Lloyd), Stone, Skerrett, L. Crooks (1t, 2g, 1dg), Norton
Referee: S. Wall (Leigh)
1982-83
Widnes 22 Burke; Linton, Hughes, Lydon (5g), Basnett (2t); A. Myler (1t), Gregory (1t) (D. Hulme); M. O'Neill, Elwell, L. Gorley, Whitfield (S. O'Neill), Prescott, Adams
Hull 10 Kemble; O'Hara (1t), Day (Solal), Leuluai, S. Evans; Topliss (1t), Dean; Skerrett, Bridges, Stone, Rose, L. Crooks (2g), Norton (Crane)
Referee: G.F. Lindop (Wakefield)
1983-84
Hull K.R. 18 Fairbairn; Clark, M. Smith (1t), Prohm (1t), Laws (1t); Dorahy (1t, 1g), Harkin; Holdstock, Rudd, Millington (Robinson), Burton (Lydiat), Broadhurst, Hall
Castleford 10 Roockley; Coen, Marchant, Hyde, Kear (1t); Robinson, R. Beardmore (3g); Ward, Horton, Connell, Crampton, Atkins, Joyner
Referee: R. Campbell (Widnes)
1984-85
St. Helens 36 Veivers (1t); Ledger (2t), Peters, Meninga (2t) (Allen), Day (4g); Arkwright, Holding; Burke (Forber), Ainsworth (1t), P. Gorley, Platt, Haggerty, Pinner (1t)

Hull K.R. 16 Fairbairn (1t, 2g); Clark, Robinson (1t), Prohm, Laws (1t); M. Smith, G. Smith (Harkin); Broadhurst, Watkinson, Ema (Lydiat), Kelly, Hogan, Hall
Referee: S. Wall (Leigh)

1985-86
Warrington 38 Paul Ford (Johnson 1t); Forster (1t), Cullen, R. Duane, Carbert; Bishop (1t, 5g), A. Gregory; Boyd (2t), Tamati (1t), Jackson (1t), Sanderson (McGinty), Roberts, M. Gregory
Halifax 10 Whitfield (3g) (Smith); Riddlesden, T. Anderson, C. Anderson (1t), S. Wilson; Crossley, Stephens; Scott, McCallion, G. Robinson, Juliff, James (Bond), Dixon
Referee: G.F. Lindop (Wakefield)

1986-87
Wigan 8 Hampson; Gill (1g), Stephenson (1g), Bell, Lydon (1t) (Russell); Edwards, Gregory; Case, Kiss, Wane (West), Goodway, Potter, Hanley
Warrington 0 Johnson; Drummond, Ropati, B. Peters, Forster; Cullen, Bishop; Tamati, Roberts (Eccles), Jackson, Humphries (M. Gregory), Sanderson, R. Duane
Referee: K. Allatt (Southport)

1987-88
Widnes 38 Platt (1g); Thackray (Tait 1t), Currier (4g), Wright (2t), Offiah; Dowd, D. Hulme (2t); Sorensen (1t), McKenzie (1t), Grima (S. O'Neill), M. O'Neill, P. Hulme, R. Eyres
St. Helens 14 Loughlin (3g); Ledger (1t), Tanner, Elia, Quirk; Bailey, Holding; Burke, Groves, Evans (Dwyer), Forber, Fieldhouse (Allen), Haggerty (1t)
Referee: J. Holdsworth (Kippax)

1988-89
Widnes 18 Tait; Davies (3g), Currier (1t) (Pyke), Wright (1t), Offiah (1t); D. Hulme (A. Myler), P. Hulme; Sorensen, McKenzie, Grima, M. O'Neill, Koloto, R. Eyres
Hull 10 Fletcher; Eastwood, Blacker, Price (Wilby), O'Hara; Pearce (3g), Windley (R. Nolan); Dannatt, L. Jackson, S. Crooks, Welham (1t), Sharp, Divorty
Referee: J. Holdsworth (Kippax)

1989-90
Widnes 28 Tait (2t); Davies (4g), Currier (2t), Wright, Offiah; D. Hulme, P. Hulme; Sorensen (A. Myler), McKenzie, M. O'Neill, Koloto (Grima), R. Eyres, Holliday (1t)
Bradford N. 6 Wilkinson; Cordle, McGowan (Cooper), Marchant (1t), Francis; Simpson, Harkin; Skerrett, Noble (Richards), Hobbs, Medley, Fairbank, Mumby (1g)
Referee: C. Morris (Huddersfield)

1990-91
Hull 14 Gay (1t); Eastwood (1g), McGarry (G. Nolan 1t), Webb, Turner; Mackey, Entat; Harrison, L. Jackson, Dannatt, Marlow (D. Busby), Walker (1t), Sharp
Widnes 4 Tait; Devereux, Currier, Davies, Offiah (1t); Dowd, D. Hulme; Sorensen, McKenzie (Wright), Grima, P. Hulme, Koloto (Howard), McCurrie
Referee: J. Holdsworth (Kippax)

1991-92
Wigan 48 Hampson (Myers 1t); Lydon, Bell, Miles (1t), Offiah (2t); Botica (10g), Edwards; Cowie, Dermott, Platt (1t), Betts (2t), McGinty (Panapa), Clarke
St. Helens 16 Veivers; Hunte, Connolly (Griffiths), Loughlin (1t, 2g), Sullivan (2t); Ropati, Bishop; Neill (Groves), Dwyer, Ward, Nickle, Mann, Cooper
Referee: J. Holdsworth (Kippax)

PREMIERSHIP TROPHY FINAL PLAYERS' REGISTER
The following is an index of players who have appeared in the Premiership final since the first in 1975. W — winners, L — losers. Substitute appearances in lower case letters. The year denotes the second half of the season.

ADAMS, Bryan: Leeds 79w
ADAMS, Mick: Widnes 78L, 80W, 82W, 83W
AINSWORTH, Gary: St. Helens 85W
ALLEN, Shaun: St. Helens 85w, 88l
ANDERSON, Chris: Halifax 86L
ANDERSON, Tony: Halifax 86L
ARKWRIGHT, Chris: St. Helens 85W
ASHTON, Alan: St. Helens 77l
ASPEY, Malcolm: Widnes 78L, 80W
ATCHESON, Paul: Wigan 93L
ATKINS, Brett: Castleford 84L
ATKINSON, John: Leeds 75W, 79W
AUSTIN, Jack: Bradford N. 78W

BAILEY, Mark: St. Helens 88L
BANKS, Barry: Hull 81L
BARENDS, David: Bradford N. 78W
BASNETT, John: Widnes 82W, 83W
BATTEN, Ray: Leeds 75W
BEARDMORE, Bob: Castleford 84L
BELL, Dean: Wigan 87W, 92W
BENTLEY, Keith: Widnes 80W
BENYON, Billy: St. Helens 76W, 77W
BETTS, Denis: Wigan 92W
BEVAN, John: Warrington 77L
BISHOP, Paul: Warrington 86W, 87L; St. Helens 92L
BLACKER, Brian: Hull 89L
BOND, Steve: Halifax 86l
BOTICA, Frano: Wigan 92W, 93L
BOWDEN, Reg: Widnes 78L, 80W
BOYD, Les: Warrington 86W

BRIDGES, John "Keith": Bradford N. 79L, 80L; Hull 83L
BROADHURST, Mark: Hull K.R. 84W, 85L
BURKE, Mick: Widnes 80W, 82W, 83W
BURKE, Tony: St. Helens 85W, 88L
BURTON, Chris: Hull K.R. 81w, 84W
BUSBY, Dean: Hull 91w
BUTLER, John: Salford 76L

CARBERT, Brian: Warrington 86W
CASE, Brian: Warrington 77L; Wigan 87W
CASEY, Len: Bradford N. 79L; Hull K.R. 81W
CASSIDY, Mick: Wigan 93L
CHISNALL, Dave: St. Helens 77W
CHISNALL, Eric: St. Helens 75L, 76W, 77W
CLARK, Garry: Hull K.R. 84W, 85L
CLARKE, Phil: Wigan 92W, 93L
CLARKSON, Geoff: Bradford N. 80L
COEN, Darren: Castleford 84L
CONNELL, Gary: Castleford 84L
CONNOLLY, Gary: St. Helens 92L, 93W
COOKSON, Phil: Leeds 75W, 79W
COOPER, David: Bradford N. 90l
COOPER, Shane: St. Helens 92L, 93W
CORDLE, Gerald: Bradford N. 90L
COSLETT, Kel: St. Helens 75L, 76W
COULMAN, Mike: Salford 76L
COWIE, Neil: Wigan 92W, 93L
CRAMPTON, Jimmy: Castleford 84L
CRANE, Mick: Hull 81L, 83l
CROOKS, Lee: Hull 82L, 83L
CROOKS, Steve: Hull 89L
CROSSLEY, John: Halifax 86L
CULLEN, Paul: Warrington 86W, 87L
CUNLIFFE, Dave: Warrington 77l
CUNNINGHAM, Eddie: St. Helens 75l, 77W; Widnes 82W
CURLING, Denis: Warrington 77L
CURRIER, Andy: Widnes 88W, 89W, 90W, 91L

DANNATT, Andy: Hull 89L, 91W
DAVIES, Jonathan: Widnes 89W, 90W, 91L
DAY, Sean: St. Helens 85W
DAY, Terry: Hull 82l, 83L
DEAN, Tony: Hull 81L, 83L
DERMOTT, Martin: Wigan 92W, 93L
DEVEREUX, John: Widnes 91L
DICK, Kevin: Leeds 79W
DICKINSON, Roy: Leeds 75W
DIVORTY, Gary: Hull 89L
DIXON, Colin: Salford 76L
DIXON, Paul: Halifax 86L
DORAHY, John: Hull K.R. 84W
DOWD, Barry: Widnes 88W, 91L
DRUMMOND, Des: Warrington 87L
DUANE, Ronnie: Warrington 86W, 87L
DWYER, Bernard: St. Helens 88l, 92L, 93W
DYL, Les: Leeds 75W, 79W

EASTWOOD, Paul: Hull 89L, 91W
ECCLES, Bob: Warrington 87l
ECCLES, Graham: Leeds 75w, 79W
ECKERSLEY, David: Widnes 78L, 80W

EDWARDS, Shaun: Wigan 87W, 92W, 93L
ELIA, Mark: St. Helens 88L
ELLIOTT, David: Hull 81L
ELWELL, Keith: Widnes 78L, 80W, 82W, 83W
EMA, Asuquo: Hull K.R. 85L
ENTAT, Patrick: Hull 91W
EVANS, Steve: Hull 82L, 83L
EVANS, Stuart: St. Helens 88L
EYRES, Richard: Widnes 88W, 89W, 90W

FAIRBAIRN, George: Hull K.R. 84W, 85L
FAIRBANK, Karl: Bradford N. 90L
FARRAR, Andrew: Wigan 93L
FARRELL, Andrew: Wigan 93L
FERRES, Steve: Bradford N. 79L, 80l
FIELDHOUSE, John: St. Helens 88L
FIELDING, Keith: Salford 76L
FINNEGAN, Derek: Warrington 77L
FLETCHER, Paul: Hull 89L
FLETCHER, Paul: Leeds 79w
FORBER, Paul: St. Helens 85w, 88L
FORD, Paul: Warrington 86W
FORSHAW, Mike: Wigan 93l
FORSTER, Mark: Warrington 86W, 87L
FORSYTH, Colin: Bradford N. 78w, 79L, 80L
FOX, Neil: Bradford N. 78w
FRANCIS, Richard: Bradford N. 90L

GANT, Les: Bradford N. 79L, 80L
GAY, Richard: Hull 91W
GEORGE, Derek "Mick": Widnes 78l, 80W
GILDART, Ian: Wigan 93l
GILL, Henderson: Wigan 87W
GILL, Ken: Widnes 78L
GLYNN, Peter: St. Helens 76W, 77W
GOODWAY, Andy: Wigan 87W
GORDON, Parry: Warrington 77L
GORLEY, Les: Widnes 80W, 82W, 83W
GORLEY, Peter: St. Helens 85W
GRAHAM, Gordon: Salford 76L
GRAYSHON, Jeff: Bradford N. 79L, 80L
GREGORY, Andy: Widnes 82W, 83W; Warrington 86W; Wigan 87W
GREGORY, Mike: Warrington 86W, 87l
GRIFFITHS, Jonathan: St. Helens 92l, 93w
GRIMA, Joe: Widnes 88W, 89W, 90w, 91L
GROVES, Paul: St. Helens 88L, 92l
GWILLIAM, Alan: Warrington 77L
GWILLIAM, Ken: St. Helens 75l, 76w, 77W

HAGGERTY, Roy: St. Helens 85W, 88L
HAGUE, Neil: Leeds 79W
HAIGH, Bob: Leeds 75W; Bradford N. 78W
HALE, Gary: Bradford N. 80L
HALL, David: Hull K.R. 81W, 84W, 85L
HAMPSON, Steve: Wigan 87W, 92W
HANLEY, Ellery: Wigan 87W
HARKIN, Kevin: Hull 82L
HARKIN, Paul: Hull K.R. 81W, 84W, 85l; Bradford N. 90L
HARRISON, Karl: Hull 91W
HARRISON, Mick: Leeds 79W
HARTLEY, Steve: Hull K.R. 81W

HEATON, Jeff: St. Helens 75L, 76W
HEPWORTH, Keith: Leeds 75W
HESFORD, Steve: Warrington 77L
HESKETH, Chris: Salford 76L
HOBBS, David: Bradford N. 90L
HOGAN, Brian: Widnes 80w
HOGAN, Phil: Hull K.R. 81W, 85L
HOLDING, Neil: St. Helens 85W, 88L
HOLDSTOCK, Roy: Hull K.R. 81W, 84W
HOLLIDAY, Les: Widnes 90W
HOLMES, John: Leeds 75W
HORTON, Stuart: Castleford 84L
HOWARD, Harvey: Widnes 91l
HUBBARD, Steve: Hull K.R. 81W
HUGHES, Eric: Widnes 78L, 82W, 83W
HULL, David: St. Helens 75L; Widnes 78L, 80W
HULME, David: Widnes 83w, 88W, 89W, 90W, 91L
HULME, Paul: Widnes 88W, 89W, 90W, 91L
HUMPHRIES, Tony: Warrington 87L
HUNTE, Alan: St. Helens 92L, 93W
HYDE, Gary: Castleford 84L
HYNES, Syd: Leeds 75W

JACKSON, Bob: Warrington 86W, 87L
JACKSON, Lee: Hull 89L, 91W
JAMES, Mel: St. Helens 76W, 77W
JAMES, Neil: Halifax 86L
JOHNSON, Brian: Warrington 86w, 87L
JONES, Les: St. Helens 75L, 76W, 77W
JOYCE, Graham: Bradford N. 78W; Leeds 79W
JOYNER, John: Castleford 84L
JOYNT, Chris: St. Helens 93W
JULIFF, Brian: Halifax 86L

KARALIUS, Tony: St. Helens 75L, 76W, 77w
KEAR, John: Castleford 84L
KELLY, Andy: Hull K.R. 85L
KELLY, Mike: Warrington 77L
KEMBLE, Gary: Hull 82L, 83L
KISS, Nicky: Wigan 87W
KNIGHTON, John: Salford 76L
KOLOTO, Emosi: Widnes 89W, 90W, 91L

LAUGHTON, Doug: Widnes 78L
LAWS, David: Hull K.R. 84W, 85L
LEDGER, Barry: St. Helens 85W, 88L
LESTER, Roy: Warrington 77L
LEULUAI, James: Hull 82L, 83L
LINTON, Ralph: Widnes 83W
LIPTROT, Graham: St. Helens 77W
LLOYD, Geoff "Sammy": Hull 82l
LOCKWOOD, Brian: Widnes 82W
LOUGHLIN, Paul: St. Helens 88L, 92L, 93W
LOWE, Phil: Hull K.R. 81W
LYDIAT, John: Hull K.R. 84w, 85l
LYDON, Joe: Widnes 83W; Wigan 87W, 92W
LYON, David: St. Helens 93W

McCALLION, Seamus: Halifax 86L
McCURRIE, Steve: Widnes 91L
McGARRY, Damien: Hull 91W
McGINTY, Billy: Warrington 86w; Wigan 92W
McGOWAN, Steve: Bradford N. 90W

McKENZIE, Phil: Widnes 88W, 89W, 90W, 91L
MACKEY, Greg: Hull 91W
MacLEAN, Ian: Bradford N. 80L
MADLEY, Ian: Hull 81l
MANN, George: St. Helens 92L, 93W
MANTLE, John: St. Helens 75L, 76W
MARCHANT, Tony: Castleford 84L;
    Bradford N. 90L
MARLOW, Ian: Hull 91W
MARSHALL, David: Leeds 75w
MARTYN, Tommy: Warrington 77L
MASON, Mel: Leeds 75W
MATHIAS, Roy: St. Helens 75L, 76W, 77W
MEDLEY, Paul: Bradford N. 90L
MENINGA, Mal: St. Helens 85W
MILES, Gene: Wigan 92W
MILLINGTON, John: Hull K.R. 81W, 84W
MILLS, Jim: Widnes 78L
MORDUE, David: Bradford N. 79l
MUMBY, Keith: Bradford N. 78W, 79L, 80L, 90L
MUSCROFT, Peter: Hull K.R. 81W
MYERS, David: Wigan 92w
MYLER, Tony: Widnes 82w, 83W, 89w, 90w

NASH, Steve: Salford 76L
NEILL, Jonathan: St. Helens 92L, 93W
NICHOLLS, George: St. Helens 75L, 76W, 77W
NICKLE, Sonny: St. Helens 92L, 93W
NOBLE, Brian: Bradford N. 90L
NOLAN, Gary: Hull 91w
NOLAN, Rob: Hull 891
NOONAN, Derek: St. Helens 76W
NORTON, Steve: Hull 81L, 82L, 83L

O'DONNELL, Gus: St. Helens 93W
OFFIAH, Martin: Widnes 88W, 89W, 90W, 91L;
    Wigan 92W, 93L
O'HARA, Dane: Hull 82L, 83L, 89L
OKULICZ, Eddie: Bradford N. 79L
O'LOUGHLIN, Kieron: Widnes 82W
O'NEILL, Mike: Widnes 80W, 82W, 83W,
    88W, 89W, 90W
O'NEILL, Steve: Widnes 83w, 88w

PANAPA, Sam: Wigan 92w, 93L
PARKER, Derek: Bradford N. 79L, 80L
PEACHAM, Gary: Hull 81L
PEARCE, Gary: Hull 89L
PEERS, Mike: Warrington 77l
PETERS, Barry: Warrington 87L
PETERS, Steve: St. Helens 85W
PHILBIN, Barry: Warrington 77L
PIMBLETT, Geoff: St. Helens 75L, 76W, 77W
PINNER, Harry: St. Helens 77W, 85W
PITCHFORD, Steve: Leeds 75W, 79W
PLATT, Andy: St. Helens 85W; Wigan 92W
PLATT, Duncan: Widnes 88W
POTTER, Ian: Wigan 87W
PRENDIVILLE, Paul: Hull 81L, 82L
PRESCOTT, Eric: Salford 76L; Widnes 82W, 83W
PRICE, Joe: Warrington 77L
PRICE, Richard; Hull 89L

203

PROCTOR, Paul: Hull K.R. 81W
PROHM, Gary: Hull K.R. 84W, 85L
PYKE, Derek: Widnes 89w

QUIRK, Les: St. Helens 88L

RAISTRICK, Dean: Salford 76L; Bradford N. 78W
RAMSEY, Bill: Widnes 78l
REDFEARN, Alan: Bradford N. 78W, 79L, 80L
REDFEARN, David: Bradford N. 78W, 80L
RICHARDS, Craig: Bradford N. 90l
RICHARDS, Maurice: Salford 76L
RIDDLESDEN, Eddie: Halifax 86L
RILEY, Mike: St. Helens 93W
ROBERTS, Mark: Warrington 86W, 87L
ROBINSON, Geoff: Halifax 86L
ROBINSON, Ian: Hull K.R. 84w, 85L
ROBINSON, Jason: Wigan 93L
ROBINSON, Steve: Castleford 84L
ROE, Peter: Bradford N. 78W
ROOCKLEY, David: Castleford 84L
ROPATI, Joe: Warrington 87L
ROPATI, Tea: St. Helens 92L, 93W
ROSE, Paul: Hull 83L
RUDD, Chris: Hull K.R. 84W
RUSSELL, Richard: Wigan 87w

SANDERSON, Gary: Warrington 86W, 87L
SANDERSON, John "Sammy": Leeds 79W
SCOTT, Mick: Halifax 86L
SHARP, Jon: Hull 89L, 91W
SHAW, Glyn: Widnes 78L, 80W
SHEFFIELD, Bill: Salford 76L
SIMPSON, Roger: Bradford N. 90L
SKERRETT, Kelvin: Bradford N. 90L; Wigan 93L
SKERRETT, Trevor: Hull 81L, 82L, 83L
SMITH, Alan: Leeds 75W, 79W
SMITH, David: Leeds 79W
SMITH, Gordon: Hull K.R. 85L
SMITH, Mike: Hull K.R. 81W, 84W, 85L
SMITH, Steve: Halifax 86l
SOLAL, Patrick: Hull 83l
SORENSEN, Kurt: Widnes 88W, 89W, 90W, 91L
SPENCER, Alan: Bradford N. 79L
STEPHENS, Gary: Halifax 86L
STEPHENSON, David: Wigan 87W
STEPHENSON, Nigel: Bradford N. 80L
STONE, Richard "Charlie": Hull 81L, 82L, 83L
SULLIVAN, Anthony: St. Helens 92L

TAIT, Alan: Widnes 88w, 89W, 90W, 91L
TAMATI, Kevin: Warrington 86W, 87L
TANNER, David: St. Helens 88L
THACKRAY, Rick: Widnes 88W
THOMPSON, Jimmy: Bradford N. 78W, 79L, 80L
TINDALL, Keith: Hull 81L, 82L
TOPLISS, David: Hull 82L, 83L
TROTTER, Dennis: Bradford N. 78W, 79L
TURNBULL, Sam: Salford 76l
TURNER, Neil: Hull 91W

VAN BELLEN, Gary: Bradford N. 80l
VAN BELLEN, Ian: Bradford N. 78W, 79l
VEIVERS, Phil: St. Helens 85W, 92L

David Watkinson, who made two Premiership final appearances with Hull K.R. in 1981 and 1985.

WALKER, Russ: Hull 91W
WALSH, John: St. Helens 75L
WANE, Shaun: Wigan 87W
WARD, David: Leeds 75W, 79W
WARD, Kevin: Castleford 84L; St. Helens 92L
WARLOW, John: St. Helens 75L
WATKINS, David: Salford 76L
WATKINSON, David: Hull K.R. 81W, 85L
WEAVILL, Dave: Warrington 77L
WEBB, Brad: Hull 91W
WELHAM, Paul: Hull 89L
WEST, Graeme: Wigan 87w
WHITFIELD, Colin: Halifax 86L
WHITFIELD, Fred: Widnes 82w, 83W
WILBY, Tim: Hull 81L, 89l
WILEMAN, Ronnie: Hull 81L, 82L
WILKINSON, Ian: Bradford N. 90L
WILSON, Frank: St. Helens 75L
WILSON, Scott: Halifax 86L
WINDLEY, Phil: Hull 89L
WOLFORD, John: Bradford N. 78W
WOODS, Paul: Widnes 78L; Hull 81L
WRIGHT, Darren: Widnes 88W, 89W, 90W, 911
WRIGHT, Stuart: Widnes 78L, 80W, 82W

THE HARRY SUNDERLAND TROPHY

The trophy, in memory of the famous Queenslander, a former Australian Tour Manager, broadcaster and journalist, is presented to the Man of the Match in the end of season Championship or Premiership final.

The award is donated and judged by the Rugby League Writers' Association and is sponsored by Stones Bitter.

The Harry Sunderland Trophy Roll of Honour

Year	Winner	Team	Position
1965	Terry Fogerty	Halifax (v. St. Helens)	Second row
1966	Albert Halsall	St. Helens (v. Halifax)	Prop
1967	Ray Owen	Wakefield T. (v. St. Helens)	Scrum half
1968	Gary Cooper	Wakefield T. (v. Hull K.R.)	Full back
1969	Bev Risman	Leeds (v. Castleford)	Full back
1970	Frank Myler	St. Helens (v. Leeds)	Stand off
1971	Bill Ashurst	Wigan (v. St. Helens)	Second row
1972	Terry Clawson	Leeds (v. St. Helens)	Prop
1973	Mick Stephenson	Dewsbury (v. Leeds)	Hooker
1974	Barry Philbin	Warrington (v. St. Helens)	Loose forward
1975	Mel Mason	Leeds (v. St. Helens)	Stand off
1976	George Nicholls	St. Helens (v. Salford)	Second row
1977	Geoff Pimblett	St. Helens (v. Warrington)	Full back
1978	Bob Haigh	Bradford N. (v. Widnes)	Loose forward
1979	Kevin Dick	Leeds (v. Bradford N.)	Stand off
1980	Mal Aspey	Widnes (v. Bradford N.)	Centre
1981	Len Casey	Hull K.R. (v. Hull)	Second row
1982	Mick Burke	Widnes (v. Hull)	Full back
1983	Tony Myler	Widnes (v. Hull)	Stand off
1984	John Dorahy	Hull K.R. (v. Castleford)	Stand off
1985	Harry Pinner	St. Helens (v. Hull K.R.)	Loose forward
1986	Les Boyd	Warrington (v. Halifax)	Prop
1987	Joe Lydon	Wigan (v. Warrington)	Winger
1988	David Hulme	Widnes (v. St. Helens)	Scrum half
1989	Alan Tait	Widnes (v. Hull)	Full back
1990	Alan Tait	Widnes (v. Bradford N.)	Full back
1991	Greg Mackey	Hull (v. Widnes)	Stand off
1992	Andy Platt	Wigan (v. St. Helens)	Prop
1993	Chris Joynt	St. Helens (v. Wigan)	Second row

PREMIERSHIP RECORDS First staged 1975

ALL ROUNDS

TEAM

Highest score: Wigan 74 v. Leeds 6 1992
(Also widest margin)
Biggest attendance: 42,043 Hull v. Widnes
.... Final at Old Trafford 1991

INDIVIDUAL

Most goals:
10 by Frano Botica (Wigan) v. St. Helens ...... Final 1992
Most tries:
10 by Martin Offiah (Wigan) v. Leeds
...... Semi-Final 1992
Most points:
40 (10t) by Martin Offiah (Wigan) v. Leeds
...... Semi-Final 1992

PREMIERSHIP FINAL

TEAM

Most appearances: 8 by Widnes
Most wins: 6 by Widnes
Highest score:
Wigan 48 v. St. Helens 16 (also widest margin) 1992
Biggest attendance:
42,043 Hull v. Widnes
(at Old Trafford, Man'r) 1991

INDIVIDUAL

Most tries:
No player has scored 3 or more
Most goals:
10 by Frano Botica (Wigan) v. St. Helens 1992
Most points:
20 (10g) by Frano Botica (Wigan) v. St. Helens 1992

DIVISIONAL PREMIERSHIP TROPHY

1993 Final

Out-of-contract Test centre Paul Newlove confirmed his market value by scoring two powerful tries to earn Man of the Match rating in Featherstone Rovers' 20-16 victory over Workington Town.

The Cumbrians, the first Third Division side to reach Old Trafford, belied the divisional gap and made the Second Division champions fight hard for victory.

While Town resisted most of what Featherstone could hurl at them, they found newly crowned Stones Bitter Second Division Player of the Year Newlove virtually unstoppable near the line.

The centre scored the first two of the Colliers' three touchdowns, each time barging through a mass of defenders to clinch the Tom Bergin Trophy as Man of the Match.

Newlove, the first centre to score 50 tries in a season, almost completed a hat-trick but the Town defence ganged up to prevent him getting the ball down.

It was Newlove's 10th successive tryscoring match and ensured that he finished top of the try chart with 52 touchdowns to pick up a £1,560 cheque from the £30-a-try prize offered by Stones Bitter.

His first try came off Brendon Tuuta's pass in the 20th minute and helped the Yorkshiremen to a 6-2 lead. But Rovers could not shake off the persistent Cumbrians, seeking a third Division Two scalp having beaten Huddersfield and Rochdale Hornets en route to Old Trafford.

Revitalised Town, boosted by the introduction of seasoned campaigners Des Drummond, Ged Byrne and Phil McKenzie, seemed to be heading for a shock victory when they led 10-8 until Newlove struck again to force his way over off scrum half Brett Daunt's pass in the 65th minute.

It came only a few minutes after Newlove had been injured, his hobbling back into position giving rise to fears that he would not be able to continue.

Having cracked against Newlove's power, the Town defence then creaked open three minutes later when Neil Roebuck's well-timed pass sent the ever-alert Francis Maloney romping in.

Full back Martin Pearson added the goal and a penalty soon after to lift Featherstone 20-10 clear, only to be left clinging on as Workington stormed back to be rewarded with a try from substitute Martin Oglanby.

Scrum half Dean Marwood added his fourth goal to give Featherstone an anxious last three minutes. Town had given them plenty of trouble throughout, having been expected to fold in the last quarter. They held a well deserved 8-6 half-time lead after on-loan hooker McKenzie pounced to touch down when Pearson spilled Marwood's high kick behind the posts in the 24th minute.

The Rovers-Town encounter continued the tradition of entertaining Stones Bitter curtain-raisers, Featherstone making amends for their narrow defeat by Oldham in the 1988 Second Division Premiership final.

Veteran wingman Des Drummond, on service for Workington Town six years after playing at Old Trafford for Warrington in the Premiership final.

Tryscoring Workington Town hooker Phil McKenzie wreaks havoc in the Featherstone Rovers rearguard.

Featherstone Rovers stand off Francis Maloney evades Workington Town defenders Wayne Kitchin and Ged Byrne (right).

STONES BITTER DIVISIONAL PREMIERSHIP FINAL

16 May   **Old Trafford, Manchester**

FEATHERSTONE ROVERS 20   **WORKINGTON TOWN** 16

Featherstone Rovers	No.	Workington Town
Martin Pearson	1.	Mark Mulligan
Ikram Butt	2.	Des Drummond
Terry Manning	3.	Tony Kay
Paul Newlove	4.	Brad Hepi
Owen Simpson	5.	Gary Smith
Francis Maloney	6.	Ged Byrne
Brett Daunt	7.	Dean Marwood
Leo Casey	8.	James Pickering
Mark Wilson, Capt.	9.	Phil McKenzie
Wayne Taekata	10.	Peter Riley
Gary Price	11.	Ian Scott
Ian Smales	12.	Colin Armstrong, Capt.
Brendon Tuuta	13.	Wayne Kitchin
Neil Roebuck	14.	Gary Schubert
Richard Gunn	15.	Martin Oglanby

T: Newlove (2), Maloney   T: McKenzie, Oglanby
G: Pearson (4)   G: Marwood (4)
Substitutions: Substitutions:
Roebuck for Simpson (30 min.)   Schubert for Riley (36 min.)
Gunn for Casey (75 min.)   Oglanby for Kitchin (Half-time)
Half-time: 6-8   Referee: John Connolly (Wigan)

1993 Round by Round

In the second Stones Bitter Divisional Premiership, the top eight Third Division sides played off in the first round. Dewsbury won the Heavy Woollen derby with landlords Batley, registering a 22-18 victory. Dewsbury led 18-6 at half-time before the Gallant Youths drew level at 18-all, Kenyan winger Eddie Rombo scoring the winning try. Champions Keighley Cougars led Hunslet 28-0 at the break, the visitors having scrum half Paul Harkin sent off after 35 minutes for verbal abuse of the referee before rallying in the second period to go down 34-6. Workington Town opened the scoring in the home tie with Doncaster with a try by former Great Britain winger Des Drummond. Doncaster were still in the game at 24-14 before the title runners-up added another 20 points for a 44-14 victory. Neighbours Whitehaven travelled to Ryedale-York, who ran in five tries to one in a 31-6 success.

In the second round, the top four in the Second Division entertained the Third Division victors. Workington Town and Dewsbury sprung surprises with away success. Town delighted their travelling army with a convincing 24-10 victory over Alex Murphy's Huddersfield, the visitors scoring four tries to two. Dewsbury loose forward Greg Pearce missed a goal kick from by the side of the posts as the final whistle blew, having to settle for a 14-14 draw at Second Division runners-up Oldham. In the replay at Batley's Mount Pleasant, scrum half Paul Shuttleworth was the hero with two drop goals in the final minutes to secure a 20-18 success. Oldham had led 10-0 before the home side ran in three glorious tries. Champions Featherstone Rovers defeated Ryedale-York 46-8 at Post Office Road, full back Martin Pearson contributing three tries and seven goals in an eight-try rout. Keighley squandered a 14-0 lead to go down 26-18 at Rochdale Hornets. Kiwi Joe Grima led the Cougars' early charges before Hornets winger Jason Green scored the match-winning try.

In the semis, Featherstone Rovers reached Old Trafford for the second time with a comfortable 35-12 home victory over Dewsbury, three records being broken on the way. Paul Newlove became the first centre to score 50 tries in a season, Pearson broke the club points in a season tally and Ian Smales broke the club record for most tries in a season by a forward. Workington Town became the first Third Division side to reach Old Trafford with a convincing 30-16 triumph at Rochdale. Drummond opened the scoring as Town took a lead they never lost, though Hornets pulled back to 18-16 before Town's extra power produced another 12 points in a late burst.

1993 Results

First Round
Dewsbury	22	Batley	18
Keighley C.	34	Hunslet	6
Ryedale-York	31	Whitehaven	6
Workington T.	44	Doncaster	14

Second Round
Featherstone R.	46	Ryedale-York	8
Huddersfield	10	Workington T.	24
Oldham	14	Dewsbury	14
Rochdale H.	26	Keighley C.	18

Replay
Dewsbury	20	Oldham	18

Semi-Finals
Featherstone R.	35	Dewsbury	12
Rochdale H.	16	Workington T.	30

Final
Featherstone R.	20	Workington T.	16

(at Old Trafford, Manchester)

1993 Prizes
Winners: £10,000
Runners-up: £4,000

SECOND DIVISION/DIVISIONAL PREMIERSHIP. . . . A REVIEW

1986-87
Swinton 27 Viller; Bate (1t), Topping (Ratcliffe), Brown, Rippon (3g); Snape, Lee (1t); Grima (1t), Ainsworth (1t), Muller, Derbyshire (1t), M. Holliday (Allen), L. Holliday (1dg)
Hunslet 10 Kay; Tate, Penola, Irvine, Wilson; Coates, King; Sykes, Gibson (Senior), Bateman (2t), Platt (1g) (Mason), Bowden, Jennings
Referee: J. McDonald (Wigan)

1987-88
Oldham 28 Burke (Irving); Round, D. Foy (2t), McAlister (4g), Meadows (1t); Walsh (1t), Ford; Sherratt (Warnecke), Sanderson, Waddell, Hawkyard, Graham, Flanagan (1t)
Featherstone R. 26 Quinn (5g); Bannister (1t), Sykes (1t), Banks, Marsh (Crossley); Steadman (2t), Fox; Siddall (Bastian), K. Bell, Harrison, Hughes, Smith, Lyman
Referee: R. Whitfield (Widnes)

1988-89
Sheffield E. 43 Gamson; Cartwright, Dickinson, Powell (3t), Young; Aston (1t, 7g, 1dg), Close (Evans); Broadbent (1t), Cook (1t), Van Bellen, Nickle, Fleming (McDermott 1t), Smiles
Swinton 18 Topping; Ranson (1t), Viller (Maloney), Snape, Bate; Frodsham (1t), Hewitt; Mooney, Melling (1t), S. O'Neill, Ainsworth, Allen (Horrocks), J. Myler (3g)
Referee: R. Whitfield (Widnes)

1989-90
Oldham 30 Platt (1g) (Martyn 1t); Irving (1t), Hyde (2g), Henderson (1t), Lord (1t); Clark, Ford (1t); Casey (Newton), Ruane (1t), Fieldhouse, Round, McAlister, Russell
Hull K.R. 29 Lightfoot; Clark (1t), M. Fletcher (4g), Austin, Sullivan; Parker (2t, 1dg), Bishop (Irvine); Niebling, Rudd, Ema, D. Harrison (1t) (Armstrong), Thompson, Lyman (1t)
Referee: R. Whitfield (Widnes)

1990-91
Salford 27 Gibson; Evans (1t), Gilfillan (1t), Birkett, Hadley (Dean); Cassidy (1dg), Kerry (2t, 4g, 1dg), Worrall, Lee (1dg), Hansen, Bradshaw (Sherratt), Blease, Burgess
Halifax 20 Smith; Wood (1t), Wilson (1t), Austin, Silva (Platt 2g); Lyons, R. Southernwood (1t); Hill (1t), Ramshaw, Bell (Scott), Brown, Milner, Keebles
Referee: B. Galtress (Bradford)

1991-92
Sheffield E. 34 Mycoe (1t); Gamson, McAlister, Powell (3t), Plange; Price, Aston (5g); Broadbent, Cook, Waddell, Laughton (Lumb 1t), Hughes (Mumby 1t), Farrell
Oldham 20 Platt (1t); Ranson (1t), Nicklin, Ropati, Tyrer; Russell (Warburton), Martyn (2g); Sherratt, Pachniuk, Newton (1t), Joynt, Tupaea (Street), Byrne (1t)
Referee: S. Cummings (Widnes)

209

ROLL OF HONOUR
SECOND DIVISION PREMIERSHIP

Year	Winners	Runners-up	Venue
1987	Swinton (2)..............27	Hunslet (1)..............10	Old Trafford, Manchester
1988	Oldham (1)..............28	Featherstone R. (2)....26	Old Trafford, Manchester
1989	Sheffield E. (3).........43	Swinton (5)..............18	Old Trafford, Manchester
1990	Oldham (3)..............30	Hull K.R. (1)...........29	Old Trafford, Manchester
1991	Salford (1)...............27	Halifax (2)...............20	Old Trafford, Manchester

DIVISIONAL PREMIERSHIP

Year	Winners	Runners-up	Venue
1992	Sheffield E. (1).........34	Oldham (3)..............20	Old Trafford, Manchester
1993	Featherstone R. (1)....20	Workington T. (*2)....16	Old Trafford, Manchester

( ) Denotes Second Division position
(*) Denotes Third Division position

THE TOM BERGIN TROPHY

The trophy, in honour of the President of the Rugby League Writers' Association and former Editor of the *Salford City Reporter*, is presented to the Man of the Match in the end of season Second Division, later Divisional, Premiership final. The award is donated and judged by the Association and sponsored by Stones Bitter.

Year	Winner	Team	Position
1987	Gary Ainsworth	Swinton (v. Hunslet)	Hooker
1988	Des Foy	Oldham (v. Featherstone R.)	Centre
1989	Mark Aston	Sheffield E. (v. Swinton)	Stand off
1990	Mike Ford	Oldham (v. Hull K.R.)	Scrum half
1991	Steve Kerry	Salford (v. Halifax)	Scrum half
1992	Daryl Powell	Sheffield (v. Oldham)	Centre
1993	Paul Newlove	Featherstone R. (v. Workington T.)	Centre

Workington Town captain Colin Armstrong is held by Featherstone Rovers duo Gary Price (left) and skipper Mark Wilson.

LANCASHIRE CUP

1992 Final

In his final season as coach of Wigan, John Monie collected the winner's medal which had eluded him during a four-year stay at Central Park.

St. Helens had won the toss for ground advantage and the capacity 20,534 crowd — paying a competition record £122,327 — saw a contest that was as close as the 5-4 scoreline suggested. Frano Botica of Wigan and St. Helens hooker Bernard Dwyer each struck two penalty goals, but a 12th-minute drop goal from former New Zealand RU All Black Botica separated the sides.

Despite the lack of a try, the Greenalls Lancashire Cup final was a fine advertisement for British club Rugby League. Possibly the only spectator not thrilled by the bone-jarring contest was Great Britain coach Malcolm Reilly who had protested against the staging of the derby clash only six days before the Stones Bitter World Cup final with reigning title holders Australia.

Reilly had pleaded for the Saints-Wigan encounter to be held two days earlier to allow a weekend recovery period before the World Cup build-up, or even a postponement until after the big Wembley date.

Instead, the international supremo had to sit in the Knowsley Road stand and witness a no-holds-barred confrontation of Britain's top two sides containing 11 of his World Cup final squad.

Ace tryscoring winger Martin Offiah became his only major concern, when he failed to reappear after the interval, coming back on 15 minutes from time only to finish the afternoon with an ice pack strapped to the back of his injured thigh.

Wigan's triumph was attributable to their organisation and to one of the most secure defences in the business. St. Helens could not create any significant gaps, coming close on a couple of occasions through summer signing Chris Joynt.

The Saints defence was every bit as good, though their general organisation was less impressive and their tactics often misguided.

Botica augmented his crucial 30-yard drop goal with a brace of penalty goals to give the visitors a well-earned 5-0 cushion at half-time. But Dwyer celebrated his call-up for the Great Britain World Cup squad with successful shots at goal after first Joe Lydon and then Neil Cowie conceded penalties.

The ceaseless tension sometimes spilled over and there were a number of flashpoints, effectively dealt with by Widnes referee Stuart Cummings. Shortly before the interval, Shaun Edwards went to the sin bin for the second successive week, along with Kevin Ward. A minute from time, St. Helens forward Sonny Nickle and Wigan skipper Dean Bell were also sent to the sin bin.

Wigan second row man Denis Betts was selected as Greenalls Man of the Match in a defence oriented encounter.

While giving the Australians notice of the standard of British Rugby League, the enthralling contest also gave Wigan revenge for the CIS Insurance Charity Shield defeat by St. Helens two months earlier.

Two goals for St. Helens hooker Bernard Dwyer.

GREENALLS LANCASHIRE CUP FINAL
18 October   **St. Helens**

WIGAN 5		ST. HELENS 4
Steve Hampson	1.	Phil Veivers
Jason Robinson	2.	Alan Hunte
Joe Lydon	3.	Gary Connolly
Andrew Farrar	4.	Jarrod McCracken
Martin Offiah	5.	Anthony Sullivan
Frano Botica	6.	Tea Ropati
Shaun Edwards	7.	Jonathan Griffiths
Kelvin Skerrett	8.	John Harrison
Martin Dermott	9.	Bernard Dwyer
Andy Platt	10.	Kevin Ward
Denis Betts	11.	Chris Joynt
Billy McGinty	12.	Sonny Nickle
Dean Bell, Capt.	13.	Shane Cooper, Capt.
Martin Crompton	14.	Gus O'Donnell
Neil Cowie	15.	Paul Forber

G: Botica (2, 1dg)
Substitutions:
Cowie for Hampson (24 min.)
Crompton for Offiah (Half-time)
Half-time: 5-0
Attendance: 20,534

G: Dwyer (2)
Substitutions:
O'Donnell for Veivers (50 min.)
Forber for Harrison (65 min.)
Referee: Stuart Cummings (Widnes)

Wigan coach John Monie, second from the left on the front row, joins in Lancashire Cup celebrations, completing his haul of British medals.

1992 Round by Round

Second Division leaders Oldham sprung the shock of the first round by defeating First Division Warrington 33-20 at Watersheddings. Oldham's Kiwi centre Iva Ropati notched a hat-trick of tries, Warrington having prop Neil Harmon sent off when already trailing 18-10. Holders St. Helens travelled to troubled Barrow with a mammoth score forecast. But the Cumbrians limited the visitors to 2-36, tourist Alan Hunte grabbing a hat-trick of touchdowns. Rochdale Hornets held out for half an hour before visitors Wigan ran away to a 36-8 success, post-interval tries from Martin Crompton and Shaun Edwards setting the seal. Five-try Welsh winger Phil Ford was the star of Salford's 60-8 home victory over Whitehaven, Australian Craig Coleman adding two tries in three minutes just before the break.

Wales captain Jonathan Davies tallied 20 points with a spectacular try and eight goals in the 52-8 Widnes rout of visitors Carlisle. Lowly Highfield trailed by only six points at half-time at Swinton, who opened up in the second half to register a 40-10 victory, marked by a Steve Garner hat-trick of tries. Blackpool Gladiators made a disappointing debut at Blackpool Mechanics FC ground with a 22-8 defeat by Workington Town, half back Dean Marwood contributing 14 points. Leigh's post-match celebrations for a 50-9 home success over Chorley Borough were spoiled by the resignation of coach Jim Crellin after only his third match in charge.

In the second round, Second Division pacesetters Oldham continued their giant-killing act by winning 26-14 at First Division Leigh, Tommy Martyn demoralising his home-town team with four goals and two drop goals. Wigan hammered Swinton at Gigg Lane 78-0, Edwards equalling the club record with a 10-try haul. In the tie of the round, St. Helens entertained Widnes and claimed a 10-8 victory with a Tea Ropati try only three minutes from time. Salford gained a 42-20 home win over Workington Town, who were only four points behind at half-time.

In the semi-finals, Salford bounced back from a recent 48-8 hammering against St. Helens to be the better side for the first hour of the Knowsley Road contest before being hit by tries from Gary Connolly and Hunte in an 18-5 reversal. Wigan set up a derby encounter in the final by disposing of Second Division Oldham 48-8 at Central Park, the eight-try performance featuring an 80-yard effort from teenager Jason Robinson, his second touchdown.

St. Helens full back Phil Veivers off-loads despite the efforts of Martin Offiah and Neil Cowie (above).

1992 RESULTS

First Round

Barrow	2	St. Helens	36
Blackpool G.	8	Workington T.	22
Leigh	50	Chorley B.	9
Oldham	33	Warrington	20
Rochdale H.	8	Wigan	36
Salford	60	Whitehaven	8
Swinton	40	Highfield	10
Widnes	52	Carlisle	8

Second Round

Leigh	14	Oldham	26
St. Helens	10	Widnes	8
Salford	42	Workington T.	20
Swinton	0	Wigan	78

Semi-Finals

St. Helens	18	Salford	5
Wigan	48	Oldham	8

Final

Wigan	5	St. Helens	4
(at St. Helens)			

LANCASHIRE CUP ROLL OF HONOUR

Season	Winners		Runners-up		Venue	Attendance	Receipts
1905-06	Wigan	0	Leigh	0	Broughton	16,000	£400
(replay)	Wigan	8	Leigh	0	Broughton	10,000	£200
1906-07	Broughton R.	15	Warrington	6	Wigan	14,048	£392
1907-08	Oldham	16	Broughton R.	9	Rochdale	14,000	£340
1908-09	Wigan	10	Oldham	9	Broughton	20,000	£600
1909-10	Wigan	22	Leigh	5	Broughton	14,000	£296
1910-11	Oldham	4	Swinton	3	Broughton	14,000	£418
1911-12	Rochdale H.	12	Oldham	5	Broughton	20,000	£630
1912-13	Wigan	21	Rochdale H.	5	Salford	6,000	£200
1913-14	Oldham	5	Wigan	0	Broughton	18,000	£610
1914-15	Rochdale H.	3	Wigan	2	Salford	4,000	£475
1915-16 to 1917-18 *Competition suspended*							
1918-19	Rochdale H.	22	Oldham	0	Salford	18,617	£1,365
1919-20	Oldham	7	Rochdale H.	0	Salford	19,000	£1,615
1920-21	Broughton R.	6	Leigh	3	Salford	25,000	£1,800
1921-22	Warrington	7	Oldham	5	Broughton	18,000	£1,200
1922-23	Wigan	20	Leigh	2	Salford	15,000	£1,200
1923-24	St. Helens Recs.	17	Swinton	0	Wigan	25,656	£1,450
1924-25	Oldham	10	St. Helens Recs.	0	Salford	15,000	£1,116
1925-26	Swinton	15	Wigan	11	Broughton	17,000	£1,115
1926-27	St. Helens	10	St. Helens Recs.	2	Warrington	19,439	£1,192
1927-28	Swinton	5	Wigan	2	Oldham	22,000	£1,275
1928-29	Wigan	5	Widnes	4	Warrington	19,000	£1,150
1929-30	Warrington	15	Salford	2	Wigan	21,012	£1,250
1930-31	St. Helens Recs.	18	Wigan	3	Swinton	16,710	£1,030
1931-32	Salford	10	Swinton	8	Broughton	26,471	£1,654
1932-33	Warrington	10	St. Helens	9	Wigan	28,500	£1,675
1933-34	Oldham	12	St. Helens Recs.	0	Swinton	9,085	£516
1934-35	Salford	21	Wigan	12	Swinton	33,544	£2,191
1935-36	Salford	15	Wigan	7	Warrington	16,500	£950
1936-37	Salford	5	Wigan	2	Warrington	17,500	£1,160
1937-38	Warrington	8	Barrow	4	Wigan	14,000	£800
1938-39	Wigan	10	Salford	7	Swinton	27,940	£1,708

Season	Winners		Runners-up		Venue	Attendance	Receipts
1939-40*	Swinton	5	Widnes	4	Widnes	5,500	£269
	Swinton	16	Widnes	11	Swinton	9,000	£446
	Swinton won on aggregate 21-15						
1940-41 to 1944-45 *Competition suspended during war-time*							
1945-46	Widnes	7	Wigan	3	Warrington	28,184	£2,600
1946-47	Wigan	9	Belle Vue R.	3	Swinton	21,618	£2,658
1947-48	Wigan	10	Belle Vue R.	7	Warrington	23,110	£3,043
1948-49	Wigan	14	Warrington	8	Swinton	39,015	£5,518
1949-50	Wigan	20	Leigh	7	Warrington	33,701	£4,751
1950-51	Wigan	28	Warrington	5	Swinton	42,541	£6,222
1951-52	Wigan	14	Leigh	6	Swinton	33,230	£5,432
1952-53	Leigh	22	St. Helens	5	Swinton	34,785	£5,793
1953-54	St. Helens	16	Wigan	8	Swinton	42,793	£6,918
1954-55	Barrow	12	Oldham	2	Swinton	25,204	£4,603
1955-56	Leigh	26	Widnes	9	Wigan	26,507	£4,090
1956-57	Oldham	10	St. Helens	3	Wigan	39,544	£6,274
1957-58	Oldham	13	Wigan	8	Swinton	42,497	£6,918
1958-59	Oldham	12	St. Helens	2	Swinton	38,780	£6,933
1959-60	Warrington	5	St. Helens	4	Wigan	39,237	£6,424
1960-61	St. Helens	15	Swinton	9	Wigan	31,755	£5,337
1961-62	St. Helens	25	Swinton	9	Wigan	30,000	£4,850
1962-63	St. Helens	7	Swinton	4	Wigan	23,523	£4,122
1963-64	St. Helens	15	Leigh	4	Swinton	21,231	£3,857
1964-65	St. Helens	12	Swinton	4	Wigan	17,383	£3,393
1965-66	Warrington	16	Rochdale H.	5	St. Helens	21,360	£3,800
1966-67	Wigan	16	Oldham	13	Swinton	14,193	£3,558
1967-68	St. Helens	2	Warrington	2	Wigan	16,897	£3,886
(replay)	St. Helens	13	Warrington	10	Swinton	7,577	£2,485
1968-69	St. Helens	30	Oldham	2	Wigan	17,008	£4,644
1969-70	Swinton	11	Leigh	2	Wigan	13,532	£3,651
1970-71	Leigh	7	St. Helens	4	Swinton	10,776	£3,136
1971-72	Wigan	15	Widnes	8	St. Helens	6,970	£2,204
1972-73	Salford	25	Swinton	11	Warrington	6,865	£3,321
1973-74	Wigan	19	Salford	9	Warrington	8,012	£2,750
1974-75	Widnes	6	Salford	2	Wigan	7,403	£2,833
1975-76	Widnes	16	Salford	7	Wigan	7,566	£3,880
1976-77	Widnes	16	Workington T.	11	Wigan	8,498	£6,414
1977-78	Workington T.	16	Wigan	13	Warrington	9,548	£5,038
1978-79	Widnes	15	Workington T.	13	Wigan	10,020	£6,261
1979-80	Widnes	11	Workington T.	0	Salford	6,887	£7,100
1980-81	Warrington	26	Wigan	10	St. Helens	6,442	£8,629
1981-82	Leigh	8	Widnes	3	Wigan	9,011	£14,029
1982-83	Warrington	16	St. Helens	0	Wigan	6,462	£11,732
1983-84	Barrow	12	Widnes	8	Wigan	7,007	£13,160
1984-85	St. Helens	26	Wigan	18	Wigan	26,074	£62,139
1985-86	Wigan	34	Warrington	8	St. Helens	19,202	£56,030
1986-87	Wigan	27	Oldham	6	St. Helens	20,180	£60,329
1987-88	Wigan	28	Warrington	16	St. Helens	20,237	£67,339
1988-89	Wigan	22	Salford	17	St. Helens	19,154	£71,879
1989-90	Warrington	24	Oldham	16	St. Helens	9,990	£41,804
1990-91	Widnes	24	Salford	18	Wigan	7,485	£36,867
1991-92	St. Helens	24	Rochdale H.	14	Warrington	9,269	£44,278
1992-93	Wigan	5	St. Helens	4	St. Helens	20,534	£122,327

*Emergency War-time competition

215

LANCASHIRE CUP FINAL .... A REVIEW
1970-71
Leigh 7 Ferguson (2g); Tickle (Canning),
L. Chisnall, Collins, Walsh; Eckersley (1t),
Murphy; D. Chisnall, Ashcroft, Watts, Grimes,
Clarkson, Mooney
St. Helens 4 F. Barrow; L. Jones, Benyon,
Walsh, Wilson; Myler, Whittle; Halsall,
A. Karalius, Rees (Prescott), Mantle,
E. Chisnall, Coslett (2g)
Referee: W.H. Thompson (Huddersfield)
1971-72
Wigan 15 Tyrer (3g); Eastham (1t), Francis (1t),
Fuller, Wright (Gandy); D. Hill, Ayres (1t);
Ashcroft, Clarke, Fletcher, Ashurst, Kevin
O'Loughlin, Laughton
Widnes 8 Dutton; Brown, McLoughlin, Aspey
(1g), Gaydon (1t); D. O'Neill (1t), Bowden;
Warlow, Foran, Doughty, Kirwan, Walsh
(Lowe), Nicholls
Referee: W.H. Thompson (Huddersfield)
1972-73
Salford 25 Charlton (1t); Eastham (1t),
Watkins (1t, 5g), Hesketh, Richards (1t); Gill,
Banner (1t); Mackay, Walker, Ward,
Whitehead, Dixon, Prescott
Swinton 11 Jackson; Fleay (1t), Cooke,
Buckley, Gomersall; Kenny (1g) (M. Philbin),
Gowers (3g); Halsall, Evans, Bate, R. Smith
(Holliday), Hoyle, W. Pattinson
Referee: W.H. Thompson (Huddersfield)
1973-74
Wigan 19 Francis; Vigo, D. Hill, Keiron
O'Loughlin (2t), Wright (1t); Cassidy,
Ayres (1g); Smethurst, Clarke, Gray (4g),
Irving, D. Robinson, Cunningham
Salford 9 Charlton; Fielding, Watkins (1t, 3g),
Hesketh, Holland; Gill, Banner; Mackay,
Walker, Davies (Grice), Dixon, Kear
(Knighton), E. Prescott
Referee: W.H. Thompson (Huddersfield)
1974-75
Widnes 6 Dutton (1g); George (1t),
D. O'Neill, Aspey, A. Prescott; Hughes (1dg),
Bowden; Mills, Elwell, J. Stephens, Adams,
Blackwood, Laughton
Salford 2 Charlton; Fielding (1g), Dixon,
Graham, Richards; Taylor, Banner; Mackay,
Devlin, Grice, Knighton, Coulman, E. Prescott
Referee: G.F. Lindop (Wakefield)
1975-76
Widnes 16 Dutton (3g, 1dg); A. Prescott (1t),
George (1t), Aspey (1t), Jenkins; Hughes,
Bowden; Mills, Elwell, Nelson, Foran,
Fitzpatrick (Sheridan), Adams

Salford 7 Watkins (2g); Fielding, Butler,
Hesketh, Richards (1t); Gill, Nash; Fiddler,
Hawksley, Dixon (Mackay), Turnbull,
Knighton, E. Prescott
Referee: W.H. Thompson (Huddersfield)
1976-77
Widnes 16 Dutton (4g, 1dg); Wright (1t),
Aspey, George (1t), A. Prescott; Eckersley,
Bowden (1dg); Ramsey, Elwell, Nelson,
Dearden, Adams, Laughton
Workington T. 11 Charlton; Collister,
Wilkins (1t), Wright, MacCorquodale (4g);
Lauder, Walker; Mills, Banks, Calvin,
Bowman, L. Gorley, W. Pattinson (P. Gorley)
Referee: W.H. Thompson (Huddersfield)
1977-78
Workington T. 16 Charlton (Atkinson);
Collister, Risman, Wright (1t), MacCorquodale
(4g); Wilkins (1t), Walker (2dg); Watts, Banks,
Bowman, L. Gorley, W. Pattinson, P. Gorley
Wigan 13 Swann; Vigo, Davies (Burke 1g),
Willicombe (1t), Hornby; Taylor, Nulty (1t, 1g);
Hogan, Aspinall, Irving, Ashurst (1t),
Blackwood, Melling (Regan)
Referee: W.H. Thompson (Huddersfield)
1978-79
Widnes 15 Eckersley; Wright (1t), Aspey,
George, Burke (3g); Hughes, Bowden; Mills,
Elwell, Shaw, Adams, Dearden (Hull),
Laughton (2t)
Workington T. 13 Charlton; Collister, Risman,
Wilkins (1t), MacCorquodale (1t, 2g), McMillan,
Walker; Beverley, Banks, Bowman, Blackwood,
P. Gorley, W. Pattinson (L. Gorley 1t)
Referee: W.H. Thompson (Huddersfield)
1979-80
Widnes 11 Eckersley; Wright, Aspey, Hughes
(George), Burke (2g); Moran (1t), Bowden;
Hogan, Elwell (1dg), Shaw, L. Gorley, Dearden,
Adams (1t)
Workington T. 0 Charlton; MacCorquodale,
Maughan, Thompson, Beck; Rudd, Walker
(Roper); Beverley, Banks, Wallbanks (Varty),
W. Pattinson, Lewis, Dobie
Referee: W.H. Thompson (Huddersfield)
1980-81
Warrington 26 Finnegan; Thackray (1t),
I. Duane, Bevan (1t), Hesford (1t, 7g);
K. Kelly, A. Gwilliam; Courtney, Waller, Case,
Martyn (1t), Eccles (Potter), Hunter
Wigan 10 Fairbairn (1t, 2g); Ramsdale (1t),
Willicombe, Davies, Hornby; M. Foy, Bolton
(Coyle); Breheny, Pendlebury (M. Smith),
S. O'Neill, Melling, Clough, Hollingsworth
Referee: D.G. Kershaw (York)

1981-82
Leigh 8 Hogan; Drummond, Bilsbury (1t),
Donlan (1dg), Worgan; Woods (2g), Green;
Wilkinson, Tabern, Cooke, Martyn (Platt),
Clarkson, McTigue
Widnes 3 Burke; George, Hughes,
Cunningham, Bentley (1t); Moran, Gregory;
M. O'Neill, Elwell, Lockwood, L. Gorley,
E. Prescott, Adams
Referee: W.H. Thompson (Huddersfield)
1982-83
Warrington 16 Hesford (2g); Fellows (1t),
R. Duane, Bevan, M. Kelly (1t); Cullen,
K. Kelly (1t); Courtney, Webb, Cooke
(D. Chisnall), Eccles (1t), Fieldhouse, Gregory
St. Helens 0 Parkes (Smith); Ledger,
Arkwright, Haggerty, Litherland; Peters,
Holding; James, Liptrot, Bottell (Mathias),
Moorby, P. Gorley, Pinner
Referee: J. Holdsworth (Leeds)
1983-84
Barrow 12 Tickle (1dg); Moore, Whittle,
Ball (3g, 1dg), Milby; McConnell (1t), Cairns;
Hodkinson, Wall, McJennett, Herbert, Szymala,
Mossop
Widnes 8 Burke; Lydon (1t, 2g), Hughes,
Keiron O'Loughlin, Basnett; A. Myler,
Gregory; S. O'Neill, Elwell, K. Tamati,
Whitfield, E. Prescott, Adams
Referee: K. Allatt (Southport)
1984-85
St. Helens 26 Veivers (Haggerty 1t); Ledger,
Allen, Meninga (2t), Day (1t, 5g); Arkwright,
Holding; Burke, Liptrot, P. Gorley, Platt,
Round, Pinner
Wigan 18 Edwards; Ferguson, Stephenson,
Whitfield (3g), Gill (1t) (Pendlebury); Cannon,
Fairhurst; Courtney, Kiss (1t), Case, West (1t),
Wane, Potter
Referee: R. Campbell (Widnes)
1985-86
Wigan 34 Edwards (1t); Henley-Smith
Hampson), Stephenson (7g), Hanley (1t),
Whitfield; Ella (2t), M. Ford; Dowling, Kiss
(1t), Wane (Case), Du Toit, Goodway, Potter
Warrington 8 Johnson (1t); Carbert (2g), Cullen,
Blake (Forster), Thackray; Kelly, A. Gregory;
Eccles, Webb, Jackson, Boyd (Tamati),
M. Gregory, Rathbone
Referee: J. Holdsworth (Kippax)
1986-87
Wigan 27 Edwards (2t); Lydon (1t, 1dg),
Stephenson, Bell, Gill (5g); Hanley, M. Ford
(1t); West, Dermott, Case, Roberts (Louw),
Potter, Goodway

Oldham 6 M'Barki; Sherman, Bridge (1t),
Warnecke, Taylor; Topliss, Kirwan; Clark,
Flanagan, Hobbs (1g), Nadiole, Worrall, Raper
(Hawkyard)
Referee: J.E. Smith (Halifax)
1987-88
Wigan 28 Hampson; Russell, Stephenson (1g)
(Bell), Lydon (5g), Gill (1t); Edwards,
A. Gregory; Case, Kiss, Wane (West 1t),
Goodway, Potter, Hanley (2t)
Warrington 16 Johnson; Drummond, Forster
(2t), Peters, Carbert; Woods (2g), Holden;
K. Tamati, Webb (Harmon), Humphries,
Sanderson, Roberts, M. Gregory (1t)
Referee: G.F. Lindop (Wakefield)
1988-89
Wigan 22 Hampson; T. Iro, K. Iro (2t, 3g),
Bell (1t), Lydon (Byrne); Edwards, Gregory;
Lucas (Betts), Dermott, Shelford (1t), Platt,
Goodway, Hanley
Salford 17 Williams (Blease); Evans (1t),
Bentley (1t), Jones, Hadley; Shaw, Cairns;
Herbert (1t), Moran, Brown (2g), Gormley,
M. Worrall (1dg), Horo (McTigue)
Referee: K. Allatt (Southport)
1989-90
Warrington 24 Lyon (Darbyshire); Drummond,
J. Ropati (1t), Thorniley, Forster (1t); Turner
(4g), Mackey; Burke, Roskell, Molloy, Jackson
(2t), Sanderson (Duane), M. Gregory
Oldham 16 Platt (1g) (Russell); Robinson (1t),
Hyde (1g), Irving (1t), Lord (1t); Clark,
M. Ford; Casey (J. Fairbank), A. Ruane,
Fieldhouse, Allen, Newton, Cogger
Referee: R. Tennant (Castleford)
1990-91
Widnes 24 Tait; Wright, Currier (1t), Davies
(4g), Offiah (1t); A. Myler (1t), D. Hulme;
Sorensen, McKenzie, Ashurst (Smith 1t),
Eyres, Koloto, Holliday
Salford 18 Gibson; Evans, Birkett, Williams
(1t), Hadley; Fell (1t), Kerry (3g) (Cassidy);
Sherratt, Lee, Whiteley (Hansen), Bradshaw,
Blease (1t), Burgess
Referee: A. Burke (Oldham)
1991-92
St Helens 24 Tanner; Riley, Connolly (Bailey),
Ropati, Sullivan; Veivers (2t), Bishop (1t, 2g);
Neill (Forber), Groves, Ward, Harrison, Mann
(2t), Cooper
Rochdale H. 14 Whitfield (1g); Fox (Calland),
Abram (1t), Duane (1t), Garritty; Clark, Gartland;
Humphries, M. Hall, Marsden, C. Eccles
(Bamber), Okesene, Kuiti (1t)
Referee: D. Campbell (Widnes)

217

MAN OF THE MATCH AWARDS

An award for the adjudged man of the match in the Lancashire Cup final was first presented in 1974-75. For four years the award was sponsored by the *Rugby Leaguer* newspaper. From 1978-85 the trophy was presented by Burtonwood Brewery, then from 1986 by Greenall Whitley, as part of their sponsorship of the Lancashire Cup. Under the auspices of the *Rugby Leaguer*, the choice was made by the Editor, while the breweries invited a panel of the Press to make the decision.

Season	Winner	Team	Position
1974-75	Mike Coulman	Salford (v. Widnes)	Second row
1975-76	Mick George	Widnes (v. Salford)	Centre
1976-77	David Eckersley	Widnes (v. Workington T.)	Stand off
1977-78	Arnold Walker	Workington T. (v. Wigan)	Scrum half
1978-79	Arnold Walker	Workington T. (v. Widnes)	Scrum half
1979-80	Mick Adams	Widnes (v. Workington T.)	Loose forward
1980-81	Tony Waller	Warrington (v. Wigan)	Hooker
1981-82	Ray Tabern	Leigh (v. Widnes)	Hooker
1982-83	Steve Hesford	Warrington (v. St. Helens)	Full back
1983-84	David Cairns	Barrow (v. Widnes)	Scrum half
1984-85	Mal Meninga	St. Helens (v. Wigan)	Centre
1985-86	Steve Ella	Wigan (v. Warrington)	Stand off
1986-87	Mike Ford	Wigan (v. Oldham)	Scrum half
1987-88	Shaun Edwards	Wigan (v. Warrington)	Stand off
1988-89	Paul Shaw	Salford (v. Wigan)	Stand off
1989-90	Bob Jackson	Warrington (v. Oldham)	Second row
1990-91	David Fell	Salford (v. Widnes)	Stand off
1991-92	Bob Marsden	Rochdale H. (v. St. Helens)	Prop
1992-93	Denis Betts	Wigan (v. St. Helens)	Second row

LANCASHIRE CUP FINAL RECORDS
TEAM
Most appearances: 35 by Wigan
Most wins: 21 by Wigan
Highest score: Wigan 34 v. Warrington 8 1985
Widest margin: St. Helens 30 v. Oldham 2 1968
Biggest attendance:
42,793 St. Helens v. Wigan (at Swinton) 1953

INDIVIDUAL
Most tries:
4 by Brian Nordgren (Wigan) v. Leigh 1949
Most goals:
7 by Jim Ledgard (Leigh) v. Widnes 1955
Steve Hesford (Warrington) v. Wigan 1980
David Stephenson (Wigan) v. Warrington 1985
Most points:
17 (1t, 7g) by Steve Hesford (Warrington) v. Wigan
.... 1980

Denis Betts, 1992 Lancashire Cup final Man of the Match

YORKSHIRE CUP

1992 Final

Wakefield Trinity's teenage stand off Nigel Wright came of age in his first final, becoming the youngest-ever winner of the White Rose Trophy as Man of the Match in the John Smiths Yorkshire Cup final as Trinity lifted the county trophy for the first time in 28 years.

Debutant finalists Sheffield Eagles could not contain the 18-year-old sensation as the youngster created three tries, added a goal to one and popped over a drop goal to steer Trinity to a 29-16 success.

Wright's outstanding contribution confirmed Trinity's high opinion of him since giving him his debut at 16, though his career had been hampered by injury.

The rich potential shone through almost every time the 6ft teenager had the ball in the Elland Road county showpiece. There was even the touch of luck that blesses rare talent.

That good fortune came in the fifth minute when Wright's kick through bounced off a defender's foot for Richard Slater to collect and swerve round Australian full back Garry Jack for the opening score. Peter Benson added the goal.

Wright's drop goal came 11 minutes later, two minutes before skipper Geoff Bagnall sneaked an 18th-minute touchdown by taking a quick tap penalty while Sheffield were expecting the Australian to open up play.

Trinity kicked off the second half with an 11-0 lead. Wright then produced two touches of class within five minutes of the restart to put the game out of the Eagles' reach.

A slicing midfield run and sidestep produced a try between the posts for full back Gary Spencer and then Wright slipped out a nugget of a pass as he seemed to be well tackled for centre Andy Mason to go over.

Wright made a rare mistake by hitting an upright with the kick at goal after Spencer's try, adding the goal to Mason's touchdown to open a 21-0 lead after only 45 minutes.

It was another five minutes before Sheffield contributed to the scoresheet with two quick tries from Australian import Bruce McGuire, both goaled by David Mycoe, to raise faint hopes of a dramatic finish.

The South Yorkshire revival soon collapsed and, inevitably, it was Wright who was at the centre of Trinity's reply. He made another midfield run and when the Eagles held him down centre Benson added the resulting penalty goal.

Substitute Billy Conway then moved smartly from a play-the-ball to send in Gary Price and Benson's goal completed Trinity's scoring in the 68th minute.

Sheffield saved their best until last when swift crossfield passing gave winger Mark Gamson the chance to beat two defenders on a 25-yard touchline dash for the final try.

Trinity were impressive up front, props Mark Webster and John Glancy always gaining valuable ground, aided by Australian back row man Darren Fritz. Wright and Bagnall added the subtle touches at half back to leave Sheffield beaten in all phases of the game.

The disappointing Eagles enjoyed flashes of form from half backs Tim Lumb and Mark Aston, plus full back Jack, who had a spell in the sin bin with fellow countryman Benson after a brief 39th-minute brawl, a rare loss of temper by either side despite a frustrating succession of penalties.

Man of the Match Nigel Wright.

JOHN SMITHS YORKSHIRE CUP FINAL

18 October   Elland Road, Leeds

WAKEFIELD TRINITY 29

Gary Spencer	1.	Garry Jack
David Jones	2.	Mark Gamson
Andy Mason	3.	Richard Price
Peter Benson	4.	David Mycoe
Andy Wilson	5.	David Plange
Nigel Wright	6.	Mark Aston
Geoff Bagnall, Capt.	7.	Tim Lumb
Mark Webster	8.	Paul Broadbent
Nigel Bell	9.	Mick Cook
John Glancy	10.	Dale Laughton
Gary Price	11.	Bruce McGuire, Capt.
Darren Fritz	12.	Paul Carr
Richard Slater	13.	Anthony Farrell
Richard Goddard	14.	Andy Young
Billy Conway	15.	Hugh Waddell

SHEFFIELD EAGLES 16

T: Slater, Bagnall, Spencer, Mason, Price
G: Benson (3), Wright (1, 1dg)
Substitutions:
Conway for Webster (56 min.)
Goddard for Wilson (77 min.)
Referee: Russell Smith (Castleford)

T: McGuire (2), Gamson
G: Mycoe (2)
Substitutions:
Waddell for Laughton (24 min.)
Young for Carr (56 min.)
Half-time: 11-0
Attendance: 7,918

Sheffield Eagles' David Mycoe, scorer of two goals.

1992 Round by Round

In a two-tie preliminary round, holders Castleford were knocked out by visitors Bradford Northern, the previous season's beaten finalists. Debutant winger Brimah Kebbie was the two-try star of the 16-10 victory in which former Leeds back row Paul Medley, Roy Powell and Dave Heron were outstanding. In an emotional encounter, Huddersfield marked their last appearance at Fartown with a 36-12 success over Ryedale-York, urged on from the stand by coach Alex Murphy, starting a month-long ban from sitting on the touchline.

In the preliminary round draw, Nottingham City were drawn to play Scarborough Pirates, who went out of existence a few weeks before the season opened. Nottingham were given a walkover to the first round.

In the first round, Hull got the upper hand in the Humberside derby clash with Hull K.R., Australian import Scott Gale scoring the crucial try in a 14-6 success at the start of his second spell at the Boulevard. In a Leeds derby, Third Division visitors Hunslet gave big-spending Leeds a fright before they collected their first win of the season, 28-20, sealed by a late solo try from Paul Dixon. A David Plange hat-trick of tries and a debutant touchdown by Australian full back Garry Jack were the highlights of a 34-14 Sheffield Eagles victory over visitors Halifax, who opened the scoring with a try from Gary Divorty. Bradford Northern's new record signing Deryck Fox came on as a substitute after only four minutes of the home tie with Bramley, who came close to spoiling the party, winger Kebbie clinching a 34-22 success with his fourth consecutive brace of tries.

Wakefield Trinity ran in 10 tries in the 54-14 hammering of Doncaster at Belle Vue, Nigel Bell, Andy Wilson, Andy Mason and Gary Spencer each collecting two tries. Now sharing with Huddersfield Town FC at Leeds Road stadium, Huddersfield were made to work hard for a 16-8 victory over Batley, the only side to pull off the double against them in the previous season's Third Division. Great Britain centre Paul Newlove was the star of Featherstone Rovers' 40-8 triumph at home to Dewsbury, scoring two tries, a feat matched by packman Gary Price. Keighley Cougars travelled to lowly Nottingham City to register a 30-4 victory, marked by a seven-goal haul by winger John Wasyliw.

In the second round, Hull were helped by a series of blunders by visitors Leeds, sweeping to an 18-4 lead before the Loiners pulled back to 18-16. Test winger Paul Eastwood struck a crucial penalty goal before Dean Busby forced his way over to seal a 26-16 success. Having been knocked out of the county competition by Bradford Northern for the past three seasons, Sheffield Eagles gained revenge with a 17-8 away victory, marked by a two-try performance from Plange. Wakefield Trinity gained a semi-final spot for the third successive season but only after an injury-time try from full back

Spencer clinched a 22-16 win over battling Third Division side Keighley. Featherstone Rovers clinched an 18-8 victory at home to Huddersfield, scoring two tries to one with Tim Sharp adding five valuable goals.

In the semi-finals, Sheffield Eagles went through to the final stage for the first time with a 12-8 home victory over Hull. Lee Jackson scored a try in nine seconds after a blunder by Sheffield full back Jack, who recovered in fine style to take the Man of the Match award. Wakefield Trinity went through to a second final in three years with a 22-8 win at Featherstone, who were depleted by the dismissal of skipper Brendon Tuuta four minutes before the interval.

1992 RESULTS

Preliminary Round

Castleford	10	Bradford N.	16
Huddersfield	36	Ryedale-York	12

First Round

Bradford N.	34	Bramley	22
Featherstone R.	40	Dewsbury	8
Huddersfield	16	Batley	8
Hull	14	Hull K.R.	6
Leeds	28	Hunslet	20
Nottingham C.	4	Keighley C.	30
Sheffield E.	34	Halifax	14
Wakefield T.	54	Doncaster	14

Second Round

Bradford N.	8	Sheffield E.	17
Featherstone R.	18	Huddersfield	8
Hull	26	Leeds	16
Wakefield T.	22	Keighley C.	16

Semi-Finals

Featherstone R.	8	Wakefield T.	22
Sheffield E.	12	Hull	8

Final

Wakefield T.	29	Sheffield E.	16
(at Elland Road, Leeds)			

YORKSHIRE CUP ROLL OF HONOUR

Year	Winners		Runners-up		Venue	Attendance	Receipts
1905-06	Hunslet	13	Halifax	3	Bradford P.A.	18,500	£465
1906-07	Bradford	8	Hull K.R.	5	Wakefield	10,500	£286
1907-08	Hunslet	17	Halifax	0	Leeds	15,000	£397
1908-09	Halifax	9	Hunslet	5	Wakefield	13,000	£356
1909-10	Huddersfield	21	Batley	0	Leeds	22,000	£778
1910-11	Wakefield T.	8	Huddersfield	2	Leeds	19,000	£696
1911-12	Huddersfield	22	Hull K.R.	10	Wakefield	20,000	£700
1912-13	Batley	17	Hull	3	Leeds	16,000	£523
1913-14	Huddersfield	19	Bradford N.	3	Halifax	12,000	£430
1914-15	Huddersfield	31	Hull	0	Leeds	12,000	£422
1918-19	Huddersfield	14	Dewsbury	8	Leeds	21,500	£1,309
1919-20	Huddersfield	24	Leeds	5	Halifax	24,935	£2,096
1920-21	Hull K.R.	2	Hull	0	Leeds	20,000	£1,926
1921-22	Leeds	11	Dewsbury	3	Halifax	20,000	£1,650
1922-23	York	5	Batley	0	Leeds	33,719	£2,414
1923-24	Hull	10	Huddersfield	4	Leeds	23,300	£1,728
1924-25	Wakefield T.	9	Batley	8	Leeds	25,546	£1,912
1925-26	Dewsbury	2	Huddersfield	0	Wakefield	12,616	£718
1926-27	Huddersfield	10	Wakefield T.	3	Leeds	11,300	£853
1927-28	Dewsbury	8	Hull	2	Leeds	21,700	£1,466
1928-29	Leeds	5	Featherstone R.	0	Wakefield	13,000	£838
1929-30	Hull K.R.	13	Hunslet	7	Leeds	11,000	£687
1930-31	Leeds	10	Huddersfield	2	Halifax	17,812	£1,405
1931-32	Huddersfield	4	Hunslet	2	Leeds	27,000	£1,764
1932-33	Leeds	8	Wakefield T.	0	Huddersfield	17,685	£1,183
1933-34	York	10	Hull K.R.	4	Leeds	22,000	£1,480
1934-35	Leeds	5	Wakefield T.	5	Dewsbury	22,598	£1,529
Replay	Leeds	2	Wakefield T.	2	Huddersfield	10,300	£745
Replay	Leeds	13	Wakefield T.	0	Hunslet	19,304	£1,327
1935-36	Leeds	3	York	0	Halifax	14,616	£1,113
1936-37	York	9	Wakefield T.	2	Leeds	19,000	£1,294
1937-38	Leeds	14	Huddersfield	8	Wakefield	22,000	£1,508
1938-39	Huddersfield	18	Hull	10	Bradford	28,714	£1,534
1939-40	Featherstone R.	12	Wakefield T.	9	Bradford	7,077	£403
1940-41	Bradford N.	15	Dewsbury	5	Huddersfield	13,316	£939
1941-42	Bradford N.	24	Halifax	0	Huddersfield	5,989	£635
1942-43	Dewsbury	7	Huddersfield	0	Dewsbury	11,000	£680
	Huddersfield	2	Dewsbury	0	Huddersfield	6,252	£618
	Dewsbury won on aggregate 7-2						
1943-44	Bradford N.	5	Keighley	2	Bradford	10,251	£757
	Keighley	5	Bradford N.	5	Keighley	8,993	£694
	Bradford N. won on aggregate 10-7						
1944-45	Hunslet	3	Halifax	12	Hunslet	11,213	£744
	Halifax	2	Hunslet	0	Halifax	9,800	£745
	Halifax won on aggregate 14-3						
1945-46	Bradford N.	5	Wakefield T.	2	Halifax	24,292	£1,934
1946-47	Wakefield T.	10	Hull	0	Leeds	34,300	£3,718

Year	Winners		Runners-up		Venue	Attendance	Receipts
1947-48	Wakefield T.	7	Leeds	7	Huddersfield	24,344	£3,461
Replay	Wakefield T.	8	Leeds	7	Bradford	32,000	£3,251
1948-49	Bradford N.	18	Castleford	9	Leeds	31,393	£5,053
1949-50	Bradford N.	11	Huddersfield	4	Leeds	36,000	£6,365
1950-51	Huddersfield	16	Castleford	3	Leeds	28,906	£5,152
1951-52	Wakefield T.	17	Keighley	3	Huddersfield	25,495	£3,347
1952-53	Huddersfield	18	Batley	8	Leeds	14,705	£2,471
1953-54	Bradford N.	7	Hull	2	Leeds	22,147	£3,833
1954-55	Halifax	22	Hull	14	Leeds	25,949	£4,638
1955-56	Halifax	10	Hull	10	Leeds	23,520	£4,385
Replay	Halifax	7	Hull	0	Bradford	14,000	£2,439
1956-57	Wakefield T.	23	Hunslet	5	Leeds	30,942	£5,609
1957-58	Huddersfield	15	York	8	Leeds	22,531	£4,123
1958-59	Leeds	24	Wakefield T.	20	Bradford	26,927	£3,833
1959-60	Featherstone R.	15	Hull	14	Leeds	23,983	£4,156
1960-61	Wakefield T.	16	Huddersfield	10	Leeds	17,456	£2,937
1961-62	Wakefield T.	19	Leeds	9	Bradford	16,329	£2,864
1962-63	Hunslet	12	Hull K.R.	2	Leeds	22,742	£4,514
1963-64	Halifax	10	Featherstone R.	0	Wakefield	13,238	£2,471
1964-65	Wakefield T.	18	Leeds	2	Huddersfield	13,527	£2,707
1965-66	Bradford N.	17	Hunslet	8	Leeds	17,522	£4,359
1966-67	Hull K.R.	25	Featherstone R.	12	Leeds	13,241	£3,482
1967-68	Hull K.R.	8	Hull	7	Leeds	16,729	£5,515
1968-69	Leeds	22	Castleford	11	Wakefield	12,573	£3,746
1969-70	Hull	12	Featherstone R.	9	Leeds	11,089	£3,419
1970-71	Leeds	23	Featherstone R.	7	Bradford	6,753	£1,879
1971-72	Hull K.R.	11	Castleford	7	Wakefield	5,536	£1,589
1972-73	Leeds	36	Dewsbury	9	Bradford	7,806	£2,659
1973-74	Leeds	7	Wakefield T.	2	Leeds	7,621	£3,728
1974-75	Hull K.R.	16	Wakefield T.	13	Leeds	5,823	£3,090
1975-76	Leeds	15	Hull K.R.	11	Leeds	5,743	£3,617
1976-77	Leeds	16	Featherstone R.	12	Leeds	7,645	£5,198
1977-78	Castleford	17	Featherstone R.	7	Leeds	6,318	£4,528
1978-79	Bradford N.	18	York	8	Leeds	10,429	£9,188
1979-80	Leeds	15	Halifax	6	Leeds	9,137	£9,999
1980-81	Leeds	8	Hull K.R.	7	Huddersfield	9,751	£15,578
1981-82	Castleford	10	Bradford N.	5	Leeds	5,852	£10,359
1982-83	Hull	18	Bradford N.	7	Leeds	11,755	£21,950
1983-84	Hull	13	Castleford	2	Elland Rd, Leeds	14,049	£33,572
1984-85	Hull	29	Hull K.R.	12	Hull C. FC	25,237	£68,639
1985-86	Hull K.R.	22	Castleford	18	Leeds	12,686	£36,327
1986-87	Castleford	31	Hull	24	Leeds	11,132	£31,888
1987-88	Bradford N.	12	Castleford	12	Leeds	10,947	£40,283
Replay	Bradford N.	11	Castleford	2	Elland Rd, Leeds	8,175	£30,732
1988-89	Leeds	33	Castleford	12	Elland Rd, Leeds	22,968	£76,658
1989-90	Bradford N.	20	Featherstone R.	14	Leeds	12,607	£50,775
1990-91	Castleford	11	Wakefield T.	8	Elland Rd, Leeds	12,420	£61,432
1991-92	Castleford	28	Bradford N.	6	Elland Rd, Leeds	8,916	£54,183
1992-93	Wakefield T.	29	Sheffield E.	16	Elland Rd, Leeds	7,918	£49,845

YORKSHIRE CUP FINAL .... A REVIEW
1971-72
Hull K.R. 11 Markham; Stephenson, Coupland, Kirkpatrick, Longstaff (1t); Millward (4g), Daley; Wiley, Flanagan, Millington, Wallis, Palmer (Cooper), Brown
Castleford 7 Edwards; Foster (1t), S. Norton, Worsley, Lowndes; Hargrave, Stephens; Hartley, Miller, I. Van Bellen (Ackroyd 2g), A. Dickinson, Lockwood, Blakeway
Referee: A. Givvons (Oldham)
1972-73
Leeds 36 Holmes (3t); Alan Smith, Hynes (1g), Dyl (2t), Atkinson (1t); Hardisty (1t), Hepworth (Langley); Clawson (5g) (Fisher), Ward, Ramsey, Cookson, Eccles (1t), Batten
Dewsbury 9 Rushton; Ashcroft (1t), Childe, Day, Yoward; Agar (3g), A. Bates; Bell (Beverley), M. Stephenson, Lowe, Grayshon, J. Bates (Lee), Hankins
Referee: M.J. Naughton (Widnes)
1973-74
Leeds 7 Holmes; Langley (1t) (Marshall 1g), Hynes (1g), Dyl, Atkinson; Hardisty, Hepworth (Jeanes (Ramsey), Ward, Clarkson, Eccles, Cookson, Batten
Wakefield T. 2 Wraith (Sheard); D. Smith, Crook (1g), Hegarty, B. Parker; Topliss, Bonnar; Valentine, Morgan, Bratt, Knowles (Ballantyne), Endersby, Holmes
Referee: M.J. Naughton (Widnes)
1974-75
Hull K.R. 16 Smithies; Sullivan (Dunn 1t), Watson (2t), Coupland, Kirkpatrick (1t); Millward, Stephenson; Millington, Heslop, Rose, Wallis, N. Fox (2g) (Madley), Brown
Wakefield T. 13 Sheard; D. Smith (1t), Crook (2g), Hegarty (1t), Archer; Topliss, Bonnar; Ballantyne, Handscombe, Bratt (1t), Skerrett, A. Tonks (Goodwin), (Holmes), Morgan
Referee: M.J. Naughton (Widnes)
1975-76
Leeds 15 Marshall; Alan Smith, Hague, Dyl (1t), Atkinson; Holmes (4g, 1dg), Hynes; Harrison, Payne, Pitchford, (Dickinson), Eccles, Batten, Cookson (1t)
Hull K.R. 11 Wallace; Dunn, A. Burwell, Watson, Sullivan (1t); Turner, Millward (1dg); Millington, Dickinson, Lyons, Rose, N. Fox (2g, 1t), Hughes (Holdstock)
Referee: J.V. Moss (Manchester)
1976-77
Leeds 16 Marshall (2g); Hague, Hynes, Dyl (2t), D. Smith; Holmes, Banner; Dickinson, Ward, Pitchford, Eccles (1t), Burton, Cookson (1t)

Featherstone R. 12 Box; Bray (1t), Coventry, Quinn (3g), K. Kellett; Newlove, Fennell; Gibbins, Bridges, Farrar, Stone, P. Smith (1t), Bell (Spells)
Referee: M.J. Naughton (Widnes)
1977-78
Castleford 17 Wraith; Richardson, Joyner, P. Johnson, Fenton; Burton (2t, 1dg), Pickerill (Stephens); Fisher (Woodall), Spurr, Weston, Huddlestone, Reilly, Lloyd (5g)
Featherstone R. 7 Marsden; Evans, Gilbert, Quinn (1g) (N. Tuffs), K. Kellett; Newlove, Butler; Townend (1g), Bridges, Farrar, Gibbins, Stone (P. Smith 1t), Bell
Referee: M.J. Naughton (Widnes)
1978-79
Bradford N. 18 Mumby; Barends, Gant (1t), D. Parker (1t), D. Redfearn; Slater (Wolford), A. Redfearn (1t); Thompson, Fisher, Forsyth (Joyce), Fox (3g), Trotter, Haigh (1t)
York 8 G. Smith (1t); T. Morgan, Day (Crossley), Foster, Nicholson; Banks (2g), Harkin; Dunkerley, Wileman, Harris, Rhodes, Hollis (1dg) (Ramshaw), Cooper
Referee: M.J. Naughton (Widnes)
1979-80
Leeds 15 Hague; Alan Smith (2t), D. Smith (1t), Dyl, Atkinson; Holmes (J. Sanderson), Dick (3g); Dickinson, Ward, Pitchford, Eccles, D. Heron (Adams), Cookson
Halifax 6 Birts (3g); Howard (Snee), Garrod, Cholmondeley, Waites; Blacker, Langton; Jarvis (Callon), Raistrick, Wood, Scott, Sharp, Busfield
Referee: M.J. Naughton (Widnes)
1980-81
Leeds 8 Hague; Alan Smith (1t), D. Smith, Atkinson, Oulton; Holmes, Dick (2g, 1dg); Harrison, Ward, Pitchford, Eccles, Cookson (Carroll), D. Heron
Hull K.R. 7 Robinson; McHugh (1t), M. Smith, Hogan (2g), Youngman; Hall, Harkin; Holdstock, Price, Crooks (Rose), Lowe, Casey, Crane
Referee: R. Campbell (Widnes)
1981-82
Castleford 10 Claughton; Richardson, Fenton, Hyde (1t), Morris; Joyner (1t), R. Beardmore; Hardy (P. Norton), Spurr, B. Johnson, Finch (2g), Ward, Timson
Bradford N. 5 Mumby; Barends, Hale, A. Parker (1t), Gant; Hanley (1g), A. Redfearn; Grayshon, Noble, Sanderson (D. Redfearn), G. Van Bellen (Jasiewicz), Idle, Rathbone
Referee: M.R. Whitfield (Widnes)

1982-83
Hull 18 Kemble; S. Evans (1t), Day, Leuluai, Prendiville (1t); Topliss, Harkin; Skerrett, Bridges, Stone, Rose (2t), L. Crooks (2g, 2dg), Crane (Norton)
Bradford N. 7 Mumby; Barends, Gant, A. Parker, Pullen (Smith); Whiteman (1t), Carroll (1g, 2dg); Grayshon, Noble, G. Van Bellen (Sanderson), Idle, Jasiewicz, Hale
Referee: S. Wall (Leigh)
1983-84
Hull 13 Kemble; Solal, Schofield, Leuluai, O'Hara (1t); Topliss, Dean; Edmonds, Wileman, Skerrett, Proctor (1t), L. Crooks, Crane (1t, 1dg)
Castleford 2 Coen; Fenton, Marchant, Hyde (Orum), Kear; Joyner, R. Beardmore (1g); Connell, Horton, Reilly, Timson, James, England
Referee: W.H. Thompson (Huddersfield)
1984-85
Hull 29 Kemble (2t); Leuluai, Schofield (4g, 1dg), S. Evans (1t), O'Hara; Ah Kuoi, Sterling; Edmonds, Patrick, L. Crooks (1t), Norton (1t), Proctor, Divorty (Rose)
Hull K.R. 12 Fairbairn (1t); Clark, Robinson (1t), Prohm, Laws; M. Smith, Harkin (Rudd); Broadhurst, Watkinson, Ema (Hartley), Burton, Kelly, Hall (1t)
Referee: G.F. Lindop (Wakefield)
1985-86
Hull K.R. 22 Fairbairn (Lydiat); Clark (1t), Dorahy (5g), Prohm, Laws; G. Smith, Harkin; Des Harrison, Watkinson, Ema, Burton, Hogan (Kelly), Miller (2t)
Castleford 18 Lord; Plange, Marchant (2t), Hyde, Spears; Diamond (1g), R. Beardmore (1t, 2g); Ward, K. Beardmore, B. Johnson, England, Ketteridge, Joyner
Referee: R. Campbell (Widnes)
1986-87
Castleford 31 Scott; Plange, Marchant, Johns, Hyde (Lord); Joyner, R. Beardmore (1dg); Ward (1t), K. Beardmore (2t), B. Johnson, Ketteridge (1t, 5g), Atkins (1t) (Shillito), England
Hull 24 Kemble; Brand (2t), Schofield, O'Hara (2t), Eastwood; Ah Kuoi, Windley; Brown (Puckering), S. Patrick, Dannatt, Norton (Divorty), L. Crooks (4g), Sharp
Referee: J. McDonald (Wigan)
1987-88
Bradford N. 12 Mercer; Ford, McGowan, Simpson, Francis; Mumby (2g), Harkin; Grayshon (Hobbs 2g), Noble, Hill, Skerrett, Fairbank (1t), Holmes (Roebuck)

Castleford 12 Roockley; Plange (1t), Marchant, Beattie, Hyde; Joyner, R. Southernwood; Shillito (R. Beardmore), K. Beardmore (Sampson), Ward, Ketteridge (2g), Fifita, Lindner (1t)
Referee: K. Allatt (Southport)
Replay
Bradford N. 11 Mumby; Ford, McGowan, Mercer, Simpson; Stewart, Harkin; Hobbs (1g, 1dg), Noble, Hill (1t), Skerrett, Fairbank, Heron (1t)
Castleford 2 Roockley; Plange, Marchant, Beattie, Hyde; R. Southernwood, R. Beardmore; Ward, Hill, Fifita (Sampson), Ketteridge (1g), England (Boothroyd), Joyner
Referee: K. Allatt (Southport)
1988-89
Leeds 33 Spencer; Ettingshausen, Schofield (2t, 1dg), Stephenson (6g), Gibson (2t); C. Lyons, Ashton; Crooks, Maskill, Waddell (Backo), Powell, Brooke-Cowden (Medley 1t), Heron
Castleford 12 Belcher; Plange, Marchant, Boothroyd (1t), Chapman (Roockley) (Sampson); Anderson, R. Beardmore; Ward, K. Beardmore, England, Ketteridge (2g), Gibbs, Joyner (1t)
Referee: R. Whitfield (Widnes)
1989-90
Bradford N. 20 Wilkinson; Cordle (2t), McGowan, Simpson, Francis; Henjak (Mumby), Harkin (2t); Skerrett, Barraclough, Hamer (Medley), Hobbs (2g), Fairbank, Pendlebury
Featherstone R. 14 Bibb; Drummond, I. Ropati (1t), Newlove, Banks; Smales, Fox (3g); Grayshon, Clark, G. Bell (Dakin), Price, Booth (Fisher), Smith (1t)
Referee: R. Whitfield (Widnes)
1990-91
Castleford 11 Larder; Ellis, Irwin, Anderson, Plange (1t); Steadman, Atkins (1t) (England); Crooks (1g), G. Southernwood, Sampson, Battye (Ketteridge), Hardy, Roebuck (1dg)
Wakefield T. 8 Harcombe (2g); Jones, Mason (1t), Eden, Wilson; Lazenby, M. Conway; Shelford, B. Conway (Slater), Thompson, Kelly (Perry), G. Price, Bell
Referee: J. Smith (Halifax)
1991-92
Castleford 28 Steadman (2t, 4g); Ellis, Bradley, Blackmore, Nelson; Smith (1t), Ford (1t); Sampson (Ketteridge), G. Southernwood, England, Battye (1t), Irwin, Nikau
Bradford N. 6 Simpson; D. Powell (1t), Shelford, McGowan, Marchant; Anderson, Iti (Croft); Hobbs (1g), Noble, Hamer, Medley (Richards), Fairbank, Barnett
Referee: J. Holdsworth (Kippax)

THE WHITE ROSE TROPHY

First awarded in 1966, the trophy is presented to the adjudged man of the match in the Yorkshire Cup final.

Donated by the late T.E. Smith, of York, the award is organised by the Yorkshire

Federation of Rugby League Supporters' Clubs and judged by a panel of the Press.

The trophy is not awarded in replays, although Bradford Northern's Brendan Hill was named Man of the Match in the second game against Castleford in 1987.

Season	Winner	Team	Position
1966-67	Cyril Kellett	Hull K.R. (v. Featherstone R.)	Full back
1967-68	Chris Davidson	Hull (v. Hull K.R.)	Scrum half
1968-69	Barry Seabourne	Leeds (v. Castleford)	Scrum half
1969-70	Joe Brown	Hull (v. Featherstone R.)	Loose forward
1970-71	Syd Hynes	Leeds (v. Featherstone R.)	Centre
1971-72	Ian Markham	Hull K.R. (v. Castleford)	Full back
1972-73	John Holmes	Leeds (v. Dewsbury)	Full back
1973-74	Keith Hepworth	Leeds (v. Wakefield T.)	Scrum half
1974-75	Roger Millward	Hull K.R. (v. Wakefield T.)	Stand off
1975-76	Neil Fox	Hull K.R. (v. Leeds)	Second row
1976-77	Les Dyl	Leeds (v. Featherstone R.)	Centre
1977-78	Bruce Burton	Castleford (v. Featherstone R.)	Stand off
1978-79	Bob Haigh	Bradford N. (v. York)	Loose forward
1979-80	Alan Smith	Leeds (v. Halifax)	Winger
1980-81	Kevin Dick	Leeds (v. Hull K.R.)	Scrum half
1981-82	Barry Johnson	Castleford (v. Bradford N.)	Prop
1982-83	Keith Mumby	Bradford N. (v. Hull)	Full back
1983-84	Mick Crane	Hull (v. Castleford)	Loose forward
1984-85	Peter Sterling	Hull (v. Hull K.R.)	Scrum half
1985-86	Gavin Miller	Hull K.R. (v. Castleford)	Loose forward
1986-87	Kevin Beardmore	Castleford (v. Hull)	Hooker
1987-88	Paul Harkin	Bradford N. (v. Castleford)	Scrum half
1988-89	Cliff Lyons	Leeds (v. Castleford)	Stand off
1989-90	Paul Harkin	Bradford N. (v. Featherstone R.)	Scrum half
1990-91	Tracy Lazenby	Wakefield T. (v. Castleford)	Stand off
1991-92	Graham Steadman	Castleford (v. Bradford N.)	Full back
1992-93	Nigel Wright	Wakefield T. (v. Sheffield E.)	Stand off

YORKSHIRE CUP FINAL RECORDS

TEAM
Most appearances: 21 Leeds
Most wins: 17 Leeds
Highest score: Leeds 36 v. Dewsbury 9 1972
Widest margin win: Huddersfield 31 v. Hull 0 1914
Biggest attendance:
36,000 Bradford N. v. Huddersfield (at Leeds) 1949

INDIVIDUAL
Most tries:
4 by Stan Moorhouse (Huddersfield) v. Leeds 1919
Most goals:
6 by David Stephenson (Leeds) v. Castleford 1988
Most points:
16 (2t, 4g) by Graham Steadman (Castleford)
v. Bradford N. 1991

1992 CHARITY SHIELD

St. Helens tasted success on their CIS Insurance Charity Shield debut, registering a comfortable 17-0 victory over arch rivals Wigan at Gateshead.

Scoring three tries without reply, the Saints' triumph in front of a disappointing crowd of 7,364 ended Wigan's winning run of 25 games, including the first-ever spring treble of Championship, Challenge Cup and Premiership.

Wigan's treble meant that St. Helens qualified for the Charity Shield match as Championship runners-up.

The North-East development mission, staged at Gateshead International Stadium for the second successive year, was marred by the controversy of Wigan Test duo Martin Offiah and Kelvin Skerrett failing to collect their runners-up mementoes in the presentation ceremony immediately after the final whistle.

St. Helens collected the shield and a £14,000 prize cheque without having to hit the heights, a decisive factor being the dominance of half backs Jonathan Griffiths and debutant scrum half Gus O'Donnell, an £80,000 summer buy from Wigan.

O'Donnell celebrated his conversion to a Saint by opening the scoring with a 17th-minute drop goal. But it was not until captain Shane Cooper brushed aside the weak challenges of four defenders in the 29th minute to go over near the posts that a St. Helens victory looked a probability. Tea Ropati added the goal.

The Saints went on to clinch the trophy in a five-minute spell before half-time. After a knock on by full back Steve Hampson, O'Donnell's slick pass from the resultant scrum sent Great Britain and Wales winger Anthony Sullivan over for an unconverted touchdown.

Two minutes before the break, Ropati drifted through for the Saints' third try, tacking on the goal for an interval scoreline of 17-0.

Putting behind them the humiliation of the 48-16 Stones Bitter Premiership final hammering in the last match of the previous season, St. Helens seemed to be content to ensure the Riversiders did not score in the second period, though Wigan's defence did show a marked improvement. Playing into a strong wind, the Saints featured strongly in the scoreless half to secure a success which was as sweet as it was deserved.

The significance of the victory, with the start of the Stones Bitter Championship campaign only five days away, was always going to be debatable. Both sides' passing lacked the timing which comes with competitive games.

At virtual full strength, St. Helens overcame the 11th-hour loss through injury of full back Phil Veivers by moving winger Alan Hunte into the number one jersey. The British Lion responded by becoming the first full back to win the Jack Bentley Memorial Trophy as Man of the Match. With New Zealand Test centre Jarrod McCracken and Great Britain Under-21 back row forward Chris Joynt expected to join their ranks within weeks, the Saints gave notice of their right to be serious Championship title contenders.

Wigan, while well beaten, rued the permanent loss of international backs Gene Miles and Andy Gregory, and the temporary absence of the injured Shaun Edwards and Test colleague Andy Platt, subject of a contract dispute.

Their afternoon of misfortune was typified by two tries going begging, Sullivan intercepting Dean Bell's trymaking pass to substitute David Myers and Offiah knocking on as he was crossing the line in the last minute. However, there was consolation in the successful return of former Test packman Andy Goodway a year after breaking his arm in the corresponding fixture.

CIS INSURANCE CHARITY SHIELD

23 August   **Gateshead International Stadium**

ST. HELENS   17   **WIGAN   0**

Alan Hunte	1.	Steve Hampson
Mike Riley	2.	Sam Panapa
Gary Connolly	3.	Dean Bell, Capt.
Tea Ropati	4.	Joe Lydon
Anthony Sullivan	5.	Martin Offiah
Jonathan Griffiths	6.	Frano Botica
Gus O'Donnell	7.	Martin Crompton
Jonathan Neill	8.	Ian Lucas
Bernard Dwyer	9.	Mick Cassidy
Kevin Ward	10.	Kelvin Skerrett
John Harrison	11.	Denis Betts
George Mann	12.	Billy McGinty
Shane Cooper, Capt.	13.	Phil Clarke
Les Quirk	14.	David Myers
Paul Forber	15.	Andy Goodway

T: Cooper, Sullivan, Ropati
G: Ropati (2), O'Donnell (dg)
Substitutions:
Forber for Mann (25 min.)
Quirk for O'Donnell (77 min.)
Referee: Stuart Cummings (Widnes)

Substitutions:
Goodway for Skerrett (27 min.)
Myers for Lydon (51 min.)
Half-time: 17-0
Attendance: 7,364

● The Charity Shield is contested between the previous season's Challenge Cup winners and Division One Champions. When Wigan won both trophies in 1990 and 1991 they met the previous season's Premiership final winners. When Wigan won the Championship, Challenge Cup and Premiership in 1992 they met the previous season's Division One title runners-up.

CHARITY SHIELD ROLL OF HONOUR

Year	Winners		Runners-up		Venue	Attendance
1985-86	Wigan	34	*Hull K.R.	6	Isle of Man	4,06●
1986-87	*Halifax	9	Castleford	8	Isle of Man	3,27●
1987-88	*Wigan	44	Halifax	12	Isle of Man	4,80●
1988-89	*Widnes	20	Wigan	14	Isle of Man	5,04●
1989-90	*Widnes	27	Wigan	22	Liverpool FC	17,26.
1990-91	†Widnes	24	*Wigan	8	Swansea C. FC	11,17●
1991-92	*Wigan	22	†Hull	8	Gateshead	10,24●
1992-93	#St. Helens	17	*Wigan	0	Gateshead	7,36●

*Denotes previous season's Champions; † Premiership winners; unmarked, Challenge Cup winners; # Championship runners-up

CHARITY SHIELD …. A REVIEW

1985-86
Wigan 34 Hampson; P. Ford, Stephenson (7g), Donlan (2t), Gill (2t); Edwards, M. Ford (1t); Courtney (Mayo), Kiss, Campbell, West (Lucas), Du Toit, Wane
Hull K.R. 6 Fairbairn (Lydiat 1g); Clark (1t), Robinson, Prohm, Laws; M. Smith, G. Smith;

Des Harrison, Watkinson, Ema, Kelly (Rudd), Burton, Hogan
Referee: R. Campbell (Widnes)

1986-87
Halifax 9 Smith (Wilson); Riddlesden, Whitfield (1t), Hague (1dg), George (1t); C. Anderson, Stephens; Dickinson, McCallion, Juliff, Scott (James), Bell, Dixon

Castleford 8 Roockley; Plange, Lord (1t), Irwin (R. Southernwood), Spears; Joyner (Fletcher), R. Beardmore; Ward, K. Beardmore, Johnson, Ketteridge (2g), Mountain, England
Referee: G.F. Lindop (Wakefield)
1987-88
Wigan 44 Hampson (2t); Stephenson (8g), Byrne (Russell), Bell (2t), Gill (1t); Edwards (2t), Gregory; West, Kiss, Case, Gildart (Wane), Potter, Goodway
Halifax 12 Eadie (2g); Taylor, Wilson, T. Anderson, George; Simpson (Juliff 1t), Stephens; Dickinson, Pendlebury, Beevers, James, Scott (Bell), Dixon (1t)
Referee: J. Holdsworth (Kippax)
1988-89
Widnes 20 Tait; Thackray, Currier (4g), Wright (1t), Offiah (1t); Dowd, D. Hulme; Sorensen, McKenzie (1t), Grima (Pyke), M. O'Neill, P. Hulme, Eyres
Wigan 14 Hampson; Gill, Lydon (1t, 1g), Bell, Preston (Lucas); Byrne, Gregory; Shelford (Betts), Kiss, Case, T. Iro (2t), Wane, Goodway
Referee: R. Tennant (Castleford)
1989-90
Widnes 27 Tait (1dg); Kebbie (1t), Davies 1t, 5g), Wright, Offiah (1t); A. Myler, D. Hulme (1t); Sorensen, P. Hulme, Grima Pyke), M. O'Neill, Koloto, Eyres
Wigan 22 Hampson; Bell (Gilfillan), K. Iro 1t), Lydon (1t, 5g), Preston; Byrne, Gregory; Lucas, Kiss, Platt (1t) (Stazicker), Betts, Gildart, Goodway
Referee: J. Holdsworth (Kippax)

1990-91
Widnes 24 Tait; Devereux (1t), Currier, Davies (3t, 2g), Offiah (1t); A. Myler, D. Hulme; Ashurst (Wright), McKenzie, Grima, P. Hulme (Sorensen), Koloto, Holliday
Wigan 8 Gilfillan; Myers, Bell, Byrne, Preston; Botica (1t, 2g) (Edwards), Goulding; Skerrett, Bridge, Wane, Gildart (Forshaw), Platt, Betts
Referee: C. Morris (Huddersfield)
1991-92
Wigan 22 Hampson; Myers (1t), Bell (2t), Lydon, Botica (3g); Edwards (1t), Gregory; Lucas (Gildart), Dermott, Skerrett, Betts, Platt (Forshaw), Goodway
Hull 8 Feather; Eastwood (2g), Blacker, G. Nolan (1t), Turner; Hanlan, Mackey; Durham (Dixon), L. Jackson, Marlow, McNamara (Jones), Walker, D. Busby
Referee: R. Whitfield (Widnes)

CHARITY SHIELD RECORDS

TEAM
Most appearances: 7 Wigan
Most wins: 3 Widnes, Wigan
Highest score: Wigan 44 v. Halifax 12 1987
(Also widest margin)
Biggest attendance:
17,263 Widnes v. Wigan (at Liverpool FC) 1989

INDIVIDUAL
Most tries:
3 by Jonathan Davies (Widnes) v. Wigan 1990
Most goals:
8 by David Stephenson (Wigan) v. Halifax 1987
Most points:
16 (8g) by David Stephenson (Wigan) v. Halifax ... 1987
   (3t,2g) Jonathan Davies (Widnes) v. Wigan 1990

MAN OF THE MATCH AWARDS

Season	Winner	Team	Position
1985-86	Shaun Edwards	Wigan (v. Hull K.R.)	Stand off
1986-87	Chris Anderson	Halifax (v. Castleford)	Stand off
1987-88	Shaun Edwards	Wigan (v. Halifax)	Stand off
1988-89	Phil McKenzie	Widnes (v. Wigan)	Hooker
1989-90	Denis Betts	Wigan (v. Widnes)	Second row
1990-91	Jonathan Davies	Widnes (v. Wigan)	Centre
1991-92	Dean Bell	Wigan (v. Hull)	Centre
1992-93	Alan Hunte	St. Helens (v. Wigan)	Full back

● From 1987 it became the Jack Bentley Trophy in memory of the former *Daily Express* Rugby League journalist.

1992 WORLD CLUB CHALLENGE

Six days after Australia's victory over Great Britain in the World Cup final at Wembley, Brisbane Broncos became the first side from Down Under to win the World Club Challenge by beating Wigan 22-8 on their own ground.

The Sydney Grand Final victors succeeded where Manly, Canberra and Penrith had failed, recording the first Australian success in the five-year-old competition against the reigning British champions.

Broncos skipper Allan Langer received the World Challenge Trophy from David Oxley, performing his last official duty before retirement as the League's Chief Executive. Australia's second world crown in a week was gained in more flamboyant style than the national side's success, with Terry Matterson taking the Man of the Match award after an outstanding loose forward display.

Brisbane's triumph was well deserved and comprehensive. The Broncos kept their pre-match promise to attack and play their traditional open game at high speed.

The Australians were superb after some early skirmishes. Andrew Gee appeared to punch Wigan's Billy McGinty on the floor in the third minute, prompting Martin Dermott to retaliate and start a brawl involving a dozen players.

The visitors fully deserved their four tries, with Wigan's only reply coming after an error from full back Julian O'Neill, who was otherwise one of their best performers.

Wigan were unfortunate to lose the cornerstone of their pack, Test prop Andy Platt, taken off after only 15 minutes with a shoulder injury. Platt's absence clearly affected Wigan's composure and the foundations for a Broncos victory were laid midway through the first half when they scored two tries in six minutes. Wigan never looked likely to recover.

Wigan had started promisingly, taking the lead through a Frano Botica penalty goal after Kerrod Walters was pulled up for obstruction in the seventh minute. The opening Brisbane try came two minutes after Platt's departure.

It came straight from a scrum after South African full back Andre Stoop fumbled Langer's kick. Scrum half Langer whipped the ball out to Kevin Walters, who spread-eagled the Wigan defence to send O'Neill over.

The goal was added by Matterson, who six minutes later set up their second try with a delightful dummy before serving Steve Renouf, Australia's tryscoring hero at Wembley. His drive down the middle set up second row man Mark Hohn, whose well-timed pass gave Kerrod Walters an easy touchdown. Matterson again obliged with the kick.

Wigan tried to get back into the game but their handling was suspect and their defence vulnerable. Gee clashed with Kelvin Skerrett, while Stoop prevented Test winger Michael Hancock from scoring with a touchline tackle, but Wigan could not reduce the 12-2 arrears before the break.

Hancock was not to be denied five minutes into the second half, touching down after impressive handling by Matterson, Kevin Walters and the outstanding Renouf.

Wigan's sole reply came in the 64th minute, the Shaun Edwards try being too little, too late. Dermott chipped over the defence, Edwards hacked on and O'Neill failed to grasp the ball before the Great Britain half back touched down. Botica added the goal.

Brisbane succeeded in scoring again to reflect their superiority in the scoreline. They needed a bad decision from New Zealand referee Dennis Hale, who failed to spot Renouf's forward pass to Hancock for the winger's second try four minutes from time.

The referee, who was also in charge of the Wembley Anglo-Aussie showdown, was loudly jeered by the Wigan faithful.

Brisbane provided a free-flowing style of rugby as their testimony for being crowned world club champions and Wigan's Australian coach John Monie was first to endorse their newly gained status.

Brisbane Broncos' substitute John Plath holds off the challenge of Wigan prop Neil Cowie.

WORLD CLUB CHALLENGE

30 October 1992   **Wigan**

BRISBANE BRONCOS   22   **WIGAN   8**

Julian O'Neill	1.	Andre Stoop
Willie Carne	2.	Jason Robinson
Steve Renouf	3.	Dean Bell, Capt.
Chris Johns	4.	Andrew Farrar
Michael Hancock	5.	Martin Offiah
Kevin Walters	6.	Frano Botica
Allan Langer, Capt.	7.	Shaun Edwards
Glenn Lazarus	8.	Kelvin Skerrett
Kerrod Walters	9.	Martin Dermott
Andrew Gee	10.	Andy Platt
Trevor Gillmeister	11.	Denis Betts
Mark Hohn	12.	Billy McGinty
Terry Matterson	13.	Phil Clarke
John Plath	14.	Sam Panapa
Tony Currie	15.	Ian Lucas
Brett Plowman	16.	Martin Crompton
Peter Ryan	17.	Neil Cowie

T: Hancock (2), O'Neill, Kerrod Walters   T: Edwards
G: Matterson (3)   G: Botica (2)
Substitutions: Substitutions:
Currie for Johns (32 min.)   Cowie for Platt (15 min.)
Plath for Langer (45 min.)   Lucas for Skerrett (31 min.)
Ryan for Gee (63 min.)   Crompton for Stoop (47 min.)
Plowman for O'Neill (78 min.)   Panapa for McGinty (58 min.)
Half-time: 12-2   Attendance: 17,746
Referee: Dennis Hale (New Zealand)

Top of the world . . . Brisbane Broncos celebrate being the first Australian side to win the World Club Challenge.

WORLD CLUB CHALLENGE ROLL OF HONOUR

Year	Winners*		Runners-up		Venue	Attendance	Receipts
1987	Wigan	8	Manly-Warringah	2	Wigan	36,895	£131,000
1989	Widnes	30	Canberra	18	Old Trafford, Man'r	30,786	£207,764
1991	Wigan	21	Penrith	4	Anfield, Liverpool	20,152	£179,797
1992	Brisbane B.	22	Wigan	8	Wigan	17,746	£170,911

WORLD CLUB CHALLENGE . . . .
A REVIEW
1987-88
Wigan 8 Hampson; Russell, Stephenson (4g), Lydon, Gill; Edwards, Gregory; Case (Lucas), Kiss, Wane, Goodway, Potter, Hanley
Manly 2 Shearer; Ronson, Williams (Ticehurst), O'Connor (1g), Davis; Lyons, Hasler; Daley, Cochrane, Gately (Brokenshire), Gibbs, Cunningham (Shaw), Vautin
Referee: J. Holdsworth (Kippax)
1989-90
Widnes 30 Tait; Currier, Davies (1t, 3g), Wright (1t), Offiah (2t); A. Myler (Dowd), D. Hulme; Grima (Moriarty), McKenzie, Pyke, Sorensen, P. Hulme (1t), Eyres (1t)
Canberra 18 Belcher; Wood (2g), Meninga (1t) (Martin), Daley, Ferguson; O'Sullivan (1t, 1g), Stuart; Jackson (Lowry), Walters (1t), Lazarus, Lance, Coyne, Clyde
Referee: F. Desplas (France)
1991-92
Wigan 21 Hampson; Myers (1t), Panapa (1t), Lydon (1dg), Botica (6g); Edwards, Gregory; Skerrett (Cowie) (Lucas), Dermott, Platt, Betts, McGinty (Gildart), Clarke (Forshaw)
Penrith 4 Barwick (B. Alexander); Willis (it) (Smith), Bradley, B. Izzard, Mackay; Carter, G. Alexander; Lee (G. Izzard), Simmons, Dunn, Clarke, Cartwright, Van Der Voort (Xuereb)
Referee: A. Sablayrolles (France)

MAN OF THE MATCH AWARDS
1987: Shaun Wane (Wigan)
1989: David Hulme (Widnes)
1991: Frano Botica (Wigan)
1992: Terry Matterson (Brisbane B.)

Victorious Broncos skipper Allan Langer with the World Club Challenge Trophy.

BBC-2 FLOODLIT TROPHY

The BBC-2 Floodlit Trophy competition was launched in 1965. Eight clubs competed in the first year and the total had grown to 22 by 1980 when the competition was abolished as part of the BBC's financial cut-backs.

For 15 years the matches became a regular television feature on Tuesday evenings throughout the early winter months.

Although the format changed slightly over the years, it was basically a knockout competition on the lines of the Challenge Cup.

In 1966 the Floodlit Competition was used to introduce the limited tackle rule, then four tackles, which proved such a great success it was adopted in all other matches before the end of the year.

BBC-2 FLOODLIT TROPHY FINALS
(Only the 1967, at Leeds, and 1972, at Wigan, finals were played on neutral grounds)

Season	Winners		Runners-up		Venue	Attendance	Receipts
1965-66	Castleford	4	St. Helens	0	St. Helens	11,510	£1,548
1966-67	Castleford	7	Swinton	2	Castleford	8,986	£1,692
1967-68	Castleford	8	Leigh	5	Leeds	9,716	£2,099
1968-69	Wigan	7	St. Helens	4	Wigan	13,479	£3,291
1969-70	Leigh	11	Wigan	6	Wigan	12,312	£2,854
1970-71	Leeds	9	St. Helens	5	Leeds	7,612	£2,189
1971-72	St. Helens	8	Rochdale H.	2	St. Helens	9,300	£2,493
1972-73	Leigh	5	Widnes	0	Wigan	4,691	£1,391
1973-74	Bramley	15	Widnes	7	Widnes	4,422	£1,538
1974-75	Salford	0	Warrington	0	Salford	4,473	£1,913
Replay	Salford	10	Warrington	5	Warrington	5,778	£2,434
1975-76	St. Helens	22	Dewsbury	2	St. Helens	3,858	£1,747
1976-77	Castleford	12	Leigh	4	Leigh	5,402	£2,793
1977-78	Hull K.R.	26	St. Helens	11	Hull K.R.	10,099	£6,586
1978-79	Widnes	13	St. Helens	7	St. Helens	10,250	£7,017
1979-80	Hull	13	Hull K.R.	3	Hull	18,500	£16,605

BBC2 FLOODLIT TROPHY . . . . A REVIEW
1965-66
Castleford 4 Edwards; C. Battye, M. Battye, Willett (2g), Briggs; Hardisty, Millward; Terry, J. Ward, C. Dickinson, Bryant, Taylor, Small
St. Helens 0 F. Barrow; Vollenhoven, Wood, Benyon, Killeen; Murphy, Prosser; French, Dagnall, Watson, Hicks, Mantle, Laughton
Referee: L. Gant (Wakefield)
1966-67
Castleford 7 Edwards; Howe, Stenton, Willett (1g), Austin (1t); Hardisty, Hepworth (1g); Hartley, C. Dickinson, McCartney, Bryant, Small, Walker
Swinton 2 Gowers; Whitehead (1g), Gomersall, Buckley, Davies; Fleet, G. Williams; Halliwell, D. Clarke, Scott (Cummings), Rees, Simpson, Robinson
Referee: J. Manley (Warrington)
1967-68
Castleford 8 Edwards; Harris, Thomas, Stenton, Willett (4g); Hardisty, Hepworth; Hartley, J. Ward, Walton, Bryant (C. Dickinson), Redfearn, Reilly

Leigh 5 Grainey; Tickle (1t), Lewis, Collins, Walsh; Entwistle, A. Murphy; Whitworth, Ashcroft, Major, Welding, M. Murphy, Gilfedder (1g)
Referee: G.F. Lindop (Wakefield)
1968-69
Wigan 7 Tyrer (2g); Francis, Ashton, Ashurst, Rowe; C. Hill (1t), Jackson; J. Stephens, Clarke, Mills, Fogerty (Lyon), Kevin O'Loughlin, Laughton
St. Helens 4 Williams; Wilson, Benyon, Myler, Wills; Whittle, Bishop; Warlow, Sayer, Watson, Mantle, Hogan, Coslett (2g)
Referee: E. Clay (Leeds)
1969-70
Leigh 11 Ferguson (3g) (Lewis); Tickle (1t), Dorrington, Collins, Walsh; Eckersley, Murphy (1g); D. Chisnall, Ashcroft, Watts, Welding, Grimes, Lyon
Wigan 6 C. Hill; Wright, Francis (2g), Rowe, Kevin O'Loughlin; D. Hill (1g), Jackson; J. Stephens, Clarke, Ashcroft, Ashurst, Mills, Laughton
Referee: W.H. Thompson (Huddersfield)

1970-71
Leeds 9 Holmes (2g); Alan Smith, Hynes (1t, 1g), Cowan, Atkinson; Wainwright, Shoebottom; J. Burke, Fisher, Barnard, Haigh, Ramsey, Batten
St. Helens 5 F. Barrow; L. Jones (1t), Benyon, Walsh, Wilson; Whittle, Heaton; Rees, A. Karalius, E. Chisnall, Mantle, E. Prescott, Coslett (1g)
Referee: E. Lawrinson (Warrington)
1971-72
St. Helens 8 G. Pimblett; L. Jones, Benyon, Walsh, Wilson; Kelly, Heaton; Rees, A. Karalius, E. Chisnall, E. Prescott, Mantle, Coslett (4g)
Rochdale H. 2 Chamberlain (1g); Brelsford, Crellin, Taylor, Glover; Myler, Gartland; Birchall, P. Clarke, Brown, Welding, Sheffield (Hodkinson), Delooze
Referee: E. Clay (Leeds)
1972-73
Leigh 5 Hogan; Lawson (1t) (Lester), Atkin, Collins, Stacey; A. Barrow, Sayer (Ryding); Grimes, D. Clarke, Fletcher, Fiddler (1g), F. Barrow, Martyn
Widnes 0 Dutton; A. Prescott, Aspey, Blackwood, McDonnell; Lowe, Ashton; Mills, Elwell, Warlow, Foran, Sheridan, Nicholls
Referee: G.F. Lindop (Wakefield)
1973-74
Bramley 15 Keegan; Goodchild (1t), Bollon, Hughes, Austin (1t); T. Briggs, Ward (1g) (Ashman); D. Briggs, Firth, Cheshire, D. Sampson (1t), Idle, Wolford (2g)
Widnes 7 Dutton (2g); D. O'Neill, Hughes, Aspey, Macko (1t); Warburton, Bowden; Hogan, Elwell, Nelson, Sheridan, Blackwood (Foran) Laughton
Referee: D.G. Kershaw (York)
1974-75
Salford 0 Charlton; Fielding, Hesketh, Graham, Richards; Brophy (Taylor), Banner; Coulman, Devlin, Grice, Knighton, Dixon, E. Prescott
Warrington 0 Whitehead; Sutton, Cunliffe (Lowe), Whittle, Bevan; Briggs, Gordon; D. Chisnall, Ashcroft, Wright, Gaskell, Conroy, B. Philbin (Jewitt)
Referee: W.H. Thompson (Huddersfield)
Replay
Salford 10 Stead; Fielding (1t), Watkins (2g), Hesketh, Richards (1t); Gill, Banner; Grice, Walker, Mackay, Dixon, Knighton, E. Prescott

Warrington 5 Cunliffe; Whitehead (1g), Pickup, Whittle, Bevan (1t); Noonan (Briggs), Gordon; D. Chisnall, Ashcroft, Wanbon, Conroy, Nicholas (Brady), B. Philbin
Referee: W.H. Thompson (Huddersfield)
1975-76
St. Helens 22 G. Pimblett (2g); L. Jones, Benyon (1t), Hull (1t), Mathias (2t); Wilson (1t), Heaton (1dg); Mantle, A. Karalius, James, Nicholls, E. Chisnall, Coslett (1g)
Dewsbury 2 Langley; Hegarty, Chalkley, Simpson, Mitchell; N. Stephenson (1g) (Lee), A. Bates; Beverley, Price, Hankins, Halloran (Artis), Bell, Grayshon
Referee: W.H. Thompson (Huddersfield)
1976-77
Castleford 12 Wraith; Fenton, Joyner, P. Johnson, Walsh (1t); Burton (1t), Stephens; Khan, Spurr, A. Dickinson, Reilly, Lloyd (3g), S. Norton
Leigh 4 Hogan; A. Prescott, Stacey, Woods, Walsh (1t); Taylor, Sayer; D. Chisnall, Ashcroft (1dg), Fletcher, Macko, Grimes, Boyd
Referee: J.E. Jackson (Pudsey)
1977-78
Hull K.R. 26 Hall (4g); Dunn (2t), M. Smith (1t), Watson, Sullivan (1t); Hartley (1t), Millward; Millington, Watkinson, Cunningham (Hughes), Lowe, Rose (1t), Casey
St. Helens 11 G. Pimblett (Platt); L. Jones (Courtney), Noonan, Cunningham (1t), Glynn (2t, 1g); Francis, K. Gwilliam; D. Chisnall, Liptrot, James, Hope, A. Karalius, Pinner
Referee: M.J. Naughton (Widnes)
1978-79
Widnes 13 Eckersley; Wright (2t), Hughes, Aspey, P. Shaw; Burke (1t, 2g), Bowden; Hogan, Elwell, Mills, Adams, Dearden, Laughton
St. Helens 7 G. Pimblett (2g); L. Jones, Glynn, Cunningham, Mathias; Francis, Holding; D. Chisnall (1t), Liptrot, James, Nicholls, Knighton (E. Chisnall), Pinner
Referee: J. McDonald (Wigan)
1979-80
Hull 13 Woods; Bray, G. Evans (1t), Coupland, Dennison (1t, 2g); Newlove, Hepworth; Tindall, Wileman, Farrar, Stone, Boxall (Birdsall 1t), Norton
Hull K.R. 3 Robinson; Hubbard (1t), M. Smith, Watson, Sullivan; Hall, Agar; Holdstock, Tyreman, Lockwood, Clarkson (Hartley), Lowe, Hogan (Millington)
Referee: W.H. Thompson (Huddersfield)

CAPTAIN MORGAN TROPHY

This sponsored competition, with a winners' prize of £3,000, lasted only one season. Entry was restricted to the 16 clubs who won their Yorkshire and Lancashire Cup first round ties. The Lancashire contingent was made up to eight by including the side which lost their first round county Cup-tie by the narrowest margin. The first round of the Captain Morgan Trophy was zoned with clubs being drawn against those in their own county. The remainder of the competition was integrated. The final was on a neutral ground as follows:

1973-74	Warrington	4	Featherstone R.	0	Salford	5,259	£2,265

1973-74

Warrington 4 Whitehead (2g); M. Philbin, Noonan, Reynolds (Pickup), Bevan; Whittle, Gordon; D. Chisnall, Ashcroft, Brady, Wanbon (Price), Wright, Mather

Featherstone R. 0 Box; Coventry, M. Smith, Hartley, Bray; Mason, Wood; Tonks, Bridges, Harris, Gibbins (Stone), Rhodes, Bell
Referee: G.F. Lindop (Wakefield)

Double club record-breaker Frano Botica, who was the First Division's top goals and points scorer as Wigan lifted their record-extending fourth successive Stones Bitter Championship title.

LEAGUE

1992-93 CHAMPIONSHIP

For the first time, the Division One Championship race was decided on points scoring difference, with Wigan claiming their record-extending fourth successive title, edging out arch rivals St. Helens in a thrilling finale. Both finished with 41 points.

The on-field action was in danger of being overshadowed by the off-field politics when a special meeting of clubs on 10 March voted by 28-6 to scrap the three-division system after two seasons and introduce two divisions of 16 from the start of 1993-94, demoting the bottom three clubs into the Second Division of the Younger's Alliance. The controversial decision meant that three of the four promotion/relegation issues became irrelevant, only the Second Division leaders having anything to play for.

The 1992-93 league campaign was in the balance until the final weekend, Wigan needing to beat Castleford to clinch the £46,000 Stones Bitter prize cheque. Ironically, it was the Yorkshiremen who two weeks earlier had beaten the Riversiders 26-17 at Wheldon Road to open up the chase for the Stones Bitter Championship Trophy.

But Wigan clinched a 25-18 victory in front of nearly 20,000 fans as St. Helens could only watch, having finished their programme four days earlier.

The Saints, seeking their first Championship title since 1975, had missed the opportunity to have a say in their own destiny a week earlier, visiting Wigan in a Good Friday derby encounter. Despite scoring two tries to one, St. Helens could only draw 8-8. Wigan almost snatched victory with a Joe Lydon drop goal attempt a couple of minutes before the final whistle, the ball going over but being judged by referee John Holdsworth to have touched Saints player Gus O'Donnell's hand, thus being disallowed.

The two Lancashire giants dominated the Stones Bitter Championship, finishing 11 points ahead of nearest rivals Bradford Northern, Widnes and Leeds, who finished jointly on 30

points. They were followed by fellow Stones Bitter Premiership qualifiers Castleford, Halifax and Warrington.

At the foot of the table, Leigh were early favourites for relegation, losing their opening eight league matches before Australian Steve Simms celebrated his November appointment with an 11-6 shock success over St. Helens at Hilton Park, a reversal which was to cost Saints the title.

Simms, a reserve grade coach Down Under, became a folk hero in Leigh as the club went on to win a total of nine games and draw two to finish fourth from bottom, while battling off the field to stay at Hilton Park.

Hull K.R. ended the 26-match campaign at the foot of the table with seven victories, four points behind Salford and Wakefield Trinity, the former having the poorer points scoring difference. The special general meeting of clubs in March, as detailed later, saved Hull K.R. and Salford from the drop.

In the Stones Bitter Second Division, Featherstone Rovers made an immediate return to the upper echelon with only three defeats in 28 league games under new coach, Australian Steve Martin. While celebrating the receipt of a £23,000 Stones Bitter prize cheque, finishing eight points ahead of runners-up Oldham, Rovers pointed out the irony of six clubs in the 1992-93 First Division finishing with fewer than the 22 points they had been relegated with the previous campaign.

It was a two-horse race in the Second Division, third-placed Huddersfield being 11 points adrift of Oldham, although this was a creditable performance from the previous season's Third Division champions. Featherstone and Oldham reaped their reward by being promoted to the new 16-strong First Division for the 1993-94 season.

At the other end of the table, Bramley and Carlisle shared bottom spot with 15 points each, the Cumbrians having the superior points scoring difference. The abandonment of the Third Division in favour of a 16-member

Second Division made relegation unnecessary.

Rejuvenated Keighley Cougars won a trophy for the first time in 90 years, clinching the Stones Bitter Third Division title by four points from Workington Town. Having finished seventh the previous season, Peter Roe's men lost only three matches en route to the £11,000 Stones Bitter prize cheque, presented at their final home league match in front of a 5,226 capacity crowd, a Third Division record.

After the March decision of clubs, five clubs at the bottom of the Third Division were unexpectedly ordered to fight for survival.

Barrow, Blackpool Gladiators, Chorley Borough, Highfield and Nottingham City were the candidates for the three demotion places, to be decided with only a handful of matches left unplayed.

Barrow, the longest established of the quintet having been formed in 1900, duly clinched a safe position but only after being overtaken by Highfield, who finished highest of the threatened five after a mini spending spree.

The recruitment drive paid off with four victories in their last five matches, including successes over Chorley, Blackpool and Nottingham, plus a shock 14-8 triumph at Barrow.

Chorley finished on equal points with Barrow, but inferior points scoring difference sealed their fate along with Blackpool and Nottingham, the Outlaws winning only once, at Barrow in their second match of the season.

The headline-grabbing political scene, centred on 10 March 1993 which was to be dubbed "Black Wednesday" by critics, had its roots in a special meeting of clubs on 12 April 1992.

Clubs met to discuss a proposal from the Board of Directors for a new three-division structure of 16-14-12, with six leading Alliance teams making up the balance needed for the third tier. The plan was withdrawn and replaced on the day by a proposal from Salford and Hull K.R. for a return to two divisions with 16 in the first and the rest in the second. The proposal needed 21 votes but gained only 18.

However, it was agreed that the league structure would continue to be debated, with the eight-club Second Division being the main drawback, a decision being sought by January 1993. During the summer, Scarborough Pirates disbanded after only one season.

The Board of Directors put forward a new plan for discussion by the Council on 2 December. It mooted the formation of two divisions of 16, with three clubs being demoted to the Younger's Alliance First Division, plus the County Cups being played in midweek on a voluntary basis. The timetable was for two divisions of 16 and 19 in 1993-94, the bottom three clubs being demoted for season 1994-95.

Council gave the plan their approval except that the County Cups should be mandatory and played pre-season, while there should be automatic promotion from the Alliance for a demoted club finishing in the top two.

When the plan came up for a formal vote at a special meeting of clubs on 6 January, a spell of frost had caused the postponement of a significant number of fixtures and this factor, combined with the extra number of fixtures in the new formula, caused the proposal to be withdrawn. The meeting did succeed in agreeing that First Division clubs would be exempt from the preliminary round of both the Regal Trophy and the Silk Cut Challenge Cup.

At the Council meeting of 3 February, Workington Town and Dewsbury suggested a three-division format of 14-14-7, with the third tier playing each other four times. London Crusaders put forward a plan for a structure of 14-10-11, with the two lower divisions playing each other three times. The Board of Directors were asked to consider these suggestions, plus any other formats.

A month later on 3 March, Batley and Leeds introduced a new idea of two divisions of 16, with the bottom three clubs demoted to the Second Division of the Alliance and the County Cups scrapped. A main feature of the proposal was its immediate introduction in the 1993-94 season.

A special meeting of clubs followed a week later on 10 March when the two-division structure was given the go-ahead by 28-6. Keighley, who were against it, arrived too late to vote. The three-division system was followed into extinction after only two years by the 96-year-old County Cup competitions.

The decisions were met by wholesale public outcry, forcing Chief Executive Maurice Lindsay to reveal details of the bottom clubs' affairs to justify their potential demotion on the grounds of minimum standards. Meanwhile, Blackpool, Chorley, Highfield and Nottingham launched a fighting fund for a possible legal battle with the League.

In the aftermath of the special meeting, the League announced plans for the formation of a new National Conference League, involving top amateur clubs and the demoted three professional teams at a projected cost of £250,000 over three years. A seven-point plan also provided for the three clubs to retain the benefits of League membership, plus an automatic route back from the Conference set-up to the Second Division.

Four on the trot . . . Wigan coach John Monie (left) and captain Dean Bell hold the Stones Bitter Championship Trophy after their title-clinching 25-18 success over Castleford on the final League weekend of the season.

Featherstone Rovers coach Steve Martin (left) joins in the Stones Bitter Second Division title celebrations, complete with £23,000 prize cheque.

The Stones Bitter Second Division Bowl is held aloft by the trio of 1992-93 skippers, from the left, Mark Wilson, Brett Daunt and Richard Gunn.

FINAL TABLES 1992-93

STONES BITTER CHAMPIONSHIP

	P.	W.	D.	L.	Dg.	Gls.	Trs.	Pts.	Dg.	Gls.	Trs.	Pts.	Pts.
						FOR				AGAINST			
Wigan	26	20	1	5	6	123	123	744	3	48	57	327	41
St. Helens	26	20	1	5	6	95	109	632	7	57	56	345	41
Bradford N.	26	15	0	11	5	78	98	553	4	65	75	434	30
Widnes	26	15	0	11	1	80	97	549	2	76	73	446	30
Leeds	26	14	2	10	3	80	108	595	6	72	93	522	30
Castleford	26	14	1	11	0	94	89	544	5	68	65	401	29
Halifax	26	13	0	13	1	88	95	557	3	73	89	505	26
Warrington	26	12	1	13	11	68	85	487	10	68	76	450	25
Hull	26	10	1	15	1	64	63	381	3	86	90	535	21
Sheffield E.	26	10	1	15	5	66	67	405	1	99	107	627	21
Leigh	26	9	2	15	8	63	69	410	2	94	110	630	20
Wakefield T.	26	8	2	16	3	53	74	405	5	81	92	535	18
Salford	26	9	0	17	4	69	89	498	1	108	127	725	18
Hull K.R.	26	7	0	19	3	61	49	321	5	87	105	599	14

SECOND DIVISION

	P.	W.	D.	L.	Dg.	Gls.	Trs.	Pts.	Dg.	Gls.	Trs.	Pts.	Pts.
						FOR				AGAINST			
Featherstone R.	28	24	1	3	0	128	185	996	2	55	60	352	49
Oldham	28	20	1	7	5	122	126	753	3	76	87	503	41
Huddersfield	28	15	0	13	9	82	98	565	4	82	95	548	30
Rochdale H.	28	14	0	14	4	91	109	622	3	90	106	607	28
London C.	28	12	2	14	2	76	95	534	6	82	98	562	26
Swinton	28	10	0	18	5	58	72	409	4	82	117	636	20
Carlisle	28	6	3	19	2	68	79	454	5	100	129	721	15
Bramley	28	7	1	20	4	46	58	328	4	104	130	732	15

THIRD DIVISION

	P.	W.	D.	L.	Dg.	Gls.	Trs.	Pts.	Dg.	Gls.	Trs.	Pts.	Pts.
						FOR				AGAINST			
Keighley C.	24	21	0	3	5	146	155	917	4	38	52	288	42
Workington T.	24	19	0	5	3	134	141	835	5	38	39	237	38
Dewsbury	24	18	0	6	10	88	133	718	7	48	47	291	36
Ryedale-York	24	17	0	7	5	109	131	747	7	52	56	335	34
Whitehaven	24	16	0	8	4	94	126	696	4	54	54	328	32
Batley	24	16	0	8	0	60	97	508	4	40	46	268	32
Doncaster	24	14	0	10	2	91	95	564	7	67	82	469	28
Hunslet	24	14	0	10	6	82	96	554	2	78	85	498	28
Highfield	24	6	0	18	8	47	52	310	5	135	160	915	12
Barrow	24	5	0	19	0	64	87	476	5	94	108	625	10
Chorley B.	24	5	0	19	7	47	54	317	9	104	141	781	10
Blackpool G.	24	4	0	20	8	43	52	302	2	132	173	958	8
Nottingham C.	24	1	0	23	7	27	30	181	4	152	206	1132	2

1992-93 PRE-SEASON BETTING FOR THE CHAMPIONSHIPS

Corals pre-season betting:

For the 1992-93 Stones Bitter Championship: 4-7 Wigan; 7-2 St. Helens; 15-2 Castleford; 8-1 Leeds; 12-1 Widnes; 25-1 Warrington; 66-1 Wakefield T.; 80-1 Halifax, Hull; 100-1 Bradford N., Salford, Sheffield E.; 150-1 Hull K.R.; 500-1 Leigh.

For the Second Division Championship: 8-13 Featherstone R.; 11-4 Oldham; 15-2 Rochdale H.; 8-1 Huddersfield; 12-1 Swinton; 33-1 London C.; 50-1 Carlisle; 66-1 Bramley.

For the Third Division Championship: 2-1 Dewsbury; 5-2 Batley; 4-1 Keighley C.; 11-2 Workington T.; 8-1 Hunslet; 10-1 Ryedale-York; 12-1 Doncaster; 33-1 Whitehaven; 66-1 Barrow, Blackpool G.; 100-1 Highfield; 200-1 Chorley B.; 1,000-1 Nottingham C.

TWO DIVISION CHAMPIONSHIP ROLL OF HONOUR

	FIRST DIVISION	SECOND DIVISION
1902-03	Halifax	Keighley
1903-04	Bradford	Wakefield Trinity
1904-05	Oldham	Dewsbury
1962-63	Swinton	Hunslet
1963-64	Swinton	Oldham
1973-74	Salford	Bradford Northern
1974-75	St. Helens	Huddersfield
1975-76	Salford	Barrow
1976-77	Featherstone Rovers	Hull
1977-78	Widnes	Leigh
1978-79	Hull Kingston Rovers	Hull
1979-80	Bradford Northern	Featherstone Rovers
1980-81	Bradford Northern	York
1981-82	Leigh	Oldham
1982-83	Hull	Fulham
1983-84	Hull Kingston Rovers	Barrow
1984-85	Hull Kingston Rovers	Swinton
1985-86	Halifax	Leigh
1986-87	Wigan	Hunslet
1987-88	Widnes	Oldham
1988-89	Widnes	Leigh
1989-90	Wigan	Hull Kingston Rovers
1990-91	Wigan	Salford

THREE DIVISION CHAMPIONSHIP ROLL OF HONOUR

	FIRST DIVISION	SECOND DIVISION	THIRD DIVISION
1991-92	Wigan	Sheffield Eagles	Huddersfield
1992-93	Wigan	Featherstone Rovers	Keighley Cougars

THE UPS AND DOWNS OF TWO DIVISION FOOTBALL
Since reintroduction of two divisions in 1973-74.

●Figure in brackets indicates position in division.

	RELEGATED	PROMOTED
1973-74	Oldham (13) Hull K.R. (14) Leigh (15) Whitehaven (16)	Bradford Northern (1) York (2) Keighley (3) Halifax (4)
1974-75	York (13) Bramley (14) Rochdale Hornets (15) Halifax (16)	Huddersfield (1) Hull K.R. (2) Oldham (3) Swinton (4)
1975-76	Dewsbury (13) Keighley (14) Huddersfield (15) Swinton (16)	Barrow (1) Rochdale Hornets (2) Workington Town (3) Leigh (4)
1976-77	Rochdale Hornets (13) Leigh (14) Barrow (15) Oldham (16)	Hull (1) Dewsbury (2) Bramley (3) New Hunslet (4)
1977-78	Hull (13) New Hunslet (14) Bramley (15) Dewsbury (16)	Leigh (1) Barrow (2) Rochdale Hornets (3) Huddersfield (4)
1978-79	Barrow (13) Featherstone Rovers (14) Rochdale Hornets (15) Huddersfield (16)	Hull (1) New Hunslet (2) York (3) Blackpool Borough (4)
1979-80	Wigan (13) Hunslet (14) York (15) Blackpool Borough (16)	Featherstone Rovers (1) Halifax (2) Oldham (3) Barrow (4)
1980-81	Halifax (13) Salford (14) Workington Town (15) Oldham (16)	York (1) Wigan (2) Fulham (3) Whitehaven (4)
1981-82	Fulham (13) Wakefield Trinity (14) York (15) Whitehaven (16)	Oldham (1) Carlisle (2) Workington Town (3) Halifax (4)
1982-83	Barrow (13) Workington Town (14) Halifax (15) Carlisle (16)	Fulham (1) Wakefield Trinity (2) Salford (3) Whitehaven (4)
1983-84	Fulham (13) Wakefield Trinity (14) Salford (15) Whitehaven (16)	Barrow (1) Workington Town (2) Hunslet (3) Halifax (4)

1984-85	Barrow (13) Leigh (14) Hunslet (15) Workington Town (16)	Swinton (1) Salford (2) York (3) Dewsbury (4)
1985-86	York (14) Swinton (15) Dewsbury (16)	Leigh (1) Barrow (2) Wakefield Trinity (3)
1986-87	Oldham (13) Featherstone Rovers (14) Barrow (15) Wakefield Trinity (16)	Hunslet (1) Swinton (2)
1987-88	Leigh (12) Swinton (13) Hunslet (14)	Oldham (1) Featherstone Rovers (2) Wakefield Trinity (3)
1988-89	Oldham (12) Halifax (13) Hull K.R. (14)	Leigh (1) Barrow (2) Sheffield Eagles (3)
1989-90	Leigh (12) Salford (13) Barrow (14)	Hull K.R. (1) Rochdale Hornets (2) Oldham (3)
1990-91	Oldham (12) Sheffield Eagles (13) Rochdale Hornets (14)	Salford (1) Halifax (2) Swinton (3)

THE UPS AND DOWNS OF THREE DIVISION FOOTBALL
Since introduction in 1991-92.

	FIRST DIVISION	SECOND DIVISION	THIRD DIVISION
1991-92	Down: Featherstone R. (13) Swinton (14)	Up: Sheffield E. (1) Leigh (2) Down: Ryedale-York (7) Workington Town (8)	Up: Huddersfield (1) Bramley (2)
1992-93	—	Up: Featherstone R. (1) Oldham (2)	—

The Stones Bitter Third Division Championship Trophy with two of Keighley Cougars' key players, scrum half Andy Eyres and skipper Joe Grima.

FIRST DIVISION RECORDS
Since reintroduction in 1973

INDIVIDUAL
Match records

Most tries:
6 Shane Cooper (St. Helens) v. Hull, 17 February 1988

Most goals: 13 Geoff Pimblett (St. Helens) v. Bramley, 5 March 1978

Most points: 38 (4t,11g) Bob Beardmore (Castleford) v. Barrow, 22 March 1987

Season records

Most tries: 44 Ellery Hanley (Wigan)   1986-87
Most goals: 130 Steve Hesford (Warrington)   1978-79
Most points: 295 (23t,101g,1dg) John Woods (Leigh) 1983-84

TEAM

Highest score and widest margin: Leeds 90 v. Barrow 0, 11 February 1990

Highest away score: Rochdale H. 12 v. Castleford 76, 3 March 1991

Widest away margin: Wakefield T. 6 v. Wigan 72, 29 March 1987; Barrow 0 v. Wigan 66, 1 October 1989

Most points by losing team: Hunslet 40 v. Barrow 41, 9 September 1984

Scoreless draw: Wigan 0 v. Castleford 0, 26 January 1974

Highest score draw: Hunslet 32 v. Swinton 32, 20 September 1987

Best opening sequence: 13 wins then a draw by Widnes 1981-82

Longest winning run: 25 by St. Helens. Won last 13 of 1985-86 and first 12 of 1986-87 (Also longest unbeaten run.)

Longest losing run: 20 by Whitehaven   1983-84; Rochdale H. 1990-91

Longest run without a win: 23, including 3 draws, by Whitehaven 1981-82 (Also worst opening sequence)

Biggest attendance: 29,839 Wigan v. St. Helens, 9 April 1993

Top ten Division One career tries
231 Ellery Hanley (Bradford N., Wigan, Leeds)
165 Keith Fielding (Salford)
155 Phil Ford (Warrington, Wigan, Bradford N., Leeds, Salford)
148 Martin Offiah (Widnes, Wigan)
148 Garry Schofield (Hull, Leeds)
144 David Smith (Wakefield T., Leeds, Bradford N.)
139 Stuart Wright (Wigan, Widnes)
136 Roy Mathias (St. Helens)
133 John Joyner (Castleford)
130 John Bevan (Warrington)
Most Division One career goals
862 John Woods (Leigh, Bradford N., Warrington)

Most Division One career points
2,150 John Woods (Leigh, Bradford N., Warrington)

20 Division One tries in a season
1973-74 36 Keith Fielding (Salford)
        29 Roy Mathias (St. Helens)
        21 David Smith (Wakefield T.)
1974-75 21 Maurice Richards (Salford)
        21 Roy Mathias (St. Helens)
1975-76 26 Maurice Richards (Salford)
        20 David Smith (Wakefield T.)
1976-77 22 David Topliss (Wakefield T.)
        21 Keith Fielding (Salford)
        21 Ged Dunn (Hull K.R.)
        20 David Smith (Leeds)
        20 Stuart Wright (Widnes)
1977-78 26 Keith Fielding (Salford)
        25 Steve Fenton (Castleford)
        24 Stuart Wright (Widnes)
        20 David Smith (Leeds)
        20 Bruce Burton (Castleford)
        20 John Bevan (Warrington)
1978-79 28 Steve Hartley (Hull K.R.)
1979-80 24 Keith Fielding (Salford)
        21 Roy Mathias (St. Helens)
        21 Steve Hubbard (Hull K.R.)
        20 David Smith (Leeds)
1980-81 20 Steve Hubbard (Hull K.R.)
1981-82   David Hobbs (Featherstone R.) was top scorer with 19 tries.
1982-83 22 Bob Eccles (Warrington)
        20 Steve Evans (Hull)
1983-84 28 Garry Schofield (Hull)
        23 John Woods (Leigh)
        20 James Leuluai (Hull)
1984-85 40 Ellery Hanley (Bradford N.)
        34 Gary Prohm (Hull K.R.)
        23 Henderson Gill (Wigan)
        22 Barry Ledger (St. Helens)
        22 Mal Meninga (St. Helens)
1985-86 22 Ellery Hanley (Wigan)
1986-87 44 Ellery Hanley (Wigan)
        24 Phil Ford (Bradford N.)
        24 Henderson Gill (Wigan)
        23 Garry Schofield (Hull)
        21 John Henderson (Leigh)
1987-88 33 Martin Offiah (Widnes)
        22 Ellery Hanley (Wigan)
1988-89 37 Martin Offiah (Widnes)
        20 Grant Anderson (Castleford)
1989-90 28 Martin Offiah (Widnes)
        25 Mark Preston (Wigan)
        20 Steve Larder (Castleford)
1990-91 22 Martin Offiah (Widnes)
        22 Les Quirk (St. Helens)
        20 Ellery Hanley (Wigan)
1991-92 31 John Devereux (Widnes)
        27 Greg Austin (Halifax)
        25 Shaun Edwards (Wigan)
        23 Mark Preston (Halifax)
1992-93 24 Shaun Edwards (Wigan)
        23 Ellery Hanley (Leeds)
        20 Martin Offiah (Wigan)
        20 Alan Hunte (St. Helens)

Top Division One goalscorers

1973-74	126	David Watkins (Salford)
1974-75	96	Sammy Lloyd (Castleford)
1975-76	118	Sammy Lloyd (Castleford)
1976-77	113	Steve Quinn (Featherstone R.)
1977-78	116	Steve Hesford (Warrington)
1978-79	130	Steve Hesford (Warrington)
1979-80	104	Steve Hubbard (Hull K.R.)
1980-81	96	Steve Diamond (Wakefield T.)
1981-82	110	Steve Quinn (Featherstone R.)
		John Woods (Leigh)
1982-83	105	Bob Beardmore (Castleford)
1983-84	106	Steve Hesford (Warrington)
1984-85	114	Sean Day (St. Helens)
1985-86	85	David Stephenson (Wigan)
1986-87	120	Paul Loughlin (St. Helens)
1987-88	95	John Woods (Warrington)
1988-89	95	David Hobbs (Bradford N.)
1989-90	96	Paul Loughlin (St. Helens)
1990-91	85	Paul Eastwood (Hull)
1991-92	86	Frano Botica (Wigan)
1992-93	107	Frano Botica (Wigan)

Top Division One points-scorer 1992-93
248 (9t,105g,2dg) Frano Botica (Wigan)

SECOND DIVISION RECORDS
Since reintroduction in 1973

INDIVIDUAL

Match records

Most tries: 6 Ged Dunn (Hull K.R.) v. New Hunslet, 2 February 1975; David Kettlestring (Ryedale-York) at Keighley, 11 March 1990; Greg Austin (Halifax) v. Trafford B., 7 April 1991

Most goals: 15 Mick Stacey (Leigh) v. Doncaster, 28 March 1976

Most points: 38 (4t,13g) John Woods (Leigh) v. Blackpool B., 11 September 1977; 38 (4t,11g) John Woods (Leigh) v. Ryedale-York, 12 January 1992

Season records

Most tries: 48 Steve Halliwell (Leigh) 1985-86

Most goals: 167 Mike Fletcher (Hull K.R.) 1989-90

Most points: 395 (22t,163g,3dg) Lynn Hopkins (Workington T.) 1981-82

TEAM

Highest score: Leigh 92 v. Keighley 2, 30 April 1986; Hull K.R. 92 v. Whitehaven 10, 18 March 1990; Rochdale H. 92 v. Runcorn H. 0, 5 November 1989 (Also widest margin)

Highest away: Runcorn H. 2 v. Leigh 88, 15 January 1989 (Also widest margin)

Most points by losing team:
Dewsbury 36 v. Rochdale H. 34, 9 October 1988; Oldham 50 v. Keighley 34, 12 November 1989

Highest score draw: Huddersfield B. 32 v. Keighley 32, 17 April 1986

Scoreless draw: Dewsbury 0 v. Rochdale H. 0, 30 January 1983

Longest winning run: 30 by Leigh in 1985-86. Hull won all 26 matches in 1978-79

Longest losing run: 55 by Runcorn H. (9 in 1988-89, all 28 in 1989-90 and 18 in 1990-91)

Longest run without a win: 67, inc 2 draws, by Runcorn H. (19 in 1988-89, all 28 in 1989-90 and 20 in 1990-91)

Biggest attendance: 12,424 Hull v. New Hunslet, 18 May 1979

1992-93 Top Division Two scorers

Most tries: 39 Paul Newlove (Featherstone R.)

Most goals: 111 Martin Pearson (Featherstone R.)

Most points: 306 (21t,111g) Martin Pearson (Featherstone R.)

THIRD DIVISION RECORDS
Two seasons only, 1991-92 and 1992-93

INDIVIDUAL

Match records

Most tries: 6 Steve Rowan (Barrow) at Nottingham C., 15 November 1992

Most goals: 15 John Wasyliw (Keighley C.) v. Nottingham C., 1 November 1992

Most points: 42 (4t,13g) Dean Marwood (Workington T.) v. Highfield, 1 November 1992

Season records

Most tries: 31 Vince Gribbin (Whitehaven) 1991-92

Most goals: 146 John Wasyliw (Keighley C.) 1992-93

Most points: 380 (22t,146g) John Wasyliw (Keighley C.) 1992-93

TEAM

Highest score: Blackpool G. 5 v. Dewsbury 90, 14 April 1993 (Also highest away score)

Widest margin: Keighley C. 86 v. Nottingham C. 0, 1 November 1992

Most points by losing team: Hunslet 33 v. Doncaster 32, 16 February 1992

Highest score draw: None of 20-20 or more

Scoreless draw: None

Longest winning run: 14 by Keighley C. 1992-93 (Also longest unbeaten)

Longest losing run: 27 by Nottingham C. All 26 in 1991-92 and first of 1992-93 (Also longest without win)

Biggest attendance: 5,226 Keighley C. v. Batley, 9 April 1993

● League match records do not include scores in abandoned matches that were replayed.

TWENTY-SEASON TABLE

St. Helens have been the most consistently successful club over 20 seasons of Division One rugby in terms of total points gained. Although St. Helens have won the title only once since the reintroduction of two divisions in 1973 they head a 20-season table with 759 points from 576 matches.

The Saints are also the only club to finish in the top eight throughout the 20 seasons. The only other clubs to have remained in Division One are Widnes, Leeds, Warrington and Castleford.

Bradford Northern, Hull and Leigh were all Division Two champions who went on to win the Division One title a few years after being promoted, while Hull Kingston Rovers, Halifax and Wigan are other former lower grade clubs who later won the major championship.

The highest place gained by a newly-promoted club is third by Hull in 1979-80 after winning the Division Two title with a 100 per cent record the previous season.

Division One champions who were relegated a few seasons after winning the Division One title were Salford, Featherstone Rovers, Leigh, Halifax and Hull K.R.

The records of the five clubs who have appeared in Division One throughout the 20 seasons are as follows:

FIRST DIVISION SCORING

The following table shows the scoring totals for each season since the inauguration of two divisions in 1973-74:

DIVISION ONE

Season	Matches each club played	Goals	1-Point drop goals	Tries	Pts
1973-74	30	1,508	—	1,295	6,901
1974-75	30	1,334	48	1,261	6,499
1975-76	30	1,498	53	1,331	7,042
1976-77	30[1]	1,435	91	1,423	7,230
1977-78	30[2]	1,402	99	1,443	7,232
1978-79	30	1,367	119	1,448	7,197
1979-80	30	1,389	131	1,349	6,956
1980-81	30	1,439	147	1,342	7,051
1981-82	30	1,486	132	1,354	7,166
1982-83	30	1,369	64	1,386	6,960
1983-84	30	1,472	108	1,479	8,968
1984-85	30	1,464	84	1,595	9,392
1985-86	30	1,296	80	1,435	8,412
1986-87	30	1,412	90	1,607	9,342
1987-88	26	1,070	75	1,170	6,895
1988-89	26	1,107	80	1,154	6,910
1989-90	26	1,198	80	1,295	7,656
1990-91	26	1,115	58	1,189	7,044
1991-92	26	1,026	46	1,178	6,810
1992-93	26	1,082	57	1,215	7,081

[1] Salford & Leeds played 29 matches — their final match was abandoned and not replayed. This match was expunged from league records.
[2] Featherstone R. & Bradford N. played 29 matches — their final match was cancelled following Featherstone's strike.

	P.	W.	D.	L.	F.	A.	Pts
1. St. Helens	576	368	23	185	12,172	8,164	759
2. Widnes	576	365	20	191	10,891	7,665	750
3. Leeds	575	332	24	219	11,057	8,687	688
4. Warrington	576	310	21	245	9,844	8,502	641
5. Castleford	576	301	28	247	11,037	9,200	630

●Although Wigan have had only 19 seasons in Division One they have totalled 711 points from 546 matches.

CHAMPIONSHIP PLAY-OFFS

Following the breakaway from the English Rugby Union, 22 clubs formed the Northern Rugby Football League. Each club played 42 matches and Manningham won the first Championship as league leaders in 1895-96.

This format was then abandoned and replaced by the Yorkshire Senior and Lancashire Senior Combination leagues until 1901-02 when 14 clubs broke away to form the Northern Rugby League with Broughton Rangers winning the first Championship.

The following season two divisions were formed with Division One title going to Halifax (1902-03), Bradford (1903-04), who won a play-off against Salford 5-0 at Halifax after both teams tied with 52 points, and Oldham (1904-05).

In 1905-06 the two divisions were merged with Leigh taking the Championship as league leaders. They won the title on a percentage basis as the 31 clubs did not play the same number of matches. The following season the top four play-off was introduced as a fairer means of deciding the title.

The top club played the fourth-placed, the second meeting the third, with the higher club having home advantage. The final was staged at a neutral venue.

It was not until 1930-31 that all clubs played the same number of league matches, but not all against each other, the top four play-off being a necessity until the reintroduction of two divisions in 1962-63.

This spell of two division football lasted only two seasons and the restoration of the one-league Championship table brought about the introduction of a top-16 play-off, this format continuing until the reappearance of two divisions in 1973-74.

Since then the Championship Trophy has been awarded to the leaders of the First Division, with the Second Division champions receiving a silver bowl. A Third Division was introduced for two years from 1991-92.

Slalom Lager launched a three-year sponsorship deal of the Championship and the Premiership in 1980-81 in a £215,000 package, extending the deal for another three years from 1983-84 for £270,000. From 1986-87, the sponsorship was taken over by brewers Bass, under the Stones Bitter banner, in a new £400,000 three-year deal, renewed for a further three years from 1989-90 for £750,000.

CHAMPIONSHIP PLAY-OFF FINALS

Season	Winners		Runners-up		Venue	Attendance	Receipts
Top Four Play-Offs							
1906-07	Halifax	18	Oldham	3	Huddersfield	13,200	£722
1907-08	Hunslet	7	Oldham	7	Salford	14,000	£690
Replay	Hunslet	12	Oldham	2	Wakefield	14,054	£800
1908-09	Wigan	7	Oldham	3	Salford	12,000	£630
1909-10	Oldham	13	Wigan	7	Broughton	10,850	£520
1910-11	Oldham	20	Wigan	7	Broughton	15,543	£717
1911-12	Huddersfield	13	Wigan	5	Halifax	15,000	£591
1912-13	Huddersfield	29	Wigan	2	Wakefield	17,000	£914
1913-14	Salford	5	Huddersfield	3	Leeds	8,091	£474
1914-15	Huddersfield	35	Leeds	2	Wakefield	14,000	£750
COMPETITION SUSPENDED DURING WARTIME							
1919-20	Hull	3	Huddersfield	2	Leeds	12,900	£1,615
1920-21	Hull	16	Hull K.R.	14	Leeds	10,000	£1,320
1921-22	Wigan	13	Oldham	2	Broughton	26,000	£1,825
1922-23	Hull K.R.	15	Huddersfield	5	Leeds	14,000	£1,370
1923-24	Batley	13	Wigan	7	Broughton	13,729	£968
1924-25	Hull K.R.	9	Swinton	5	Rochdale	21,580	£1,504
1925-26	Wigan	22	Warrington	10	St. Helens	20,000	£1,100
1926-27	Swinton	13	St. Helens Recs.	8	Warrington	24,432	£1,803
1927-28	Swinton	11	Featherstone R.	0	Oldham	15,451	£1,136
1928-29	Huddersfield	2	Leeds	0	Halifax	25,604	£2,028
1929-30	Huddersfield	2	Leeds	2	Wakefield	32,095	£2,111
Replay	Huddersfield	10	Leeds	0	Halifax	18,563	£1,319
1930-31	Swinton	14	Leeds	7	Wigan	31,000	£2,100
1931-32	St. Helens	9	Huddersfield	5	Wakefield	19,386	£943
1932-33	Salford	15	Swinton	5	Wigan	18,000	£1,053
1933-34	Wigan	15	Salford	3	Warrington	31,564	£2,114
1934-35	Swinton	14	Warrington	3	Wigan	27,700	£1,710
1935-36	Hull	21	Widnes	2	Huddersfield	17,276	£1,208

249

Season	Winners		Runners-up		Venue	Attendance	Receipts
1936-37	Salford	13	Warrington	11	Wigan	31,500	£2,000
1937-38	Hunslet	8	Leeds	2	Elland Rd., Leeds	54,112	£3,572
1938-39	Salford	8	Castleford	6	Man. C. FC	69,504	£4,301

WARTIME EMERGENCY PLAY-OFFS
For the first two seasons the Yorkshire League and Lancashire League champions met in a two-leg final as follows:

1939-40	Swinton	13	Bradford N.	21	Swinton	4,800	£237
	Bradford N.	16	Swinton	9	Bradford	11,721	£570

Bradford N. won 37-22 on aggregate

1940-41	Wigan	6	Bradford N.	17	Wigan	11,245	£640
	Bradford N.	28	Wigan	9	Bradford	20,205	£1,148

Bradford N. won 45-15 on aggregate
For the remainder of the War the top four in the War League played-off as follows:

1941-42	Dewsbury	13	Bradford N.	0	Leeds	18,000	£1,121
1942-43	Dewsbury	11	Halifax	3	Dewsbury	7,000	£400
	Halifax	13	Dewsbury	22	Halifax	9,700	£683

Dewsbury won 33-16 on aggregate but the Championship was declared null and void because they had played an ineligible player

1943-44	Wigan	13	Dewsbury	9	Wigan	14,000	£915
	Dewsbury	5	Wigan	12	Dewsbury	9,000	£700

Wigan won 25-14 on aggregate

1944-45	Halifax	9	Bradford N.	2	Halifax	9,426	£955
	Bradford N.	24	Halifax	11	Bradford	16,000	£1,850

Bradford N. won 26-20 on aggregate

1945-46	Wigan	13	Huddersfield	4	Man. C. FC	67,136	£8,387
1946-47	Wigan	13	Dewsbury	4	Man. C. FC	40,599	£5,895
1947-48	Warrington	15	Bradford N.	5	Man. C. FC	69,143	£9,792
1948-49	Huddersfield	13	Warrington	12	Man. C. FC	75,194	£11,073
1949-50	Wigan	20	Huddersfield	2	Man. C. FC	65,065	£11,500
1950-51	Workington T.	26	Warrington	11	Man. C. FC	61,618	£10,993
1951-52	Wigan	13	Bradford N.	6	Huddersfield Town FC	48,684	£8,215
1952-53	St. Helens	24	Halifax	14	Man. C. FC	51,083	£11,503
1953-54	Warrington	8	Halifax	7	Man. C. FC	36,519	£9,076
1954-55	Warrington	7	Oldham	3	Man. C. FC	49,434	£11,516
1955-56	Hull	10	Halifax	9	Man. C. FC	36,675	£9,179
1956-57	Oldham	15	Hull	14	Bradford	62,199	£12,054
1957-58	Hull	20	Workington T.	3	Bradford	57,699	£11,149
1958-59	St. Helens	44	Hunslet	22	Bradford	52,560	£10,146
1959-60	Wigan	27	Wakefield T.	3	Bradford	83,190	£14,482
1960-61	Leeds	25	Warrington	10	Bradford	52,177	£10,475
1961-62	Huddersfield	14	Wakefield T.	5	Bradford	37,451	£7,979

TWO DIVISIONS 1962-63 and 1963-64

Top Sixteen Play-Offs

1964-65	Halifax	15	St. Helens	7	Swinton	20,786	£6,141
1965-66	St. Helens	35	Halifax	12	Swinton	30,634	£8,750
1966-67	Wakefield T.	7	St. Helens	7	Leeds	20,161	£6,702
Replay	Wakefield T.	21	St. Helens	9	Swinton	33,537	£9,800
1967-68	Wakefield T.	17	Hull K.R.	10	Leeds	22,586	£7,697
1968-69	Leeds	16	Castleford	14	Bradford	28,442	£10,130
1969-70	St. Helens	24	Leeds	12	Bradford	26,358	£9,791
1970-71	St. Helens	16	Wigan	12	Swinton	21,745	£10,200
1971-72	Leeds	9	St. Helens	5	Swinton	24,055	£9,513
1972-73	Dewsbury	22	Leeds	13	Bradford	18,889	£9,479

CHAMPIONSHIP FINAL . . . . A 10-YEAR REVIEW

1961-62   HUDDERSFIELD 14   Dyson (4g); Breen, Deighton, Booth, Wicks (1t); Davies, Smales (1t); Slevin, Close, Noble, Kilroy, Bowman, Ramsden
WAKEFIELD T. 5   Round; F. Smith, Skene, N. Fox (1t, 1g), Hirst; Poynton, Holliday; Wilkinson, Kosanovic, Firth, Briggs, Vines, Turner
Referee: N. T. Railton (Wigan)

TWO DIVISIONS — NO PLAY-OFFS 1963 and 1964

1964-65   HALIFAX 15   James (3g); Jackson (1t), Burnett (2t), Kellett, Freeman; Robinson, Daley; Roberts, Harrison, Scroby, Fogerty, Dixon, Renilson
ST. HELENS 7   F. Barrow; Harvey, Vollenhoven, Northey, Killeen (1t, 2g); Murphy, Smith; Tembey (Warlow), Dagnall, Watson, French, Mantle, Laughton
Referee: D. S. Brown (Dewsbury)

1965-66   ST. HELENS 35   F. Barrow; A. Barrow (1t), Murphy (1g), Benyon, Killeen (3t, 6g); Harvey, Bishop; Halsall (3t), Sayer, Watson, French, Warlow (Hitchen), Mantle
HALIFAX 12   Cooper (3g); Jones, Burnett, Dixon, Freeman; Robinson, Baker (1t); Roberts, Harrison, Scroby, Ramshaw (Duffy), Fogerty (1t), Renilson
Referee: J. Manley (Warrington)

1966-67   WAKEFIELD T. 7   Cooper; Hirst, Brooke, N. Fox (2g), Coetzer; Poynton, Owen (1t); Bath, Prior, Campbell, Clarkson, Haigh, D. Fox
ST. HELENS 7   F. Barrow; Vollenhoven, A. Barrow, Smith, Killeen (2g); Douglas, Bishop; Warlow, Sayer, Watson (1t), French, Hogan (Robinson), Mantle
Referee: G. Philpott (Leeds)

Replay: WAKEFIELD T. 21   Cooper; Hirst (1t), Brooke (2t), N. Fox (3g), Coetzer; Poynton (1t), Owen (1t); Bath, Prior, Campbell, Clarkson, Haigh, D. Fox
ST. HELENS 9   F. Barrow; Vollenhoven (1t), A. Barrow, Smith, Killeen (2g); Douglas, Bishop (1g); Warlow, Sayer, Watson, French, Hogan, Mantle
Referee: J. Manley (Warrington)

1967-68   WAKEFIELD T. 17   G. Cooper; Coetzer, Brooke, N. Fox (1t, 2g), Batty; Poynton (1g), Owen (1t); Jeanes (1t), Shepherd, D. Fox (1g), Haigh, McLeod, Hawley
HULL K.R. 10   Wainwright; C. Young, Moore (1t), A. Burwell, Longstaff (1t); Millward (2g), C. Cooper; L. Foster, Flanagan, Mennell, Lowe, Major, F. Foster
Referee: D. S. Brown (Preston)

1968-69   LEEDS 16   Risman (4g); Cowan (1t), Hynes, Watson, Atkinson (1t); Shoebottom, Seabourne (Langley); Clark (Hick), Crosby, K. Eyre, Joyce, Ramsey (1g), Batten
CASTLEFORD 14   Edwards; Briggs, Howe, Thomas, Lowndes; Hardisty (1t, 1g), Hepworth; Hartley, C. Dickinson (1t), J. Ward, Redfearn (3g), Lockwood, Reilly (Fox)
Referee: W. H. Thompson (Huddersfield)

1969-70   ST. HELENS 24   F. Barrow; L. Jones, Benyon, Walsh (1t, 2g), E. Prescott (2t); Myler, Heaton; Halsall, Sayer (1t), Watson, Mantle, E. Chisnall, Coslett (4g)
LEEDS 12   Holmes (3g); Alan Smith (1t), Hynes, Cowan (1t), Atkinson; Shoebottom, Seabourne; J. Burke, Crosby, A. Eyre, Ramsey (Hick), Eccles, Batten
Referee: W. H. Thompson (Huddersfield)

1970-71   ST. HELENS 16   Pimblett; L. Jones, Benyon (1t), Walsh, Blackwood (1t); Whittle, Heaton; J. Stephens, A. Karalius, Rees (Wanbon), Mantle, E. Chisnall, Coslett (5g)
WIGAN 12   Tyrer (1g); Kevin O'Loughlin, Francis, Rowe, Wright; D. Hill, Ayres; Hogan, Clarke, Fletcher, Ashurst (1t, 2g), Robinson (1t) (Cunningham), Laughton
Referee: E. Lawrinson (Warrington)

1971-72   LEEDS 9   Holmes (Hick); Alan Smith, Langley, Dyl, Atkinson (1t); Hardisty, Barham; Clawson (3g), Ward, Fisher (Pickup), Cookson, Eccles, Batten
ST. HELENS 5   Pimblett; L. Jones (Whittle), Benyon, Walsh (1g), Wilson; Kelly, Heaton; Rees, Greenall (1t), J. Stephens, Mantle, E. Chisnall, Coslett
Referee: S. Shepherd (Oldham)

1972-73   DEWSBURY 22   Rushton; Ashcroft, Clark, N. Stephenson (1t, 5g), Day; Agar (1t), A. Bates; Beverley (Taylor), M. Stephenson (2t), Lowe, Grayshon, J. Bates, Whittington
LEEDS 13   Holmes; Alan Smith, Hynes (1g), Dyl (1t), Atkinson; Hardisty, Hepworth; Clawson (1g), Fisher (Ward), Clarkson (Langley), Cookson (1t), Eccles (1t), Haigh
Referee: H. G. Hunt (Prestbury)

LEAGUE LEADERS TROPHY
While the top 16 play-off decided the Championship between 1964 and 1973 it was decided to honour the top club in the league table with a League Leaders Trophy. The winners were:

1964-65 St. Helens
1965-66 St. Helens
1966-67 Leeds
1967-68 Leeds
1968-69 Leeds
1969-70 Leeds
1970-71 Wigan
1971-72 Leeds
1972-73 Warrington

CLUB CHAMPIONSHIP (Merit Table)
With the reintroduction of two divisions, a complicated merit table and Division Two preliminary rounds system produced a 16-club play-off with the Club Championship finalists as follows:

Season	Winners		Runners-up		Venue	Attendance	Receipts
1973-74	Warrington	13	St. Helens	12	Wigan	18,040	£10,032

This format lasted just one season and was replaced by the Premiership.

CLUB CHAMPIONSHIP FINAL . . . . A REVIEW
1973-74   WARRINGTON 13   Whitehead (2g); M. Philbin (1t), Noonan (1t), Pickup (Lowe), Bevan; Whittle, A. Murphy; D. Chisnall, Ashcroft, Brady (1t), Wanbon (Gaskell), Mather, B. Philbin
ST. HELENS 12   Pimblett; Brown, Wills, Wilson (2t), Mathias; Eckersley, Heaton; Mantle, Liptrot, M. Murphy, E. Chisnall (Warlow), Nicholls, Coslett (3g)
Referee: P. Geraghty (York)

PREMIERSHIP
With the further reintroduction of two divisions in 1973-74, it was declared that the title of Champions would be awarded to the leaders of the First Division.

However, it was also decided to continue the tradition of an end-of-season competition, the winners to receive the newly instituted Premiership Trophy.
*For full details of the Premiership Trophy see the CUPS section.

David Eckersley, stand off for 1974 Club Championship runners-up St. Helens.

COUNTY LEAGUE
In the early seasons of the code the Lancashire Senior and Yorkshire Senior Competitions, not to be confused with the later reserve leagues, were major leagues. The winners were:

	Lancashire SC	Yorkshire SC
1895-96	Runcorn	Manningham
1896-97	Broughton Rangers	Brighouse Rangers
1897-98	Oldham	Hunslet
1898-99	Broughton Rangers	Batley
1899-00	Runcorn	Bradford
1900-01	Oldham	Bradford
1901-02	Wigan	Leeds

With the introduction of two divisions in 1902-03, the county league competitions were scrapped until they reappeared as the Lancashire League and Yorkshire League in 1907-08. Clubs from the same county played each other home and away to decide the titles. These games were included in the main championship table along with inter-county fixtures. The county leagues continued until 1970, with the exception of war-time interruptions and two seasons when regional leagues with play-offs operated during the 1960s two-division era. They were then abolished when a more integrated fixture formula meant clubs did not play all others from the same county, this system later being replaced by the two-division structure.

LEAGUE LEADERS .... A REVIEW

The following is a list of the League leaders since the formation of the Northern Union, with the exception of the three eras of two-division football. From 1896 to 1901, the League was divided into a Lancashire Senior Competition and a Yorkshire Senior Competition, winners of both leagues being listed for those seasons. From 1905 to 1930 not all the clubs played each other, the League being determined on a percentage basis.

LSC — Lancashire Senior Competition
LL — Lancashire League
YSC — Yorkshire Senior Competition
YL — Yorkshire League
WEL — War Emergency League
* Two points deducted for breach of professional rules
† Decided on a percentage basis after Belle Vue Rangers withdrew shortly before the start of the season.

		P.	W.	D.	L.	F.	A.	Pts.	
1895-96	Manningham	42	33	0	9	367	158	66	
1896-97	Broughton R.	26	19	5	2	201	52	43	LSC
	Brighouse R.	30	22	4	4	213	68	48	YSC
1897-98	Oldham	26	23	1	2	295	94	47	LSC
	Hunslet	30	22	4	4	327	117	48	YSC
1898-99	Broughton R.	26	21	0	5	277	74	42	LSC
	Batley	30	23	2	5	279	75	48	YSC
1899-00	Runcorn	26	22	2	2	232	33	46	LSC
	Bradford	30	24	2	4	324	98	50	YSC
1900-01	Oldham	26	22	1	3	301	67	45	LSC
	Bradford	30	26	1	3	387	100	51*	YSC
1901-02	Broughton R.	26	21	1	4	285	112	43	
1902-05	Two Divisions								
1905-06	Leigh	30	23	2	5	245	130	48	80.00%
1906-07	Halifax	34	27	2	5	649	229	56	82.35%
1907-08	Oldham	32	28	2	2	396	121	58	90.62%
1908-09	Wigan	32	28	0	4	706	207	56	87.50%
1909-10	Oldham	34	29	2	3	604	184	60	88.23%
1910-11	Wigan	34	28	1	5	650	205	57	83.82%
1911-12	Huddersfield	36	31	1	4	996	238	63	87.50%
1912-13	Huddersfield	32	28	0	4	732	217	56	87.50%
1913-14	Huddersfield	34	28	2	4	830	258	58	85.29%
1914-15	Huddersfield	34	28	4	2	888	235	60	88.24%
1915-18	Competitive matches suspended during First World War								
1918-19	Rochdale H.	12	9	0	3	92	52	18	75.00% LL
	Hull	16	13	0	3	392	131	26	81.25% YL
1919-20	Huddersfield	34	29	0	5	759	215	58	85.29%
1920-21	Hull K.R.	32	24	1	7	432	233	49	76.56%
1921-22	Oldham	36	29	1	6	521	201	59	81.94%
1922-23	Hull	36	30	0	6	587	304	60	83.33%
1923-24	Wigan	38	31	0	7	824	228	62	81.57%
1924-25	Swinton	36	30	0	6	499	224	60	83.33%
1925-26	Wigan	38	29	3	6	641	310	61	80.26%
1926-27	St. Helens R.	38	29	3	6	544	235	61	80.26%
1927-28	Swinton	36	27	3	6	439	189	57	79.16%

		P.	W.	D.	L.	F.	A.	Pts.	
1928-29	Huddersfield	38	26	4	8	476	291	56	73.68%
1929-30	St. Helens	40	27	1	12	549	295	55	68.75%
1930-31	Swinton	38	31	2	5	504	156	64	
1931-32	Huddersfield	38	30	1	7	636	368	61	
1932-33	Salford	38	31	2	5	751	165	64	
1933-34	Salford	38	31	1	6	715	281	63	
1934-35	Swinton	38	30	1	7	468	175	61	
1935-36	Hull	38	30	1	7	607	306	61	
1936-37	Salford	38	29	3	6	529	196	61	
1937-38	Hunslet	36	25	3	8	459	301	53	
1938-39	Salford	40	30	3	7	551	191	63	
1939-40	Swinton	22	17	0	5	378	158	34	WEL LL
	Bradford N.	28	21	0	7	574	302	42	WEL YL
1940-41	Wigan	16	15	1	0	297	71	31	WEL LL
	Bradford N.	25	23	1	1	469	126	47	WEL YL
1941-42	Dewsbury	24	19	1	4	431	172	39	81.25% WEL
1942-43	Wigan	16	13	0	3	301	142	26	81.25% WEL
1943-44	Wakefield T.	22	19	0	3	359	97	38	86.36% WEL
1944-45	Bradford N.	20	17	0	3	337	69	34	85.00% WEL
1945-46	Wigan	36	29	2	5	783	219	60	
1946-47	Wigan	36	29	1	6	567	196	59	
1947-48	Wigan	36	31	1	4	776	258	63	
1948-49	Warrington	36	31	0	5	728	247	62	
1949-50	Wigan	36	31	1	4	853	320	63	
1950-51	Warrington	36	30	0	6	738	250	60	
1951-52	Bradford N.	36	28	1	7	758	326	57	
1952-53	St. Helens	36	32	2	2	769	273	66	
1953-54	Halifax	36	30	2	4	538	219	62	
1954-55	Warrington	36	29	2	5	718	321	60	
1955-56	Warrington	34	27	1	6	712	349	55	80.88% †
1956-57	Oldham	38	33	0	5	893	365	66	
1957-58	Oldham	38	33	1	4	803	415	67	
1958-59	St. Helens	38	31	1	6	1,005	450	63	
1959-60	St. Helens	38	34	1	3	947	343	69	
1960-61	Leeds	36	30	0	6	620	258	60	
1961-62	Wigan	36	32	1	3	885	283	65	
1962-64	Two Divisions								
1964-65	St. Helens	34	28	0	6	621	226	56	
1965-66	St. Helens	34	28	1	5	521	275	57	
1966-67	Leeds	34	29	0	5	704	373	58	
1967-68	Leeds	34	28	0	6	720	271	56	
1968-69	Leeds	34	29	2	3	775	358	60	
1969-70	Leeds	34	30	0	4	674	314	60	
1970-71	Wigan	34	30	0	4	662	308	60	
1971-72	Leeds	34	28	2	4	750	325	58	
1972-73	Warrington	34	27	2	5	816	400	56	

Studious Australian Steve Martin marked his debut season on the British club scene with trophy success in the Stones Bitter Second Division and Divisional Premiership.

COACHES

COACHES

INDEX OF COACHES

The following is an index of the 258 coaches who have held first team coaching posts since the start of the 1974-75 season to the end of May 1993.

It includes the alphabetical listing of British clubs they coached in the period.

Fifteen new coaches were added to the list during the past 12 months when 17 clubs made at least one change.

Although some clubs appoint team managers with a coach as his assistant, the list refers only to the man generally recognised as being in overall charge of team affairs.

A caretaker coach, who stands in while the club is seeking a permanent appointment, is only listed if he takes charge for more than a few matches.

For a list of each club's appointments since 1974 see CLUBS section.

Ray Abbey (Dewsbury)
Jack Addy (Dewsbury, Huddersfield B.)
Allan Agar (Bramley, Carlisle, Featherstone R., Rochdale H.)
Gary Ainsworth (Trafford B.)
Dave Alred (Bridgend)
Chris Anderson (Halifax)
Harry Archer (Workington T.)
Chris Arkwright (Highfield)
Kevin Ashcroft (Leigh, Salford, Warrington)
Eric Ashton (St. Helens)
Ray Ashton (Workington T.)
Bill Ashurst (Runcorn H., Wakefield T.)
Mal Aspey (Salford)
John Atkinson (Carlisle)
Jack Austin (Hunslet)

Trevor Bailey (Scarborough P., Wakefield T.)
Maurice Bamford (Bramley, Dewsbury, Halifax, Huddersfield, Leeds, Wigan, Workington T.)
Frank Barrow (Oldham, Swinton)
Tony Barrow (Oldham, Swinton, Warrington)
Ray Batten (Wakefield T.)
Jeff Bawden (Whitehaven)
Mel Bedford (Huddersfield)
Cameron Bell (Carlisle)
Billy Benyon (Leigh, St. Helens, Warrington)
Les Bettinson (Salford)
Charlie Birdsall (Rochdale H.)

Alan Bishop (Runcorn H.)
Tommy Bishop (Barrow, Leigh, Workington T.)
Mick Blacker (Halifax, Huddersfield, Mansfield M.)
Tommy Blakeley (Blackpool B.)
Dick Bonser (Rochdale H.)
Reg Bowden (Fulham, Warrington)
Carl Briscoe (Chorley B.)
Drew Broatch (Hunslet)
Ian Brooke (Bradford N., Huddersfield, Wakefield T.)
Arthur Bunting (Hull, Hull K.R.)
Mark Burgess (Nottingham C.)
Dave Busfield (Dewsbury)

Len Casey (Hull, Scarborough P., Wakefield T.)
Jim Challinor (Oldham)
Paul Charlton (Workington T.)
Eddie Cheetham (Leigh)
Dave Chisnall (Runcorn H.)
Colin Clarke (Leigh, Wigan)
Terry Clawson (Featherstone R.)
Noel Cleal (Hull)
Malcolm Clift (Leeds)
Joe Coan (Wigan)
John Cogger (Runcorn H.)
Gary Cooper (York)
Kel Coslett (Rochdale H., St. Helens, Wigan)
Gordon Cottier (Whitehaven)
Keith Cotton (Featherstone R.)
Mike Coulman (Salford)
Les Coulter (Keighley)
Dave Cox (Batley, Castleford, Dewsbury, Huyton, Oldham, Workington T.)
Jim Crellin (Blackpool B., Halifax, Leigh, Mansfield M., Rochdale H., Swinton)
Terry Crook (Batley, Dewsbury)
Steve Crooks (Ryedale-York)

Arthur Daley (Runcorn H.)
Paul Daley (Batley, Featherstone R., Hunslet, York)
Jackie Davidson (Whitehaven, Workington T.)
Keith Davies (Workington T.)
Tommy Dawes (Barrow, Carlisle, Whitehaven)
Harry Dawson (Widnes)
Tony Dean (Hull, Wakefield T.)
Henry Delooze (Rochdale H.)
Steve Dennison (Mansfield M.)
Robin Dewhurst (Leeds)
Bakary Diabira (Blackpool B., Keighley)
Tommy Dickens (Blackpool B., Leigh)
Roy Dickinson (Bramley)

Colin Dixon (Halifax, Keighley, Salford)
Mal Dixon (York)
John Dorahy (Halifax, Wigan)
David Doyle-Davidson (Hull, York)
Ray Dutton (Whitehaven)

Graham Eadie (Halifax)
Bob Eccles (Blackpool G., Chorley)
Derek Edwards (Doncaster)
Joe Egan Jnr. (Blackpool B.)

George Fairbairn (Hull K.R., Wigan)
Vince Farrar (Featherstone R.)
Albert Fearnley (Batley, Blackpool B., Keighley)
John Fieldhouse (Oldham)
Tony Fisher (Bramley, Doncaster, Keighley)
Eric Fitzsimons (Oldham, Rochdale H.,
    Whitehaven)
Bob Fleet (Swinton)
Geoff Fletcher (Huyton, Runcorn H.)
Terry Fogerty (Rochdale H.)
Chris Forster (Bramley, Huddersfield B.)
Derek Foster (Ryedale-York)
Frank Foster (Barrow, Whitehaven)
Kenny Foulkes (Hull)
Don Fox (Batley)
Harry Fox (Halifax)
Neil Fox (Huddersfield)
Peter Fox (Bradford N., Bramley, Featherstone R.,
    Leeds, Wakefield T.)
Bill Francis (Oldham)
Roy Francis (Bradford N., Leeds)

Paul Gamble (Blackpool G.)
Bill Gardner (Sheffield E.)
Brian Gartland (Oldham)
Stan Gittins (Blackpool B., Chorley, Rochdale H.,
    Springfield B.)
Bill Goodwin (Fulham, Kent Invicta)
Tony Gordon (London C.)
Terry Gorman (Huyton, Swinton)
Keith Goulding (Featherstone R., Huddersfield,
    York)
Mal Graham (Oldham)
Tom Grainey (Leigh, Swinton)
Jeff Grayshon (Dewsbury)
Lee Greenwood (Keighley, Mansfield M./
    Nottingham C.)
Geoff Gunney (Wakefield T.)

Bob Haigh (Wakefield T.)
Derek Hallas (Halifax)

Former New Zealand Test coach Tony Gordon, who took charge of London Crusaders in February 1993.

Ken Halliwell (Swinton)
Alan Hardisty (Dewsbury, Halifax, York)
Arnold Hema (Nottingham C.)
Graham Heptinstall (Doncaster)
Alan Hepworth (Batley)
Keith Hepworth (Bramley, Hull)
Gary Hetherington (Sheffield E.)
Ron Hill (Dewsbury)
David Hobbs (Bradford N.)
Neil Holding (Rochdale H.)
Bill Holliday (Swinton)
Eric Hughes (Rochdale H., Widnes)
Syd Hynes (Leeds)

Bob Irving (Blackpool B.)
Keith Irving (Workington T.)

Dennis Jackson (Barrow)
Francis Jarvis (Huddersfield)
Peter Jarvis (Bramley, Hunslet)
Graeme Jennings (Hunslet)
Barry Johnson (Bramley)
Brian Johnson (Warrington)
Willie Johnson (Highfield)
Allen Jones (Huddersfield B.)
Lewis Jones (Dewsbury)
John Joyner (Castleford)

Vince Karalius (Widnes, Wigan)
Paul Kavanagh (Barrow)
John Kear (Bramley)
Arthur Keegan (Bramley)
Ivor Kelland (Barrow)
Alan Kellett (Carlisle, Halifax, Keighley)
Bill Kenny (Doncaster)
Bill Kindon (Leigh)
Bill Kirkbride (Mansfield M., Rochdale H.,
   Wakefield T., York)
Phil Kitchin (Whitehaven, Workington T.)

Dave Lamming (Wakefield T.)
Steve Lane (Kent Invicta)
Phil Larder (Widnes)
Doug Laughton (Leeds, Widnes)
Roy Lester (Carlisle, Fulham)
Alan Lockwood (Dewsbury)
Brian Lockwood (Batley, Huddersfield,
   Wakefield T.)
Paul Longstaff (Rochdale H.)
Graham Lowe (Wigan)
Phil Lowe (York)
Trevor Lowe (Batley, Doncaster)
Ken Loxton (Bramley)
Geoff Lyon (Blackpool B.)

Mike McClennan (St. Helens)
Stan McCormick (Salford)
John McFarlane (Whitehaven)
Alan McInnes (Salford, Wigan)
John Mantle (Blackpool B., Cardiff C., Leigh)
Steve Martin (Featherstone R.)
Jack Melling (Blackpool G.)
Roger Millward (Halifax, Hull K.R.)
John Monie (Wigan)
Mick Morgan (Carlisle)
Geoff Morris (Doncaster)
David Mortimer (Huddersfield)
Alex Murphy (Huddersfield, Leigh, St. Helens,
   Salford, Warrington, Wigan)
Frank Myler (Oldham, Rochdale H., Swinton,
   Widnes)

Steve Nash (Mansfield M.)
Steve Norton (Barrow)

Chris O'Sullivan (Swinton)

Les Pearce (Bramley, Halifax)
Mike Peers (Blackpool G., Chorley B./Trafford B.,
   Highfield, Swinton)
Geoff Peggs (Keighley)

Australian Peter Regan, appointed coach of Rochdale Hornets in January 1993.

George Pieniazek (Batley, Featherstone R.)
Billy Platt (Mansfield M.)
Harry Poole (Hull K.R.)

Denis Ramsdale (Barrow)
Bill Ramsey (Hunslet)
Terry Ramshaw (Oldham)
Keith Rayne (Batley)
Rod Reddy (Barrow)
Graham Rees (Blackpool B.)
Peter Regan (Rochdale H.)
Malcolm Reilly (Castleford, Halifax, Leeds)
Alan Rhodes (Doncaster, Sheffield E.)
Austin Rhodes (Swinton)
Bev Risman (Fulham)
Ken Roberts (Halifax)
Don Robinson (Bramley)
Don Robson (Doncaster)
Peter Roe (Halifax, Keighley)
Sol Roper (Workington T.)

Roy Sabine (Keighley)
Dave Sampson (Castleford, Doncaster,
   Nottingham C.)
Barry Seabourne (Bradford N., Huddersfield,
   Keighley)
Les Sheard (Huddersfield)
Danny Sheehan (York)
John Sheridan (Doncaster)
Royce Simmons (Hull)
Steve Simms (Leigh)

Tommy Smales [*Scrum half*] (Featherstone R.)
Tommy Smales [*Forward*] (Batley, Bramley,
    Dewsbury, Doncaster, Featherstone R.)
Peter Smethurst (Leigh, Oldham)
Barry Smith (Whitehaven)
Bill Smith (Whitehaven, Workington T.)
Brian Smith (Huddersfield)
Brian Smith [*Australian*] (Hull)
Kurt Sorensen (Whitehaven)
Ike Southward (Whitehaven, Workington T.)
Graham Starkey (Oldham, Rochdale H.)
Gary Stephens (York)
Nigel Stephenson (Huddersfield, Hunslet)
Dave Stockwell (Batley, Bramley)
John Stopford (Swinton)
Ted Strawbridge (Doncaster)
Ross Strudwick (Fulham/London C., Halifax)
Clive Sullivan (Doncaster, Hull)
Phil Sullivan (Fulham)
Kevin Tamati (Salford)
John Taylor (Chorley B.)
Bob Tomlinson (Huddersfield)
Ted Toohey (Wigan)
David Topliss (Wakefield T.)
Peter Tunks (Oldham)
Norman Turley (Trafford B., Whitehaven,
    Workington T.)
Derek Turner (Wakefield T.)
Colin Tyrer (Widnes)
Darryl Van de Velde (Castleford)
Don Vines (Doncaster)
Arnold Walker (Whitehaven)
Trevor Walker (Batley)
Peter Walsh (Workington T.)
David Ward (Batley, Hunslet, Leeds)
John Warlow (Bridgend)
David Watkins (Cardiff C.)
Bernard Watson (Dewsbury)
Neil Whittaker (Huddersfield B.)
Mel Wibberley (Nottingham C.)
Ron Willey (Bradford N.)
Dean Williams (Workington T.)
Frank Wilson (Runcorn H.)
John Wolford (Hunslet)
Jeff Woods (Bridgend)
John Woods (Leigh)
Paul Woods (Runcorn H.)
Geoff Worrall (Barrow)
Geoff Wraith (Wakefield T.)
Billy Yates (Doncaster)

DOSSIER OF 1992-93 COACHES

The following is a dossier of the British coaching and playing careers of coaches holding first team posts from June 1992 to the end of May 1993. Overseas details are not included.
● BF — beaten finalist.

JACK ADDY

Dewsbury:	Feb. 84 - Jan. 87 (Promotion)
Huddersfield B:	Jan. 87 - Mar. 88
Dewsbury:	Dec. 90 -

Played for: Dewsbury

ALLAN AGAR

Carlisle:	May 81 - June 82 (Promotion)
Featherstone R.:	Dec. 82 - Oct. 85
	(RL Cup winners)
Bramley:	Dec. 85 - Apr. 87
Rochdale H.:	July 89 - Jan. 91 (Promotion)
Featherstone R.:	Oct. 91 - Aug. 92

Played for: Featherstone R., Dewsbury, New Hunslet, Hull K.R., Wakefield T., Carlisle, Bramley

KEVIN ASHCROFT

Leigh:	June 75 - Jan. 77 (Promotion)
	Floodlit Trophy (BF)
Salford:	Nov. 80 - Mar. 82
Warrington:	Mar. 82 - May 84
	(Lancs. Cup winners & BF)
Salford:	May 84 - Oct. 89 (Promotion)
Leigh:	Sep. 91 - June 92 (Promotion)

Played for: Dewsbury, Rochdale H., Leigh, Warrington, Salford

MAURICE BAMFORD

Dewsbury:	Aug. 74 - Oct. 74
Halifax:	Feb. 78 - May 80
	(Yorks. Cup BF, Promotion)
Huddersfield:	May 80 - May 81
Wigan:	May 81 - May 82
Bramley:	May 82 - Oct. 83
Leeds:	Nov. 83 - Feb. 85
	(John Player winners)
Leeds:	Dec. 86 - Apr. 88
	(John Player BF)
Workington T.:	July 88 - Dec. 88
Dewsbury:	Dec. 88 - Dec. 90
Bramley:	Apr. 92 - (Promotion)
Great Britain &	
Under-21s:	Oct. 84 - Dec. 86

Played for: Dewsbury, Batley

TONY BARROW

Warrington:	Mar. 86 - Nov. 88 (Premier winners & BF, John Player BF, Lancs. Cup BF)
Oldham:	Nov. 88 - Jan. 91 (Promotion, Lancs. Cup BF, Div. 2 Premier winners)
Swinton:	Jan. 92 -

Played for: St. Helens, Leigh

CAMERON BELL (New Zealander)

Carlisle:	Feb. 90 -

CARL BRISCOE

Chorley B.:	Jan. 93 -

Played for: Wigan, Springfield B./Chorley B.

MARK BURGESS

Nottingham C.:	June 91 - May 92
Nottingham C.:	Nov. 92 -

Played for: Rochdale H., Hunslet, Dewsbury, Nottingham C.

GORDON COTTIER

Whitehaven:	June 92 - May 93
Cumbria:	1992-93

Played for: Barrow, Whitehaven, Workington T.

JIM CRELLIN

Blackpool B.:	May 76 - Mar. 77 (John Player BF)
Halifax:	June 77 - Oct. 77
Swinton:	Nov. 83 - May 86 (Div. 2 champs)
Mansfield M.:	Dec. 86 - June 88
Rochdale H.:	June 88 - June 89
Swinton:	July 89 - July 91 (Promotion)
Leigh:	June 92 - Sep. 92

Played for: Workington T., Oldham, Rochdale H.

STEVE CROOKS

Ryedale-York	Nov. 92 -

Played for: Hull K.R., Hull, York

PAUL DALEY

New Hunslet:	Apr. 74 - Aug. 78 (Promotion)
York:	Jan. 79 - May 79 (Promotion)
Featherstone R.:	May 79 - Jan. 81 (Div. 2 champs)
Hunslet:	Apr. 81 - Nov. 85 (Promotion)
Featherstone R.:	Nov. 86 - Apr. 87
Batley:	July 87 - Apr. 90
Hunslet:	May 90 -

Played for: Halifax, Bradford N., Hull K.R., Hunslet

JACKIE DAVIDSON

Workington T.:	Apr. 85 - Jan. 86
Whitehaven:	May 91 - June 92
Cumbria:	1985-86

Played for: Whitehaven

JOHN DORAHY (Australian)

Halifax:	June 89 - Aug. 90 (Regal Trophy BF)
Wigan:	June 93 -

Played for: Leigh, Hull K.R., Halifax

BOB ECCLES

Chorley B.:	May 90 - Sep. 91
Blackpool G.:	Nov. 92 - Jan. 93

Played for: Warrington, Springfield B./Chorley B., Trafford B.

GEORGE FAIRBAIRN

Wigan:	Apr. 80 - May 81 (Promotion)
Hull K.R.:	May 91 -

Played for: Wigan, Hull K.R.

TONY FISHER

Bramley:	Nov. 87 - Feb. 89
Keighley:	June 90 - Sep. 91
Doncaster:	Nov. 92 -

Played for: Bradford N., Leeds, Castleford

DEREK FOSTER

Ryedale-York:	July 91 - Nov. 92

Played for: Castleford, York

PETER FOX

Featherstone R.:	Jan. 71 - May 74 (RL Cup winners & BF)
Wakefield T.:	June 74 - May 76 (Yorks. Cup BF)
Bramley:	Sep. 76 - Apr. 77 (Promotion)
Bradford N.:	Apr. 77 - May 85 (Div. 1 champs (2), Yorks. Cup winners & BF (2), Premier winners & BF (2), John Player winners)
Leeds:	May 85 - Dec. 86
Featherstone R.:	May 87 - Oct. 91 (Promotion, Div. 2 Premier BF, Yorks. Cup BF)
Bradford N.:	Oct. 91 - (Regal Trophy BF)
England:	1977 (2 matches)
Great Britain:	1978 (3 Tests v. Australia)
Yorkshire:	1985-86 to 1991-92

Played for: Featherstone R., Batley, Hull K.R., Wakefield T.

PAUL GAMBLE

Blackpool G.:	Feb. 93 -

Played for: Blackpool B.

Runners-up at Wembley and fourth in the League, a debutant season's achievement for Widnes coach Phil Larder.

BILL GARDNER (Australian)
Sheffield E.:   May 93 -

STAN GITTINS
Blackpool B./
Springfield B.:   Nov. 85 - June 88
Chorley: June 89 - Apr. 90
Rochdale H.:   Apr. 91 - Jan. 93 (Lancs. Cup BF)
Played for: Batley, Swinton, Chorley

TONY GORDON (New Zealander)
London C.:   Feb. 93 -

GARY HETHERINGTON
Sheffield E.:   July 86 - May 93 (Div. 2 champs,
                Promotion (2),
                Div. 2 Premier winners,
                Divisional Premier winners,
                Yorks. Cup BF)
Played for: York, Leeds, Kent I., Sheffield E.

BRIAN JOHNSON (Australian)
Warrington: Nov. 88 - (Lancs. Cup winners,
              RL Cup BF, Regal winners)
Played for: Warrington

WILLIE JOHNSON
Highfield: Aug. 91 - Apr. 93
Played for: Dewsbury, Swinton, Highfield

JOHN JOYNER
Castleford: May 93 -
Played for: Castleford

PAUL KAVANAGH
Barrow: Feb. 91 - July 92
Played for: Barrow, Workington T.

PHIL LARDER
Widnes: May 92 - (RL Cup BF)
Great Britain
  Under-21s: 1990-91, 1991-92
Played for: Oldham, Whitehaven

DOUG LAUGHTON
Widnes: May 78 - Mar. 83
              (RL Cup winners (2) & BF,
              Lancs. Cup winners (2) & BF,
              John Player winners & BF,
              Premier winners (2), Floodlit
              Trophy winners)
Widnes: Jan. 86 - May 91 (Div. 1
              champs (2), Premier winners
              (3) & BF, Charity Shield
              winners (3), John Player BF,
              Lancs. Cup winners, World
              Club Challenge winners)
Leeds: May 91 - (Regal Trophy BF)
Lancashire: 1982-83, 1988-89, 1989-90
Played for: Wigan, St. Helens, Widnes

MIKE McCLENNAN (New Zealander)
St. Helens: Feb. 90 - (RL Cup BF, Premier
              winners & BF, Lancs.
              Cup winners & BF, Charity
              Shield winners)

STEVE MARTIN (Australian)
Featherstone R.: Sep 92 - (Div. 2 champs,
                 Divisional Premier winners)
Played for: Barrow, Leeds

JACK MELLING
Blackpool G.:   July 92 - Nov. 92
Played for: Warrington

ROGER MILLWARD
Hull K.R.:   Mar. 77 - May 91 (Div. 1
              champs (3), RL Cup winners &
              BF (2), John Player winners &
              BF (2), Premier winners (2) &
              BF, Yorks. Cup winners & BF
              (2), Floodlit Trophy winners &
              BF, Charity Shield BF, Div. 2
              champs, Div. 2 Premier BF)
Halifax: May 91 - Dec. 92
Played for: Castleford, Hull K.R.

JOHN MONIE (Australian)
Wigan: Sep. 89 - May 93

Wigan: (Div. 1 champs (4), RL Cup
winners (4), Regal winners (2),
Premier winners & BF, Lancs.
Cup winners, World Club
Challenge winners & BF, Charity
Shield winners & BF (2))

GEOFF MORRIS
Doncaster: Jan. 92 - Nov. 92
Played for: Castleford, Rochdale H., Doncaster

ALEX MURPHY
Leigh: Nov. 66 - May 71
(RL Cup winners, Lancs. Cup
winners & BF, Floodlit Trophy
winners & BF)

Warrington: May 71 - May 78 (League
Leaders, Club Merit winners,
RL Cup winners & BF,
John Player winners (2),
Floodlit Trophy BF,
Capt. Morgan winners,
Premier BF)

Salford: May 78 - Nov. 80
Leigh: Nov. 80 - June 82 (Div. 1
champs, Lancs. Cup winners)
Wigan: June 82 - Aug. 84 (John Player
winners, RL Cup BF)
Leigh: Feb. 85 - Nov. 85
St. Helens: Nov. 85 - Jan. 90 (RL Cup BF
(2), John Player winners,
Premier BF)
Leigh: Mar. 90 - Aug. 91
Huddersfield: Sep. 91 - (Div. 3 champs)
Lancashire: 1973-74 to 1977-78 Champions
(2); 1985-86 to 1987-88
England: 1975 (including World
Championship (European
Champions))
Played for: St. Helens, Leigh, Warrington

MIKE PEERS
Swinton: June 86 - Oct. 87 (Promotion,
Div. 2 Premier winners)
Springfield B./
Chorley B./
Trafford B.: Aug. 87 - May 91
Blackpool G.: Jan. 93 - Feb. 93
Highfield: Apr. 93 -
Played for: Warrington, Swinton

DENIS RAMSDALE
Barrow: May 93 -
Played for: Wigan

PETER REGAN (Australian)
Rochdale H.: Jan. 93 -

MALCOLM REILLY
Castleford: Dec. 74 - May 87
(RL Cup winners, John Player
winners, Premier BF, Yorks. Cup
winners (3) & BF (2), Charity
Shield BF, Floodlit Trophy
winners)
Leeds: Aug. 88 - Sep. 89
(Yorks. Cup winners)
Halifax: Jan. 93 -
Great Britain: Jan. 87 -
Under-21s: 1986-87, 1987-88, 1989-90,
1991-92, 1992-93
Played for: Castleford

PETER ROE
Keighley: Sep. 85 - July 86
Halifax: Aug. 90 - May 91 (Promotion,
Div. 2 Premier BF)
Keighley C.: Sep. 91 - (Div. 3 champs)
Played for: Keighley, Bradford N., York, Hunslet

DAVE SAMPSON
Castleford: Apr. 87 - Apr. 88 (Yorks. Cup
BF)
Doncaster: May 89 - Jan. 92
Nottingham C.: May 92 - Oct. 92
Played for: Wakefield T., Bramley, Castleford

ROYCE SIMMONS (Australian)
Hull: May 92 -

STEVE SIMMS (Australian)
Leigh: Nov. 92 -

KURT SORENSEN (New Zealander)
Whitehaven: May 93 -
Played for: Widnes, Wigan

ROSS STRUDWICK (Australian)
Halifax: Aug. 88 - Feb. 89
Fulham/
London C.: June 89 - Feb. 93

KEVIN TAMATI (New Zealander)
Salford: Oct. 89 -(Lancs. Cup BF, Div.
2 champs, Div. 2 Premier
winners)
Played for: Widnes, Warrington, Salford

JOHN TAYLOR
Chorley B.: Sep. 91 - Jan. 93
Played for: Salford, Leigh, Widnes

DAVID TOPLISS
Wakefield T.:   May 87 - (Promotion, Yorks.
                   Cup winners & BF)
GB Under-21s: 1988-89
Played for: Wakefield T., Hull, Oldham

PETER TUNKS (Australian)
Oldham: Apr. 91 - (Promotion, Div. 2
                   Premier BF)
Played for: Leeds, Salford, Sheffield E.

DARRYL VAN DE VELDE (Australian)
Castleford: July 88 - May 93 (Yorks. Cup
                   winners (2) & BF, Challenge Cup
                   BF)

PETER WALSH (Australian)
Workington T.:   Apr. 92 - (Divisional Premier BF)
Played for: Oldham

DAVID WARD
Hunslet: July 86 - Apr. 88 (Div. 2
                   champs, Div. 2 Premier BF)
Hunslet: Jan. 89 - May 89
Leeds: Sep. 89 - May 91
Batley: May 91 -
Played for: Leeds, Workington T.

GEOFF WORRALL
Barrow: July 92 - Apr. 93
Played for: Barrow, Huyton

The old and the new . . . Castleford coach Darryl Van de Velde (left) and, after a five-year stay, his successor, ex-Test centre John Joyner.

REPRESENTATIVE REGISTER

The following is a list of international and county coaches since 1974-75.

GREAT BRITAIN

Jim Challinor	Dec. 71 - Aug. 74
	(Inc. tours)
David Watkins	1977 World Championship
Peter Fox	1978
Eric Ashton	1979 tour
Johnny Whiteley	Aug. 80 - Nov. 82
Frank Myler	Dec. 82 - Aug. 84
	(Inc. tour)
Maurice Bamford	Oct. 84 - Dec. 86
Malcolm Reilly	Jan. 87 -
	(Inc. tours)

ENGLAND

Alex Murphy	Jan. 75 - Nov. 75
	(Inc. World Championship tour)
Peter Fox	1976-77
Frank Myler	1977-78
Eric Ashton	1978-79 & 1979-80
Johnny Whiteley	1980-81 & 1981-82
Reg Parker	1984-85
(Mgr)	
Malcolm Reilly	1992-93

WALES

Les Pearce	Jan. 75 - Nov. 75
	(Inc. World Championship tour)
David Watkins Bill Francis	} 1976-77
Kel Coslett Bill Francis	} 1977-78
Kel Coslett	1978-79 to 1981-82
David Watkins	1982-83, 1984-85
Clive Griffiths	1991-92, 1992-93

GREAT BRITAIN UNDER-24s

Johnny Whiteley	1976-82
Frank Myler	1983-84

GREAT BRITAIN UNDER-21s

Maurice Bamford	Oct. 84 - Dec. 86
Malcolm Reilly	1986-87, 1987-88, 1989-90, 1991-92, 1992-93
David Topliss	1988-89
Phil Larder	1990-91, 1991-92

CUMBRIA

Ike Southward	1975-76
Frank Foster	1976-77 to 1977-78
Sol Roper	1978-79
Frank Foster	1979-80
Phil Kitchin	1980-81 to 1981-82
Frank Foster	1982-83
Jackie Davidson	1985-86
Phil Kitchin	1986-87 to 1991-92
Gordon Cottier	1992-93

LANCASHIRE

Alex Murphy	1973-74 to 1977-78
Eric Ashton	1978-79 to 1979-80
Tom Grainey	1980-81 to 1981-82
Doug Laughton	1982-83
Alex Murphy	1985-86 to 1987-88
Doug Laughton	1988-89 to 1989-90
Ray Ashton	1991-92

YORKSHIRE

Johnny Whiteley	1970-71 to 1979-80
Arthur Keegan	1980-81
Johnny Whiteley	1981-82 to 1982-83
Peter Fox	1985-86 to 1991-92

OTHER NATIONALITIES

Dave Cox	1974-75 to 1975-76

Tom Van Vollenhoven, holder of the St. Helens records for most tries in a match, season and career.

SOUTH AFRICA

The re-emergence of Rugby League in South Africa took a big step forward with their hosting of a three-match tour by Russia (C.I.S.) in 1992, including two international matches.

On the domestic front, clubs playing regularly were South Africa Barbarians, Cape Town Coasters, Durban, Johannesburg Nomads, Port Elizabeth, Pretoria Bulls, Centurians (Pretoria), Longdale Lions (Johannesburg), Nomads (Johannesburg) and West Rand Unicorns.

The first competitive match under the new South African RFL took place on 21 November 1991 when Pretoria Bulls beat Johannesburg Nomads 33-18.

Hopes are high that the latest venture will be more successful than previous attempts to establish the game in South Africa.

The first significant move to get Rugby League started there came in 1957 when local promoter Ludwig Japhet discussed the possibility with Bill Fallowfield, the British League Secretary.

It was agreed that Great Britain and France would play exhibition matches on their way home from the 1957 World Cup in Australia.

But the matches were farcical high-scoring matches which did nothing to enhance the game's reputation. Britain won the matches 61-41, 32-11 and 69-11 with Lewis Jones totalling 73 points from 29 goals and five tries. These matches do not count towards scoring records.

The attendances dwindled from 13,000 to 6,000, with many spectators streaming from the grounds long before the finish.

A far more serious attempt to establish Rugby League in South Africa followed four years later.

Then, two organisations were set up — Rugby League South Africa and the National League. Unfortunately, the divided efforts were counter-productive and weakened the fight against strong Rugby Union opposition.

But, for a while, the prospects looked promising and the National League invited Wakefield Trinity to make a six-match tour in July 1962. Including four guest South Africans from other English clubs, Wakefield won all their six matches by wide margins. These matches also do not count towards official records.

Rugby League South Africa then hosted a brief tour by a Great Britain squad returning from Australasia but the matches against representative sides were again lacking in competitive spirit with the tourists winning 49-30, 39-33 and 45-23.

However, the matches were given official tour status and Neil Fox boosted his record career total with 50 points.

Colin Hutton, Britain's trainer, came out of retirement to assist the injury-hit squad and scored four tries in one substitute appearance.

Attendances for the tour games were reasonably encouraging with about 10,000 at Pretoria and Johannesburg, but only 3,000 at Durban.

Despite problems on the home front, a bold step was taken to send a tour squad to Australia and New Zealand.

Captained by Dawie Ackerman, a former Springbok Rugby Union international, the squad included players who had played for English Rugby League clubs — Alan Skene, Oupa Coetzer and Colin Greenwood (Wakefield T.), Fred Griffiths (Wigan) and Johnny Gaydon (Widnes).

Although they won only four of their 13 matches and were well beaten in two international matches against Australia, the tourists scored a remarkable 4-3 win over New Zealand.

But that was to be the height of the 1960s venture and players began to drift back to the 15-a-side code when the South Africa Rugby Union authorities granted an amnesty to those who had switched codes.

They included several former Springbok RU internationals, among them Martin Pelser, Dawie Ackerman, Natie Rens, Hennie Van Zyl, Mannetjie Gericke and Chris Bezuidenhout.

The difficulty in obtaining grounds because of RU opposition also proved to be a major stumbling block and Rugby League faded away.

BRITISH XIII v. FRENCH XIII 1957

20 July. At Willowmore Park, Benoni. Attendance 13,000
British XIII won 61-41.
British XIII: G. Moses; G. Gunney, L. Jones (3t, 11g), E. Ashton (2t), M. Sullivan (3t); A. Rhodes (3t), J. Stevenson; A. Prescott (Capt), T. Harris, S. Little, J. Grundy (1t), J. Whiteley (1t), D. Turner.

24 July. At Kingsmead, Durban. Attendance 8,000
British XIII won 32-11.
British XIII: G. Moses; G. Gunney, L. Jones (6g), E. Ashton (2t), M. Sullivan (2t); A. Rhodes (1t), J. Stevenson; A. Prescott (Capt), T. Harris, T. McKinney, S. Little (1t), J. Grundy, D. Turner (1g).

27 July. At Jan Smuts Ground, East London. Attendance 6,000
British XIII won 69-11.
British XIII: G. Moses (1t); G. Gunney (2t), L. Jones (2t, 12g), E. Ashton, M. Sullivan (1t); A. Rhodes (3t), J. Stevenson (1t); A. Prescott (Capt), T. Harris (1t), T. McKinney (1t), S. Little, J. Grundy, D. Turner (3t).

GREAT BRITAIN TOUR OF SOUTH AFRICA 1962

All matches against Rugby League South Africa.

23 August. At Pretoria. Attendance 10,000
Great Britain won 49-30.
Great Britain: G. Cooper (1t); F. Carlton (1t), P. Small (2t), N. Fox (2t, 8g), M. Sullivan; D. Bolton, H. Poynton; J. Wilkinson, J. Shaw, J. Taylor (1t), L. Gilfedder (1t), R. Huddart (2t), D. Turner. Sub: E. Fraser (1t).

25 August. At Durban. Attendance 3,000
Great Britain won 39-33.
Great Britain: E. Fraser; I. Southward, P. Small (1t), N. Fox (1t, 6g), M. Sullivan (2t); D. Bolton, H. Poynton; J. Wilkinson, J. Shaw, K. Noble, L. Gilfedder, R. Huddart (1t), D. Turner. Sub: C. Hutton (4t).

31 August. At Johannesburg. Attendance 10,000
Great Britain won 45-23.
Great Britain: E. Fraser; P. Small, G. Cooper (3t), N. Fox (1t, 5g), M. Sullivan (3t); D. Bolton (1t), H. Poynton (1t); J. Wilkinson, J. Shaw, J. Taylor, L. Gilfedder (2t, 1g), R. Huddart, D. Turner.

Centre Alan Skene, scorer of 69 tries in 136 games for Wakefield Trinity.

Winger Jan Prinsloo, who turned professional in 1958 and served St. Helens and Wakefield Trinity.

SOUTH AFRICAN RUGBY UNION INTERNATIONALS WHO PLAYED FOR ENGLISH CLUBS

TOMMY GENTLES
Six matches for South Africa RU. Scrum half. Signed for Wigan and had his debut against Salford on Christmas Day 1958, but made only six more appearances. Joined Leeds in January 1960 and never played in the first team. At 5ft 3in was one of the smallest to play senior rugby.

COLIN GREENWOOD
One match for South Africa RU. Centre. Signed for Wakefield Trinity in June 1961 and went on to make 75 appearances, scoring 32 tries. Was on the right wing when Wakefield won the Challenge Cup at Wembley in 1963. Toured Australia and New Zealand with the 1963 South Africa RL squad.

ARTHUR LARARD
Two matches for South Africa RU. Half back. Born at Hull in 1877 and went to South Africa at 17. Signed for Huddersfield in September 1901 and made 100 appearances, mostly in the centre, scoring 14 tries. Captain of Huddersfield in his last season of 1904-05.

ROB LOUW
Nineteen matches for South Africa RU. Forward. The most-capped South African to play Rugby League in England. Signed for Wigan, along with fellow Springbok Ray Mordt, in December 1985 for a reported £75,000 the pair. At 30, Louw had left it too late to make an impact and made only 30 appearances, including 14 as substitute, scoring four tries. He was a non-playing substitute for Wigan's 1986-87 John Player Special Trophy final victory and made a substitute appearance in the Lancashire Cup final win that season.

RAY MORDT
Eighteen matches for South Africa RU. Wing. Signed for Wigan, along with fellow Springbok Rob Louw, in December 1985 for a reported £75,000 the pair. Gained a Cup-winner's medal in only his second match — the John Player Special Trophy final defeat of Hull K.R. With 17 tries in only 25 appearances, including four as substitute, showed a lot of promise but was hampered by a knee injury after only five matches.

CHARLIE NIMB
One match for South Africa RU. Stand off. Signed by Hull in October 1962, having switched codes with Johannesburg City in the newly formed South

African Rugby League. Never looked like making the grade with Hull and played only 26 matches, scoring one try and 19 goals.

JAN PRINSLOO
Two matches for South Africa RU. Winger. Signed for St. Helens in October 1958 and was an immediate success. Scored two tries on his debut and finished with 76 in 91 matches. Moved to Wakefield Trinity in January 1961 for £9,000. Scored 45 tries in 48 matches for Wakefield.

Threequarter Wilf Rosenberg, serving Leeds and Hull with 115 tries in a 168-match career.

WILF ROSENBERG
Five matches for South Africa RU. Centre. Signed for Leeds in February 1959. Made little initial impact at centre but became an outstanding winger. His 44 tries in 1960-61 is the best Leeds total for more than 50 years. Finished with 73 in 81 appearances. Transferred to Hull in November 1961 for £5,750. Scored two tries on his debut with future Great Britain captain Clive Sullivan grabbing a hat-trick on the other wing as an unnamed trialist in his first match. Rosenberg scored 42 tries in 87 matches for Hull.

ALAN SKENE
One match for South Africa RU. Wing. Signed for Wakefield Trinity and made his debut on Christmas Day 1958. Formed a brilliant centre partnership with Neil Fox. Gained winner's medals on his two Challenge Cup final appearances at Wembley of 1960, when he scored two tries, and 1962. Scored 69 tries in 136 matches for Trinity. Toured Australia and New Zealand with the 1963 South African RL squad. Also played club rugby in Australia.

ADRIAN VAN HEERDEN
Two matches for South Africa RU. Winger. Signed for Wigan in October 1923. Gained a Challenge Cup winner's medal in his first season and folklore status with a remarkable try when it is claimed he rounded a policeman's horse at the packed Rochdale Hornets ground to touch down in the defeat of Oldham. Scored 107 tries in 127 matches for Wigan. Became a great favourite at Wigan before moving to Leigh in 1927, where he played only 14 matches, scoring two tries.

George Van Rooyen, a 1922 debutant in Hull K.R.'s first game at the old Craven Park ground.

GEORGE VAN ROOYEN
Two matches for South Africa RU. Forward. Signed for Hull Kingston Rovers and made his debut in their first match at the old Craven Park ground on 2 September 1922. After being involved in a dispute over pay and living conditions, transferred to Wigan in November 1923. Won a Challenge Cup winner's medal in his first season. Totalled 178 appearances for Wigan, scoring 26 tries in five successful years. Aged 37, was given a free transfer to Widnes in 1929. At the end of his first season was the only non-local player in the Widnes side which gained a shock 1930 Challenge Cup final win over St. Helens at Wembley. Made 98 appearances, scoring four tries, for Widnes before retiring in 1933 at 41.

TOM VAN VOLLENHOVEN
Seven matches for South Africa RU. Centre/winger. A sensational signing for St. Helens in October 1957 for a then substantial £7,230. Made a tryscoring debut at home to Leeds on 26 October before a crowd of 23,000 and went on to become one of the greatest wingers in the game's history. Headed the tryscoring chart three times with 62, 54 and 59. Holds club records of most tries in a match (six) achieved twice; in a season (62) and career (392), plus three representative match touchdowns. They included

memorable touchdowns at Wembley in 1961 and the 1959 Championship final at Bradford. Received a second Wembley winner's medal in 1966. Later became captain and totalled 409 appearances for St. Helens. Retired at the end of 1967-68 after receiving a then record £2,800 testimonial cheque.

OTHER NOTABLE SOUTH AFRICANS WITH BRITISH CLUBS
Many more South Africans have played for British clubs, the boom period being in the 1960s when over 50 were signed with varying success. In 1992-93 Jamie Bloem played several matches for Oldham after one trial game with Castleford. A former RU player he played for the South Africa RL against Russia. Andre Stoop, a South African-born Namibia RU international, played for Wigan.

The following is a list of other South Africans who made notable contributions to British Rugby League:

Winger David Barends, the only South African to play for Great Britain.

DAVID BARENDS
Winger. Played for South Africa Coloured National RU side. Signed for Wakefield Trinity in November 1970. Transferred to York in August 1973 and moved to Bradford Northern in October 1977. Became the only South African to play for Great Britain when he went on the 1979 tour of Australia and New Zealand, playing in two Tests. Finished his career with a brief spell at Featherstone Rovers after signing in September 1983.

OUPA COETZER
Winger. Played top-class Rugby Union before joining the new South African Rugby League with Johannesburg Celtic. Signed for Wakefield Trinity in January 1963 after trials and impressing against them on their 1962 tour. Scored two tries in the 1963 Wembley victory. His last match for Wakefield was the 1968

Wembley "watersplash" final when they lost to Leeds. Member of the 1963 South Africa RL tour squad to Australia and New Zealand.

FRED GRIFFITHS

Full back. Born in Rhodesia but became a South Africa RU trialist. Nicknamed "Poensie", pronounced "Punchie". Signed for Wigan in December 1957 and had five outstanding years. Until 1992-93 held club records of most goals, 176, and points, 394, in a season in 1958-59 when he finished at top of the British points chart. Had a career total of 161 appearances, scoring 1,455 points from 663 goals and 43 tries. Kicked six goals in Wigan's 1959 Wembley victory over Hull and three when they lost to St. Helens two years later. Emigrated to Australia in 1963 and became captain-coach of North Sydney. A member of the 1963 South Africa tour squad to Australia and New Zealand.

Len Killeen with the 1966 Lance Todd Trophy.

LEN KILLEEN

Winger. In line for a Springbok tour of Britain when he signed for St. Helens in May 1962. Had five outstanding seasons, making 187 appearances for St. Helens and totalling 1,161 points from 408 goals and 115 tries. Won the Lance Todd Trophy when he scored five goals and a try in the 21-2 defeat of Wigan at Wembley in 1966. Credited with the longest goal ever scored at Wembley with a 65-yard penalty eight yards from the touchline. The only player to finish at the top of all three scoring charts with 32 tries, 120 goals and 336 points in 1965-66. Went to Australia and still holds the Balmain record of 207 points in a season.

GREEN VIGO

Winger. Played for the South African National Coloured RU side and was being tipped to become the first coloured player to appear for the Springboks when Wigan signed him in July 1973. A great personality, equalled the then club record of seven tries against St. Helens in 1976. Scored 86 tries and a goal in 168 appearances for Wigan. Played for Other Nationalities in the County Championship. Moved to Swinton in 1980 and to Oldham a year later before fading out of the game.

Two Wembley appearances for Oupa Coetzer.

SOUTH AFRICANS AT WEMBLEY

The following South Africans have played in the Rugby League Challenge Cup final at Wembley, W-Won, L-Lost:

Oupa Coetzer (Wakefield T: 1963W, 1968L)
Colin Greenwood (Wakefield T: 1963W)
Fred Griffiths (Wigan: 1959W, 1961L)
Len Killeen (St. Helens: 1966W)
Jack Pansegrouw (Halifax: 1949L)
Alan Skene (Wakefield T: 1960W, 1962W)
George Van Rooyen (Widnes: 1930W)
Tom Van Vollenhoven (St. Helens: 1961W, 1966W)

WAKEFIELD TRINITY TOUR OF SOUTH AFRICA 1962

Wakefield were without five players who were with Great Britain's squad in Australasia and they included the following South Africans from British clubs: Fred Griffiths (Wigan), Tom Van Vollenhoven (St. Helens), Wilf

Rosenberg (Hull) and Eddie Brophy (Leigh).

Trinity also had their own South African signings in the squad — Alan Skene, Jan Prinsloo and Colin Greenwood. Skene captained the squad in the absence of Derek Turner, who was with the British Lions.

The tour led to Wakefield signing another top class South African — Oupa Coetzer, who played against them for Johannesburg Celtic and later joined Trinity after trials.

Wakefield's squad: Alan Skene, Fred Smith, Jan Prinsloo, Ken Hirst, Colin Greenwood, Keith Rollin, Ken Holliday, Dennis Williamson, Milan Kosanovic, Geoff Oakes, Brian Briggs, Alan Firth, Don Vines, Fred Griffiths (Wigan), Tom Van Vollenhoven (St. Helens), Wilf Rosenberg (Hull), Eddie Brophy (Leigh). Coach: Ken Traill.

Featherstone referee Laurie Gant accompanied the party and took charge of matches.

Date	Result	Score	Opposition	Venue
June 30	W	52-6	Johannesburg Celtic	Milner Park, Johannesburg
July 3	W	42-15	Johannesburg Vikings	Rand Stadium, Johannesburg
July 6	W	48-9	Bloemfontein Aquilas	Springbok Park, Bloemfontein
July 9	W	59-3	South African XIII	Kingsmead, Durban
July 14	W	38-25	South African XIII	Willowmore Park, Benoni
July 17	W	42-8	South African XIII	Pretoria

SOUTH AFRICA TOUR OF AUSTRALIA AND NEW ZEALAND 1963

Result	Score	Opposition	Venue	Attendance
W	20-10	Northern N.S.W.	Tamworth	5,750
W	41-2	Monaro	Canberra	3,500
L	5-49	Sydney	Sydney	18,219
L	16-32	Queensland	Brisbane	6,752
L	6-34	AUSTRALIA	Brisbane	10,210
L	21-30	South Queensland	Brisbane	2,187
L	21-54	AUSTRALIA	Sydney	16,995
L	17-27	Newcastle	Newcastle	7,634
L	18-39	Parramatta	Sydney	5,372

IN NEW ZEALAND

W	21-12	Wellington	Wellington	
L	8-12	South Island	Christchurch	
L	4-10	Auckland	Auckland	
W	4-3	NEW ZEALAND	Auckland	

TOUR SUMMARY

	P	W	L	F	A
In Australia	9	2	7	165	277
In New Zealand	4	2	2	37	37
Totals	13	4	9	202	314

Tour squad: D. Ackerman (capt), H. Bennett, O. Coetzer, B. Erazmus, F. Gericke, C. Greenwood, F. Griffiths, O. Odendaal, O. Oosthuizan, B. Overholzer, R. Peacock, K. Pelser, M. Pelser, J. Pieterse, N. Rens, A. Skene, G. Smit, G. van Dyl, W. Vermaas, J. Verwey, G. de Waal.

Australians G. Wilson (Newtown) and F. Anderson (Canterbury-Bankstown) were loaned to South Africa for the New Zealand tour.

Smith was the top scorer with 23 goals, two tries and 52 points. De Waal was top tryscorer with six and Pieterse made the most appearances with 11.

THE C.I.S. TOUR OF SOUTH AFRICA 1992

Date	Result	Score	Opposition	Venue	Attendance
13 Nov.	W	30-26	**SOUTH AFRICA**	Johannesburg	2,000

South Africa:
Bloem (3g); Johnson, J. Assor (1t), Mahoney (2t), Cupido; Steemag (1t), Tate; Van Dyke, Webb, Mulder, Jacobs, P. Assor, Willard. Subs: Scholtz, Coopman, Duvenhage, Jordaan, Peterson (1t).
C.I.S:
Schlimmer; Savihin, Piskunov, Vinohodov (1t, 3g), Xramchenko (3t); Zotov, Olar (1t); Bolonkin, Smirnov, Romanov, Ermolaev, Sokolov, Taran (1t).
Subs: Not available.
Referee: B. Haslam (South Africa)

Date	Result	Score	Opposition	Venue	Attendance
18 Nov.	L	12-22	**West Province**	Cape Town	1,500

T: Nechaev (2)
G: Vinohodov (2)

Date	Result	Score	Opposition	Venue	Attendance
20 Nov.	W	22-19	**SOUTH AFRICA**	Pretoria	3,000

South Africa:
Bloem (3g, 1dg); Johnson (1t), J. Assor, Mahoney, Jordaan; Steemag, Scholtz; Van Dyke, Webb, Mulder, P. Assor (2t), Willard, Jacobs.
Subs: Peterson, Tate, McHugh, Duvenhage, Tran.
C.I.S:
Schlimmer; Savihin, Piskunov, Vinohodov, Xramchenko (1t); Zotov, Olar (3g); Bolonkin, Smirnov (1t), Romanov, Ermolaev, Glotikov, Taran.
Subs: Orlenko, Dunalkin, Kiriakov (1t), Sokolov (1t).
Referee: B. Haslam (South Africa)

TOUR SUMMARY

P	W	L	F	A
3	2	1	64	67

TOUR REGISTER

Captain: Andrei Olar
Managers: Edgard Tatourian, Boris Borkov
Coach: Eugniy Klebanov

Player	Club	App	Sub	T	G	Pts
BOLONKIN, Sergy	Red Arrows, Moscow	2	1	—	—	—
DUNALKIN, Andrei	Red Arrows, Moscow	—	1	—	—	—
ERMOLAEV, Andrei	Sheela, Kazan	3	—	—	—	—
GAVRILIN, Igor	Red Arrows, Moscow	1	—	—	—	—
GLOTIKOV, Andrei	Minkas, Moscow	2	—	—	—	—
KIRIAKOV, Leonid	Magicians, Moscow	1	1	1	—	4
NECHAEV, Igor	Red Arrows, Moscow	1	—	2	—	8
OLAR, Andrei	Tiraspol	3	—	1	3	10
ORLENKO, Sergei		—	2	—	—	—
PISKONOV, Mikhail	Tiraspol	3	—	—	—	—
ROMANOV, Valeri	Minkas, Moscow	2	—	—	—	—
SAVIHIN, Valeri	Minkas, Moscow	2	—	—	—	—
SCHLIMMER, Dimitri	Red Arrows, Moscow	3	—	—	—	—
SHARKOV, Mikhail	Red Arrows, Moscow	1	—	—	—	—
SMIRNOV, Viktor		3	—	1	—	4
SOKOLOV, Andrei	Red Arrows, Moscow	2	1	1	—	4
TARAN, Andrei		2	—	1	—	4
VINOHODOV, Dimitri	Red Arrows, Moscow	2	1	1	5	14
XRAMCHENKO, Maxim	Magicians, Moscow	3	—	4	—	16
ZOTOV, Oleg	Magicians, Moscow	3	—	—	—	—

Utility back Dave Watson, scorer of six tries in six appearances on the 1989 Kiwi tour of Britain.

NEW ZEALAND

NEW ZEALAND

The following is a list of Test matches involving New Zealand. For matches against Great Britain see the GREAT BRITAIN section.

New Zealand v. Australia Tests

Date	Result	Score	Venue
9 May 1908	W	11-10	Sydney
30 May 1908	W	24-12	Brisbane
6 Jun. 1908	L	9-14	Sydney
12 Jun. 1909	W	19-11	Sydney
26 Jun. 1909	L	5-10	Brisbane
3 Jul. 1909	L	5-25	Sydney
23 Aug. 1919	L	21-44	Wellington
30 Aug. 1919	W	26-10	Christchurch
6 Sep. 1919	L	23-34	Auckland
13 Sep. 1919	L	2-32	Auckland
28 Sep. 1935	W	22-14	Auckland
2 Oct. 1935	L	8-29	Auckland
5 Oct. 1935	L	8-31	Auckland
7 Aug. 1937	L	8-12	Auckland
14 Aug. 1937	W	16-15	Auckland
29 May 1948	W	21-19	Sydney
12 Jun. 1948	L	4-13	Brisbane
17 Sep. 1949	W	26-21	Wellington
8 Oct. 1949	L	10-13	Auckland
9 Jun. 1952	L	13-25	Sydney
28 Jun. 1952	W	49-25	Brisbane
2 Jul. 1952	W	19-9	Sydney
27 Jun. 1953	W	25-5	Christchurch
4 Jul. 1953	W	12-11	Wellington
18 Jul. 1953	L	16-18	Auckland
9 Jun. 1956	L	9-12	Sydney
23 Jun. 1956	L	2-8	Brisbane
30 Jun. 1956	L	14-31	Sydney
13 Jun. 1959	L	8-9	Sydney
27 Jun. 1959	L	10-38	Brisbane
4 Jul. 1959	W	28-12	Sydney
1 Jul. 1961	W	12-10	Auckland
8 Jul. 1961	L	8-10	Auckland
8 Jun. 1963	L	3-7	Sydney
22 Jun. 1963	W	16-13	Brisbane
29 Jun. 1963	L	0-14	Sydney
19 Jun. 1965	L	8-13	Auckland
26 Jun. 1965	W	7-5	Auckland
10 Jun. 1967	L	13-22	Sydney
1 Jul. 1967	L	22-35	Brisbane
8 Jul. 1967	L	9-13	Sydney
1 Jun. 1969	L	10-20	Auckland
7 Jun. 1969	W	18-14	Auckland
26 Jun. 1971	W	24-3	Auckland
8 Jul. 1972	L	11-36	Sydney
15 Jul. 1972	L	7-31	Brisbane
24 Jun. 1978	L	2-24	Sydney
15 Jul. 1978	L	7-38	Brisbane
22 Jul. 1978	L	16-33	Sydney
1 Jun. 1980	L	6-27	Auckland
15 Jun. 1980	L	6-15	Auckland
3 Jul. 1982	L	8-11	Brisbane
17 Jul. 1982	L	2-20	Sydney
12 Jun. 1983	L	4-16	Auckland
9 Jul. 1983	W	19-12	Brisbane
18 Jun. 1985	L	20-26	Brisbane
30 Jun. 1985	L	6-10	Auckland
★7 Jul. 1985	W	18-0	Auckland
6 Jul. 1986	L	8-22	Auckland
19 Jul. 1986	L	12-29	Sydney
★29 Jul. 1986	L	12-32	Brisbane
21 Jul. 1987	W	13-6	Brisbane
9 Jul. 1989	L	6-26	Christchurch
16 Jul. 1989	L	0-8	Rotorua
★23 Jul. 1989	L	14-22	Auckland
19 Aug. 1990	L	6-24	Wellington
3 Jul. 1991	W	24-8	Melbourne
24 Jul. 1991	L	0-44	Sydney
★31 Jul. 1991	L	12-40	Brisbane

★Also World Cup match.

	P	W	D	L	F	A
TOTALS	69	22	0	47	862	1311

New Zealand v. Australia World Cup

Date	Result	Score	Venue
7 Nov. 1954	L	15-34	Marseilles
15 Jun. 1957	L	5-25	Brisbane
1 Oct. 1960	L	15-21	Leeds
1 Jun. 1968	L	12-31	Brisbane
21 Oct. 1970	L	11-47	Wigan
1 Nov. 1972	L	5-9	Paris
1 Jun. 1975	L	8-36	Brisbane
27 Sep. 1975	L	8-24	Auckland
29 May 1977	L	12-27	Auckland
9 Oct. 1988	L	12-25	Auckland

● Tests on 7 July 1985, 29 July 1986, 23 July 1989 and 31 July 1991 World Cup matches.

New Zealand v. Australia other matches
19 Nov. 1954   L   5-18   Leigh

New Zealand v. France Tests

28 Dec. 1947	W	11-7	Paris
25 Jan. 1948	L	7-25	Bordeaux
4 Aug. 1951	W	16-15	Auckland
23 Dec. 1951	L	3-8	Paris
30 Dec. 1951	L	7-17	Bordeaux
6 Aug. 1955	L	9-19	Auckland
15 Aug. 1955	W	11-6	Auckland
8 Jan. 1956	L	7-24	Toulouse
15 Jan. 1956	W	31-22	Lyons
21 Jan. 1956	L	3-24	Paris
23 Jul. 1960	W	9-2	Auckland
6 Aug. 1960	W	9-3	Auckland
11 Nov. 1961	D	6-6	Bordeaux
18 Nov. 1961	W	23-2	Perpignan
9 Dec. 1961	D	5-5	St. Ouen
25 Jul. 1964	W	24-16	Auckland
1 Aug. 1964	W	18-8	Christchurch
15 Aug. 1964	W	10-2	Auckland
14 Nov. 1965	L	3-14	Marseilles
28 Nov. 1965	L	2-6	Perpignan
12 Dec. 1965	L	5-28	Toulouse
11 Nov. 1971	W	27-11	Perpignan
21 Nov. 1971	W	24-2	Carcassonne
28 Nov. 1971	D	3-3	Toulouse
22 Nov. 1980	L	5-6	Perpignan
7 Dec. 1980	W	11-3	Toulouse
7 Jun. 1981	W	26-3	Auckland
21 Jun. 1981	W	25-2	Auckland
23 Nov. 1985	W	22-0	Marseilles
7 Dec. 1985	W	22-0	Perpignan
19 Nov. 1989	W	16-14	Carcassonne
3 Dec. 1989	W	34-0	Carcassonne
13 Jun. 1991	W	60-6	Auckland
23 Jun. 1991	W	32-10	Christchurch

Also World Cup match.

	P	W	D	L	F	A
TOTALS	34	21	3	10	526	319

Current New Zealand coach Howie Tamati, in action on the 1985 Kiwi tour of Britain.

New Zealand v. France World Cup

30 Oct. 1954	L	13-22	Paris
17 Jun. 1957	L	10-14	Brisbane
8 Oct. 1960	W	9-0	Wigan
25 May 1968	L	10-15	Auckland
25 Oct. 1970	W	16-15	Hull
28 Oct. 1972	L	9-20	Marseilles
15 Jun. 1975	W	27-0	Christchurch
17 Oct. 1975	D	12-12	Marseilles
19 Jun. 1977	W	28-20	Auckland

● Tests on 7 December 1985, 3 December 1989 and 23 June 1991 also World Cup matches.

New Zealand v. France other matches

13 Oct. 1960	L	11-22	Paris
15 Nov. 1970	L	2-16	Carcassonne

New Zealand's 18st Maori prop Henry Maxwell off-loads in the first Test against France at Auckland in July 1960.

New Zealand v. Great Britain Tests

see GREAT BRITAIN section

New Zealand v. Great Britain World Cup

11 Nov. 1954	L	6-26	Bordeaux
25 Jun. 1957	W	29-21	Sydney
24 Sep. 1960	L	8-23	Bradford
8 Jun. 1968	L	14-38	Sydney
31 Oct. 1970	L	17-27	Swinton
4 Nov. 1972	L	19-53	Pau
12 Jun. 1977	L	12-30	Christchurch

● The Third Test in 1985 and one in 1988, 1989, 1990 were also World Cup matches.

New Zealand v. Papua New Guinea Tests

25 Jul. 1982	W	56-5	Port Moresby
2 Oct. 1983	W	60-20	Auckland
10 Aug. 1986	W	36-26	Goroka
*17 Aug. 1986	L	22-24	Port Moresby
12 Jul. 1987	W	36-22	Port Moresby
*10 Jul. 1988	W	66-14	Auckland
5 Aug. 1990	W	36-4	Goroka
*11 Aug. 1990	W	18-10	Port Moresby
*5 Jul. 1992	W	66-10	Auckland

*Also World Cup match.

New Zealand v. Papua New Guinea other matches

30 Jul. 1978	W	30-21	Port Moresby

New Zealand v. England World Cup

21 Jun. 1975	D	17-17	Auckland
25 Oct. 1975	L	12-27	Bradford

New Zealand v. England other matches

11 Jan. 1908	L	16-18	Wigan

New Zealand v. Wales World Cup

28 Jun. 1975	W	13-8	Auckland
2 Nov. 1975	L	24-25	Swansea

New Zealand v. Wales other matches

1 Jan. 1908	L	8-9	Aberdare
4 Dec. 1926	L	8-34	Pontypridd
18 Oct. 1947	W	28-20	Swansea
7 Dec. 1951	W	15-3	Bradford

New Zealand v. other international sides

23 Jan. 1952	British Empire	L	2-26	Chelsea
7 Dec. 1955	RL XIII	L	11-24	Bradford
12 Dec. 1955	RL XIII (Charity)	W	28-15	Castleford
8 Jul. 1957	Northern Hemisphere	L	31-34	Auckland
20 Sep. 1961	RL XIII	L	20-22	Manchester
10 Aug. 1963	South Africa	L	3-4	Auckland
18 Aug. 1965	Commonwealth XIII	W	15-7	Crystal Palace
5 Nov. 1980	Britain Under-24	W	18-14	Fulham
9 Oct. 1985	Britain Under-21	W	16-12	Bradford

NEW ZEALAND TEAMS

A 20-year review

The following is a compendium of New Zealand Test and World Cup teams since 1972. Only playing substitutes are included on the teamsheets.

Key: *: Captain   (WC): World Cup   t: try   g: goal   dg: drop goal

1972 Australia
Sydney: 8 July
Lost 11-36
Whittaker 1t
Orchard, P
*Christian
Williams, Dennis
Brereton
Sorensen, Dave
Stirling
Gailey
Fisher, J
Orchard, R 4g
Eade
Greengrass
Kriletich
Sub: O'Sullivan

1972 Australia
Brisbane: 15 July
Lost 7-31
Collicoat 2g
Orchard, P
*Christian
O'Sullivan
Brereton
Williams, Dennis
Dowsett
Paul
Fisher, J
Gailey
Eade 1t
Greengrass
Kriletich
Sub: Bolton

1972 France (WC)
Marseilles: 28 Oct
Lost 9-20
Whittaker
Orchard, P 2t
O'Sullivan
*Christian
Brereton 1t
Williams, Dennis
Tracey
Mohi
Burgoyne
Paul
Gailey
Gurnick
Eade
Subs: Cooksley
       Coll

1972 Australia (WC)
Paris: 1 Nov
Lost 5-9
Wilson, J 1g
Orchard, P
Brereton
*Christian
Whittaker 1t
Williams, Dennis
Tracey
Mann, Donald
Burgoyne
Gailey
Eade
Paul
Gurnick
Sub: Walker

1972 Great Britain (WC)
Pau: 4 Nov
Lost 19-53
Wilson, J 2g
Orchard, P
Brereton
*Christian
Whittaker 1t
Williams, Dennis 1t
Tracey
Mann, Donald
Burgoyne 1t
Gailey
Eade 1t
Coll 1t
Gurnick
Subs: Collicoat
       Walker

1974 Great Britain
Auckland: 27 July
Won 13-8
Collicoat 5g
Brereton
Johnsen
Kerrigan
O'Sullivan
Williams, Dennis
*Stirling 1t
Proctor
Burgoyne
Gailey
Coll
Greengrass
Eade
Sub: Robertson

1974 Great Britain
Christchurch: 4 Aug
Lost 8-17
Collicoat 4g
Brereton
O'Sullivan
Johnsen
Kerrigan
Williams, Dennis
*Stirling
Gailey
Hibbs
Greengrass
Coll
Robertson
Eade
Sub: Mann, Donald

1974 Great Britain
Auckland: 10 Aug
Lost 0-20
Collicoat
Brereton
Johnsen
O'Sullivan
Kerrigan
Williams, Dennis
*Stirling
Gailey
Hibbs
Mann, Donald
Robertson
Greengrass
Eade
Subs: Jarvis
      Gurnick

1975 Australia (WC)
Brisbane: 1 June
Lost 8-36
Collicoat 1g
Brereton
O'Sullivan
Whittaker 1t
Orchard, P
Williams, Dennis
*Stirling 1t
West
Conroy
Hibbs
Coll
Baxendale
Eade

1975 France (WC)
Christchurch: 15 June
Won 27-0
Whittaker
Orchard, P
O'Sullivan
Williams, Dennis
Munro
Jarvis 2t
*Stirling 1t
Greengrass
Conroy 1t
Sorensen, Dane 6g
Coll
Baxendale
Eade 1t
Subs: Collicoat
      Proctor

1975 England (WC)
Auckland: 21 June
Drew 17-17
Whittaker
Orchard, P 1t
O'Sullivan
Williams, Dennis 2t
Munro
Jarvis
*Stirling
Greengrass
Conroy
Sorensen, Dane 4g
Coll
Baxendale
Eade
Subs: Collicoat
      Proctor

1975 Wales (WC)
Auckland: 28 June
Won 13-8
Collicoat 5g
Orchard, P 1t
O'Sullivan
Williams, Dennis
Munro
Jarvis
*Stirling
Proctor
Conroy
Sorensen, Dane
Coll
Baxendale
Eade

1975 Australia (WC)
Auckland: 27 Sept
Lost 8-24
Collicoat 4g
Orchard, P
Matete
Williams, Dennis
Ah Kuoi
Jarvis
*Stirling
Greengrass
Conroy
Sorensen, Dane
Coll
Baxendale
Eade
Subs: Smith, J
      Sorensen, K

1975 France (WC)
Marseilles: 17 Oct
Drew 12-12
Collicoat 3g
Orchard, P
Williams, Dennis
Smith, J
Dickison
Jarvis 1t
*Stirling
Greengrass
Conroy
Proctor 1t
Coll
Baxendale
Gurnick
Sub: Gordon

1975 England (WC)
Bradford: 25 Oct
Lost 12-27
Collicoat 2g
Orchard, P
Smith, J 1t
Williams, Dennis
Dickison
Jarvis
*Stirling
Proctor
Conroy
Greengrass
Baxendale
Coll
Eade
Subs: Gordon 1t, 1g
      Gurnick

1975 Wales (WC)
Swansea: 2 Nov
Lost 24-25
Collicoat 1g
Orchard, P 1t
Ah Kuoi
*Williams, Dennis
Gordon 1t, 5g
Jarvis
Smith, J
Sorensen, Dane
Conroy
Greengrass 1t
Sorensen, K
Coll 1t
Gurnick
Subs: Proctor
      Dickison

1977 France (WC)
Auckland: 19 June
Won 28-20
O'Donnell
Fisher, K 1t
Ah Kuoi
Williams, Dennis
Whittaker
Jordan 1t, 8g
Smith, J 1t
Proctor
Rushton
Henry, Whetu
*Coll
Sorensen, K
Graham 1t

1978 Australia
Sydney: 22 July
Lost 16-33
Jordan 1t, 5g
Ah Kuoi
Filipaina
Williams, Dennis
O'Hara 1t
Smith, J
*Stirling
Bell, I
Rushton
Proctor
Prohm
Coll
Graham

1977 Australia (WC)
Auckland: 29 May
Lost 12-27
Collicoat 3g
O'Hara
Filipaina
Jordan
Fisher, K
Williams, Dennis
Smith, J 1t
Henry, Whetu
Rushton 1t
Sorensen, Dane
Sorensen, K
*Coll
Henry, Whare

1978 Australia
Sydney: 24 June
Lost 2-24
Jordan 1g
Ah Kuoi
Filipaina
Williams, Dennis
O'Hara
Smith, J
*Stirling
Baxendale
Rushton
Proctor
Coll
Taylor, G
Eade
Sub: Prohm

1979 Great Britain
Auckland: 21 July
Lost 8-16
Collicoat 1g
Uluave 1t
Leuluai
Filipaina
O'Hara
Ah Kuoi 1t
Smith, G
Broadhurst
Tamati, H
Sorensen, Dane
*West
Tamati, K
Coll

1977 Great Britain (WC)
Christchurch: 12 June
Lost 12-30
Collicoat 3g
Fisher, K 1t
Ah Kuoi
Filipaina
Whittaker 1t
Williams, Dennis
Smith, J
Proctor
Rushton
Henry, Whetu
Sorensen, K
*Coll
Henry, Whare
Sub: Graham

1978 Australia
Brisbane: 15 July
Lost 7-38
Jordan 2g
Varley
Filipaina
Williams, Dennis
O'Hara 1t
Smith, J
*Stirling
Baxendale
Rushton
Proctor
Prohm
Coll
Graham
Sub: Henry, Whetu

1979 Great Britain
Christchurch: 5 Aug
Lost 7-22
Leuluai
O'Hara
Filipaina 1t, 2g
Hudson
Uluave
Ah Kuoi
Smith, G
Broadhurst
Tamati, H
Sorensen, Dane
Tamati, K
*West
Coll

1979 Great Britain
Auckland: 11 Aug
Won 18-11
Leuluai 1t
Fisher, K 1t
Filipaina 3g
Hudson
O'Hara 1t
*Ah Kuoi
Varley
Broadhurst
Tamati, H
Tamati, K
Edkins
Coll
Graham 1t
Subs: Smith, J
     Ravlich

1980 Great Britain
Wigan: 18 Oct
Drew 14-14
O'Donnell
Fisher, K
Leuluai
Dickison
O'Hara
Ah Kuoi 1t
Smith, G 4g
Broadhurst
Rushton
Tamati, K
West
Coll 1t
*Graham
Sub: Baxendale

1980 France
Perpignan: 22 Nov
Lost 5-6
Kemble
Prohm 1t
O'Donnell
Whittaker
O'Hara
Ah Kuoi
Smith, G 1g
Broadhurst
Rushton
Tamati, K
West
Baxendale
*Graham
Subs: Dickison
     Tamati, H

1980 Australia
Auckland: 1 June
Lost 6-27
O'Donnell 3g
Fisher, K
Filipaina
Leuluai
*O'Hara
Smith, G
Varley
Broadhurst
Tamati, H
Te Ariki
Tamati, K
Edkins
Graham

1980 Great Britain
Bradford: 2 Nov
Won 12-8
O'Donnell 1t
Prohm
Whittaker
Leuluai
O'Hara 1t
Ah Kuoi
Smith, G 3g
Broadhurst
Rushton
Tamati, K
West
Coll
*Graham
Sub: Baxendale

1980 France
Toulouse: 7 Dec
Won 11-3
O'Donnell
Prohm 1t
Whittaker
Leuluai
O'Hara 1t
Ah Kuoi
Smith, G 1t, 1g
Broadhurst
Tamati, H
Tamati, K
West
Coll
*Graham

1980 Australia
Auckland: 15 June
Lost 6-15
O'Donnell 3g
Fisher, K
Filipaina
Leuluai
*O'Hara
Williams, Dennis
Smith, G
Broadhurst
Tamati, H
Tamati, K
Coll
Edkins
Graham

1980 Great Britain
Leeds: 15 Nov
Lost 2-10
O'Donnell
Prohm
Whittaker
Dickison
O'Hara
Ah Kuoi
Smith, G 1g
Broadhurst
Rushton
Tamati, K
West
Edkins
*Graham
Sub: Tamati, H

1981 France
Auckland: 7 June
Won 26-3
O'Donnell 1t
Prohm 1t
Williams, Dennis 4g
Leuluai 1t
O'Hara
Ah Kuoi
Varley 1t
Broadhurst
Rushton
Tamati, K
Coll 1t
West
*Graham 1t

1981 France
Auckland: 21 June
Won 25-2
O'Donnell
Prohm
Filipaina 5g
Leuluai 1t
O'Hara 1t
Ah Kuoi 1t
Varley
Broadhurst
Rushton
Baxendale
Coll
West
*Graham 1t
Subs: Tamati, H 1t
    Wilson, W

1982 Australia
Brisbane: 3 July
Lost 8-11
Kemble
Prohm
Filipaina
Leuluai
O'Hara
Ah Kuoi
Smith, G 4g
Broadhurst
Tamati, H
Tamati, K
West
Gall
*Graham
Sub: Whittaker

1982 Australia
Sydney: 17 July
Lost 2-20
Kemble
Prohm
Filipaina
Leuluai
O'Hara
Ah Kuoi
Smith, G 1g
Broadhurst
Tamati, H
Tamati, K
West
Gall
*Graham
Subs: Whittaker
    McGahan

1982 Papua New Guinea
Port Moresby: 25 July
Won 56-5
Leuluai 2t
Fisher, K 2t
Prohm 1t
Whittaker
O'Hara
Smith, G 9g
Friend 1t
Broadhurst
Tamati, H 1t
Tamati, K 1t
*West 1t
Gall 1t
McGahan 2t
Subs: Wright, O
    Coll 1g

1983 Australia
Auckland: 12 June
Lost 4-16
Kemble
Ropati, J
Leuluai 1t
O'Regan
Bell, D
Ah Kuoi
Smith, G
Broadhurst
Tamati, H
Sorensen, Dane
*Graham
Sorensen, K
Prohm
Subs: Varley
    West

1983 Australia
Brisbane: 9 July
Won 19-12
Wright, N 3g, 1dg
Ropati, J 1t
Leuluai 1t
Ah Kuoi
Bell, D
Smith, G
Varley
Broadhurst
Tamati, H
Sorensen, Dane
*West 1t
Sorensen, K
Prohm
Subs: O'Regan
    Bell, I

1983 Papua New Guinea
Auckland: 2 Oct
Won 60-20
Wright, N 8g
Alfeld
Bell, D 3t
O'Regan
Crequer 1t
Varley
Friend
Tinitelia
*Tamati, H
Bell, I
Wright, O 1t
Sorensen, K
McGahan 6t
Subs: Orr
    Ackland

1984 Great Britain
Auckland: 14 July
Won 12-0
Kemble
Bell, D
Leuluai 1t
*Ah Kuoi 1t
O'Hara
Filipaina 2g
Varley
Tamati, K
Tamati, H
Sorensen, Dane
Wright, O
Sorensen, K
McGahan
Sub: Friend

1984 Great Britain
Christchurch: 22 July
Won 28-12
Kemble
Bell, D 1t
Leuluai 1t
*Ah Kuoi 1t
O'Hara 2t
Filipaina 4g
Varley
Tamati, K
Tamati, H
Sorensen, Dane
Wright, O
Sorensen, K
McGahan
Subs: Friend
    Cowan

1984 Great Britain
Auckland: 28 July
Won 32-16
Kemble
Bell, D
Leuluai 2t
*Ah Kuoi
O'Hara 1t
Filipaina 6g
Varley
Tamati, K
Tamati, H
Sorensen, Dane
Wright, O
Sorensen, K
McGahan
Subs: Friend 2t
    Cowan

1985 Australia
Brisbane: 18 June
Lost 20-26
Kemble
Bell, D 1t
Prohm
Leuluai
O'Hara
Filipaina 1t, 4g
Friend
Wright, O
Tamati, H
Tamati, K
*Graham
Sorensen, K
McGahan 1t
Subs: Elia
    Cowan

1985 Australia
Auckland: 30 June
Lost 6-10
Kemble
Bell, D
Prohm
Leuluai 1t
O'Hara
Filipaina 1g
Friend
Wright, O
Tamati, H
Tamati, K
*Graham
Sorensen, K
McGahan
Subs: Ropati, J
    Cowan

1985 Australia (Also WC)
Auckland: 7 July
Won 18-0
Kemble
Bell, D
Prohm
Leuluai 1t
O'Hara
Filipaina 3g
Friend 2t
Sorensen, K
Tamati, H
Tamati, K
*Graham
Wright, O
McGahan
Subs: Ropati, J
    Cowan

1985 Great Britain
Leeds: 19 Oct
Won 24-22
Leuluai 1t
Bell, D 1t
Ah Kuoi
Prohm
O'Hara 1t
Filipaina 2g
Friend
Sorensen, K 1t
Tamati, H
Sorensen, Dane
*Graham 1t
Wright, O
McGahan
Subs: Kemble
    Tamati, K

1985 Great Britain
Wigan: 2 Nov
Lost 8-25
Kemble
Bell, D 1t
Leuluai
Prohm
O'Hara
*Filipaina 2g
Friend
Sorensen, K
Tamati, H
Sorensen, Dane
West
Stewart
McGahan
Subs: Ah Kuoi
    Cowan

1985 Great Britain (Also WC)
Elland Rd, Leeds: 9 Nov
Drew 6-6
Kemble
Williams, Darrell
Leuluai
Bell, D
O'Hara
Ah Kuoi
Friend
Tamati, K
Wallace
Sorensen, Dane 1g
*Graham 1t
Sorensen, K
Prohm
Subs: Filipaina
    McGahan

1985 France
Marseilles: 23 Nov
Won 22-0
Kemble
Williams, Darrell
Leuluai
Bell, D
O'Hara 1t
Cooper
Friend
Sorensen, Dane 2g
Wallace
Sorensen, K 2t
Wright, O
Goulding
*McGahan 1t
Subs: Ah Kuoi
    Filipaina 1g

1985 France (Also WC)
Perpignan: 7 Dec
Won 22-0
Kemble 1t
Bell, D
Leuluai
Ah Kuoi
O'Hara
Filipaina 3g
Friend
Sorensen, Dane
Wallace
Sorensen, K 1t
*McGahan 2t
Wright, O
O'Regan
Subs: Elia
    Todd

1986 Australia
Auckland: 6 July
Lost 8-22
Williams, Darrell
Ropati, J
Bell, D 1t
Leuluai
O'Hara
Filipaina 2g
Cooper
Wright, O
Wallace
Sorensen, K
*Graham
McGahan
Prohm
Subs: Elia
    O'Regan

1986 Papua New Guinea
Goroka: 10 Aug
Won 36-26
Kemble
Ropati, J 1t, 3g
Williams, Darrell
Elia 1t
O'Hara 1t
Leuluai
Freeman 1t
Shelford, A
Wallace
Brown 2t, 1g
Wright, O
*McGahan 1t
O'Regan
Subs: Crequer
    Stewart

1987 Australia
Brisbane: 21 July
Won 13-6
Williams, Darrell
Elia
Iro, K 2g
Bell, D
Mercer 1t
Cooper 1dg
Friend
Taylor, R 1t
Wallace
Shelford, A
Horo, M
Stewart
*McGahan
Subs: Freeman
    Lonergan

1986 Australia
Sydney: 19 July
Lost 12-29
Kemble
Bell, D
Ropati, J
Elia
O'Hara 1t
Filipaina 1t, 2g
Freeman
Wright, O
Harvey
Sorensen, K
*Graham
McGahan
Prohm
Sub: Cooper

1986 Papua New Guinea (Also WC)
Port Moresby: 17 Aug
Lost 22-24
Kemble
Crequer
Williams, Darrell
Ropati, J 1t
O'Hara
Cooper
Freeman
Shelford, A
Wallace 1t
Brown 1t, 3g
Wright, O
*McGahan 1t
O'Regan
Subs: Leuluai
    Stewart

1988 Papua New Guinea (Also WC)
Auckland: 10 July
Won 66-14
Williams, Darrell 1t
Horo, S 3t
*Bell, D
Iro, K 3t
Mercer 2t
Cooper
Friend
Brown 9g
Wallace 1t
Shelford, A 1t
Graham 1t
Stewart
Horo, M
Subs: Freeman
    Faimalo

1986 Australia (Also WC)
Brisbane: 29 July
Lost 12-32
Kemble
Williams, Darrell 2t
Ropati, J
Prohm
O'Hara
Filipaina 2g
Freeman
Todd
Harvey
Sorensen, K
*Graham
McGahan
O'Regan
Subs: Cooper
    Wright, O

1987 Papua New Guinea
Port Moresby: 12 July
Won 36-22
Mercer
Elia 2t
Iro, K 3t, 4g
*Bell, D 2t
Horo, S
Freeman
Friend
Taylor, R
Wallace
Todd
Shelford, A
Horo, M
Cooper
Subs: Stewart
    Lonergan

1988 Great Britain (Also WC)
Christchurch: 17 July
Won 12-10
Williams, Darrell
Horo, S
*Bell, D
Iro, K
Mercer
Cooper
Friend
Brown 2g
Wallace
Shelford, A
Graham
Stewart
Horo, M
Sub: Freeman 2t

283

1988 Australia (WC)
Auckland: 9 Oct
Lost 12-25
Mercer
Iro, T 1t
*Bell, D
Iro, K 1t
Elia
Freeman
Friend
Brown 2g
Wallace
Shelford, A
Sorensen, K
Graham
Horo, M
Subs: Cooper
Stewart

1989 Australia
Christchurch: 9 July
Lost 6-26
Williams, Darrell
Iro, T
Iro, K 1g
Kemp
Elia 1t
Cooper
Friend
Todd
Harvey
Goulding
*McGahan
Stewart
Tuuta
Sub: Freeman

1989 Australia
Rotorua: 16 July
Lost 0-8
Williams, Darrell
Iro, T
Iro, K
Kemp
Mercer
Cooper
Freeman
Todd
Mann, Duane
Goulding
*McGahan
Stewart
Tuuta
Subs: Bancroft
Horo, M

1989 Australia (Also WC)
Auckland: 23 July
Lost 14-22
Williams, Darrell
Mercer 1t
Iro, K
Kemp
Elia 1t
Shelford, K 3g
Freeman
Todd
Mann, Duane
Goulding
Horo, M
Stewart
*McGahan
Subs: Sherlock
Tuuta

1989 Great Britain
Old Trafford: 21 Oct
Won 24-16
Williams, Darrell
Iro, K 1t
Bell, D
Sherlock 2g
Mercer
Shelford, K 1t
Freeman 1t
Goulding 1t
Mann, Duane
Todd
Sorensen, K
Stewart
*McGahan 1t
Sub: Kemp

1989 Great Britain
Elland Rd, Leeds: 28 Oct
Lost 6-26
Williams, Darrell
Iro, K
Bell, D
Sherlock 1g
Mercer
Shelford, K
Freeman
Shelford, A
Mann, Duane
Todd
Sorensen, K
Stewart
*McGahan 1t
Subs: Faimalo
Kemp

1989 Great Britain (Also WC)
Wigan: 11 Nov
Lost 6-10
Kemp
Iro, K
Bell, D
Williams, Darrell
Mercer
Shelford, K 1t, 1g
Freeman
Todd
Mann, Duane
Faimalo
Sorensen, K
Stewart
*McGahan
Subs: Leota
Clark

1989 France
Carcassonne: 19 Nov
Won 16-14
Kemp
Iro, K 1t
Bell, D
Williams, Darrell
Mercer
Shelford, K 1t, 2g
Freeman 1t
Todd
Mann, Duane
Faimalo
Sorensen, K
Stewart
*McGahan
Subs: Leota
Kuiti

1989 France (Also WC)
Carcassonne: 3 Dec
Won 34-0
Kemp 1t
Watson 3t
Bell, D 1t
Williams, Darrell 1t
Mercer
Clark
Freeman
Todd
Mann, Duane
Mann, G
Kuiti 1t
Stewart
*McGahan
Subs: Sherlock 3g
Shelford, K

1990 Great Britain
Palmerston N: 24 June
Lost 10-11
Williams, Darrell
Iro, T
Iro, K 1t
Kemp
Panapa 1t
Clark
Freeman
Brown 1g
Mann, Duane
Todd
Nikau
Horo, M
*McGahan
Subs: Mann, G
     Edwards

1990 Papua New Guinea
Goroka: 5 Aug
Won 36-4
Edwards 2g
Panapa 1t
Watson
Tuimavave
Iro, T 1t
Kemp 1t
*Freeman
Brown 1t, 2g
Mann, Duane 1t
Todd
Nikau
Kuiti
Horo, M
Subs: Nixon
     Mann, G
     Lonergan 2t

1991 France
Auckland: 13 June
Won 60-6
Botica 8g
Panapa 1t
McCracken 2t
Watson
Blackmore 2t
Shelford, K 1t
*Freeman 1t
Todd 1t
Mann, Duane 1t
Brown
Koloto
Lonergan 1t
Nikau 1t
Subs: Patton
     Friend
     Mann, G
     Mercer

1990 Great Britain
Auckland: 8 July
Lost 14-16
Ridge 5g
Panapa
Iro, K
Williams, Darrell
Iro, T
Clark
Freeman
Brown
Mann, Duane
Todd
Nikau
Horo, M 1t
*McGahan
Subs: Kemp
     Lonergan

1990 Papua New Guinea (Also WC)
Port Moresby: 11 Aug
Won 18-10
Ridge 3g
Panapa 1t
Watson 1t
Tuimavave
Iro, T
Nixon
*Freeman
Brown
Mann, Duane
Todd
Nikau
Lonergan 1t
Kuiti
Subs: Edwards
     Patton
     Mann, G
     Leota

1991 France (Also WC)
Christchurch: 23 June
Won 32-10
Botica 6g
Panapa 1t
McCracken
Watson 1t
Blackmore 1t
Shelford, K 1t
*Freeman
Todd
Mann, Duane
Brown
Koloto
Lonergan
Nikau
Subs: Patton
     Friend 1t
     Mann, G
     Mercer

1990 Great Britain (Also WC)
Christchurch: 15 July
Won 21-18
Ridge 6g
Panapa
Iro, K
Williams, Darrell
Iro, T
Kemp 1t
Freeman
Brown
Mann, Duane
Todd
Nikau 1t
Horo, M
*McGahan 1dg
Subs: Edwards
     Lonergan

1990 Australia
Wellington: 19 Aug
Lost 6-24
Ridge 1g
Edwards
Williams, Darrell
Watson
Panapa 1t
Shelford, K
Freeman
Todd
Mann, Duane
Brown
Nikau
Lonergan
*McGahan

Hooker Duane Mann.

285

1991 Australia
Melbourne: 3 July
Won 24-8
Botica 4g
Blackmore 1t
McCracken 1t
Watson
Williams, J
Kemp
*Freeman
Todd
Mann, Duane
Brown
Koloto
Lonergan
Nikau 1t
Subs: Patton
     Friend 1t
     Mann, G
     Mercer

1991 Australia
Sydney: 24 July
Lost 0-44
Botica
Blackmore
McCracken
Iro, K
Williams, J
Watson
*Freeman
Todd
Mann, Duane
Brown
Koloto
Lonergan
Nikau
Subs: Patton
     Friend
     Mann, G
     Mercer

1991 Australia (Also WC)
Brisbane: 31 July
Lost 12-40
Botica 2g
Blackmore 1t
McCracken 1t
Iro, K
Watson
*Freeman
Friend
Todd
Mann, Duane
Brown
Mann, G
Mercer
Nikau
Subs: Patton
     Williams, J
     Koloto
     Faimalo

1992 Papua New Guinea (Also WC)
Auckland: 5 July
Won 66-10
Ridge 1t, 4g
Hoppe 1t
Iro, K 1t
Kemp 1t
Blackmore 3t
Clark 2t
*Freeman 1t
Stuart 1t
Mann, Duane 1t
Todd
Hill 1t
Pongia
Nikau
Subs: Halligan 3g
     Tuuta
     Ropati, T
     Woods

1992 Great Britain
Palmerston N: 12 July
Won 15-14
Ridge 2g
Hoppe
Iro, K
Kemp 1t
Blackmore 1t
Clark
*Freeman
Stuart
Mann, Duane
Todd
Hill 1g
Pongia
Tuuta
Subs: Halligan 1dg
     Ropati, T
     Woods
     Kuiti

1992 Great Britain
Auckland: 19 July
Lost 16-19
Ridge 2g
Hoppe 1t
Iro, K
Kemp
Blackmore
Clark
*Freeman 1t
Stuart
Mann, Duane
Todd 1t
Hill
Pongia
Tuuta
Subs: Halligan
     Ropati, T
     Woods
     Kuiti

Stand off Dean Clark.

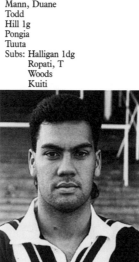

Centre Kevin Iro.

Loose forward Brendon Tuuta.

NEW ZEALAND REGISTER
1972-93

The following is an index of players who have appeared for New Zealand, toured or been members of a World Cup squad from 1972 to 1 June 1993.
Appearances refer to Test and World Cup matches only. World Cup matches are given in bold letters. Substitute appearances are in lower case letters.
Key: A — Australia, B — Britain, E — England, F — France, P — Papua New Guinea, W — Wales.

ACKLAND, John (+1)
Appearances: 1983 p
AH KUOI, Fred (26+2)
Appearances: 1975 **A,W**; 1977 **B,F**; 1978 A2; 1979 B3; 1980 B3,F2; 1981 F2; 1982 A2; 1983 A2; 1984 B3; 1985 B2b, Ff
Tours: 1978 A,P; 1980 B; 1982 A,P
World Cup: 1975, 1977
ALFELD, Robin (1)
Appearances: 1983 P

BANCROFT, Phil (+1)
Appearances: 1989 a
Tours: 1989 B
BARRY, Kevin
Tours: 1975 A
World Cup: 1975
BAXENDALE, Ray (11+2)
Appearances: 1975 **A2,F2,E2,W**; 1978 A2; 1980 b2,F; 1981 F
Tours: 1975 A; 1978 A,P; 1980 B
World Cup: 1975, 1977
BEEHRE, Les
World Cup: 1975
BELL, Dean (26)
Appearances: 1983 A2,P; 1984 B3; 1985 A3,B3,F2; 1986 A2; 1987 P,A; 1988 P,B,**A**; 1989 B3,F2
Tours: 1985 B; 1986 A,P; 1987 A,P
BELL, Ian (2+1)
Appearances: 1978 A; 1983 a,P
Tours: 1978 A,P
BLACKMORE, Richard (8)
Appearances: 1991 F2,A3; 1992 P,B2
BOLTON, Dick (+1)
Appearances: 1972 a
Tours: 1972 A
BOTICA, Frano (5)
Appearances: 1991 F2,A3

BOURNEVILLE, Mark
Tours: 1985 B
BRERETON, Maurice (24)
Appearances: 1969 A2; 1970 B3,**A,F,B**; 1971 A,B3,F3; 1972 A2,**F,A,B**; 1974 B3; 1975 **A**
Tours: 1971 B; 1972 A; 1975 A
World Cup: 1970, 1972, 1975
BROADHURST, Mark (17)
Appearances: 1979 B3; 1980 A2,B3,F2; 1981 F2; 1982 A2,P; 1983 A2
Tours: 1980 B; 1982 A,P
BROWN, Peter (16)
Appearances: 1986 A2; 1988 P,B,**A**; 1990 B3,P2,A; 1991 F2,A3
Tours: 1986 A,P; 1987 A,P
BURGOYNE, William (4)
Appearances: 1972 **F,A,B**; 1974 B
Tours: 1971 B
World Cup: 1970, 1972

CAMPBELL, Danny
Tours: 1980 1 guest app. while with Wigan
CHRISTIAN, Roy (19)
Appearances: 1969 A; 1970 B3,**A,F,B**; 1971 A,B3,F3; 1972 **F,A,B**
Tours: 1965 B; 1971 B; 1972 A
World Cup: 1970, 1972
CLARK, Dean (6+1)
Appearances: 1989 b,F; 1990 B2; 1992 P,B2
Tours: 1989 B
COLL, Tony (26+2)
Appearances: 1972 f,**B**; 1974 B2; 1975 **A2,F2,E2,W2**; 1977 **A,B,F**; 1978 A3; 1979 B3; 1980 A,B2,F; 1981 F2; 1982 p
Tours: 1975 A; 1978 A,P; 1980 B; 1982 A,P
World Cup: 1972, 1975, 1977
COLLICOAT, Warren (13+3)
Appearances: 1972 A,b; 1974 B3; 1975 **A2,fF,eE,W2**; 1977 **A,B**; 1979 B
Tours: 1972 A; 1975 A
World Cup: 1972, 1975, 1977
CONROY, Tom (8)
Appearances: 1975 **A2,F2,E2,W2**
Tours: 1975 A
World Cup: 1975
COOKSLEY, Graeme (5+2)
Appearances: 1969 A2; 1970 **A,F,B**; 1971 b; 1972 f
Tours: 1971 B
World Cup: 1970, 1972
COWAN, Ricky (+6)
Appearances: 1984 b2; 1985 a3,b
Tours: 1985 B
CREQUER, Marty (2+1)
Appearances: 1983 P; 1986 Pp
Tours: 1985 B; 1986 A,P

DICKISON, Bruce (5+1)
Appearances: 1975 **F,E,W**; 1980 B2,f
Tours: 1980 B
World Cup: 1975
DONALDSON, Glen
Tours: 1986 A,P
DOWSETT, Shane (1)
Appearances: 1972 A
Tours: 1971 B; 1972 A
DWYER, Wayne
Tours: 1982 A,P
DYER, Barrie
Tours: 1975 A
World Cup: 1975

EADE, Murray (15+1)
Appearances: 1971 b; 1972 A2,**F,A,B**; 1974 B3; 1975
    A2,F,E2,W; 1978 A
Tours: 1971 B; 1972 A; 1975 A; 1978 A,P
World Cup: 1972, 1975
EDKINS, Barry (4)
Appearances: 1979 B; 1980 A2,B
Tours: 1978 A,P; 1980 B
EDWARDS, Morvin (2+3)
Appearances: 1990 b2, Pp,A
Tours: 1989 B
ELIA, Mark (7+3)
Appearances: 1985 a,f; 1986 aA,P; 1987 P,A; 1988 **A**;
    1989 A2
Tours: 1985 B; 1986 A,P; 1987 A,P; 1989 B
EWE, David
Tours: 1989 B

FAIMALO, Esene (2+3)
Appearances: 1988 p; 1989 Bb,F; 1991 a
Tours: 1989 B
FEPULEAI, Toa
Tours: 1978 A,P
FIELD, David
Tours: 1982 A,P
FILIPAINA, Olsen (25+2)
Appearances: 1977 **A,B**; 1978 A3; 1979 B3; 1980 A2;
    1981 F; 1982 A2; 1984 B3; 1985 A3,B2b,Ff; 1986 A3
Tours: 1978 A,P; 1982 A,P; 1985 B; 1986 A,P
World Cup: 1977
FISHER, James (8)
Appearances: 1971 B3,F3; 1972 A2
Tours: 1971 B; 1972 A; 1982 A,P
FISHER, Kevin (8)
Appearances: 1977 **A,F,B**; 1979 B; 1980 A2,B; 1982 P
Tours: 1980 B; 1982 A,P
World Cup: 1977
FREEMAN, Gary (27+4)
Appearances: 1986 A2,P2; 1987 P,a; 1988 p,b,**A**;
    1989 A2a,B3,F2; 1990 B3,P2,A; 1991 F2,A3; 1992 P,B2
Tours: 1986 A,P; 1987 A,P; 1989 B

FRIEND, Clayton (17+7)
Appearances: 1982 P; 1983 P; 1984 b3; 1985 A3,B3,F2;
    1987 P,A; 1988 P,B,**A**; 1989 A; 1991 f2,Aa2
Tours: 1982 A,P; 1985 B; 1987 A,P

GAILEY, Doug (19)
Appearances: 1969 A; 1970 B3,**A,F**; 1971 B2,F3;
    1972 A2,**F,A,B**; 1974 B3
Tours: 1971 B; 1972 A
World Cup: 1970, 1972
GALL, Bruce (3)
Appearances: 1982 A2,P
Tours: 1980 B; 1982 A,P
GIBB, Glen
Tours: 1985 B
GILLESPIE, Mark
Tours: 1982 A,P
GORDON, Tony (1+2)
Appearances: 1975 f,e,**W**
World Cup: 1975
GOULDING, James (5)
Appearances: 1985 F; 1989 A3,B
Tours: 1985 B; 1986 A,P; 1989 B
GRAHAM, Mark (27+1)
Appearances: 1977 **b,F**; 1978 A2; 1979 B; 1980 A2,B3,F2;
    1981 F2; 1982 A2; 1983 A; 1985 A3,B2; 1986 A3;
    1988 P,B,**A**
Tours: 1978 A,P; 1980 B; 1982 A,P; 1985 B; 1986 A,P
World Cup: 1977
GREEN, Bernard
Tours: 1980 B
GREENGRASS, John (17+1)
Appearances: 1970 **a,F,B**; 1971 B3,F; 1972 A2; 1974 B3;
    1975 **F2,E2,A,W**
Tours: 1971 B; 1972 A
World Cup: 1970, 1975
GRIFFIN, John
Tours: 1982 A,P
GURNICK, Peter (5+2)
Appearances: 1972 **F,A,B**; 1974 b; 1975 **F,e,W**
Tours: 1975 A
World Cup: 1972, 1975

HALLIGAN, Daryl (+3)
Appearances: 1992 p,b2
HARVEY, Barry (3)
Appearances: 1986 A2; 1989 A
Tours: 1986 A, P; 1987 A,P
HENRY, Whare (2)
Appearances: 1977 **A,B**
World Cup: 1977
HENRY, Whetu (3+1)
Appearances: 1977 **A,B,F**; 1978 a
Tours: 1978 A,P
World Cup: 1977

HIBBS, John (6)
Appearances: 1969 A; 1970 B2; 1974 B2; 1975 **A**
Tours: 1975 A
World Cup: 1975
HILL, Gavin (3)
Appearances: 1992 P,B2
HOPPE, Sean (3)
Appearances: 1992 P,B2
HORO, Mark (10+1)
Appearances: 1987 P; 1987 A; 1988 P,B,**A**; 1989 Aa;
  1990 B3,P
Tours: 1987 A,P
HORO, Shane (3)
Appearances: 1987 P; 1988 P,B
Tours: 1985 B; 1987 A,P
HUDSON, Lewis (2)
Appearances: 1979 B2
Tours: 1982 A,P

IRO, Kevin (20)
Appearances: 1987 P,A; 1988 P,B,**A**; 1989 A3,B3,F;
  1990 B3; 1991 A2; 1992 P,B2
Tours: 1987, A,P; 1989 B
IRO, Tony (8)
Appearances: 1988 **A**; 1989 A2; 1990 B3,P2

JARVIS, Robert (7+1)
Appearances: 1974 b; 1975 **F2,E2,W2,A**
Tours: 1975 A
World Cup: 1975
JOHNSEN, Bill (3)
Appearances: 1974 B3
JORDAN, Chris (5)
Appearances: 1977 **A,F**; 1978 A3
Tours: 1978 A,P
World Cup: 1977

KELLS, Bill
Tours: 1980 B
KEMBLE, Gary (18+1)
Appearances: 1980 F; 1982 A2; 1983 A; 1984 B3;
  1985 A3,B2b,F2; 1986 A2,P2
Tours: 1980 B; 1982 A,P; 1986 A,P
KEMP, Tony (13+3)
Appearances: 1989 A3,Bb2,F2; 1990 B2b,P; 1991 A;
  1992 P,B2
Tours: 1989 B
KERRIGAN, Eddie (3)
Appearances: 1974 B3
KOLOTO, Emosi (4+1)
Appearances: 1991 F2, A2a
KRILETICH, Tony (17)
Appearances: 1969 A2; 1970 B3,**A,F,B**; 1971 A,B3,F3;
  1972 A2
Tours: 1971 B; 1972 A
World Cup: 1970

KUITI, Mike (3+3)
Appearances: 1989 Ff; 1990 P2; 1992 b2
Tours: 1989 B

LAJPOLD, George
Tours: 1987 A,P
LEOTA, Francis (+3)
Appearances: 1989 b,f; 1990 p
Tours: 1989 B
LEULUAI, James (28+1)
Appearances: 1979 B3; 1980 A2,B2,F; 1981 F2;
  1982 A2,P; 1983 A2; 1984 B3;
  1985 A3,B3,F2; 1986 A,Pp
Tours: 1978 A,P; 1980 B; 1982 A,P; 1986 A,P
LIAVAA, Josh
Tours: 1975 A
World Cup: 1975
LONERGAN, Dean (6+5)
Appearances: 1987 p,a; 1990 b2,Pp,A; 1991 F2,A2
Tours: 1986 A,P; 1987 A,P

McCRACKEN, Jarrod (5)
Appearances: 1991 F2,A3
McGAHAN, Hugh (30+2)
Appearances: 1982 a,P; 1983 P; 1984 B3; 1985 A3,B2b,F2;
  1986 A3,P2; 1987 A; 1989 A3,B3,F2; 1990 B3,A
Tours: 1982 A,P; 1985 B; 1986 A,P; 1987 A,P; 1989 B
McGREGOR, Steve
Tours: 1978 A,P
MANN, Donald (3+1)
Appearances: 1972 **A,B**; 1974 Bb
Tours: 1971 B
World Cup: 1972
MANN, Duane (21)
Appearances: 1989 A2,B3,F2; 1990 B3,P2,A; 1991 F2,A3;
  1992 P,B2
Tours: 1989 B
MANN, George (1+7)
Appearances: 1990 b,p2; 1991 f2,Aa2
Tours: 1989 B
MATETE, Paul (1)
Appearances: 1975 **A**
World Cup: 1975
MELLARS, Peter
Tours: 1982 A,P
MERCER, Gary (13+4)
Appearances: 1987 P,A; 1988 P,B,**A**; 1989 A2,B3,F2;
  1991 f2,Aa2
Tours: 1986A,P; 1987 A,P; 1989 B
MOHI, Mita (1)
Appearances: 1972 **F**
World Cup: 1972
MUNRO, Don (3)
Appearances: 1975 **F,E,W**
Tours: 1975 A
World Cup: 1975
MURU, Rick
Tours: 1980 B

NIKAU, Tawera (12)
Appearances: 1990 B3,P2,A; 1991 F2,A3; 1992 P
Tours: 1989 B
NIXON, Mark (1+1)
Appearances: 1990 pP

O'CALLAGHAN, Vaun
Tours: 1985 B
O'DONNELL, Michael (10)
Appearances: 1977 **F**; 1980 A2; 1980 B3,F2; 1981 F2
Tours: 1978 A,P; 1980 B
World Cup: 1977
O'HARA, Dane (35)
Appearances: 1977 **A**; 1978 A3; 1979 B3; 1980 A2,B3,F2;
    1981 F2; 1982 A2,P; 1984 B3; 1985 A3,B3,F2;
    1986 A3,P2
Tours: 1978 A,P; 1980 B; 1982 A,P; 1986 A,P
World Cup: 1977
ORCHARD, Phil (20)
Appearances: 1969 A; 1970 B2; 1971 B2,F3;
    1972 A,**F,A,B**; 1975 **A2,F2,E2,W2**
Tours: 1971 B; 1972 A; 1975 A
World Cup: 1972, 1975
ORCHARD, Robert (9+3)
Appearances: 1970 B3; 1971 A,Bb2,F2f; 1972 A2
Tours: 1965 B; 1971 B; 1972 A
O'REGAN, Ron (6+2)
Appearances: 1983 Aa,P; 1985 F; 1986 Aa,P2
Tours: 1985 B; 1986 A,P
ORR, Dean (+1)
Appearances: 1983 p
O'SULLIVAN, John (10+1)
Appearances: 1969 A; 1972 aA,F; 1974 B3; 1975 **A,F,E,W**
Tours: 1971 B; 1972 A; 1975 A
World Cup: 1972, 1975

PANAPA, Sam (8)
Appearances: 1990 B3,P2,A; 1991 F2
Tours: 1987 A,P
PATTON, Mike (3+3)
Appearances: 1990 p; 1991 f2,A3
PAUL, Bob (4)
Appearances: 1972 A2,**F,A**
Tours: 1972 A
World Cup: 1972
PONGIA, Quentin (3)
Appearances: 1992 P,B2
POTTER, Kevin
Tours: 1975 A
World Cup: 1975
PROCTOR, Lyndsey (9+3)
Appearances: 1974 B; 1975 Ff,Ee,Ww; 1977 **B,F**; 1978 A3
Tours: 1978 A,P; 1975 A
World Cup: 1975, 1977
PROHM, Gary (22+1)
Appearances: 1978 aA2; 1980 B2,F2; 1981 F2; 1982 A2,P;
    1983 A2; 1985 A3,B3; 1986 A3
Tours: 1978 A,P; 1980 B; 1982 A,P; 1986 A,P

RAVLICH, Paul (+1)
Appearances: 1979 b
RIDGE, Matthew (7)
Appearances: 1990 B2,P2; 1992 P,B2
ROBERTSON, Wayne (2+1)
Appearances: 1974 B2b
ROPATI, Joe (7+2)
Appearances: 1983 A2; 1985 a2; 1986 A3,P2
Tours: 1985 B; 1986 A,P; 1987 A,P
ROPATI, Tea (+3)
Appearances: 1992 p,b2
Tours: 1986 A,P; 1989 B
RUSHTON, Alan (12)
Appearances: 1977 **A,B.F**; 1978 A3; 1980 B3,F; 1981 F2
Tours: 1978 A,P; 1980 B
World Cup: 1977

SHELFORD, Adrian (8)
Appearances: 1986 P2; 1987 P,A; 1988 P,B,**A**; 1989 B
Tours: 1985 B; 1986 A,P; 1987 A,P; 1989 B
SHELFORD, Kelly (7+1)
Appearances: 1989 A,B3,Ff; 1991 F2
Tours: 1989 B
SHERLOCK, Kurt (2+2)
Appearances: 1989 a,B2,f
Tours: 1989 B
SMITH, Gordon (13)
Appearances: 1979 B2; 1980 A2,B3,F2; 1982 A2,P;
    1983 A
Tours: 1980 B; 1982 A,P
SMITH, John (9+2)
Appearances: 1975 **a,F,E,W**; 1977 **A,B,F**; 1978 A3; 1979 b
Tours: 1978 A,P
World Cup: 1975, 1977
SORENSEN, Dane (18)
Appearances: 1975 **F,E,W2,A**; 1977 **A**; 1979 B2; 1983 A2;
    1984 B3; 1985 B3,F2
Tours: 1985 B
World Cup: 1975, 1977
SORENSEN, Dave (1)
Appearances: 1972 A
Tours: 1971 B; 1972 A
SORENSEN, Kurt (26+1)
Appearances: 1975, a,**W**; 1977 **A,B,F**; 1983 A2,P;
    1984 B3; 1985 A3,B3,F2; 1986 A3; 1988 **A**;
    1989 B3,F
Tours: 1985 B; 1986 A,P
World Cup: 1975, 1977
STEWART, Sam (12+4)
Appearances: 1985 B; 1986 p2; 1987 p,A; 1988 P,B,a;
    1989 A3,B3,F2
Tours: 1985 B; 1986 A,P; 1987 A,P; 1989 B
STIRLING, Ken (21)
Appearances: 1971 A,B3,F3; 1972 A; 1974 B3;
    1975 **A2,F2,E2,W**; 1978 A3
Tours: 1971 B; 1972 A; 1975 A; 1978 A,P
World Cup: 1975

STOKES, Gerard
Tours: 1982 A,P
STUART, Brent (3)
Appearances: 1992 P,B2

TAEWA, Whetu
Tours: 1989 B
TAMATI, Howie (20+3)
Appearances: 1979 B3; 1980 A2,b,Ff; 1981 f; 1982 A2,P;
1983 A2,P; 1984 B3; 1985 A3,B2
Tours: 1980 B; 1982 A,P; 1985 B
TAMATI, Kevin (21+1)
Appearances: 1979 B3; 1980 A2,B3,F2; 1981 F;
1982 A2,P; 1984 B3; 1985 A3,Bb
Tours: 1980 B; 1982 A,P
TAYLOR, Glen (1)
Appearances: 1978 A
Tours: 1978 A,P
TAYLOR, Ross (2)
Appearances: 1987 P,A
Tours: 1985 B; 1987 A,P
TE ARIKI, Paul (1)
Appearances: 1980 A
Tours: 1980 B
THOMPSON, Angus
Tours: 1972 A
TINITELIA, Frank (1)
Appearances: 1983 P
TODD, Brent (24+1)
Appearances: 1985 f; 1986 A; 1987 P; 1989 A3,B3,F2;
1990 B3,P2,A; 1991 F2,A3; 1992 P,B2
Tours: 1985 B; 1986 A,P; 1987 A,P; 1989 B
TRACEY, Brian (3)
Appearances: 1972 **F,A,B**
World Cup: 1972
TUIMAVAVE, Paddy (2)
Appearances: 1990 P2
TUPAEA, Nolan
Tours: 1980 B
TUUTA, Brendon (4+2)
Appearances: 1989 A2a; 1992 p,B2
Tours: 1989 B

ULUAVE, Dick (2)
Appearances: 1979 B2

VARLEY, Shane (10+1)
Appearances: 1978 A; 1979 B; 1980 A; 1981 F2;
1983 aA,P; 1984 B3
Tours: 1978 A,P; 1980 B; 1982 A,P

WALKER, Rodney (1+3)
Appearances: 1969 A; 1970 b; 1972 **a,b**
World Cup: 1972
WALLACE, Wayne (11)
Appearances: 1985 B,F2; 1986 A,P2; 1987 P,A;
1988 P,B,**A**
Tours: 1985 B; 1986 A,P; 1987 A,P; 1989 B
WATSON, Dave (9)
Appearances: 1989 F; 1990 P2,A; 1991 F2,A3
Tours: 1989 B

WEST, Graeme (15+1)
Appearances: 1975 **A**; 1979 B2; 1980 B3,F2; 1981 F2;
1982 A2,P; 1983 aA; 1985 B
Tours: 1975 A; 1980 B; 1982 A,P
World Cup: 1975
WHITTAKER, John (23+2)
Appearances: 1970 **F,B**; 1971 A,B3,F3; 1972 A,**F,A,B**;
1975 **A,F,E**; 1977 **B,F**; 1980 B2,F2; 1982 a2,P
Tours: 1971 B; 1972 A; 1975 A; 1980 B; 1982 A,P
World Cup: 1970, 1972, 1975, 1977
WILLIAMS, Darrell (21)
Appearances: 1985 B,F; 1986 A2,P2; 1987 A; 1988 P,B;
1989 A3,B3,F2; 1990 B3,A
Tours: 1985 B; 1986 A,P; 1987 A,P; 1989 B
WILLIAMS, Dennis (30)
Appearances: 1971 B3,F3; 1972 A2,**F,A,B**; 1974 B3;
1975 **A2,F2,E2,W2**; 1977 **A,B,F**; 1978 A3; 1980 A;
1981 F
Tours: 1971 B; 1972 A; 1975 A; 1978 A,P
World Cup: 1972, 1975, 1977
WILLIAMS, Jason (2+1)
Appearances: 1991 A2a
WILSON, John (2)
Appearances: 1972 **A,B**
World Cup: 1972
WILSON, Ray (1)
Appearances: 1969 A
Tours: 1972 A
WILSON, Wally (+1)
Appearances: 1981 f
WINTER, Warren
Tours: 1978 A,P
WOODS, Mark (+3)
Appearances: 1992 p,b2
WRIGHT, John
Tours: 1975 A; 1978 A,P
World Cup: 1975
WRIGHT, Murray
Tours: 1975 A
World Cup: 1975
WRIGHT, Nick (2)
Appearances: 1983 A,P
Tours: 1978 A,P
WRIGHT, Owen (14+2)
Appearances: 1982 p; 1983 P; 1984 B3; 1985 A3,B,F2;
1986 A2a,P2
Tours: 1982 A,P; 1985 B; 1986 A,P

NEW ZEALAND TOURS OF BRITAIN

1907-08 TOUR

MATCH RESULTS

Bramley	W	25-6	6,000
Huddersfield	W	19-8	9,000
Widnes	W	26-11	7,000
Broughton R.	W	20-14	24,000
Wakefield T.	D	5-5	5,800
Leeds	W	8-2	12,321
St. Helens	W	24-5	8,000
Merthyr Tydfil	W	27-9	7,000
Keighley	W	9-7	8,000
Wigan	L	8-12	30,000
Barrow	L	3-6	7,500
Hull	W	18-13	12,000
Leigh	L	9-15	8,000
Oldham	L	7-8	12,000
Runcorn	L	0-9	4,500
Dewsbury & Batley	W	18-8	7,000
Swinton	W	11-2	4,000
Rochdale H.	W	19-0	8,000
Bradford N.	L	2-7	2,000
Halifax	L	4-9	11,000
Yorkshire (Wakefield)	**W**	**23-4**	**3,000**
Warrington	L	7-8	8,000
Hunslet	D	11-11	19,000
Salford	W	9-2	12,000
Wales (Aberdare)	**L**	**8-9**	**15,000**
Hull K.R.	W	6-3	10,000
Cumberland (Workington)	**L**	**9-21**	**4,000**
England (Wigan)	**L**	**16-18**	**10,000**
Lancashire (Oldham)	**L**	**4-20**	**6,500**
GREAT BRITAIN (Leeds)	**L**	**6-14**	**8,182**
York	L	3-5	4,500
Ebbw Vale	W	3-2	8,000
GREAT BRITAIN (Chelsea)	**W**	**18-6**	**14,000**
GREAT BRITAIN (Cheltenham)	**W**	**8-5**	**4,000**
St. Helens	W	21-10	4,000

SUMMARY

Played 35   Won 19   Drew 2   Lost 14

For
Tries 90   Goals 72   Points 414

Against
Tries 70   Goals 42   Points 294

Won Test series 2-1

TOUR PARTY

Manager: H.J. Palmer   Captain: H.R. Wright

	App	Tries	Gls	Pts
A.H Baskerville	1	1	0	3
C.A. Byrne	17	2	0	6
A. Callum	1	0	0	0
T.W. Cross	29	2	0	6
C. Dunning	7	0	0	0
D. Gilchrist	24	0	0	0
J.G. Gleeson	2	0	0	0
W. Johnston	30	7	0	21
A.F. Kelly	12	1	0	3
J.A. Lavery	8	2	0	6
A. Lile	14	1	0	3
D. McGregor	6	2	0	6
W. Mackrell	10	0	0	0
H.H. Messenger	29	7	60	141
C.J. Pearce	30	0	0	0
H.F. Rowe	24	10	0	30
G.W. Smith	24	7	0	21
L.B. Todd	22	10	0	30
W.M. Trevarthen	16	1	0	3
H.S. Turtill	33	1	5	13
W.T. Tyler	15	4	0	12
H. Tyne	9	2	0	6
H.R. Wright	21	5	0	15
E. Wrigley	31	7	7	35
R.J. Wynard	31	15	0	45
W.T. Wynard	9	3	0	9

MEMO

First match on 9 October, last match on 22 February.

The first-ever tour by any country 12 years after the game was born. Organised by Albert H. Baskerville and made up of Rugby Union players, including four of the New Zealand RU squad which toured Britain in 1905. Regarded as mercenaries by RU authorities, who labelled them the *All Golds*, the breakaway group were the pioneers of Rugby League in New Zealand.

They also helped to found the game in Australia, playing matches there en route to Britain and on their return. The great Australian player Dally Messenger joined the squad as a guest player and did much to make the tour a success.

Several tourists signed for British clubs, including Lance Todd who joined Wigan and later became manager of Salford.

Tragedy hit the squad on the way home when Baskerville died of pneumonia, aged 25.

The first-ever tour game was at Bramley on Wednesday 9 October.

1926-27 TOUR

MATCH RESULTS

Dewsbury	W	13-9	13,000
Leigh	W	23-16	12,000
Halifax	L	13-19	13,000
Rochdale H.	W	11-9	7,590
Barrow	W	19-16	5,500
Widnes	W	15-5	6,000
GREAT BRITAIN (Wigan)	**L**	**20-28**	**14,500**
York	W	19-11	3,099
Warrington	L	5-17	5,000
Bramley	W	35-12	
Hull	W	15-13	13,000
Bradford N.	W	38-17	4,000
Oldham	L	10-15	16,000
Leeds	W	13-11	4,000
St. Helens Rec.	L	14-28	6,000
Salford	W	18-10	3,500
Huddersfield	L	10-12	5,000
GREAT BRITAIN (Hull)	**L**	**11-21**	**7,000**
Wigan Highfield	W	14-2	2,000
Batley	L	17-19	3,000
Keighley	W	21-3	3,861
Swinton	L	14-16	12,000
Wales (Pontypridd)	**L**	**8-34**	**18,000**
St. Helens	L	12-22	2,000
Wigan	L	15-36	9,000
Yorkshire (Huddersfield)	**L**	**16-17**	**3,000**
Hunslet	L	12-13	
Pontypridd	W	17-8	
Broughton R.	W	32-8	5,000
Wakefield T.	W	29-24	6,000
Hull K.R.	L	15-20	7,500
Lancashire (Leigh)	**L**	**3-28**	**7,000**
Cumberland (Workington)	**W**	**18-3**	**4,200**
GREAT BRITAIN (Leeds)	**L**	**17-32**	**6,000**

SUMMARY

Played 34   Won 17   Lost 17

For
Tries 132   Goals 83   Points 562

Against
Tries 126   Goals 88   Points 554

Lost Test series 3-0

TOUR PARTY

Manager: G.H. Ponder   Team Manager: E.H. Mair
Captain: H. Avery

	App	Tries	Gls	Pts
H. Avery	29	23	0	69
H. Brisbane	27	6	0	18
L. Brown	27	15	0	45
A. Carroll	17	3	0	9
H. Cole	14	1	0	3
B. Davidson	23	14	0	42
F. Delgrosso	20	4	6	24
W.L. Desmond	15	8	0	24
W.W. Devine	9	2	0	6
C. Dufty	19	2	42	90
G. Gardiner	20	10	10	50
E.C. Gregory	15	0	6	12
A.W. Hall	22	4	0	12
F. Henry	12	2	0	6
E. Herring	30	6	0	18
J. Kirwan	18	5	0	15
L. Mason	26	8	3	30
J. Menzies	12	1	0	3
N. Mouat	10	3	16	41
J. Parkes	17	5	0	15
L. Peterson	8	2	0	6
J. Sanders	15	5	0	15
A. Singe	6	1	0	3
H. Thomas	18	2	0	6
C. Webb	7	0	0	0
J. Wright	6	0	0	0

MEMO

First match on 11 September, last match on 15 January.

Following their 2-1 Test series defeat of the 1924 British Lions, New Zealand replaced Australia as the 1926 tourists to Britain. But the high hopes were dashed by a long-running dispute between players and management which resulted in seven tourists being sent home in December.

At the centre of the dispute was the coach-manager E.H. Mair, an Australian with revolutionary playing tactics who was a strict disciplinarian.

The players were all amateurs receiving only expenses and this led to further protests when the English Rugby League gave the suspended players £10 to assist them on their passage home.

Despite the disputes, Bert Avery was a worthy captain with the forward's 23 tries still a record for a New Zealand tourist in Britain.

All three Tests against Britain were lost and only half of the 34 tour games won, with a big financial loss also reported.

1939 TOUR

MATCH RESULTS

St. Helens	W	19-3	4,000
Dewsbury	W	22-10	6,200

SUMMARY
Played 2   Won 2

For
Tries 7   Goals 10   Points 41

Against
Tries 3   Goals 2   Points 13

MEMO

The tour was abandoned because of the outbreak of the Second World War the day after the first match was played at St. Helens on 2 September.

While arrangements were being made to send the squad home safely, a second game was played against Dewsbury on 9 September.

Both games were won, which suggests that the tour would have been one of their best.

Lou Brown, who signed for Wigan after the 1926-27 tour, returned with the tourists and played in one of the matches to complete a span of 13 years between tours.

This was the first tour on which the New Zealanders adopted the Kiwis title, having previously been the All Blacks.

TOUR PARTY

Managers: J.A. Redwood and R. Doble
Captain: R.K. King

	App	Tries	Gls	Pts
J.R. Banham	2	1	0	3
G.W. Beadle	1	1	0	3
G.R. Bellaney	1	0	0	0
L. Brown	1	0	0	0
J.J. Campbell	1	0	0	0
T.H. Chase	1	0	0	0
J. Clark	1	0	0	0
J.G. Cootes	0	0	0	0
C.H. Davidson	0	0	0	0
J. Hemi	2	0	10	20
R.D. Jones	2	1	0	3
A.G. Kay	1	1	0	3
R.K. King	1	1	0	3
B. Leatherbarrow	1	1	0	3
A.J. McInnarney	0	0	0	0
H. Mataira	1	0	0	0
H.M. Milliken	2	0	0	0
L.D. Mills	1	0	0	0
G.G. Mitchell	0	0	0	0
G.A. Orman	1	0	0	0
P. Ririnui	1	0	0	0
V.J. Scott	0	0	0	0
J. Smith	1	0	0	0
D. Solomon	2	1	0	3
I. Sterling	1	0	0	0
W.H. Tittleton	1	0	0	0

The Kiwis perform their traditional war dance before the first Test at Swinton in 1955.

1947-48 TOUR

MATCH RESULTS

St. Helens	W	11-5	22,000
Swinton	L	6-8	12,148
York	W	29-0	4,500
GREAT BRITAIN (Leeds)	**L**	**10-11**	**28,445**
Castleford	W	17-3	11,000
Hull K.R.	L	7-13	12,000
Bradford N.	W	17-7	17,519
Leigh	W	10-5	15,000
Wales (Swansea)	**W**	**28-20**	**18,283**
Wigan	W	10-8	24,089
Oldham	W	18-8	17,239
Hunslet	L	10-18	5,533
Hull	L	7-13	16,113
Batley	L	18-19	3,510
GREAT BRITAIN (Swinton)	**W**	**10-7**	**29,031**
Leeds	W	23-16	8,864
Warrington	L	5-7	20,682
Halifax	W	21-5	5,276
Huddersfield	L	7-12	8,872
Widnes	L	0-7	11,900
Dewsbury	W	24-5	7,270
Workington T.	W	12-7	10,722
Barrow	D	2-2	5,565
Wakefield T.	W	30-3	11,595
Bramley	W	31-3	3,100
Belle Vue R.	W	19-3	10,000
GREAT BRITAIN (Bradford)	**L**	**9-25**	**42,680**

Eight-try tourist Ron McGregor, who went on to become secretary of the International Board.

SUMMARY
Played 27   Won 16   Drew 1   Lost 10

For
Tries 83   Goals 71   Points 391

Against
Tries 52   Goals 42   Points 240

Lost Test series 2-1

TOUR PARTY

Managers: J.A. Redwood and L. Hunter
Captain: P.A. Smith   Coach: T.A. McClymont

	App	Tries	Gls	Pts
H.D. Anderson	15	8	0	24
R. Aynsley	13	3	0	9
D.A. Barchard	13	3	0	9
R.J. Clark	14	1	2	7
S.W. Clarke	19	2	52	110
R. Cunningham	10	1	0	3
W.G. Davidson	9	1	0	3
J.A. Forrest	18	9	0	27
A.E.C. Gillman	10	1	0	3
A.H. Graham	2	0	0	0
J.S. Haig	7	0	0	0
C.C. Hancox	9	1	0	3
T.H. Hardwick	18	7	0	21
J.J. Johnson	16	0	0	0
L.R. Jordan	19	10	0	30
C. McBride	20	5	0	15
R.G. McGregor	18	8	0	24
A.J. McInnarney	15	4	0	12
A.W. McKenzie	5	0	0	0
K. Mountford	19	3	0	9
J. Newton	19	7	0	21
R. Nuttall	7	0	16	32
L.R. Pye	14	2	1	8
M.W. Robertson	21	6	0	18
P.A. Smith	21	1	0	3

MEMO
First match on 25 September, last match on 20 December.

A dock strike in Auckland delayed the tourists' departure by three weeks, forcing them to open with four matches in 10 days, including the first Test on 4 October.

Another setback was Sandy Hurndell being taken ill en route and the second row forward returned home without being replaced.

The post-war boom was at its height and over 375,000 saw the 27 matches, with 42,680 at Bradford for the third Test, which remains a record for a New Zealand game in this country.

Arthur McInnarney was the only player from the war-hit 1939 squad to return for a full tour.

For the first time the New Zealanders extended their tour to France and played eight matches including two Tests in a four-week trip.

1951-52 TOUR

MATCH RESULTS

Rochdale H.	W	13-9	4,000
Halifax	L	12-18	15,000
Workington T.	W	17-15	8,935
Oldham	L	18-21	15,174
Castleford	W	10-9	6,600
GREAT BRITAIN (Bradford)	**L**	**15-21**	**37,475**
Huddersfield	W	34-12	9,859
Warrington	W	19-13	18,889
Batley	W	20-13	5,087
Bramley	W	24-20	2,100
St. Helens	W	33-10	17,000
Leigh	W	31-5	9,000
Barrow	L	5-9	13,319
Bradford N.	L	8-13	29,072
Wigan	W	15-8	13,500
York	W	15-12	4,183
GREAT BRITAIN (Swinton)	**L**	**19-20**	**29,938**
Wakefield T.	W	26-18	8,850
Leeds	W	19-4	16,000
Lancashire (Warrington)	**L**	**12-13**	**7,313**
Belle Vue R.	L	5-7	5,000
Hull	W	28-8	9,000
Salford	W	27-12	10,000
Yorkshire (Wakefield)	**W**	**10-3**	**2,910**
Wales (Bradford)	**W**	**15-3**	**8,568**
Cardiff	W	18-10	2,000
GREAT BRITAIN (Leeds)	**L**	**12-16**	**18,649**
British Empire (Chelsea)	**L**	**2-26**	**6,800**

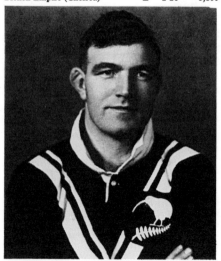

Fifteen points from 14 appearances for J.S. Haig on his second successive Kiwi tour of Britain.

SUMMARY

Played 28   Won 18   Lost 10

For
Tries 110   Goals 76   Points 482

Against
Tries 72   Goals 66   Points 348

Lost Test series 3-0

TOUR PARTY

Managers: D.A. Wilkie and T.F. McKenzie
Captain: M.W. Robertson   Coach: T.A. McClymont

	App	Tries	Gls	Pts
A.J. Atkinson	19	5	0	1!
D.A. Barchard	16	1	0	?
T.O. Baxter	20	9	0	2?
A. Berryman	5	3	0	ç
D.L. Blanchard	12	1	0	3
G.J. Burgoyne	6	1	0	?
R.J. Cranch	7	2	0	(
J.J. Curtain	7	1	0	?
W.G. Davidson	20	2	0	(
J.F. Dodd	8	4	0	12
C.A. Eastlake	18	9	6	3ç
J.R. Edwards	14	6	0	18
K. English	10	3	0	ç
J.A. Forrest	10	7	0	2!
J.S. Haig	14	3	3	1!
B.K. Hough	19	12	0	3(
C.R. Johnson	19	7	0	2?
C. McBride	22	6	0	1?
W.R. McLennan	20	2	0	(
G. Menzies	7	1	0	?
F.G. Mulcare	19	4	0	12
D. Richards-Jolley	7	1	0	?
B.E. Robertson	14	13	0	3ç
M.W. Robertson	22	4	0	12
W. Sorensen	7	1	4	1!
D.H. White	22	2	63	13?

MEMO

First match on 18 September, last match on 23 January.

The second Test at Swinton made history as the first to be televised, Britain winning 20-19 with a late penalty goal by Jim Ledgard.

Des White was New Zealand's goalkicking star with 63 which remains a Kiwi record for a tour of Britain.

A young squad arrived with great expectations after a series of good performances against Australia, France and Britain, but never fully recovered from a poor start.

All three Test matches were lost and after making a 12-match trip to France the Kiwis ended their Britain tour with a 26-2 defeat against a British Empire side at Chelsea soccer ground.

1955 TOUR

MATCH RESULTS

Blackpool B.	D	24-24	12,015
York	L	16-20	8,174
Halifax	L	17-18	12,492
Yorkshire (Hull K.R.)	**W**	**33-17**	**7,907**
Wigan	L	15-17	19,386
Hull	W	17-12	10,167
Barrow	L	13-17	7,098
Workington T.	W	26-16	11,043
GREAT BRITAIN (Swinton)	**L**	**6-25**	**21,937**
Lancashire (Warrington)	**W**	**17-15**	**6,887**
Leeds	W	18-16	15,738
Featherstone R.	W	7-6	5,100
Huddersfield	L	16-25	11,271
St. Helens	L	8-16	14,000
Oldham	W	15-13	15,000
Leigh	L	13-14	3,400
Warrington	L	15-22	14,462
GREAT BRITAIN (Bradford)	**L**	**12-27**	**24,443**
Castleford	W	31-7	2,440
Rochdale H.	W	17-16	9,300
Bradford N.	W	11-6	5,271
Salford	W	21-5	4,000
Wakefield T.	W	27-16	4,838
Rugby League XIII (Bradford)	**L**	**11-24**	**3,643**
Keighley	D	11-11	4,200
GREAT BRITAIN (Leeds)	**W**	**28-13**	**10,438**

SUMMARY
Played 26   Won 13   Drew 2   Lost 11

For
Tries 95   Goals 80   Points 445

Against
Tries 94   Goals 68   Points 418

Lost Test series 2-1

Tour manager H. Tetlow.

TOUR PARTY

Managers: H. Tetlow and C. Siddle
Captain: T.O. Baxter

	App	Tries	Gls	Pts
A. Atkinson	19	11	0	33
V. Bakalich	21	20	0	60
T.O. Baxter	22	1	0	3
S.E. Belsham	2	1	0	3
D.L. Blanchard	13	1	0	3
J.E. Bond	6	1	0	3
J.R. Butterfield	13	1	0	3
P.J. Creedy	18	1	5	13
N.L. Denton	6	3	0	9
I.N. Grey	7	2	0	6
R. Haggie	18	6	48	114
R.P. Hawes	6	3	0	9
T.T. Kilkelly	10	0	0	0
G.S. MacDonald	20	0	0	0
R.J. McKay	16	4	7	26
B. McLennan	18	2	2	10
L.J. McNicol	11	8	0	24
H.D. Maxwell	19	4	0	12
G. Menzies	14	3	0	9
R.L. Moore	6	1	17	37
R.W. Percy	18	10	1	32
J. Riddell	5	0	0	0
N.K. Roberts	10	2	0	6
B.E. Robertson	9	4	0	12
W. Sorensen	22	5	0	15
J.E. Yates	9	1	0	3

MEMO

First match on 10 September, last match on 17 December.

The Kiwis flew to Britain for the first time but were slow to find form, opening with a draw at Blackpool Borough and losing their next two matches.

But after being well beaten in the first two Test matches New Zealand finished the tour with a shock 28-13 win over a complacent Great Britain at Headingley.

During the game at Castleford, home prop Dennis Norton complained of chest pains and died 12 days later. A benefit game was played at Castleford in aid of Norton's dependants.

The tourists, with Halifax's Tony Lynch making a guest appearance, beat an RL XIII 28-15 but the game is not included in tour records.

1961 TOUR

MATCH RESULTS

Widnes-Liverpool	L	6-9	9,050
Manchester XIII	L	7-19	6,926
Castleford-Featherstone	W	31-20	5,744
Leeds XIII	W	24-9	7,085
Oldham-Rochdale H.	L	8-10	8,795
Yorkshire (Hull K.R.)	**L**	**11-21**	**6,750**
Barrow	W	36-11	6,647
Lancashire (Warrington)	**L**	**13-15**	**9,332**
Huddersfield-Halifax	W	31-11	7,251
Rugby League XIII			
(Manchester)	**L**	**20-22**	**5,271**
Warrington	W	21-9	8,959
GREAT BRITAIN (Leeds)	**W**	**29-11**	**16,540**
Hull-Hull K.R.	L	6-17	8,125
Wigan	L	6-28	25,483
Cumberland (Whitehaven)	**W**	**10-9**	**4,970**
St. Helens	L	10-25	21,680
GREAT BRITAIN (Bradford)	**L**	**10-23**	**19,980**
Leigh	W	15-4	6,584
Wakefield T.	L	7-20	16,558
GREAT BRITAIN (Swinton)	**L**	**19-35**	**22,536**

SUMMARY
Played 20   Won 8   Lost 12

For
Tries 60   Goals 70   Points 320

Against
Tries 62   Goals 71   Points 328

Lost Test series 2-1

Most tour appearances for packman H.K. Emery,
17 games from a possible 20.

TOUR PARTY

Manager: C. Siddle   Coach: W. Telford
Captain: R.D. Hammond

	App	Tries	Gls	Pts
A.N. Amer	10	5	0	15
G.R. Bailey	3	0	0	0
R.W. Bailey	15	12	0	36
J.A. Bond	14	5	0	15
J.R. Butterfield	17	1	0	3
B.E. Castle	11	4	0	12
M.I. Cooke	13	3	0	9
R.S. Cooke	16	4	24	60
R.H.G. Duffy	5	1	0	3
S.K. Edwards	15	2	0	6
H.K. Emery	17	0	0	0
J.E. Fagan	14	1	43	89
G.S. Farrar	8	2	0	6
J.P. Ford	5	0	0	0
B.T. Hadfield	9	6	0	18
R.D. Hammond	14	2	0	6
R.W. Harrison	6	0	0	0
W.R. Harrison	6	0	0	0
R.G. Hart	3	0	0	0
G.M. Kennedy	7	0	3	6
B.S. Lee	11	1	0	3
K.R. McCracken	5	1	0	3
J.G. Patterson	5	0	0	0
B.T. Reidy	15	9	0	27
W.L. Snowden	13	1	0	3
N.T. Tiller	3	0	0	0

MEMO
First match on 19 August, last match on 4 November.

The shortest tour so far, with the schedule cut to just 20 matches with seven of them against combined club sides such as Swinton and Salford. None of these matches attracted attendances of 10,000 or more.

They finished with the worst record of all, still being the only Kiwi squad to lose more matches than they won. Yet the tourists shocked Great Britain by winning the first Test 29-11, which remains their highest Test score in this country.

Britain made seven changes for the next Test which they won 23-10 and clinched the series with a 35-15 final Test win, which was their biggest home score over New Zealand.

1965 TOUR

MATCH RESULTS

Commonwealth XIII (Crystal			
Palace)	W	15-7	1,200
Bradford N.	L	15-28	8,373
Warrington	W	14-7	8,162
Halifax	W	24-12	6,730
Oldham	W	5-2	13,021
Wigan	W	17-12	12,853
Widnes	L	3-8	9,450
Hull K.R.	W	21-11	7,540
St. Helens	L	7-28	11,270
Leeds	W	28-13	5,782
Yorkshire (Castleford)	L	8-15	14,814
GREAT BRITAIN (Swinton)	L	2-7	8,541
Leigh	W	10-5	4,840
Barrow	W	20-10	5,081
Whitehaven	L	7-12	3,208
Castleford	W	7-6	5,702
Hull	W	11-8	6,591
Lancashire (St. Helens)	W	21-10	8,781
Rochdale H.	W	10-4	7,075
GREAT BRITAIN (Bradford)	L	9-15	15,740
Swinton	L	7-14	8,345
Wakefield T.	L	4-16	7,484
GREAT BRITAIN (Wigan)	D	9-9	7,919

Most tour appearances with 19 from a possible 23,
G.M. Kennedy.

SUMMARY
Played 23   Won 13   Drew 1   Lost 9

For
Tries 48   Goals 65   Points 274

Against
Tries 41   Goals 68   Points 259

Lost Test series 2-0, one drawn

TOUR PARTY

Managers: W.L. O'Callaghan and T. Wellsmore
Captain: W.L. Snowden   Coach: W. Telford

	App	Sub	Tries	Gls	Pts
R.W. Bailey	18	0	5	0	15
L.P. Brown	6	1	2	0	6
R.F. Christian	14	0	2	0	6
W.G. Deacon	13	0	2	0	6
J.K. Dixon	9	0	2	0	6
S.K. Edwards	15	1	0	0	0
H.R. Emery	18	0	7	0	21
J.E. Fagan	12	1	0	28	56
R.D. Hammond	14	1	2	0	6
R.S. Irvine	8	2	1	0	3
G.M. Kennedy	19	0	1	7	17
B.W. Langton	8	0	1	0	3
G. Mattson	11	1	5	0	15
E. Moore	12	0	1	0	3
C. O'Neil	10	0	1	0	3
R.I. Orchard	10	1	2	0	6
B.T. Reidy	15	1	5	0	15
R.O. Scholefield	7	0	0	0	0
P. Shultz	12	0	3	0	9
W.T. Shultz	13	0	1	0	3
W.L. Snowden	13	0	0	0	0
R. Strong	8	0	0	0	0
R. Tait	14	1	3	30	69
J.D.M. Walshe	6	1	1	0	3
J.L. White	6	0	0	0	0
P.M. White	8	0	1	0	3

MEMO
First match on 18 August, last match on 6 November.

The tour opened with a 15-7 victory over a Commonwealth XIII at Crystal Palace, London. There was a crowd of only 1,200, with the receipts going to the Central Council for Physical Recreation.

Another disappointing tour with the Kiwis' lack of flair reflected in a total of only 48 tries scored in 23 matches and no player scoring more than seven.

It was the last tour under the old unlimited play-the-ball rule and Britain clinched a dull Test series with two wins and then a draw.

The slump in New Zealand rugby continued in France where they lost all three Test matches.

1971 TOUR

MATCH RESULTS

Rochdale H.	W	23-8	2,374
St. Helens	L	8-18	8,169
Hull K.R.	L	10-12	5,746
Widnes	W	18-15	5,787
Castleford	L	8-25	5,889
Warrington	L	2-13	6,295
GREAT BRITAIN (Salford)	**W**	**18-13**	**3,764**
Barrow	W	25-15	4,839
Whitehaven	W	21-8	3,105
Swinton	L	15-26	3,280
Wigan	W	24-10	12,187
GREAT BRITAIN (Castleford)	**W**	**17-14**	**4,108**
Huddersfield	L	10-11	3,495
Leigh	L	5-10	4,012
Salford	L	30-31	7,127
Wakefield T.	W	23-12	5,367
Oldham	W	24-13	2,172
Bradford N.	W	30-23	6,362
York	L	5-11	2,803
GREAT BRITAIN (Leeds)	**L**	**3-12**	**5,479**

SUMMARY

Played 20   Won 10   Lost 10

For
Tries 68   Goals 57   Drop goal 1   Points 319

Against
Tries 62   Goals 55   Drop goals 4   Points 300

Won Test series 2-1

Kiwi tour skipper Roy Christian, scorer of four tries in 13 appearances.

TOUR PARTY

Managers: W. O'Callaghan and J. Williams
Captain: R.F. Christian   Coach: D.L. Blanchard

	App	Sub	Tries	Gls	Pts
M.P. Brereton	12	2	10	0	30
W.J. Burgoyne	9	0	0	0	0
R.F. Christian	13	0	4	0	12
G.R. Cooksley	7	1	1	0	3
W.G. Deacon	9	1	0	6	12
D.S. Dowsett	1	0	0	0	0
M.K. Eade	9	1	2	0	6
J.H. Fisher	11	1	0	0	0
D. Gailey	9	1	1	0	3
J. Greengrass	11	0	3	0	9
A.P. Kriletich	14	2	2	0	6
B.R. Lowther	9	0	2	0	6
M.J.McClennan	9	0	1	0	3
R.C. McGuinn	11	1	1	0	3
D.K. Mann	4	1	0	0	0
P.C. Orchard	14	1	20	0	60
R.I. Orchard	10	3	2	5	16
J.C. O'Sullivan	8	3	2	0	6
G.M. Smith	12	1	1	0	3
Dave Sorensen	6	0	1	0	3
K.L. Stirling	9	1	1	0	3
H. Tatanah	15	0	4	46	104
J.A. Whittaker	16	0	3	0	9
Dennis Williams	13	1	6	(1)	19
R.F. Williams	7	1	1	0	3
G.F. Woollard	12	3	0	0	0

(1) Drop goal — one point

MEMO

First match on 4 September, last match on 6 November.

Before travelling north, the Kiwis played two matches against Southern Amateur XIIIs, winning 67-6 on 29 August and 66-0 the following day, but these games are not included in the tour records.

Although the Kiwis showed only modest form against club sides they made it a memorable tour by winning the Test series 2-1, the first time they had achieved it since the inaugural tour of 1907.

The squad was captained by Roy Fletcher Christian, who had toured in 1965 and gained additional publicity as a direct descendant of Fletcher Christian of *Mutiny on the Bounty* fame.

Success on the field was not reflected in attendances with a total of fewer than 14,000 seeing the three Test matches.

1980 TOUR

MATCH RESULTS

Blackpool B.	W	23-5	1,312
Hull	W	33-10	15,945
Cumbria (Whitehaven)	**L**	**3-9**	**4,070**
St. Helens	L	6-11	6,000
Bradford N.	L	10-15	4,553
GREAT BRITAIN (Wigan)	**D**	**14-14**	**7,031**
Hull K.R.	W	20-12	9,516
Leeds	W	25-5	5,662
Warrington	L	7-11	5,680
GREAT BRITAIN (Bradford)	**W**	**12-8**	**10,946**
Great Britain Under-24s			
(Fulham)	**W**	**18-14**	**2,397**
Widnes	L	7-14	6,416
Leigh	W	22-5	3,166
GREAT BRITAIN (Leeds)	**L**	**2-10**	**8,210**

SUMMARY

Played 14   Won 7   Drew 1   Lost 6

For

Tries 42   Goals 38   Points 202

Against

Tries 23   Goals 35   Drop goals 4   Points 143

Drew Test series 1-1, one drawn

Stand off Fred Ah Kuoi, who played in nine of the 14 Kiwi tour matches.

TOUR PARTY

Manager-coach: C. Mountford
Business Manager: W. Nesbitt
Captain: M. Graham

	App	Sub	Tries	Gls	Pts
F. Ah Kuoi	9	0	1	0	3
R. Baxendale	6	3	1	0	3
M. Broadhurst	9	0	0	0	0
T. Coll	6	0	4	0	12
B. Dickison	8	0	2	0	6
B. Edkins	7	0	0	9	18
K. Fisher	6	1	0	0	0
B. Gall	7	1	3	0	9
M. Graham	6	0	4	0	12
B. Green	5	0	2	0	6
B. Kells	4	0	0	0	0
G. Kemble	7	0	2	9	24
J. Leuluai	9	0	3	0	9
R. Muru	4	1	1	0	3
M. O'Donnell	8	0	1	5	13
D. O'Hara	9	2	6	0	18
G. Prohm	8	1	0	0	0
A. Rushton	7	1	1	0	3
G. Smith	7	0	1	15	33
H. Tamati	8	1	1	0	3
K. Tamati	8	0	1	0	3
P. Te Ariki	4	2	0	0	0
N. Tupaea	6	0	3	0	9
S. Varley	6	1	1	0	3
G. West	9	0	2	0	6
J. Whittaker	8	1	2	0	6

D. Campbell (Wigan) played one game on loan, a non-scorer.

MEMO

First match on 29 September, last match on 15 November.

The tour programme was cut to 14 matches and though the Kiwis won only half of them, several players emerged who were to have a long stay on the international scene.

Hull signed three of them in one of the biggest-ever signing coups — Gary Kemble, James Leuluai and Dane O'Hara. Many more were to join other clubs as restrictions on overseas signings were lifted.

The Test series was drawn for the first time in this country, with New Zealand's second Test win their first-ever at Bradford.

Although attendances for Test matches were well above those of 1971 they were still disappointing and the biggest crowd was 15,945 for the match against Hull at Hull City's soccer ground.

1985 TOUR

MATCH RESULTS

Wigan	L	8-14	12,856
Great Britain Under-21s			
(Bradford)	**W**	**16-12**	2,285
Hull K.R.	**W**	**20-10**	6,630
Cumbria (Whitehaven)	**W**	**32-6**	5,212
GREAT BRITAIN (Leeds)	**W**	**24-22**	12,591
Yorkshire (Bradford)	L	8-18	3,745
St. Helens	**W**	**46-8**	7,897
Leeds	**W**	**16-10**	4,829
GREAT BRITAIN (Wigan)	L	8-25	15,506
Widnes	**W**	**32-12**	5,181
GREAT BRITAIN			
(Elland Rd, Leeds)	**D**	**6-6**	22,209
Hull	**W**	**33-10**	8,406

SUMMARY

Played 12 Won 8 Drew 1 Lost 3

For
Tries 42 Goals 40 Drop goal 1 Points 249

Against
Tries 20 Goals 35 Drop goals 3 Points 153

Drew Test series 1-1, one drawn

Scrum half Clayton Friend, scorer of three tries in eight matches.

TOUR PARTY

Manager: J. Campbell. Business Manager: T. McKeown
Captain: M. Graham Coach: G. Lowe

	App	Sub	Tries	Gls	Pts
D. Bell	7	1	2	0	8
M. Bourneville	9	0	3	0	12
S. Cooper	5	3	3	0	12
R. Cowan	5	1	0	0	0
M. Crequer	1	0	1	0	4
M. Elia	8	0	8	0	32
O. Filipaina	7	2	0	20	40
C. Friend	8	0	3	0	12
G. Gibb	3	0	0	0	0
J. Goulding	6	0	0	0	0
M. Graham	4	0	3	0	12
S. Horo	5	0	3	0	12
H. McGahan	7	1	3	0	12
V. O'Callaghan	3	0	1	7	18
R. O'Regan	5	2	1	0	4
J. Ropati	5	1	0	8	16
A. Shelford	4	3	2	0	8
Dane Sorensen	5	1	0	1	2
K. Sorensen	6	1	2	0	8
S. Stewart	7	0	4	0	16
H. Tamati	6	0	0	0	0
R. Taylor	3	0	1	0	4
*B. Todd	0	1	0	0	0
W. Wallace	6	0	0	0	0
Darrell Williams	8	0	0	0	0
O. Wright	6	2	0	4(1)	9
British-based players					
F. Ah Kuoi (Hull)	2	1	0	0	0
G. Kemble (Hull)	2	1	0	0	0
J. Leuluai (Hull)	3	0	1	0	4
D. O'Hara (Hull)	3	0	1	0	4
G. Prohm (Hull K.R.)	3	0	0	0	0
K. Tamati (Warrington)	2	1	0	0	0
G. West (Wigan)	2	0	0	0	0

*Replacement
( )drop goal — one point

MEMO

First match on 6 October, last match on 17 November.

The shortest tour on record was reduced even further when the game against Lancashire at Oldham was postponed because of frost. Interest in the 12 remaining matches, however, produced the best Kiwi tour attendances for 20 years.

After an opening defeat at Wigan, the tourists won all five of their other club matches. They ran up their highest-ever score on tour with a 46-8 defeat of St. Helens, including a record nine penalty goals by Olsen Filipaina.

A late equalising penalty goal by Britain's Lee Crooks in the third Test squared the series.

The squad of 24 tourists was strengthened by several British-based New Zealanders, mostly for the Test matches.

1989 TOUR

MATCH RESULTS

St. Helens	L	26-27	7,040
Castleford	W	22-20	5,993
Wigan	L	14-24	15,013
Bradford N.	W	26-8	3,498
Leeds	W	34-4	9,632
Cumbria (Whitehaven)	W	28-2	3,983
GREAT BRITAIN (Man. U. FC)	W	**24-16**	18,273
GREAT BRITAIN			
(Elland Rd, Leeds)	L	6-26	13,073
Hull	W	44-8	5,894
Widnes	W	26-18	9,905
Featherston R.	W	44-20	2,773
GREAT BRITAIN (Wigan)	L	**6-10**	20,346

SUMMARY

Played 12   Won 8   Lost 4

For
Tries 50   Goals 49   Drop goals 2   Points 300

Against
Tries 30   Goals 31   Drop goal 1   Points 183

Lost Test series 2-1

MEMO

First match on 1 October, last match on 11 November.

The Kiwis lost their first Test series in Britain since 1965, but their 66 per cent success rate over the 12-match tour equalled their best-ever figures.

They also attracted the highest crowd aggregate since the 23-match tour of 1965 and the best for a Kiwi Test series since 1961.

The Test series was decided in the final game with Britain winning 10-6 after widely fluctuating form in the two previous games.

New Zealand were convincing 24-16 winners of the first Test with Britain's only highlight being a 75-yard touchdown by Martin Offiah, which won Rothmans' solo try of the decade award.

A week later, Britain pulled off one of the most remarkable wins in Test history after being reduced to 12 men inside two minutes when full back Steve Hampson was sent off by Australian referee Greg McCallum for butting Gary Freeman.

Britain's already much-changed side regrouped and strode to a magnificent 26-6 victory.

The third Test was a titanic tussle full of controversial refereeing decisions, sweeping attacks and fierce tackling, with Britain hanging on to their 10-6 interval lead to win the series.

Gary Mercer won New Zealand's man of the series award.

Although 10 Kiwis were sent to the sin bin during the tour, Tawera Nikau was the only tourist to be dismissed permanently, for dissent.

TOUR PARTY

Managers: I. Jenkins and T. McKeown
Captain: H. McGahan   Coach: T. Gordon

	App	Sub	Tries	Gls	Pts
P. Bancroft	5	1	0	29	58
D. Clark	5	1	1	0	4
M. Edwards	5	0	2	0	8
M. Elia	3	1	4	0	16
*D. Ewe	2	0	0	1	2
E. Faimalo	6	1	1	0	4
G. Freeman	7	1	5	0	20
J. Goulding	4	1	1	0	4
K. Iro	7	0	4	0	16
T. Kemp	6	2	1	0	4
M. Kuiti	6	1	4	0	16
F. Leota	5	3	2	0	8
H. McGahan	7	0	3	0(1)	13
D. Mann	7	0	0	0	0
*G. Mann	1	1	0	0	0
G. Mercer	8	0	2	0	8
T. Nikau	5	1	2	0	8
T. Ropati	2	0	0	0	0
A. Shelford	4	0	0	0	0
K. Shelford	7	0	3	12(1)	37
K. Sherlock	6	1	1	7	18
S. Stewart	7	2	1	0	4
W. Taewa	5	0	3	0	12
B. Todd	7	0	0	0	0
B. Tuuta	5	1	1	0	4
W. Wallace	5	0	1	0	4
D. Watson	6	1	6	0	24
Darrell Williams	7	1	2	0	8
British-based players					
D. Bell (Wigan)	3	0	0	0	0
K. Sorensen (Widnes)	3	0	0	0	0

()drop goal — one point
*Replacement

Top goals and points scorer, Phil Bancroft.

NEW ZEALAND APPENDIX

In addition to full tours, World Cup squads made occasional appearances against club sides as follows, Kiwis' score first:

1960
Halifax	W	18-12	1,960

1970
Salford	W	8-7	2,226
Bradford N.	W	28-17	2,542
Barrow	W	14-10	5,118

1972
Leeds	L	6-11	3,510
Huddersfield	W	32-2	1,069
Salford	L	4-50	3,572

1975
Barrow	W	24-0	4,150
Keighley	W	20-8	2,125

RECORDS AGAINST CLUB SIDES
Highest score: 46-8 v. St. Helens in 1985
(Also *widest margin win*)
Biggest defeat: 4-50 v. Salford (1972 World Cup tour)
Biggest attendance: 30,000 v. Wigan in 1907-08

INDIVIDUAL RECORDS
(Club and representative matches)
Most tries on tour: 23 by Bert Avery in 1926-27
Most goals on tour: 63 by Des White in 1951-52
Most points on tour: 141 (7t, 60g) by Herbert Messenger in 1907-08
Most appearances on tour: 33 by H. Turtill in 1907-08
Most tries in a match: 5 by Bert Avery v. Broughton Rangers in 1926-27
Most goals in a match: 9 by Olsen Filipaina v. St. Helens in 1985
Most points in a match: 18 by Olsen Filipaina v. St. Helens in 1985

NEW ZEALAND TOURS OF PAPUA NEW GUINEA

	P	W	D	L	F	A
1978	2	2	0	0	79	33
1982	3	3	0	0	136	30
1986	4	2	0	2	104	82

NEW ZEALAND TOURS OF AUSTRALIA

	P	W	D	L	F	A
1907-08	13	9	1	3	275	131
1909	10	5	0	5	181	182
1911	8	5	0	3	94	67
1912	7	4	0	3	84	83
1913	9	5	0	4	199	161
1919	11	5	0	6	211	187
1921	7	2	0	5	103	147
1925	12	5	0	7	223	230
1930	13	6	0	7	211	276
1938	9	5	1	3	182	161
1948	8	6	0	2	118	99
1952	13	10	0	3	368	149
1956	15	9	0	6	353	244
1959	15	13	0	2	488	205
1963	16	12	0	4	258	157
1967	17	11	0	6	369	216
1972	3	0	0	3	28	93
1975*	6	3	0	3	154	124
1978	16	10	0	6	358	241
1982	8	3	0	5	145	147
1986	6	3	0	3	138	105
1987	3	3	0	0	79	34

*Including one World Cup match.

NEW ZEALAND TOURS OF FRANCE

Each tour immediately followed trip to Britain.

	P	W	D	L	F	A
	8	4	1	3	118	104
1947-48						
Drew Test series 1-1						
1951-52	12	7	1	4	181	93
Lost Test series 2-0						
1955-56	8	3	1	4	107	143
Lost Test series 2-1						
1961	9	6	2	1	150	57
Won Test series 1-0, drew 2						
1965	8	3	1	4	67	80
Lost Test series 3-0						
1971	6	5	1	0	108	43
Won Test series 2-0, drew 1						
1980	7	6	1	0	119	34
Drew Test series 1-1						
1985	7	7	0	0	192	41
Won Test series 2-0						
1989	5	5	0	0	218	28
Won Test series 2-0						

● Two World Cup squads also played extra matches. In 1970 New Zealand played twice, winning and losing. The defeat was 16-2 against France in an unofficial Test. In 1975 they won two and drew one of three matches.

1985 Kiwis to Britain and France. Left to right: Back row: H. Tamati, Wallace, Taylor, Stewart, O'Callaghan, Ropati, K. Sorensen, Cooper, Bell. Middle row: Graham Lowe (Coach), Bourneville, Shelford, O'Regan, McGahan, Wright, Coxван, Williams, Elia, Horo, Glen Gallagher (Physio). Front row: Jim Campbell (Manager), Gibb, D. Sorensen, Graham (Captain), Filipaina, Goulding, Friend, Tom McKeown (Business Manager).

RECORDS IN TEST AND WORLD CUP MATCHES

For New Zealand
Highest score: 66-14 v. Papua New Guinea, Test and
World Cup match at Auckland 10 July 1988
66-10 v. Papua New Guinea, Test and World Cup
match at Auckland 5 July 1992 (Also *widest margin win*)
Most tries in a match: 6 by Hugh McGahan v. Papua
New Guinea, Test at Auckland 2 Oct. 1983
Most points in a match: 24 by Hugh McGahan (as above)
Most goals in a match: 11 by Des White v. Australia,
Second Test at Brisbane 28 June 1952
Most appearances: 36 by Jock Butterfield (1954-63)
Most career tries: 16 by Hugh McGahan (1982-90)
Most career goals: 62 by Des White (1950-56)
Most career points: 130 by Des White (1950-56)
Biggest attendance: 47,363 v. Australia, World Cup final
at Eden Park, Auckland 9 October 1988

Against New Zealand
Highest score: 53-19 v. Great Britain, World Cup at Pau
4 November 1972
Widest margin: 44-0 v. Australia, Second Test at Sydney
24 July 1991
Most tries in a match: 4 by Billy Boston (Britain), First
Test at Auckland 24 July 1954
4 by Garry Schofield (Britain),
Second Test at Wigan 2 November 1985
Most goals in a match: 10 by John Holmes (Britain),
World Cup at Pau 4 November 1972
Most points in a match: 26 (2t,10g) by John Holmes
(Britain) as above

*Hugh McGahan, Kiwi record-holder for most tries and points
in a match and most tries in a career, in rainswept action
on the 1985 tour of Britain.*

*British Lions Player of the Tour Andy Platt, promoted to
vice-captain after the departure of Ellery Hanley.*

1992 LIONS

1992 TOUR REVIEW

Despite winning only three of the six Tests, the 1992 British Lions returned from a 10-week tour of Papua New Guinea, Australia and New Zealand to be hailed as the most successful outfit since the Ashes-winning squad of 1970.

The biggest-ever 32-man tour party, who called up seven replacements, undertook the shortest-ever itinerary of 17 fixtures and lost four. But the reduced timetable included a record five games against Sydney Premiership sides.

The lengthy casualty list featured tour captain Ellery Hanley, who was plagued by foot and hamstring injuries. Having last played for Leeds on 26 April, Hanley eventually made his first appearance of the tour on 23 June in the 10th match, to last only nine minutes before being withdrawn from the match and the tour.

Off the field, the tour was a commercial success, with record profits of £233,645 swelled by three capacity Test gates in Australia and television rights sales.

Wigan prop forward Andy Platt was adjudged to be the player of the tour; winger Martin Offiah confirmed his rating as the world's deadliest finisher; and Garry Schofield — making a record fourth tour — proved to be an inspirational deputy captain, especially in the darkest hour after the first Test defeat in Sydney.

The squad that left England in May included 13 Wigan players, a record number from one club. A 14th Wigan player, David Myers, joined the squad in mid-June, while injured club colleagues Andy Gregory, Neil Cowie and Ian Lucas returned home at the same time.

The most Wigan players to be in a starting line-up was eight on three occasions, including the second and third Tests against Australia. Wigan had 10 players on duty for the first Test, with seven in the starting line-up plus three substitutes and had nine on the field at one stage. The three above feats were all British

Test records.

The Lions, having replaced original selections Jonathan Davies (injured) and Bobby Goulding (suspended) with Alan Hunte and Deryck Fox before departure, were hit by injuries throughout the tour. Having been called up for his Test debut against Papua New Guinea at Port Moresby, St. Helens second row man Sonny Nickle was the first to return home, followed by Paul Loughlin, Les Holliday and the Wigan trio.

Into the touring party came Paul Hulme, Karl Harrison, Myers, Steve McNamara and Dean Sampson. Sheffield Eagles duo Mark Aston and Paul Broadbent, due to undertake a sabbatical visit to Winfield Cup side South Sydney, were called in as replacements. Broadbent was utilised for just two appearances, with Aston being invited to join the tourists for the remainder of the trip.

The 10-match Australian segment of the tour had been specially requested by the British management as preparation for the Tests. The record number of Winfield Cup opponents were Canberra, Illawarra, Parramatta, Newcastle Knights and Gold Coast.

A Brett Kenny-inspired Parramatta were the only non-Test team to beat the Lions, the midweek side providing much-needed confidence by going through the tour undefeated. Scrum half Deryck Fox was the captain and star of the second string, being denied a reward of Test selection for the last encounter in New Zealand by injury.

In the Test arena, Great Britain overcame the heat barrier in Papua New Guinea to snatch a late 20-14 success thanks to two tries by Offiah. After being steam-rollered by the powerful Australian pack in the first Test at Sydney, Britain recorded one of the most memorable of Test victories with a 33-10 rout at Melbourne in the first-ever staging of an Anglo-Aussie game in the southern outpost.

As in 1990 in Britain, Australia enjoyed the deeper reserves of mental and physical strength in the decider to retain the Ashes with a 16-10 success, a scoreline which flattered the Lions.

The anti-climax of two Tests in New Zealand hit the Britons' concentration levels and the weary Lions paid the price in the first Test at Palmerston North, going down 15-14 after leading 14-6 on the hour. The development of professionalism and team spirit during 10 weeks on the road was reflected in the second Test a week later, the Lions gaining a 19-16 victory to square the series.

The Hanley saga was the chief negative element of the successful tour. Although declared fit before departure, it became obvious that the Leeds captain was unable to train flat out and often undertook fitness tests behind closed doors. The make-or-break trial came after the demoralising first Test defeat in Sydney and the reversal at lowly Parramatta.

With the British camp at its lowest ebb, Hanley was being lined up for his first appearance at Newcastle when a major row broke out regarding his negotiations for an Australian television commentary role. After an outburst from the British team management, it was resolved that representatives of Hanley had been discussing a lucrative contract, said to be worth more than £10,000, only if he was ruled out of the tour.

His much-publicised comeback after a two-month lay-off came against Newcastle Knights. Hanley fell awkwardly taking a pass from Kevin Ellis in the seventh minute, tried to continue, but gave up the struggle within two minutes and limped off.

The Lions went on to give one of the best displays of the tour in a 22-0 victory. Hanley was ruled out of the rest of the tour, Leeds giving him permission to stay on to fulfil his television commentary contract which was eventually cut short, the Australians claiming they had difficulty deciphering his Yorkshire accent. Acting captain Schofield was confirmed as official Test captain and went on to inspire Britain to their 33-10 night of glory in Melbourne three days later.

Schofield also continued to be involved in helping to boost the tour by his willing co-operation with the media, in contrast to Hanley's refusal to talk to the Press.

In the scoring charts, Paul Eastwood emerged as the main striking force following the return home of broken arm victim Paul Loughlin. Eastwood kicked 23 goals from 28 attempts to top the goals chart, adding four tries to be top points scorer with 62. The Hull winger was also the holder of the tour record for most goals and points in a match.

Stones Bitter Young Player of the Year Gary Connolly came of age on the tour by making most appearances, 13 including five as substitute.

The record tour profits, easily beating the £92,000 haul in 1974, included gate receipts of £514,426, of which £346,652 came from the three sell-out Australian Tests. The British share of television receipts was just short of £200,000.

In his tour report to the Rugby League Council, manager Maurice Lindsay recommended a turn around of the tour itinerary for future visits. He advocated opening in New Zealand, on to Australia and rounding off in Papua New Guinea, thus minimising the effects of the tropical humidity and living conditions.

Garry Schofield, skipper of Great Britain in all six Tests on tour.

TOUR RESULTS

Date	Result	Score	Opposition	Venue	Attendance
In Papua New Guinea					
May 24	W	24-15	Highlands Zone	Goroka	4,591
27	W	38-20	Islands Zone	Rabaul	3,408
31	W	20-14	PAPUA NEW GUINEA	Port Moresby	7,294
In Australia					
June 2	W	14-10	Queensland Residents	Townsville	4,181
6	W	24-12	Canberra	Canberra	4,728
8	W	11-10	Illawarra	Wollongong	10,021
12	L	6-22	AUSTRALIA	Sydney	40,141
16	W	24-6	NSW Country	Parkes	8,014
19	L	16-22	Parramatta	Parramatta	18,220
23	W	22-0	Newcastle Knights	Newcastle	9,758
26	W	33-10	AUSTRALIA	Melbourne	30,257
30	W	28-10	Gold Coast	Tweed Heads	9,573
July 3	L	10-16	AUSTRALIA	Brisbane	32,313
In New Zealand					
8	W	14-8	Auckland	Auckland	5,485
12	L	14-15	NEW ZEALAND	Palmerston North	11,548
15	W	17-6	Canterbury	Christchurch	3,026
19	W	19-16	NEW ZEALAND	Auckland	10,223

TOUR SUMMARY

	P	W	D	L	T	G	Dr	Pts	T	G	Dr	Pts
						FOR				**AGAINST**		
In Papua New Guinea	3	3	0	0	15	11	0	82	8	8	1	49
In Australia	10	7	0	3	32	29	2	188	20	19	0	118
In New Zealand	4	3	0	1	10	11	2	64	7	8	1	45
Tour totals	17	13	0	4	57	51	4	334	35	35	2	212

TEST SUMMARY

	P	W	D	L	T	G	Dr	Pts	T	G	Dr	Pts
						FOR				**AGAINST**		
In Papua New Guinea	1	1	0	0	4	2	0	20	3	1	0	14
In Australia	3	1	0	2	7	10	1	49	8	8	0	48
In New Zealand	2	1	0	1	5	6	1	33	5	5	1	31
Test totals	6	3	0	3	16	18	2	102	16	14	1	93

TOUR RECORDS

Biggest attendance: 40,141 first Test v. Australia at Sydney
Highest score: 38-20 v. Islands Zone
Widest margin: 33-10 v. Australia, second Test at Melbourne
Highest score against: Lost to Australia 22-6, first Test at Sydney *(widest margin defeat)* Lost to Parramatta 22-16
Most tries in a match: No player scored three or more
Most goals in a match: 6 by Paul Eastwood v. NSW Country v. Australia, second Test
Most points in a match: 16 by Paul Eastwood v. NSW Country
Most tries on tour: 7 by Martin Offiah

Most goals on tour: 23 by Paul Eastwood
Most points on tour: 62 by Paul Eastwood
Most appearances: 13 (including five as substitute) by Gary Connolly
Most full appearances: 9 by Denis Betts, Phil Clarke, Paul Eastwood, Shaun Edwards, Billy McGinty, Paul Newlove, Andy Platt, Daryl Powell, Garry Schofield
Sent off: Sonny Nickle v. Highlands Zone
Sin bin: John Devereux v. Highlands Zone
Kelvin Skerrett v. Highlands Zone
Andy Gregory v. Australia (1st Test)
Gary Connolly v. NSW Country
Shaun Edwards v. Parramatta
Opponents' sin bin: Gigmai Ongogo (Highlands Zone)
Nere Launa (Highlands Zone)

Test debutant Sonny Nickle is subjected to a double Papuan tackle at Port Moresby.

TOUR PARTY

Manager: Maurice Lindsay
Coach: Malcolm Reilly
Assistant Coach: Phil Larder/John Kear
Doctor: David Graham
Physiotherapist: Dave Fevre

Player	Club	IN PAPUA NEW GUINEA					IN AUSTRALIA					IN NEW ZEALAND					TOUR TOTALS				
		App	Sub	T	G	Pts	App	Sub	T	G	Pts	App	Sub	T	G	Pts	App	Sub	T	G	Pts
†ASTON, Mark	Sheffield E.	–	–	–	–	–	1	1	–	–	–	–	2	2	–	8	1	3	2	–	8
BETTS, Denis	Wigan	2	–	1	–	4	5	–	1	–	4	2	1	–	2	4	9	1	2	2	12
†BROADBENT, Paul	Sheffield E.	–	–	–	–	–	1	–	3	–	12	–	–	–	–	–	1	–	3	–	12
CLARKE, Phil	Wigan	2	–	1	–	4	5	3	1	–	4	2	2	1	–	4	9	5	3	–	12
CONNOLLY, Gary	St. Helens	–	2	–	–	–	6	–	3	1	14	2	–	–	–	–	8	2	3	1	14
*COWIE, Neil	Wigan	1	1	–	–	–	2	–	–	1	2	–	–	–	–	–	3	1	–	1	2
CROOKS, Lee	Castleford	2	–	–	–	–	3	–	–	1	2	1	–	–	–	–	6	–	–	1	2
DERMOTT, Martin	Wigan	2	–	–	–	–	5	–	–	–	–	1	–	–	–	–	8	–	–	–	–
DEVEREUX, John	Widnes	1	–	2	–	8	5	–	–	1	2	1	2	–	–	–	7	2	2	1	10
EASTWOOD, Paul	Hull	2	–	2	–	8	5	–	2	17	42	2	–	–	6	12	9	–	4	23	62
EDWARDS, Shaun	Wigan	2	–	1	–	4	5	1	3	–	12	2	–	–	–	–	9	1	4	–	16
ELLIS, Kevin	Warrington	1	–	1	–	4	5	–	–	(1)	1	2	–	2	–	8	8	–	3	(1)	13
FAIRBANK, Karl	Bradford N.	2	–	2	–	8	4	2	1	–	4	2	1	–	–	–	8	3	3	–	12
FOX, Deryck	Featherstone R.	–	1	–	2	4	3	3	–	7	14	2	–	–	5	10	5	4	–	14	28
*GREGORY, Andy	Wigan	1	–	–	–	–	3	–	–	–	–	–	–	–	–	–	4	–	–	–	–
HALLAS, Graeme	Hull K.R.	1	1	1	–	4	4	–	–	–	–	1	1	1	1	6	6	2	2	1	10
HAMPSON, Steve	Wigan	2	–	–	–	–	4	–	1	–	4	1	–	–	–	–	7	–	1	–	4
*HANLEY, Ellery	Leeds	–	–	–	–	–	1	–	1	–	4	–	–	–	–	–	1	–	1	–	4
†HARRISON, Karl	Halifax	–	–	–	–	–	2	3	–	–	–	2	1	–	–	–	4	4	–	–	–
*HOLLIDAY, Les	Widnes	–	–	–	–	–	2	1	–	–	–	–	–	–	–	–	2	1	–	–	–
†HULME, Paul	Widnes	–	–	–	–	–	3	3	–	–	–	1	1	–	–	–	4	4	–	–	–
HUNTE, Alan	St. Helens	1	–	1	–	4	5	1	3	–	12	2	–	2	–	8	8	1	6	–	24
JACKSON, Lee	Hull	1	–	1	–	4	5	–	–	–	–	2	–	–	–	–	8	–	1	–	4
JACKSON, Michael	Wakefield T.	–	–	–	–	–	2	3	–	–	–	2	1	–	–	–	4	4	–	–	–
*LOUGHLIN, Paul	St. Helens	2	–	–	6	12	2	1	–	1	2	–	–	–	–	–	4	1	–	7	14
*LUCAS, Ian	Wigan	–	–	–	–	–	2	1	–	–	–	–	–	–	–	–	2	–	–	–	–
LYDON, Joe	Wigan	1	1	1	–	4	2	4	2	–	8	1	2	–	(1)	1	4	7	3	(1)	13
McGINTY, Billy	Wigan	2	–	–	–	–	5	1	1	–	4	2	–	–	–	–	9	–	1	–	4
†McNAMARA, Steve	Hull	–	1	–	–	–	2	–	1	–	4	2	2	–	–	–	4	3	1	–	4
†MYERS, David	Wigan	–	–	–	–	–	–	2	–	–	–	1	1	–	–	–	1	3	–	–	–
NEWLOVE, Paul	Featherstone R.	2	1	1	–	4	5	1	2	–	8	2	1	–	–	–	9	3	3	–	12

Player	Club	App	Sub	T	G	Pts	App	Sub	T	G	Pts	App	Sub	T	G	Pts
*NICKLE, Sonny	St. Helens	—	3	—	—	—	2	1	—	—	—	—	3	—	—	—
OFFIAH, Martin	Wigan	1	—	2	—	8	2	—	4	—	16	7	1	7	—	28
PLATT, Andy	Wigan	2	—	—	—	—	2	—	2	—	8	9	—	2	—	8
POWELL, Daryl	Sheffield E.	2	—	—	—	—	2	—	—	—	—	9	—	—	—	—
†SAMPSON, Dean	Castleford	—	—	—	—	—	2	—	—	—	—	2	—	—	—	—
SCHOFIELD, Garry	Leeds	2	—	2	—	8	2	—	1	(1)	5	9	—	3	(2)	14
SKERRETT, Kelvin	Wigan	1	2	1	—	4	1	1	—	—	—	6	3	1	—	4
STEADMAN, Graham	Castleford	1	—	—	3	6	2	—	2	1	10	7	1	2	4	16

(1) Indicates drop goal

* Sent home injured: Nickle (11 June), Gregory, Holliday, Loughlin, Lucas (26 June), Cowie (6 July)

† Arrived as replacement: Hulme (11 June), Harrison (16 June), McNamara and Myers (18 June), Aston and Broadbent (19 June), Sampson (6 July)

Karl Fairbank scores one of his two tries in the 38-20 victory over Islands Zone.

MATCH BY MATCH

24 May
Goroka
HIGHLANDS ZONE	**15**
GREAT BRITAIN	**24**

1. Hampson
2. Devereux (Hallas, 63 min.)
3. Loughlin
4. Newlove (Connolly, 29 min.)
5. Eastwood
6. Schofield, Capt.
7. Edwards
8. Cowie (Skerrett, 55 min.)
9. Dermott
10. Platt
11. Betts
12. McGinty (Nickle, 29 min.)
13. Clarke

T: Schofield (2), Eastwood, Betts
G: Loughlin (4)

Highlands Zone:
Singapar; Gonia, Nema, Tete, Yako; Soga, Ongogo; Launa, Togola (Singiso), Sare (Kepo), Tiri (Capt.), Olik (Kuso), Kamiak

T: Singapar, Ongogo
G: Ongogo (2, 1dg), Tete

Half-time: 9-10

Referee: Luxie Metta
Attendance: 4,591

27 May
Rabaul
ISLANDS ZONE	**20**
GREAT BRITAIN	**38**

1. Steadman
2. Hunte
3. Lydon
4. Newlove (Connolly, half-time)
5. Hallas
6. Ellis
7. Gregory, Capt. (Fox, 43 min.)
8. Crooks (Cowie, 52 min.)
9. L. Jackson
10. Skerrett (Nickle, 56 min.)
11. Fairbank
12. McGinty
13. Powell

T: Fairbank (2), Lydon, Ellis, Hunte, Hallas, Skerrett
G: Steadman (3), Fox (2)

Islands Zone:
Eremas; Palangat, Johnson, Vovono, Kapia (Sine); Langa (Capt.), Ngatia; Maveo (Alunga), Bate, Rich, Peter, Kennedy (Marnara), Pangas

· T: Alunga (2), Langa
G: Eremas (4)

Half-time: 4-24

Referee: Graham Ainui
Attendance: 3,408

St. Helens packman Nickle was sent off on his Lions debut, with two players from each side sin-binned, in a controversial start to the 17-match tour. The performance of whistle-happy referee Metta was described by the Great Britain management as "bizarre".

Nickle came on as a 29th-minute substitute and was dismissed six minutes from the end for swinging a punch in retaliation at scrum half Ongogo after being tackled without the ball. Ongogo was a tormentor in every sense, scoring a try, two goals and a drop goal, as well as creating the home side's other touchdown.

Britain's Devereux and Skerrett were despatched to the sin bin, as were Highlands duo Ongogo and Launa. Centre Newlove shone for the visitors before being taken off with heat exhaustion, while Platt and Dermott were outstanding in defence.

The Lions were kept standing around for 23 minutes in the sweltering midday sun, waiting for the Islands team to turn up. When the match eventually kicked off, temperatures soared to 94 degrees. Britain responded with a scorching performance in a fixture reduced to 35 minutes each way so the tourists could leave the primitive airstrip before dark.

With no explanation forthcoming for the delayed start, the Lions roared into a 24-4 half-time lead. Prop Crooks put in a strong claim for a Test spot in his first game since Wembley, despite a dramatic weight-loss in training.

Also impressive were fellow prop Skerrett and back row men Fairbank, scorer of two tries, and Powell, well supported by half backs Ellis and Gregory.

Recalled Great Britain prop Lee Crooks powers into a three-man Kumul tackle at Port Moresby.

Stand off Daryl Powell kicks ahead in the Port Moresby Test, supported by Andy Platt (left) and Garry Schofield.

TEST MATCH v. PAPUA NEW GUINEA
Try-scoring hero Martin Offiah came to Great
Britain's rescue at the double as Papua New
Guinea led 14-12 with only eight minutes
remaining of a mistake-ridden Test at Port
Moresby.

Offiah saved the Lions with two tries in two
minutes to clinch a 20-14 victory but this was
not enough to spare his colleagues from a
verbal lashing from coach Malcolm Reilly.

His charges were blasted for losing possession
on the first tackle seven times, while twice
failing to win scrums with the advantage of
head and ball. Excuses of the erratic behaviour
of the light ball were dismissed by an angry
Reilly who pointed out that the local product
had been used in two previous fixtures and
more than a week of training.

Offiah took his Test tally to 21 tries in as
many matches in his first game of the tour after
recovering from a calf injury, then praised his
centre partner Paul Loughlin for some classic
service.

In their third game of the tour, the Lions
struggled from the start against a Papua team
who controlled the Test at half back through
Aquil Emil and skipper Ngala Lapan. As the
visitors repeatedly lost possession, the Kumuls
were able to build pressure and momentum.

Outstanding prop Kera Ngaffin and Lapan
were prominent in a six-man move before the
captain's sharp pass sent loose forward Mathew
Elara striding through for the opening try after
11 minutes.

The Papuans then put together a sweeping
65-yard attack to dismantle Britain once again.
Emil's short kick split the visiting defence for
full back Philip Boge to pick up the ball and
serve centre August Joseph, who set up a
touchdown for Kini Tani.

The Lions showed tremendous character in
countering the heat and partisan crowd,
producing a touchdown with their first positive
attack after 25 minutes. Scrum half Shaun
Edwards changed the direction of play, switching
the ball to skipper Garry Schofield, selected in
his former centre role. He gave his replacement
at stand off, Daryl Powell, room to put in a
well-judged short kick over the line for winger
Paul Eastwood to win the race to touch down.

Loughlin failed with the difficult conversion
attempt but levelled the score with two
well-struck penalties before the Lions edged in
front two minutes from half-time.

When the Kumuls lost the ball on their own
22 metre, Wigan duo Steve Hampson and
Edwards spread the ball right to send over
clubmate Phil Clarke on his first full appearance for Great Britain.

But a four-point lead hardly looked good
enough as the visitors turned into a strong
wind. Their hesitancy with the light ball
proved costly on the hour when Lapan's lofted
kick bounced over the try line between
Eastwood and Hampson for centre Richard
Wagambie to sweep between them to touch
down. Emil's angled goal kick meant that the
Papuans were poised to secure a shock victory
with eight minutes left on the clock.

Britain then found their touch at last.
Martin Dermott, Edwards, Schofield and
substitute Joe Lydon combined before Loughlin
timed his pass perfectly for Offiah to finish off.
Then Loughlin burst on to a Schofield pass to
supply Offiah again and spare Britain's blushes.

Two-try rescue hero, Martin Offiah.

TEST MATCH

31 May

Port Moresby

PAPUA NEW GUINEA 14

GREAT BRITAIN 20

Philip Boge	1.	Steve Hampson
Joshua Kouoro	2.	Paul Eastwood
Richard Wagambie	3.	Garry Schofield, Capt.
August Joseph	4.	Paul Loughlin
Kini Tani	5.	Martin Offiah
Aquil Emil	6.	Daryl Powell
Ngala Lapan, Capt.	7.	Shaun Edwards
Ben Bire	8.	Lee Crooks
Michael Matmillo	9.	Martin Dermott
Kera Ngaffin	10.	Andy Platt
Bobby Ako	11.	Denis Betts
Joe Gispe	12.	Karl Fairbank
Mathew Elara	13.	Phil Clarke
Korul Sinemau	14.	Joe Lydon
Michael Angra	15.	Kelvin Skerrett
Steven Kapan	16.	Paul Newlove
Nande Yer	17.	Sonny Nickle

T: Tani, Elara, Wagambie
G: Emil
Substitutions:
Angra for Elara (28 min.)
Yer for Ako (34 min.)
Sinemau for Tani (45 min.)
Kapan for Emil (57 min.)
Half-time: 8-12
Referee: Eddie Ward (Australia)
Attendance: 7,294

T: Offiah (2), Eastwood, Clarke
G: Loughlin (2)
Substitutions:
Skerrett for Crooks (47 min.)
Nickle for Fairbank (47 min.)
Lydon for Hampson (60 min.)
Newlove for Powell (60 min.)

Scorechart

Minute	Score	PNG	GB
11:	Elara (T)	4	0
21:	Tani (T)	8	0
25:	Eastwood (T)	8	4
30:	Loughlin (P)	8	6
33:	Loughlin (P)	8	8
38:	Clarke (T)	8	12
50:	Wagambie (T)		
	Emil (G)	14	12
72:	Offiah (T)	14	16
74:	Offiah (T)	14	20

First of three Test tries on tour for Phil Clarke.

2 June
Townsville
QUEENSLAND RESIDENTS 10
GREAT BRITAIN 14

1. Lydon (Betts, half-time)
2. Devereux (Newlove, 28 min.)
3. Connolly
4. Ellis
5. Hunte
6. Edwards
7. Gregory, Capt. (Fox, 65 min.)
8. Lucas (Skerrett, 58 min.)
9. L. Jackson
10. Cowie
11. Fairbank
12. Hallas
13. McGinty

T: Devereux, McGinty, Edwards
G: Hallas

Queensland Residents:
Schultz; White, Hamilton (Smith), Robertson, Kerr (Fisher); Hetherington, Grauf (Capt.); Kennedy, Marty, Pike, Retchless (Mills), Clifford (Bella), Spark

T: Hamilton
G: Kerr (3)

Half-time: 6-4

Referee: John Willey
Attendance: 4,181

The injury-hit British, with seven forwards unavailable, retained their unbeaten record — but only just — against the best of Queensland outside of the Premiership.

The Residents, featuring two former London Crusaders in Craig Grauf and Eric Kennedy, led 6-4 at the interval. Although falling behind 10-14, they were pressing on the British line when the final whistle went.

The Lions paid the price for going into the game without a recognised kicker, missing out on 10 points as Lydon, Edwards and Hampson all missed simple chances before makeshift forward Hallas finally hit the target on the sixth and final attempt.

Connolly was the best of a disappointing Lions side. Gregory showed a lack of match practice, teammate Lucas was rusty in his first game for two months and winger Devereux fumbled a high ball to give Queensland their only try.

British coach Reilly denied post-match Queensland gouging claims.

6 June
Canberra
CANBERRA 12
GREAT BRITAIN 24

1. Steadman
2. Eastwood
3. Newlove
4. Loughlin
5. Hunte
6. Schofield, Capt. (Connolly, 66 min.)
7. Gregory (Fox, 38 min.)
8. Skerrett
9. Dermott
10. Platt
11. Betts
12. M. Jackson (Holliday, 31 min.)
13. Clarke

T: Platt (2), Newlove, Hunte, Eastwood
G: Loughlin, Steadman

Canberra:
Mullins; Hoppe, Norton, Gale, Croker; O'Sullivan, Stuart (Capt.); McDonnell, Stone, Woods, Graham, G. Coyne, Bellamy. Subs: Friend, Hunt, Pickering, Spinks, plus Jones, Nages and Cannon used on interchange system

T: Croker, Spinks
G: Stuart, Friend

Half-time: 6-20

Referee: Greg McCallum
Attendance: 4,728

Great Britain manager Maurice Lindsay accused Canberra of "insulting international rugby" by fielding a virtual reserve side and sending on a total of seven substitutes, three more than the permitted quota.

The Raiders, scheduled to play a Winfield Cup game 24 hours later, devalued the Lions' last major preparation for the first Test against Australia, although the visitors did gain heart from a five-try victory.

Britain also suffered injury scares to Test veterans Gregory and Platt, a two-try hero. Four of their tries came in the first half with Gregory and skipper Schofield at their creative best, helping build a 20-6 interval lead.

8 June
Wollongong
ILLAWARRA   **10**
GREAT BRITAIN   **11**

1. Hampson
2. Devereux
3. Connolly (Hunte, half-time)
4. Powell
5. Hallas
6. Ellis
7. Edwards, Capt.
8. Lucas (Fox, 66 min.)
9. L. Jackson
10. Crooks
11. Fairbank (M. Jackson, 47 min.)
12. Holliday (Cowie, 55 min.)
13. McGinty

T: Hallas, Edwards
G: Devereux, Ellis (dg)

Illawarra:
Docherty (Pauls); O'Meara, Girdler, McGregor, Britten
(Piccinelli); Whittaker, Neil; Waddell (Dunn), Schifilliti,
Teitzel (Walsh), Cross (Capt.), Gallagher, Russell

T: Girdler, Whittaker
G: Girdler

Half-time: 4-10

Referee: Graham Annesley
Attendance: 10,021

Crooks powered his way into contention for a first Test place
as Britain staved off the determined challenge of Illawarra to
extend their unbeaten start to the tour to six matches.

The Lions performed defensive heroics, especially in a
nerve-tingling final quarter, to clinch the one-point victory.
Castleford skipper Crooks, seeking a way out of the Test
wilderness, took the ball up in fearless style and emerged as
the visitors' top tackler.

Winger Hallas gave the Lions an early lead with a
spectacular try after 13 minutes, outstripping a stunned
Steelers' defence in an 80-yard touchline run. Wigan full
back Hampson, returning to the club he played for in 1989,
brought off two awesome try-saving tackles before Illawarra
pulled back from 11-4 down when Whittaker scored a try
with eight minutes left.

Paul Sironen, tryscorer in the first Anglo-Aussie Test at Sydney.

FIRST TEST v. AUSTRALIA

Great Britain displayed power and pace to rock Australia in the opening quarter before the green-and-gold machine steam-rollered the Lions into submission.

A capacity 40,141 Sydney Football Stadium crowd saw Britain start in great style, shaking the mighty home forwards with a series of bone-shattering tackles. Even the formidable Glenn Lazarus failed to recover from a fifth-minute body collision and had to be replaced.

The pace inevitably came from Martin Offiah, who was tactically unleashed from as early as the third minute.

But the Kangaroos cut the supply line to Wigan's flying winger and relentlessly gained ground in the war of forward attrition in a convincing 22-6 triumph.

Home supremacy was confirmed in the power battle. With 10 minutes still to go, Britain were battered down to 12 men as Ian Lucas became their fifth casualty and could not be replaced because all four permitted substitutes had been utilised for injured players.

The catalogue of injury victims emphasised Britain's efforts. During that promising opening spell, the Lions also outwitted Australia with a series of well-planned tactical moves involving strike force Offiah.

Within three minutes, long passes from half-back duo Andy Gregory and Garry Schofield sent Offiah sprinting 60 yards down the wing. He looked to be heading for a stunning long-range try only for the stadium's giant television screen to confirm that he had touched a few blades of the touchline as he edged past Australian full back Andrew Ettingshausen.

Then a planned long kick from a scrum deep inside Britain's half again set Australian alarm bells ringing as Offiah gave chase from deep, albeit too far back, as full back Graham Steadman sped forward to force the home defence into desperate cover action.

Yet another marvellous touchline run by Offiah almost brought a try again as he pulled away from a high tackle, sweeping from the cover. This time, Ettingshausen's flying tackle managed to put Offiah into touch.

Injuries plus an early 10-minute spell in the sin bin for scrum half Gregory following a high tackle helped to break the Lions' gameplan. Among the enforced changes was the switch of skipper Schofield from stand off to centre, sending on Shaun Edwards to partner Gregory after 44 minutes. Soon after the reshuffle, Schofield made Britain's best second half break and later he produced the pass for substitute Joe Lydon to score their only try.

It was Mal Meninga who led the Kangaroo charge, powering in for the first two tries. Allan Langer had an outstanding game at scrum half while every one of the Australian forwards drove deep wedges into the British defence. Loose forward Bradley Clyde took the Man of the Match award as the main creator of two of Australia's four tries.

The opening touchdown came in scintillating style as Britain were still threatening an upset, despite trailing to a Rod Wishart penalty goal. Meninga was involved three times and completed the bewildering 70-yard raid with a 30th-minute touchdown, Wishart's goal providing an 8-2 interval lead. Prop Lee Crooks contributed a penalty goal for Britain.

The second half saw the Kangaroos roll relentlessly to victory with further tries from Meninga, Paul Sironen and winger Michael Hancock.

The penalty count favoured Britain and included one for the foul by Paul Harragon which resulted in Lucas being taken to hospital with concussion. Despite that incident and Gregory's sin bin, it was a night of controlled aggression regardless of the pre-match "big fight" hype.

Wigan had a British club record 10 players on Test duty with seven in the starting line-up, plus three substitutes. For a brief period there were a record nine Wigan players on the field.

FIRST TEST

12 June   Sydney

AUSTRALIA 22   GREAT BRITAIN 6

Australia		Great Britain
Andrew Ettingshausen	1.	Graham Steadman
Rod Wishart	2.	Paul Newlove
Laurie Daley	3.	Daryl Powell
Mal Meninga, Capt.	4.	Paul Loughlin
Michael Hancock	5.	Martin Offiah
Peter Jackson	6.	Garry Schofield, Capt.
Allan Langer	7.	Andy Gregory
Glenn Lazarus	8.	Kelvin Skerrett
Steve Walters	9.	Martin Dermott
Paul Harragon	10.	Lee Crooks
Paul Sironen	11.	Denis Betts
Bob Lindner	12.	Andy Platt
Bradley Clyde	13.	Phil Clarke
Brad Mackay	14.	Shaun Edwards
David Gillespie	15.	Michael Jackson
Brad Fittler	16.	Joe Lydon
Kevin Walters	17.	Ian Lucas

T: Meninga (2), Sironen, Hancock
G: Wishart (3)
Substitutions:
Gillespie for Lazarus (5 min.)
Fittler for Lindner (73 min.)
Mackay for Sironen (73 min.)
K. Walters for Jackson (75 min.)
Half-time: 8-2
Referee: Dennis Hale (New Zealand)
Attendance: 40,141

T: Lydon
G: Crooks
Substitutions:
Lydon for Loughlin (17 min.)
Edwards for Newlove (44 min.)
Lucas for Skerrett (53 min.)
M. Jackson for Dermott (56 min.)

Scorechart

Minute	Score	Aus	GB
26:	Wishart (P)	2	0
30:	Meninga (T)		
	Wishart (G)	8	0
39:	Crooks (P)	8	2
47:	Meninga (T)	12	2
63:	Sironen (T)		
	Wishart (G)	18	2
71:	Lydon (T)	18	6
75:	Hancock (T)	22	6
	Scrums	7	4
	Penalties	13	16

Hooker Martin Dermott, part of a record Wigan Test contingent.

16 June
Parkes
NSW COUNTRY   **6**
GREAT BRITAIN   **24**

1. Hampson (Steadman, 73 min.)
2. Eastwood
3. Devereux (Loughlin, 31 min.)
4. Connolly
5. Hunte
6. Ellis
7. Fox, Capt.
8. Cowie (Lydon, 64 min.)
9. L. Jackson
10. Fairbank
11. Holliday (Gregory, half-time)
12. Hulme
13. McGinty

T: Eastwood, Connolly, Steadman
G: Eastwood (6)

NSW Country:
Beath; Roskell, Connelly, Krause (Linnane), Quinton; Twigg, Price; Corvo, Crowe (Capt.), Marr, Tutt (Breen), Stephan (Oldfield), Wilson (Crooks)

T: Connelly
G: Quinton

Half-time: 0-8

Referee: Steve Albert
Attendance: 8,014

The continuation of a wretched run of injuries overshadowed a seventh tour victory in eight outings and an impressive 16-point haul from winger Eastwood.

The latest trio of victims was Holliday (Achilles' tendon), Cowie (groin), and in-form centre Loughlin (arm), who all failed to finish the scrappy match.

The luckless Lions finished with only three recognised forwards, including new arrival Hulme, playing his first match for two months. Such was their plight that Fox was forced to play most of the second half as emergency loose forward, for the first time in his career, while Lydon played the last quarter in the second row for only the second time.

Eastwood staked a claim for Test selection with six goals and a try, plus the prevention of two tries with timely touchdowns behind his own line.

An often ill-tempered match flared up in the 70th minute and Britain's Connolly was sent to the sin bin, although he appeared to be the victim of a dangerously high tackle.

19 June
Parramatta
PARRAMATTA   **22**
GREAT BRITAIN   **16**

1. Connolly
2. Eastwood
3. Powell
4. Newlove
5. Offiah
6. Schofield, Capt.
7. Edwards
8. Harrison (Crooks, 54 min.)
9. Dermott (Fairbank, 20 min.)
10. Platt
11. Betts
12. Hulme
13. Clarke

T: Offiah (2), Edwards
G: Eastwood (2)

Parramatta:
Crnkovitch; Oudenryn, Mahon, Buettner, Erickson (Muchmore); Kenny (Capt.), Galbraith; Fearnley (Schofield), Flanagan (Horo), Drake (Tiernan), Blair, King, Laurie

T: Laurie, Buettner, Mahon, Galbraith
G: Buettner (3)

Half-time: 12-6

Referee: Eddie Ward
Attendance: 18,220

Britain's hopes of a morale-boosting win a week before the second Test crashed to a Parramatta side struggling near the bottom of the Sydney Premiership.

Veteran skipper Kenny, though now lacking pace, produced a vintage stand off performance at 31, instigating the try that set up a 12-6 interval lead and shrugging off a handful of defenders to send Mahon racing 40 yards to the posts for a vital 18-16 lead on the hour.

Mahon's try came while Britain were down to 12 men, with Edwards having been sent to the sin bin for dissent.

Forty minutes before the kick-off, Offiah suffered a blow to his ego when he was beaten by Parramatta winger Lee Oudenryn in a length of the field £1,000 cash challenge. The roles were reversed in the match as Offiah outshone his opposite number to race in for two well-taken tries.

23 June
Newcastle
NEWCASTLE KNIGHTS   **0**
GREAT BRITAIN   **22**

1. Lydon (Myers, 60 min.)
2. Hunte
3. Connolly
4. Devereux
5. Hallas
6. Ellis
7. Fox
8. Harrison
9. L. Jackson
10. Broadbent (Fairbank, half-time)
11. M. Jackson
12. McNamara (Aston, 50 min.)
13. Hanley, Capt. (Hulme, 9 min.)

T: Hunte (2), Lydon, Fairbank
G: Fox (3)

Newcastle Knights:
O'Davis (Fulmer); Herman, Schuster, Smith, Mackley; Hagan (Capt.) (McCormack), Rodwell; Sargent, Chapman, Stewart, Miller, Mullane (Crowe), Glanville (Richards)

Half-time: 0-4

Referee: Bill Harrigan
Attendance: 9,758

Skipper Hanley, who last played on 26 April, made his long-awaited return from injury in the 10th match of the tour ... to limp off after only nine minutes. In what was to be his only appearance on a third tour Down Under, Hanley played for seven minutes before crashing to the ground in pain, spending a further two minutes trying to recover before bowing out of a calculated comeback attempt.

Against a strong Newcastle side, Britain kept a clean sheet for the first time and looked fluent on attack despite the inclusion of four tour debutants — Broadbent, McNamara, Myers and Aston.

Harrison, Lee Jackson, Fox, Connolly, Lydon and Devereux all made serious claims for squad inclusion in the Test line-up.

Australian loose forward Bradley Clyde takes on British Lions duo Paul Newlove (left) and Martin Dermott.

SECOND TEST v. AUSTRALIA

Garry Schofield celebrated his official appointment as tour captain by inspiring Great Britain to a record-equalling 23-point margin victory over Australia in Melbourne's first-ever Anglo-Aussie Test.

Another first — the fielding of a Test pack from the same club — paid off handsomely as the Wigan six laid the foundations for a five-try success, cohesion overcoming a lack of bulk.

Wigan also had two players in the back to equal the Test record of eight players from one club in a Test starting line-up.

The Melbourne mauling was Britain's best performance on Australian soil since the record 40-17 win in 1958.

The levelling of the series left the Australian hierarchy regretting the pioneering choice of Melbourne as the second Test venue. The conditions of a cool night and a soggy pitch were more suitable for the visitors. The capacity 30,257 crowd included an army of about 8,000 travelling British supporters, plus a massive contingent of expatriate Britons and New Zealanders, providing the Lions with nearly 50 per cent of the vocal backing.

The five superb tries against the best-drilled defence in the world told the story of the Test, the green-and-golds being forced into the basic errors which allowed Britain to dominate from the start, apart from a 20-minute spell in the second half when Australia threatened to hit back.

Andy Platt, back in his most effective position at prop, set the example up front, refusing to concede an inch. He had an inspirational effect on Kelvin Skerrett and lightweight debutant Billy McGinty, whose mobility and industry was in sharp contrast to Australia's forwards.

The hosts looked leaden-footed on the slippery surface and were always prone to errors against British tackling which never relaxed apart from the short spell during the second half when Allan Langer sparked a home revival.

The Australian retaliation consisted of two tries around the hour. Otherwise, the game belonged to Britain, with winger Paul Eastwood, playing only because of Paul Loughlin's injury, kicking six goals from seven attempts.

Eastwood's part in calming nerves with two penalty goals in the opening 10 minutes cannot be underestimated. Both were given for offside as Australia moved up too quickly to snuff out the danger of Britain's incisive passing.

The Lions' first touchdown came in the 18th minute when loose forward Phil Clarke danced past two challenges, Eastwood adding the goal to open a 10-0 lead. The alert Shaun Edwards, who formed a productive half-back pairing with Schofield, set up the second try 12 minutes later with a delicate kick over Kangaroo full back Andrew Ettingshausen. Winger Martin Offiah over-ran the ball, but centre Paul Newlove was following up to score.

Schofield cheekily chipped the ball through away from the grasp of Ettingshausen to add a third try five minutes before the break, Eastwood maintaining his 100 per cent goalkicking record to give Britain an amazing 22-0 interval lead.

Schofield extended that superiority with a 49th-minute drop goal before fatigue and a lack of concentration allowed the Kangaroos to creep back into the game through tries from Bob Lindner and Chris Johns. But the Lions were determined to have the last word.

Full back Graham Steadman, whose defence was impeccable throughout the game, showed his renowned attacking flair in the 73rd minute when latching on to Offiah's pass to score in the corner. The reliable boot of Eastwood re-opened a 19-point lead for the visitors.

It was Offiah who rounded off a memorable evening, curving round Ettingshausen with a minute left for an unconverted try to level the three-match series with only the Brisbane encounter to come.

SECOND TEST

26 June

Melbourne

AUSTRALIA 10

GREAT BRITAIN 33

Australia	No.	Great Britain
Andrew Ettingshausen	1.	Graham Steadman
Rod Wishart	2.	Paul Eastwood
Laurie Daley	3.	Paul Newlove
Mal Meninga, Capt.	4.	Daryl Powell
Michael Hancock	5.	Martin Offiah
Peter Jackson	6.	Garry Schofield, Capt.
Allan Langer	7.	Shaun Edwards
David Gillespie	8.	Kelvin Skerrett
Steve Walters	9.	Martin Dermott
Paul Harragon	10.	Andy Platt
Paul Sironen	11.	Denis Betts
Bob Lindner	12.	Billy McGinty
Bradley Clyde	13.	Phil Clarke
Brad Mackay	14.	Gary Connolly
Glenn Lazarus	15.	Paul Hulme
Chris Johns	16.	Joe Lydon
Kevin Walters	17.	Karl Harrison

T: Johns, Lindner
G: Meninga
Substitutions:
K. Walters for Jackson (8 min.)
Johns for Wishart (half-time)
Lazarus for Sironen (56 min.)
Mackay for Harragon (67 min.)
Half-time: 0-22
Referee: Dennis Hale (New Zealand)
Attendance: 30,257

T: Clarke, Schofield, Steadman,
Newlove, Offiah
G: Eastwood (6), Schofield (dg)
Substitutions:
Harrison for Skerrett (61 min.)
Hulme for McGinty (61 min.)
Connolly for Newlove (65 min.)
Lydon for Powell (73 min.)

Scorechart

Minute	Score	Aus	GB
6:	Eastwood (P)	0	2
10:	Eastwood (P)	0	4
18:	Clarke (T)		
	Eastwood (G)	0	10
30:	Newlove (T)		
	Eastwood (G)	0	16
35:	Schofield (T)		
	Eastwood (G)	0	22
49:	Schofield (DG)	0	23
56:	Lindner (T)		
	Meninga (G)	6	23
60:	Johns (T)	10	23
73:	Steadman (T)		
	Eastwood (G)	10	29
79:	Offiah (T)	10	33
	Scrums	6	11
	Penalties	10	5

Six-goal hero, Hull winger Paul Eastwood.

Scorer of Britain's fifth and final try, Martin Offiah again torments Australia full back Andrew Ettingshausen.

Celebrating the record-equalling 33-10 victory over Australia are British trio, from the left, Martin Dermott, Joe Lydon and Daryl Powell.

30 June
Tweed Heads
GOLD COAST 10
GREAT BRITAIN 28

1. Hampson
2. Hunte
3. Devereux
4. Connolly (Myers, 47 min.)
5. Hallas
6. Ellis
7. Fox, Capt.
8. Crooks (Harrison, half-time)
9. L. Jackson (Broadbent, 63 min.)
10. Fairbank
11. McNamara
12. Hulme (M. Jackson, 33 min.)
13. Aston

T: Connolly (2), Devereux, Hampson, McNamara
G: Fox (4)

Gold Coast:
Peacock; Bouveng, Cook (Goddard), Vowles, Mohr (Thorne); Donovan, Davys; Stains, Herring (Capt.), Neller (Sattler), Galea (Campion), McLean, Bartrim

T: Herring (2)
G: Bartrim

Half-time: 4-10

Referee: David Manson
Attendance: 9,573

The Lions' second string side maintained their unbeaten midweek record, skipper Fox earning wholesome praise from coach Reilly despite not being able to clinch a Test role.

Fox's smart distribution and darting runs sparked many of the British attacks in an often scrappy encounter played in pouring rain. And his long, accurate kicks repeatedly pushed Gold Coast into deep defensive positions from which they could not escape.

Gold Coast missed the organising ability of player-coach Lewis, ruled out with a hamstring injury. The Lions were well served by loose forward Aston, two-try Connolly and centre Devereux, who showed a welcome return to form with touches of strength and speed.

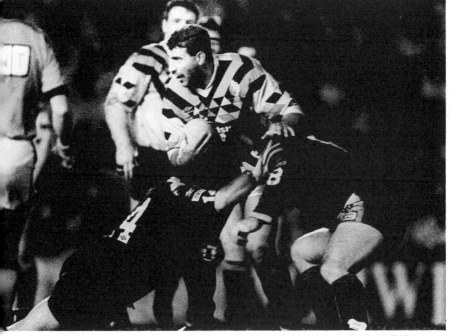

His second half performance against Gold Coast earned Karl Harrison a substitute role in the third Test at Brisbane.

THIRD TEST v. AUSTRALIA

With the stage set for an Ashes-deciding third Test at Brisbane's Lang Park, Australia skipper Mal Meninga stepped forward to take the starring role in record-breaking fashion.

Meninga celebrated a record 37th Test cap by extending his record points tally to 242 with four goals and a series-clinching try. His personal triumph was to be one of the few highlights of a disappointing encounter, an anti-climax to the pre-match hype.

Without disgracing themselves, Great Britain never looked likely to lift the Ashes for the first time in 22 years.

Australia deserved recognition for regrouping within a week of the 33-10 hammering at Melbourne, the return of Brad Fittler and switch to stand off by Laurie Daley proving vital. The green-and-golds were back to being determined and business-like, while Britain made too many unforced errors.

The Kangaroos also made handling errors in a tense atmosphere, but usually in the visitors' half. Inspired by scrum half Allan Langer and then loose forward Bradley Clyde, the home side dominated the centre of the field and employed an excellent kicking game.

After a tryless first half, Australia punished Britain with two early second half touchdowns, Martin Offiah's try four minutes from time coming too late to inspire a rally.

The Lions were unable to revive memories of Melbourne, despite the attempts of skipper Schofield, Andy Platt, Phil Clarke and Kelvin Skerrett. Fluency, support and distribution evaded the visitors against Australia's resolute defence. A positive kicking game was also absent.

The first half was a tale of penalties. Meninga and Eastwood each kicked two goals before the Australian captain earned an 8-4 half-time lead with two further successful kicks after Skerrett obstructed Langer and hooker Martin Dermott was pulled up following a flare-up with opposite number Steve Walters.

The first score in the second half was always going to be decisive and when a vastly improved Daley shrugged off the challenge of Shaun Edwards and Daryl Powell to stretch over from Fittler's pass in the 47th minute, Britain were struggling.

Inevitably, it was Meninga who clinched the Ashes eight minutes later when he regathered Daley's hopeful kick through and forced his massive frame over.

Britain never attacked with confidence and it took a rare error from Meninga, who spilled the ball as Dermott tackled, before they scored. Offiah fully capitalised on his only break of the night to sprint over from 70 yards, Eastwood adding the 76th-minute goal.

The Meninga-inspired victory brought back memories of the 1990 series in Britain. Coming into the deciding Test on level terms, the Australians again showed the capacity to call on greater reserves of mental and physical strength at the crucial time. Having been taught a lesson at Melbourne, the Australians showed that they were talented enough to immediately revert to the role of master.

Wigan again equalled the record of eight appearances from one club in a Test starting line-up.

Positive lead from prop forward Kelvin Skerrett.

THIRD TEST

3 July   **Brisbane**

AUSTRALIA 16   GREAT BRITAIN 10

Australia	No.	Great Britain
Andrew Ettingshausen	1.	Graham Steadman
Willie Carne	2.	Paul Eastwood
Brad Fittler	3.	Daryl Powell
Mal Meninga, Capt.	4.	Paul Newlove
Michael Hancock	5.	Martin Offiah
Laurie Daley	6.	Garry Schofield, Capt.
Allan Langer	7.	Shaun Edwards
Glenn Lazarus	8.	Kelvin Skerrett
Steve Walters	9.	Martin Dermott
Paul Harragon	10.	Andy Platt
Paul Sironen	11.	Denis Betts
Bob Lindner	12.	Billy McGinty
Bradley Clyde	13.	Phil Clarke
David Gillespie	14.	Gary Connolly
Kevin Walters	15.	Paul Hulme
Chris Johns	16.	Joe Lydon
John Cartwright	17.	Karl Harrison

T: Daley, Meninga
G: Meninga (4)
Substitutions:
Gillespie for Sironen (half-time)
K. Walters for Ettingshausen (74 min.)
Cartwright for Lindner (75 min.)
Johns for Carne (75 min.)
Half-time: 8-4
Referee: Dennis Hale (New Zealand)
Attendance: 32,313

T: Offiah
G: Eastwood (3)
Substitutions:
Hulme for McGinty (50 min.)
Harrison for Skerrett (50 min.)
Connolly for Newlove (62 min.)
Lydon for Schofield (74 min.)

Scorechart

Minute	Score	Aus	GB
5:	Meninga (P)	2	0
13:	Eastwood (P)	2	2
17:	Meninga (P)	4	2
23:	Eastwood (P)	4	4
28:	Meninga (P)	6	4
38:	Meninga (P)	8	4
47:	Daley (T)	12	4
55:	Meninga (T)	16	4
76:	Offiah (T)		
	Eastwood (G)	16	10
	Scrums	10	10
	Penalties	8	9

Australian captain Mal Meninga lifts the 1992 Ashes Trophy after scoring a try and four goals in Brisbane.

FIRST TEST v. NEW ZEALAND

A young and unrated New Zealand side were dubbed underdogs by the bookmakers against a Great Britain side who had come close to taking Australia's world crown. Trailing 14-6 with 20 minutes to go, punters could have named their own odds for a Kiwi victory.

The Lions totally dominated the first hour of an absorbing contest, lacking fluency but possessing enough individual skill and power to hold New Zealand's attack and make yardage at will through their forwards.

For all the pressure, Britain became pedestrian and unimaginative, being unable to increase their eight-point lead into a decisive margin. As the visitors relaxed, the inexperienced Kiwi side battled back to secure an improbable victory with a drop goal by Daryl Halligan five minutes from time.

At the start of the last quarter, New Zealand camped in the British half of the field. They still needed either a British mistake or a slice of luck to break the Lions' stranglehold. They got both.

With the score at 14-6 to the visitors, Kiwi full back Matthew Ridge sparked a revival with a towering kick, putting pressure on opposite number Graham Steadman, who succumbed by dropping the ball. Winger Paul Eastwood had ample time to make the runaway ball safe, but his wild kick missed completely and a grateful Richard Blackmore fell on it for a try.

Ridge's goal closed the margin to only two points which were soon wiped out by a Gavin Hill penalty. It followed a controversial incident in which Ridge claimed he was grabbed by the testicles.

The slice of luck came five minutes later. A kick from Halligan, substitute for Ridge, touched a British player before a wicked bounce left Steadman floundering as he tried to gather the ball. The Kiwis regathered possession and had ample time to set up Halligan, who coolly dropped the winning goal.

New Zealand opened the scoring against the run of play. Former Doncaster centre Tony Kemp touched down after good approach work from Man of the Match Gary Freeman and Kevin Iro.

The Lions quickly replied with a Shaun Edwards try, created by a shrewd pass from Garry Schofield and a brilliant burst and offload from Phil Clarke.

Two goals from Paul Eastwood put the visitors ahead at the break and they stretched their lead with a magnificent try early in the second half. Martin Offiah was twice involved in the move, the second time scraping a flicked pass from Schofield off his bootlaces to send Clarke striding in at the corner.

The Lions then mounted another spell of intense pressure on the Kiwis, who were missing inspirational loose forward Tawera Nikau for family reasons. Lack of further points was compounded by the loss of concentration and the tourists were forced to pay the ultimate price of defeat.

Tryscoring scrum half Shaun Edwards.

FIRST TEST

12 July   **Palmerston North**

NEW ZEALAND 15   ### GREAT BRITAIN 14

Matthew Ridge	1.	Graham Steadman
Sean Hoppe	2.	Paul Eastwood
Kevin Iro	3.	Daryl Powell
Tony Kemp	4.	Gary Connolly
Richard Blackmore	5.	Martin Offiah
Dean Clark	6.	Garry Schofield, Capt.
Gary Freeman, Capt.	7.	Shaun Edwards
Brent Stuart	8.	Kelvin Skerrett
Duane Mann	9.	Lee Jackson
Brent Todd	10.	Andy Platt
Gavin Hill	11.	Denis Betts
Quentin Pongia	12.	Billy McGinty
Brendon Tuuta	13.	Phil Clarke
Daryl Halligan	14.	Joe Lydon
Mike Kuiti	15.	Paul Hulme
Tea Ropati	16.	John Devereux
Mark Woods	17.	Karl Harrison

T: Kemp, Blackmore
G: Ridge (2), Hill, Halligan (dg)
Substitutions:
Ropati for Clark (51 min.)
Woods for Stuart (55 min.)
Kuiti for Pongia (70 min.)
Halligan for Ridge (70 min.)
Referee: Bill Harrigan (Australia)

T: Edwards, Clarke
G: Eastwood (3)
Substitutions:
Harrison for Skerrett (half-time)
Lydon for Connolly (65 min.)
Hulme for Jackson (76 min.)
Half-time: 6-8
Attendance: 11,548

Scorechart

Minute	Score	NZ	GB
13:	Kemp (T)	4	0
18:	Edwards (T)		
	Eastwood (G)	4	6
26:	Eastwood (P)	4	8
32:	Ridge (P)	6	8
47:	Clarke (T)		
	Eastwood (G)	6	14
66:	Blackmore (T)		
	Ridge (G)	12	14
71:	Hill (P)	14	14
75:	Halligan (DG)	15	14
	Scrums	8	4
	Penalties	4	8

● For 8 July v. Auckland see end of section.

Fifth successive Test substitute role for Joe Lydon.

SECOND TEST v. NEW ZEALAND

Great Britain called on the professionalism and spirit developed during the 10-week tour to register a 19-16 victory over the confident Kiwis and square the two-match Test series.

The battling Lions earned rich praise from coach Malcolm Reilly as the 17-match tour finished on a high note after the shock 15-14 Test defeat a week earlier.

Britain silenced a volatile 10,000-plus Auckland crowd with a superb comeback after trailing 10-0 midway through the first half. The Lions had to call on all their character and steel, responding to Garry Schofield's leadership and a great pack performance.

Kiwi captain Gary Freeman started this Auckland Test as he had finished in Palmerston North seven days earlier. His brilliance inspired New Zealand into early supremacy, Freeman opening the scoring with a superb touchdown.

Winger Sean Hoppe then grabbed a second Kiwi try after intercepting a Schofield pass, full back Matthew Ridge adding a goal to open up the 10-0 lead.

After weathering the Kiwi storm, the Lions struck back five minutes before the break. Schofield's pass was perfectly timed this time, sending through Denis Betts in fine style for the Wigan second row man to feed hooker Lee Jackson for a touchdown by the posts.

Paul Eastwood added the goal to leave Britain trailing 10-6 at half-time and then repeated the dose five minutes after the interval with a brilliant touchline conversion after a try in the corner from Betts.

Winger Martin Offiah switched from some impressive defensive work to seize on Daryl Powell's shrewd, short pass and race through the Kiwi rearguard for his 24th try in 26 Tests.

It left Eastwood with an easy kick at goal and tactical thinking by Schofield brought him a timely drop goal with eight minutes left.

The foundation of Britain's victory was laid up front. Wigan trio Andy Platt, Betts and Clarke were outstanding, along with front row men Karl Harrison and Lee Jackson.

Centre Gary Connolly fully justified his call-up to the Test arena in preference to Paul Newlove, while full back Graham Steadman was always prominent. Half backs Schofield and Shaun Edwards combined well to capitalise on the pack's superiority.

The Kiwis showed that they were building strongly for the future and came back with a Brent Todd try and Matthew Ridge goal to leave a final margin that scarcely did Britain's late superiority justice.

Graham Steadman, British full back in both Kiwi Tests.

SECOND TEST

19 July   Auckland

NEW ZEALAND 16   GREAT BRITAIN 19

Matthew Ridge	1.	Graham Steadman
Sean Hoppe	2.	Paul Eastwood
Kevin Iro	3.	Daryl Powell
Tony Kemp	4.	Gary Connolly
Richard Blackmore	5.	Martin Offiah
Dean Clark	6.	Garry Schofield, Capt.
Gary Freeman, Capt.	7.	Shaun Edwards
Brent Stuart	8.	Karl Harrison
Duane Mann	9.	Lee Jackson
Brent Todd	10.	Andy Platt
Gavin Hill	11.	Denis Betts
Quentin Pongia	12.	Billy McGinty
Brendon Tuuta	13.	Phil Clarke
Daryl Halligan	14.	Paul Newlove
Mike Kuiti	15.	Michael Jackson
Tea Ropati	16.	John Devereux
Mark Woods	17.	Karl Fairbank

T: Freeman, Hoppe, Todd
G: Ridge (2)
Substitutions:
Ropati for Iro (37 min.)
Woods for Hill (49 min.)
Kuiti for Tuuta (56 min.)
Halligan for Clark (67 min.)
Referee: Bill Harrigan (Australia)
Attendance: 10,223

T: L. Jackson, Betts, Offiah
G: Eastwood (3), Schofield (dg)
Substitutions:
Devereux for Offiah (8 min., blood bin)
M. Jackson for McGinty (28 min.)
Fairbank for M. Jackson (56 min.)
Newlove for Harrison (71 min.)
Half-time: 10-6

Scorechart

Minute	Score	NZ	GB
10:	Freeman (T)		
	Ridge (G)	6	0
22:	Hoppe (T)	10	0
33:	L. Jackson (T)		
	Eastwood (G)	10	6
45:	Betts (T)		
	Eastwood (G)	10	12
57:	Offiah (T)		
	Eastwood (G)	10	18
71:	Schofield (DG)	10	19
77:	Todd (T)		
	Ridge (G)	16	19
	Scrums	10	8
	Penalties	7	4

● For 12 July v. Canterbury see overleaf.

Denis Betts, one of Great Britain's three tryscorers.

8 July
Auckland
AUCKLAND   **8**
GREAT BRITAIN   **14**

1. Hampson
2. Hunte
3. Lydon (Devereux, 54 min.)
4. Newlove
5. Hallas (Myers, 72 min.)
6. Ellis
7. Fox, Capt.
8. Harrison
9. Dermott (Aston, half-time)
10. Sampson
11. M. Jackson (Betts, 72 min.)
12. Fairbank
13. McNamara

T: Hunte, Ellis
G: Fox (3)

Auckland:

Mackintosh (Tuisamoa); Patton, Elia, I. Ropati, Campbell; McIntosh (Kini), Friend (Capt.); Afoa, Malam, Pickering (Lowrie), Leota, Tatupu (Robarts), Ramsay

T: Mackintosh
G: Mackintosh (2)

Half-time: 8-14

Referee: Jim Stokes
Attendance: 5,485

The Lions' midweek side continued their winning ways with one of the most satisfying victories of the tour against a strong Auckland side.

Seeking a fourth consecutive victory over the tourists, Auckland were aided by a 2-1 penalty count from Christchurch referee Stokes, who was severely criticised by British coach Reilly.

Britain's tremendous defence restricted Auckland to only one touchdown, which opened the tryscoring in the 22nd minute. Hunte started and finished the Lions' reply four minutes later.

Skipper Fox, who was involved in Hunte's try, was a vital cog in the second touchdown five minutes later, putting through a delightful low kick for Ellis to follow up and score, Fox adding three goals to the points tally.

15 July
Christchurch
CANTERBURY   **6**
GREAT BRITAIN   **17**

1. Hampson
2. Myers
3. Devereux (Lydon, 66 min.)
4. Newlove
5. Hunte
6. Ellis
7. Fox, Capt. (Aston, 66 min.)
8. Sampson
9. Hulme
10. Crooks (Hallas, 68 min.)
11. Fairbank
12. M. Jackson
13. McNamara

T: Newlove, Ellis, Hunte
G: Fox (2), Lydon (dg)

Canterbury:

Atkinson; Dorreen, M. David (Kerrigan), Vincent (Wallace), Taewa; Nixon (Capt.), Bergman; Rangiaho (R. David), Culley, Simanu (Duff), Neame, Hermansson, Setu

T: M. David
G: Culley

Half-time: 6-8

Referee: Des O'Sullivan
Attendance: 3,026

The Lions' midweek side completed the tour unbeaten after overcoming a farcical build-up to the penultimate fixture. The party was delayed for five hours at a fog-bound Auckland airport, delaying the Christchurch kick-off for an hour.

Britain arrived one man short as substitute Skerrett had to be left behind when the much-delayed flight was overbooked.

Teeming rain and a mud-heap of a pitch still could not dampen British spirits and they handled the ball superbly.

The creative leadership of Fox was again impressive, and the Featherstone Rovers scrum half staked a claim for a place in the second Kiwi Test line-up, along with Devereux and Michael Jackson.

Substitute full back Alan Tait bombards the Australian try line as Great Britain launch a last bid to secure the Stones Bitter World Cup at Wembley.

WORLD CUP

WORLD CUP

1989-92 WORLD CUP

Final

Great Britain's safety-first bid to wrest world supremacy from the Australians just failed. Rugby League's super powers were separated by a solitary try conceded during a lapse of concentration in a tense Stones Bitter World Cup final at Wembley.

The Lions matched the Kangaroos tackle for tackle, pass for pass, kick for kick, in front of a world record international crowd of 73,631. But the mental durability of the reigning world title-holders was the deciding factor.

Britain were leading 6-4 with only 12 minutes left when they relaxed their grip, freeing Australia to register the only touchdown of a thrilling if unspectacular encounter.

A knock-on by Alan Hunte enabled the visitors to gain possession 25 yards from the British line. From the resultant scrum, Australia moved up and when John Devereux mistimed his tackle on opposite number Steve Renouf, the Brisbane Bronco sped to score the deciding try, skipper Mal Meninga adding his third successful kick.

Earlier, stand off Shaun Edwards paid the price for indiscipline by being sent to the sin bin, his absence undoubtedly helping the visitors gain the initiative.

The holders of the Ashes in the last nine series and winners of the past three World Cup competitions retained their number one rating with a display of ruthless efficiency.

British pundits were left ruing two contributory factors: why Martin Offiah was again starved of possession, and the effects of a hectic club fixture programme.

All the other scoring was in the first half, with five penalty goals inside the opening 33 minutes. Deryck Fox kicked all Britain's points, starting with a third-minute penalty when Renouf was offside, Meninga equalising after Ellery Hanley held down Bob Lindner.

Fox put the home side back in the lead after 23 minutes when Kevin Ward was held down and Meninga levelled the scores again four minutes later after being fouled by Hanley. Fox's third penalty goal put Britain into a half-time lead after Paul Sironen was caught offside.

British coach Malcolm Reilly's gameplan relied on top-class tactical kicking, with no risks on attack. The Lions did not attempt to break out of this self-built fortress until the last few minutes when making a desperate run for glory.

It almost paid off with handsome dividends as for the first time Australia looked vulnerable. There was little method in Britain's final fling, but that only added to the sudden uncertainty in Australia's defence.

Fox epitomised the home performance, which earned reviews of what might have been, especially if the shackles had been released earlier. The linchpin of the 1992 Lions unbeaten midweek side carried out his duties to perfection, trying nothing fancy on attack and finishing second in the tackle count with 27.

Fox hardly put a foot wrong as he landed three raking touchfinders and kicked the three penalty goals from four attempts which kept Britain in the lead for so long.

It was Fox who hoisted an up-and-under in the final flurry, almost bringing a decisive touchdown for substitute full back Alan Tait, who collected the ball near the posts but could not get it down. Victory was that close for the home side, although there could be no doubting the Kangaroos' right to the world crown.

The Lions did a good job in closing down scrum half Allan Langer, strangely subdued after an award-winning domestic season, hooker Steve Walters earning the Stones Bitter Man of the Match rating.

Offiah — the subject of a much-praised, pre-match London tube station poster campaign — handled the ball fewer than 10 times and never on the run, while Britain's props received a total of nearly 40 passes to grind out a few yards at a time. In doing so, Kevin Ward did all that was asked of him on his recall and farewell to international football at 35.

While there was some sadness in watching Hanley struggle to recapture the form of a once-great champion, he went down battling before retiring with five minutes left, still topping the tackle count with 32 and leading from the front by example.

There were only isolated examples of indiscipline in a relentless show of physical commitment. Edwards continued his pre-match verbal assault on New Zealand referee Dennis Hale, despite his 11-8 penalty count in favour of the home side. British hooker Martin Dermott was lucky to stay on after his late high tackle smashed Brad Fittler's cheekbone. Fittler himself might have been sin-binned for a first-half obstruction on British skipper Garry Schofield, who was generally unproductive in his switch from stand off to centre.

But it was mostly vigorous, fair tackling which restricted Australia to only one try for the first time since 1974. Set against that highly satisfactory fact was Britain's failure to score even one try in their last two home matches against the Kangaroos.

The Australians duly climbed the famous Wembley steps to receive the Stones Bitter World Cup trophy, a fitting reward for topping the qualifying table with a 100 per cent record and taking the gamble of conceding home advantage for the lure of a share of world record receipts for an international fixture of £1,848,056.

Great Britain's Man of the Match, scrum half Deryck Fox.

ADDITIONAL MATCHES

Australia played three matches in Britain as part of their preparations for the Stones Bitter World Cup final at Wembley.

9 October Huddersfield 2 Australians 66
Huddersfield Laurence; Naidole, Hellewell, Chapman, Thomas; Blacker (Davies) (Pearson), Flanagan; Fogerty (Simpson), St. Hilaire, Pearce, Pucill, Coulter (Sewell), Senior
G: Hellewell
Australians Godden (Kevin Walters); Brasher, Renouf, Meninga, Mackay; Fittler, Stuart; Sargent (Harragon), S. Walters, Lazarus (Gillespie), Sironen, Cartwright (Lindner), Clyde
T: Mackay (4), Clyde (2), Brasher (2), Harragon, S. Walters, Renouf, Lindner, Gillespie
G: Meninga (5), Brasher (2)
Referee: John Holdsworth (Kippax)
Attendance: 4,716

14 October Sheffield E. 22 Australians 52
Sheffield E. Jack (Sheridan); Simpson, Price, Gamson, Plange; Mycoe, Lumb; James (Broadbent) (Thompson), Cook (Robertson), Waddell, Laughton, Young, Aston
T: Broadbent, Jack, Plange, Simpson
G: Mycoe (3)
Australians Brasher (Godden); Carne, Renouf, Johns, Hancock; Kevin Walters (Fittler); Langer; Lazarus, Kerrod Walters, Harragon (Sargent), Sironen (Cartwright), Gillespie, Lindner
T: Brasher (2), Langer (2), Hancock, Sargent, Lindner, Renouf, Kevin Walters, Carne
G: Brasher (3), Carne (2), Fittler
Referee: Robin Whitfield (Widnes)
Attendance: 5,500

18 October Cumbria 0 Australians 44 at Workington
Cumbria Lightfoot (Whitehaven); Burns (Workington T.), Pape (Carlisle), Birkett (Salford), Beckwith (Whitehaven); Routledge (Whitehaven), Murdock (Carlisle); Armstrong (Workington T.), McCurrie (Widnes), D. Kendall (Whitehaven), Williams (Carlisle), Vannett (Hull K.R.), Walker, Capt. (Hull)
Substitutes, all played: Kitchin (Workington T.), Marwood (Workington T.), Crarey (Barrow), Riley (Workington T.)
Australians Brasher; Carne (Mackay), Renouf, Meninga, Mackay (Hancock); Fittler, Langer (Stuart); Lazarus (Cartwright), S. Walters, Sargent, Gillespie, (Sironen), Cartwright (Lindner), Clyde
T: Meninga (2), Hancock (2), Renouf, S. Walters, Fittler, Clyde, Gillespie, Sargent
G: Brasher, Mackay
Referee: Colin Morris (Huddersfield)
Attendance: 5,156
Sin bin: John Cartwright v. Cumbria
Opponents' sending off: Peter Riley (Cumbria)
Sin bin: Shaun Edwards (Great Britain)

STONES BITTER WORLD CUP FINAL

24 October 1992   **Wembley**

AUSTRALIA 10   GREAT BRITAIN 6

Tim Brasher (Balmain)	1.	Joe Lydon (Wigan)
Willie Carne (Brisbane B.)	2.	Alan Hunte (St. Helens)
Steve Renouf (Brisbane B.)	3.	Gary Connolly (St. Helens)
Mal Meninga (Canberra), Capt.	4.	Garry Schofield (Leeds), Capt.
Michael Hancock (Brisbane B.)	5.	Martin Offiah (Wigan)
Brad Fittler (Penrith)	6.	Shaun Edwards (Wigan)
Allan Langer (Brisbane B.)	7.	Deryck Fox (Bradford N.)
Glenn Lazarus (Brisbane B.)	8.	Kevin Ward (St. Helens)
Steve Walters (Canberra)	9.	Martin Dermott (Wigan)
Mark Sargent (Newcastle)	10.	Andy Platt (Wigan)
Paul Sironen (Balmain)	11.	Denis Betts (Wigan)
Bob Lindner (Wests)	12.	Phil Clarke (Wigan)
Bradley Clyde (Canberra)	13.	Ellery Hanley (Leeds)
John Cartwright (Penrith)	14.	John Devereux (Widnes)
David Gillespie (Wests)	15.	Kelvin Skerrett (Wigan)
Chris Johns (Brisbane B.)	16.	Alan Tait (Leeds)
Kevin Walters (Brisbane B.)	17.	Richard Eyres (Widnes)

T: Renouf
G: Meninga (3)
Substitutions:
Gillespie for Sironen (half-time)
K. Walters for Clyde (45 min.)
Cartwright for Sargent (63 min.)
Managers: Geoff Carr and Ted Weber
Coach: Bobby Fulton
Half-time: 4-6
Referee: Dennis Hale (New Zealand)
Attendance: 73,631

G: Fox (3)
Substitutions:
Devereux for Connolly (half-time)
Tait for Lydon (48 min.)
Skerrett for Ward (52 min.)
Eyres for Hanley (75 min.)
Manager: Maurice Lindsay
Coach: Malcolm Reilly

Scorechart

Minute	Score	Aus	GB
3:	Fox (P)	0	2
11:	Meninga (P)	2	2
23:	Fox (P)	2	4
27:	Meninga (P)	4	4
33:	Fox (P)	4	6
68:	Renouf (T)		
	Meninga (G)	10	6
	Scrums	14	6
	Penalties	8	11

Australia hooker Steve Walters with the Stones Bitter Man of the Match award.

Australia World Cup final squad 1992
Left to right: Back row: Allan Langer, Bradley Clyde, John Cartwright, Paul Sironen, Paul Harragon, Graham Mackay, Glenn Lazarus, Willie Carne.
Middle row: Nathan Gibbs (Doctor), Shaun McRae (Conditioner), Ricky Stuart, Tim Brasher, Steve Renouf, Brad Fittler, Brad Godden, Bob Lindner, Steve Walters,
Michael Hancock, Brian Hollis (Trainer), Dave Ryan (Trainer).
Front row: Kevin Walters, David Gillespie, Bobby Fulton (Coach), Geoff Carr (Manager), Mal Meninga (Capt.), Ted Weber (Manager), Kerrod Walters,
Chris Johns, Mark Sargent.

Great Britain World Cup final squad 1992
Left to right: Back row: Gary Connolly, Alan Hunte, Ellery Hanley, Denis Betts, Kevin Ward, John Devereux, Martin Offiah, Phil Clarke.
Middle row: Alan Tait, Shaun Edwards, Joe Lydon, Dave Feere (Physio), Richard Eyres, Andy Platt, Graham Steadman.
Front row: Bernard Dwyer, Deryck Fox, Malcolm Reilly (Coach), Garry Schofield (Capt.) Maurice Lindsay (Manager), Martin Dermott, Kelvin Skerrett.

1989-92 WORLD CUP RESULTS

23 JULY 1989
Auckland
15,000

NEW ZEALAND 14
T: Mercer, Elia
G: K. Shelford (3)

AUSTRALIA 22
T: Shearer, O'Connor,
Meninga, Clyde
G: O'Connor (2), Meninga

11 NOVEMBER 1989
Wigan
20,346

GREAT BRITAIN 10
T: Offiah, Tait
G: Loughlin

NEW ZEALAND 6
T: K. Shelford
G: K. Shelford

3 DECEMBER 1989
Carcassonne
4,208

FRANCE 0

NEW ZEALAND 34
T: Watson (3), Kemp, Bell,
Williams, Kuiti
G: Sherlock (3)

2 JUNE 1990
Port Moresby
5,969

PAPUA NEW GUINEA 8
T: Ongogo
G: Numapo (2)

GREAT BRITAIN 40
T: Gibson (2), Eastwood, Goulding,
Dixon, D. Powell, Schofield
G: Davies (6)

27 JUNE 1990
Parkes
12,384

AUSTRALIA 34
T: Mackay (3), McGaw (2),
Shearer, Daley, Meninga
G: Belcher

FRANCE 2
G: Dumas

15 JULY 1990
Christchurch
3,133

NEW ZEALAND 21
T: Kemp, Nikau
G: Ridge (6), McGahan (dg)

GREAT BRITAIN 18
T: Schofield, R. Powell, Offiah
G: Davies (3)

11 AUGUST 1990
Port Moresby
10,000

PAPUA NEW GUINEA 10
T: Soga, Waine
G: Numapo

NEW ZEALAND 18
T: Panapa, Watson, Lonergan
G: Ridge (3)

24 NOVEMBER 1990
Elland Road, Leeds
32,500

GREAT BRITAIN 0

AUSTRALIA 14
T: Ettingshausen, Meninga, Elias
G: Meninga

9 DECEMBER 1990
Perpignan
3,428

FRANCE 10
T: Pons, Entat
G: Tisseyre

AUSTRALIA 34
T: Mackay (2), Alexander, Meninga,
Shearer, Ettingshausen, Roach
G: Alexander (3)

27 JANUARY 1991
Perpignan
3,965

FRANCE 10
T: Auroy, Fraisse
G: Tisseyre

GREAT BRITAIN 45
T: Schofield (2), Offiah (2),
Edwards (2), Betts, Platt
G: Eastwood (6), Schofield (dg)

23 JUNE 1991
Christchurch
2,000

NEW ZEALAND 32
T: Panapa, Watson, Friend,
Blackmore, K. Shelford
G: Botica (6)

FRANCE 10
T: Verdes
G: Dumas (3)
G: Dumas (3)

7 JULY 1991
Goroka
11,485

PAPUA NEW GUINEA 18
T: Gela, Naipao
G: Wanega (5)

FRANCE 20
T: Garcia, Despin, Bienes
G: Torreilles (4)

31 JULY 1991
Brisbane
29,139

AUSTRALIA 40
T: Ettingshausen, Carne, Meninga,
Daley, Wishart, Clyde, S. Walters
G: Meninga (6)

NEW ZEALAND 12
T: Blackmore, McCracken
G: Botica (2)

341

13 OCTOBER 1991
Port Moresby
14,500

PAPUA NEW GUINEA 6
T: Haru
G: Boge

AUSTRALIA 40
T: Carne (3), Belcher, Clyde,
Wishart, Meninga, Jackson,
Ettingshausen
G: Meninga (2)

9 NOVEMBER 1991
Wigan
4,193

GREAT BRITAIN 56
T: M. Jackson (2), Moriarty (2),
Schofield, D. Powell, Sullivan,
Betts, Newlove, Fairbank
G: Davies (8)

PAPUA NEW GUINEA 4
G: Karu (2)

24 NOVEMBER 1991
Carcassonne
1,440

FRANCE...........................28
T: Garcia, Pons, Dumas, Divet,
Bonnafous
G: Dumas (4)

PAPUA NEW GUINEA 14
T: Itam, Haru
G: Karu (2), Haru

7 MARCH 1992
Hull
5,250

GREAT BRITAIN 36
T: Eastwood, Holliday, Fox, Platt,
Hunte, Dermott
G: Eastwood (6)

FRANCE........................... 0

3 JULY 1992
Brisbane
32,313

AUSTRALIA 16
T: Daley, Meninga
G: Meninga (4)

GREAT BRITAIN 10
T: Offiah
G: Eastwood (3)

5 JULY 1992
Auckland
3,000

NEW ZEALAND 66
T: Blackmore (3), Clark (2),
Kemp, Stuart, Hoppe, Hill, Ridge,
Freeman, D. Mann, Iro
G: Ridge (4), Halligan (3)

PAPUA NEW GUINEA 10
T: Uradok (2)
G: Boge

15 JULY 1992
Townsville
12,470

AUSTRALIA 36
T: Mackay (2), Fittler, Daley,
Carne, Sargent, Johns
G: Meninga (4)

PAPUA NEW GUINEA 14
T: Joseph, Babago, Emil
G: Boge

1989-92 FINAL WORLD CUP TABLE

	P.	W.	D.	L.	F.	A.	Diff.	Pts
Australia	8	8	0	0	236	68	+168	16
Great Britain	8	5	0	3	215	79	+136	10
New Zealand	8	5	0	3	203	120	+83	10
France	8	2	0	6	80	247	-167	4
Papua New Guinea	8	0	0	8	84	304	-220	0

WORLD CUP ROLL OF HONOUR

Year	Host Country	Winners	Runners-up
1954	France	Great Britain	France
1957	Australia	Australia	Great Britain
1960	England	Great Britain	Australia
1968	Australia and New Zealand	Australia	France
1970	England	Australia	Great Britain
1972	France	Great Britain	Australia
1975	Both Hemispheres	Australia	England★
1977	Australia and New Zealand	Australia	Great Britain
1985-88	Both Hemispheres	Australia	New Zealand
1989-92	Both Hemispheres	Australia	Great Britain

The Rugby Football League entered England and Wales into the tournament, rather than Great Britain.

*Test scrum half Allan Langer, Australia's Player of the Year
1992 and captain of Grand Final victors Brisbane Broncos.*

DOWN UNDER

DOWN UNDER

WINFIELD CUP
1992 Sydney Premiership Grand Final
Queensland's Brisbane Broncos became the first club to take the Winfield Cup outside New South Wales with a 28-8 defeat of St. George at a packed Sydney Football Stadium.

It was a fitting finale to a wonderful season for the Broncos, who had cantered to the top of the league table and finished six points clear of second placed St. George.

Their spectacular attacking play was in thrilling contrast to much of the stereotyped rugby adopted by Sydney clubs and St. George did well to restrict them to a 6-4 half-time lead before being left trailing in the closing stages.

Brisbane captain Allan Langer crowned a memorable season, in which he was acclaimed Australia's outstanding player, by winning the Clive Churchill Medal as the final's Man of the Match.

The Test scrum half scored the opening try of each half and stamped his authority on the final with a superb all-round game.

Alan Cann also scored two tries in an impressive second row display, but the most memorable touchdown was the one by Steve Renouf in the 61st minute. The young Brisbane centre broke through just a few yards from his own line to race almost the length of the field for a glorious try.

Many believed it clinched his place in Australia's World Cup squad to visit Britain along with seven of his final teammates.

Terry Matterson added the goals to take Brisbane 22-4 clear and added his fourth to complete Brisbane's scoring after Cann charged over for his second try.

St. George had some consolation in scoring the last try as Scott Gourley touched down in the closing seconds, but they had been outplayed for most of the game.

Ricky Walford's 16th-minute try made it 4-6 and they battled on to stay only two points behind until the last half-hour before Brisbane's class told.

Their efforts brought general praise for former Hull coach Brian Smith, who had got the most out of a side which did not have a player selected for the World Cup squad.

There were no British players appearing in the final for a third successive year.

Brisbane Broncos threequarters in the 1992 Grand Final, Willie Carne (left) and Steve Renouf.

WINFIELD CUP GRAND FINAL

27 September 1992   Sydney Football Stadium

BRISBANE BRONCOS 28   ST. GEORGE 8

Brisbane	No.	St. George
Julian O'Neill	1.	Michael Potter
Michael Hancock	2.	Ricky Walford
Steve Renouf	3.	Mark Coyne
Chris Johns	4.	Michael Beattie, Capt.
Willie Carne	5.	Ian Herron
Kevin Walters	6.	Peter Coyne
Allan Langer, Capt.	7.	Noel Goldthorpe
Glenn Lazarus	8.	Tony Priddle
Kerrod Walters	9.	Wayne Collins
Gavin Allen	10.	Neil Tierney
Trevor Gillmeister	11.	David Barnhill
Alan Cann	12.	Scott Gourley
Terry Matterson	13.	Jeff Hardy

T: Langer (2), Cann (2), Renouf
G: Matterson (4)
Substitutions:
Mark Hohn for Allen
Tony Currie for O'Neill
John Plath for Cann
Andrew Gee for Lazarus
Coach: Wayne Bennett
Half-time: 6-4
Referee: Greg McCallum
Scrums: 4-7
Penalties: 6-4

T: Walford, Gourley
Substitutions:
Brad Mackay for Tierney
Rex Terp for Beattie
Tony Smith for Peter Coyne
Matthew Elliott for Tierney
Coach: Brian Smith
Clive Churchill Medal for Man of the Match: Allan Langer (Brisbane)
Attendance: 41,560

1992 WINFIELD CUP

	P.	W.	D.	L.	F.	A.	Pts
Brisbane Broncos	22	18	0	4	506	311	36
St. George	22	15	0	7	401	283	30
Illawarra	22	13	1	8	318	259	27
Newcastle	22	12	2	8	363	267	26
Western Suburbs	22	12	1	9	356	327	25
Eastern Suburbs	22	12	0	10	392	319	24
Canterbury-Bankstown	22	10	2	10	423	417	22
Manly-Warringah	22	10	2	10	334	335	22
Penrith	22	11	0	11	274	309	22
Balmain	22	10	1	11	402	398	21
North Sydney	22	10	1	11	376	381	21
Canberra	22	10	0	12	435	409	20
Cronulla-Sutherland	22	8	0	14	284	395	16
South Sydney	22	7	0	15	429	533	14
Parramatta	22	6	1	15	276	491	13
Gold Coast	22	6	1	15	288	423	11*

*Deducted two points for breaking the player replacement rule.

WINFIELD CUP PLAY-OFF
Minor preliminary semi-final
Newcastle 21 v. Western Suburbs 2
Major preliminary semi-final
Illawarra 18 v. St. George 16
Minor semi-final
St. George 3 v. Newcastle 2
Major semi-final
Brisbane Broncos 22 v. Illawarra 12
Preliminary final
St. George 4 v. Illawarra 0
Grand Final
Brisbane Broncos 28 v. St. George 8

● All matches played at the Sydney Football Stadium.

LEADING SCORERS
● Not including play-offs.

Tries
16 Mark Bell (Western Suburbs)
   Tim Brasher (Balmain)
Goals (inc. drop goals)
76 Eion Crossan (South Sydney)
Points
168 Daryl Halligan (North Sydney)

BRITISH PLAYERS IN GRAND FINALS
British players who have appeared in the
Sydney Grand Final are:
Dick Huddart (St. George) 1966 winners, 1 try
Dave Bolton (Balmain) 1966 losers; 1969
   winners, 2 drop goals
Mervyn Hicks (Canterbury) 1967 losers
Ken Batty (St. George) 1971 losers
Malcolm Reilly (Manly) 1972 winners, 1973
   winners
Tommy Bishop (Cronulla) 1973 losers
Bob Wear (Cronulla) 1973 losers
Cliff Watson (Cronulla) 1973 losers
Brian Lockwood (Canterbury) 1974 losers
Gary Stephens (Manly) 1976 winners
Steve Norton (Manly) 1976 winners
Phil Lowe (Manly) 1976 winners, 1 try
Kevin Ward (Manly) 1987 winners
Ellery Hanley (Balmain) 1988 losers
Andy Currier (Balmain) 1989 losers, 3 goals
Shaun Edwards (Balmain) 1989 losers, sub
   Apart from Hicks, all the above also appeared in
a Challenge Cup final at Wembley. In addition Len

Killeen, the South African winger who began his
league career with St. Helens, also played at
Wembley and got a Grand Final winners' medal with
Balmain in 1969 when he kicked two goals.

Australians who have achieved the big double
since the Grand Final became mandatory in 1954
are: Chris Anderson, Harry Bath, Graham Eadie,
Andrew Farrar, John Ferguson, Kerry Hemsley,
Brett Kenny, John Muggleton, Michael O'Connor,
Peter Sterling and Paul Vautin.

There were a record four British players in the
1973 Grand Final. Reilly got a winners' medal with
Manly, while Bishop, Watson and Wear were in the
beaten Cronulla side.

Three British players — Stephens, Norton and
Lowe — were also in the Manly side which won the
final in 1976.

Ellery Hanley was the first player to appear in both
major finals in the same year. In 1988 he led Wigan
to success at Wembley and four months later was in
Balmain's beaten Grand Final team.

Shaun Edwards is the only other player to play in
both finals in the same year. He was stand off when
Wigan beat St. Helens at Wembley in 1989 and made
a late substitute appearance for Balmain when they
were beaten by Canberra at Sydney.

*Test threequarter Michael O'Connor, one of only 11 Australian
players to have appeared in the British Challenge Cup final
and the Australian Grand Final.*

**BRITISH PLAYERS IN 1992 WINFIELD CUP
SYDNEY PREMIERSHIP**
No British players appeared in the Winfield Cup
competition for the first time in several seasons.

The British Lions tour of Australia and New
Zealand restricted the opportunities for Britain's
best players to join Sydney clubs.

STATE OF ORIGIN

The State of Origin matches between New South Wales and Queensland began in 1980 and are now established as a major part of the Australian Rugby League scene.

Their introduction revived interest in the inter-state matches which had been dominated by New South Wales, who had won the last 15 matches by mainly wide margins.

Under the old system, players appeared for the state in which they were playing club rugby at the time and this gave a big advantage to New South Wales because many of Queensland's best players were with Sydney clubs.

But in State of Origin matches players appear for the state in which they first played senior rugby and this has resulted in the matches becoming more fiercely and evenly fought before increased attendances.

NEW SOUTH WALES v. QUEENSLAND RESULTS State of Origin only.

Date	Winner	Score	Venue	Attendance
8 July 1980	Queensland	20-10	Brisbane	31,000
28 July 1981	Queensland	22-15	Brisbane	25,613
1 June 1982	New South Wales	20-16	Brisbane	27,326
8 June 1982	Queensland	11-7	Brisbane	19,435
22 June 1982	Queensland	10-5	Sydney	20,242
7 June 1983	Queensland	24-12	Brisbane	29,412
21 June 1983	New South Wales	10-6	Sydney	21,620
28 June 1983	Queensland	43-22	Brisbane	26,084
29 May 1984	Queensland	29-12	Brisbane	33,662
19 June 1984	Queensland	14-2	Sydney	29,088
17 July 1984	New South Wales	22-12	Brisbane	16,599
28 May 1985	New South Wales	18-2	Brisbane	33,011
11 June 1985	New South Wales	21-14	Sydney	39,068
23 July 1985	Queensland	20-6	Brisbane	18,825
27 May 1986	New South Wales	22-16	Brisbane	33,000
10 June 1986	New South Wales	24-20	Sydney	40,707
1 July 1986	New South Wales	18-16	Brisbane	21,097
2 June 1987	New South Wales	20-16	Brisbane	33,411
16 June 1987	Queensland	12-6	Sydney	42,048
15 July 1987	Queensland	10-8	Brisbane	33,000
*6 Aug. 1987	New South Wales	30-18	California	12,349
17 May 1988	Queensland	26-18	Sydney	26,441
31 May 1988	Queensland	16-6	Brisbane	31,817
21 June 1988	Queensland	38-22	Sydney	16,910
23 May 1989	Queensland	36-6	Brisbane	33,000
14 June 1989	Queensland	16-12	Sydney	40,000
28 June 1989	Queensland	36-16	Brisbane	33,000
9 May 1990	New South Wales	8-0	Sydney	41,235
30 May 1990	New South Wales	12-6	Melbourne	25,800
13 June 1990	Queensland	14-10	Brisbane	31,000
8 May 1991	Queensland	6-4	Brisbane	31,500
29 May 1991	New South Wales	14-12	Sydney	41,520
12 June 1991	Queensland	14-12	Brisbane	32,500
6 May 1992	New South Wales	14-6	Sydney	40,039
20 May 1992	Queensland	5-4	Brisbane	32,000
3 June 1992	New South Wales	16-4	Sydney	41,878

*Not part of 1987 series.

SUMMARY

New South Wales won 15; Queensland won 21. Since it became a three-match series in 1982, Queensland have won seven series to New South Wales' four.

ENGLISH REFEREES English referees who have taken charge of State of Origin matches are: Billy Thompson on 8 July 1980 and Robin Whitfield on 28 June 1983.

1992 STATE OF ORIGIN MATCHES *Denotes captain

6 May
Sydney
New South Wales 14

Ettingshausen (Cronulla) 1t
G. Mackay (Penrith)
Fittler (Penrith)
McGregor (Illawarra)
Wishart (Illawarra) 3g
*Daley (Canberra)
Simon (Illawarra)
Lazarus (Brisbane B.)
Elias (Balmain)
Harragon (Newcastle)
Sironen (Balmain)
Cartwright (Penrith)
Clyde (Canberra) 1t

Subs: B. Mackay (St. George)
Gillespie (Wests)
McCormack (Newcastle)
Salvatori (Easts) 1t

20 May
Brisbane
New South Wales 4

Ettingshausen (Cronulla)
G. Mackay (Penrith)
Fittler (Penrith)
McGregor (Illawarra)
Wishart (Illawarra) 2g
*Daley (Canberra)
Stuart (Canberra)
Lazarus (Brisbane B.)
Elias (Balmain)
Harragon (Newcastle)
Sironen (Balmain)
Cartwright (Penrith)
Clyde (Canberra)

Subs: B. Mackay (St. George)
Carter (Penrith)
Salvatori (Easts)
Gillespie (Wests)

3 June
Sydney
New South Wales 16

Ettingshausen (Cronulla) 1t
Wishart (Illawarra)
McGregor (Illawarra)
Fittler (Penrith)
Johns (Brisbane B.)
*Daley (Canberra)
Stuart (Canberra) 1t
Lazarus (Brisbane B.)
Elias (Balmain)
Harragon (Newcastle)
Sironen (Balmain)
Cartwright (Penrith) 1t
Clyde (Canberra)

Subs: Salvatori (Easts)
Gillespie (Wests)
Brasher (Balmain) 2g
B. Mackay (St. George)

Queensland 6

Shearer (Gold Coast)
Carne (Brisbane B.)
*Meninga (Canberra) 1g
P. Jackson (Norths)
Hancock (Brisbane B.)
Kevin Walters (Brisbane B.)
Langer (Brisbane B.) 1t
S. Jackson (Gold Coast)
S. Walters (Canberra)
Bella (Manly)
Gillmeister (Brisbane B.)
Lindner (Wests)
Larson (Norths)

Subs: Allen (Brisbane B.)
M. Coyne (St. George)
G. Coyne (Canberra)
Renouf (Brisbane B.)

Referee: David Manson
Man of the Match: Elias

Queensland 5

Shearer (Gold Coast)
Brunker (Newcastle)
*Meninga (Canberra)
M. Coyne (St. George)
Hancock (Brisbane B.)
P. Jackson (Norths)
Langer (Brisbane B.) 1dg
Allen (Brisbane B.)
S. Walters (Canberra)
Bella (Manly)
Larson (Norths)
Lindner (Wests)
Moore (Norths) 1t

Subs: Kevin Walters (Brisbane B.)
McLean (Gold Coast)
Gillmeister (Brisbane B.)
D. Smith (Canterbury)

Referee: Bill Harrigan
Man of the Match: Lindner

Queensland 4

Shearer (Gold Coast)
Hancock (Brisbane B.)
M. Coyne (St. George)
*Meninga (Canberra) 2g
Brunker (Newcastle)
P. Jackson (Norths)
Langer (Brisbane B.)
Bella (Manly)
S. Walters (Canberra)
Allen (Brisbane B.)
Larson (Norths)
McLean (Gold Coast)
Moore (Norths)

Subs: Kevin Walters (Brisbane B.) 1
D. Smith (Canterbury)
S. Jackson (Gold Coast)
G. Coyne (Canberra)

Referee: Eddie Ward
Man of the Match: Stuart

NEW SOUTH WALES v. QUEENSLAND RECORDS
State of Origin only

NEW SOUTH WALES

Highest score:	30-18 at California, 6 August 1987
Widest margin:	18-2 at Brisbane, 28 May 1985
Most full appearances:	19 by Michael O'Connor (St. George, Manly)
Most tries in a match:	3 by Chris Anderson (Canterbury), 28 June 1983
Most goals in a match:	No player has kicked more than five
Most points in a match:	18 (2t,5g) Michael O'Connor (Manly), 28 May 1985
Biggest home attendance:	42,048, 16 June 1987

QUEENSLAND

Highest score:	43-22 at Brisbane, 28 June 1983
Widest margin:	36-6 at Brisbane, 23 May 1989
Most full appearances:	31 by Wally Lewis (Fortitude Valley, Wynnum Manly, Brisbane Broncos, Gold Coast)
Most tries in a match:	3 by Kerry Boustead (Manly), 29 May 1984
Most goals in a match:	7 by Mal Meninga (Souths, B), 8 July 1980
Most points in a match:	16 (2t,4g) by Mal Meninga (Canberra), 23 May 1989 and Dale Shearer (Manly), 28 June 1989
Biggest home attendance:	33,662, 29 May 1984

Coaches:

New South Wales:	Ted Glossop (1980, 1981, 1983); Frank Stanton (1982, 1984); Terry Fearnley (1985); Ron Willey (1986, 1987); John Peard (1988); Jack Gibson (1989, 1990); Tim Sheens (1991); Phil Gould (1992)
Queensland:	John McDonald (1980); Arthur Beetson (1981, 1982, 1983, 1984, 1989, 1990); Des Morris (1985); Wayne Bennett (1986, 1987, 1988); Graham Lowe (1991, 1992)

NEW SOUTH WALES REGISTER

The following is a register of players who have appeared for New South Wales in the State of Origin series plus the match against Queensland in the United States of America, up to and including 1992.
+ indicates number of matches played as a substitute. B-Brisbane, S-Sydney.

ALEXANDER, Greg (4+2) Penrith
ANDERSON, Chris (4) Canterbury
AYLIFFE, Royce (1+2) Easts, S

BLAKE, Phil (+1) Souths, S
BOWDEN, Steve (1) Newtown
BOYD, Les (3) Manly
BOYLE, David (2+2) Souths, S
BRASHER, Tim (+1) Balmain
BRENTNALL, Greg (4) Canterbury
BROOKS, David (1) Balmain
BROWN, Ray (1+2) Manly
BUGDEN, Geoff (2) Parramatta

CARTER, Steve (+1) Penrith
CARTWRIGHT, John (5+3) Penrith
CLEAL, Noel (11+1) Manly
CLYDE, Bradley (10) Canberra
CONLON, Ross (3) Canterbury
COOPER, Bob (1) Wests, S
COVENEY, John (2) Canterbury
CRONIN, Mick (6) Parramatta

DALEY, Laurie (8) Canberra
DALEY, Phil (3) Manly
DAVIDSON, Les (5) Souths, S
DOCKING, Jonathan (2) Cronulla
DUKE, Phillip (1) Moree
DUNN, Paul (2+1) Canterbury

EADIE, Graham (1) Manly
EDGE, Steve (1) Parramatta
ELIAS, Ben (14) Balmain
ELLA, Steve (3+4) Parramatta
ETTINGSHAUSEN, Andrew (15+1) Cronulla

FAHEY, Terry (2) Easts, S
FAIRLEIGH, David (+1) Norths, S
FARRAR, Andrew (5+2) Canterbury
FENECH, Mario (2) Souths, S
FERGUSON, John (8) Easts, S 3; Canberra 5

FIELD, Paul (2) Cootamundra
FITTLER, Brad (4+2) Penrith
FLORIMO, Greg (+1) Norths, S
FOLKES, Steve (8+1) Canterbury

GERARD, Geoff (2) Manly
GEYER, Mark (3) Penrith
GILLESPIE, David (5+7) Canterbury 3+3, Wests 2+4
GROTHE, Eric (9) Parramatta
GURR, Marty (2) Easts, S

HAMBLY, Gary (1) Souths, S
HANSON, Steve (1) Norths, S
HARRAGON, Paul (3) Newcastle
HASLER, Des (6+6) Manly
HASTINGS, Kevin (+1) Easts, S
HETHERINGTON, Brian (1+1) Illawarra
HILDITCH, Ron (1) Parramatta
HUNT, Neil (2) Parramatta

IZZARD, Brad (2+2) Penrith

JACK, Garry (17) Balmain
JARVIS, Pat (6+2) St. George 4+2, Canterbury 2
JENSEN, Barry (1) Newtown
JOHNS, Chris (7) Brisbane Broncos
JOHNSTON, Brian (8) St. George
JOHNSTON, Lindsey (2) Norths, S
JURD, Stan (1+1) Parramatta

KELLY, Peter (2) Penrith
KENNY, Brett (16+1) Parramatta
KRILICH, Max (5) Manly

LAMB, Terry (4+3) Canterbury 3+3, Wests, S 1
LANGMACK, Paul (3+1) Canterbury
LAZARUS, Glenn (4+4) Canberra 1+4, Brisbane Broncos 3
LEIS, Jim (1) Wests, S
LYONS, Cliff (6) Manly
LYONS, Graham (2+1) Souths, S

McCORMACK, Robbie (+1) Newcastle
McGAW, Mark (10+3) Cronulla
McGREGOR, Paul (3) Illawarra
McGUIRE, Bruce (5) Balmain
MACKAY, Brad (4+4) St. George
MACKAY, Graham (2) Penrith
McKINNON, Don (1) Norths, S
MATTERSON, Terry, (+1) Brisbane Broncos
MELROSE, Tony (1) Souths, S
MERLO, Paul (1) Wests, S
MILLER, Gavin (5) Cronulla
MORRIS, Steve (2) St. George
MORTIMER, Chris (8+1) Canterbury 7, Penrith 1+1
MORTIMER, Steve (8) Canterbury
MUGGLETON, John (2) Parramatta

NISZCOTT, Ziggy (2) Souths, S

O'CONNOR, Michael (19) St. George 6, Manly 13

PEARCE, Wayne (15) Balmain
POTTER, Michael (+1) Canterbury
PRICE, Ray (8) Parramatta

RAMPLING, Tony (2+1) Souths, S
RAUDONIKIS, Tom (1) Newtown
ROACH, Steve (17) Balmain

ROBERTS, Ian (5) Manly
ROGERS, Steve (4) Cronulla

SALVATORI, Craig (+4) Easts, S
SARGENT, Mark (+1) Newcastle
SIGSWORTH, Phil (3) Newtown 2, Manly 1
SIMMONS, Royce (10) Penrith
SIMON, John (1) Illawarra
SIRONEN, Paul (5+3) Balmain
STERLING, Peter (13) Parramatta
STONE, Robert (+1) St. George
STUART, Ricky (8) Canberra

THOMPSON, Alan (5+1) Manly
TOOVEY, Geoff (+1) Manly
TREWHELLA, David (1+1) Easts, S
TUNKS, Peter (7+1), Souths 1, Canterbury 6+1

WALFORD, Ricky (1) St. George
WALSH, Chris (1) St. George
WILSON, Alan (+2) Cronulla
WISHART, Rod (8) Illawarra
WRIGHT, Rex (1) N. Newcastle
WYNN, Graeme (1) St. George
WYNN, Peter (4) Parramatta

YOUNG, Craig (4+1) St. George

QUEENSLAND REGISTER

The following is a register of players who have appeared for Queensland in the State of Origin series plus the match against New South Wales in the United States of America, up to and including 1992. + indicates number of matches played as a substitute. B-Brisbane, S-Sydney.

ALLEN, Gavin (2+3) Brisbane Broncos
ASTILL, Bruce (+1) Souths, B

BACKER, Brad (3) Easts, B
BACKO, Sam (7) Canberra 3; Brisbane Broncos 4
BEETSON, Arthur (1) Parramatta
BELCHER, Gary (15) Canberra
BELLA, Martin (17) Norths, S 8; Manly 9
BOUSTEAD, Kerry (6) Easts, S 3; Manly 3
BRENNAN, Mitch (4) Souths, S 3; Redcliffe 1
BROHMAN, Darryl (2) Penrith
BROWN, Dave (9+1) Manly 5+1; Easts, S 4
BRUNKER, Adrian (2) Newcastle
BUTLER, Terry (1) Wynnum Manly

CARNE, Willie (5) Brisbane Broncos
CARR, Norm (2) Wests, B
CLOSE, Chris (9) Manly 7; Redcliffe 2
CONESCU, Greg (20) Norths, B 4; Redcliffe 10;
    Gladstone Brothers 3; Brisbane Broncos 3
COYNE, Gary (2+9) Canberra
COYNE, Mark (2+3) St. George
CURRIE, Tony (8+3) Wests, B +1; Redcliffe +1;
    Canterbury 5+1; Brisbane Broncos 3

DOWLING, Greg (11) Wynnum Manly 7; Norths, B 4
DOWLING, John (3) St. George

FRENCH, Brett (1+3) Wynnum Manly; Norths, S +3
FRENCH, Ian (3+6) Wynnum Manly 2+3;
    Norths, S 1+3
FULLERTON-SMITH, Wally (12) Redcliffe 8;
    St. George 4

GEE, Andrew (3+1) Brisbane Broncos
GILLMEISTER, Trevor (6+6) Easts, S 5+5;
    Brisbane Broncos 1+1

HAGAN, Michael (2+3) Newcastle
HANCOCK, Michael (9) Brisbane Broncos
HANCOCK, Rohan (5) Easts, B 1; Toowoomba
    Wattles 4
HAUFF, Paul (3) Brisbane Broncos
HENRICK, Ross (2) Norths, B 1; Fortitude Valley 1
HEUGH, Cavill (2+1) Easts, B

JACKSON, Peter (14+2) Canberra 7; Souths, B +1;
    Brisbane Broncos 1+1; Norths, S 6
JACKSON, Steve (4+2) Wests, S 3+1; Gold Coast 1+1
JONES, Gavin (3) Norths, S

KELLAWAY, Bob (+1) Souths, B
KHAN, Paul (4) Easts, B 3; Cronulla 1
KILROY, Joe (2) Brisbane Broncos
KISS, Les (4) Norths, S

LANG, John (1) Easts, S
LANGER, Allan (18) Ipswich 4, Brisbane Broncos 14
LARSON, Gary (6) Norths, S
LEWIS, Wally (31) Wynnum Manly 13;
    Fortitude Valley 8; Brisbane Broncos 7;
    Gold Coast 3
LINDNER, Bob (19+1) Souths, B 1; Wynnum
    Manly 5; Parramatta 6; Gold Coast 2; Wests, S 5+1

McCABE, Paul (5) Easts, S 1; Manly 4
McINDOE, Alan (9) Illawarra 3; Penrith 6
McLEAN, Mike (4+1) Newcastle 3; Gold Coast 1+1
MENINGA, Mal (26) Souths, B 13; Canberra 13
MILES, Gene (19) Wynnum Manly 14;
    Brisbane Broncos 5
MOORE, Billy (2) Norths, S
MORRIS, Rod (4) Balmain 2; Wynnum Manly 2
MURRAY, Mark (14) Fortitude Valley 3, Redcliffe 11

NIEBLING, Bryan (9) Fortitude Valley 3; Redcliffe 6

OLIPHANT, Greg (1) Balmain

PHELAN, Chris (2) Souths, B 1; Parramatta 1

QUINN, Graham (1) St. George

REDDY, Rod (1) St. George
RENOUF, Steve (+2) Brisbane Broncos
RIBOT, John (8) Manly 5; Redcliffe 3

SCOTT, Colin (16+1) Wynnum Manly 15+1;
    Easts, B 1

SHEARER, Dale (17+4) Manly 11+2;
    Brisbane Broncos 3+2; Gold Coast 3
SMITH, Allan (1) Norths, S
SMITH, Darren (+2) Canterbury
SMITH, Gary (+1) Brothers
STACEY, Steve (2) Easts, B
STAINS, Danny (4) Cronulla

TESSMAN, Brad (4+1) Souths, B 3; Easts, S 1+1
TRONC, Scott (+1) Wests, S

VAUTIN, Paul (20+1) Manly 19+1; Easts, S 1

WALKER, Bruce (1) Manly
WALTERS, Kerrod (5) Brisbane Broncos
WALTERS, Kevin (1+7) Canberra +1;
    Brisbane Broncos 1+6
WALTERS, Steve (7) Canberra

PAPUA NEW GUINEA TOUR OF NEW ZEALAND AND AUSTRALIA 1992

Date	Result	Score	Opposition	Venue	Attendance
IN NEW ZEALAND					
24 June	Lost	10-14	**Hawkes Bay** T: Emil, Lakur G: Eremas	Hastings	
28 June	Won	36-16	**Kiwi Colts** T: Kouoru, Bire, Matmillo, Karu, Ngaffin, Naipao, Emil G: Boge (2), Karu, Emil	New Plymouth	
1 July	Lost	26-43	**Northland** T: Wagambie, Togola, Babago, Tani, Angra G: Eremas (3)	Whamgarei	
5 July	Lost	10-66	**NEW ZEALAND** **New Zealand:**	Auckland	3,000

Matthew Ridge (1t, 4g); Sean Hoppe (1t), Kevin Iro (1t),
Tony Kemp (1t), Richard Blackmore (3t); Dean Clark (2t),
Gary Freeman (Capt) (1t); Brent Stuart (1t), Duane Mann (1t),
Brent Todd, Gavin Hill (1t), Quentin Pongia, Tawera Nikau.
Subs: Daryl Halligan (3g), Brendon Tuuta, Tea Ropati,
Mark Woods (all played)
Papua New Guinea:
Philip Boge (1g); Kini Tani, August Joseph, Richard Wagambie,
Jack Uradok (2t); Tuksy Karu, Aquil Emil; Ben Bire, Michael
Matmillo, Kera Ngaffin (Capt), Nande Yer, James Naipao, Joe Gispe.
Subs: John Piel, Korul Sinemau, Michael Angra, Ngala Lapan
(all played)
Referee: Greg McCallum (Australia)

351

IN AUSTRALIA

8 July   Drew   24-24   **Gold Coast Vikings**   Tweed Heads
T: Piel, Kapia, Eremas, Uradok
G: Karu (2), Eremas (2)

11 July   Lost   26-32   **Queensland Country**   Rockhampton
T: Kapia (2), Bire, Babago
G: Eremas (4), Emil

15 July   Lost   14-36   **AUSTRALIA**   Townsville   12,470
Australia:
Willie Carne (1t); Graham Mackay (2t), Brad Fittler (1t),
Mal Meninga (Capt) (4g), Michael Hancock; Laurie Daley (1t),
Allan Langer; Glenn Lazarus, Steve Walters, David Gillespie,
Paul Sironen, Bob Lindner, Brad Mackay.
Subs: Mark Sargent (1t), Chris Johns (1t), Kevin Walters,
John Cartwright (all played)
Papua New Guinea:
Philip Boge (1g); Jack Uradok, August Joseph (1t), Korul Sinemau,
Richard Wagambie; Tuksy Karu (1t), Aquil Emil (1t); Ben Bire,
Michael Matmillo, Kera Ngaffin (Capt), Daroa Ben-Moide,
James Naipao, Joe Gispe.
Subs: Nande Yer, Michael Angra, Normyle Eremas, Ngala Lapan
(all played)
Referee: Dennis Hale (New Zealand)

TOUR SUMMARY

P	W	D	L	F	A
7	1	1	5	146	231

TOUR REGISTER

Captain: Kera Ngaffin
Coach: John Wagambie
Manager: Andrew Terry

*Includes substitute appearances
†Replacements due to injury: Ben-Moide for Hoffman,
Uradok for Kouoru.

Player	App*	T	G	Pts
ANGRA, Michael	4	1	—	4
BABAGO, Sauna	6	3	—	12
†BEN-MOIDE, Daroa	2	—	—	—
BIRE, Ben	5	2	—	8
BOGE, Philip	6	—	4	8
EMIL, Aquil	5	3	2	16
EREMAS, Normyle	5	1	10	24
HOFFMAN, Leslee	2	—	—	—
GISPE, Joe	5	—	—	—
JOSEPH, August	7	1	—	4
KAPIA, James	5	3	—	12
KARU, Tuksy	6	1	3	10
KOUORU, Joshua	1	1	—	4
LAKUR, Ben	3	1	—	4
LAPAN, Ngala	3	—	—	—
LAUNA, Nere	5	—	—	—
MATMILLO, Michael	5	1	—	4
NAIPAO, James	5	1	—	
NGAFFIN, Kera	6	1	—	4
PIEL, John	4	1	—	4
SINEMAU, Korul	6	—	—	—
TANI, Kini	3	1	—	
TOGOLA, John	3	1	—	
†URADOK, Jack	4	3	—	12
WAGAMBIE, Richard	6	1	—	
YER, Nande	7	—	—	
TOTALS		**27**	**19**	**14**

Tour skipper Kera Ngaffin.

*Second row man Denis Betts, who took his Test ca
tally to 21 in 199*

GREAT BRITAIN

1992-93 TEST REVIEW

While failing to reach the ultimate pinnacle of world number-one rating, Great Britain peaked during a hectic 10-month international tour of duty by hammering Australia in Melbourne by a record-equalling margin, narrowly losing the World Cup final at Wembley and demolishing France in a double record rout.

Britain played nine Test and World Cup matches, registering five victories, including the scalp of each rival country. But Malcolm Reilly's charges were unable to provide the final finish.

The magnificent 33-10 victory, at a wet Princes Park, Melbourne, was the only win in the three-Test Anglo-Aussie series as the green-and-golds extended their supremacy to 19 years.

After the heady heights of a sell-out series in Australia, the Lions came down to earth with a 14-15 defeat in the first New Zealand Test before squaring the series with a hard-fought 19-16 success a week later.

Back on home soil, Great Britain prepared for the Stones Bitter World Cup final, having qualified by points difference from New Zealand. Unbeaten table-toppers Australia opted to take a calculated gamble and swap home advantage for the greater financial returns from Wembley Stadium. The gamble paid off twice . . . the Kangaroos took back the World Cup Trophy and a £500,000 profit. Britain just missed glory in a tense 10-6 contest.

The 10-week trip Down Under is fully chronicled in the section 1992 LIONS, while the Wembley culmination of a three-year tournament is documented in the section WORLD CUP.

Great Britain prepared for the 1993 autumn series with the touring New Zealanders by running up record scores against France, home and away.

In the opening encounter at Carcassonne, skipper Garry Schofield led the way with a hat-trick of tries, to take his personal tally to 30 touchdowns in 40 appearances, leaving him within striking distance of Mick Sullivan's records of 41 tries in 46 games.

Even allowing for the weak opposition, Schofield gave a first-class display of creative skills and finishing power and could have added two more touchdowns, but instead he was unselfish and fed Ellery Hanley and Mike Ford for easy scores.

The record tally of 48 points beat the previous best on French soil, a 45-10 success at Perpignan in 1991, and was achieved despite being without six of the original line-up and after little more than 90 minutes of training because of the League controversially bending the rules to allow Test players to take part in midweek club matches.

It took Britain only 11 minutes to open their nine-try account, Schofield touching down to be followed by Hanley and John Devereux as the Lions opened an 18-0 lead. Ironically, it was Schofield who created the only French try of the game, opposite number and captain Gilles Dumas intercepting his long pass to scamper 60 unopposed yards to the posts. Fages added the goal for an interval scoreline of 18-6 to Britain.

Schofield completed his hat-trick in the 67th minute, Britain's other tries coming from Richard Eyres, Shaun Edwards and Hanley, his second completing the rout a minute from time, his 20th try for Great Britain.

Andy Currier celebrated his return to Test duty after a nightmare debut against New Zealand in 1989, successfully taking on the goalkicking responsibility to land six from 10 attempts.

A month later, Great Britain showed no mercy by racing to a world record score, inflicting a 72-6 defeat on the demoralised French at Headingley, Leeds.

The relentless Lions passed the previous best British score of 60-4 against France, established on the same ground only two years arlier, and went on to surpass Australia's world record 70-8 hammering of Papua New Guinea at Wagga in July 1988.

Jonathan Davies kicked a British record-qualling 10 goals from 13 attempts.

There was a pre-match sensation when Ellery Hanley was withdrawn from the side ight hours before kick-off as a disciplinary measure. Manager Steve Watson and coach Malcolm Reilly pulled Hanley out of the loose forward berth after he left the team hotel on he outskirts of Leeds without permission, eturning to his home in the city for a lengthy period on the day of the Friday evening fixture.

Denis Betts was promoted from the ubstitute bench, with Wigan clubmate Phil Clarke moving back to fill the number 13 ersey, Bradford Northern's Karl Fairbank tepping up from travelling reserve.

The no-contest nature of the record rout was eflected by the penalty count of Australian eferee Graham Annesley — just one to Britain.

Paul Newlove took the British Coal Man of he Match award as the centre swept through ackles with ease to go in for three tries, his hird successive hat-trick after scoring two for Featherstone Rovers. He also provided the final ass for three other British touchdowns in an mpressive performance, even allowing for the vholesale weakness of the downhearted pposition.

Leeds full back Alan Tait scored two quick ries in the first half and linked up at will, aving very little to do in defence. The Lions an in seven tries before the break to lead 8-0. The last try of the half was probably he best solo effort with majestic wingman Devereux pounding 60 yards down the right ving, brushing off one defender and bowling ver the full back with a mighty hand-off efore going round to the posts.

Britain had piled up their 72 points before France replied in the 70th minute, full back Eric Van Brussel passing two defenders in a 0-yard run to the line.

Shaun Edwards was totally involved at scrum half and sparked off several raids in addition to scoring two tries with great support play.

The record-breaking double, while achieved in fine style, set alarm bells ringing among internationalists. The British League responded to the crisis by arranging courses for French players and coaches and inviting young Gallic players to stay with British clubs for pre-season training.

Great Britain centre Paul Newlove, a hat-trick try hero against France in April.

BRITISH COAL TESTS

7 March   Carcassonne

GREAT BRITAIN 48   FRANCE 6

Stuart Spruce (Widnes)	1.	Jean Frison (Villefranche)
John Devereux (Widnes)	2.	Jean-Marc Garcia (St. Esteve)
Andy Currier (Widnes)	3.	Pierre Chamorin (St. Esteve)
Gary Connolly (St. Helens)	4.	Pascal Fages (Pia)
Alan Hunte (St. Helens)	5.	Claude Sirvent (St. Gaudens)
Garry Schofield (Leeds), Capt.	6.	Gilles Dumas (St. Gaudens), Capt.
Shaun Edwards (Wigan)	7.	Lucien de Macedo (Avignon)
Neil Cowie (Wigan)	8.	Theo Anast (St. Gaudens)
Steve McCurrie (Widnes)	9.	Bernard Cartier (St. Esteve)
Steve Molloy (Leeds)	10.	Thierry Buttignol (Avignon)
Richard Eyres (Widnes)	11.	Ezzedine Attia (Cannes)
Phil Clarke (Wigan)	12.	Didier Cabestany (XIII Catalan)
Ellery Hanley (Leeds)	13.	David Amat (Lezignan)
Mike Ford (Castleford)	14.	Eric Castel (Albi)
Chris Joynt (St. Helens)	15.	Pascal Bomati (XIII Catalan)
Allan Bateman (Warrington)	16.	Richard Clarke (Cannes)
Steve McNamara (Hull)	17.	Patrick Torreilles (Pia)

T: Schofield (3), Hanley (2),
Devereux, Eyres, Ford, Edwards
G: Currier (6)
Substitutions:
Bateman for Spruce (47 min.)
McNamara for Cowie (53 min.)
Joynt for Clarke (60 min.)
Ford for Eyres (66 min.)
Manager: Steve Watson
Coach: Malcolm Reilly

T: Dumas
G: Fages
Substitutions:
Castel for Chamorin (14 min.)
Bomati for Frison (20 min.)
Torreilles for de Macedo (50 min.)
Clarke for Dumas (63 min.)
Half-time: 18-6
Referee: Graham Annesley (Australi
Attendance: 5,500

Scorechart

Minute	Score	GB	France	Minute	Score	GB	Franc
10:	Schofield (T)	4	0	67:	Schofield (T)		
16:	Currier (P)	6	0		Currier (G)	32	
19:	Devereux (T)			73:	Ford (T)	36	
	Currier (G)	12	0	74:	Edwards (T)		
32:	Hanley (T)				Currier (G)	42	
	Currier (G)	18	0	79:	Hanley (T)		
35:	Dumas (T)				Currier (G)	48	
	Fages (G)	18	6		Scrums	9	
55:	Schofield (T)	22	6		Penalties	4	
62:	Eyres (T)	26	6				

2 April   **Leeds**

GREAT BRITAIN 72   FRANCE 6

Alan Tait (Leeds)	1.	Eric Van Brussel (Carcassonne)
John Devereux (Widnes)	2.	Claude Sirvent (St. Gaudens)
Paul Newlove (Featherstone R.)	3.	Pascal Mons (Carcassonne)
Gary Connolly (St. Helens)	4.	Adolphe Alesina (XIII Catalan)
Alan Hunte (St. Helens)	5.	Jean-Marc Garcia (St. Esteve)
Jonathan Davies (Widnes)	6.	Gilles Dumas (St. Gaudens), Capt.
Shaun Edwards (Wigan)	7.	Pascal Fages (Pia)
Karl Harrison (Halifax)	8.	Theo Anast (St. Gaudens)
Martin Dermott (Wigan)	9.	Patrick Torreilles (Pia)
Andy Platt (Wigan), Capt.	10.	Thierry Buttignol (Avignon)
Denis Betts (Wigan)	11.	Bernard Cartier (St. Esteve)
Richard Eyres (Widnes)	12.	Didier Cabestany (XIII Catalan)
Phil Clarke (Wigan)	13.	Jean-Luc Combettes (Pia)
Mike Ford (Castleford)	14.	David Amat (Lezignan)
Karl Fairbank (Bradford N.)	15.	Abdrajah Baba (XIII Catalan)
Daryl Powell (Sheffield E.)	16.	David Fraisse (Carpentras)
Jonny Nickle (St. Helens)	17.	Fabien Beranger (Lyon)

T: Newlove (3), Tait (2), Hunte (2), Edwards (2), Betts, Powell, Ford, Devereux. G: Davies (10)
Substitutions:
Powell for Connolly (40 min.)
Nickle for Betts (50 min.)
Fairbank for Harrison (63 min.)
Ford for Edwards (64 min.)
Manager: Steve Watson
Coach: Malcolm Reilly

T: Van Brussel
G: Dumas
Substitutions:
Amat for Combettes (9 min.)
Baba for Buttignol (40 min.)
Beranger for Cabestany (49 min.)
Fraisse for Mons (75 min.)
Half-time: 38-0
Referee: Graham Annesley (Australia)
Attendance: 8,196

Scorechart

Minute	Score	GB	France	Minute	Score	GB	France
4:	Hunte (T)	4	0	42:	Edwards (T)		
10:	Newlove (T)	8	0		Davies (G)	44	0
13:	Hunte (T)			45:	Powell (T)		
	Davies (G)	14	0		Davies (G)	50	0
19:	Betts (T)			52:	Newlove (T)		
	Davies (G)	20	0		Davies (G)	56	0
22:	Tait (T)			55:	Edwards (T)	60	0
	Davies (G)	26	0	61:	Newlove (T)		
28:	Tait (T)				Davies (G)	66	0
	Davies (G)	32	0	67:	Ford (T)		
35:	Devereux (T)				Davies (G)	72	0
	Davies (G)	38	0	70:	Van Brussel (T)		
					Dumas (G)	72	6
					Scrums	5	8
					Penalties	1	0

TESTS

● Although early Tests were played under the titles of Northern Union or England, it is acceptable to regard them as Great Britain.
W-Won, D-Drawn, L-Lost refer to Great Britain.

GREAT BRITAIN v. AUSTRALIA

Date	Result	Score	Venue	Attendance
12 Dec. 1908	D	22-22	QPR, London	2,000
23 Jan. 1909	W	15-5	Newcastle	22,000
15 Feb. 1909	W	6-5	Birmingham	9,000
18 Jun. 1910	W	27-20	Sydney	42,000
2 Jul. 1910	W	22-17	Brisbane	18,000
8 Nov. 1911	L	10-19	Newcastle	6,500
16 Dec. 1911	D	11-11	Edinburgh	6,000
1 Jan. 1912	L	8-33	Birmingham	4,000
27 Jun. 1914	W	23-5	Sydney	40,000
29 Jun. 1914	L	7-12	Sydney	55,000
4 Jul. 1914	W	14-6	Sydney	34,420
26 Jun. 1920	L	4-8	Brisbane	28,000
3 Jul. 1920	L	8-21	Sydney	40,000
10 Jul. 1920	W	23-13	Sydney	32,000
1 Oct. 1921	W	6-5	Leeds	32,000
5 Nov. 1921	L	2-16	Hull	21,504
14 Jan. 1922	W	6-0	Salford	21,000
23 Jun. 1924	W	22-3	Sydney	50,000
28 Jun. 1924	W	5-3	Sydney	33,842
12 Jul. 1924	L	11-21	Brisbane	36,000
23 Jun. 1928	W	15-12	Brisbane	39,200
14 Jul. 1928	W	8-0	Sydney	44,548
21 Jul. 1928	L	14-21	Sydney	37,000
5 Oct. 1929	L	8-31	Hull K.R.	20,000
9 Nov. 1929	W	9-3	Leeds	31,402
4 Jan. 1930	D	0-0	Swinton	34,709
15 Jan. 1930	W	3-0	Rochdale	16,743
6 Jun. 1932	W	8-6	Sydney	70,204
18 Jun. 1932	L	6-15	Brisbane	26,500
16 Jul. 1932	W	18-13	Sydney	50,053
7 Oct. 1933	W	4-0	Belle Vue, Manchester	34,000
11 Nov. 1933	W	7-5	Leeds	29,618
16 Dec. 1933	W	19-16	Swinton	10,990
29 Jun. 1936	L	8-24	Sydney	63,920
4 Jul. 1936	W	12-7	Brisbane	29,486
18 Jul. 1936	W	12-7	Sydney	53,546
16 Oct. 1937	W	5-4	Leeds	31,949
13 Nov. 1937	W	13-3	Swinton	31,724
18 Dec. 1937	L	3-13	Huddersfield	9,093
17 Jun. 1946	D	8-8	Sydney	64,527
6 Jul. 1946	W	14-5	Brisbane	40,500
20 Jul. 1946	W	20-7	Sydney	35,294
9 Oct. 1948	W	23-21	Leeds	36,529
6 Nov. 1948	W	16-7	Swinton	36,354
29 Jan. 1949	W	23-9	Bradford	42,000
12 Jun. 1950	W	6-4	Sydney	47,215
1 Jul. 1950	L	3-15	Brisbane	35,000
22 Jul. 1950	L	2-5	Sydney	47,178
4 Oct. 1952	W	19-6	Leeds	34,505
8 Nov. 1952	W	21-5	Swinton	32,421
13 Dec. 1952	L	7-27	Bradford	30,509
12 Jun. 1954	L	12-37	Sydney	65,884
3 Jul. 1954	W	38-21	Brisbane	46,355
17 Jul. 1954	L	16-20	Sydney	67,577
17 Nov. 1956	W	21-10	Wigan	22,473
1 Dec. 1956	L	9-22	Bradford	23,634
15 Dec. 1956	W	19-0	Swinton	17,542
14 Jun. 1958	L	8-25	Sydney	68,777
5 Jul. 1958	W	25-18	Brisbane	32,965
19 Jul. 1958	W	40-17	Sydney	68,720
17 Oct. 1959	L	14-22	Swinton	35,224
21 Nov. 1959	W	11-10	Leeds	30,184
12 Dec. 1959	W	18-12	Wigan	26,089
9 Jun. 1962	W	31-12	Sydney	70,174
30 Jun. 1962	W	17-10	Brisbane	34,766
14 Jul. 1962	L	17-18	Sydney	42,104
16 Oct. 1963	L	2-28	Wembley	13,946
9 Nov. 1963	L	12-50	Swinton	30,833
30 Nov. 1963	W	16-5	Leeds	20,497
25 Jun. 1966	W	17-13	Sydney	57,962
16 Jul. 1966	L	4-6	Brisbane	45,057
23 Jul. 1966	L	14-19	Sydney	63,503
21 Oct. 1967	W	16-11	Leeds	22,293
3 Nov. 1967	L	11-17	White City, London	17,445
9 Dec. 1967	L	3-11	Swinton	13,615
6 Jun. 1970	L	15-37	Brisbane	42,807
20 Jun. 1970	W	28-7	Sydney	60,962
4 Jul. 1970	W	21-17	Sydney	61,258
3 Nov. 1973	W	21-12	Wembley	9,874
24 Nov. 1973	L	6-14	Leeds	16,674
1 Dec. 1973	L	5-15	Warrington	10,019
15 Jun. 1974	L	6-12	Brisbane	30,280
6 Jul. 1974	W	16-11	Sydney	48,006
20 Jul. 1974	L	18-22	Sydney	55,505
21 Oct. 1978	L	9-15	Wigan	17,644
5 Nov. 1978	W	18-14	Bradford	26,447
18 Nov. 1978	L	6-23	Leeds	29,627
16 Jun. 1979	L	0-35	Brisbane	23,051
30 Jun. 1979	L	16-24	Sydney	26,837
14 Jul. 1979	L	2-28	Sydney	16,844
30 Oct. 1982	L	4-40	Hull C. FC	26,771
20 Nov. 1982	L	6-27	Wigan	23,216
28 Nov. 1982	L	8-32	Leeds	17,318
9 Jun. 1984	L	8-25	Sydney	30,190

26 Jun. 1984	L	6-18	Brisbane	26,534	27 Oct. 1990	W	19-12	Wembley	54,569
7 Jul. 1984	L	7-20	Sydney	18,756	10 Nov. 1990	L	10-14	Man U. FC	46,615
25 Oct. 1986	L	16-38	Man U. FC	50,583	* 24 Nov. 1990	L	0-14	Elland Rd,	
8 Nov. 1986	L	4-34	Elland Rd,					Leeds	32,500
			Leeds	30,808	12 Jun. 1992	L	6-22	Sydney	40,141
* 22 Nov. 1986	L	15-24	Wigan	20,169	26 Jun. 1992	W	33-10	Melbourne	30,257
11 Jun. 1988	L	6-17	Sydney	24,202	* 3 Jul. 1992	L	10-16	Brisbane	32,313
28 Jun. 1988	L	14-34	Brisbane	27,103	* Also World Cup match.				
* 9 Jul. 1988	W	26-12	Sydney	15,994					

	Played	Won	Drawn	Lost	Tries	Goals	Dr	Pts for
Great Britain	108	52	4	52	262	270	7	1362
Australia	108	52	4	52	309	333	6	1653

GREAT BRITAIN-AUSTRALIA TEST MATCH RECORDS

Britain

Highest score: 40-17 Third Test at Sydney, 19 July 1958

Widest margin win: As above and
33-10 Second Test at Melbourne, 26 June 1992

Most tries in a match: 4 by Jim Leytham (Wigan) Second Test at Brisbane, 2 July 1910

Most goals in a match: 10 by Lewis Jones (Leeds) Second Test at Brisbane, 3 July 1954

Most points in a match: 20 by Lewis Jones (as above)
20 (2t, 7g) by Roger Millward (Hull K.R.) Second Test at Sydney, 20 June 1970

Biggest attendance: 54,569 First Test at Wembley, London, 27 October 1990

For the World Cup final at Wembley on 24 October 1992, there was an attendance of 73,631

Australia

Highest score: 50-12 Second Test at Swinton, 9 Nov 1963 (Also widest margin win)

Most tries in a match: 3 by Jimmy Devereux, First Test at QPR, London, 12 December 1908
3 by Reg Gasnier, First Test at Swinton, 17 October 1959
3 by Reg Gasnier, First Test at Wembley, 16 October 1963
3 by Ken Irvine, Second Test at Swinton, 9 November 1963
3 by Ken Irvine, Third Test at Sydney, 23 July 1966
3 by Gene Miles, First Test at Old Trafford, Manchester, 25 October 1986
3 by Michael O'Connor, First Test at Old Trafford, Manchester, 25 October 1986

Most goals in a match: 10 by Mick Cronin, First Test at Brisbane, 16 June 1979

Most points in a match: 22 (3t, 5g) by Michael O'Connor, First Test at Old Trafford, Manchester, 25 October 1986

Biggest attendance: 70,204 First Test at Sydney, 6 June 1932

In a World Cup match at Perpignan, France, on 29 October 1972, Bobby Fulton scored 3 tries

GREAT BRITAIN v. NEW ZEALAND

Date	Res	Score	Venue	Crowd
25 Jan. 1908	W	14-6	Leeds	8,182
8 Feb. 1908	L	6-18	Chelsea	14,000
15 Feb. 1908	L	5-8	Cheltenham	4,000
30 Jul. 1910	W	52-20	Auckland	16,000
1 Aug. 1914	W	16-13	Auckland	15,000
31 Jul. 1920	W	31-7	Auckland	34,000
7 Aug. 1920	W	19-3	Christchurch	10,000
14 Aug. 1920	W	11-10	Wellington	4,000
2 Aug. 1924	L	8-16	Auckland	22,000
6 Aug. 1924	L	11-13	Wellington	6,000
9 Aug. 1924	W	31-18	Dunedin	14,000
2 Oct. 1926	W	28-20	Wigan	14,500
13 Nov. 1926	W	21-11	Hull	7,000
15 Jan. 1927	W	32-17	Leeds	6,000
4 Aug. 1928	L	13-17	Auckland	28,000
18 Aug. 1928	W	13-5	Dunedin	12,000
25 Aug. 1928	W	6-5	Christchurch	21,000
30 Jul. 1932	W	24-9	Auckland	25,000
13 Aug. 1932	W	25-14	Christchurch	5,000
20 Aug. 1932	W	20-18	Auckland	6,500
8 Aug. 1936	W	10-8	Auckland	25,000
15 Aug. 1936	W	23-11	Auckland	17,000
10 Aug. 1946	L	8-13	Auckland	10,000
4 Oct. 1947	W	11-10	Leeds	28,445
8 Nov. 1947	L	7-10	Swinton	29,031
20 Dec. 1947	W	25-9	Bradford	42,680
29 Jul. 1950	L	10-16	Christchurch	10,000
12 Aug. 1950	L	13-20	Auckland	20,000
6 Oct. 1951	W	21-15	Bradford	37,475
10 Nov. 1951	W	20-19	Swinton	29,938
15 Dec. 1951	W	16-12	Leeds	18,649
24 Jul. 1954	W	27-7	Auckland	22,097
31 Jul. 1954	L	14-20	Greymouth	4,240
14 Aug. 1954	W	12-6	Auckland	6,186
8 Oct. 1955	W	25-6	Swinton	21,937
12 Nov. 1955	W	27-12	Bradford	24,443
17 Dec. 1955	L	13-28	Leeds	10,438
26 Jul. 1958	L	10-15	Auckland	25,000
9 Aug. 1958	W	32-15	Auckland	25,000
30 Sep. 1961	L	11-29	Leeds	16,540
21 Oct. 1961	W	23-10	Bradford	19,98...
4 Nov. 1961	W	35-19	Swinton	22,53...
28 Jul. 1962	L	0-19	Auckland	14,97...
11 Aug. 1962	L	8-27	Auckland	16,41...
25 Sep. 1965	W	7-2	Swinton	8,54...
23 Oct. 1965	W	15-9	Bradford	15,74...
6 Nov. 1965	D	9-9	Wigan	7,91...
6 Aug. 1966	W	25-8	Auckland	14,49...
20 Aug. 1966	W	22-14	Auckland	10,65...
11 Jul. 1970	W	19-15	Auckland	15,948
19 Jul. 1970	W	23-9	Christchurch	8,60...
25 Jul. 1970	W	33-16	Auckland	13,13...
25 Sep. 1971	L	13-18	Salford	3,76...
16 Oct. 1971	L	14-17	Castleford	4,10...
6 Nov. 1971	W	12-3	Leeds	5,47...
27 Jul. 1974	L	8-13	Auckland	10,46...
4 Aug. 1974	W	17-8	Christchurch	6,31...
10 Aug. 1974	W	20-0	Auckland	11,57...
21 Jul. 1979	W	16-8	Auckland	9,00...
5 Aug. 1979	W	22-7	Christchurch	8,50...
11 Aug. 1979	L	11-18	Auckland	7,00...
18 Oct. 1980	D	14-14	Wigan	7,03...
2 Nov. 1980	L	8-12	Bradford	10,94...
15 Nov. 1980	L	10-2	Leeds	8,21...
14 Jul. 1984	L	0-12	Auckland	10,23...
22 Jul. 1984	L	12-28	Christchurch	3,82...
28 Jul. 1984	L	16-32	Auckland	7,96...
19 Oct. 1985	L	22-24	Leeds	12,59...
2 Nov. 1985	W	25-8	Wigan	15,50...
* 9 Nov. 1985	D	6-6	Elland Rd, Leeds	22,20...
* 17 Jul. 1988	L	10-12	Christchurch	8,52...
21 Oct. 1989	L	16-24	Man U. FC	18,27...
28 Oct. 1989	W	26-6	Elland Rd, Leeds	13,07...
* 11 Nov. 1989	W	10-6	Wigan	20,34...
24 Jun. 1990	W	11-10	Palmerston N.	8,07...
8 Jul. 1990	W	16-14	Auckland	7,84...
* 15 Jul. 1990	L	18-21	Christchurch	3,13...
12 Jul. 1992	L	14-15	Palmerston N.	11,54...
19 Jul. 1992	W	19-16	Auckland	10,22...

*Also World Cup match.

	Played	Won	Drawn	Lost	Tries	Goals	Dr	Pts for
Great Britain	79	48	3	28	278	226	5	1326
New Zealand	79	28	3	48	182	227	2	1040

GREAT BRITAIN-NEW ZEALAND TEST MATCH RECORDS

Britain

Highest score:	52-20 First Test at Auckland, 30 July 1910 (Also widest margi... win)
Most tries in a match:	4 by Billy Boston (Wigan) First Test at Auckland, 24 July 1954
	4 by Garry Schofield (Hull) Second Test at Wigan, 2 November 198...

Most goals in a match: 7 by Eric Fraser (Warrington) Second Test at Auckland, 9 August 1958
                         7 by Neil Fox (Wakefield T.) Third Test at Swinton, 4 November 1961
Most points in a match: 16 (4t) by Garry Schofield (Hull) Second Test at Wigan, 2 November
                         1985
Biggest attendance: 42,680 Third Test at Bradford, 20 December 1947

● In a World Cup match at Pau, France, on 4 November 1972, Britain won 53-19 with John
Holmes (Leeds) scoring 26 points from 10 goals and two tries.
In a World Cup match at Sydney on 8 June 1968, Bev Risman scored 7 goals.

New Zealand
Highest score: 32-16 Third Test at Auckland, 28 July 1984
Widest margin win: 19-0 First Test at Auckland, 28 July 1962
                         27-8 Second Test at Auckland, 11 August 1962
No player has scored three tries or more in a Test.
Most goals and points: 7g-14pts by Des White, Second Test at Greymouth, 31 July 1954
                         Jack Fagan, First Test at Headingley, 30 September 1961
                         Ernie Wiggs, Second Test at Auckland, 20 August 1966
Biggest attendance: 34,000 First Test at Auckland, 31 July 1920
● In a World Cup match at Sydney, Australia, on 25 June 1957, Bill Sorensen also scored
7 goals, 14 points.

GREAT BRITAIN v. FRANCE
● Results since France were given Test match
status.

Date	Result	Score	Venue	Attendance
26 Jan. 1957	W	45-12	Leeds	20,221
3 Mar. 1957	D	19-19	Toulouse	16,000
10 Apr. 1957	W	29-14	St. Helens	23,250
3 Nov. 1957	W	25-14	Toulouse	15,000
23 Nov. 1957	W	44-15	Wigan	19,152
2 Mar. 1958	W	23-9	Grenoble	20,000
14 Mar. 1959	W	50-15	Leeds	22,000
5 Apr. 1959	L	15-24	Grenoble	8,500
6 Mar. 1960	L	18-20	Toulouse	15,308
26 Mar. 1960	D	17-17	St. Helens	14,000
11 Dec. 1960	W	21-10	Bordeaux	8,000
28 Jan. 1961	W	27-8	St. Helens	18,000
17 Feb. 1962	L	15-20	Wigan	17,277
11 Mar. 1962	L	13-23	Perpignan	14,000
2 Dec. 1962	L	12-17	Perpignan	5,000
3 Apr. 1963	W	42-4	Wigan	19,487
8 Mar. 1964	W	11-5	Perpignan	4,326
18 Mar. 1964	W	39-0	Leigh	4,750
6 Dec. 1964	L	8-18	Perpignan	15,000
23 Jan. 1965	W	17-7	Swinton	9,959
16 Jan. 1966	L	13-18	Perpignan	6,000
5 Mar. 1966	L	4-8	Wigan	14,004
22 Jan. 1967	W	16-13	Carcassonne	10,650
4 Mar. 1967	L	13-23	Wigan	7,448
11 Feb. 1968	W	22-13	Paris	8,000
2 Mar. 1968	W	19-8	Bradford	14,196
30 Nov. 1968	W	34-10	St. Helens	6,080
2 Feb. 1969	L	9-13	Toulouse	10,000
7 Feb. 1971	L	8-16	Toulouse	14,960
17 Mar. 1971	W	24-2	St. Helens	7,783
6 Feb. 1972	W	10-9	Toulouse	11,508
12 Mar. 1972	W	45-10	Bradford	7,313
20 Jan. 1974	W	24-5	Grenoble	5,500
17 Feb. 1974	W	29-0	Wigan	10,105
6 Dec. 1981	W	37-0	Hull	13,173
20 Dec. 1981	L	2-19	Marseilles	6,500
20 Feb. 1983	W	20-5	Carcassonne	3,826
6 Mar. 1983	W	17-5	Hull	6,055
29 Jan. 1984	W	12-0	Avignon	4,000
17 Feb. 1984	W	10-0	Leeds	7,646
1 Mar. 1985	W	50-4	Leeds	6,491
17 Mar. 1985	L	16-24	Perpignan	5,000
* 16 Feb. 1986	D	10-10	Avignon	4,000
1 Mar. 1986	W	24-10	Wigan	8,112
* 24 Jan. 1987	W	52-4	Leeds	6,567
8 Feb. 1987	W	20-10	Carcassonne	2,000
24 Jan. 1988	W	28-14	Avignon	6,500
6 Feb. 1988	W	30-12	Leeds	7,007
21 Jan. 1989	W	26-10	Wigan	8,266
5 Feb. 1989	W	30-8	Avignon	6,500
18 Mar. 1990	W	8-4	Perpignan	6,000
7 Apr. 1990	L	18-25	Leeds	6,554
* 27 Jan. 1991	W	45-10	Perpignan	3,965
16 Feb. 1991	W	60-4	Leeds	5,284
16 Feb. 1992	W	30-12	Perpignan	5,688
* 7 Mar. 1992	W	36-0	Hull	5,250
7 Mar. 1993	W	48-6	Carcassonne	5,500
2 Apr. 1993	W	72-6	Leeds	8,196

*Also World Cup match.

	Played	Won	Drawn	Lost	Tries	Goals	Dr	Pts for
Great Britain	58	41	3	14	280	256	1	1461
France	58	14	3	41	105	137	4	621

GREAT BRITAIN-FRANCE TEST MATCH RECORDS

Britain

Highest score:	72-6 at Leeds, 2 April 1993 (Also widest margin win)
Most tries in a match:	5 by Martin Offiah (Widnes) at Leeds, 16 February 1991
Most goals in a match:	10 by Bernard Ganley (Oldham) at Wigan, 23 November 1957
	10 by Jonathan Davies (Widnes) at Leeds, 2 April 1993
Most points in a match:	21 (1t, 9g) by Lewis Jones (Leeds) at Leeds, 26 January 1957
	21 (1t, 9g) by Neil Fox (Wakefield T.) at Wigan, 3 April 1963
	21 (1t, 9g) by Neil Fox (Wakefield T.) at Leigh, 18 March 1964
Biggest attendance:	23,250 at St. Helens, 10 April 1957

France

Highest score:	25-18 at Leeds, 7 April 1990
Widest margin win:	19-2 at Marseilles, 20 December 1981
Most tries in a match:	3 by Didier Couston at Perpignan, 17 March 1985
Most goals in a match:	7 by Pierre Lacaze at Wigan, 4 March 1967
Most points in a match:	14 by Pierre Lacaze (as above)
	14 (2t, 4g) by Gilbert Benausse at Wigan, 17 February 1962
Biggest attendance:	20,000 at Grenoble, 2 March 1958

● In a World Cup match at Toulouse on 7 November 1954, there were 37,471

Additional Great Britain v. France

Pre-Test status

22 May 1952	L 12-22	Paris	16,466
24 May 1953	L 17-28	Lyons	
27 Apr. 1954	W 17-8	Bradford	14,153
11 Dec. 1955	L 5-17	Paris	18,000
11 Apr. 1956	W 18-10	Bradford	10,453

Other match

31 July 1982	L 7-8	Venice	1,500

GREAT BRITAIN v. PAPUA NEW GUINEA

5 Aug. 1984	W 38-20	Mt. Hagen	7,510
*24 Oct. 1987	W 42-0	Wigan	9,121
*22 May 1988	W 42-22	Port Moresby	12,107
27 May 1990	L 18-20	Goroka	11,598
*2 Jun. 1990	W 40-8	Port Moresby	5,969
*9 Nov. 1991	W 56-4	Wigan	4,193
31 May 1992	W 20-14	Port Moresby	7,294

*Also World Cup match.

Great Britain's Garry Schofield receives the cold towel treatment in the 1992 Papua Test at Port Moresby.

	Played	Won	Lost	Tries	Goals	Dr	Pts for
Great Britain	7	6	1	45	38	0	256
Papua New Guinea	7	1	6	14	15	2	88

GREAT BRITAIN-PAPUA NEW GUINEA TEST MATCH RECORDS

Britain

Highest score:	56-4 at Wigan, 9 November 1991 (Also widest margin win)
Most tries in a match:	No player has scored 3 or more
Most goals in a match:	8 by Jonathan Davies (Widnes) at Wigan, 9 November 1991
Most points in a match:	16 by Jonathan Davies (Widnes) as above
Biggest attendance:	9,121 at Wigan, 24 October 1987

Papua New Guinea

Highest score:	22-42 at Port Moresby, 22 May 1988
Only win:	20-18 at Goroka, 27 May 1990
Most tries in a match:	No player has scored 3 or more
Most goals in a match:	6 by Bal Numapo at Goroka, 27 May 1990
Most points in a match:	11 (5g, 1dg) by Bal Numapo as above
Biggest attendance:	12,107 at Port Moresby, 22 May 1988

Great Britain centre Gary Connolly on the attack in the world record rout of France at Leeds in April 1993.

CLUB REPRESENTATION

Wigan hold the record for most players supplied by one club for a Test or World Cup match. They have had eight in Great Britain's starting line-up on three occasions as follows:

v. Papua New Guinea at Wigan on 24 October 1987. Won 42-0: Steve Hampson, David Stephenson, Joe Lydon, Shaun Edwards, Andy Gregory, Brian Case, Andy Goodway and Ellery Hanley (capt).

v. Australia at Melbourne on 26 June 1992. Won 33-10: Martin Offiah, Shaun Edwards, Kelvin Skerrett, Martin Dermott, Andy Platt, Denis Betts, Billy McGinty and Phil Clarke.

v. Australia at Brisbane on 3 July 1992. Lost 10-16: As above.

In the second and third Tests of 1992 Wigan became the first club to provide all six forwards.

Wigan had a record 10 players on duty for the first 1992 Test against Australia, seven in the starting line-up plus three substitutes, all of whom played. For a brief period, there were a record nine Wigan players in action.

Wigan also hold the record for the total of players selected from one club over the years with 81.

Billy Boston, the former Wigan winger, holds the record for most Tests with one club, making all of his 31 appearances while at Central Park.

Only six of last season's clubs have not had a player selected for Great Britain — Blackpool Gladiators, Bramley, Carlisle, Chorley Borough, Doncaster and Nottingham City.

Of the extinct clubs only Broughton Rangers (later Belle Vue Rangers), Merthyr Tydfil, St. Helens Recs and Runcorn had players selected for Britain.

*A register of each club's representation for Great Britain is featured in the CLUBS section.

GREAT BRITAIN TEAMS
...A 20-year review

The following is a compendium of Great Britain Test and World Cup teams since the start of the 1973-74 season.

Initials are included where more than one celebrated player shared a surname in the same era. Only playing substitutes are included on the teamsheet.

(WC): World Cup t: try g: goal dg: drop goal * captain

Hull K.R. second row man Phil Lowe, who appeared in all three Tests against Australia in 1973.

1973 Australia

Wembley: 3 Nov

Won 21-12

Charlton (Salford)
*Sullivan, C (Hull)
Hynes (Leeds)
Hesketh (Salford)
Atkinson, J (Leeds)
Topliss (Wakefield)
Nash (Featherstone) 1dg
Clawson (Oldham) 4g
Clarke (Wigan) 1t
Lockwood (Castleford) 1t
Nicholls (St. Helens)
Lowe, P (Hull KR) 2t
Batten, R (Leeds)

1973 Australia

Leeds: 24 Nov

Lost 6-14

Charlton (Salford)
*Sullivan, C (Hull)
Hynes (Leeds)
Hesketh (Salford)
Atkinson, J (Leeds)
Topliss (Wakefield)
Nash (Featherstone)
Clawson (Oldham) 3g
Clarke (Wigan)
Lockwood (Castleford)
Mantle (St. Helens)
Lowe, P (Hull KR)
Batten, R (Leeds)
Sub: Eckersley (St. Helens)
Dixon, C (Salford)

1973 Australia

Warrington: 1 Dec

Lost 5-15

Charlton (Salford)
Smith, A (Leeds)
Hynes (Leeds)
Hesketh (Salford)
*Sullivan, C (Hull)
Eckersley (St. Helens)
Millward (Hull KR) 1t, 1g
Clawson (Oldham)
Clarke (Wigan)
Harrison, M (Hull)
Nicholls (St. Helens)
Lowe, P (Hull KR)
Laughton (Widnes)
Sub: Watkins, D (Salford)
Dixon, C (Salford)

1974 France

Grenoble: 20 Jan

Won 24-5

Charlton (Salford)
Fielding (Salford) 3t
Willicombe (Halifax) 1t
Hesketh (Salford)
Redfearn, D (Bradford)
Gill, K (Salford) 1t
Bates, A (Dewsbury)
Clawson (Oldham) 3g
Bridges (Featherstone)
Lockwood (Castleford)
Dixon, C (Salford)
Nicholls (St. Helens)
*Laughton (Widnes) 1t
Sub: Watkins, D (Salford)
Gray (Wigan)

1974 France

Wigan: 17 Feb

Won 29-0

Charlton (Salford) 2t
Fielding (Salford)
Willicombe (Wigan) 1t
Hesketh (Salford)
Redfearn, D (Bradford) 2t
Gill, K (Salford)
Bates, A (Dewsbury)
Clawson (Oldham) 2g
Bridges (Featherstone)
Fogerty (Rochdale)
Dixon, C (Salford)
Nicholls (St. Helens)
*Laughton (Widnes) 1t
Sub: Watkins, D (Salford) 1g
Gray (Wigan) 1t, 1g

1974 Australia

Brisbane: 15 June

Lost 6-12

Charlton (Salford)
Redfearn, D (Bradford)
Watkins, D (Salford) 1g
*Hesketh (Salford)
Bevan, J (Warrington)
Millward (Hull KR)
Nash (Featherstone)
Clawson (Oldham) 2g
Bridges (Featherstone)
Mills (Widnes)
Dixon, C (Salford)
Thompson, J (Featherstone)
Nicholls (St. Helens)
Sub: Eckersley (St. Helens)
Gray (Wigan)

1974 Australia

Sydney: 6 July

Won 16-11

Charlton (Salford)
Dyl (Leeds)
Eckersley (St. Helens)
*Hesketh (Salford)
Millward (Hull KR)
Gill, K (Salford) 1t
Nash (Featherstone)
Mills (Widnes)
Gray (Wigan) 3g, 1dg
Thompson, J (Featherstone)
Dixon, C (Salford) 1t
Chisnall, E (St. Helens) 1t
Nicholls (St. Helens)
Sub: Norton (Castleford)

1974 Australia

Sydney: 20 July

Lost 18-22

Charlton (Salford)
Richards (Salford) 1t
Dyl (Leeds) 1t
*Hesketh (Salford)
Bevan, J (Warrington)
Gill, K (Salford)
Nash (Featherstone)
Clawson (Oldham)
Gray (Wigan) 6g
Thompson, J (Featherstone)
Dixon, C (Salford)
Chisnall, E (St. Helens)
Nicholls (St. Helens)
Sub: Millward (Hull KR)
Rose, P (Hull KR)

1974 New Zealand

Auckland: 27 July

Lost 8-13

Charlton (Salford)
Redfearn, D (Bradford)
Dyl (Leeds)
*Hesketh (Salford)
Bevan, J (Warrington) 1t
Gill, K (Salford)
Nash (Featherstone) 1t
Clawson (Oldham) 1g
Gray (Wigan)
Thompson, J (Featherstone)
Dixon, C (Salford)
Norton (Castleford)
Nicholls (St. Helens)
Sub: Ashcroft (Warrington)

1974 New Zealand

Christchurch: 4 Aug

Won 17-8

Charlton (Salford)
Redfearn, D (Bradford) 1t
Dyl (Leeds) 1t
Dixon, C (Salford)
Richards (Salford)
*Hesketh (Salford) 1t
Nash (Featherstone)
Mills (Widnes)
Gray (Wigan) 4g
Thompson, J (Featherstone)
Chisnall, E (St. Helens)
Norton (Castleford)
Nicholls (St. Helens)
Sub: Bates, A (Dewsbury)

1974 New Zealand

Auckland: 10 Aug

Won 20-0

Charlton (Salford)
Redfearn, D (Bradford)
Willicombe (Wigan)
Dyl (Leeds) 1t
Bevan, J (Warrington) 2t
*Hesketh (Salford) 1t
Nash (Featherstone)
Clawson (Oldham)
Gray (Wigan) 4g
Thompson, J (Featherstone)
Chisnall, E (St. Helens)
Dixon, C (Salford)
Nicholls (St. Helens)
Sub: Bates, A (Dewsbury)
       Ramsey (Bradford)

1977 France (WC)

Auckland: 5 June

Won 23-4

Fairbairn (Wigan) 7g
Fielding (Salford)
Holmes (Leeds)
Dyl (Leeds) 1t
Wright, S (Widnes) 1t
*Millward (Hull KR) 1t
Nash (Salford)
Thompson, J (Featherstone)
Ward, D (Leeds)
Pitchford, S (Leeds)
Bowman, E (Workington)
Nicholls (St. Helens)
Hogan (Barrow)
Sub: Gill, K (Salford)
       Casey (Hull KR)

1977 New Zealand (WC)

Christchurch: 12 June

Won 30-12

Fairbairn (Wigan) 6g
Wright, S (Widnes) 2t
Holmes (Leeds)
Dyl (Leeds)
Francis, W (Wigan)
*Millward (Hull KR) 1t
Nash (Salford)
Thompson, J (Featherstone)
Ward, D (Leeds)
Pitchford, S (Leeds)
Bowman, E (Workington) 1t
Nicholls (St. Helens) 1t
Hogan (Barrow) 1t
Sub: Casey (Hull KR)

1977 Australia (WC)

Brisbane: 18 June

Lost 5-19

Fairbairn (Wigan) 1g
Wright, S (Widnes)
Francis, W (Wigan)
Dyl (Leeds)
Fielding (Salford)
*Millward (Hull KR) 1t
Nash (Salford)
Thompson, J (Featherstone)
Ward, D (Leeds)
Pitchford, S (Leeds)
Bowman, E (Workington)
Nicholls (St. Helens)
Hogan (Barrow)
Sub: Holmes (Leeds)
       Smith, P (Featherstone)

1977 Australia (WC)

Sydney: 25 June

Lost 12-13

Fairbairn (Wigan) 3g
Wright, S (Widnes)
Holmes (Leeds)
Dyl (Leeds)
Francis, W (Wigan)
*Millward (Hull KR)
Nash (Salford)
Thompson, J (Featherstone)
Elwell (Widnes)
Pitchford, S (Leeds) 1t
Bowman, E (Workington)
Casey (Hull KR)
Hogan (Barrow)
Sub: Gill, K (Salford) 1t
       Smith, P (Featherstone)

1978 Australia

Wigan: 21 Oct

Lost 9-15

Fairbairn (Wigan) 3g
Wright, S (Widnes)
Hughes (Widnes)
Cunningham (St. Helens)
Bevan, J (Warrington) 1t
*Millward (Hull KR)
Nash (Salford)
Thompson, J (Featherstone)
Ward, D (Leeds)
Rose, P (Hull KR)
Nicholls (St. Helens)
Casey (Hull KR)
Norton (Hull)
Sub: Holmes (Leeds)
       Hogan (Barrow)

1978 Australia

Bradford: 5 Nov

Won 18-14

Fairbairn (Wigan) 6g
Wright, S (Widnes) 2t
Joyner (Castleford)
Dyl (Leeds)
Atkinson, J (Leeds)
*Millward (Hull KR)
Nash (Salford)
Mills (Widnes)
Fisher (Bradford)
Lockwood (Hull KR)
Nicholls (St. Helens)
Lowe, P (Hull KR)
Norton (Hull)
Sub: Holmes (Leeds)
       Rose, P (Hull KR)

1978 Australia

Leeds: 18 Nov

Lost 6-23

Fairbairn (Wigan)
Wright, S (Widnes)
Joyner (Castleford)
Bevan, J (Warrington) 1t
Atkinson, J (Leeds)
*Millward (Hull KR) 1t
Nash (Salford)
Mills (Widnes)
Fisher (Bradford)
Farrar (Hull)
Nicholls (St. Helens)
Lowe, P (Hull KR)
Norton (Hull)
Sub: Holmes (Leeds)
       Rose, P (Hull KR)

1979 Australia
Brisbane: 16 June
Lost 0-35
Woods, J (Leigh)
Barends (Bradford)
Joyner (Castleford)
Hughes (Widnes)
Mathias (St. Helens)
Holmes (Leeds)
Stephens (Castleford)
Mills (Widnes)
Ward, D (Leeds)
Skerrett (Wakefield)
Nicholls (St. Helens)
*Laughton (Widnes)
Norton (Hull)
Sub: Evans, S (Featherstone)
     Hogan (Hull KR)

1979 Australia
Sydney: 30 June
Lost 16-24
Fairbairn (Wigan)
Barends (Bradford)
Joyner (Castleford) 1t
Woods, J (Leigh) 5g
Hughes (Widnes) 1t
Holmes (Leeds)
Stephens (Castleford)
*Nicholls (St. Helens)
Ward, D (Leeds)
Skerrett (Wakefield)
Casey (Bradford)
Grayshon (Bradford)
Adams, M (Widnes)
Sub: Evans, S (Featherstone)
     Watkinson (Hull KR)

1979 Australia
Sydney: 14 July
Lost 2-28
Fairbairn (Wigan) 1g
Evans, S (Featherstone)
Joyner (Castleford)
Woods, J (Leigh)
Hughes (Widnes)
Topliss (Wakefield)
Redfearn, A (Bradford)
*Nicholls (St. Helens)
Ward, D (Leeds)
Casey (Bradford)
Hogan (Hull KR)
Grayshon (Bradford)
Norton (Hull)
Sub: Holmes (Leeds)
     Adams, M (Widnes)

1979 New Zealand
Auckland: 21 July
Won 16-8
Fairbairn (Wigan) 1t, 2g
Evans, S (Featherstone) 1t
Joyner (Castleford)
Smith, M (Hull KR) 1t
Hughes (Widnes) 1t
Holmes (Leeds)
Stephens (Castleford)
Casey (Bradford)
Ward, D (Leeds)
*Nicholls (St. Helens)
Hogan (Hull KR)
Grayshon (Bradford)
Adams, M (Widnes)
Sub: Lockwood (Hull KR)

1979 New Zealand
Christchurch: 5 Aug
Won 22-7
Fairbairn (Wigan) 5g
Evans, S (Featherstone) 1t
Joyner (Castleford)
Smith, M (Hull KR)
Hughes (Widnes) 1t
Holmes (Leeds)
Stephens (Castleford)
*Nicholls (St. Helens)
Ward, D (Leeds)
Skerrett (Wakefield)
Casey (Bradford) 1t
Grayshon (Bradford) 1t
Adams, M (Widnes)

1979 New Zealand
Auckland: 11 Aug
Lost 11-18
Fairbairn (Wigan) 1g
Evans, S (Featherstone)
Joyner (Castleford)
Smith, M (Hull KR) 1t
Hughes (Widnes) 1t
Holmes (Leeds)
Stephens (Castleford) 1t
Skerrett (Wakefield)
Ward, D (Leeds)
*Nicholls (St. Helens)
Casey (Bradford)
Grayshon (Bradford)
Adams, M (Widnes)
Sub: Woods, J (Leigh)
     Hogan (Hull KR)

1980 New Zealand
Wigan: 18 Oct
Drew 14-14
*Fairbairn (Wigan) 4g
Camilleri (Barrow) 1t
Joyner (Castleford)
Smith, M (Hull KR) 1t
Bentley (Widnes)
Hartley, S (Hull KR)
Dick (Leeds)
Holdstock (Hull KR)
Watkinson (Hull KR)
Skerrett (Hull)
Gorley, L (Widnes)
Grayshon (Bradford)
Casey (Hull KR)
Sub: Pinner (St. Helens)

1980 New Zealand
Bradford: 2 Nov
Lost 8-12
*Fairbairn (Wigan) 4g
Drummond (Leigh)
Joyner (Castleford)
Smith, M (Hull KR)
Camilleri (Barrow)
Kelly, K (Warrington)
Dick (Leeds)
Holdstock (Hull KR)
Elwell (Widnes)
Shaw, G (Widnes)
Casey (Hull KR)
Grayshon (Bradford)
Pinner (St. Helens)
Sub: Evans, S (Featherstone)
     Gorley, L (Widnes)

1980 New Zealand
Leeds: 15 Nov
Won 10-2
Burke (Widnes) 2g
Drummond (Leigh) 2t
Joyner (Castleford)
Evans, S (Featherstone)
Atkinson, J (Leeds)
Woods, J (Leigh)
Walker (Whitehaven)
Skerrett (Hull)
Elwell (Widnes)
*Casey (Hull KR)
Gorley, P (St. Helens)
Adams, M (Widnes)
Norton (Hull)

1981 France
Hull: 6 Dec
Won 37-0
Fairbairn (Hull KR) 1g
Drummond (Leigh) 2t
Smith, M (Hull KR)
Woods, J (Leigh) 1t, 7g
Gill (Wigan) 3t
Hartley, S (Hull KR) 1t
Gregory, A (Widnes)
Grayshon (Bradford)
*Ward, D (Leeds)
Skerrett (Hull)
Gorley, L (Widnes)
Gorley, P (St. Helens)
Norton (Hull)
Sub: Burke (Widnes)
     Szymala (Barrow)

1981 France
Marseilles: 20 Dec
Lost 2-19
Burke (Widnes)
Drummond (Leigh)
Smith, M (Hull KR)
Woods, J (Leigh) 1g
Gill (Wigan)
Hartley, S (Hull KR)
Gregory, A (Widnes)
*Grayshon (Bradford)
Watkinson (Hull KR)
Skerrett (Hull)
Gorley, L (Widnes)
Szymala (Barrow)
Norton (Hull)
Sub: Gorley, P (St. Helens)

1982 Australia
Hull City FC: 30 Oct
Lost 4-40
Fairbairn (Hull KR)
Drummond (Leigh)
Hughes (Widnes)
Dyl (Leeds)
Evans, S (Hull)
Woods, J (Leigh)
*Nash (Salford)
Grayshon (Bradford)
Ward, D (Leeds)
Skerrett (Hull)
Gorley, L (Widnes)
Crooks, L (Hull) 2g
Norton (Hull)
Sub: Heron, D (Leeds)

1982 Australia
Wigan: 20 Nov
Lost 6-27
Mumby (Bradford) 3g
Drummond (Leigh)
Smith, M (Hull KR)
Stephenson (Wigan)
Gill (Wigan)
Holmes (Leeds)
Kelly, K (Warrington)
*Grayshon (Bradford)
Dalgreen (Fulham)
Skerrett (Hull)
Eccles (Warrington)
Burton (Hull KR)
Heron, D (Leeds)
Sub: Woods, J (Leigh)
     Rathbone (Bradford)

1982 Australia
Leeds: 28 Nov
Lost 8-32
Fairbairn (Hull KR)
Drummond (Leigh)
Stephenson (Wigan)
Smith, M (Hull KR)
Evans, S (Hull) 1t
*Topliss (Hull)
Gregory, A (Widnes)
O'Neill, M (Widnes)
Noble (Bradford)
Rose, P (Hull)
Smith, P (Featherstone)
Crooks, L (Hull) 2g, 1dg
Crane (Hull)
Sub: Courtney (Warrington)

1983 France
Carcassonne: 20 Feb
Won 20-5
Burke (Widnes) 1g
Drummond (Leigh)
Joyner (Castleford) 1t
Duane, R (Warrington)
Lydon (Widnes) 1t, 3g
Myler, A (Widnes)
Gregory, A (Widnes)
O'Neill, M (Widnes)
Noble (Bradford) 1t
Goodway (Oldham) 1t
*Casey (Hull KR)
Rathbone (Bradford)
Flanagan (Oldham)
Sub: Woods, J (Leigh)
     Smith, P (Featherstone)

1983 France
Hull: 6 March
Won 17-5
Mumby (Bradford) 4g
Drummond (Leigh)
Joyner (Castleford)
Duane, R (Warrington) 1t
Lydon (Widnes)
Myler, A (Widnes)
Gregory, A (Widnes) 1t
O'Neill, M (Widnes)
Noble (Bradford)
Goodway (Oldham)
*Casey (Hull KR)
Rathbone (Bradford)
Flanagan (Oldham)
Sub: Smith, P (Featherstone) 1t

1984 France
Avignon: 29 Jan
Won 12-0
*Mumby (Bradford)
Drummond (Leigh)
Duane, R (Warrington)
Foy, D (Oldham) 1t
Clark (Hull KR)
Lydon (Widnes)
Cairns (Barrow)
Rayne, Keith (Leeds)
Watkinson (Hull KR)
Goodway (Oldham) 1t
Worrall, M (Oldham)
Hobbs, D (Featherstone)
Hall (Hull KR)
Sub: Hanley (Bradford)
     Crooks, L (Hull) 2g

1984 France
Leeds: 17 Feb
Won 10-0
Mumby (Bradford)
Clark (Hull KR)
Joyner (Castleford)
Schofield (Hull)
Basnett (Widnes)
Hanley (Bradford)
Cairns (Barrow)
Rayne, Keith (Leeds)
*Noble (Bradford)
Ward, K (Castleford)
Jasiewicz (Bradford)
Hobbs, D (Featherstone) 5g
Hall (Hull KR)
Sub: Smith, M (Hull KR)
     Smith, P (Featherstone)

1984 Australia
Sydney: 9 June
Lost 8-25
Burke (Widnes) 2g
Drummond (Leigh)
Schofield (Hull) 1t
Mumby (Bradford)
Hanley (Bradford)
Foy, D (Oldham)
Holding (St. Helens)
Crooks, L (Hull)
*Noble (Bradford)
Goodway (Oldham)
Burton (Hull KR)
Worrall, M (Oldham)
Adams, M (Widnes)
Sub: Lydon (Widnes)
    Hobbs, D (Featherstone)

1984 Australia
Brisbane: 26 June
Lost 6-18
Burke (Widnes) 1g
Drummond (Leigh)
Schofield (Hull) 1t
Mumby (Bradford)
Hanley (Bradford)
Myler, A (Widnes)
Holding (St. Helens)
Rayne, Keith (Leeds)
*Noble (Bradford)
Crooks, L (Hull)
Burton (Hull KR)
Goodway (Oldham)
Worrall, M (Oldham)
Sub: Gregory, A (Widnes)
    Adams, M (Widnes)

1984 Australia
Sydney: 7 July
Lost 7-20
Burke (Widnes) 1g
Drummond (Leigh)
Schofield (Hull)
Mumby (Bradford)
Hanley (Bradford) 1t
Myler, A (Widnes)
Holding (St. Helens) 1dg
Hobbs, D (Featherstone)
*Noble (Bradford)
Case (Wigan)
Burton (Hull KR)
Goodway (Oldham)
Adams, M (Widnes)

1984 New Zealand
Auckland: 14 July
Lost 0-12
Burke (Widnes)
Drummond (Leigh)
Schofield (Hull)
Mumby (Bradford)
Hanley (Bradford)
Smith, M (Hull KR)
Holding (St. Helens)
Hobbs, D (Featherstone)
*Noble (Bradford)
Case (Wigan)
Burton (Hull KR)
Goodway (Oldham)
Adams, M (Widnes)

1984 New Zealand
Christchurch: 22 July
Lost 12-28
Burke (Widnes) 2g
Drummond (Leigh)
Hanley (Bradford) 1t
Mumby (Bradford)
Lydon (Widnes)
Myler, A (Widnes) 1t
Gregory, A (Widnes)
Hobbs, D (Featherstone)
*Noble (Bradford)
Case (Wigan)
Burton (Hull KR)
Goodway (Oldham)
Adams, M (Widnes)
Sub: Joyner (Castleford)
    Beardmore, K (Castleford)

1984 New Zealand
Auckland: 28 July
Lost 16-32
Burke (Widnes) 4g
Drummond (Leigh)
Hanley (Bradford) 1t
Mumby (Bradford) 1t
Lydon (Widnes)
Myler, A (Widnes)
Gregory, A (Widnes)
Hobbs, D (Featherstone)
*Noble (Bradford)
Case (Wigan)
Adams, M (Widnes)
Goodway (Oldham)
Flanagan (Oldham)
Sub: Donlan (Leigh)
    Joyner (Castleford)

1984 Papua New Guinea
Mount Hagen: 5 Aug
Won 38-20
Burke (Widnes) 1t, 5g
Drummond (Leigh) 2t
Hanley (Bradford) 1t
Mumby (Bradford) 1t
Lydon (Widnes)
Myler, A (Widnes)
Gregory, A (Widnes)
Rayne, Keith (Leeds) 1t
*Noble (Bradford)
Goodway (Oldham)
Flanagan (Oldham)
Hobbs, D (Featherstone) 1t
Adams, M (Widnes)
Sub: Donlan (Leigh)
    Proctor (Hull)

1985 France
Leeds: 1 March
Won 50-4
Edwards (Wigan)
Ledger (St. Helens)
Creasser (Leeds) 8g
Gribbin (Whitehaven) 1t
Gill (Wigan) 1t
Hanley (Bradford) 2t
Fox (Featherstone) 2t, 1g
Dickinson (Leeds)
Watkinson (Hull KR) 1t
Dannatt (Hull)
*Goodway (Oldham)
Rathbone (Bradford)
Divorty (Hull) 1t
Sub: Gibson (Batley)
    Platt (St. Helens)

1985 France
Perpignan: 17 March
Lost 16-24
Johnson, C (Leigh)
Clark (Hull KR)
Creasser (Leeds) 1g
Foy, D (Oldham) 1t
Ford, P (Wigan) 2t
*Hanley (Bradford)
Fox (Featherstone)
Dickinson (Leeds)
Kiss (Wigan)
Wane (Wigan)
Dannatt (Hull)
Rathbone (Bradford)
Divorty (Hull) 1g
Sub: Harkin (Hull KR)
    Powell, R (Leeds)

1985 New Zealand
Leeds: 19 Oct
Lost 22-24
Burke (Widnes) 3g
Drummond (Leigh)
Schofield (Hull)
Hanley (Wigan) 1t
Lydon (Widnes) 1t, 2g
Myler, A (Widnes)
Fox (Featherstone)
Crooks, L (Hull)
Watkinson (Hull KR)
Fieldhouse (Widnes)
Goodway (Wigan) 1t
Potter (Wigan)
*Pinner (St. Helens)
Sub: Arkwright (St. Helens)

1985 New Zealand
Wigan: 2 Nov
Won 25-8
Burke (Widnes)
Drummond (Leigh)
Schofield (Hull) 4t
Hanley (Wigan)
Lydon (Widnes) 4g
Myler, A (Widnes)
Fox (Featherstone)
Grayshon (Leeds)
Watkinson (Hull KR)
Fieldhouse (Widnes)
Goodway (Wigan)
Potter (Wigan)
*Pinner (St. Helens) 1dg
Sub: Edwards (Wigan)
    Burton (Hull KR)

1985 New Zealand (Also WC)
Elland Rd, Leeds: 9 Nov
Drew 6-6
Burke (Widnes)
Drummond (Leigh)
Schofield (Hull)
Edwards (Wigan)
Lydon (Widnes)
Hanley (Wigan)
Fox (Featherstone)
Grayshon (Leeds)
Watkinson (Hull KR)
Fieldhouse (Widnes)
Goodway (Wigan)
Potter (Wigan)
*Pinner (St. Helens)
Sub: Arkwright (St. Helens)
    Crooks, L (Hull) 3g

1986 France (Also WC)
Avignon: 16 Feb
Drew 10-10
Burke (Widnes)
Drummond (Leigh)
Schofield (Hull)
Hanley (Wigan) 1t
Gill (Wigan)
Myler, A (Widnes)
Fox (Featherstone)
Crooks, L (Hull) 3g
Watkinson (Hull KR)
Wane (Wigan)
Potter (Wigan)
Fieldhouse (Widnes)
*Pinner (St. Helens)

1986 France
Wigan: 1 March
Won 24-10
Lydon (Wigan)
Drummond (Leigh) 1t
Schofield (Hull) 1t, 2g
Marchant (Castleford) 1t
Laws (Hull KR)
Myler, A (Widnes)
Fox (Featherstone)
Crooks, L (Hull) 2g
*Watkinson (Hull KR)
Fieldhouse (Widnes)
Rayne, Kevin (Leeds)
James (Halifax) 1t
Potter (Wigan)
Sub: Platt (St. Helens)

1986 Australia
Man. U. FC: 25 Oct
Lost 16-38
Lydon (Wigan) 1t
Marchant (Castleford)
Schofield (Hull) 2t
Hanley (Wigan)
Gill (Wigan) 1g
Myler, A (Widnes)
Fox (Featherstone)
Ward (Castleford)
*Watkinson (Hull KR)
Fieldhouse (Widnes)
Crooks, L (Hull) 1g
Potter (Wigan)
Goodway (Wigan)

1986 Australia
Elland Rd, Leeds: 8 Nov
Lost 4-34
Lydon (Wigan)
Ledger (St. Helens)
Schofield (Hull) 1t
Marchant (Castleford)
Gill (Wigan)
Myler, A (Widnes)
Fox (Featherstone)
Ward (Castleford)
*Watkinson (Hull KR)
Fieldhouse (St. Helens)
Crooks, L (Hull)
Potter (Wigan)
Goodway (Wigan)
Sub: Edwards (Wigan)
    Platt (St. Helens)

1986 Australia (Also WC)
Wigan: 22 Nov
Lost 15-24
Lydon (Wigan) 2g
Gill (Wigan) 1g
Schofield (Hull) 2t, 1dg
Stephenson (Wigan)
Basnett (Widnes)
Myler, A (Widnes)
Gregory, A (Warrington)
Ward (Castleford)
*Watkinson (Hull KR)
Crooks, L (Hull)
Burton (Hull KR)
Goodway (Wigan)
Pinner (Widnes)
Sub: Potter (Wigan)

1987 France (Also WC)
Leeds: 24 Jan
Won 52-4
Lydon (Wigan) 1t, 8g
Forster (Warrington) 1t
Schofield (Hull)
Stephenson (Wigan)
Gill (Wigan)
*Hanley (Wigan) 2t
Edwards (Wigan) 2t
Hobbs, D (Oldham)
Beardmore, K (Castleford)
Crooks, L (Hull)
Goodway (Wigan) 1t
Haggerty (St. Helens)
Gregory, M (Warrington) 2t
Sub: Creasser (Leeds)
    England (Castleford)

1987 France
Carcassonne: 8 Feb
Won 20-10

Lydon (Wigan) 4g
Forster (Warrington)
Schofield (Hull)
*Hanley (Wigan) 1t
Gill (Wigan) 1t
Edwards (Wigan)
Gregory, A (Wigan)
Hobbs, D (Oldham)
Beardmore, K (Castleford) 1t
England (Castleford)
Burton (Hull KR)
Haggerty (St. Helens)
Gregory, M (Warrington)
Sub: Dixon (Halifax)

1988 France
Leeds: 6 Feb
Won 30-12

Hampson (Wigan)
Plange (Castleford) 1t
Schofield (Leeds) 1t, 5g
*Hanley (Wigan) 2t
Ford, P (Bradford)
Edwards (Wigan)
Gregory, A (Wigan) 1t
Ward (Castleford)
Beardmore, K (Castleford)
Waddell (Oldham)
Powell, R (Leeds)
Dixon (Halifax)
Platt (St. Helens)
Sub: Stephenson (Leeds)
Medley (Leeds)

1988 Australia
Brisbane: 28 June
Lost 14-34

Loughlin (St. Helens) 3g
Gill (Wigan)
Ford, P (Bradford) 1t
*Hanley (Wigan)
Offiah (Widnes) 1t
Hulme, D (Widnes)
Gregory, A (Wigan)
Ward (Castleford)
Beardmore, K (Castleford)
Powell, R (Leeds)
Dixon (Halifax)
Platt (St. Helens)
Gregory, M (Warrington)
Sub: Wright (Widnes)
Hulme, P (Widnes)

1987 Papua New Guinea (Also WC)
Wigan: 24 Oct
Won 42-0

Hampson (Wigan)
Drummond (Warrington)
Stephenson (Wigan) 7g
Lydon (Wigan) 1t
Ford, P (Bradford) 1t
Edwards (Wigan) 2t
Gregory, A (Wigan) 1t
Ward (Castleford)
Groves (St. Helens)
Case (Wigan)
Medley (Leeds) 1t
Goodway (Wigan)
*Hanley (Wigan) 1t
Sub: Woods, J (Warrington)
Fairbank (Bradford)

1988 Papua New Guinea (Also WC)
Port Moresby: 22 May
Won 42-22

Loughlin (St. Helens) 7g
Ford, P (Bradford)
Schofield (Leeds) 2t
Stephenson (Leeds) 1t
Gill (Wigan) 2t
Edwards (Wigan)
Gregory, A (Wigan)
Ward (Castleford)
Beardmore, K (Castleford)
Case (Wigan)
Medley (Leeds) 1t
Gregory, M (Warrington) 1t
*Hanley (Wigan)
Sub: Hulme, D (Widnes)
Dixon (Halifax)

1988 Australia (Also WC)
Sydney: 9 July
Won 26-12

Ford, P (Bradford) 1t
Gill (Wigan) 2t
Stephenson (Leeds)
Loughlin (St. Helens) 3g
Offiah (Widnes) 1t
Hulme, D (Widnes)
Gregory, A (Wigan)
Ward (Castleford)
Hulme, P (Widnes)
Waddell (Oldham)
Gregory, M (Warrington) 1t
Powell, R (Leeds)
*Hanley (Wigan)
Sub: Case (Wigan)

1988 France
Avignon: 24 Jan
Won 28-14

Hampson (Wigan)
Drummond (Warrington) 1t
Schofield (Leeds) 2t
Loughlin (St. Helens) 3g
Offiah (Widnes) 1t
*Hanley (Wigan) 1t
Edwards (Wigan)
Ward (Castleford)
Beardmore, K (Castleford)
Waddell (Oldham)
Powell, R (Leeds)
Medley (Leeds)
Platt (St. Helens)
Sub: Creasser (Leeds) 1g
Dixon (Halifax)

1988 Australia
Sydney: 11 June
Lost 6-17

Loughlin (St. Helens) 1g
Ford, P (Bradford)
Schofield (Leeds)
Stephenson (Leeds)
Offiah (Widnes)
Hulme, D (Widnes)
Gregory, A (Wigan)
Ward (Castleford)
Beardmore, K (Castleford)
Dixon (Halifax)
Gregory, M (Warrington)
Platt (St. Helens)
*Hanley (Wigan) 1t
Sub: Gill (Wigan)
Powell, R (Leeds)

1988 New Zealand (Also WC)
Christchurch: 17 July
Lost 10-12

Ford, P (Bradford)
Gill (Wigan)
Stephenson (Leeds)
Loughlin (St. Helens) 1t, 1g
Offiah (Widnes)
Hulme, D (Widnes) 1t
Gregory, A (Wigan)
Ward (Castleford)
Beardmore, K (Castleford)
Waddell (Oldham)
Gregory, M (Warrington)
Powell, R (Leeds)
*Hanley (Wigan)
Sub: Hulme, P (Widnes)

1989 France
Wigan: 21 Jan
Won 26-10
Tait (Widnes)
Ford, P (Leeds) 1t
Loughlin (St. Helens) 3g
Lydon (Wigan) 1t
Offiah (Widnes) 1t
Edwards (Wigan) 1t
Gregory, A (Wigan)
Ward (Castleford)
Beardmore, K (Castleford)
Waddell (Leeds)
Gregory, M (Warrington)
Powell, R (Leeds)
*Hanley (Wigan) 1t
Sub: Williams (Salford)
    Eyres (Widnes)

1989 France
Avignon: 5 Feb
Won 30-8
Tait (Widnes) 1t
Ford, P (Leeds) 2t
Williams (Salford) 1t
Lydon (Wigan) 3g
Offiah (Widnes)
Edwards (Wigan) 1t
Gregory, A (Wigan)
Ward (Castleford)
Beardmore, K (Castleford)
Crooks, L (Leeds)
Gregory, M (Warrington)
Powell, R (Leeds)
*Hanley (Wigan) 1t
Sub: Hampson (Wigan)
    England (Castleford)

1989 New Zealand
Man. U. FC: 21 Oct
Lost 16-24
Tait (Widnes) 1t
Ford, P (Leeds) 1t
Currier (Widnes)
Loughlin (St. Helens) 2g
Offiah (Widnes) 1t
Hulme, D (Widnes)
Gregory, A (Wigan)
Skerrett (Bradford)
Beardmore, K (Castleford)
Hobbs, D (Bradford)
Goodway (Wigan)
Platt (Wigan)
*Gregory, M (Warrington)
Sub: Edwards (Wigan)
    Newlove (Featherstone)

1989 New Zealand
Elland Rd, Leeds: 28 Oct
Won 26-6
Hampson (Wigan)
Ford, P (Leeds)
Newlove (Featherstone)
Loughlin (St. Helens) 5g
Offiah (Widnes) 1t
Edwards (Wigan) 1t
Hulme, D (Widnes)
Skerrett (Bradford)
Hulme, P (Widnes)
Platt (Wigan)
Goodway (Wigan) 2t
Powell, R (Leeds)
*Gregory, M (Warrington)
Sub: Hobbs (Bradford)
    Fox (Featherstone)

1989 New Zealand (Also WC)
Wigan: 11 Nov
Won 10-6
Tait (Widnes) 1t
Ford, P (Leeds)
Newlove (Featherstone)
Loughlin (St. Helens) 1g
Offiah (Widnes) 1t
Edwards (Wigan)
Hulme, D (Widnes)
Skerrett (Bradford)
Hulme, P (Widnes)
Platt (Wigan)
Goodway (Wigan)
Powell, R (Leeds)
*Gregory, M (Warrington)
Sub: Lydon (Wigan)
    England (Castleford)

1990 France
Perpignan: 18 March
Won 8-4
Tait (Widnes)
Lydon (Wigan)
Schofield (Leeds) 2g
Loughlin (St. Helens)
Offiah (Widnes) 1t
Edwards (Wigan)
Gregory, A (Wigan)
Skerrett (Bradford)
Beardmore, K (Castleford)
Platt (Wigan)
Gregory, M (Warrington)
Goodway (Wigan)
*Hanley (Wigan)
Sub: Powell, D (Sheffield)
    Betts (Wigan)

1990 France
Leeds: 7 April
Lost 18-25
Tait (Widnes) 1t
Cordle (Bradford) 1t
Schofield (Leeds)
Gibson (Leeds)
Offiah (Widnes) 1t
Steadman (Castleford) 3g
*Edwards (Wigan)
Skerrett (Bradford)
Beardmore, K (Castleford)
England (Castleford)
Betts (Wigan)
Fairbank (Bradford)
Gregory, M (Warrington)
Sub: Irwin (Castleford)
    Bishop (Hull KR)

1990 Papua New Guinea
Goroka: 27 May
Lost 18-20
Tait (Widnes)
Eastwood (Hull) 1t
Powell, D (Sheffield)
Davies (Widnes) 1t, 3g
Gibson (Leeds)
Schofield (Leeds)
Goulding (Wigan) 1t
Powell, R (Leeds)
Jackson, L (Hull)
Dixon (Leeds)
Betts (Wigan)
Fairbank (Bradford)
*Gregory, M (Warrington)
Sub: Irwin (Castleford)
    England (Castleford)

1990 Papua New Guinea (Also WC)
Port Moresby: 2 June
Won 40-8
Tait (Widnes)
Eastwood (Hull) 1t
Davies (Widnes) 6g
Powell, D (Sheffield) 1t
Gibson (Leeds) 2t
Schofield (Leeds) 1t
Goulding (Wigan) 1t
Powell, R (Leeds)
Jackson, L (Hull)
England (Castleford)
Betts (Wigan)
Dixon (Leeds) 1t
*Gregory, M (Warrington)
Sub: Fox (Featherstone)
    Clarke (Wigan)

1990 New Zealand
Palmerston North: 24 June
Won 11-10
Bibb (Featherstone)
Davies (Widnes) 1t, 1g
Lydon (Wigan)
Gibson (Leeds) 1t
Offiah (Widnes)
Schofield (Leeds) 1dg
Goulding (Wigan)
Skerrett (Bradford)
Dermott (Wigan)
England (Castleford)
Betts (Wigan)
Dixon (Leeds)
*Gregory, M (Warrington)
Sub: Powell, D (Sheffield)
    Powell, R (Leeds)

1990 Australia
Wembley: 27 Oct
Won 19-12
Hampson (Wigan)
Eastwood (Hull) 2t, 3g
Powell, D (Sheffield)
Gibson (Leeds)
Offiah (Widnes) 1t
Schofield (Leeds) 1dg
Gregory, A (Wigan)
Harrison (Hull)
Jackson, L (Hull)
Dixon (Leeds)
Betts (Wigan)
Powell, R (Leeds)
*Hanley (Wigan)
Sub: Fairbank (Bradford)
    Ward (St. Helens)

1991 France (Also WC)
Perpignan: 27 Jan
Won 45-10
Hampson (Wigan)
Eastwood (Hull) 6g
Powell, D (Sheffield)
Gibson (Leeds)
Offiah (Widnes) 2t
Schofield (Leeds) 2t, 1dg
Edwards (Wigan) 2t
Lucas (Wigan)
Jackson, L (Hull)
Platt (Wigan) 1t
Betts (Wigan) 1t
Holliday (Widnes)
*Hanley (Wigan)
Sub: Aston (Sheffield)
    Ellis, S (Castleford)
    Fairbank (Bradford)

1990 New Zealand
Auckland: 8 July
Won 16-14
Lydon (Wigan)
Davies (Widnes) 2g
Powell, D (Sheffield)
Gibson (Leeds)
Offiah (Widnes) 1t
Schofield (Leeds) 1t
Goulding (Wigan)
Skerrett (Bradford)
Jackson, L (Hull)
England (Castleford)
Betts (Wigan) 1t
Dixon (Leeds)
*Gregory, M (Warrington)
Sub: Irwin (Castleford)
    Powell, R (Leeds)

1990 Australia
Man. U. FC: 10 Nov
Lost 10-14
Hampson (Wigan)
Eastwood (Hull) 1g
Powell, D (Sheffield)
Gibson (Leeds)
Offiah (Widnes)
Schofield (Leeds)
Gregory, A (Wigan)
Harrison (Hull)
Jackson, L (Hull)
Platt (Wigan)
Betts (Wigan)
Dixon (Leeds) 1t
*Hanley (Wigan)
Sub: Loughlin (St. Helens) 1t
    Ward (St. Helens)

1991 France
Leeds: 16 Feb
Won 60-4
Hampson (Wigan) 1t
Eastwood (Hull) 1t, 8g
Powell, D (Sheffield)
Loughlin (St. Helens)
Offiah (Widnes) 5t
Schofield (Leeds) 3t
Edwards (Wigan) 1t
Dannatt (Hull)
Jackson, L (Hull)
Platt (Wigan)
Eyres (Widnes)
Fairbank (Bradford)
*Hanley (Wigan)
Sub: Ellis, K (Warrington)
    Ellis, S (Castleford)
    England (Castleford)
    Powell, R (Leeds)

1990 New Zealand (Also WC)
Christchurch: 15 July
Lost 18-21
Lydon (Wigan)
Davies (Widnes) 3g
Gibson (Leeds)
Powell, D (Sheffield)
Offiah (Widnes) 1t
Schofield (Leeds) 1t
Goulding (Wigan)
Skerrett (Bradford)
Dermott (Wigan)
England (Castleford)
Betts (Wigan)
Powell, R (Leeds) 1t
*Gregory, M (Warrington)
Sub: Irwin (Castleford)
    Dixon (Leeds)

1990 Australia (Also WC)
Elland Rd, Leeds: 24 Nov
Lost 0-14
Hampson (Wigan)
Eastwood (Hull)
Powell, D (Sheffield)
Gibson (Leeds)
Offiah (Widnes)
Schofield (Leeds)
Gregory, A (Wigan)
Harrison (Hull)
Jackson, L (Hull)
Platt (Wigan)
Betts (Wigan)
Dixon (Leeds)
*Hanley (Wigan)
Sub: Davies (Widnes)
    Gregory, M (Warrington)
    Powell, R (Leeds)

1991 Papua New Guinea (Also WC)
Wigan: 9 Nov
Won 56-4
Hampson (Wigan)
Newlove, P (Featherstone) 1t
Powell, D (Sheffield) 1t
Davies (Widnes) 8g
Sullivan (St. Helens) 1t
*Schofield (Leeds) 1t
Edwards (Wigan)
Harrison (Halifax)
Dermott (Wigan)
Platt (Wigan)
Betts (Wigan) 1t
Moriarty (Widnes) 2t
Jackson, M (Wakefield) 2t
Sub: Connolly (St. Helens)
    Fox (Featherstone)
    Fairbank (Bradford) 1t
    Price (Wakefield)

1992 France
Perpignan: 16 Feb
Won 30-12
Tait (Widnes)
Devereux (Widnes) 1t
Connolly (St. Helens)
*Davies (Widnes) 3g
Bentley (Leeds) 1t
Griffiths (St. Helens) 1t
Goulding (Leeds)
Crooks, L (Castleford)
Jackson, L (Hull)
Dixon (Leeds)
Fairbank (Bradford)
Jackson, M (Wakefield)
Holliday (Widnes)
Sub: Powell, D (Sheffield)
　　Steadman (Castleford) 2t
　　Jones (Hull)
　　Eyres (Widnes) 1t

1992 Australia
Sydney: 12 June
Lost 6-22
Steadman (Castleford)
Newlove (Featherstone)
Powell, D (Sheffield)
Loughlin (St. Helens)
Offiah (Wigan)
*Schofield (Leeds)
Gregory, A (Wigan)
Skerrett (Wigan)
Dermott (Wigan)
Crooks, L (Castleford) 1g
Betts (Wigan)
Platt (Wigan)
Clarke (Wigan)
Sub: Edwards (Wigan)
　　Jackson, M (Wakefield)
　　Lydon (Wigan) 1t
　　Lucas (Wigan)

1992 New Zealand
Palmerston North: 12 July
Lost 14-15
Steadman (Castleford)
Eastwood (Hull) 3g
Powell, D (Sheffield)
Connolly (St. Helens)
Offiah (Wigan)
*Schofield (Leeds)
Edwards (Wigan) 1t
Skerrett (Wigan)
Jackson, L (Hull)
Platt (Wigan)
Betts (Wigan)
McGinty (Wigan)
Clarke (Wigan) 1t
Sub: Lydon (Wigan)
　　Hulme, P (Widnes)
　　Harrison (Halifax)

1992 France (Also WC)
Hull: 7 March
Won 36-0
Steadman (Castleford)
Eastwood (Hull) 1t, 6g
Connolly (St. Helens)
Bateman (Warrington)
Hunte (St. Helens) 1t
Powell, D (Sheffield)
*Edwards (Wigan)
Crooks, L (Castleford)
Dermott (Wigan) 1t
Skerrett (Wigan)
Betts (Wigan)
Fairbank (Bradford)
Holliday (Widnes) 1t
Sub: Fox (Featherstone) 1t
　　Platt (Wigan) 1t
　　McNamara (Hull)

1992 Australia
Melbourne: 26 June
Won 33-10
Steadman (Castleford) 1t
Eastwood (Hull) 6g
Newlove (Featherstone) 1t
Powell, D (Sheffield)
Offiah (Wigan) 1t
*Schofield (Leeds) 1t, 1dg
Edwards (Wigan)
Skerrett (Wigan)
Dermott (Wigan)
Platt (Wigan)
Betts (Wigan)
McGinty (Wigan)
Clarke (Wigan) 1t
Sub: Connolly (St. Helens)
　　Hulme, P (Widnes)
　　Lydon (Wigan)
　　Harrison (Halifax)

1992 New Zealand
Auckland: 19 July
Won 19-16
Steadman (Castleford)
Eastwood (Hull) 3g
Powell, D (Sheffield)
Connolly (St. Helens)
Offiah (Wigan) 1t
*Schofield (Leeds) 1dg
Edwards (Wigan)
Harrison (Halifax)
Jackson, L (Hull) 1t
Platt (Wigan)
Betts (Wigan) 1t
McGinty (Wigan)
Clarke (Wigan)
Sub: Newlove (Featherstone)
　　Jackson, M (Wakefield)
　　Devereux (Widnes)
　　Fairbank (Bradford)

1992 Papua New Guinea
Port Moresby: 31 May
Won 20-14
Hampson (Wigan)
Eastwood (Hull) 1t
*Schofield (Leeds)
Loughlin (St. Helens) 2g
Offiah (Wigan) 2t
Powell, D (Sheffield)
Edwards (Wigan)
Crooks, L (Castleford)
Dermott (Wigan)
Platt (Wigan)
Betts (Wigan)
Fairbank (Bradford)
Clarke (Wigan) 1t
Sub: Lydon (Wigan)
　　Skerrett (Wigan)
　　Newlove (Featherstone)
　　Nickle (St. Helens)

1992 Australia
Brisbane: 3 July
Lost 10-16
Steadman (Castleford)
Eastwood (Hull) 3g
Powell, D (Sheffield)
Newlove (Featherstone)
Offiah (Wigan) 1t
*Schofield (Leeds)
Edwards (Wigan)
Skerrett (Wigan)
Dermott (Wigan)
Platt (Wigan)
Betts (Wigan)
McGinty (Wigan)
Clarke (Wigan)
Sub: Connolly (St. Helens)
　　Hulme, P (Widnes)
　　Lydon (Wigan)
　　Harrison (Halifax)

1992 Australia (WC Final)
Wembley: 24 Oct
Lost 6-10
Lydon (Wigan)
Hunte (St. Helens)
Connolly (St. Helens)
*Schofield (Leeds)
Offiah (Wigan)
Edwards (Wigan)
Fox (Bradford) 3g
Ward (St. Helens)
Dermott (Wigan)
Platt (Wigan)
Betts (Wigan)
Clarke (Wigan)
Hanley (Leeds)
Sub: Devereux (Widnes)
　　Tait (Leeds)
　　Skerrett (Wigan)
　　Eyres (Widnes)

1993 France
Carcassonne: 7 March
Won 48-6
Spruce (Widnes)
Devereux (Widnes) 1t
Currier (Widnes) 6g
Connolly (St. Helens)
Hunte (St. Helens)
*Schofield (Leeds) 3t
Edwards (Wigan) 1t
Cowie (Wigan)
McCurrie (Widnes)
Molloy (Leeds)
Eyres (Widnes) 1t
Clarke (Wigan)
Hanley (Leeds) 2t
Sub: Ford, M (Castleford) 1t
Joynt (St. Helens)
Bateman (Warrington)
McNamara (Hull)

1993 France
Leeds: 2 April
Won 72-6
Tait (Leeds) 2t
Devereux (Widnes) 1t
Newlove (Featherstone) 3t
Connolly (St. Helens)
Hunte (St. Helens) 2t
Davies (Widnes) 10g
Edwards (Wigan) 2t
Harrison (Halifax)
Dermott (Wigan)
*Platt (Wigan)
Betts (Wigan) 1t
Eyres (Widnes)
Clarke (Wigan)
Sub: Ford, M (Castleford) 1t
Fairbank (Bradford)
Powell, D (Sheffield) 1t
Nickle (St. Helens)

Alan Tait, two tries against France in April 1993.

GREAT BRITAIN REGISTER

The following is a record of the 612 players who have appeared for Great Britain in 278 Test and World Cup matches.

It does not include matches against France before 1957, the year they were given official Test match status.

Figures in brackets are the total of appearances, with the plus sign indicating substitute appearances, e.g. (7+3).

For matches against touring teams, the year given is for the first half of the season.

World Cup matches are in bold letters except when also classified as Test matches. Substitute appearances are in lower case letters.

A - Australia, F - France, NZ - New Zealand, P - Papua New Guinea.

ACKERLEY, Alvin (2) Halifax: 1952 A; 1958 NZ
ADAMS, Les (1) Leeds: 1932 A
ADAMS, Mick (11+2) Widnes: 1979 Aa,NZ3; 1980 NZ; 1984 A2a,NZ3,P
ARKWRIGHT, Chris (+2) St. Helens: 1985 nz2
ARKWRIGHT, Jack (6) Warrington: 1936 A2,NZ; 1937 A3
ARMITT, Tom (8) Swinton: 1933 A; 1936 A2,NZ2; 1937 A3
ASHBY, Ray (2) Liverpool: 1964 F; Wigan: 1965 F
ASHCROFT, Ernest (11) Wigan: 1947 NZ2; 1950 A3,NZ; 1954 A3,NZ2
ASHCROFT, Kevin (5+1) Leigh: **1968 A**; 1968 F; 1969 F; **1970 F,NZ**; Warrington: 1974 nz
ASHTON, Eric (26) Wigan: **1957 A,NZ**; 1958 A2,NZ2; 1959 F, A3; 1960 F2; **1960 NZ,A**; 1961 NZ3; 1962 F3,A3; 1963 F,A2
ASHURST, Bill (3) Wigan: 1971 NZ; 1972 F2
ASKIN, Tom (6) Featherstone R: 1928 A3,NZ3
ASPINALL, Willie (1) Warrington: 1966 NZ
ASTON, Len (3) St. Helens: 1947 NZ3
ASTON, Mark (+1) Sheffield E: 1991 f

ATKINSON, Arthur (11) Castleford: 1929 A3; 1932 A3,NZ3; 1933 A; 1936 A
ATKINSON, John (26) Leeds: **1968 F,NZ**; 1970 A3,NZ3; **1970 A2,F,NZ**; 1971 F2,NZ; 1972 F2; **1972 A2,F,NZ**; 1973 A2; 1978 A2; 1980 NZ
AVERY, Albert (4) Oldham: 1910 A,NZ; 1911 A2

BACON, Jim (11) Leeds: 1920 A3,NZ3; 1921 A3; 1924 A; 1926 NZ
BARENDS, David (2) Bradford N: 1979 A2
BARTON, Frank (1) Wigan: 1951 NZ
BARTON, John (2) Wigan: 1960 F; 1961 NZ
BASNETT, John (2) Widnes: 1984 F; 1986 A
BASSETT, Arthur (2) Halifax: 1946 A2
BATEMAN, Allan (1+1) Warrington: 1992 F; 1993 f
BATES, Alan (2+2) Dewsbury: 1974 F2,nz2
BATTEN, Billy (10) Hunslet: 1907 NZ; 1908 A3; 1910 A2,NZ; 1911 A2; Hull: 1921 A
BATTEN, Eric (4) Bradford N: 1946 A2,NZ; 1947 NZ
BATTEN, Ray (3) Leeds: 1969 F; 1973 A2
BAXTER, Johnnie (1) Rochdale H: 1907 NZ
BEAMES, Jack (2) Halifax: 1921 A2

BEARDMORE, Kevin (13+1) Castleford: 1984 nz; 1987 F2; 1988 F2,P,A2,NZ; 1989 F2,NZ; 1990 F2

BELSHAW, Billy (8) Liverpool S: 1936 A3,NZ2; 1937 A; Warrington: 1937 A2

BENNETT, Jack (7) Rochdale H: 1924 A3,NZ3; Wigan: 1926 NZ

BENTHAM, Billy (2) Broughton R: 1924 NZ2

BENTHAM, Nat (10) Wigan H: 1928 A3,NZ3; Halifax: 1929 A2; Warrington: 1929 A2

BENTLEY, John (1) Leeds: 1992 F

BENTLEY, Keith (1) Widnes: 1980 NZ

BENYON, Billy (5+1) St. Helens: 1971 F2,NZnz; 1972 F2

BETTS, Denis (20+1) Wigan: 1990 fF,P2,NZ3,A3; 1991 F,P; 1992 F,P,A3,NZ2, **A**; 1993F

BEVAN, Dai (1) Wigan: 1952 A

BEVAN, John (6) Warrington: 1974 A2,NZ2; 1978 A2

BEVERLEY, Harry (6) Hunslet: 1936 A3; 1937 A; Halifax: 1937 A2

BIBB, Chris (1) Featherstone R: 1990 NZ

BIRCH, Jim (1) Leeds: 1907 NZ

BISHOP, David (+1) Hull KR: 1990 f

BISHOP, Tommy (15) St. Helens: 1966 A3,NZ2; 1967 A3; 1968 F3; **1968 A,F,NZ**; 1969 F

BLAN, Billy (3) Wigan: 1951 NZ3

BLINKHORN, Tom (1) Warrington: 1929 A

BOLTON, Dave (23) Wigan: 1957 F3; 1958 F,A2; 1959 F,A3; 1960 F2; 1961 NZ3; 1962 F2,A,NZ2; 1963 F,A2

BOSTON, Billy (31) Wigan: 1954 A2,NZ3; 1955 NZ; 1956 A3; 1957 F5; **1957 F,A**; 1958 F; 1959 A; 1960 F; **1960 A**; 1961 F,NZ3; 1962 F2,A3,NZ; 1963 F

BOTT, Charlie (1) Oldham: 1966 F

BOWDEN, Jim (3) Huddersfield: 1954 A2,NZ

BOWEN, Frank (3) St. Helens Recs: 1928 NZ3

BOWERS, Joe (1) Rochdale H: 1920 NZ

BOWMAN, Eddie (4) Workington T: **1977 F,NZ,A2**

BOWMAN, Harold (8) Hull: 1924 NZ2; 1926 NZ2; 1928 A2,NZ; 1929 A

BOWMAN, Ken (3) Huddersfield: 1962 F; 1963 F,A

BOYLEN, Frank (1) Hull: 1908 A

BRADSHAW, Tommy (6) Wigan: 1947 NZ2; 1950 A3,NZ

BRIDGES, John "Keith" (3) Featherstone R: 1974 F2,A

BRIGGS, Brian (1) Huddersfield: 1954 NZ

BROGDEN, Stan (16) Huddersfield: 1929 A; 1932 A3,NZ3; 1933 A2; Leeds: 1936 A3,NZ2; 1937 A2

BROOKE, Ian (13) Bradford N: 1966 A3,NZ2; Wakefield T: 1967 A3; 1968 F2; **1968 A,F,NZ**

BROOKS, Ernie (3) Warrington: 1908 A3

BROUGH, Albert (2) Oldham: 1924 A,NZ

BROUGH, Jim (5) Leeds: 1928 A2,NZ2; 1936 A

BROWN, Gordon (6) Leeds: **1954 F2,NZ,A**; 1955 NZ2

BRYANT, Bill (4+1) Castleford: 1964 F2; 1966 Aa; 1967 F

BUCKLEY, Alan (7) Swinton: 1963 A; 1964 F; 1965 NZ; 1966 F,A2,NZ

BURGESS, Bill (16) Barrow: 1924 A3,NZ3; 1926 NZ3; 1928 A3,NZ2; 1929 A2

BURGESS, Bill (14) Barrow: 1962 F; 1963 A; 1965 NZ2; 1966 F,A3,NZ2; 1967 F,A; 1968 F; Salford: 1969 F

BURGHAM, Oliver (1) Halifax: 1911 A

BURKE, Mick (14+1) Widnes: 1980 NZ; 1981 fF; 1983 F; 1984 A3,NZ3,P; 1985 NZ3; 1986 F

BURNELL, Alf (3) Hunslet: 1951 NZ2; 1954 NZ

BURTON, Chris (8+1) Hull KR: 1982 A; 1984 A3,NZ2; 1985 nz; 1986 A; 1987 F

BURWELL, Alan (7+1) Hull KR: 1967 a; 1968 F3; **1968 A,F,NZ**; 1969 F

BUTTERS, Fred (2) Swinton: 1929 A2

CAIRNS, David (2) Barrow: 1984 F2

CAMILLERI, Chris (2) Barrow: 1980 NZ2

CARLTON, Frank (2) St. Helens: 1958 NZ; Wigan: 1962 NZ

CARR, Charlie (7) Barrow: 1924 A2,NZ2; 1926 NZ3

CARTWRIGHT, Joe (7) Leigh: 1920 A,NZ3; 1921 A3

CASE, Brian (6+1) Wigan: 1984 A,NZ3; 1987 P; 1988 P,a

CASEY, Len (12+2) Hull KR: **1977 f,nz,A**; 1978 A; Bradford N: 1979 A2,NZ3; Hull KR: 1980 NZ3; 1983 F2

CASTLE, Frank (4) Barrow: 1952 A3; 1954 A

CHALLINOR, Jim (3) Warrington: 1958 A,NZ; **1960 F**

CHARLTON, Paul (18+1) Workington T: 1965 NZ; Salford: **1970 nz**; 1972 F2; **1972 A2,F,NZ**; 1973 A3; 1974 F2,A3,NZ3

CHERRINGTON, Norman (1) Wigan: 1960 F

CHILCOTT, Jack (3) Huddersfield: 1914 A3

CHISNALL, Dave (2) Leigh: 1970 A; **1970 NZ**

CHISNALL, Eric (4) St. Helens: 1974 A2,NZ2

CLAMPITT, Jim (3) Broughton R: 1907 NZ; 1911 A; 1914 NZ

CLARK, Doug (11) Huddersfield: 1911 A2; 1914 A3; 1920 A3,NZ3

CLARK, Garry (3) Hull KR: 1984 F2; 1985 F

CLARK, Mick (5) Leeds: 1968 F2; **1968 A,F,NZ**

CLARKE, Colin (7) Wigan: 1965 NZ; 1966 F,NZ; 1967 F; 1973 A3

CLARKE, Phil (9+1) Wigan: 1990 p; 1992 P,A3,NZ2, **A**; 1993 F2

CLAWSON, Terry (14) Featherstone R: 1962 F2; Leeds: **1972 A2,F**; Oldham: 1973 A3; 1974 F2,A2,NZ2

CLOSE, Don (1) Huddersfield: 1967 F
COLDRICK, Percy (4) Wigan: 1914 A3,NZ
COLLIER, Frank (2) Wigan: 1963 A; Widnes: 1964 F
CONNOLLY, Gary (7+3) St. Helens: 1991 p; 1992 F2,a2,NZ2,**A**; 1993 F2
CORDLE, Gerald (1) Bradford N: 1990 F
COULMAN, Mike (2+1) Salford: 1971 f,NZ2
COURTNEY, Neil (+1) Warrington: 1982 a
COVERDALE, Bob (4) Hull: **1954 F2,NZ,A**
COWIE, Neil (1) Wigan: 1993 F
CRACKNELL, Dick (2) Huddersfield: 1951 NZ2
CRANE, Mick (1) Hull: 1982 A
CREASSER, David (2+2) Leeds: 1985 F2; 1987 f; 1988 f
CROOKS, Lee (16+2) Hull: 1982 A2; 1984 f,A2; 1985 NZnz; 1986 F2,A3; 1987 F; Leeds: 1989 F; Castleford: 1992 F2,P,A
CROSTON, Jim (1) Castleford: 1937 A
CROWTHER, Hector (1) Hunslet: 1929 A
CUNLIFFE, Billy (11) Warrington: 1920 A,NZ2; 1921 A3; 1924 A3,NZ; 1926 NZ
CUNLIFFE, Jack (4) Wigan: 1950 A,NZ; 1951 NZ; 1954 A
CUNNIFFE, Bernard (1) Castleford: 1937 A
CUNNINGHAM, Eddie (1) St. Helens: 1978 A
CURRAN, George (6) Salford: 1946 A,NZ; 1947 NZ; 1948 A3
CURRIER, Andy (2) Widnes: 1989 NZ; 1993 F
CURZON, Ephraim (1) Salford: 1910 A

DAGNALL, Bob (4) St. Helens: 1961 NZ2; 1964 F; 1965 F
DALGREEN, John (1) Fulham: 1982 A
DANBY, Tom (3) Salford: 1950 A2,NZ
DANIELS, Arthur (3) Halifax: 1952 A2; 1955 NZ
DANNATT, Andy (3) Hull: 1985 F2; 1991 F
DARWELL, Joe (5) Leigh: 1924 A3,NZ2
DAVIES, Alan (20) Oldham: 1955 NZ; 1956 A3; **1957 F,A**; 1957 F2; 1958 F,A2,NZ2; 1959 F2,A; **1960 NZ,F,A**; 1960 F
DAVIES, Billy (1) Swinton: 1968 F
DAVIES, Billy J (1) Castleford: 1933 A
DAVIES, Evan (3) Oldham: 1920 NZ3
DAVIES, Jim (2) Huddersfield: 1911 A2
DAVIES, Jonathan (8+1) Widnes: 1990 P2,NZ3,a; 1991 P; 1992 F; 1993 F
DAVIES, Will T (1) Halifax: 1911 A
DAVIES, Willie A (2) Leeds: 1914 A,NZ
DAVIES, Willie T.H (3) Bradford N: 1946 NZ; 1947 NZ2
DAWSON, Edgar (1) York: 1956 A
DERMOTT, Martin (10) Wigan: 1990 NZ2; 1991 P; 1992 F,P,A3,**A**; 1993 F
DEVEREUX, John (3+2) Widnes: 1992 F,nz,a; 1993 F2
DICK, Kevin (2) Leeds: 1980 NZ2
DICKENSON, George (1) Warrington: 1908 A
DICKINSON, Roy (2) Leeds: 1985 F2

DINGSDALE, Billy (3) Warrington: 1929 A2; 1933 A
DIVORTY, Gary (2) Hull: 1985 F2
DIXON, Colin (12+2) Halifax: 1968 F; Salford: 1969 F; 1971 NZ; **1972 F**; 1973 a2; 1974 F2,A3,NZ3
DIXON, Malcolm (2) Featherstone R: 1962 F; 1964 F
DIXON, Paul (11+4) Halifax: 1987 f; 1988 fF,p,A2; Leeds: 1990 P2,NZ2nz,A3; 1992 F
DOCKAR, Alec (1) Hull KR: 1947 NZ
DONLAN, Steve (+2) Leigh: 1984 nz,p
DRAKE, Bill (1) Hull: 1962 F
DRAKE, Jim (1) Hull: 1960 F
DRUMMOND, Des (24) Leigh: 1980 NZ2; 1981 F2; 1982 A3; 1983 F2; 1984 F,A3,NZ3,P; 1985 NZ3; 1986 F2; Warrington: 1987 P; 1988 F
DUANE, Ronnie (3) Warrington: 1983 F2; 1984 F
DUTTON, Ray (6) Widnes: 1970 NZ2; **1970 A2,F,NZ**
DYL, Les (11) Leeds: 1974 A2,NZ3; **1977 F,NZ,A2**; 1978 A; 1982 A
DYSON, Frank (1) Huddersfield: 1959 A

EASTWOOD, Paul (13) Hull: 1990 P2,A3; 1991 F2; 1992 F,P,A2,NZ2
ECCLES, Bob (1) Warrington: 1982 A
ECCLES, Percy (1) Halifax: 1907 NZ
ECKERSLEY, David (2+2) St. Helens: 1973 Aa; 1974 Aa
EDGAR, Brian (11) Workington T: 1958 A,NZ; 1961 NZ; 1962 A3,NZ; 1965 NZ; 1966 A3
EDWARDS, Alan (7) Salford: 1936 A3,NZ2; 1937 A2
EDWARDS, Derek (3+2) Castleford: 1968 f; 1970 A; 1971 NZ2nz
EDWARDS, Shaun (26+4) Wigan: 1985 F,nzNZ; 1986 a; 1987 F2,P; 1988 F2,P; 1989 F2,nzNZ2; 1990 F2; 1991 F2,P; 1992 F,P,aA2,NZ2,**A**; 1993 F2
EGAN, Joe (14) Wigan: 1946 A3; 1947 NZ3; 1948 A3; 1950 A3,NZ2
ELLABY, Alf (13) St. Helens: 1928 A3,NZ2; 1929 A2; 1932 A3,NZ2; 1933 A
ELLIS, Kevin (+1) Warrington: 1991 f
ELLIS, St. John (+2) Castleford: 1991 f2
ELWELL, Keith (3) Widnes: **1977 A;** 1980 NZ2
ENGLAND, Keith (6+5) Castleford: 1987 fF; 1989 f,nz; 1990 F,pP,NZ3; 1991 f
EVANS, Bryn (10) Swinton: 1926 NZ; 1928 NZ; 1929 A; 1932 A2,NZ3; 1933 A2
EVANS, Frank (4) Swinton: 1924 A2,NZ2
EVANS, Jack (4) Hunslet: 1951 NZ; 1952 A3
EVANS, Jack (3) Swinton: 1926 NZ3
EVANS, Roy (4) Wigan: 1961 NZ2; 1962 F,NZ
EVANS, Steve (7+3) Featherstone R: 1979 Aa2,NZ3; 1980 NZnz; Hull: 1982 A2
EYRE, Ken (1) Hunslet: 1965 NZ

EYRES, Richard (3+4) Widnes: 1989 f; 1991 fF; 1992 f,a; 1993 F2

FAIRBAIRN, George (17) Wigan: **1977 F,NZ,A2**; 1978 A3; 1979 A2,NZ3; 1980 NZ2; Hull KR: 1981 F; 1982 A2

FAIRBANK, Karl (6+6) Bradford N: 1987 p; 1990 F,P,a; 1991 fF,p; 1992 F2,P,nz; 1993 f

FAIRCLOUGH, Les (6) St. Helens: 1926 NZ; 1928 A2,NZ2; 1929 A

FARRAR, Vince (1) Hull: 1978 A

FEATHERSTONE, Jim (6) Warrington: 1948 A; 1950 NZ2; 1952 A3

FEETHAM, Jack (8) Hull KR: 1929 A; Salford: 1932 A2,NZ2; 1933 A3

FIELD, Harry (3) York: 1936 A,NZ2

FIELD, Norman (1) Batley: 1963 A

FIELDHOUSE, John (7) Widnes: 1985 NZ3; 1986 F2,A; St. Helens: 1986 A

FIELDING, Keith (3) Salford: 1974 F2; **1977 F**

FILDES, Alec (15) St. Helens Recs: 1926 NZ2; 1928 A3,NZ3; 1929 A3; St. Helens: 1932 A,NZ3

FISHER, Tony (11) Bradford N: 1970 A2,NZ3; **1970 A**; Leeds: **1970 A;** 1971 F2; Bradford N: 1978 A2

FLANAGAN, Peter (14) Hull KR: 1962 F; 1963 F; 1966 A3,NZ; 1967 A3; 1968 F2; **1968 F,NZ**; 1970 A

FLANAGAN, Terry (4) Oldham: 1983 F2; 1984 NZ,P

FOGERTY, Terry (2+1) Halifax: 1966 nz; Wigan: 1967 F; Rochdale H: 1974 F

FORD, Mike (+2) Castleford: 1993 f2

FORD, Phil (13) Wigan: 1985 F; Bradford N: 1987 P; 1988 F,P,A3,NZ; Leeds: 1989 F2,NZ3

FORSTER, Mark (2) Warrington: 1987 F2

FOSTER, Frank (1) Hull KR: 1967 A

FOSTER, Peter (3) Leigh: 1955 NZ3

FOSTER, Trevor (3) Bradford N: 1946 NZ; 1948 A2

FOX, Deryck (10+4) Featherstone R: 1985 F2, NZ3; 1986 F2,A2; 1989 nz; 1990 p; 1991 p; 1992 f; Bradford N: 1992 **A**

FOX, Don (1) Featherstone R: 1963 A

FOX, Neil (29) Wakefield T: 1959 F,A2; 1960 F3; 1961 NZ2; 1962 F3,A3,NZ2; 1963 A2,F; 1964 F; 1965 F; 1966 F; 1967 F2,A; 1968 F3; 1969 F

FOY, Des (3) Oldham: 1984 F,A; 1985 F

FRANCIS, Bill (4) Wigan: 1967 A; **1977 NZ,A2**

FRANCIS, Roy (1) Barrow: 1947 NZ

FRASER, Eric (16) Warrington: 1958 A3,NZ2; 1959 F2,A; 1960 F3; **1960 F,NZ**; 1961 F,NZ2

FRENCH, Ray (4) Widnes: 1968 F2; **1968 A,NZ**

FRODSHAM, Alf (3) St. Helens: 1928 NZ2; 1929 A

GABBITAS, Brian (1) Hunslet: 1959 F

GALLAGHER, Frank (12) Dewsbury: 1920 A3; 1921 A; Batley: 1924 A3,NZ3; 1926 NZ2

GANLEY, Bernard (3) Oldham: 1957 F2; 1958 F

GARDINER, Danny (1) Wigan: 1965 NZ

GEE, Ken (17) Wigan: 1946 A3,NZ; 1947 NZ3; 1948 A3; 1950 A3,NZ2; 1951 NZ2

GEMMELL, Dick (3) Leeds: 1964 F; Hull: 1968 F; 1969 F

GIBSON, Carl (10+1) Batley: 1985 f; Leeds: 1990 F,P2,NZ3,A3; 1991 F

GIFFORD, Harry (2) Barrow: 1908 A2

GILFEDDER, Laurie (5) Warrington: 1962 A,NZ2,F; 1963 F

GILL, Henderson (14+1) Wigan: 1981 F2; 1982 A; 1985 F; 1986 F,A3; 1987 F2; 1988 P,A2a,NZ

GILL, Ken (5+2) Salford: 1974 F2,A2,NZ; **1977 f,a**

GOODWAY, Andy (23) Oldham: 1983 F2; 1984 F,A3,NZ3,P; 1985 F; Wigan: 1985 NZ3; 1986 A3; 1987 F,P; 1989 NZ3; 1990 F

GOODWIN, Dennis (5) Barrow: 1957 F2; 1958 F,NZ2

GORE, Jack (1) Salford: 1926 NZ

GORLEY, Les (4+1) Widnes: 1980 NZnz; 1981 F2; 1982 A

GORLEY, Peter (2+1) St. Helens: 1980 NZ; 1981 Ff

GOULDING, Bobby (6) Wigan: 1990 P2,NZ3; Leeds: 1992 F

GOWERS, Ken (14) Swinton: 1962 F; 1963 F,A3; 1964 F2; 1965 NZ2; 1966 F2,A,NZ2

GRAY, John (5+3) Wigan: 1974 F2,A2a,NZ3

GRAYSHON, Jeff (13) Bradford N: 1979 A2,NZ3; 1980 NZ2; 1981 F2; 1982 A2; Leeds: 1985 NZ2

GREENALL, Doug (6) St. Helens: 1951 NZ3; 1952 A2; 1954 NZ

GREENALL, Johnny (1) St. Helens Recs: 1921 A

GREENOUGH, Bobby (1) Warrington: **1960 NZ**

GREGORY, Andy (25+1) Widnes: 1981 F2; 1982 A; 1983 F2; 1984 a,NZ2,P; Warrington: 1986 A; Wigan: 1987 F,P; 1988 F,P,A3,NZ; 1989 F2,NZ; 1990 F,A3; 1992 A

GREGORY, Mike (19+1) Warrington: 1987 F2; 1988 P,A3,NZ; 1989 F2,NZ3; 1990 F2,P2,NZ3,a

GRIBBIN, Vince (1) Whitehaven: 1985 F

GRIFFITHS, Jonathan (1) St. Helens: 1992 F

GRONOW, Ben (7) Huddersfield: 1911 A2; 1920 A2,NZ3

GROVES, Paul (1) St. Helens: 1987 P

GRUNDY, Jack (12) Barrow: 1955 NZ3; 1956 A3; 1957 F3; **1957 F,A,NZ**

GUNNEY, Geoff (11) Hunslet: 1954 NZ3; 1956 A; 1957 F3; **1957 F,NZ**; 1964 F; 1965 F

GWYNNE, Emlyn (3) Hull: 1928 A,NZ; 1929 A

GWYTHER, Elwyn (6) Belle Vue R: 1947 NZ2; 1950 A3; 1951 NZ

HAGGERTY, Roy (2) St. Helens: 1987 F2

HAIGH, Bob (5+1) Wakefield T: **1968 A,F**; Leeds: **1970 NZ,a;** 1971 F,NZ

HALL, Billy (4) Oldham: 1914 A3,NZ

HALL, Dave (2) Hull KR: 1984 F2

HALLAS, Derek (2) Leeds: 1961 F,NZ
HALMSHAW, Tony (1) Halifax: 1971 NZ
HALSALL, Hector (1) Swinton: 1929 A
HAMPSON, Steve (11+1) Wigan: 1987 P; 1988 F2; 1989 f,NZ; 1990 A3; 1991 F2,P; 1992 P
HANLEY, Ellery (35+1) Bradford N: 1984 fF,A3,NZ3,P; 1985 F2; Wigan: 1985 NZ3; 1986 F,A; 1987 F2,P; 1988 F2,P,A3,NZ; 1989 F2; 1990 F,A3; 1991 F2; Leeds: 1992 **A**; 1993 F
HARDISTY, Alan (12) Castleford: 1964 F3; 1965 F,NZ; 1966 A3,NZ; 1967 F2; 1970 A
HARE, Ian (1) Widnes: 1967 F
HARKIN, Paul (+1) Hull KR: 1985 f
HARRIS, Tommy (25) Hull: 1954 NZ2; 1956 A3; 1957 F5; **1957 F,A**; 1958 A3,NZ,F; 1959 F2,A3; 1960 F2; **1960 NZ**
HARRISON, Fred (3) Leeds: 1911 A3
HARRISON, Karl (6+3) Hull: 1990 A3; Halifax: 1991 P; 1992 a2,nzNZ; 1993 F
HARRISON, Mick (7) Hull: 1967 F2; 1971 NZ2; 1972 F2; 1973 A
HARTLEY, Dennis (11) Hunslet: 1964 F2; Castleford: 1968 F; 1969 F; 1970 A2,NZ2; **1970 A2,F**
HARTLEY, Steve (3) Hull KR: 1980 NZ; 1981 F2
HELME, Gerry (12) Warrington: 1948 A3; 1954 A3,NZ2; **1954 F2,A,NZ**
HEPWORTH, Keith (11) Castleford: 1967 F2; 1970 A3,NZ2; **1970 A2,F,NZ**
HERBERT, Norman (6) Workington T: 1961 NZ; 1962 F,A3,NZ
HERON, David (1+1) Leeds: 1982 aA
HESKETH, Chris (21+2) Salford: 1970 NZ; **1970 NZ,a**; 1971 Ff,NZ3; **1972 A2,F,NZ**; 1973 A3; 1974 F2,A3,NZ3
HICKS, Mervyn (1) St. Helens: 1965 NZ
HIGGINS, Fred (6) Widnes: 1950 A3,NZ2; 1951 NZ
HIGGINS, Harold (2) Widnes: 1937 A2
HIGSON, John (2) Hunslet: 1908 A2
HILL, Cliff (1) Wigan: 1966 F
HILL, David (1) Wigan: 1971 F
HILTON, Herman (7) Oldham: 1920 A3,NZ3; 1921 A
HILTON, Jack (4) Wigan: 1950 A2,NZ2
HOBBS, David (10+2) Featherstone R: 1984 F2,Aa,NZ3,P; Oldham: 1987 F2; Bradford N: 1989 NZnz
HODGSON, Martin (16) Swinton: 1929 A2; 1932 A3,NZ3; 1933 A3; 1936 A3,NZ3; 1937 A
HOGAN, Phil (6+3) Barrow: **1977 F,NZ,A2**; 1978 a; Hull KR: 1979 Aa,NZnz
HOGG, Andrew (1) Broughton R: 1907 NZ
HOLDEN, Keith (1) Warrington: 1963 A
HOLDER, Billy (1) Hull: 1907 NZ
HOLDING, Neil (4) St. Helens: 1984 A3,NZ
HOLDSTOCK, Roy (2) Hull KR: 1980 NZ2
HOLLAND, Dave (4) Oldham: 1914 A3,NZ

HOLLIDAY, Bill (9+1) Whitehaven: 1964 F; Hull KR: 1965 F,NZ3; 1966 Ff; 1967 A3
HOLLIDAY, Les (3) Widnes: 1991 F; 1992 F2
HOLLINDRAKE, Terry (1) Keighley: 1955 NZ
HOLMES, John (14+6) Leeds: 1971 NZ; 1972 F2; **1972 Aa,NZ**; **1977 F,NZ,Aa**; 1978 a3; 1979 A2a,NZ3; 1982 A
HORNE, Willie (8) Barrow: 1946 A3; 1947 NZ; 1948 A; 1952 A3
HORTON, Bill (14) Wakefield T: 1928 A3,NZ3; 1929 A; 1932 A3,NZ; 1933 A3
HOWLEY, Tommy (6) Wigan: 1924 A3,NZ3
HUDDART, Dick (16) Whitehaven: 1958 A2,NZ2; St. Helens: 1959 A; 1961 NZ3; 1962 F2,A3,NZ2; 1963 A
HUDSON, Barney (8) Salford: 1932 NZ; 1933 A2; 1936 A,NZ2; 1937 A2
HUDSON, Bill (1) Wigan: 1948 A
HUGHES, Eric (8) Widnes: 1978 A; 1979 A3,NZ3; 1982 A
HULME, David (7+1) Widnes: 1988 p,A3,NZ; 1989 NZ3
HULME, Paul (3+5) Widnes: 1988 aA,nz; 1989 NZ2; 1992 a2,nz
HUNTE, Alan (4) St. Helens: 1992 F,A; 1993 F2
HURCOMBE, Danny (8) Wigan: 1920 A2,NZ; 1921 A; 1924 A2,NZ2
HYNES, Syd (12+1) Leeds: 1970 A2,NZ2nz; **1970 A2,F,NZ**; 1971 F; 1973 A3

IRVING, Bob (8+3) Oldham: 1967 F2,A3; 1970 a,NZ; 1971 NZ; 1972 f; **1972 NZ,a**
IRWIN, Shaun (+4) Castleford: 1990 f,p,nz2

JACKSON, Ken (2) Oldham: 1957 F2
JACKSON, Lee (11) Hull: 1990 P2,NZ,A3; 1991 F2; 1992 F,NZ2
JACKSON, Michael (2+2) Wakefield T: 1991 P; 1992 F,a,nz
JACKSON, Phil (27) Barrow: 1954 A3,NZ3; **1954 F2,A,NZ**; 1955 NZ3; 1956 A3; **1957 F,NZ**; 1957 F5; 1958 F,A2,NZ
JAMES, Neil (1) Halifax: 1986 F
JARMAN, Billy (2) Leeds: 1914 A2
JASIEWICZ, Dick (1) Bradford N: 1984 F
JEANES, David (8) Wakefield T: 1971 F,NZ2; 1972 F2; Leeds: **1972 A2,NZ**
JENKINS, Bert (12) Wigan: 1907 NZ3; 1908 A3; 1910 A,NZ; 1911 A2; 1914 A,NZ
JENKINS, Dai (1) Hunslet: 1929 A
JENKINS, Dai (1) Leeds: 1947 NZ
JENKINS, Emlyn (9) Salford: 1933 A; 1936 A3,NZ2; 1937 A3
JENKINSON, Albert (2) Hunslet: 1911 A2
JOHNSON, Albert (4) Widnes: 1914 A,NZ; 1920 A2
JOHNSON, Albert (6) Warrington: 1946 A2,NZ; 1947 NZ3

JOHNSON, Chris (1) Leigh: 1985 F
JOLLEY, Jim (3) Runcorn: 1907 NZ3
JONES, Berwyn (3) Wakefield T: 1964 F; 1965 F; 1966 F
JONES, Dai (2) Merthyr: 1907 NZ2
JONES, Ernest (4) Rochdale H: 1920 A,NZ3
JONES, Joe (1) Barrow: 1946 NZ
JONES, Keri (2) Wigan: **1970 F,NZ**
JONES, Les (1) St. Helens: 1971 NZ
JONES, Lewis (15) Leeds: 1954 A3,NZ3; 1955 NZ3; 1957 F3; **1957 F,A,NZ**
JONES, Mark (+1) Hull: 1992 f
JORDAN, Gary (2) Featherstone R: 1964 F; 1967 A
JOYNER, John (14+2) Castleford: 1978 A2; 1979 A3,NZ3; 1980 NZ3; 1983 F2; 1984 F,nz2
JOYNT, Chris (+1) St. Helens: 1993 f
JUBB, Ken (2) Leeds: 1937 A2
JUKES, Bill (6) Hunslet: 1908 A3; 1910 A2,NZ

KARALIUS, Tony (4+1) St. Helens: 1971 NZ3; 1972 F; **1972 nz**
KARALIUS, Vince (12) St. Helens: 1958 A2,NZ2; 1959 F; **1960 NZ,F,A**; 1960 F; 1961 F; Widnes: 1963 A2
KEEGAN, Arthur (9) Hull: 1966 A2; 1967 F2,A3; 1968 F; 1969 F
KELLY, Ken (4) St. Helens: 1972 F2; Warrington: 1980 NZ; 1982 A
KEMEL, George (2) Widnes: 1965 NZ2
KERSHAW, Herbert (2) Wakefield T: 1910 A,NZ
KINNEAR, Roy (1) Wigan: 1929 A
KISS, Nicky (1) Wigan: 1985 F
KITCHEN, Frank (2) Leigh: **1954 A,NZ**
KITCHIN, Phil (1) Whitehaven: 1965 NZ
KITCHING, Jack (1) Bradford N: 1946 A
KNAPMAN, Ernest (1) Oldham: 1924 NZ
KNOWELDEN, Bryn (1) Barrow: 1946 NZ

LAUGHTON, Doug (15) Wigan: 1970 A3,NZ2; **1970 A2,F,NZ**; 1971 F2; Widnes: 1973 A; 1974 F2; 1979 A
LAWRENSON, John (3) Wigan: 1948 A3
LAWS, David (1) Hull KR: 1986 F
LEDGARD, Jim (11) Dewsbury: 1947 NZ2; Leigh: 1948 A; 1950 A2,NZ; 1951 NZ; **1954 F2,A,NZ**
LEDGER, Barry (2) St. Helens: 1985 F; 1986 A
LEWIS, Gordon (1) Leigh: 1965 NZ
LEYTHAM, Jim (5) Wigan: 1907 NZ2; 1910 A2,NZ
LITTLE, Syd (10) Oldham: 1956 A; 1957 F5; **1957 F,A,NZ**; 1958 F
LLEWELLYN, Tom (2) Oldham: 1907 NZ2
LLOYD, Robbie (1) Halifax: 1920 A
LOCKWOOD, Brian (8+1) Castleford: **1972 A2,F,NZ**; 1973 A2; 1974 F; Hull KR: 1978 A; 1979 nz
LOMAS, Jim (7) Salford: 1908 A2; 1910 A2,NZ; Oldham: 1911 A2

LONGSTAFF, Fred (2) Huddersfield: 1914 A,NZ
LONGWORTH, Bill (3) Oldham: 1908 A3
LOUGHLIN, Paul (14+1) St. Helens: 1988 F,P,A3,NZ; 1989 F,NZ3; 1990 F,a; 1991 F; 1992 P,A
LOWE, John (1) Leeds: 1932 NZ
LOWE, Phil (12) Hull KR: 1970 NZ; 1972 F2; **1972 A2,F,NZ**; 1973 A3; 1978 A2
LOXTON, Ken (1) Huddersfield: 1971 NZ
LUCAS, Ian (1+1) Wigan: 1991 F; 1992 a
LYDON, Joe (23+7) Widnes: 1983 F2; 1984 F,a,NZ2,P; 1985 NZ3; Wigan: 1986 F,A3; 1987 F2,P; 1989 F2,nz; 1990 F,NZ3; 1992 p,a3,nz,**A**

McCORMICK, Stan (3) Belle Vue R: 1948 A2; St. Helens: 1948 A
McCUE, Tommy (6) Widnes: 1936 A; 1937 A; 1946 A3,NZ
McCURRIE, Steve (1) Widnes: 1993 F
McGINTY, Billy (4) Wigan: 1992 A2,NZ2
McINTYRE, Len (1) Oldham: 1963 A
McKEATING, Vince (2) Workington T: 1951 NZ2
McKINNEY, Tom (11) Salford: 1951 NZ; 1952 A2; 1954 A3,NZ; Warrington: 1955 NZ3; St. Helens: **1957 NZ**
McNAMARA, Steve (+2) Hull: 1992 f; 1993 f
McTIGUE, Brian (25) Wigan: 1958 A2,NZ2; 1959 F2,A3; 1960 F2; **1960 NZ,F,A**; 1961 F,NZ3; 1962 F,A3,NZ2; 1963 F
MANN, Arthur (2) Bradford N: 1908 A2
MANTLE, John (13) St. Helens: 1966 F2,A3; 1967 A2; 1969 F; 1971 F2,NZ2; 1973 A
MARCHANT, Tony (3) Castleford: 1986 F,A2
MARTIN, Billy (1) Workington T: 1962 F
MARTYN, Mick (2) Leigh: 1958 A; 1959 A
MATHIAS, Roy (1) St. Helens: 1979 A
MEASURES, Jim (2) Widnes: 1963 A2
MEDLEY, Paul (3+1) Leeds: 1987 P; 1988 Ff,P
MIDDLETON, Alf (1) Salford: 1929 A
MILLER, Joe (1) Wigan: 1911 A
MILLER, Joe (6) Warrington: 1933 A3; 1936 A,NZ2
MILLS, Jim (6) Widnes: 1974 A2,NZ; 1978 A2; 1979 A
MILLWARD, Roger (28+1) Castleford: 1966 F; Hull KR: 1967 A3; 1968 F2; **1968 A,F,NZ**; 1970 A2,NZ3; 1971 F,NZ3; 1973 A; 1974 A2a; **1977 F,NZ,A2**; 1978 A3
MILNES, Alf (2) Halifax: 1920 A2
MOLLOY, Steve (1) Leeds: 1993 F
MOONEY, Walter (2) Leigh: 1924 NZ2
MOORHOUSE, Stan (2) Huddersfield: 1914 A,NZ
MORGAN, Arnold (4) Featherstone R: 1968 F2; **1968 F,NZ**
MORGAN, Edgar (2) Hull: 1921 A2
MORGAN, Ron (2) Swinton: 1963 F,A
MORIARTY, Paul (1) Widnes: 1991 P
MORLEY, Jack (2) Wigan: 1936 A; 1937 A

MORTIMER, Frank (2) Wakefield T: 1956 A2
MOSES, Glyn (9) St. Helens: 1955 NZ2; 1956 A;
1957 F3; **1957 F,A,NZ**
MUMBY, Keith (11) Bradford N: 1982 A; 1983 F;
1984 F2,A3,NZ3,P
MURPHY, Alex (27) St. Helens: 1958 A3,NZ; 1959
F2,A; **1960 NZ,F,A**; 1960 F; 1961 F,NZ3;
1962 F,A3; 1963 A2; 1964 F; 1965 F,NZ; 1966
F2; Warrington: 1971 NZ
MURPHY, Harry (1) Wakefield T: 1950 A
MYLER, Frank (23+1) Widnes: **1960 NZ,F,A**;
1960 F; 1961 F; 1962 F; 1963 A; 1964 F; 1965
F,NZ; 1966 A,NZnz; 1967 F2; St. Helens:
1970 A3,NZ3; **1970 A2,F**
MYLER, Tony (14) Widnes: 1983 F2; 1984 A2,NZ2,P;
1985 NZ2; 1986 F2,A3

NASH, Steve (24) Featherstone R: 1971 F,NZ; 1972
F2; **1972 A2,F,NZ**; 1973 A2; 1974 A3,NZ3;
Salford: **1977 F,NZ,A2**; 1978 A3; 1982 A
NAUGHTON, Albert (2) Warrington: **1954 F2**
NEWBOULD, Tommy (1) Wakefield T: 1910 A
NEWLOVE, Paul (7+3) Featherstone R: 1989
nzNZ2; 1991 P; 1992 p,A3,nz; 1993 F
NICHOLLS, George (29) Widnes: 1971 NZ; 1972
F2; **1972 A2,F,NZ**; St. Helens: 1973 A2; 1974
F2,A3,NZ3; **1977 F,NZ,A**; 1978 A3; 1979
A3,NZ3
NICHOLSON, Bob (3) Huddersfield: 1946 NZ
1948 A2
NICKLE, Sonny (+2) St. Helens: 1992 p; 1993 f
NOBLE, Brian (11) Bradford N: 1982 A; 1983 F2;
1984 F,A3,NZ3,P
NORTON, Steve (11+1) Castleford: 1974 a,NZ2;
Hull: 1978 A3; 1979 A2; 1980 NZ; 1981 F2;
1982 A

OFFIAH, Martin (27) Widnes: 1988 F,A3,NZ; 1989
F2,NZ3; 1990 F2,NZ3,A3; 1991 F2; Wigan 1992
P,A3,NZ2,**A**
O'GRADY, Terry (6) Oldham: 1954 A2,NZ3;
Warrington: 1961 NZ
OLIVER, Joe (1) Batley: 1928 A3,NZ
O'NEILL, Denis (2+1) Widnes: 1971 nz; **1972 A,F**
O'NEILL, Mike (3) Widnes: 1982 A; 1983 F2
OSTER, Jack (1) Oldham: 1929 A
OWEN, Jim (1) St. Helens Recs: 1921 A
OWEN, Stan (1) Leigh: 1958 F
OWENS, Ike (4) Leeds: 1946 A3,NZ

PADBURY, Dick (1) Runcorn: 1908 A
PALIN, Harold (2) Warrington: 1947 NZ2
PARKER, Dave (2) Oldham: 1964 F2
PARKIN, Jonty (17) Wakefield T: 1920 A2,NZ3;
1921 A2; 1924 A3,NZ; 1926 NZ2; 1928 A,NZ;
1929 A2
PARR, Ken (1) Warrington: 1968 F
PAWSEY, Charlie (7) Leigh: 1952 A3; 1954 A2,NZ2

PEPPERELL, Albert (2) Workington T: 1950 NZ;
1951 NZ
PHILLIPS, Doug (4) Oldham: 1946 A3; Belle Vue
R: 1950 A
PIMBLETT, Albert (3) Warrington: 1948 A3
PINNER, Harry (6+1) St. Helens: 1980 nzNZ;
1985 NZ3; 1986 F; Widnes: 1986 A
PITCHFORD, Frank (2) Oldham: 1958 NZ;
1962 F
PITCHFORD, Steve (4) Leeds: **1977 F,NZ,A2**
PLANGE, David (1) Castleford: 1988 F
PLATT, Andy (21+4) St. Helens: 1985 f; 1986 f,a;
1988 F2,A2; Wigan: 1989 NZ3; 1990 F,A2;
1991 F2,P; 1992 f,P,A3,NZ2,**A**; 1993 F
POLLARD, Charlie (1) Wakefield T: 1924 NZ
POLLARD, Ernest (2) Wakefield T: 1932 A2
POLLARD, Roy (1) Dewsbury: 1950 NZ
POOLE, Harry (3) Hull KR: 1964 F; Leeds:
1966 NZ2
POTTER, Ian (7+1) Wigan: 1985 NZ3;
1986 F2,A2a
POWELL, Daryl (17+4) Sheffield E: 1990
f,P,nzNZ2,A3; 1991 F2,P; 1992 fF,P,A3,NZ2;
1993 f
POWELL, Roy (13+6) Leeds: 1985 f; 1988
F2,A2a,NZ; 1989 F2,NZ2; 1990 P2,nz2NZ,Aa;
1991 f
POYNTON, Harold (3) Wakefield T: 1962 A2,NZ
PRESCOTT, Alan (28) St. Helens: 1951 NZ2; 1952
A3; 1954 A3,NZ3; 1955 NZ3; 1956 A3; 1957
F5; **1957 F,A,NZ**; 1958 F,A2
PRICE, Gary (+1) Wakefield T: 1991 p
PRICE, Jack (6) Broughton R: 1921 A2; Wigan:
1924 A2,NZ2
PRICE, Malcolm (2) Rochdale H: 1967 A2
PRICE, Ray (9) Warrington: 1954 A,NZ2; 1955
NZ; 1956 A3; 1957 F2
PRICE, Terry (1) Bradford N: 1970 A
PRIOR, Bernard (1) Hunslet: 1966 F
PROCTOR, Wayne (+1) Hull: 1984 p
PROSSER, Dai (1) Leeds: 1937 A
PROSSER, Stuart (1) Halifax: 1914 A

RAE, Johnny (1) Bradford N: 1965 NZ
RAMSDALE, Dick (8) Wigan: 1910 A2; 1911 A2;
1914 A3,NZ
RAMSEY, Bill (7+1) Hunslet: 1965 NZ2; 1966
F,A2,NZ2; Bradford N; 1974 nz
RATCLIFFE, Gordon (3) Wigan: 1947 NZ;
1950 A2
RATHBONE, Alan (4+1) Bradford N: 1982 a;
1983 F2; 1985 F2
RAYNE, Keith (4) Leeds: 1984 F2,A,P
RAYNE, Kevin (1) Leeds: 1986 F
REDFEARN, Alan (1) Bradford N: 1979 A
REDFEARN, David (6+1) Bradford N: **1972 nz**;
1974 F2,A,NZ3

REES, Billo (11) Swinton: 1926 NZ2; 1928 A3,NZ3; 1929 A3

REES, Dai (1) Halifax: 1926 NZ

REES, Tom (1) Oldham: 1929 A

REILLY, Malcolm (9) Castleford: 1970 A3,NZ3; **1970 A2,F**

RENILSON, Charlie (7+1) Halifax: 1965 NZ; 1967 a; 1968 F3; **1968 A,F,NZ**

RHODES, Austin (4) St. Helens: **1957 NZ; 1960 F,A**; 1961 NZ

RICHARDS, Maurice (2) Salford: 1974 A,NZ

RILEY, Joe (1) Halifax: 1910 A

RING, Johnny (2) Wigan: 1924 A; 1926 NZ

RISMAN, Gus (17) Salford: 1932 A,NZ3; 1933 A3; 1936 A2,NZ2; 1937 A3; 1946 A3

RISMAN, Bev (5) Leeds: 1968 F2; **1968 A,F,NZ**

RIX, Sid (9) Oldham: 1924 A3,NZ3; 1926 NZ3

ROBERTS, Ken (10) Halifax: 1963 A; 1964 F2; 1965 F,NZ3; 1966 F,NZ2

ROBINSON, Asa (3) Halifax: 1907 NZ; 1908 A2

ROBINSON, Bill (2) Leigh: 1963 F,A

ROBINSON, Dave (13) Swinton: 1965 NZ; 1966 F2,A3,NZ2; 1967 F2,A2; Wigan: 1970 A

ROBINSON, Don (10) Wakefield T: **1954 F2,NZ,A**; 1955 NZ; Leeds: 1956 A2; 1959 A2; 1960 F

ROBINSON, Jack (2) Rochdale H: 1914 A2

ROGERS, Johnny (7) Huddersfield: 1914 A; 1920 A3; 1921 A3

ROSE, David (4) Leeds: **1954 F2,A,NZ**

ROSE, Paul (2+3) Hull KR: 1974 a; 1978 Aa2; Hull: 1982 A

ROUND, Gerry (8) Wakefield T: 1959 A; 1962 F2,A3,NZ2

RUDDICK, George (3) Broughton R: 1907 NZ2; 1910 A

RYAN, Bob (5) Warrington: 1950 A,NZ2; 1951 NZ; 1952 A

RYAN, Martin (4) Wigan: 1947 NZ; 1948 A2; 1950 A

RYDER, Ron (1) Warrington: 1952 A

SAYER, Bill (7) Wigan: 1961 NZ; 1962 F,A3,NZ; 1963 A

SCHOFIELD, Derrick (1) Halifax: 1955 NZ

SCHOFIELD, Garry (40) Hull: 1984 F,A3,NZ; 1985 NZ3; 1986 F2,A3; 1987 F2; Leeds: 1988 F2,P,A; 1990 F2,P2,NZ3,A3; 1991 F2,P; 1992 P,A3,NZ2,**A**; 1993 F

SEABOURNE, Barry (1) Leeds: 1970 NZ

SENIOR, Ken (2) Huddersfield: 1965 NZ; 1967 F

SHARROCK, Jim (4) Wigan: 1910 A2,NZ; 1911 A

SHAW, Brian (6) Hunslet: 1956 A2; **1960 F,A**; 1960 F; Leeds: 1961 F

SHAW, Glyn (1) Widnes: 1980 NZ

SHAW, John (5) Halifax: **1960 F,A**; 1960 F; 1961 F; 1962 NZ

SHELTON, Geoff (7) Hunslet: 1964 F2; 1965 NZ3; 1966 F2

SHOEBOTTOM, Mick (10+2) Leeds: **1968 A,nz**; 1969 F; 1970 A2a,NZ; **1970 A2,F,NZ**; 1971 F

SHUGARS, Frank (1) Warrington: 1910 NZ

SILCOCK, Dick (1) Wigan: 1908 A

SILCOCK, Nat (12) Widnes: 1932 A2,NZ2; 1933 A3; 1936 A3; 1937 A2

SILCOCK, Nat (3) Wigan: 1954 A3

SIMMS, Barry (1) Leeds: 1962 F

SKELHORNE, George (7) Warrington: 1920 A,NZ3; 1921 A3

SKERRETT, Kelvin (13+2) Bradford N: 1989 NZ3; 1990 F2,NZ3; Wigan: 1992 F,p,A3,NZ,a

SKERRETT, Trevor (10) Wakefield T: 1979 A2,NZ2; Hull: 1980 NZ2; 1981 F2; 1982 A2

SLOMAN, Bob (5) Oldham: 1928 A3,NZ2

SMALES, Tommy (8) Huddersfield: 1962 F; 1963 F,A; 1964 F2; Bradford N: 1965 NZ3

SMALL, Peter (1) Castleford: 1962 NZ

SMITH, Alan (10) Leeds: 1970 A2,NZ3; **1970 A2**; 1971 F2; 1973 A

SMITH, Arthur (6) Oldham: 1907 NZ3; 1908 A3

SMITH, Bert (2) Bradford N: 1926 NZ2

SMITH, Fred (9) Hunslet: 1910 A,NZ; 1911 A3; 1914 A3,NZ

SMITH, Geoff (3) York: 1963 A; 1964 F2

SMITH, Mike (10+1) Hull KR: 1979 NZ3; 1980 NZ2; 1981 F2; 1982 A2; 1984 f,NZ

SMITH, Peter (1+5) Featherstone R: **1977 a2**; 1982 A; 1983 f2; 1984 f

SMITH, Sam (4) Hunslet: **1954 A,NZ,F2**

SMITH, Stanley (11) Wakefield T: 1929 A; Leeds: 1929 A2; 1932 A3,NZ3; 1933 A2

SOUTHWARD, Ike (11) Workington T: 1958 A3,NZ; Oldham: 1959 F2,A2; 1960 F2; 1962 NZ

SPENCER, Jack (1) Salford: 1907 NZ

SPRUCE, Stuart (1) Widnes: 1993 F

STACEY, Cyril (1) Halifax: 1920 NZ

STEADMAN, Graham (7+1) Castleford: 1990 F; 1992 fF,A3,NZ2

STEPHENS, Gary (5) Castleford: 1979 A2,NZ3

STEPHENSON, David (9+1) Wigan: 1982 A2; 1986 A; 1987 F,P; Leeds: 1988 f,P,A2,NZ

STEPHENSON, Mick (5+1) Dewsbury: 1971 nz; 1972 F; **1972 A2,F,NZ**

STEVENSON, Jeff (19) Leeds: 1955 NZ3; 1956 A3; 1957 F5; **1957 F,A,NZ**; 1958 F; York: 1959 A2; 1960 F2

STOCKWELL, Squire (3) Leeds: 1920 A; 1921 A2

STONE, Billy (8) Hull: 1920 A3,NZ3; 1921 A2

STOPFORD, John (12) Swinton: 1961 F; 1963 F,A2; 1964 F2; 1965 F,NZ2; 1966 F2,A

STOTT, Jim (1) St. Helens: 1947 NZ

STREET, Harry (4) Dewsbury: 1950 A3,NZ

SULLIVAN, Anthony (1) St. Helens: 1991 P

SULLIVAN, Clive (17) Hull: 1967 F; **1968 A,F,NZ**; 1970 A; 1971 NZ3; 1972 F2; **1972 A2,F,NZ**; 1973 A3

SULLIVAN, Jim (25) Wigan: 1924 A3,NZ; 1926 NZ3; 1928 A3,NZ3; 1929 A3; 1932 A3,NZ3; 1933 A3
SULLIVAN, Mick (46) Huddersfield: **1954 F2,NZ,A**; 1955 NZ3; 1956 A3; 1957 F3; **1957 F,A,NZ**; Wigan: 1957 F2; 1958 F,A3,NZ2; 1959 F2,A3; 1960 F3; **1960 F,NZ,A**; St. Helens: 1961 F,NZ2; 1962 F3,A3,NZ; York: 1963 A
SZYMALA, Eddie (1+1) Barrow: 1981 fF

TAIT, Alan (10+1) Widnes: 1989 F2,NZ2; 1990 F2,P2; 1992 F; Leeds: 1992 a; 1993 F
TAYLOR, Bob (2) Hull: 1921 A; 1926 NZ
TAYLOR, Harry (3) Hull: 1907 NZ3
TEMBEY, John (2) St. Helens: 1963 A; 1964 F
TERRY, Abe (11) St. Helens: 1958 A2; 1959 F2,A3; 1960 F; 1961 F,NZ; Leeds: 1962 F
THOMAS, Arthur "Ginger" (4) Leeds: 1926 NZ2; 1929 A2
THOMAS, George (1) Warrington: 1907 NZ
THOMAS, Gwyn (9) Wigan: 1914 A; Huddersfield: 1920 A3,NZ2; 1921 A3
THOMAS, Johnny (8) Wigan: 1907 NZ; 1908 A3; 1910 A2,NZ; 1911 A
THOMAS, Les (1) Oldham: 1947 NZ
THOMAS, Phil (1) Leeds: 1907 NZ
THOMPSON, Cecil (2) Hunslet: 1951 NZ2
THOMPSON, Jim (20+1) Featherstone R: 1970 A2,NZ2; **1970 A2,F,NZ**; 1971 Ff; 1974 A3,NZ3; **1977 F,NZ,A2**; Bradford N: 1978 A
THOMPSON, Joe (12) Leeds: 1924 A,NZ2; 1928 A,NZ; 1929 A; 1932 A3,NZ3
THORLEY, John (4) Halifax: **1954 F2,NZ,A**
TOOHEY, Ted (3) Barrow: 1952 A3
TOPLISS, David (4) Wakefield T: 1973 A2; 1979 A; Hull: 1982 A
TRAILL, Ken (8) Bradford N: 1950 NZ2; 1951 NZ; 1952 A3; 1954 A,NZ
TROUP, Alec (2) Barrow: 1936 NZ2
TURNBULL, Andrew (1) Leeds: 1951 NZ
TURNER, Derek (24) Oldham: 1956 A2; 1957 F5; **1957 F,A,NZ**; 1958 F; Wakefield T: 1959 A; 1960 F3; **1960 NZ,A**; 1961 F,NZ; 1962 A2,NZ2,F
TYSON, Brian (3) Hull KR: 1963 A; 1965 F; 1967 F
TYSON, George (4) Oldham: 1907 NZ; 1908 A3

VALENTINE, Bob (1) Huddersfield: 1967 A
VALENTINE, Dave (15) Huddersfield: 1948 A3; 1951 NZ; 1952 A2; 1954 A3,NZ2; **1954 F2,NZ,A**
VINES, Don (3) Wakefield T: 1959 F2,A

WADDELL, Hugh (5) Oldham: 1988 F2,A,NZ; Leeds: 1989 F
WAGSTAFF, Harold (12) Huddersfield: 1911 A2; 1914 A3,NZ; 1920 A2,NZ2; 1921 A2

WALKER, Arnold (1) Whitehaven: 1980 NZ
WALLACE, Jim (1) St. Helens Recs: 1926 NZ
WALSH, Joe (1) Leigh: 1971 NZ
WALSH, John (4+1) St. Helens: 1972 f; **1972 A2,F,NZ**
WALTON, Doug (1) Castleford: 1965 F
WANE, Shaun (2) Wigan: 1985 F; 1986 F
WARD, Billy (1) Leeds: 1910 A
WARD, David (12) Leeds: **1977 F,NZ,A**; 1978 A; 1979 A3,NZ3; 1981 F; 1982 A
WARD, Edward (3) Wigan: 1946 A2; 1947 NZ
WARD, Ernest (20) Bradford N: 1946 A3,NZ; 1947 NZ2; 1948 A3; 1950 A3,NZ2; 1951 NZ3; 1952 A3
WARD, Johnny (4) Castleford: 1963 A; 1964 F2; Salford: 1970 NZ
WARD, Kevin (15+2) Castleford: 1984 F; 1986 A3; 1987 P; 1988 F2,P,A3,NZ; 1989 F2; St. Helens: 1990 a2; 1992 **A**
WARLOW, John (6+1) St. Helens: 1964 F; **1968 f,NZ**; 1968 F; Widnes: 1971 F2,NZ
WARWICK, Silas (2) Salford: 1907 NZ2
WATKINS, Billy (7) Salford: 1933 A; 1936 A2,NZ2; 1937 A2
WATKINS, David (2+4) Salford: 1971 f,NZ; 1973 a; 1974 f2,A
WATKINSON, David (12+1) Hull KR: 1979 a; 1980 NZ; 1981 F; 1984 F; 1985 F,NZ3; 1986 F2,A3
WATSON, Cliff (29+1) St. Helens: 1963 A2; 1966 F2,A3,NZ2; 1967 F,A3; 1968 F2; **1968 A,F,nz**; 1969 F; 1970 A3,NZ3; **1970 A2,F,NZ**; 1971 F
WATTS, Basil (5) York: **1954 F2,NZ,A**; 1955 NZ
WEBSTER, Fred (3) Leeds: 1910 A2,NZ
WHITCOMBE, Frank (2) Bradford N: 1946 A2
WHITE, Les (7) Hunslet: 1932 A3,NZ2; 1933 A2
WHITE, Les (6) York: 1946 A3,NZ; Wigan: 1947 NZ2
WHITE, Tommy (1) Oldham: 1907 NZ
WHITEHEAD, Derek (3) Warrington: 1971 F2,NZ
WHITELEY, Johnny (15) Hull: **1957 A**; 1958 A3,NZ; 1959 F2,A2; 1960 F; **1960 NZ,F**; 1961 NZ2; 1962 F
WILKINSON, Jack (13) Halifax: 1954 A,NZ2; 1955 NZ3; Wakefield T: 1959 A; 1960 F2; **1960 NZ,F,A**; 1962 NZ
WILLIAMS, Billy (2) Salford: 1929 A; 1932 A
WILLIAMS, Dickie (12) Leeds: 1948 A2; 1950 A2,NZ2; 1951 NZ3; Hunslet: 1954 A2,NZ
WILLIAMS, Frank (2) Halifax: 1914 A2
WILLIAMS, Peter (1+1) Salford: 1989 fF
WILLICOMBE, David (3) Halifax: 1974 F; Wigan: 1974 F,NZ
WILSON, George (3) Workington T: 1951 NZ3
WILSON, Harry (3) Hunslet: 1907 NZ3
WINSLADE, Charlie (1) Oldham: 1959 F
WINSTANLEY, Billy (5) Leigh: 1910 A,NZ; Wigan: 1911 A3

383

WOOD, Alf (4) Oldham: 1911 A2; 1914 A,NZ
WOODS, Harry (6) Liverpool S: 1936 A3,NZ2;
    Leeds: 1937 A
WOODS, Jack (1) Barrow: 1933 A
WOODS, John (7+4) Leigh: 1979 A3,nz; 1980 NZ;
    1981 F2; 1982 Aa; 1983 f; Warrington: 1987 p
WOODS, Tommy (2) Rochdale H: 1911 A2
WORRALL, Mick (3) Oldham: 1984 F,A2
WRIGHT, Darren (+1) Widnes: 1988 a
WRIGHT, Joe (1) Swinton: 1932 NZ
WRIGHT, Stuart (7) Widnes: **1977 F,NZ,A2;**
    1978 A3
WRIGLESWORTH, Geoff (5) Leeds: 1965 NZ;
    1966 A2,NZ2

YOUNG, Chris (5) Hull KR: 1967 A3; 1968 F2
YOUNG, Frank (1) Leeds: 1908 A
YOUNG, Harold (1) Huddersfield: 1929 A

Five-cap Hull K.R. winger Chris Young.

GREAT BRITAIN TOUR SUMMARIES

						For			Against	
1910	P	W	D	L	T	G	Pts	T	G	Pts
In Australia	14	9	1	4	76	56	340	51	47	247
In New Zealand	4	4	0	0	43	29	187	11	7	47
TOTAL	18	13	1	4	119	85	527	62	54	294
1914	P	W	D	L	T	G	Pts	T	G	Pts
In Australia	12	9	0	3	77	55	341	24	31	134
In New Zealand	6	6	0	0	46	28	194	12	13	62
TOTAL	18	15	0	3	123	83	535	36	44	196
1920	P	W	D	L	T	G	Pts	T	G	Pts
In Australia	15	12	0	3	83	64	377	48	42	228
In New Zealand	10	9	0	1	89	47	361	24	16	104
TOTAL	25	21	0	4	172	111	738	72	58	332
1924	P	W	D	L	T	G	Pts	T	G	Pts
In Australia	18	14	0	4	104	77	466	56	45	255
In New Zealand	9	7	0	2	64	40	272	25	21	117
TOTAL	27	21	0	6	168	117	738	81	66	375
1928	P	W	D	L	T	G	Pts	T	G	Pts
In Australia	16	11	1	4	67	60	321	43	45	219
In New Zealand	8	7	0	1	55	36	237	16	12	72
TOTAL	24	18	1	5	122	96	558	59	57	291
1932	P	W	D	L	T	G	Pts	T	G	Pts
In Australia	18	15	1	2	105	84	483	32	38	172
In New Zealand	8	8	0	0	65	52	299	17	18	87
TOTAL	26	23	1	2	170	136	782	49	56	259

1936

	P	W	D	L	For			Against		
					T	G	Pts	T	G	Pts
In Australia	17	14	0	3	79	82	401	38	45	204
In New Zealand	8	8	0	0	52	27	210	8	16	56
TOTAL	25	22	0	3	131	109	611	46	61	260

1946

	P	W	D	L	T	G	Pts	T	G	Pts
In Australia	20	16	1	3	146	100	638	36	45	198
In New Zealand	7	5	0	2	35	20	145	12	21	78
TOTAL	27	21	1	5	181	120	783	48	66	276

1950

	P	W	D	L	T	G	Pts	T	G	Pts
In Australia	19	15	0	4	133	102	603	22	56	178
In New Zealand	6	4	0	2	37	25	161	16	20	88
TOTAL	25	19	0	6	170	127	764	38	76	266

1954

	P	W	D	L	T	G	Pts	T	G	Pts
In Australia	*22	13	1	7	133	114	627	78	96	426
In New Zealand	10	8	0	2	60	56	292	14	32	106
TOTAL	*32	21	1	9	193	170	919	92	128	532

*One match abandoned. Scores included in points total.

1958

	P	W	D	L	T	G	Pts	T	G	Pts
In Australia	21	19	1	1	184	129	810	64	93	378
In New Zealand	9	8	0	1	88	61	386	18	27	108
TOTAL	30	27	1	2	272	190	1,196	82	120	486

1962

	P	W	D	L	T	G	Pts	T	G	Pts
In Australia	21	18	0	3	151	113	679	61	60	303
In New Zealand	9	6	0	3	73	50	319	35	28	161
TOTAL	30	24	0	6	224	163	998	96	88	464

1966

	P	W	D	L	T	G	Pts	T	G	Pts
In Australia	22	13	0	9	112	85	506	47	83	307
In New Zealand	8	8	0	0	57	47	265	10	24	78
TOTAL	30	21	0	9	169	132	771	57	107	385

1970

	P	W	D	L	T	G	Pts	T	G	Pts
In Australia	17	15	1	1	104	92	496	27	66	213
In New Zealand	7	7	0	0	61	37	257	9	24	75
TOTAL	24	22	1	1	165	129	753	36	90	288

1974

	P	W	D	L	T	G	DG	Pts	T	G	DG	Pts
In Australia	20	15	0	5	104	93	2	500	38	59	3	235
In New Zealand	8	6	0	2	37	32	0	175	8	27	0	78
TOTAL	28	21	0	7	141	125	2	675	46	86	3	313

1979

	P	W	D	L	T	G	DG	Pts	T	G	Pts
In Australia	18	13	1	4	66	73	3	347	39	68	253
In New Zealand	9	8	0	1	48	34	0	212	15	12	69
TOTAL	27	21	1	5	114	107	3	559	54	80	332

1984	P	W	D	L	T	G	For DG	Pts	T	G	DG	Against Pts
In Australia	15	11	0	4	70	59	1	399	40	46	2	254
In New Zealand	8	4	0	4	32	25	1	179	21	21	0	126
In Papua New Guinea	1	1	0	0	7	5	0	38	4	2	0	20
TOTAL	24	16	0	8	109	89	2	616	65	69	2	400

1988	P	W	D	L	T	G	DG	Pts	T	G	DG	Pts
In Papua New Guinea	2	2	0	0	13	13	0	78	7	6	0	40
In Australia	13	8	0	5	59	47	0	330	42	36	1	241
In New Zealand	3	1	0	2	8	8	0	48	10	10	0	60
TOTAL	18	11	0	7	80	68	0	456	59	52	1	341

1990	P	W	D	L	T	G	DG	Pts	T	G	DG	Pts
In Papua New Guinea	5	4	0	1	31	24	0	172	7	15	2	60
In New Zealand	10	6	0	4	30	28	3	179	24	32	1	161
TOTAL	15	10	0	5	61	52	3	351	31	47	3	221

1992	P	W	D	L	T	G	DG	Pts	T	G	DG	Pts
In Papua New Guinea	3	3	0	0	15	11	0	82	8	8	1	49
In Australia	10	7	0	3	32	29	2	188	20	19	0	118
In New Zealand	4	3	0	1	10	11	2	64	7	8	1	45
TOTAL	17	13	0	4	57	51	4	334	35	35	2	212

GREAT BRITAIN TOUR SQUADS TO AUSTRALIA AND NEW ZEALAND
Captains in bold

1910 Tour

J. Lomas (Salford)
A. Avery (Oldham)
J. Bartholomew (Huddersfield)
W. Batten (Hunslet)
F. Boylen (Hull)
E. Curzon (Salford)
J. Davies (Huddersfield)
F. Farrar (Hunslet)
T. Helm (Oldham)
B. Jenkins (Wigan)
T. Jenkins (Ebbw Vale)
W. Jukes (Hunslet)
H. Kershaw (Wakefield T.)
J. Leytham (Wigan)
T. Newbould (Wakefield T.)
R. Ramsdale (Wigan)
J. Riley (Halifax)
G. Ruddick (Broughton R.)
J. Sharrock (Wigan)
F. Shugars (Warrington)
F. Smith (Hunslet)
J. Thomas (Wigan)
W. Ward (Leeds)
F. Webster (Leeds)
W. Winstanley (Leigh)
F. Young (Leeds)

Managers: J. Clifford
(Huddersfield) and J.
Houghton (St. Helens)

1914 Tour

H. Wagstaff (Huddersfield)
J. Chilcott (Huddersfield)
J. Clampitt (Broughton R.)
D. Clark (Huddersfield)
A. Coldrick (Wigan)
W. Davies (Leeds)
A. Francis (Hull)
J. Guerin (Hunslet)
W. Hall (Oldham)
D. Holland (Oldham)
J. Jarman (Leeds)
B. Jenkins (Wigan)
A. Johnson (Widnes)
F. Longstaff (Huddersfield)
S. Moorhouse (Huddersfield)
J. O'Garra (Widnes)
W. Prosser (Halifax)
R. Ramsdale (Wigan)
J. Robinson (Rochdale H.)
J. Rogers (Huddersfield)
W. Roman (Rochdale H.)
J. Smales (Hunslet)
F. Smith (Hunslet)
G. Thomas (Wigan)
F. Williams (Halifax)
A. Wood (Oldham)

Managers: J. Clifford
(Huddersfield) and J.
Houghton (St. Helens)

1920 Tour

H. Wagstaff (Huddersfield)
J. Bacon (Leeds)
J. Bowers (Rochdale H.)
J. Cartwright (Leigh)
D. Clark (Huddersfield)
W. Cunliffe (Warrington)
E. Davies (Oldham)
J. Doyle (Barrow)
F. Gallagher (Dewsbury)
B. Gronow (Huddersfield)
H. Hilton (Oldham)
D. Hurcombe (Wigan)
A. Johnson (Widnes)
E. Jones (Rochdale H.)
R. Lloyd (Halifax)
A. Milnes (Halifax)
J. Parkin (Wakefield T.)
G. Rees (Leeds)
W. Reid (Widnes)
J. Rogers (Huddersfield)
G. Skelhorne (Warrington)
J. Stacey (Halifax)
S. Stockwell (Leeds)
W. Stone (Hull)
G. Thomas (Huddersfield)
A. Wood (Oldham)

Managers: S. Foster (Halifax)
and J. Wilson (Hull K.R.)

1924 Tour

J. Parkin (Wakefield T.)
J. Bacon (Leeds)
J. Bennett (Rochdale H.)
W. Bentham (Broughton R.)
H. Bowman (Hull)
A. Brough (Oldham)
W. Burgess (Barrow)
C. Carr (Barrow)
W. Cunliffe (Warrington)
J. Darwell (Leigh)
F. Evans (Swinton)
F. Gallagher (Batley)
B. Gronow (Huddersfield)
T. Howley (Wigan)
D. Hurcombe (Wigan)
E. Knapman (Oldham)
W. Mooney (Leigh)
C. Pollard (Wakefield T.)
J. Price (Wigan)
D. Rees (Halifax)
J. Ring (Wigan)
S. Rix (Oldham)
R. Sloman (Oldham)
J. Sullivan (Wigan)
J. Thompson (Leeds)
S. Whitty (Hull)

Managers: J.H. Dannatt
(Hull) and E. Osborne
(Warrington)

1928 Tour

J. Parkin (Wakefield T.)
T. Askin (Featherstone R.)
N. Bentham (Wigan Highfield)
F. Bowen (St. Helens Recs)
H. Bowman (Hull)
J. Brough (Leeds)
W. Burgess (Barrow)
O. Dolan (St. Helens Recs)
A. Ellaby (St. Helens)
B. Evans (Swinton)
J. Evans (Swinton)
L. Fairclough (St. Helens)
A. Fildes (St. Helens Recs)
A. Frodsham (St. Helens)
W. Gowers (Rochdale H.)
T. Gwynne (Hull)
B. Halfpenny (St. Helens)
W. Horton (Wakefield T.)
J. Oliver (Batley)
W. Rees (Swinton)
M. Rosser (Leeds)
R. Sloman (Oldham)
J. Sullivan (Wigan)
J. Thompson (Leeds)
W. Williams (Salford)
H. Young (Bradford N.)

Managers: G. Hutchins
(Oldham) and E. Osborne
(Warrington)

1932 Tour

J. Sullivan (Wigan)
L. Adams (Leeds)
A. Atkinson (Castleford)
S. Brogden (Huddersfield)
F. Butters (Swinton)
I. Davies (Halifax)
W. Dingsdale (Warrington)
A. Ellaby (St. Helens)
B. Evans (Swinton)
J. Feetham (Salford)
N. Fender (York)
A. Fildes (St. Helens)
M. Hodgson (Swinton)
W. Horton (Wakefield T.)
B. Hudson (Salford)
J. Lowe (Leeds)
E. Pollard (Wakefield T.)
A. Risman (Salford)
G. Robinson (Wakefield T.)
N. Silcock (Widnes)
S. Smith (Leeds)
J. Thompson (Leeds)
L. White (Hunslet)
W. Williams (Salford)
J. Woods (Barrow)
J. Wright (Swinton)

Managers: R. Anderton
(Warrington) and G. Hutchins
(Oldham)

1936 Tour

J. Brough (Leeds)
J. Arkwright (Warrington)
T. Armitt (Swinton)
A. Atkinson (Castleford)
W. Belshaw (Liverpool S.)
H. Beverley (Hunslet)
S. Brogden (Leeds)
E. Davies (Wigan)
A. Edwards (Salford)
H. Ellerington (Hull)
G. Exley (Wakefield T.)
H. Field (York)
F. Harris (Leeds)
M. Hodgson (Swinton)

B. Hudson (Salford)
E. Jenkins (Salford)
H. Jones (Keighley)
T. McCue (Widnes)
J. Miller (Warrington)
J. Morley (Wigan)
A. Risman (Salford)
N. Silcock (Widnes)
S. Smith (Leeds)
L. Troup (Barrow)
W. Watkins (Salford)
H. Woods (Liverpool S.)

Managers: R. Anderton
(Warrington) and
W. Popplewell (Bramley)

1946 Tour

A. Risman (Salford)
A. Bassett (Halifax)
E. Batten (Bradford N.)
G. Curran (Salford)
W. Davies (Bradford N.)
J. Egan (Wigan)
T. Foster (Bradford N.)
K. Gee (Wigan)
W. Horne (Barrow)
F. Hughes (Workington T.)
D. Jenkins (Leeds)
A. Johnson (Warrington)

J. Jones (Barrow)
J. Kitching (Bradford N.)
B. Knowelden (Barrow)
J. Lewthwaite (Barrow)
T. McCue (Widnes)
H. Murphy (Wakefield T.)
R. Nicholson (Huddersfield)
I. Owens (Leeds)
D. Phillips (Oldham)
M. Ryan (Wigan)
Edward Ward (Wigan)
Ernest Ward (Bradford N.)
F. Whitcombe (Bradford N.)
L. White (York)

Managers: W. Popplewell
(Bramley) and W. Gabbatt
(Barrow)

1950 Tour

E. Ward (Bradford N.)
E. Ashcroft (Wigan)
T. Bradshaw (Wigan)
J. Cunliffe (Wigan)
T. Danby (Salford)
A. Daniels (Halifax)
J. Egan (Wigan)
J. Featherstone (Warrington)
K. Gee (Wigan)
E. Gwyther (Belle Vue R.)
F. Higgins (Widnes)
J. Hilton (Wigan)
W. Horne (Barrow)
J. Ledgard (Leigh)
H. Murphy (Wakefield T.)
D. Naughton (Widnes)
F. Osmond (Swinton)
A. Pepperell (Workington T.)
D. Phillips (Belle Vue R.)
R. Pollard (Dewsbury)
G. Ratcliffe (Wigan)
M. Ryan (Wigan)
R. Ryan (Warrington)
H. Street (Dewsbury)
K. Traill (Bradford N.)
R. Williams (Leeds)

Managers: G. Oldroyd
(Dewsbury) and T. Spedding
(Belle Vue R.)

1954 Tour

R. Williams (Hunslet)
E. Ashcroft (Wigan)
W. Boston (Wigan)
J. Bowden (Huddersfield)
B. Briggs (Huddersfield)
A. Burnell (Hunslet)
E. Cahill (Rochdale H.)
F. Castle (Barrow)
J. Cunliffe (Wigan)
D. Greenall (St. Helens)
G. Gunney (Hunslet)
T. Harris (Hull)
G. Helme (Warrington)
J. Henderson (Workington T.)
P. Jackson (Barrow)
B. L. Jones (Leeds)
T. McKinney (Salford)
T. O'Grady (Oldham)
C. Pawsey (Leigh)
A. Prescott (St. Helens)
R. Price (Warrington)
N. Silcock (Wigan)
K. Traill (Bradford N.)
A. Turnbull (Leeds)
D. Valentine (Huddersfield)
J. Wilkinson (Halifax)

Managers: T. Hesketh
(Wigan) and H. Rawson
(Hunslet)

1958 Tour

A. Prescott (St. Helens)
A. Ackerley (Halifax)
H. Archer (Workington T.)
E. Ashton (Wigan)
D. Bolton (Wigan)
F. Carlton (St. Helens)
J. Challinor (Warrington)
A. Davies (Oldham)
B. Edgar (Workington T.)
E. Fraser (Warrington)
D. Goodwin (Barrow)
T. Harris (Hull)
R. Huddart (Whitehaven)
K. Jackson (Oldham)
P. Jackson (Barrow)
V. Karalius (St. Helens)

B. McTigue (Wigan)
M. Martyn (Leigh)
G. Moses (St. Helens)
A. Murphy (St. Helens)
F. Pitchford (Oldham)
I. Southward (Workington T.)
M. Sullivan (Wigan)
A. Terry (St. Helens)
J. Whiteley (Hull)
W. Wookey (Workington T.)

Managers: B. Manson
(Swinton) and T. Mitchell
(Workington T.)
Coach: J. Brough
(Workington T.)

1962 Tour

E. Ashton (Wigan)
D. Bolton (Wigan)
W. Boston (Wigan)
F. Carlton (Wigan)
G. Cooper (Featherstone R.)
B. Edgar (Workington T.)
R. Evans (Wigan)
D. Fox (Featherstone R.)
N. Fox (Wakefield T.)
E. Fraser (Warrington)
L. Gilfedder (Warrington)
N. Herbert (Workington T.)
R. Huddart (St. Helens)
B. McTigue (Wigan)
A. Murphy (St. Helens)
K. Noble (Huddersfield)
H. Poynton (Wakefield T.)
G. Round (Wakefield T.)
W. Sayer (Wigan)
J. Shaw (Halifax)
P. Small (Castleford)
I. Southward (Workington T.)
M. Sullivan (St. Helens)
J. Taylor (Hull K.R.)
D. Turner (Wakefield T.)
J. Wilkinson (Wakefield T.)

Managers: S. Hadfield
(Wakefield T.) and A. Walker
(Rochdale H.)
Coach: C. Hutton (Hull K.R.)

1966 Tour

H. Poole (Leeds)
W. Aspinall (Warrington)
T. Bishop (St. Helens)
I. Brooke (Bradford N.)
W. Bryant (Castleford)
A. Buckley (Swinton)
W. Burgess (Barrow)
C. Clarke (Wigan)
G. Crewdson (Keighley)
C. Dooler (Featherstone R.)
B. Edgar (Workington T.)
P. Flanagan (Hull K.R.)
T. Fogerty (Halifax)
K. Gowers (Swinton)
A. Hardisty (Castleford)
B. Jones (Wakefield T.)
A. Keegan (Hull)
I. Mantle (St. Helens)
F. Myler (Widnes)
W. Ramsey (Hunslet)
K. Roberts (Halifax)
D. Robinson (Swinton)
G. Shelton (Hunslet)
I. Stopford (Swinton)
C. Watson (St. Helens)
G. Wriglesworth (Leeds)

Managers: W. Spaven (Hull
K.R.) and J. Errock (Oldham)

1970 Tour

F. Myler (St. Helens)
I. Atkinson (Leeds)
D. Chisnall (Leigh)
R. Dutton (Widnes)
D. Edwards (Castleford)
A. Fisher (Bradford N.)
P. Flanagan (Hull K.R.)
A. Hardisty (Castleford)
D. Hartley (Castleford)
K. Hepworth (Castleford)
C. Hesketh (Salford)
S. Hynes (Leeds)
R. Irving (Oldham)
D. Laughton (Wigan)
P. Lowe (Hull K.R.)
R. Millward (Hull K.R.)
T. Price (Bradford N.)

M. Reilly (Castleford)
D. Robinson (Wigan)
B. Seabourne (Leeds)
M. Shoebottom (Leeds)
A. Smith (Leeds)
C. Sullivan (Hull)
J. Thompson (Featherstone R.)
J. Ward (Salford)
C. Watson (St. Helens)

Manager: J. Harding (Leigh)
Coach: J. Whiteley (Hull)

1974 Tour

C. Hesketh (Salford)
K. Ashcroft (Warrington)
J. Atkinson (Leeds)
A. Bates (Dewsbury)
J. Bates (Dewsbury)
J. Bevan (Warrington)
J. Bridges (Featherstone R.)
J. Butler (Rochdale H.)
P. Charlton (Salford)
E. Chisnall (St. Helens)
T. Clawson (Oldham)
C. Dixon (Salford)
L. Dyl (Leeds)
D. Eckersley (St. Helens)
K. Gill (Salford)
J. Gray (Wigan)
J. Mills (Widnes)
R. Millward (Hull K.R.)
S. Nash (Featherstone R.)
G. Nicholls (St. Helens)
S. Norton (Castleford)
D. Redfearn (Bradford N.)
P. Rose (Hull K.R.)
J. Thompson (Featherstone R.)
D. Watkins (Salford)
D. Willicombe (Wigan)

Replacements during tour
W. Ramsey (Bradford N.) for
J. Bates; M. Richards
(Salford) for Atkinson

Manager: R. Parker
(Blackpool B.)
Coach: J. Challinor
(St. Helens)

1979 Tour

D. Laughton (Widnes)
M. Adams (Widnes)
D. Barends (Bradford N.)
L. Casey (Bradford N.)
S. Evans (Featherstone R.)
P. Glynn (St. Helens)
J. Grayshon (Bradford N.)
P. Hogan (Hull K.R.)
J. Holmes (Leeds)
E. Hughes (Widnes)
M. James (St. Helens)
J. Joyner (Castleford)
G. Liptrot (St. Helens)
B. Lockwood (Hull K.R.)
T. Martyn (Warrington)
R. Mathias (St. Helens)
J. Mills (Widnes)
R. Millward (Hull K.R.)
K. Mumby (Bradford N.)
S. Nash (Salford)
G. Nicholls (St. Helens)
S. Norton (Hull)
A. Redfearn (Bradford N.)
T. Skerrett (Wakefield T.)
M. Smith (Hull K.R.)
G. Stephens (Castleford)
C. Stone (Hull)
D. Ward (Leeds)
D. Watkinson (Hull K.R.)
J. Woods (Leigh)

Replacements during tour
J. Burke (Wakefield T.) for
Mills; G. Fairbairn (Wigan)
for Martyn; D. Topliss
(Wakefield T.) for Millward

Managers: H. Womersley
(Bradford N.) and
R. Gemmell (Hull)
Coach: E. Ashton (St. Helens)

1984 Tour*

B. Noble (Bradford N.)
M. Adams (Widnes)
R. Ashton (Oldham)
K. Beardmore (Castleford)
M. Burke (Widnes)
C. Burton (Hull K.R.)
B. Case (Wigan)
G. Clark (Hull K.R.)
L. Crooks (Hull)
S. Donlan (Leigh)
D. Drummond (Leigh)
R. Duane (Warrington)
T. Flanagan (Oldham)
D. Foy (Oldham)
A. Goodway (Oldham)
A. Gregory (Widnes)
E. Hanley (Bradford N.)
D. Hobbs (Featherstone R.)
N. Holding (St. Helens)
J. Joyner (Castleford)
J. Lydon (Widnes)
K. Mumby (Bradford N.)
A. Myler (Widnes)
M. O'Neill (Widnes)
H. Pinner (St. Helens)
W. Proctor (Hull)
Keith Rayne (Leeds)
G. Schofield (Hull)
M. Smith (Hull K.R.)
M. Worrall (Oldham)

Replacement during tour
J. Basnett (Widnes) for Duane

Managers: R. Gemmell (Hull)
and R. Davis (RLHQ)
Coach: Frank Myler (Oldham)

*One match in Papua New
  Guinea

1988 Tour*

E. Hanley (Wigan)
K. Beardmore (Castleford)
B. Case (Wigan)
L. Crooks (Leeds)
P. Dixon (Halifax)
S. Edwards (Wigan)
K. Fairbank (Bradford N.)
M. Ford (Oldham)
P. Ford (Bradford N.)
C. Gibson (Leeds)
H. Gill (Wigan)
A. Gregory (Wigan)
M. Gregory (Warrington)
P. Groves (St. Helens)
R. Haggerty (St. Helens)
D. Hulme (Widnes)
P. Loughlin (St. Helens)
P. Medley (Leeds)
M. Offiah (Widnes)
A. Platt (St. Helens)
R. Powell (Leeds)
G. Schofield (Leeds)
D. Stephenson (Leeds)
H. Waddell (Oldham)
K. Ward (Castleford)
I. Wilkinson (Halifax)

Replacements during tour
D. Wright (Widnes) for
Edwards; A. Currier (Widnes)
and P. Hulme (Widnes) for
Schofield and Medley; R.
Eyres (Widnes) and J. Joyner
(Castleford) for Crooks, Dixon
and Platt

Managers: L. Bettinson
(Salford) and D. Howes
(RLHQ)
Coach: M. Reilly

*Including Papua New Guinea

1990 Tour*

M. Gregory (Warrington)
D. Betts (Wigan)
C. Bibb (Featherstone R.)
D. Bishop (Hull K.R.)
P. Clarke (Wigan)
J. Davies (Widnes)
M. Dermott (Wigan)
P. Dixon (Leeds)
P. Eastwood (Hull)
K. England (Castleford)
K. Fairbank (Bradford N.)
D. Fox (Featherstone R.)
C. Gibson (Leeds)
R. Goulding (Wigan)
S. Irwin (Castleford)
L. Jackson (Hull)
I. Lucas (Wigan)
J. Lydon (Wigan)
M. Offiah (Widnes)
D. Powell (Sheffield E.)
R. Powell (Leeds)
G. Price (Wakefield T.)
G. Schofield (Leeds)
R. Simpson (Bradford N.)
K. Skerrett (Bradford N.)
I. Smales (Featherstone R.)
G. Steadman (Castleford)
A. Sullivan (Hull K.R.)
A. Tait (Widnes)

Replacements during tour
J. Devereux (Widnes) for
Sullivan; D. Lyon
(Warrington) for Tait

Manager: M. Lindsay (Wigan)
Coach: M. Reilly

*Papua New Guinea and
  New Zealand only

992 Tour*

.. **Hanley (Leeds)**
). Betts (Wigan)
. Clarke (Wigan)
*. Connolly (St. Helens)
I. Cowie (Wigan)
.. Crooks (Castleford)
1. Dermott (Wigan)
. Devereux (Widnes)
. Eastwood (Hull)
. Edwards (Wigan)
:. Ellis (Warrington)
:. Fairbank (Bradford N.)
). Fox (Featherstone R.)
.. Gregory (Wigan)
*. Hallas (Hull K.R.)
. Hampson (Wigan)
. Holliday (Widnes)
.. Hunte (St. Helens)
. Jackson (Hull)
1. Jackson (Wakefield T.)
. Loughlin (St. Helens)
. Lucas (Wigan)
. Lydon (Wigan)

W. McGinty (Wigan)
P. Newlove (Featherstone R.)
S. Nickle (St. Helens)
M. Offiah (Wigan)
A. Platt (Wigan)
D. Powell (Sheffield E.)
G. Schofield (Leeds)
K. Skerrett (Wigan)
G. Steadman (Castleford)

Replacements during tour
P. Hulme (Widnes) for Nickle;
K. Harrison (Halifax),
S. McNamara (Hull), D. Myers
(Wigan), M. Aston (Sheffield E.)
and P. Broadbent (Sheffield E.)
for Gregory, Holliday, Loughlin,
Hanley and Lucas; D. Sampson
(Castleford) for Cowie

Manager: M. Lindsay (Wigan)
Coach: M. Reilly

*Including Papua New Guinea

The 1984 British Lions, left to right.
Back row: Lydon, Donlan, Case, Burke, Schofield, Goodway, Foy, Crooks, Pinner, Clark, Myler, Mumby.
Middle row: McKenzie (Conditioner), Hobbs, Rayne, Arkwright, O'Neill, Worrall, Duane, Burton, Proctor, Joyner,
Smith, Barritt (Physio).
Front row: Myler (Coach), Beardmore, Ashton, Drummond, Noble (Capt.), Gemmell (Manager), Adams, Hanley,
Gregory, Holding, Davis (Business Manager).

ALL TIME TOUR RECORDS

IN AUSTRALIA
Highest score: 101-0 v. South Australia in 1914

Biggest defeat: 42-6 v. New South Wales in 1920 (Also *widest margin*)

Fewest defeats: 1 (and 1 draw) from 21 matches in 1958 and from 17 matches in 1970

Most defeats: 9 from 22 matches in 1966

Biggest attendances: 70,419 v. New South Wales (Sydney) in 1950

IN NEW ZEALAND
Highest score: 81-14 v. Bay of Plenty in 1962

Widest margin win: 72-3 v. Buller in 1928
72-3 v. North Island in 1958

Biggest defeat: 46-13 v. Auckland in 1962 (Also *widest margin*)

Fewest defeats: The tourists have won all their matches in the following years: 1910 (4 matches), 1914 (6), 1932 (8), 1936 (8), 1966 (8), 1970 (7).

Most defeats: 4 from 8 matches in 1984

Biggest attendance: 35,000 v. Auckland in 1920

PLAYERS' FULL TOUR RECORDS
Most full appearances: 24 by Dick Huddart in 1958

Most tries: 38 by Mick Sullivan in 1958

Most goals and points: 127g, 278 pts by Lewis Jones in 1954

Most tours: 4 by Garry Schofield (1984, 1988, 1990, 1992)

Biggest club representation: 13+1 replacement by Wigan in 1992 — Denis Betts, Phil Clarke, Neil Cowie, Martin Dermott, Shaun Edwards, Andy Gregory, Steve Hampson, Ian Lucas, Joe Lydon, Billy McGinty, Martin Offiah, Andy Platt, Kelvin Skerrett, plus David Myers as a replacement

Brothers touring together: Bryn and Jack Evans (1928), Don and Neil Fox (1962), Alan and John Bates (1974), David and Paul Hulme (1988, Paul as replacement)

GREAT BRITAIN IN THE WORLD CUP

A — Australia, Fr — France, GB — Great Britain, NZ — New Zealand, PNG — Papua New Guinea

1954 in France — *Winners:* Great Britain

Date					Venue	Att
30 Oct.	Fr	22	NZ	13	Paris	13,240
31 Oct.	GB	28	A	13	Lyons	10,250
7 Nov.	GB	13	Fr	13	Toulouse	37,471
7 Nov.	A	34	NZ	15	Marseilles	20,000
11 Nov.	GB	26	NZ	6	Bordeaux	14,000
11 Nov.	A	5	Fr	15	Nantes	13,000

Play-off

13 Nov.	GB	16	Fr	12	Paris	30,368

Final Table

	P.	W.	D.	L.	F.	A.	Pts.
Great Britain	3	2	1	0	67	32	5
France	3	2	1	0	50	31	5
Australia	3	1	0	2	52	58	2
New Zealand	3	0	0	3	34	82	0

1957 in Australia — *Winners:* Australia

Date					Venue	Att
15 June	GB	23	Fr	5	Sydney	50,00
15 June	A	25	NZ	5	Brisbane	29,63
17 June	GB	6	A	31	Sydney	57,95
17 June	NZ	10	Fr	14	Brisbane	28,00
22 June	A	26	Fr	9	Sydney	35,15
25 June	GB	21	NZ	29	Sydney	14,26

Final Table

	P.	W.	D.	L.	F.	A.	Pts.
Australia	3	3	0	0	82	20	6
Great Britain	3	1	0	2	50	65	2
New Zealand	3	1	0	2	44	60	2
France	3	1	0	2	28	59	2

1960 in England   *Winners:* Great Britain

24 Sept.	GB	23	NZ	8	Bradford	20,577
24 Sept.	A	13	Fr	12	Wigan	20,278
1 Oct.	A	21	NZ	15	Leeds	10,773
1 Oct.	GB	33	Fr	7	Swinton	22,923
8 Oct.	A	3	GB	10	Bradford	32,773
8 Oct.	NZ	9	Fr	0	Wigan	2,876

Final Table

	P.	W.	D.	L.	F.	A.	Pts.
Great Britain	3	3	0	0	66	18	6
Australia	3	2	0	1	37	37	4
New Zealand	3	1	0	2	32	44	2
France	3	0	0	3	19	55	0

1968 in Australia   *Winners:* Australia
and New Zealand

25 May	A	25	GB	10	Sydney	62,256
25 May	Fr	15	NZ	10	Auckland	18,000
1 June	A	31	NZ	12	Brisbane	23,608
2 June	Fr	7	GB	2	Auckland	15,760
8 June	A	37	Fr	4	Brisbane	32,600
8 June	GB	38	NZ	14	Sydney	14,105

Final Table

	P.	W.	D.	L.	F.	A.	Pts.
Australia	3	3	0	0	93	26	6
France	3	2	0	1	26	49	4
Great Britain	3	1	0	2	50	46	2
New Zealand	3	0	0	3	36	84	0

Play-off final

| 10 June | A | 20 | Fr | 2 | Sydney | 54,290 |

Halifax forward Charlie Renilson, a 1968 World Cup squad member.

1970 in England   *Winners:* Australia

21 Oct.	A	47	NZ	11	Wigan	9,586
24 Oct.	GB	11	A	4	Leeds	15,084
25 Oct.	NZ	16	Fr	15	Hull	3,824
28 Oct.	GB	6	Fr	0	Castleford	8,958
31 Oct.	GB	27	NZ	17	Swinton	5,609
1 Nov.	Fr	17	A	15	Bradford	6,215

Final Table

	P.	W.	D.	L.	F.	A.	Pts.
Great Britain	3	3	0	0	44	21	6
Australia	3	1	0	2	66	39	2
France	3	1	0	2	32	37	2
New Zealand	3	1	0	2	44	89	2

Play-off final

| 7 Nov. | A | 12 | GB | 7 | Leeds | 18,776 |

1972 in France   *Winners:* Great Britain

28 Oct.	Fr	20	NZ	9	Marseilles	20,748
29 Oct.	GB	27	A	21	Perpignan	6,324
1 Nov.	A	9	NZ	5	Paris	8,000
1 Nov.	GB	13	Fr	4	Grenoble	5,321
4 Nov.	GB	53	NZ	19	Pau	7,500
5 Nov.	A	31	Fr	9	Toulouse	10,332

Final Table

	P.	W.	D.	L.	F.	A.	Pts.
Great Britain	3	3	0	0	93	44	6
Australia	3	2	0	1	61	41	4
France	3	1	0	2	33	53	2
New Zealand	3	0	0	3	33	82	0

Play-off final

| 11 Nov. | GB | 10 | A | 10 | Lyons | 4,231 |

No further score after extra-time so Great Britain took the championship because they had scored the greatest number of points in the qualifying League table.

1977 in Australia   *Winners:* Australia
and New Zealand

29 May	A	27	NZ	12	Auckland	18,000
5 June	GB	23	Fr	4	Auckland	10,000
11 June	A	21	Fr	9	Sydney	13,231
12 June	GB	30	NZ	12	C'church	7,000
18 June	A	19	GB	5	Brisbane	27,000
19 June	NZ	28	Fr	20	Auckland	8,000

Final Table

	P.	W.	D.	L.	F.	A.	Pts.
Australia	3	3	0	0	67	26	6
Great Britain	3	2	0	1	58	35	4
New Zealand	3	1	0	2	52	77	2
France	3	0	0	3	33	72	0

Play-off final

25 June	A	13	GB	12	Sydney	24,457

1985-88 Series   *Winners:* Australia

1985

7 July	NZ	18	A	0	Auckland	19,000
9 Nov.	GB	6	NZ	6	Leeds	22,209
7 Dec.	Fr	0	NZ	22	Perpignan	5,000

1986

16 Feb.	Fr	10	GB	10	Avignon	4,000
29 July	A	32	NZ	12	Brisbane	22,811
17 Aug.	PNG	24	NZ	22	Port Moresby	15,000
4 Oct.	PNG	12	A	62	Port Moresby	17,000
22 Nov.	GB	15	A	24	Wigan	20,169
13 Dec.	Fr	0	A	52	Carcassonne	3,000

1987

24 Jan.	GB	52	Fr	4	Leeds	6,567
24 Oct.	GB	42	PNG	0	Wigan	9,121
15 Nov.	Fr	21	PNG	4	Carcassonne	5,000

1988

22 May	PNG	22	GB	42	Port Moresby	12,077
9 July	A	12	GB	26	Sydney	15,994
10 July	NZ	66	PNG	14	Auckland	8,392
17 July	NZ	12	GB	10	Christchurch	8,525
20 July	A	70	PNG	8	Wagga Wagga	11,685

Final Table

	P.	W.	D.	L.	F.	A.	Pts.
Australia	7	5	0	2	252	91	12*
New Zealand	7	4	1	2	158	86	11*
Great Britain	8	4	2	2	203	90	10
P. N. Guinea	7	1	0	6	84	325	4*
France	5	1	1	3	35	140	3

*Awarded two points in lieu of France's non-fulfilment of fixtures Down Under.

Play-off final

1988

9 Oct.	A	25	NZ	12	Auckland	47,363

GREAT BRITAIN WORLD CUP SQUADS

Captains in bold

1954 IN FRANCE

D. Valentine (Huddersfield)
W. Banks (Huddersfield)
H. Bradshaw (Huddersfield)
G. Brown (Leeds)
R. Coverdale (Hull)
G. Helme (Warrington)
P. Jackson (Barrow)
F. Kitchen (Leigh)
J. Ledgard (Leigh)

A. Naughton (Warrington)
D. Robinson (Wakefield T)
D. Rose (Leeds)
R. Rylance (Huddersfield)
S. Smith (Hunslet)
M. Sullivan (Huddersfield)
J. Thorley (Halifax)
B. Watts (York)
J. Whiteley (Hull)

Manager: G. Shaw (Castleford)

1957 IN AUSTRALIA

A. Prescott (St. Helens)
E. Ashton (Wigan)
W. Boston (Wigan)
A. Davies (Oldham)
J. Grundy (Barrow)
G. Gunney (Hunslet)
T. Harris (Hull)
P. Jackson (Barrow)
L. Jones (Leeds)

S. Little (Oldham)
T. McKinney (St. Helens)
G. Moses (St. Helens)
R. Price (Warrington)
A. Rhodes (St. Helens)
J. Stevenson (Leeds)
M. Sullivan (Huddersfield)
D. Turner (Oldham)
J. Whiteley (Hull)

Managers: W. Fallowfield (RL Secretary) and H. Rawson (Hunslet)

1960 IN ENGLAND

E. Ashton (Wigan)
W. Boston (Wigan)
J. Challinor (Warrington)
A. Davies (Oldham)
E. Fraser (Warrington)
R. Greenough (Warrington)
T. Harris (Hull)
V. Karalius (St. Helens)
B. McTigue (Wigan)

A. Murphy (St. Helens)
F. Myler (Widnes)
A. Rhodes (St. Helens)
B. Shaw (Hunslet)
J. Shaw (Halifax)
M. Sullivan (Wigan)
D. Turner (Wakefield T)
J. Whiteley (Hull)
J. Wilkinson (Wakefield T)

Manager: W. Fallowfield (RL Secretary)

1968 IN AUSTRALIA AND NEW ZEALAND

B. Risman (Leeds)
K. Ashcroft (Leigh)
J. Atkinson (Leeds)
T. Bishop (St. Helens)
I. Brooke (Wakefield T)
A. Burwell (Hull KR)
M. Clark (Leeds)

D. Edwards (Castleford)
P. Flanagan (Hull KR)
R. French (Widnes)
R. Haigh (Wakefield T)
R. Millward (Hull KR)
A. Morgan (Featherstone R)
C. Renilson (Halifax)

M. Shoebottom (Leeds)
C. Sullivan (Hull)
J. Warlow (St. Helens)
C. Watson (St. Helens)
C. Young (Hull KR)

Manager: W. Fallowfield (RL Secretary)   Coach: C. Hutton (Hull KR)

1970 IN ENGLAND

F. Myler (St. Helens)
K. Ashcroft (Leigh)
J. Atkinson (Leeds)
P. Charlton (Salford)
D. Chisnall (Leigh)
R. Dutton (Widnes)
A. Fisher (Bradford N & Leeds)

R. Haigh (Leeds)
D. Hartley (Castleford)
K. Hepworth (Castleford)
C. Hesketh (Salford)
S. Hynes (Leeds)
K. Jones (Wigan)
D. Laughton (Wigan)

M. Reilly (Castleford)
M. Shoebottom (Leeds)
A. Smith (Leeds)
J. Thompson (Featherstone R)
C. Watson (St. Helens)

Manager: J. Harding (Leigh)   Coach: J. Whiteley (Hull KR)

1972 IN FRANCE

C. Sullivan (Hull)
J. Atkinson (Leeds)
P. Charlton (Salford)
T. Clawson (Leeds)
C. Dixon (Salford)
C. Hesketh (Salford)
J. Holmes (Leeds)

R. Irving (Oldham)
D. Jeanes (Leeds)
A. Karalius (St. Helens)
B. Lockwood (Castleford)
P. Lowe (Hull KR)
S. Nash (Featherstone R)
G. Nicholls (Widnes)

D. O'Neill (Widnes)
D. Redfearn (Bradford N)
M. Stephenson (Dewsbury)
D. Topliss (Wakefield T)
John Walsh (St. Helens)

Manager: W. Spaven (Hull KR)   Coach: J. Challinor (St. Helens)

1977 IN AUSTRALIA AND NEW ZEALAND

R. Millward (Hull KR)
E. Bowman (Workington T)
L. Casey (Hull KR)
L. Dyl (Leeds)
K. Elwell (Widnes)
G. Fairbairn (Wigan)
K. Fielding (Salford)

W. Francis (Wigan)
K. Gill (Salford)
A. Hodkinson (Rochdale H)
P. Hogan (Barrow)
J. Holmes (Leeds)
S. Lloyd (Castleford)
. S. Nash (Salford)

G. Nicholls (St. Helens)
S. Pitchford (Leeds)
P. Smith (Featherstone R)
J. Thompson (Featherstone R
D. Ward (Leeds)
S. Wright (Widnes)

Manager: R. Parker (Blackpool B)   Coach: D. Watkins (Salford)

GREAT BRITAIN RECORDS

● In Test and World Cup matches.

MOST TRIES IN CAREER

*41 Mick Sullivan (Huddersfield, Wigan, St. Helens, York)	1954-63
30 Garry Schofield (Hull, Leeds)	1984-
24 Billy Boston (Wigan)	1954-63
24 Martin Offiah (Widnes, Wigan)	1988-
20 Ellery Hanley (Bradford N., Wigan, Leeds)	1984-
17 Roger Millward (Cas'd, Hull K.R.)	1966-78
16 Alex Murphy (St. Helens, Warrington)	1958-71
14 Eric Ashton (Wigan)	1957-63
14 Shaun Edwards (Wigan)	1985-
14 Neil Fox (Wakefield T.)	1959-69
13 Clive Sullivan (Hull)	1967-73
12 John Atkinson (Leeds)	1968-80
10 Jim Leytham (Wigan)	1907-10

*Mick Sullivan also scored two tries for Great Britain against France before the matches were given Test status.
●Most tries by a forward is eight by Derek Turner (Oldham, Wakefield T.) 1956-62; and Phil Lowe (Hull K.R.) 1970-78.

MOST GOALS IN CAREER

93 Neil Fox (Wakefield T.)	1959-69
66 Lewis Jones (Leeds)	1954-57
64 Jim Sullivan (Wigan)	1924-33
53 Eric Fraser (Warrington)	1958-61
44 George Fairbairn (Wigan, Hull K.R.)	1977-82
39 Paul Eastwood (Hull)	1990-
36 Jonathan Davies (Widnes)	1990-
29 Paul Loughlin (St. Helens)	1988-
26 Joe Lydon (Widnes, Wigan)	1983-
25 Terry Clawson (Featherstone R., Leeds, Oldham)	1962-74
22 Ray Dutton (Widnes)	1970
22 John Holmes (Leeds)	1971-82
22 Ernest Ward (Bradford N.)	1946-52
21 Mick Burke (Widnes)	1980-86
21 Ken Gowers (Swinton)	1962-66

MOST POINTS IN CAREER

228 Neil Fox (Wakefield T.)	1959-69
147 Lewis Jones (Leeds)	1954-57
144 Garry Schofield (Hull, Leeds)	1984-
128 Jim Sullivan (Wigan)	1924-33
123 Mick Sullivan (Huddersfield, Wigan, St. Helens, York)	1954-63
109 Eric Fraser (Warrington)	1958-61
106 Paul Eastwood (Hull)	1990-
96 Martin Offiah (Widnes, Wigan)	1988-
91 George Fairbairn (Wigan, Hull K.R.)	1977-82
81 Roger Millward (Castleford, Hull K.R.)	1966-78
80 Jonathan Davies (Widnes)	1990-
80 Ellery Hanley (Bradford N., Wigan, Leeds)	1984-
79 Joe Lydon (Widnes, Wigan)	1983-

MOST TRIES IN A MATCH

5 by Martin Offiah (Widnes) v. France at Leeds 16 February, 1991
4 by Jim Leytham (Wigan) v. Australia at Brisbane 2 July, 1910
Billy Boston (Wigan) v. New Zealand at Auckland 24 July, 1954
Alex Murphy (St. Helens) v. France at Leeds 14 March, 1959
Garry Schofield (Hull) v. New Zealand at Wigan 2 November, 1985
3 by Bill Jukes (Hunslet) v. Australia at Sydney 18 June, 1910
Bert Avery (Oldham) v. New Zealand at Auckland 30 July, 1910
Billy Stone (Hull) v. New Zealand at Auckland 31 July, 1920
Jonty Parkin (Wakefield T.) v. New Zealand at Auckland 31 July, 1920
Charlie Carr (Barrow) v. New Zealand at Leeds 15 January, 1927
Stan Smith (Leeds) v. Australia at Sydney 16 July, 1932
Arthur Bassett (Halifax) v. Australia at Brisbane 6 July, 1946
George Wilson (Workington T.) v. New Zealand at Bradford 6 October, 1951

Mick Sullivan (Huddersfield) v. New Zealand at Bradford 12 November, 1955
Dave Bolton (Wigan) v. France at Wigan 23 November, 1957
Mick Sullivan (Wigan) v. Australia at Sydney 19 July, 1958
Mick Sullivan (Wigan) v. New Zealand at Auckland 9 August, 1958
Mick Sullivan (Wigan) v. France at Leeds 14 March, 1959
Clive Sullivan (Hull) v. New Zealand at Sydney (World Cup) 8 June, 1968
Bill Burgess (Barrow) v. France at St. Helens 30 November, 1968
Keith Fielding (Salford) v. France at Grenoble 20 January, 1974
Henderson Gill (Wigan) v. France at Hull 6 December, 1981
Garry Schofield (Leeds) v. France at Leeds 16 February, 1991
Garry Schofield (Leeds) v. France at Carcassonne 7 March, 1993
Paul Newlove (Featherstone R.) v. France at Leeds 2 April, 1993

●Bill Jukes and Bert Avery are the only forwards to have scored hat-tricks for Great Britain, both on tour in 1910.

MOST GOALS IN A MATCH

10 by Lewis Jones (Leeds) v. Australia at Brisbane 3 July, 1954
Bernard Ganley (Oldham) v. France at Wigan 23 November, 1957
John Holmes (Leeds) v. New Zealand at Pau (World Cup) 4 November, 1972
Jonathan Davies (Widnes) v. France at Leeds 2 April, 1993
9 by Lewis Jones (Leeds) v. France at Leeds 26 January, 1957
Neil Fox (Wakefield T.) v. France at Wigan 3 April, 1963
Neil Fox (Wakefield T.) v. France at Leigh 18 March, 1964

Lewis Jones, joint record for most Great Britain goals in a match.

8 by Eric Fraser (Warrington) v. Australia at Sydney 19 July, 1958
David Creasser (Leeds) v. France at Leeds 1 March, 1985
Joe Lydon (Wigan) v. France at Leeds 24 January, 1987
Paul Eastwood (Hull) v. France at Leeds 16 February, 1991
Jonathan Davies (Widnes) v. Papua New Guinea at Wigan 9 November, 1991
7 by Lewis Jones (Leeds) v. France at St. Helens 10 April, 1957
Eric Fraser (Warrington) v. New Zealand at Auckland 9 August, 1958
Eric Fraser (Warrington) v. France at Leeds 14 March, 1959
Neil Fox (Wakefield T.) v. New Zealand at Swinton 4 November, 1961
Neil Fox (Wakefield T.) v. France at Swinton 23 January, 1965
Bev Risman (Leeds) v. New Zealand at Sydney (World Cup) 8 June, 1968
Roger Millward (Hull K.R.) v. Australia at Sydney 20 June, 1970
George Fairbairn (Wigan) v. France at Auckland (World Cup) 5 June, 1977
John Woods (Leigh) v. France at Hull 6 December, 1981
David Stephenson (Wigan) v. Papua New Guinea at Wigan 24 October, 1987
Paul Loughlin (St. Helens) v. Papua New Guinea at Port Moresby 22 May, 1988

MOST POINTS IN A MATCH

26 (2t, 10g) by John Holmes (Leeds) v. New Zealand at Pau (World Cup) 4 November, 1972
21 (1t, 9g) by Lewis Jones (Leeds) v. France at Leeds 26 January, 1957
Neil Fox (Wakefield T.) v. France at Wigan 3 April, 1963
Neil Fox (Wakefield T.) v. France at Leigh 18 March, 1964
20 (10g) by Lewis Jones (Leeds) v. Australia at Brisbane 3 July, 1954
(10g) Bernard Ganley (Oldham) v. France at Wigan 23 November, 1957
(2t, 7g) Roger Millward (Hull K.R.) v. Australia at Sydney 20 June, 1970
(1t, 8g) Joe Lydon (Wigan) v. France at Leeds 24 February, 1987
(5t) Martin Offiah (Widnes) v. France at Leeds 16 February, 1991
(1t, 8g) Paul Eastwood (Hull) v. France at Leeds 16 February, 1991
(10g) Jonathan Davies (Widnes) v. France at Leeds 2 April, 1993

MOST APPEARANCES

46	Mick Sullivan*
40	Garry Schofield
36(1)	Ellery Hanley
31	Billy Boston
30(1)	Cliff Watson
30(4)	Shaun Edwards
30(7)	Joe Lydon
29	George Nicholls
29	Neil Fox
29(1)	Roger Millward
28	Alan Prescott
27	Phil Jackson
27	Alex Murphy
27	Martin Offiah
26	Eric Ashton
26	John Atkinson
26(1)	Andy Gregory
25	Brian McTigue
25	Jim Sullivan
25	Tommy Harris
25(4)	Andy Platt

( ) Indicates substitute appearance included in total

* Mick Sullivan's record number of appearances include a record run of 36 successive matches. In addition he played in two matches against France before they were given Test status.

LONGEST TEST CAREERS

14 years — Gus Risman
1932 to 1946 (17 appearances)
13 years 9 months — Billy Batten
1908 to 1921 (10 appearances)
13 years 6 months — Alex Murphy
1958 to 1971 (27 appearances)
12 years 9 months — Roger Millward
1966 to 1978 (28+1 appearances)
12 years 6 months — John Atkinson
1968 to 1980 (26 appearances)
12 years 6 months — Terry Clawson
1962 to 1974 (14 appearances)

YOUNGEST TEST PLAYER

Paul Newlove was 18 years 72 days old when he made his Great Britain Test debut as a 76th-minute substitute in the first Test against New Zealand at Old Trafford, Manchester, on 21 October 1989, making his full debut a week later. Born on 10 August 1971, he beat the previous record held by Shaun Edwards (born 17 October 1966) who was 18 years 135 days old when capped against France at Leeds on 1 March 1985.

Roger Millward (born 16 September 1947) was 18 years 37 days old when he was a non-playing substitute for the second Test against New Zealand at Bradford on 23 October 1965.

OLDEST TEST PLAYER

Jeff Grayshon (born 4 March 1949) was 36 years 8 months when he played in his last Test for Britain, against New Zealand at Elland Road, Leeds, on 9 November 1985.

RECORD TEAM CHANGES

The record number of team changes made by the Great Britain selectors is 10, on three occasions, all against Australia.

In 1929, Britain crashed 31-8 to Australia in the first Test at Hull KR and retained only three players for the second Test at Leeds, where they won 9-3.

After their biggest ever defeat of 50-12 in the 1963 second Test at Swinton, Britain dropped nine players and were forced to make another change when Vince Karalius was injured and replaced by Don Fox. Britain stopped Australia making a clean sweep of the series by winning 16-5 at Leeds in the last Test.

Following the 40-4 first Test defeat at Hull City's soccer ground in 1982, the selectors again made 10 changes, not including substitutes, Britain going down 27-6 in the second Test at Wigan.

Britain have never fielded the same team for three or more successive Tests.

Featherstone Rovers utility back Martin Pearson, top point scorer in Great Britain's 1993 defeat of France

UNDER-21s

1992-93 REVIEW

Great Britain Under-21s cantered to a 46-10 victory in their only 1992-93 meeting, staged at Rochdale Hornets' Spotland stadium to celebrate the opening of a new main stand.

Captain Steve McNamara, the Hull second row man, earned the British Coal Man of the Match rating, justifying British coach Malcolm Reilly's decision to move him up to prop.

McNamara, a replacement on the 1992 British Lions tour, drove in hard and his ability to slip out the ball from a tackle led to tries for Oldham's Gary Christie and Widnes hooker Steve McCurrie.

One disappointment was that the great expectations of Britain's exciting half-back partnership of Wakefield Trinity's Nigel Wright and Wigan's Jason Robinson were not fulfilled.

Britain's young Lions took some time to settle down in the first half before a late flourish gave them a 22-0 interval lead. The first two tries from Wigan's Paul Atcheson and Christie both came from kicks, before Christie fed Atcheson for his second touchdown and Wigan's Barrie-Jon Mather completed the first-half scoring with a 40-yard run to the line. Featherstone Rovers' Martin Pearson added four goals.

The second half became more of a procession, with a second try for Mather and touchdowns by McCurrie, Sheffield's Ian Hughes, Warrington full back Lee Penny and Pearson, to make him top points scorer for the night with 14.

BRITISH COAL INTERNATIONAL
17 February   **Rochdale**

GREAT BRITAIN 46

Lee Penny (Warrington)	1.	
James Mosley (Wakefield T.)	2.	
Gary Christie (Oldham)	3.	
Martin Pearson (Featherstone R.)	4.	
Paul Atcheson (Wigan)	5.	
Nigel Wright (Wakefield T.)	6.	
Jason Robinson (Wigan)	7.	
Paul Anderson (Leeds)	8.	
Steve McCurrie (Widnes)	9.	
Steve McNamara (Hull), Capt.	10.	
Ian Hughes (Sheffield E.)	11.	
Barrie-Jon Mather (Wigan)	12.	
Chris Joynt (St. Helens)	13.	
Jason Donohue (Leigh)	14.	
Richard Chamberlain (Hull K.R.)	15.	
Gareth Stephens (Leeds)	16.	
Mick Cassidy (Wigan)	17.	

T: Atcheson (2), Mather (2), Christie, McCurrie, Hughes, Penny, Pearson
G: Pearson (5)
Substitutes:
Chamberlain for McCurrie (46 min.)
Stephens for Mosley (46 min.)
Cassidy for Joynt (60 min.)
Donohue for Atcheson (73 min.)
Manager: Steve Watson
Coach: Malcolm Reilly

FRANCE 10

Fabien Beranger (Lyon Villeurbanne)
Philippe Ricard (Albi)
Pascal Mons (Carcassonne)
Lilian Tiburcio (St. Esteve)
Arnaud Bousquet (Carcassonne)
Frederic Abadie (Lezignan)
Patrice Satge (Carcassonne)
Sebastian Bouche (Toulouse Julien)
Laurent Garnier (Cabestany)
David Collado (Albi)
Jean-Michel Baroni (Carpentras)
Frederic Teixido (Limoux)
Patrick Acroue (Avignon)
Stephan Tena (XIII Catalan)
Jerome Azema (Carcassonne)
Mousa Loukili (Lezignan)
Stephane Revello (Lezignan)
T: Mons, Collado
G: Abadie
Substitutes:
Azema for Baroni (28 min.)
Loukili for Beranger (54 min.)
Revello for Tiburcio (62 min.)
Tena for Garnier (70 min.)
Half-time: 22-0
Referee: Jean-Louis Aribaud (France)
Attendance: 2,080

Tryscoring hooker Steve McCurrie.

Wigan's Jason Robinson, disappointing at scrum half.

GREAT BRITAIN UNDER-21s RESULTS

25 Nov.	1984	W 24-8	v. F	Castleford
16 Dec.	1984	W 8-2	v. F	Albi
9 Oct.	1985	L 12-16	v. NZ	Bradford
19 Jan.	1986	L 6-19	v. F	St. Esteve
2 Feb.	1986	W 6-2	v. F	Whitehaven
8 Mar.	1987	W 40-7	v. F	St. Jean de Luz
21 Mar.	1987	W 54-6	v. F	St. Helens
6 Mar.	1988	L 13-14	v. F	Ausillon
19 Mar.	1988	L 4-8	v. F	St. Helens
20 Jan.	1989	W 30-0	v. F	Leeds
4 Feb.	1989	L 8-16	v. F	Carpentras
20 Jan.	1990	W 22-0	v. F	Villeneuve
16 Feb.	1990	W 20-6	v. F	Doncaster
26 Jan.	1991	W 48-2	v. F	Limoux
15 Feb.	1991	L 6-16	v. F	Wigan
30 Oct.	1991	W 58-0	v. P	Leeds
6 Mar.	1992	W 56-2	v. F	Halifax
20 Mar.	1992	W 34-2	v. F	Albi
17 Feb.	1993	W 46-10	v. F	Rochdale

Key: F — France
NZ — New Zealand
P — Papua New Guinea

GREAT BRITAIN UNDER-21s REGISTER

The following is a register of appearances for Great Britain Under-21s since this classification of match was introduced in 1984.

Figures in brackets are the total appearances, with the plus sign indicating substitute appearances, e.g. (3+1).

Away matches are in bold letters. Substitute appearances are in lower case letters.

ALLEN, Shaun (1) St. Helens: 1984 F
ANDERSON, Grant (4) Castleford: 1989 F, **F**; 1990 **F**, F
ANDERSON, Paul (2) Leeds: 1992 **F**; 1993 F
ATCHESON, Paul (1) Wigan: 1993 F

BECKWITH, Mark (1+1) Whitehaven: 1986 f, F
BETTS, Denis (4) Wigan: 1989 F, **F**; 1990 **F**, F
BIBB, Chris (5) Featherstone R.: 1987 **F**, F; 1988 F; 1989 F, **F**
BISHOP, Paul (1+1) Warrington: 1987 **F**, f
BONSON, Paul (2) Featherstone R.: 1992 F, **F**
BOOTHROYD, Giles (1) Castleford: 1989 F
BURGESS, Andy (+1) Salford: 1991 f
BUSBY, Dean (2+1) Hull: 1991 P; 1992 F, f

CARBERT, Brian (3) Warrington: 1985 NZ; 1986 F, F
CASSIDY, Frank (1+1) Swinton: 1988 f, F
CASSIDY, Mick (+1) Wigan: 1993 f
CHAMBERLAIN, Richard (+1) Hull K.R.: 1993 f
CHAMBERS, Gary (2) Warrington: 1991 F, F
CHRISTIE, Gary (1) Oldham: 1993 F
CLARK, Garry (2) Hull K.R.: 1984 F, F
CLARKE, Phil (5) Wigan: 1990 F; 1991 F, F; 1992 F, F
CONNOLLY, Gary (4) St. Helens: 1990 F; 1991 F, P; 1992 F
CONWAY, Mark (1) Leeds: 1984 F
CREASSER, David (5) Leeds: 1984 F, F; 1985 NZ; 1986 F, F
CRITCHLEY, Jason (+1) Widnes: 1990 f
CROOKS, Lee (2) Hull: 1984 F, F
CURRIER, Andy (2) Widnes: 1984 F, F

DALTON, James (3) Whitehaven: 1985 NZ; 1986 F, F
DANNATT, Andy (6) Hull: 1984 F, F; 1985 NZ; 1986 F; 1987 F, F
DARBYSHIRE, Paul (1+1) Warrington: 1991 f, F
DELANEY, Paul (+2) Leeds: 1990 f, f
DERMOTT, Martin (5) Wigan: 1987 F, F; 1988 F, F; 1989 F
DISLEY, Gary (+1) Salford: 1987 f
DIVORTY, Gary (6) Hull: 1984 F; 1985 NZ; 1986 F, F; 1987 F, F
DIXON, Mike (1) Hull: 1991 P
DONOHUE, Jason (+2) Leigh: 1992 f; 1993 f

EASTWOOD, Paul (2) Hull: 1987 F, F
EDWARDS, Shaun (4) Wigan: 1984 F; 1985 NZ; 1987 F, F

FARRELL, Anthony (1+1) Huddersfield: 1989 f, F
FAWCETT, Vince (3) Leeds: 1990 F, F; 1991 F
FLETCHER, Mike (2) Hull K.R.: 1988 F, F
FORD, Mike (3+1) Wigan: 1985 NZ; 1986 F; Leigh: 1987 f, F
FORSHAW, Michael (+2) Wigan: 1991 f, f
FORSTER, Mark (3) Warrington: 1985 NZ; 1986 F, F
FOX, Deryck (1) Featherstone R.: 1984 F

GILDART, Ian (6) Wigan: 1988 F, F; 1989 F, F; 1990 F, F
GOULDING, Bobby (5) Wigan: 1990 F, F; 1991 F, F; Leeds: 1991 P
GREGORY, Mike (1) Warrington: 1984 F
GRIBBIN, Vince (1+1) Whitehaven: 1984 f, F
GROVES, Paul (3) Salford: 1984 F, F; 1985 NZ

HALLAS, Graeme (1+2) Hull K.R.: 1991 P; 1992 f, f
HARCOMBE, Kevin (1) Rochdale H.: 1986 F
HARMON, Neil (1+3) Warrington: 1988 f, F; 1989 f, f
HILL, Brendan (+1) Leeds: 1986 f
HILL, Kenny (3) Castleford: 1988 F, F; 1989 F
HUGHES, Gary (1) Leigh: 1986 F
HUGHES, Ian (1) Sheffield E.: 1993 F

HULME, David (2+1) Widnes: 1985 nz; 1986 F, F
HUNTE, Alan (2) St. Helens: 1990 F; 1991 F

IRWIN, Shaun (4) Castleford: 1988 F; 1989 F, F; 1990 F

JACKSON, Michael (+1) Hunslet: 1991 f
JOHNSON, Errol (2) Leeds: 1988 F, F
JOYNT, Chris (4) Oldham: 1991 P; 1992 F, F; St. Helens: 1993 F

LAY, Steve (+1) Hunslet: 1989 f
LORD, Gary (1) Castleford: 1988 F
LOUGHLIN, Paul (2) St. Helens: 1987 F, F
LUCAS, Ian (4) Wigan: 1988 F, F; 1989 F, F
LUMB, Tim (+1) Hunslet: 1991 f
LYMAN, Paul (3) Featherstone R.: 1985 NZ; 1986 F, F
LYON, David (2) Widnes: 1985 NZ; 1986 F

McCORMACK, Kevin (2) St. Helens: 1987 F, F
McCURRIE, Steve (2+1) Widnes: 1991 P; 1992 f; 1993 F
McNAMARA, Steve (5) Hull: 1991 F, F, P; 1992 F; 1993 F
MARTYN, Tommy (1+3) Oldham: 1991 F, f, p; 1992 F
MATHER, Barrie-Jon (1+1) Wigan: 1992 f; 1993 F
MEDLEY, Paul (2) Leeds: 1987 F, F
MOLLOY, Steve (2) Warrington: 1990 F, F
MOSLEY, James (1) Wakefield T.: 1993 F
MOUNTAIN, Dean (+1) Castleford: 1987 f
MOXON, Darren (1) Bradford N.: 1991 F
MYCOE, David (4) Sheffield E.: 1990 F; 1991 P; 1992 F, F
MYERS, David (5) Wigan: 1991 F, F, P; 1992 F, F

NEWLOVE, Paul (8) Featherstone R.: 1989 F, F; 1990 F, F; 1991 F, P; 1992 F, F
NICKLE, Sonny (1) Sheffield E.: 1990 F

O'DONNELL, Gus (2) Wigan: 1992 F, F

PARKER, Wayne (2) Hull K.R.: 1988 F, F
PARR, Chris (1) Huddersfield: 1991 P
PEARSON, Martin (4) Featherstone R.: 1991 P; 1992 F, F; 1993 F
PENNY, Lee (1) Warrington: 1993 F
PICKSLEY, Richard (1) Sheffield E.: 1992 F
PINKNEY, Nick (+1) Ryedale-York: 1991 p
POWELL, Roy (5) Leeds: 1984 F, F; 1985 NZ; 1986 F, F
PRATT, Richard (2) Leeds: 1988 F, F
PRECIOUS, Andy (+1) Hunslet: 1991 p
PRICE, Gary (5+1) Wakefield T.: 1988 f; 1989 F, F; 1990 F; 1991 F, F
PRICE, Richard (2) Hull: 1989 F, F
PROCTOR, Wayne (+1) Hull: 1984 f
PUCKERING, Neil (4) Hull: 1986 F, F; 1987 F, F

RICHARDS, Craig (2) Bradford N.: 1991 F, F
RILEY, Mike (2) St. Helens: 1992 F, F
RIPPON, Andy (1) Swinton: 1984 F
ROBINSON, Jason (1) Wigan: 1993 F

ROBINSON, Steve (1) Halifax: 1988 F
ROEBUCK, Neil (+1) Castleford: 1990 f
ROUND, Paul (1+1) St. Helens: 1984 F, f
RUDD, Chris (2) Warrington: 1991 **F, F**
RUSSELL, Richard (1+1) Wigan: 1987 F; 1988 f
SAMPSON, Dean (1) Castleford: 1988 **F**
SANDERSON, Gary (4) Warrington: 1987 **F**, F; 1988 **F, F**
SCHOFIELD, Garry (2) Hull: 1984 **F**, F
SLATER, Richard (+1) Wakefield T.: 1992 f
SMITH, Tony (1) Castleford: 1991 F
SOUTHERNWOOD, Graham (6) Castleford: 1990 **F**, F; 1991 **F**, F; 1992 F, **F**
SOUTHERNWOOD, Roy (2) Castleford: 1989 F, **F**
SPRUCE, Stuart (+1) Widnes: 1991 f
STEPHENS, Gareth (+1) Leeds: 1993 f
STREET, Tim (2) Leigh: 1989 F, **F**
SULLIVAN, Anthony (1) Hull K.R.: 1990 F
SUMNER, Phil (3) Warrington: 1990 F; 1991 P; 1992 F

TURNER, Robert (1) Warrington: 1990 F

WANE, Shaun (3) Wigan: 1984 F; 1985 NZ; 1986 **F**
WESTHEAD, John (1+2) Leigh: 1985 nz; 1986 f, **F**
WRIGHT, Darren (2) Widnes: 1987 F; 1988 **F**
WRIGHT, Nigel (1) Wakefield T.: 1993 F

GREAT BRITAIN UNDER-21 RECORDS

Highest score:	58-0 v. Papua New Guinea at Leeds, 30 October 1991
Highest against:	6-19 v. France at St. Esteve, 19 January 1986
Most tries in a match:	3 by Neil Puckering (Hull) v. France at St. Helens, 21 March 1987
	David Myers (Wigan) v. PNG at Leeds, 30 October 1991
	David Myers (Wigan) v. France at Halifax, 6 March 1992
	Martin Pearson (Featherstone R.) v. France at Halifax, 6 March 1992
	David Myers (Wigan) v. France at Albi, 20 March 1992
Most goals in a match:	8 by Chris Rudd (Warrington) v. France at Limoux, 26 January 1991
	Martin Pearson (Featherstone R.) v. PNG at Leeds, 30 October 1991
Most points in a match:	24 (3t,6g) by Martin Pearson (Featherstone R.) v. France at Halifax, 6 March 1992
Biggest attendance:	4,596 v. France at Doncaster, 16 February 1990

GREAT BRITAIN UNDER-24s RESULTS

3 Apr.	1965	W 17-9	v. F	Toulouse
20 Oct.	1965	W 12-5	v. F	Oldham
26 Nov.	1966	L 4-7	v. F	Bayonne
17 Apr.	1969	W 42-2	v. F	Castleford
14 Nov.	1976	W 19-2	v. F	Hull K.R.
5 Dec.	1976	W 11-9	v. F	Albi
12 Nov.	1977	W 27-9	v. F	Hull
18 Dec.	1977	W 8-4	v. F	Tonneins
4 Oct.	1978	L 8-30	v. A	Hull K.R.
14 Jan.	1979	W 15-3	v. F	Limoux
24 Nov.	1979	W 14-2	v. F	Leigh
13 Jan.	1980	W 11-7	v. F	Carcassonne
5 Nov.	1980	L 14-18	v. NZ	Fulham
10 Jan.	1981	W 9-2	v. F	Villeneuve
16 Jan.	1982	W 19-16	v. F	Leeds
21 Feb.	1982	W 24-12	v. F	Tonneins
16 Jan.	1983	W 19-5	v. F	Carpentras
11 Nov.	1983	W 28-23	v. F	Villeneuve
4 Dec.	1983	W 48-1	v. F	Oldham

GREAT BRITAIN UNDER-24s REGISTER
Since reintroduction in 1976

The following is a register of appearances by current players, who played at least one club game in 1992-93, for Great Britain Under-24s since this classification of match was reintroduced in 1976, until it was replaced by the new Under-21 level in 1984.

Figures in brackets are the total appearances, with the plus sign indicating substitute appearances, e.g (7+3).

Away matches are in bold letters. Substitute appearances are in lower case letters.

ASHTON, Ray (3) Oldham: 1983 **F**, F, F

BELL, Keith (2) Featherstone R.: 1977 F, **F**

CAIRNS, David (2) Barrow: 1979 F; 1982 **F**
CLARK, Garry (3) Hull K.R.: 1983 F, **F**, F
CROOKS, Lee (1) Hull: 1983 F

Under-21s loose forward Chris Joynt.

DRUMMOND, Des (5) Leigh: 1979 F; 1980 **F**; 1981 **F**; 1982 F, **F**
DUANE, Ronnie (2) Warrington: 1983 **F**, **F**
DUNN, Brian (2) Wigan: 1983 **F**, F

ECCLES, Bob (2) Warrington: 1978 A; 1979 F
ENGLAND, Keith (+1) Castleford: 1983 f

FIELDHOUSE, John (1+1) Warrington: 1983 **F**, f
FORD, Phil (1) Warrington: 1982 **F**
FOY, Des (2) Oldham: 1983 **F**, F

GOODWAY, Andy (2) Oldham: 1983 **F**, F
GREGORY, Andy (1) Widnes: 1982 F

HANLEY, Ellery (2) Bradford N.: 1982 F; 1983 F
HARKIN, Paul (1) Hull K.R.: 1981 **F**
HOBBS, David (2) Featherstone R.: 1982 F, **F**

LEDGER, Barry (2) St. Helens: 1983 **F**, F
LYDON, Joe (3) Widnes: 1983 **F**, **F**, F

MASKILL, Colin (1) Wakefield T.: 1983 **F**
MUMBY, Keith (6) Bradford N.: 1976 F, **F**; 1977 F, **F**; 1978 A; 1981 **F**
MYLER, Tony (3) Widnes: 1982 **F**; 1983 **F**, F

NOBLE, Brian (4) Bradford N.: 1982 F, **F**; 1983 **F**, F

O'NEILL, Mike (3+2) Widnes: 1980 nz; 1982 F, f; 1983 **F**, **F**

POTTER, Ian (4) Warrington: 1979 **F**; 1981 **F**; Leigh: 1982 F, **F**

SCHOFIELD, Garry (+2) Hull: 1983 f, f

THACKRAY, Rick (1) Warrington: 1980 NZ
TIMSON, Andy (2) Castleford: 1982 F, **F**

WARD, Kevin (3) Castleford: 1980 **F**, NZ; 1981 **F**
WHITFIELD, Colin (1) Salford: 1981 **F**
WOODS, John (5) Leigh: 1977 F, **F**; 1978 A; 1979 **F**, F
WORRALL, Mick (3) Oldham: 1983 **F**, **F**, F

England debutant Dean Busby falls to Welsh stand off
Kevin Ellis in the 1992 British Coal international a
rain-sodden Vetch Field, Swansea

ENGLAND AND WALES

ENGLAND AND WALES

England weathered a first-half battering from Wales to eventually run out comfortable 36-11 winners at a rain-lashed Vetch Field, Swansea, in the first Anglo-Welsh encounter for eight years.

Two weeks later, the Red Dragons rounded off a laudable return to the international arena by beating France 19-18 at Perpignan, their squad badly hit by injuries and suspension.

By surviving a second-half French onslaught after leading 19-4 inside 32 minutes, Wales registered their third victory from four internationals within 13 months, having been absent from the world scene for seven seasons.

Wales' dual commitment opened at Swansea in November, persistent torrential rain almost causing a cancellation of the Friday night fixture. England coach Malcolm Reilly paid the Welsh the compliment of fielding his strongest side, combining Test stalwarts Garry Schofield, Ellery Hanley and Martin Offiah with in-form Mike Ford, Steve Molloy and Richard Eyres.

Hanley and Schofield were the two survivors from the England side which last played Wales at Ebbw Vale in 1984.

Cheered on by a patriotic crowd of more than 10,000, the Welsh made a contest of the first half, coming back from 12-0 down after 22 minutes to trail by only one point with just 60 seconds of the half remaining. A defensive error let England in for a decisive try and they pulled away with superior mobility in the second half.

A first-minute penalty goal by Castleford's Lee Crooks gave the visitors lift off and they piled on the pressure for Hanley to go in off Ford's pass after 12 minutes.

It began to look like a runaway win for England when a sweeping move ended with Ford again providing the final pass for Stuart Spruce to nip in for a well-taken touchdown on his international debut, Crooks' goal making it 12-0.

The partisan Welsh crowd fell silent only to be back in full voice when an enterprising break by Phil Ford, the only Welsh survivor from the 1984 match, set up the first home try.

The Salford winger, playing at full back, feinted to make a clearance kick from his own line and then broke brilliantly down the right. When he eventually kicked near halfway, Spruce collected only to lose the ball in a crash tackle. Wales stand off Jonathan Griffiths snapped up possession to push off a defender and go in between the posts. John Devereux added the goal to signal a Welsh revival.

Three minutes later came a sensational try from Hull prop Mark Jones, who scattered three defenders in a short charge to the line, a power burst which inspired the fervent Welsh crowd into song.

The vocals increased when scrum half Kevin Ellis dropped a goal to cut the English lead to 12-11. Wales deserved to hold on to that margin until the interval, but in the last minute of the half Anthony Sullivan fumbled Hanley's speculative kick and Crooks pounced for a fortunate touchdown, adding the goal himself.

Much of the fire went out of the Welsh play as England doubled their score in the second period. Increasing the momentum, England moved the ball about in style despite the greasy surface, adding tries through Offiah (2), Paul Newlove and Schofield, who aggravated a hamstring injury when touching down. Daryl Powell replaced him with two minutes left.

Widnes packman Richard Eyres took the British Coal Man of the Match award with a strong-running second row performance, while Hanley worked hard to complement the playmaking Ford at the base of the scrum.

Wales, who suffered the loss of winger Gerald Cordle with a broken jaw after only nine minutes, were well served by prop Jones, who produced a towering display before retiring hurt on the hour. Makeshift hooker David Bishop belied his lack of match practice by completing the full 80 minutes with a notable contribution on both attack and defence.

Having beaten France 35-6 at Swansea the previous March, Wales travelled to Perpignan in mid-December seeking only their third success in 19 encounters on French soil. The Red

Dragons were hit by injuries to Cordle and Griffiths, plus the suspension of the barnstorming Jones.

Wales gave debuts to substitutes Peter Williams, Ian Stevens and Paul Kennett. Williams had previously represented Great Britain at Rugby League and England at Rugby Union, qualifying for Welsh selection through parentage. Depleted Wales were further hampered by the 26th-minute withdrawal of winger Sullivan with a serious knee injury.

Having built an impressive 19-4 lead with eight minutes of the first half left, Wales served up a display of resilience and brave defence to secure their immediate international future with a double over the French.

Second row man Paul Moriarty earned the British Coal Man of the Match rating, outstanding in a pack which dominated the opening half. Prop David Young played a captain's role, with Rowland Phillips, Rob Ackerman, Gary Pearce and Ellis all enjoying solid games.

Centre pairing Allan Bateman and Devereux formed an impressive partnership, while full back Ford saved two tries shortly before and after the interval.

The most significant event was Pearce's 32nd minute drop goal which was to be the only difference between the two sides. Pearce also kicked three goals, while French skipper Gilles Dumas and Marc Tisseyre could manage only one success from a combined total of five kicks.

Wales had to overcome an initial setback when Ford's kick was charged down and was heading for touch when the strong wind kept the ball in and Dumas reacted first to touch down.

Five minutes later, Bishop created a try for Bateman; a three-man move then paved the way for a Devereux touchdown; followed in the 27th minute by Ackerman taking advantage of a yawning gap to score. Pearce added all three goals to open a commanding 18-4 lead before adding the vital drop goal.

France built a platform for revival just before the break with scrum half Lucien de Macedo cutting through the Welsh threequarters for a try and a half-time scoreline of 19-8.

Driven on by Didier Cabestany, France started to dominate. Dumas's kick set up a Claude Sirvent try to reduce the gap to seven points in the 55th minute. With Dumas in full cry, it was almost inevitable that Wales would crack, Pierre Chamorin going over two minutes from time, Tisseyre adding France's only goal to set up a nail-biting finale.

Wales maintained their commitment and composure to survive the last two minutes and revel in the narrowest of away victories to add to those of 1936 and 1970.

England centre Paul Newlove falls to Allan Bateman.

BRITISH COAL INTERNATIONAL

27 November   **Vetch Field, Swansea**

WALES 11		ENGLAND 36
Phil Ford (Salford)	1.	Stuart Spruce (Widnes)
Gerald Cordle (Bradford N.)	2.	Alan Hunte (St. Helens)
Allan Bateman (Warrington)	3.	Gary Connolly (St. Helens)
John Devereux (Widnes)	4.	Paul Newlove (Featherstone R.)
Anthony Sullivan (St. Helens)	5.	Martin Offiah (Wigan)
Jonathan Griffiths (St. Helens)	6.	Garry Schofield (Leeds), Capt.
Kevin Ellis (Warrington)	7.	Mike Ford (Castleford)
Mark Jones (Hull)	8.	Lee Crooks (Castleford)
David Bishop (London C.)	9.	Lee Jackson (Hull)
David Young (Salford), Capt.	10.	Steve Molloy (Leeds)
Paul Moriarty (Widnes)	11.	Richard Eyres (Widnes)
Ian Marlow (Hull)	12.	Phil Clarke (Wigan)
Rob Ackerman (Salford)	13.	Ellery Hanley (Leeds)
Adrian Hadley (Widnes)	14.	Daryl Powell (Sheffield E.)
Rowland Phillips (Warrington)	15.	Chris Joynt (St. Helens)
Gary Pearce (Ryedale-York)	16.	Jason Critchley (Salford)
Mark Moran (Leigh)	17.	Dean Busby (Hull)

T: Griffiths, Jones
G: Devereux, Ellis (dg)
Substitutions:
Hadley for Cordle (9 min.)
Phillips for Jones (61 min.)
Pearce for Ellis (76 min.)
Moran for Ackerman (76 min.)
Manager: Jim Mills
Coach: Clive Griffiths
Half-time: 11-18
Attendance: 10,243

T: Offiah (2), Crooks, Hanley,
Spruce, Newlove, Schofield
G: Crooks (4)
Substitutions:
Joynt for Molloy (60 min.)
Critchley for Hunte (66 min.)
Busby for Eyres (71 min.)
Powell for Schofield (78 min.)
Coach: Malcolm Reilly
Referee: Alain Sablayrolles
(France)

England 1992, left to right. Back row: Spruce, Hanley, Joynt, Busby, Jackson, Betts, Offiah, Clarke.
Middle row: Molloy, Hunte, Newlove, Schofield (Capt.), Reilly (Coach), Powell, Eyres.
Front row: Tait, Fox, Connolly, Critchley, Ford, Kear (Asst. Coach).

BRITISH COAL INTERNATIONAL

13 December   Perpignan

WALES 19   FRANCE 18

Wales		France
Phil Ford (Salford)	1.	Jean Frison (Villefranche)
Adrian Hadley (Widnes)	2.	Claude Sirvent (St. Gaudens)
Allan Bateman (Warrington)	3.	Pierre Chamorin (St. Esteve)
John Devereux (Widnes)	4.	Pascal Fages (Pia)
Anthony Sullivan (St. Helens)	5.	Jean-Marc Garcia (St. Esteve)
Gary Pearce (Ryedale-York)	6.	Gilles Dumas (St. Gaudens), Capt.
Kevin Ellis (Warrington)	7.	Lucien de Macedo (Avignon)
Ian Marlow (Hull)	8.	Bernard Llong (XIII Catalan)
David Bishop (London C.)	9.	Patrick Torreilles (Pia)
David Young (Salford), Capt.	10.	Guy Delpech (Carcassonne)
Paul Moriarty (Widnes)	11.	Richard Clarke (Cannes)
Rowland Phillips (Warrington)	12.	Didier Cabestany (XIII Catalan)
Rob Ackerman (Salford)	13.	Marc Tisseyre (Carcassonne)
Ian Stevens (Hull)	14.	David Amat (Lezignan)
Mark Moran (Leigh)	15.	Christophe Grandjean (Lezignan)
Paul Kennett (Swinton)	16.	Eric Castel (Albi)
Peter Williams (Salford)	17.	David Despin (Villeneuve)

T: Bateman, Devereux, Ackerman
G: Pearce (3, 1dg)
Substitutions:
Stevens for Sullivan (25 min.)
Moran for Marlow (55 min.)
Williams for Bishop (69 min.)
Kennett for Moriarty (79 min.)
Manager: Jim Mills
Coach: Clive Griffiths

T: Dumas, de Macedo, Chamorin, Sirvent
G: Tisseyre
Substitutions:
Amat for Llong (55 min.)
Grandjean for Clarke (63 min.)
Despin for Fages (65 min.)
Half-time: 19-8
Referee: Robin Whitfield (Widnes)
Attendance: 3,700

Wales 1992, left to right. Back row: Griffiths (Coach), Bateman, Marlow, Jones, Moriarty, Hadley, Phillips, Bishop, Young (Capt.), Devereux, Ackerman, Cordle, Mills (Manager). Front row: Ford, Ellis, Moran, Stevens, Griffiths, Sullivan, Pearce, Kennett.

ENGLAND REGISTER
● Since reintroduction in 1975

The following is a register of England appearances since the reintroduction of European and World Championship matches in 1975, but does not include the challenge match against Australia played after the 1975 World Championship.

Figures in brackets are the total appearances for England since 1975, with the plus sign indicating substitute appearances, e.g. (7+3).

A few players also played in the 1969-70 European Championship and this is shown as an additional total outside bracket, e.g. (11)2.

World Championship matches are in bold letters. Substitute appearances are in lower case letters.

A - Australia, F - France,
NZ - New Zealand, W - Wales.

ADAMS, Mick (3+2) Widnes: 1975 **NZ, a**; 1978 F; 1979 W; 1981 w
ARKWRIGHT, Chris (+1) St. Helens: 1984 w
ATKINSON, John (7)4 Leeds: 1975 W, **F, W, NZ, W**; 1978 F, W

BANKS, Barry (+1) York: 1979 f
BEARDMORE, Kevin (1) Castleford: 1984 W
BEVERLEY, Harry (1) Workington T: 1979 W
BRIDGES, John "Keith" (7) Featherstone R: 1975 **NZ, A, W, F, NZ, A**; 1977 W
BURKE, Mick (1) Widnes: 1984 W
BUSBY, Dean (+1) Hull: 1992 w

CAIRNS, David (1) Barrow: 1984 W
CASE, Brian (1) Warrington: 1981 F
CASEY, Len (5) Hull KR: 1978 F, W; 1980 W; 1981 F, W
CHARLTON, Paul (1) Salford: 1975 **F**
CHISNALL, Dave (3+1) Warrington: 1975 w, **F, W, NZ**
CHISNALL, Eric (3+1) St. Helens: 1975 F, **W, NZ, a**
CLARK, Garry (1) Hull KR: 1984 W
CLARKE, Phil (1) Wigan: 1992 W
CONNOLLY, Gary (1) St. Helens: 1992 W
COOKSON, Phil (2) Leeds: 1975 **NZ, A**
COULMAN, Mike (5) Salford: 1975 F, W, **W, A**; 1977 F
CRITCHLEY, Jason (+1) Salford: 1992 w
CROOKS, Lee (1) Castleford: 1992 W
CUNNINGHAM, John (2) Barrow: 1975 F, W

DONLAN, Steve (1) Leigh: 1984 W
DRUMMOND, Des (5) Leigh: 1980 W, F; 1981 F, W; 1984 W
DUNN, Ged (6) Hull KR: 1975 W, **A, F, NZ, A**; 1977 F
DYL, Les (12+1) Leeds: 1975 F, W, **F, W, NZ, A, nz, A**; 1977 W, F; 1978 F, W; 1981 W
ECKERSLEY, Dave (+5) St. Helens: 1975 f, **w, f**; Widnes: 1977 w; 1978 w
ELWELL, Keith (2) Widnes: 1978 F, W
EVANS, Steve (3) Featherstone R: 1979 F; 1980 W, F

EYRES, Richard (1) Widnes: 1992 W

FAIRBAIRN, George (15) Wigan: 1975 **W, NZ, A, W, F, NZ, A**; 1977 W, F; 1978 F; 1980 W, F; 1981 F, W; Hull KR: 1981 W
FARRAR, Vince (1) Featherstone R: 1977 F
FENTON, Steve (2) Castleford: 1981 F, W
FIELDING, Keith (7) Salford: 1975 F, **F, W, NZ, A, W, F**
FORD, Mike (1) Castleford: 1992 W
FORSYTH, Colin (3) Bradford N: 1975 **W, F, NZ**

GILL, Henderson (1) Wigan: 1981 W
GILL, Ken (9+2) Salford: 1975 W, **F, w, NZ, a, W, F, NZ, A**; 1977 W, F
GLYNN, Peter (2) St. Helens: 1979 W, F
GOODWAY, Andy (1) Oldham: 1984 W
GORLEY, Les (1+1) Workington T: 1977 W; Widnes: 1981 w
GORLEY, Peter (2+1) St. Helens: 1980 W, f; 1981 W
GRAY, John (3) Wigan: 1975 F, W, **F**
GRAYSHON, Jeff (9+1) Dewsbury: 1975 **W, F, NZ, A**; 1977 W; Bradford N: 1979 W, F; 1980 w, F; 1981 W

HANLEY, Ellery (2) Bradford N: 1984 W; Leeds: 1992 W
HARRISON, Mick (2) Leeds: 1978 F, W
HOBBS, David (1) Featherstone R: 1984 W
HOGAN, Brian (5) Wigan: 1975 **W, F, NZ, A**; 1977 W
HOGAN, Phil (1) Hull KR: 1979 F
HOLDING, Neil (1) St. Helens: 1980 W
HOLDSTOCK, Roy (3) Hull KR: 1980 W, F; 1981 W
HOLMES, John (5+2) Leeds: 1975 **W, F, NZ, A**; 1977 W, f; 1978 f
HUDDART, Milton (1) Whitehaven: 1984 W
HUGHES, Eric (8+1) Widnes: 1975 **W, F, NZ, a**; 1977 F; 1978 F, W; 1979 W, F
HUNTE, Alan (1) St. Helens: 1992 W

IRVING, Bob (3) Wigan: 1975 **W, F, A**

JACKSON, Lee (1) Hull: 1992 W
JACKSON, Phil (2) Bradford N: 1975 W, **F**

JONES, Les (1) St. Helens: 1977 W
JOYNER, John (4) Castleford: 1980 W, F; 1981 F, W
JOYNT, Chris (+1) St. Helens: 1992 w

KELLY, Andy (1) Hull KR: 1984 W
KELLY, Ken (3) Warrington: 1979 W; 1981 F, W

LAUGHTON, Doug (1) Widnes: 1977 W
LEDGER, Barry (+1) St. Helens: 1984 w
LIPTROT, Graham (2) St. Helens: 1979 W, F
LOCKWOOD, Brian (2)+1 Hull KR: 1979 W, F
LOWE, Phil (3)2 Hull KR: 1977 F; 1978 F; 1981 W

MARTYN, Tommy (4+1) Warrington: 1975 W, **F, w**;
    1979 W, F
MILLINGTON, John (2) Hull KR: 1975 F; 1981 W
MILLWARD, Roger (13)3+1 Hull KR: 1975 F, W,
    F, W, A, W, F, NZ, A; 1977 W, F; 1978 F, W
MOLLOY, Steve (1) Leeds: 1992 W
MORGAN, Mick (3+3) Wakefield T: 1975 f, W, **f, W,
    nz, A**
MUMBY, Keith (2) Bradford N: 1979 W, F
MURPHY, Martin (1) Oldham: 1975 F

NASH, Steve (7) Featherstone R: 1975 **W, NZ, A**;
    Salford: 1978 F, W; 1981 W, W
NEWLOVE, Paul (1) Featherstone R: 1992 W
NICHOLLS, George (7+4) St. Helens: 1975 F, **F, W,
    NZ, A, w, nz, f**; 1977 f; 1978 F, W
NOONAN, Derek (3) Warrington: 1975 W, **F, W**
NORTON, Steve (11) Castleford: 1975 **W, NZ, A, W, F,
    NZ, A**; 1977 F; Hull: 1978 W; 1981 W, W

OFFIAH, Martin (1) Wigan: 1992 W
O'NEILL, Steve (1) Wigan: 1981 F

PATTINSON, Bill (1+1) Workington T: 1981 f, W
PHILBIN, Barry (1) Warrington: 1975 **F**
PIMBLETT, Geoff (1) St. Helens: 1978 W
PINNER, Harry (3) St. Helens: 1980 W, F; 1981 F
POTTER, Ian (2) Warrington: 1981 F, W
POWELL, Daryl (+1) Sheffield E: 1992 w

RAYNE, Keith (2) Wakefield T: 1980 W, F
REDFEARN, Alan (2) Bradford N: 1979 F; 1980 F
REDFEARN, Dave (2) Bradford N: 1975 F, **A**
REILLY, Malcolm (+1)2 Castleford: 1977 w
RICHARDSON, Terry (1) Castleford: 1981 W
ROSE, Paul (2) Hull KR: 1977 F; 1978 W

SCHOFIELD, Garry (2) Hull: 1984 W; Leeds: 1992 W
SHEARD, Les (1) Wakefield T: 1975 W
SMITH, David (1) Leeds: 1977 F
SMITH, Keith (1) Wakefield T: 1979 W
SMITH, Mike (5) Hull KR: 1980 W, F; 1981 F, W, W
SMITH, Peter (1) Featherstone R: 1980 F
SPRUCE, Stuart (1) Widnes: 1992 W
STEPHENS, Gary (1) Castleford: 1979 W
SZYMALA, Eddie (+1) Barrow: 1979 f

THOMPSON, Jimmy (2+1)1 Featherstone R: 1975 **A**;
    1977 W; Bradford N: 1978 w

TINDALL, Keith (1) Hull: 1979 F
TOPLISS, David (1) Wakefield T: 1975 F

WADDELL, Hugh (1) Blackpool B: 1984 W
WALKER, Arnold (1) Whitehaven: 1981 F
WALSH, John (3) St. Helens: 1975 F, **NZ, A**
WARD, David (6) Leeds: 1977 F; 1980 W, F;
    1981 F, W, W
WATKINSON, David (+1) Hull KR: 1977 w
WOODS, John (3+4) Leigh: 1979 w, F; 1980 w, F;
    1981 f, w, W
WRIGHT, Stuart (7) Wigan: 1975 **NZ**; Widnes: 1977 W;
    1978 F, W; 1979 W, F; 1980 W

Chris Joynt (St. Helens).

Steve Molloy (Leeds).

411

WALES REGISTER
● Since 1975

Figures in brackets are the total appearances for Wales since 1975, with the plus sign indicating substitute appearances, e.g. (7+3).

A few players also played in the 1969-70 European Championship and this is shown as an additional total outside bracket, e.g. (11)2.

World Championship matches are in bold letters. Substitute appearances are in lower case letters. A - Australia, E - England, F - France, NZ - New Zealand, P - Papua New Guinea.

ACKERMAN, Rob (4) Carlisle: 1991 P; 1992 F; Salford: 1992 E, F

BANNER, Peter (9) Salford: 1975 F, E, **F, E, NZ;** Featherstone R: 1975 **E, A, NZ, F**

BATEMAN, Allan (4) Warrington: 1991 P; 1992 F, E, F

BAYLISS, Steve (1) St. Helens: 1981 E

BEVAN, John (17) Warrington: 1975 F, E, **E, A, NZ, F;** 1977 E, F; 1978 A; 1979 F, E; 1980 F, E; 1981 F, E, E; 1982 A

BISHOP, David (4) Hull KR: 1991 P; 1992 F; London C: 1992 E, F

BOX, Harold (5) Featherstone R: 1979 F, E; 1980 F, E; Wakefield T: 1981 F

BUTLER, Brian (2+2) Swinton: 1975 **F, nz;** Warrington: 1975 f; 1977 F

CAMBRIANI, Adrian (3) Fulham: 1981 F, E, E

CAMILLERI, Chris (3) Barrow: 1980 F; Widnes: 1982 A; Bridgend: 1984 E

CORDLE, Gerald (1+1) Bradford N: 1991 p; 1992 E

COSLETT, Kel (8)2 St. Helens: 1975 F, E, **F, E, A, NZ, E, A**

CUNNINGHAM, Eddie (8) St. Helens: 1975 **E, A, E, A;** 1977 E; 1978 F, E, A

CUNNINGHAM, Tommy (2) Warrington: 1979 F, E

CURLING, Dennis (+1) Warrington: 1977 f

DAVID, Tommy (2) Cardiff C: 1981 E; 1982 A

DAVIES, Frank (1) New Hunslet: 1978 E

DAVIES, Jonathan (2) Widnes: 1991 P; 1992 F

DAVIES, Mike (1) Bridgend: 1984 E

DEVEREUX, John (4) Widnes: 1991 P; 1992 F, E, F

DIAMOND, Steve (2+1) Wakefield T: 1980 F, e; 1981 F

DIXON, Colin (10)3 Salford: 1975 F, E, **F, E, NZ, A;** 1977 E, F; 1978 F; Hull KR: 1981 E

ELLIS, Kevin (4) Warrington: 1991 P; 1992 F, E, F

EVANS, Richard (5) Swinton: 1975 E, **F, F;** 1978 F; Salford: 1978 E

FENWICK, Steve (2) Cardiff C: 1981 E; 1982 A

FISHER, Tony (10)4 Leeds: 1975 F, E, **A, NZ;** Castleford: 1975 **E, A, NZ;** 1977 E, F; Bradford N: 1978 A

FLOWERS, Ness (4) Wigan: 1980 F, E; 1981 E; Bridgend: 1984 E

FORD, Phil (5) Warrington: 1984 E; Leeds: 1991 P; 1992 F; Salford: 1992 E, F

FRANCIS, Bill (19) Wigan: 1975 F, E, **F, E, A, NZ, E, A, NZ, F;** 1977 E, F; St. Helens: 1978 F, E, A; 1979 F, E; Oldham: 1980 F, E

GALLACHER, Stuart (3+1) Keighley: 1975 f, E, **NZ, F**

GREGORY, Brian (3) Wigan: 1975 **E, NZ, F**

GRIFFITHS, Clive (+2) St. Helens: 1980 f; 1981 f

GRIFFITHS, Jonathan (3) St. Helens: 1991 P; 1992 F, E

HADLEY, Adrian (1+3) Salford: 1991 p; 1992 f; Widnes: e, F

HALLETT, Lynn (2) Cardiff C: 1982 A; Bridgend: 1984 E

HERDMAN, Martin (2+1) Fulham: 1981 e, E; 1982 A

HOPKINS, Lynn (1) Workington T: 1982 A

JAMES, Mel (11) St. Helens: 1975 **E;** 1978 F, E, A; 1979 F, E; 1980 F, E; 1981 F, E, E

JOHNS, Graeme (+2) Salford: 1979 f; Blackpool B: 1984 e

JONES, Clive (1+3) Leigh: 1975 **nz, F;** 1978 f, e

JONES, Mark (3) Hull: 1991 P; 1992 F, E

JULIFF, Brian (8) Wakefield T: 1979 F, E; 1980 F, E; 1981 F, E; Wigan: 1982 A; 1984 E

KENNETT, Paul (+1) Swinton: 1992 f

McJENNETT, Mark (2+1) Barrow: 1980 F; 1982 a; 1984 E

MANTLE, John (11+1)3 St. Helens: 1975 F, E, **F, e, A, NZ, E, A, NZ, F;** 1977 E; 1978 E

MARLOW, Ian (3) Hull: 1992 F, E, F

MATHIAS, Roy (20) St. Helens: 1975 F, E, **F, E, A, NZ, A, NZ, F;** 1977 E, F; 1978 F, E, A; 1979 F, E; 1980 F, E; 1981 F, E

MILLS, Jim (13)4 Widnes: 1975 F, E, **E, A, NZ, A, NZ;** 1977 E, F; 1978 F, E, A; 1979 E

MORAN, Mark (+2) Leigh: 1992 e, f

MORIARTY, Paul (3) Widnes: 1991 P; 1992 E, F

MURPHY, Mick (4+1) Bradford N: 1975 **F, NZ, F;** 1977 f; St. Jacques, France: 1979 F

NICHOLAS, Mike (4+2) Warrington: 1975 F, e; 1977 E, F; 1978 F; 1979 e

O'BRIEN, Chris (1) Bridgend: 1984 E

OWEN, Gareth (2) Oldham: 1981 E, F

OWEN, Roger (+2) St. Helens: 1981 f, e

PARRY, Donald (6) Blackpool B: 1980 F, E; 1981 F, E, E; 1982 A

PEARCE, Gary (1+3) Scarborough P: 1991 p; Ryedale-York: 1992 f, e, F

PHILLIPS, Rowland (1+3) Warrington: 1991 p; 1992 f, e, F

PREECE, Chris (1) Bradford N: 1984 E

PRENDIVILLE, Paul (4+2) Hull: 1979 e; 1980 E; 1981 F, e; 1982 A; 1984 E

PRITCHARD, Gordon (1+2) Barrow: 1978 f, e; Cardiff C: 1981 E

RICHARDS, Maurice (2)1 Salford: 1975 **F**; 1977 E

RINGER, Paul (2) Cardiff C: 1981 E; 1982 A

RISMAN, John (2+1) Workington T: 1978 F; 1979 f, E

ROWE, Peter (4+3)2 Blackpool B: 1975 **a, e, a**; Huddersfield: 1977 E, F; 1979 F, E

RULE, Steve (1) Salford: 1981 E

SELDON, Chris (1+1) St. Helens: 1980 f, E

SHAW, Glyn (7) Widnes: 1978 F, A; 1980 F, E; 1981 E; Wigan: 1982 A; 1984 E

SILVA, Matthew (+1) Halifax: 1991 p

SKERRETT, Trevor (7) Wakefield T: 1978 A; 1979 F, E; 1980 F; Hull: 1981 F, E; 1984 E

STEVENS, Ian (+1) Hull: 1992 f

SULLIVAN, Anthony (4) St. Helens: 1991 P; 1992 F, E, F

SULLIVAN, Clive (10)4 Hull KR: 1975 **E, A, NZ, E**; 1977 F; 1978 F, E, A; 1979 F, E

TREASURE, David (5) Oldham: 1975 **E, A, NZ, E**; 1977 F

TURNER, Glyn (3+3) Hull KR: 1975 e, **A, e, A, f**; Hull: 1978 E

WALLACE, Richard (+1) York: 1975 **f**

WALTERS, Graham (2+1) Hull: 1980 E; 1981 E; Bridgend 1984 e

WANBON, Bobby (3)3+1 Warrington: 1975 **E, A, NZ**

WATKINS, David (14) Salford: 1975 F, E, **F, E, A, NZ, E, A, NZ, F**; 1977 E; 1978 E, A; 1979 F

WILKINS, Ray (1+1) Workington T: 1977 e, F

WILLIAMS, Barry (2) Carlisle: 1991 P; 1992 F

WILLIAMS, Brynmor (1) Cardiff C: 1982 A

WILLIAMS, Peter (+1) Salford: 1992 f

WILLICOMBE, David (11)+2 Wigan: 1975 F, E, **F, E, A, NZ, NZ, F**; 1978 F, E, A

WILSON, Danny (4) Swinton: 1981 F, E, E; 1984 E

WILSON, Frank (7+2)4 St. Helens: 1975 F, E, **F, e, a, E, A, NZ, F**

WOODS, Paul (10) Widnes: 1977 E, F; 1978 F, E, A; Rochdale H: 1979 F, E; Hull: 1980 E; 1981 F, E

YOUNG, David (4) Salford: 1991 P; 1992 F, E, F

Wales full back Phil Ford kicks past England hooker Lee Jackson in the first Anglo-Welsh encounter for eight years.

ENGLAND RECORDS

Highest score:	60-13 v. Wales at St. Helens, 28 May 1978
	(Also widest margin win)
Highest score against:	63-13* v. Australia at Paris, 31 December 1933

*England included Welshmen. Highest score against All-England side 42-13 v. France at Marseilles, 25 November 1951 (Also widest margin defeat)

Most tries in a match:	4 by J. Leytham (Wigan) v. Other Nationalities
	at Bradford, 2 January 1905
	4 by S. Moorhouse (Huddersfield) v. Wales
	at Plymouth, 15 February 1913
	4 by P. Norburn (Swinton) v. Other Nationalities
	at Wigan, 28 November 1953
	4 by K. Fielding (Salford) v. France
	at Bordeaux, 11 October 1975
	4 by S. Wright (Widnes) v. Wales
	at St. Helens, 28 May 1978
Most goals and points in a match:	9g-21pts by G. Pimblett (St. Helens) v. Wales at St. Helens, 28 May 1978
Biggest home attendance:	27,500 v. Wales at Wigan, 1 March 1950

WALES RECORDS

Highest score:	68-0 v. Papua New Guinea at Swansea FC, 27 October 1991
	(Also widest margin win)
Highest score against:	60-13 v. England at St. Helens, 28 May 1978
	(Also widest margin defeat)
Most tries in a match:	4 by W. T. Davies (Halifax) v. Australia
	at Ebbw Vale, 7 October 1911
Most goals and points in a match:	8g-24pts by Jonathan Davies (Widnes) v. Papua New Guinea at Swansea FC, 27 October 1991
Biggest home attendance:	30,000 v. England at Swansea, 24 November 1945

Scrum half Deryck Fox, the top cash transfer in 1992-93 on goalkicking duty for Great Britain in the Stones Bitter World Cup final at Wembley.

TRANSFERS

TRANSFER REVIEW
1 June 1992 to 31 May 1993
The recession that hit all sports was reflected in the drop in major transfers, with only one straight cash deal of £100,000 or more but several player exchanges.

The top cash deal saw Deryck Fox, 27, move from Featherstone Rovers to Bradford Northern on 9 September for a £140,000 fee that was a record for both clubs. It was also the most ever paid for a scrum half, beating the £130,000 handed over when Andy Gregory transferred from Warrington to Wigan in January 1987.

A further reflection of the recession was that the Fox deal was completed only after Northern appealed to their fans and local businesses to help them raise the cash. It followed a similar move by Hull, who were the first to come up with a £140,000 offer, which Featherstone accepted but the Great Britain scrum half wanted to join Bradford.

Graeme Hallas's move from Hull Kingston Rovers to Halifax on 28 October was reckoned to be the biggest cash-plus-player deal of the year. The British Lions threequarter was listed at £180,000 when he sought a move after Rovers decided not to renew any players' cash contracts at the beginning of the season.

Hallas, 21, did not play for the club again and moved to Halifax in a six-figure deal that included Rob Hutchinson joining Rovers.

Another major player-exchange deal resulted in Widnes full back Alan Tait joining Leeds with scrum half Bobby Goulding going to Naughton Park. Leeds also paid a cash adjustment of under £10,000. Tait was on the transfer list at £230,000, while Leeds valued Goulding at the £90,000 they had paid Wigan a year earlier.

David Myers returned to Widnes when Wigan transferred him in exchange for full back Paul Atcheson plus a cash adjustment in the latter's favour. Atcheson was on the list at £120,000, while Widnes had recently agreed an £80,000 deal with Hull for Myers, who turned down the move.

There were only five transfers adjudicated by the League's tribunal compared with 10 the previous year. They were:
John Pendlebury, Bradford N. to Leigh £20,000; Martin Crompton, Warrington to Wigan, £65,000 plus £20,000 on debut for Great Britain; James Lowes, Hunslet to Leeds £30,000 plus £10,000 after 10 first-team matches, a further £15,000 after another 20 matches and £30,000 if he plays for Great Britain; Keith Waterhouse, Leigh to Warrington £1,000 plus £1,500 after five first-team matches and £2,500 after a further five appearances Dave Kendall, Barrow to Whitehaven, £12,500

There was a total of 166 transfers of player between clubs plus 129 loan transactions.

RUGBY UNION SIGNINGS
Oldham made the only signing of a Rugby Union international during the year when they signed England winger Nigel Heslop from Orrell in February. At 29, Heslop switched codes at a much later age than most top Rugby Union converts and he is one of the very few to have signed for a Division Two club.

Heslop, who played 10 times for England did not receive a big signing-on fee an Oldham said his contract of just over two year was based on incentives.

Earlier in the season, Oldham also signed England 'B' stand off Martin Strett from Orrell.

Another England 'B' player to try Rugby League was full back Steve Pilgrim, who was banned for a year by the Rugby Football Union after one trial match for Leeds reserves.

The ban brought nationwide criticism and the situation was also raised in Parliament. Pilgrim made only one first-team appearance for Leeds and had a senior game with Halifax but was not retained by either club. For more details see HEADLINES.

The total of Rugby Union signings over the year was 17 compared with 21 in the previous 12 months. The drop in major signings was continuing reflection of the 15-a-side code relaxation of their laws relating to professionalism, with many top players, especially in Wales, being financially well supported.

AMATEUR SIGNINGS

A total of 196 players was signed from amateur Rugby League clubs, including signings from Academy teams, compared with 293 in the previous period.

OVERSEAS SIGNINGS

The number of overseas players making first-team appearances during 1992-93 rose from the previous season's 151 to 162 — only six short of the record set in 1990-91.

Australia regained its position as the most popular source of imports with 91 making first-team appearances; 60 New Zealanders appeared plus 11 players from other countries.

New Zealand continued to provide more top-quality recruits, as their total included 23 Test players plus Tongan Emosi Koloto, who has played for the Kiwis.

Only three Australian Test players appeared. Although none was a current international, Sheffield Eagles' signing of all-time great full back Garry Jack was a major capture.

He joined Test man Bruce McGuire at Sheffield, while 1988 World Cup final centre Andrew Farrar went to Wigan.

Widnes also made a notable signing when utility back Julian O'Neill stayed to play 11 matches for them after coming over with the Australian World Cup squad and playing for Brisbane Broncos in the World Club Challenge match against Wigan.

O'Neill was later flown back from Australia to make a substitute appearance in the Silk Cut Challenge Cup final at Wembley.

France also provided one Test player, with Daniel Divet appearing for Hull.

The following is a list of overseas players who made at least one first-team appearance during 1992-93. The New Zealand register includes Pacific island-born players.

OVERSEAS REGISTER 1992-93

*Test players as at 1 June 1993

AUSTRALIA (91)

Tony Anderson	(Bradford N.)
Darren Appleby	(Featherstone R., Keighley C.)
Greg Austin	(Halifax)
Geoff Bagnall	(Wakefield T.)
Scott Barnes	(Batley)
Paul Beath	(Hunslet)
Peter Benson	(Wakefield T.)
Michael Booth	(Batley)
Shane Buckley	(London C.)
Terry Bullen	(Barrow)
Dave Callan	(Blackpool G.)
Mick Cameron	(Batley)
Paul Carr	(Sheffield E.)
Simon Chappell	(Highfield)
Jason Charlton	(Whitehaven)
Brett Clark	(Rochdale H.)
Troy Clarke	(Carlisle, Leigh)
Craig Coleman	(Salford)
Dale Collins	(Bramley, Doncaster)
Glen Coughlan	(Dewsbury)
Peter Coyne	(Castleford)
David Cruickshank	(Salford)
Brett Daunt	(Featherstone R.)
Bradley Davis	(Huddersfield, Nottingham C.)
Matthew Dray	(London C.)
Darryl Duncan	(London C.)
Terry Dunne	(Ryedale-York)
Steve Edwards	(Doncaster, Whitehaven)
John Elias	(Leigh)
*Andrew Farrar	(Wigan)
Paul Fisher	(London C.)
Peter Fitzgerald	(Ryedale-York)
Anthony Foy	(Nottingham C.)
Darren Fritz	(Wakefield T.)
Scott Gale	(Hull)
Ian Gateley	(Keighley C.)
Mark Gee	(Bramley)
Steve Georgallis	(Carlisle)
Steve Gibson	(Salford)
Wally Gibson	(Huddersfield, Oldham)
Troy Goldman	(Hull K.R.)
James Grant	(Hull)
Dean Hanger	(Leigh)
Duane Harp	(Nottingham C.)
Brad Hayes	(Doncaster)
Ivan Henjak	(Hull)
Cavill Heugh	(Rochdale H.)
Craig Hibberd	(Carlisle, Swinton)
Kenny Isaacs	(Nottingham C.)
*Garry Jack	(Sheffield E.)
Bob Jackson	(Warrington)

Ken Kerr	(Halifax, Huddersfield, Keighley C.)
David King	(London C.)
Jason Laurence	(Huddersfield, Nottingham C.)
Mark Laurie	(Salford)
David Liddiard	(Hull K.R.)
*Bruce McGuire	(Sheffield E.)
John McKelvie	(Hunslet)
Grant McKenzie	(London C.)
Phil McKenzie	(Rochdale H., Workington T.)
Craig McKeough	(Hull K.R.)
Mike McLean	(Halifax)
Sean McVean	(Ryedale-York)
John Machon	(Swinton)
Greg Mackey	(Warrington)
Scott Mahon	(Leigh)
Justin Maitland	(Nottingham C.)
Tony Mitchell	(Huddersfield)
Danny Mulkerin	(London C.)
Mark Mulligan	(Workington T.)
Dave Nui	(Bramley)
Julian O'Neill	(Widnes)
Matthew Parsons	(Ryedale-York)
Greg Pearce	(Dewsbury)
Rion Pearce	(Huddersfield)
Steve Pickett	(Widnes)
Darryl Pitt	(London C.)
Paul Rees	(Hunslet)
Scott Roskell	(London C.)
Steve Rosolen	(London C.)
Jeff Roy	(Carlisle)
Gary Schubert	(Workington T.)
Greg Shuttleworth	(Bramley, Doncaster)
David Smith	(Carlisle)
Paul Srama	(Barrow)
Glen Tomlinson	(Batley)
Mike Twigg	(Bramley)
Phil Veivers	(St. Helens)
Chris Winstanley	(London C.)
Graham Woods	(Nottingham C.)
Glen Workman	(London C.)

NEW ZEALAND (60)

*Dean Bell	(Wigan)
Glen Bell	(Dewsbury)
Karl Benson	(Chorley B.)
*Richard Blackmore	(Castleford)
*Frano Botica	(Wigan)
Mark Brooke-Cowden	(Keighley C.)
Steve Carey	(Barrow)
*Dean Clark	(Hull K.R.)
Trevor Clark	(Bradford N.)
*Shane Cooper	(St. Helens)
*Ricky Cowan	(St. Helens)
Reg Dunn	(Whitehaven)

*Morvin Edwards	(Leeds)
*Esene Faimalo	(Widnes)
Joe Faimalo	(Highfield)
*Clayton Friend	(Carlisle, Whitehaven)
Bernie Gilbert	(London C.)
Joe Grima	(Keighley C.)
Carl Hall	(Hull K.R.)
Shane Hansen	(Salford)
Arnold Hema	(Bramley)
Brad Hepi	(Workington T.)
Greg Hiley	(Keighley C.)
Craig Innes	(Leeds)
*Kevin Iro	(Leeds)
Brett Iti	(Bradford N., Carlisle)
Clarry Iti	(Doncaster)
Jason Kerapa	(Highfield, London C.)
Moses Keresoma	(Barrow)
Wayne Kohlhase	(Chorley B., Workington T.)
Chris Kolose	(Barrow)
*Mike Kuiti	(Rochdale H.)
Charlie McAlister	(Keighley C., Sheffield E., Whitehaven)
*Jarrod McCracken	(St. Helens)
*Duane Mann	(Warrington)
*George Mann	(St. Helens)
*Gary Mercer	(Leeds)
Craig Montford	(Carlisle)
*Tawera Nikau	(Castleford)
*Sam Panapa	(Wigan)
Neville Ramsey	(London C.)
Mark Riley	(London C.)
Iva Ropati	(Oldham)
*Tea Ropati	(St. Helens)
Darrall Shelford	(Bradford N.)
*Kelly Shelford	(Warrington)
Dennis "Joe" Smith	(Blackpool G.)
Se'e Solomona	(Oldham)
*Kurt Sorensen	(Widnes)
*Brent Stuart	(Halifax)
George Suafoa	(Whitehaven)
Peter Subritzky	(Doncaster)
Wayne Taekata	(Featherstone R.)
Lawrence Tagaloa	(Barrow)
Shane Tupaea	(Oldham)
*Brendon Tuuta	(Featherstone R.)
Vaughan Watene	(Chorley B.)
*Dave Watson	(Bradford N.)
Jason Watts	(Blackpool G.)
Sonny Whakarau	(Bramley)

FIJI (1)

James Pickering	(Workington T.)

FRANCE (2)

Dazi Abderaman	(London C.)
*Daniel Divet	(Hull)

KENYA (2)
Eric Kibe   (Nottingham C.)
Eddie Rombo   (Dewsbury)

RUSSIA (1)
Andre Sokolov   (London C.)

SOUTH AFRICA (3)
Jamie Bloem   (Castleford, Oldham)
Mark Johnson   (London C.)
Andre Stoop   (Wigan)

TONGA (2)
Lee Hansen   (Leigh)
*[1]Emosi Koloto   (Halifax, Widnes)
*[1] New Zealand Test player

*Fijian James Pickering on the rampage for Workington Town
in the 1993 Stones Bitter Divisional Premiership final at Old Trafford.*

RECORD TRANSFERS

The first £1,000 transfer came in 1921 when Harold Buck joined Leeds from Hunslet, although there were reports at the time that another player was involved in the deal to make up the four-figure transfer. Other claims for the first £1,000 transfer are attached to Stan Brogden's move from Bradford Northern to Huddersfield in 1929. The following list shows how transfer fees have grown this century in straight cash deals only:

Season	Player	Position	From	To	Fee
1901-02	Jim Lomas	Centre	Bramley	Salford	£100
1910-11	Jim Lomas	Centre	Salford	Oldham	£300
1912-13	Billy Batten	Centre	Hunslet	Hull	£600
1921-22	Harold Buck	Wing	Hunslet	Leeds	£1,000
1929-30	Stanley Smith	Wing	Wakefield T.	Leeds	£1,075
1933-34	Stanley Brogden	Wing/centre	Huddersfield	Leeds	£1,200
1937-38	Billy Belshaw	Full back	Liverpool S.	Warrington	£1,450
1946-47	Bill Davies	Full back/centre	Huddersfield	Dewsbury	£1,650

1947-48	Bill Hudson	Forward	Batley	Wigan	£2,000	
1947-48	Jim Ledgard	Full back	Dewsbury	Leigh	£2,650	
1948-49	Ike Owens	Forward	Leeds	Castleford	£2,750	
1948-49	Ike Owens	Forward	Castleford	Huddersfield	£2,750	
1948-49	Stan McCormick	Wing	Belle Vue R.	St. Helens	£4,000	
1949-50	Albert Naughton	Centre	Widnes	Warrington	£4,600	
1950-51	Bruce Ryan	Wing	Hull	Leeds	£4,750	
1950-51	Joe Egan	Hooker	Wigan	Leigh	£5,000	
1950-51	Harry Street	Forward	Dewsbury	Wigan	£5,000	
1957-58	Mick Sullivan	Wing	Huddersfield	Wigan	£9,500	
1958-59	Ike Southward	Wing	Workington T.	Oldham	£10,650	
1960-61	Mick Sullivan	Wing	Wigan	St. Helens	£11,000	
1960-61	Ike Southward	Wing	Oldham	Workington T.	£11,002 10	
1968-69	Colin Dixon	Forward	Halifax	Salford	£12,000	
1969-70	Paul Charlton	Full back	Workington T.	Salford	£12,500	
1972-73	Eric Prescott	Forward	St. Helens	Salford	£13,500	
1975-76	Steve Nash	Scrum half	Featherstone R.	Salford	£15,000	
1977-78	Bill Ashurst	Forward	Wigan	Wakefield T.	£18,000	
1978-79	Clive Pickerill	Scrum half	Castleford	Hull	£20,000	
1978-79	Phil Hogan	Forward	Barrow	Hull K.R.	£35,000	
1979-80	Len Casey	Forward	Bradford N.	Hull K.R.	£38,000	
1980-81	Trevor Skerrett	Forward	Wakefield T.	Hull	£40,000	
1980-81	George Fairbairn	Full back	Wigan	Hull K.R.	£72,500	
1985-86	Ellery Hanley	Centre/stand off	Bradford N.	Wigan	£85,000	
1985-86	Joe Lydon	Centre	Widnes	Wigan	£100,000	
1986-87	Andy Gregory	Scrum half	Warrington	Wigan	£130,000	
1987-88	Lee Crooks	Forward	Hull	Leeds	£150,000	
1987-88	Garry Schofield	Centre	Hull	Leeds	£155,000	
1989-90	Graham Steadman	Stand off	Featherstone R.	Castleford	£170,000	
1991-92	Ellery Hanley	Forward	Wigan	Leeds	£250,000	
1991-92	Martin Offiah	Winger	Widnes	Wigan	£440,000	

MOST MOVES

Geoff Clarkson extended his record number of transfers to 12 when he left Leigh for Featherstone Rovers on 27 October 1983. He played for 10 different English clubs and had a brief spell in Australia.

Clarkson, born on 12 August 1943, was 40 years old when he finished playing regular first team rugby in 1983-84. He turned professional with Wakefield Trinity in 1966 after gaining Yorkshire County forward honours with Wakefield Rugby Union Club. Clarkson's club career in England is as follows:

1966 — Wakefield T.
1968 — Bradford N.
1970 — Leigh
1971 — Warrington
1972 — Leeds
1975 — York
1976 — Bramley
1978 — Wakefield T. and Hull K.R.
1980 — Bradford N. and Oldham
1981 — Leigh
1983 — Featherstone R.

Stones Bitter Man of Steel 1993, Wigan prop Andy Pla who was chosen as Great Britain's Player of the Tour on 1992 British Lions trip Down Und

AWARDS

THE 1993 MAN OF STEEL AWARDS
Launched in the 1976-77 season, the Rugby
Football League's official awards are presented
to the Man of Steel, the personality judged to
have made the biggest impact on the season;
the First, Second and Third Division Players
of the Year, decided by a ballot of the
players; the Young Player of the Year, under-21
at the start of the season; the Coach of the
Year and Referee of the Year, all chosen by a
panel of judges, including Great Britain coach
Malcolm Reilly.

The official award scheme was sponsored
by Trumanns Steel from inception in 1977 to
1983, brewers Greenall Whitley taking over in
1984 until 1989. Stones Bitter took over
sponsorship in 1990.

Stones Bitter Man of Steel
Wigan prop **Andy Platt,** Great Britain's Player
of the Tour on the 1992 British Lions visit
Down Under, took the coveted title and a
prize of £4,000 and a £300 silver champagne
goblet, plus the new Man of Steel trophy.
Platt, recently voted the world's number one
prop, was the cornerstone of Wigan's four-
trophy side. He became only the sixth forward to
gain 25 Test caps and in April 1993 captained
Britain for the first time.

Stones Bitter First Division Player
St. Helens stand off **Tea Ropati** topped the
ballot of fellow Stones Bitter Championship
players with a record poll of votes. The club's
only ever-present with 40 appearances, scoring
134 points including 21 tries.

Stones Bitter Second Division Player
Great Britain, England and Featherstone Rovers
threequarter **Paul Newlove** was the choice of
fellow players in the eight-club Second Division.
The 1992 British Lion scored a club record 48
tries in a final tally of 52, a British record for a
centre.

Stones Bitter Third Division Player
Loose forward **Martin Wood,** an inspiration
in Keighley Cougars' title-winning side, was
the players' selection in the Third Division.
The former Halifax and Scarborough Pirates
forward scored 27 tries in 29 appearances to
finish joint ninth in the try chart.

Stones Bitter Young Player
Wigan utility player **Jason Robinson** crowned
his first season in the first team by adding the
title of Young Player of the Year to his four
winners' medals. Scorer of 13 tries in 40
appearances, Robinson played full back, wing,
stand off, scrum half and loose forward for the
Riversiders, being capped for Great Britain
Under-21s in the number seven jersey.

Stones Bitter Referee of the Year
Wigan whistler **John Connolly** took the Referee
of the Year award in only his third season as a
senior official. Connolly topped the referees'
marking chart and took charge of the Stones
Bitter Divisional Premiership Final, being denied
other top appointments by Wigan's involvement.

Stones Bitter Coach of the Year
Australian **John Monie** marked his departure
for a post with the newly-formed Auckland
Warriors by lifting the Coach of the Year title
for a fourth successive season, extending his
own record. Monie masterminded a four trophy
haul of Championship, Challenge Cup, Regal
Trophy and Lancashire Cup.

● Each of the above six category winners
received £1,000 and a £250 silver wine goblet.

	Man of Steel	First Division Player	Second Division Player	Young Player	Coach	Referee
1977	David Ward (Leeds)	Malcolm Reilly (Castleford)	Ged Marsh (Blackpool B.)	David Ward (Leeds)	Eric Ashton (St. Helens)	Billy Thompson (Huddersfield)
1978	George Nicholls (St. Helens)	George Nicholls (St. Helens)	John Woods (Leigh)	John Woods (Leigh)	Frank Myler (Widnes)	Billy Thompson (Huddersfield)
1979	Doug Laughton (Widnes)	Mick Adams (Widnes)	Steve Norton (Hull)	Steve Evans (Featherstone R.)	Doug Laughton (Widnes)	Mick Naughton (Widnes)
1980	George Fairbairn (Wigan)	Mick Adams (Widnes)	Steve Quinn (Featherstone R.)	Roy Holdstock (Hull K.R.)	Peter Fox (Bradford N.)	Fred Lindop (Wakefield)
1981	Ken Kelly (Warrington)	Ken Kelly (Warrington)	John Crossley (York)	Des Drummond (Leigh)	Billy Benyon (Warrington)	John Holdsworth (Kippax)
1982	Mick Morgan (Carlisle)	Steve Norton (Hull)	Mick Morgan (Carlisle)	Des Drummond (Leigh)	Arthur Bunting (Hull)	Fred Lindop (Wakefield)
1983	Allan Agar (Featherstone R.)	Keith Mumby (Bradford N.)	Steve Nash (Salford)	Brian Noble (Bradford N.)	Arthur Bunting (Hull)	Robin Whitfield (Widnes)
1984	Joe Lydon (Widnes)	Joe Lydon (Widnes)	David Cairns (Barrow)	Joe Lydon (Widnes)	Tommy Dawes (Barrow)	Billy Thompson (Huddersfield)
1985	Ellery Hanley (Bradford N.)	Ellery Hanley (Bradford N.)	Graham Steadman (York)	Lee Crooks (Hull)	Roger Millward (Hull K.R.)	Ron Campbell (Widnes)
1986	Gavin Miller (Hull K.R.)	Gavin Miller (Hull K.R.)	Derek Pyke (Leigh)	Shaun Edwards (Wigan)	Chris Anderson (Halifax)	Fred Lindop (Wakefield)
1987	Ellery Hanley (Wigan)	Ellery Hanley (Wigan)	John Cogger (Runcorn H.)	Shaun Edwards (Wigan)	Graham Lowe (Wigan)	John Holdsworth (Kippax)
1988	Martin Offiah (Widnes)	Steve Hampson (Wigan)	Peter Smith (Featherstone R.)	Shaun Edwards (Wigan)	Doug Laughton (Widnes)	Fred Lindop (Wakefield)
1989	Ellery Hanley (Wigan)	David Hulme (Widnes)	Daryl Powell (Sheffield E.)	Paul Newlove (Featherstone R.)	Graham Lowe (Wigan)	John Holdsworth (Kippax)
1990	Shaun Edwards (Wigan)	Andy Goodway (Wigan)	John Woods (Rochdale H.)	Bobby Goulding (Wigan)	John Monie (Wigan)	Robin Whitfield (Widnes)

	Man of Steel	1st Division Player	2nd Division Player	3rd Division Player	Young Player	Coach	Referee
1991	Garry Schofield (Leeds)	Jonathan Davies (Widnes)	Tawera Nikau (Ryedale-York)	—	Denis Betts (Wigan)	John Monie (Wigan)	John Holdsworth (Kippax)
1992	Dean Bell (Wigan)	Graham Steadman (Castleford)	Iva Ropati (Oldham)	Wally Gibson (Huddersfield)	Gary Connolly (St. Helens)	John Monie (Wigan)	Robin Whitfield (Widnes)
1993	Andy Platt (Wigan)	Tea Ropati (St. Helens)	Paul Newlove (Featherstone R.)	Martin Wood (Keighley C.)	Jason Robinson (Wigan)	John Monie (Wigan)	John Connolly (Wigan)

NOMINEES:

1977 *1st Division Player:* Bruce Burton (Castleford), Vince Farrar (Featherstone R.). *2nd Division Player:* Jeff Grayshon (Dewsbury), Keith Hepworth (Hull). *Young Player:* Jimmy Crampton (Hull), Harry Pinner (St. Helens). *Coach:* Keith Cotton (Featherstone R.), Mal Reilly (Castleford). *Referee:* Joe Jackson (Pudsey), Mick Naughton (Widnes).

1978 *1st Division Player:* Roger Millward (Hull K.R.), Harry Pinner (St. Helens). *2nd Division Player:* Phil Hogan (Barrow), Mick Morgan (York). *Young Player:* Neil Hague (Leeds), Keith Mumby (Bradford N.). *Coach:* Eric Ashton MBE (St. Helens), John Mantle (Leigh). *Referee:* Ron Campbell (Widnes), Fred Lindop (Wakefield).

1979 *1st Division Player:* Brian Lockwood (Hull K.R.), Tommy Martyn (Warrington). *2nd Division Player:* Barry Banks (York), John Wolford (Dewsbury). *Young Player:* Mick Burke (Widnes), John Woods (Leigh). *Coach:* Billy Benyon (Warrington), Arthur Bunting (Hull). *Referee:* Fred Lindop (Wakefield), Billy Thompson (Huddersfield).

1980 *1st Division Player:* Len Casey (Hull K.R.), George Fairbairn (Wigan). *2nd Division Player:* Mick Blacker (Halifax), John Wolford (Dewsbury). *Young Player:* Steve Hubbard (Hull K.R.), Harry Pinner (St. Helens). *Coach:* Maurice Bamford (Halifax), Arthur Bunting (Hull). *Referee:* Ron Campbell (Widnes), Billy Thompson (Huddersfield).

1981 *1st Division Player:* Mick Adams (Widnes), Tommy Martyn (Warrington). *2nd Division Player:* Arnie Walker (Whitehaven), Danny Wilson (Swinton). *Young Player:* Paul Harkin (Hull K.R.), Keith Mumby (Bradford N.). *Coach:* Reg Bowden (Fulham), Peter Fox (Bradford N.). *Referee:* Ron Campbell (Widnes), Fred Lindop (Wakefield).

1982 *1st Division Player:* Jeff Grayshon (Bradford N.), Andy Gregory (Widnes). *2nd Division Player:* Denis Boyd (Carlisle), Alan Fairhurst (Swinton). *Young Player:* Lee Crooks (Hull), Andy Gregory (Widnes). *Coach:* Doug Laughton (Widnes), Alex Murphy/Colin Clarke (Leigh). *Referee:* Gerry Kershaw (York), Billy Thompson (Huddersfield).

1983 *1st Division Player:* Bob Eccles (Warrington), David Topliss (Hull). *2nd Division Player:* Tommy David (Cardiff C.), Mike Lampkowski (Wakefield T.). *Young Player:* Ronnie Duane (Warrington), Andy Goodway (Oldham). *Coach:* Alex Murphy (Wigan), Frank Myler (Oldham). *Referee:* John Holdsworth (Leeds), Fred Lindop (Wakefield).

1984 *1st Division Player:* Garry Schofield (Hull), John Woods (Leigh). *2nd Division Player:* Lynn Hopkins (Workington T.), John Wolford (Hunslet). *Young Player:* Gary Divorty (Hull), Garry Schofield (Hull). *Coach:* Arthur Bunting (Hull), Roger Millward (Hull K.R.). *Referee:* Derek Fox (Wakefield), Fred Lindop (Wakefield).

1985 *1st Division Player:* Harry Pinner (St. Helens), Gary Prohm (Hull K.R.). *2nd Division Player:* Terry Langton (Mansfield M.), Peter Wood (Runcorn H.). *Young Player:* Deryck Fox (Featherstone R.), Andy Platt (St. Helens). *Coach:* Arthur Bunting (Hull), Colin Clarke/Alan McInnes (Wigan). *Referee:* Fred Lindop (Wakefield), Stan Wall (Leigh).

1986 *1st Division Player:* Steve Ella (Wigan), John Fieldhouse (Widnes). *2nd Division Player:* John Henderson (Leigh), Graham King (Hunslet). *Young Player:* Paul Lyman (Featherstone R.), Roy Powell (Leeds). *Coach:* Roger Millward (Hull K.R.), John Sheridan (Doncaster). *Referee:* John Holdsworth (Kippax), Robin Whitfield (Widnes).

1987 *1st Division Player:* Lee Crooks (Hull), Ellery Hanley (Wigan). *2nd Division Player:* Andy Bateman (Hunslet), Les Holliday (Swinton). *Young Player:* Paul Loughlin (St. Helens), Kevin McCormack (St. Helens). *Coach:* Chris Anderson (Halifax), Alex Murphy (St. Helens). *Referee:* Kevin Allatt (Southport), Fred

1988 *1st Division Player:* Martin Offiah (Widnes), Kurt Sorensen (Widnes). *2nd Division Player:* Deryck Fox (Featherstone R.), Hugh Waddell (Oldham). *Young Player:* Paul Medley (Leeds), Steve Robinson (Halifax). *Coach:* Alex Murphy (St. Helens), Barry Seabourne (Bradford N.). *Referee:* John Holdsworth (Kippax), Ray Tennant (Castleford).

1989 *1st Division Player:* Andy Gregory (Wigan), Kelvin Skerrett (Bradford N.). *2nd Division Player:* Cavill Heugh (Barrow), Chris Johnson (Leigh). *Young Player:* Grant Anderson (Castleford), Denis Betts (Wigan). *Coach:* Peter Fox (Featherstone R.), Brian Smith (Hull). *Referee:* Ray Tennant (Castleford), Robin Whitfield (Widnes).

1990 *1st Division Player:* Deryck Fox (Featherstone R.), Andy Platt (Wigan). *2nd Division Player:* David Bishop (Hull K.R.), John Cogger (Oldham). *Young Player:* Denis Betts (Wigan), Anthony Sullivan (Hull K.R.). *Coach:* Tony Barrow (Oldham), Brian Johnson (Warrington). *Referee:* John Holdsworth (Kippax), Colin Morris (Huddersfield).

1991 *1st Division Player:* Andy Gregory (Wigan), George Mann (St. Helens). *2nd Division Player:* Steve Kerry (Salford), Peter Ropati (Leigh). *Young Player:* Phil Clarke (Wigan), Craig Richards (Bradford N.). *Coach:* Ray Ashton (Workington T.), Doug Laughton (Widnes). *Referee:* Brian Galtress (Bradford), Jim Smith (Halifax).

1992 *1st Division Player:* Dean Bell (Wigan), John Devereux (Widnes). *2nd Division Player:* Clayton Friend (Carlisle), Paul Topping (Leigh). *3rd Division Player:* Steve Carroll (Bramley), Paul Delaney (Dewsbury). *Young Player:* Paul Newlove (Featherstone R.), David Myers (Wigan). *Coach:* Alex Murphy (Huddersfield), Darryl Van de Velde (Castleford). *Referee:* Stuart Cummings (Widnes), John Holdsworth (Kippax).

1993 *1st Division Player:* Phil Clarke (Wigan), Andy Platt (Wigan). *2nd Division Player:* Neil Flanagan (Huddersfield), Brendon Tuuta (Featherstone R.). *3rd Division Player:* Clayton Friend (Whitehaven), Brad Hepi (Workington T.). *Young Player:* Chris Joynt (St. Helens), Nigel Wright (Wakefield T.). *Coach:* Peter Fox (Bradford N.), Mike McClennan (St. Helens). *Referee:* John Holdsworth (Kippax), Russell Smith (Castleford).

Great Britain and Featherstone Rovers centre Paul Newlove, Stones Bitter Second Division Player of the Year and most tries award-winner.

425

STONES BITTER TEAM OF THE MONTH AWARDS 1992-93

Introduced in the 1979-80 season, the scheme acknowledges the adjudged Team of the Month in each division.

A panel of judges representing Stones Bitter and the Rugby League selected the three monthly winners, the First Division winners receiving £500, the Second Division £350, the Third Division £250, plus a framed citation.

The awards were sponsored for the first four seasons by Shopacheck before Lada Cars took over in the 1983-84 season and introduced the first-ever Team of the Year title. Stones Bitter took over the sponsorship in 1987-88, the 1993 Team of the Year, **Wigan,** receiving £1,500. A Third Division award was introduced in 1991-92.

	First Division	Second Division
Aug./Sept.	St. Helens	Oldham
Oct.	Bradford N.	Featherstone R.
Nov.	Castleford	Huddersfield
Dec.	Hull	Featherstone R.
Jan.	Widnes	Oldham
Feb.	Wigan	Featherstone R.
Mar.	Wigan	Swinton
Apr./May	Wigan	Featherstone R.

Third Division
Ryedale-York
Batley
Hunslet
Whitehaven
Keighley C.
Workington T.
Keighley C.
Workington T.

Team of the Year
1983-84: Widnes
1984-85: Hull K.R.
1985-86: Halifax
1986-87: Wigan
1987-88: Widnes
1988-89: Wigan
1989-90: Wigan
1990-91: Wigan
1991-92: Wigan
1992-93: Wigan

WALLACE ARNOLD – SUNDAY MIRROR ENTERTAINER AWARDS 1992-93

Introduced in 1986-87, the scheme was sponsored by Wallace Arnold and promoted by the *Sunday Mirror.*

Each month a player was chosen as Entertainer of the Month to receive a Wallace Arnold holiday voucher for £400. The Entertainer of the Year was awarded a £1,500 holiday voucher, the 1993 winner being Wigan half back **Frano Botica,** who broke the club goals and points records.

Entertainer of the Month

Sept.	Alan Hunte (St. Helens)
Oct.	Deryck Fox (Bradford N.)
Nov.	Mike Ford (Castleford)
Dec.	Lee Jackson (Hull)
Jan.	John Wasyliw (Keighley C.)
Feb.	Andy Currier (Widnes)
Mar.	Jason Robinson (Wigan)
Apr./May	Paul Newlove (Featherstone R.)

Entertainer of the Year

1987:	Ellery Hanley (Wigan)
1988:	Martin Offiah (Widnes)
1989:	Martin Offiah (Widnes)
1990:	Deryck Fox (Featherstone R.)
1991:	Garry Schofield (Leeds)
1992:	Shaun Edwards (Wigan)
1993:	Frano Botica (Wigan)

STONES BITTER TOP SCORERS AWARDS 1992-93

Launched in the 1976-77 season, the scheme was designed to reward the top try and goal scorers in the League. Sponsored by Stones Bitter, the 1993 awards were worth £30 a try and £10 a goal.

The top try merchant was Featherstone Rovers centre **Paul Newlove** who touched down 52 times to earn a prize cheque for £1,560.

The top marksman was Keighley Cougars winger **John Wasyliw** who hit the target 187 times to qualify for a prize pay-out of £1,870.

REFEREES

REFEREES' HONOURS 1992-93

Silk Cut Challenge Cup final:
Russell Smith

Regal Trophy final:
John Holdsworth

Stones Bitter Premiership final:
John Holdsworth

Divisional Premiership final:
John Connolly

Greenalls Lancashire Cup final:
Stuart Cummings

John Smiths Yorkshire Cup final:
Russell Smith

France v Wales:
Robin Whitfield

CIS Insurance Charity Shield:
Stuart Cummings

Cumbria v Australia:
Colin Morris

SENIOR REFEREES 1993-94

DAVID ASQUITH (York)
Date of birth: 20.6.53
Grade One: 1989-90

DAVID ATKIN (Hull)
Date of birth: 19.12.64
Grade One: 1992-93

GEOFF BERRY (Batley)
Date of birth: 26.4.54
Grade Two: 1981-82
Grade One: 1983-84

ALAN BURKE (Oldham)
Date of birth: 21.1.57
Grade One: 1987-88
Lancashire Cup 1990-91

DAVID CAMPBELL (St. Helens)
Date of birth: 9.10.54
Grade One: 1989-90
Lancashire Cup 1991-92

DAVE CARTER (Widnes)
Date of birth: 29.11.55
Grade One: 1984-85
France v Great Britain Under-21s 1988-89

JOHN CONNOLLY (Wigan)
Date of birth: 30.9.59
Grade One: 1990-91
Divisional Premiership 1992-93

ROBERT CONNOLLY (Wigan)
Date of birth: 30.9.59
Grade One: 1990-91

PAUL CRASHLEY (Wakefield)
Date of birth: 1.8.50
Grade One: 1989-90

STEVE CROSS (Hull)
Date of birth: 23.3.50
Grade One: 1986-87

STUART CUMMINGS (Widnes)
Date of birth: 17.11.60
Grade One: 1991-92
Divisional Premiership 1991-92
Lancashire Cup 1992-93
Charity Shield 1992-93

BRIAN GALTRESS (Bradford)
Date of birth: 8.10.51
Grade One: 1988-89
Regal Trophy 1991-92
Second Division Premiership 1990-91
France v Great Britain Under-21s 1990-91

STEPHEN HAIGH (Ossett)
Date of birth: 5.4.45
Grade Two: 1980-81
Grade One: 1983-84

JOHN HOLDSWORTH (Kippax)
Date of birth: 25.1.47
Grade Two: 1979-80
Grade One: 1980-81
Challenge Cup 1986-87, 1989-90
Regal Trophy 1985-86, 1986-87, 1988-89, 1992-93
Premiership Trophy 1980-81, 1987-88, 1988-89,
  1990-91, 1991-92, 1992-93
Lancashire Cup 1982-83, 1985-86
Yorkshire Cup 1991-92
World Club Challenge 1987-88
Australia v New Zealand (3) 1991
France v Australia (2) 1990-91
Wales v England 1980-81
Great Britain v Rest of World 1988-89
RL Chairman's XIII v Papua New Guinea 1987-88
Cumbria v Yorkshire 1981-82
France v Great Britain Under-24s 1982-83
War of the Roses 1987-88
Charity Shield 1987-88, 1989-90

REFEREES

JOHN KENDREW (Castleford)
Date of birth: 22.4.50
Grade Two: 1982-83
Grade One: 1983-84
Lancashire v Papua New Guinea 1987-88

GERRY KERSHAW (Easingwold)
Date of birth: 24.10.43
Grade Two: 1969-70
Grade One: 1970-71
Challenge Cup 1980-81
Lancashire Cup 1980-81
Floodlit Trophy 1973-74
Regal Trophy 1973-74, 1989-90
Wales v England 1981-82
Wales v Australia 1982-83
France v Great Britain Under-24s 1981-82
Lancashire v Yorkshire 1971-72
Lancashire v Cumbria 1972-73
Cumbria v Other Nationalities 1974-75
Cumbria v Lancashire 1978-79, 1980-81
War of the Roses 1989-90

IAN McGREGOR (Huddersfield)
Date of birth: 27.12.53
Grade One: 1993-94

COLIN MORRIS (Huddersfield)
Date of birth: 11.3.57
Grade One: 1989-90
Premiership Trophy 1989-90
Papua New Guinea v France 1991
France v Papua New Guinea 1991-92
Wales v France 1991-92
Russia v France 1992
France v Great Britain Under-21s 1989-90
Charity Shield 1990-91
Cumbria v Papua New Guinea 1991-92
Cumbria v Australia 1992-93
War of the Roses 1991-92

STEVE NICHOLSON (Whitehaven)
Date of birth: 5.4.61
Grade One: 1992-93

IAN OLLERTON (Wigan)
Date of birth: 31.3.53
Grade One: 1990-91

STEVE PRESLEY (Castleford)
Date of birth: 4.4.57
Grade One: 1993-94

JIM SMITH (Halifax)
Date of birth: 2.3.44
Grade Two: 1977-78
Grade One: 1983-84
Challenge Cup 1990-91
Regal Trophy 1990-91
Yorkshire Cup 1990-91
Lancashire Cup 1986-87

RUSSELL SMITH (Castleford)
Date of birth: 24.1.64
Grade One: 1991-92
Challenge Cup 1992-93
Yorkshire Cup 1992-93
France v Great Britain Under-21s 1991-92

COLIN STEELE (Dalton-in-Furness)
Date of birth: 11.9.60
Grade One: 1987-88
Cumbria v France 1988-89

PAUL VOLANTE (Birstall)
Date of birth: 30.6.52
Grade One: 1983-84

JOHN WHITELAM (Hull)
Date of birth: 11.5.53
Grade One: 1988-89

ROBIN WHITFIELD (Widnes)
Date of birth: 26.11.43
Grade Two: 1979-80
Grade One: 1980-81
Challenge Cup 1982-83, 1985-86, 1991-92
Yorkshire Cup 1981-82, 1988-89
Second Division Premiership 1987-88, 1988-89, 1989-90
France v Australia (2) 1982-83
France v New Zealand (2) 1989-90
New Zealand v Australia 1983
Australia v New Zealand (3) 1986
France v Wales 1992-93
Yorkshire v Lancashire 1981-82
Charity Shield 1991-92
War of the Roses 1988-89

NEIL WOOD (Keighley)
Date of birth: 12.7.62
Grade One: 1992-93

THE ALLIANCE

YOUNGER'S ALLIANCE 1992-93

FIRST DIVISION

	P.	W.	D.	L.	Dg.	FOR Gls.	FOR Trs.	FOR Pts.	Dg.	AGAINST Gls.	AGAINST Trs.	AGAINST Pts.	Pts.
Wigan	26	21	0	5	4	122	164	904	5	52	77	417	42
Castleford	26	19	2	5	0	96	120	672	6	64	71	418	40
Halifax	26	17	0	9	7	93	126	697	1	65	84	467	34
Warrington	26	15	0	11	8	84	99	572	4	58	100	520	30
Leeds	26	13	2	11	3	77	105	577	3	80	121	647	28
Widnes	26	13	0	13	0	87	119	650	3	104	123	703	26
Hull	26	13	0	13	6	90	111	630	3	83	100	569	26
Wakefield T.	26	12	1	13	1	68	113	589	5	82	115	629	25
Featherstone R.	26	12	1	13	3	82	90	527	3	79	116	625	25
Batley	26	11	0	15	7	64	73	427	5	78	122	649	22
Bradford N.	26	10	0	16	1	60	93	493	6	91	104	604	20
St. Helens	26	9	0	17	10	71	109	588	5	109	116	687	18
Hull K.R.	26	8	1	17	5	64	80	453	6	98	117	670	17
Rochdale H.	26	5	1	20	3	92	88	539	3	107	124	713	11

SECOND DIVISION

	P.	W.	D.	L.	Dg.	FOR Gls.	FOR Trs.	FOR Pts.	Dg.	AGAINST Gls.	AGAINST Trs.	AGAINST Pts.	Pts.
Salford	22	19	0	3	5	111	150	827	2	32	51	270	38
Ryedale-York	22	18	1	3	5	103	135	751	2	45	56	316	37
Workington T.	22	14	0	8	4	74	101	556	2	70	80	462	28
Dewsbury	22	13	2	7	6	62	95	510	3	56	49	311	28
Leigh	22	13	1	8	6	93	92	560	2	56	61	358	27
Sheffield E.	22	13	1	8	7	77	79	477	5	59	80	443	27
Oldham	22	11	0	11	1	95	106	615	6	74	89	510	22
Swinton	22	10	1	11	1	60	95	501	1	76	105	573	21
Bramley	22	10	0	12	2	61	71	408	6	71	91	512	20
Hemel Hempstead	22	9	1	12	3	59	70	401	3	85	105	593	19
Keighley C.	22	8	3	11	2	50	81	426	3	82	113	619	19
Hunslet	22	8	0	14	5	73	82	479	6	74	98	546	16
Huddersfield	22	8	0	14	2	56	62	362	6	80	106	590	16
Doncaster	22	7	0	15	1	53	74	403	3	80	104	579	14
London C.	22	5	2	15	2	59	66	384	2	82	110	606	12
Carlisle	22	3	2	17	1	35	70	351	1	99	131	723	8

YOUNGER'S ALLIANCE CHALLENGE CUP 1993

First Round

Batley	36	Swinton	4	Leigh	8	Halifax	4
Carlisle	18	Doncaster	22	Rochdale H.	18	Wakefield T.	28
Huddersfield	34	Hemel Hempstead	16	St. Helens	24	Ryedale-York	28
Hull	27	Castleford	14	Salford	16	Dewsbury	18
Hunslet	14	Bramley	13	Sheffield E.	22	Hull K.R.	12
Keighley C.	14	Warrington	42	Wigan	66	London C.	6
Leeds	38	Featherstone R.	22				

Walk over: Oldham
Byes: Bradford N., Widnes

Second Round

Batley	8	Warrington	17
Doncaster	12	Ryedale-York	20
Hull	40	Bradford N.	10
Hunslet	6	Leigh	46
Leeds	60	Huddersfield	16
Oldham	22	Wigan	22
Sheffield E.	12	Dewsbury	26
Widnes	42	Wakefield T.	4

Replay

Wigan	32	Oldham	14

Third Round

Dewsbury	10	Leeds	18
Ryedale-York	22	Hull	30
Warrington	19	Wigan	30
Widnes	36	Leigh	12

Semi-Finals

Leeds	18	Hull	17
Wigan	49	Widnes	22

Final

Leeds	8	Wigan	32

YOUNGER'S ALLIANCE SECOND DIVISION CUP 1993

First Round

Bramley	0	Ryedale-York	38
Carlisle	20	Workington T.	34
Huddersfield	24	Swinton	20
Hunslet	13	Sheffield E.	10
Keighley C.	8	Dewsbury	22
Leigh	16	Hemel Hempstead	6
London C.	10	Salford	38
Oldham	64	Doncaster	8

Second Round

Leigh	44	Hunslet	2
Ryedale-York	16	Huddersfield	8
Salford	22	Dewsbury	14
Workington T.	26	Oldham	16

Semi-Finals

Leigh	39	Workington T.	6
Salford	21	Ryedale-York	6

Final

Salford	56	Leigh	12

LANCASHIRE COMBINATION CHALLENGE SHIELD 1992-93

First Round

Hemel Hempstead	8	Rochdale H.	42
Oldham	26	Carlisle	22
Salford	44	Workington T.	12
Wigan	64	Swinton	14

Byes: Leigh, St. Helens, Warrington and Widnes

Second Round

Leigh	24	Warrington	28
Oldham	4	Wigan	34
Salford	20	St. Helens	10
Widnes	20	Rochdale H.	14

Semi-Finals

Widnes	18	Salford	24
Wigan	16	Warrington	20

Final

Warrington	13	Salford	30

YORKSHIRE SENIOR COMPETITION CHALLENGE CUP 1992-93

Preliminary Round

Halifax	38	Doncaster	8

First Round

Batley	19	Ryedale-York	12
Bradford N.	14	Wakefield T.	17
Bramley	26	Huddersfield	18
Halifax	20	Castleford	8
Hull K.R.	6	Hull	8
Keighley C.	8	Dewsbury	22
Leeds	26	Featherstone R.	14
Sheffield E.	16	Hunslet	12

Second Round

Batley	0	Leeds	64
Dewsbury	11	Bramley	14
Hull	24	Halifax	22
Wakefield T.	38	Sheffield E.	14

Semi-Finals

Bramley	12	Wakefield T.	22
Hull	19	Leeds	6

Final

Hull	30	Wakefield T.	4

YOUNGER'S ALLIANCE PLAYER OF THE YEAR
1993: Chris Kelly (Widnes)

POT POURRI

DIARY OF LANDMARKS

1895 August 29... the beginning. The Northern Rugby Football Union formed at The George Hotel, Huddersfield, following the breakaway from the English RU by 21 clubs who wanted to pay players for taking time off work to play.
September 7... season opens with 22 clubs.
Joseph Platt appointed Rugby League Secretary.

1897 April 24... Batley won the first Northern Union — later Rugby League — Challenge Cup final.
Line-out abolished and replaced by punt from touch.
All goals to be worth two points.

1898 Professionalism allowed but players must be in full-time employment.

1899 Scrum if player cannot release the ball after a tackle.

1901 Punt from touch replaced by 10-yard scrum when ball is carried into touch.

1902 Two divisions introduced.
Punt from touch abolished completely.
Touch-finding rule introduced with the ball having to bounce before entering touch.

1905 Two divisions scrapped.
Lancashire and Yorkshire County Cup competitions inaugurated.

1906 Thirteen-a-side introduced, from traditional 15.
Play-the-ball introduced.

1907 First tour — New Zealand to England. The tour party were RU 'rebels'.
First Top Four play-off for championship.

1908 Australia and New Zealand launch Rugby League.
First Australian tour of England.

1910 First British tour of Australia and New Zealand.

1915 Competitive rugby suspended for duration of First World War.

1919 Competitive rugby resumed in January.

1920 John Wilson appointed Rugby League Secretary.

1922 Title of Northern Rugby Football Union changed to Rugby Football League.
Goal from a mark abolished.

1927 First radio broadcast of Challenge Cup final — Oldham v. Swinton at Wigan.

1929 Wembley staged its first RL Challenge Cup final — Wigan v. Dewsbury.

1932 London exhibition match under floodlights at White City — Leeds v. Wigan.

1933 France staged its first Rugby League match — an exhibition between England and Australia in Paris.
London Highfield, formerly Wigan Highfield, became capital's first Rugby League team, also first to play regularly under floodlights.

1934 A French squad made a short tour of England before Rugby League was officially launched in France.

1935 European Championship introduced, contested by England, France and Wales.

1939 Second World War. Emergency war-time competitions introduced.

1945 War-time emergencies over.
Bill Fallowfield appointed Rugby League Secretary.

1946 First all-ticket match — Hull v. Hull K.R.

1948 King George VI became first reigning monarch to attend Rugby League match — Wigan v. Bradford Northern Cup final at Wembley.
First televised match — at Wembley — but shown only in London area.
Wembley's first all-ticket final.
International Board formed.

1949 Welsh League formed.

1950 Italian squad made brief tour of England.

1951 First televised match in the North — Britain v. New Zealand at Swinton.
First floodlights installation by Northern club, Bradford Northern.

1952 First nationally televised Challenge Cup final — Workington Town v. Featherstone Rovers.

1954 First World Cup, staged in France.

1955	London staged series of televised floodlit matches for the Independent Television Association Trophy.
	Welsh League disbanded.
1956	Sunday rugby for amateurs permitted by the Rugby Football League.
1962	Two divisions reintroduced, with Eastern and Western Divisions also formed.
1964	Substitutes allowed for injuries, but only up to half-time.
	Two divisions and regional leagues scrapped. One league system with Top-16 play-off for championship.
1965	BBC-2 Floodlit Trophy competition began with regular Tuesday night series.
	Substitutes allowed for any reason up to and including half-time.
	English Schools Rugby League formed.
1966	Four-tackle rule introduced for Floodlit Trophy competition in October, then for all games from December.
1967	First Sunday fixtures played, two matches on December 17.
1969	Substitutes allowed at any time.
	Universities and Colleges Rugby League Association formed.
1971	John Player Trophy competition launched.
1972	Six-tackle rule introduced.
	Timekeepers with hooter system to signal end of match introduced.
	Colts League formed.
1973	Two divisions reintroduced.
	March 4... British Amateur Rugby League Association formed.
1974	Drop goal value halved to one point. Had been reduced earlier in international matches.
	David Oxley appointed Rugby League Secretary.
	David Howes appointed first full-time Public Relations Officer to the Rugby Football League.
	National Coaching Scheme launched.
1975	Premiership Trophy competition launched.
1976	Differential penalty introduced for technical scrum offences.
1977	County Championship not held for first time

	since 1895, excluding war years.
	Anglo-Australian transfer ban agreed.
1978	Papua New Guinea admitted as full member of International Board.
1981	Rugby League Professional Players Association formed.
1982	County Championship scrapped.
1983	January 1... Sin bin introduced.
	Try value increased to four points.
	Handover after sixth tackle introduced among several other new or amended law following meeting of International Board
	Anglo-Australian transfer ban lifted.
1984	Alliance League introduced in reserve grade reorganisation.
1985	First Charity Shield match played in Isle of Man.
	War of the Roses launched on Lancashire v. Yorkshire county of origin basis.
	Relegation-promotion reduced to three down three up.
1986	Relegation-promotion altered for one year only to four down, two up to provide a 14 strong First Division for the 1987-88 season.
1987	Division Two Premiership Trophy competition launched.
	New players' contracts system introduced Random drug testing introduced.
1988	Colts scrapped for new youth scheme.
	Six-man League Board of Directors appointed.
1990	Russia introduced Rugby League and sent 90-man squad on three-match tour to Britain
1991	Russian eight-club league launched.
	Three divisions introduced for 1991-92 season.
	Academy Under-18 league formed.
	Blood bin introduced.
1992	Maurice Lindsay appointed Rugby League Chief Executive on retirement of David Oxley.
	Ten-metre play-the-ball rule introduced.
1993	Two divisions reintroduced with three bottom clubs demoted to non-League status National pro-am Conference League launched County Cups scrapped.

432

DISCIPLINARY RECORDS

This sub-section is a compilation of sendings off and disciplinary verdicts for first team players.

The following information is based on the workings of the League's Disciplinary Committee which meets weekly during a season.

	1992-93	1991-92	1990-91	1989-90	1988-89
Barrow	3	6	5	5	4
Batley	4	7	4	1	2
Blackpool G.	0	6	2	9	2
Bradford N.	0	4	3	5	2
Bramley	4	2	5	4	2
Carlisle	6	2	4	0	4
Castleford	3	3	4	6	4
Chorley B.	0	5	7	3	—
Dewsbury	1	1	5	3	3
Doncaster	2	3	4	2	1
Featherstone R.	3	7	1	4	1
Halifax	1	2	3	8	1
Highfield	7	7	3	3	6
Huddersfield	6	2	1	7	3
Hull	3	2	1	3	1
Hull K.R.	0	1	3	3	3
Hunslet	3	2	6	6	5
Keighley C.	2	4	5	10	3
Leeds	1	2	5	3	0
Leigh	1	3	1	7	3
London C.	5	2	1	4	0
Nottingham C.	2	2	2	5	7
Oldham	6	5	3	6	3
Rochdale H.	2	4	5	3	3
Ryedale-York	2	1	3	7	3
St. Helens	1	6	1	6	3
Salford	0	0	5	4	2
Scarborough P.	—	1	—	—	—
Sheffield E.	4	7	2	3	4
Swinton	3	4	1	4	2
Wakefield T.	1	3	2	6	1
Warrington	2	6	2	4	2
Whitehaven	1	5	3	6	3
Widnes	5	2	2	6	2
Wigan	2	2	7	8	3
Workington T.	4	6	4	8	3
Totals	**90**	**127**	**115**	**172**	**91**

DISMISSALS .... A five-year review

The following is a review of the number of first team dismissals in each season since 1988-89. The 1992-93 tally of 90 dismissals, five of whom were found not guilty, was 37 down on the previous season.

— indicates where a club was not in existence.

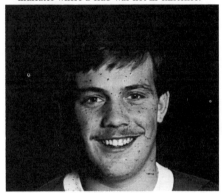

Widnes scrum half Bobby Goulding, called up twice in 1992-93 for trial by video.

DISCIPLINARY ANALYSIS 1992-93

The following is a club-by-club disciplinary record for last season, showing the players sent off in first team matches and the findings of the League's Disciplinary Committee.

The committee's verdict is featured in the brackets after the player's name, each number indicating the match ban imposed. SOS stands for sending off sufficient and NG for not guilty. A suspension reduced or increased on appeal is shown as follows, 6 to 4.

During 1988-89 the totting-up system for sin-bin suspensions was abandoned. Previously two points were issued for a 10-minute temporary dismissal, a one-match ban being imposed when the total reached six. Instead, the sin bins were recorded and taken into account when considering a full dismissal.

The 1984-85 season was the first time video action other than official BBC or ITV tapes could be offered in evidence. Seven cases were considered by the committee after viewing a video, the player not having been dismissed.

Club	Total sent off	Dismissed Player	Number of sin bins
Barrow	3	Chris Koloto (2, 2), Keith Pemberton (NG)	4
Batley	4	Jimmy Irvine (4, 4), Mark Scott (2), Steve Smith (1)	8
Blackpool G.	0		5
Bradford N.	0		7
Bramley	4	Des Drummond (3), Andy Marson (2), Andy Timson (4), Craig Whitehead (4)	3
Carlisle	6	Gary Charlton (4), Mark Doyle (4), Kevin Fox (2), Grant Harris (3), Brett Iti (4), Barry Williams (4)	14
Castleford	3	Lee Crooks (SOS), St. John Ellis (SOS), Keith England (2)	6
Chorley B.	0		6
Dewsbury	1	Gary Cocks (4)	6
Doncaster	2	Martin Rowse (2), Peter Subritzky (NG)	10
Featherstone R.	3	Richard Gunn (SOS), Brendon Tuuta (2 to 3, 6)	9
Halifax	1	Adam Fogerty (SOS)	7
Highfield	7	Michael Carr (SOS), Lee Crook (2), Geoff Dean (2), Gary Haggerty (4), Roy Haggerty (2), David Hine (6, 4)	2
Huddersfield	6	Gary Coulter (4, 2), Jason Fogerty (2), Roy Haggerty (2), Gary Senior (2, 4)	10
Hull	3	Mark Jones (SOS), Steve McNamara (4), Jon Sharp (2)	6
Hull K.R.	0		2
Hunslet	3	Steve Campling (SOS), Michael Coyle (SOS), Paul Harkin (SOS)	7
Keighley C.	2	Joe Grima (4 to SOS), Wayne Race (SOS)	9
Leeds	1	Morvin Edwards (2)	9
Leigh	1	Michael Ogden (1)	8
London C.	5	Colin Atkinson (3), Danny Mulkerin (SOS), Darryl Pitt (3), Chris Whiteley (1), Warren Mann (10)	5
Nottingham C.	2	Ken Isaacs (2), Lee Butler (2)	7
Oldham	6	Barrie McDermott (2), Iva Ropati (2), Mark Sheals (2, SOS), Ian Sherratt (1), Se'e Solomona (4)	10
Rochdale H.	2	Bob Hall (4), Karl Marriott (2)	10
Ryedale-York	2	Paul Hutchinson (4), Stuart Morris (2)	4
St. Helens	1	Kevin Ward (2)	8
Salford	0		4
Sheffield E.	4	Mark Aston (4), Mick Cook (4 to 2), Neil James (SOS), Bruce McGuire (2)	12
Swinton	3	Simon Ashcroft (3), David Barratt (4), Danny Whittle (4)	7
Wakefield T.	1	Darren Fritz (2)	10
Warrington	2	Neil Harmon (SOS), Greg Mackey (SOS)	9

Whitehaven	1	David Kendall (NG)	11
Widnes	5	John Devereux (2, 2), Harvey Howard (2), Steve McCurrie (NG), Richard Eyres (6)	8
Wigan	2	Phil Clarke (2), Kelvin Skerrett (5)	9
Workington T.	4	Brad Hepi (NG, 4), Paul Penrice (SOS), Peter Riley (SOS)	8

In addition, the Disciplinary Committee carried out seven trials by video, calling up after viewing a video tape players who had not been dismissed by the referee. The following match bans were imposed: Bobby Goulding of Widnes (2); Alan Hunte of St. Helens (3); Paul Hutchinson of Ryedale-York (2); Mark Jones of Hull (6); Neil Rudd of Nottingham City (10); Kevin Sanders of Whitehaven (4); Gary Senior of Huddersfield (2); David Hine of Highfield (10); Bobby Goulding of Widnes (£1,000, half suspended for 12 months).

Rain-drenched St. Helens celebrate Stones Bitter Premiership success at Manchester United's Old Trafford, the showpiece being part of Stones Bitter's £300,000 annual sponsorship.

SPONSORSHIP

This updated sub-section is a record of the sponsorship programme under the control of the Rugby Football League.

1992-93 COMPETITIONS:

Silk Cut Challenge Cup	£340,000
Regal Trophy	£330,000
Stones Bitter Championship and Premiership	£300,000
British Coal Tests	£190,000
Stones Bitter World Cup Final	£ 75,000
CIS Insurance Charity Shield	£ 25,000
GRAND TOTAL	**£1,260,000**

QUEEN'S HONOURS

Eight Rugby League players have been awarded the MBE by Her Majesty the Queen for their services to the game. Former Castleford player-coach Malcolm Reilly was awarded the OBE in June 1991, while Great Britain's full-time coach.

Player	Awarded MBE	GB Caps	Career	Clubs
Eric Ashton	June 1966	26	1955-69	Wigan
Geoff Gunney	June 1970	11	1951-73	Hunslet
Clive Sullivan	January 1974	17	1961-85	Hull, Hull K.R., Oldham, Doncaster
Chris Hesketh	January 1976	21+2	1963-79	Wigan, Salford
Roger Millward	January 1983	28+1	1963-80	Castleford, Hull K.R.
Neil Fox	June 1983	29	1956-79	Wakefield T., Bradford N., Hull K.R., York, Bramley, Huddersfield
David Watkins	January 1986	2+4	1967-82	Salford, Swinton, Cardiff C.
Ellery Hanley	January 1990	33+1	1978-	Bradford N., Wigan, Leeds
Jeff Grayshon	June 1992	13	1970-	Dewsbury, Bradford N., Leeds, Featherstone R., Batley
	Awarded OBE			
Malcolm Reilly	June 1991	9	1967-87	Castleford

Honoured by Her Majesty the Queen, Ellery Hanley (left) and Malcolm Reilly.

ATTENDANCES

CLUB ATTENDANCE REVIEW

The following is a review of clubs' home attendances for league matches from 1984-85.

The main figure is the individual club's average gate for league games during that season. The figure in brackets indicates an upward or downward trend compared with the previous season.

Also indicated is the division the club competed in that season, i.e.

1 — First Division, 2 — Second Division, 3 — Third Division.

Club	84-85	85-86	86-87	87-88	88-89	89-90	90-91	91-92	92-93
Barrow	1 2728 (−490)	2 1926 (−802)	1 2664 (+738)	2 1624 (−1040)	2 1594 (−30)	1 1997 (+403)	2 962 (−1035)	3 1003 (+41)	3 786 (−217)
Batley	2 1015 (+151)	2 930 (−85)	2 744 (−186)	2 859 (+115)	2 924 (+65)	2 1506 (+582)	2 1188 (−318)	3 1145 (−43)	3 925 (−220)
Blackpool G.	2 555 (−70)	2 534 (−21)	2 475 (−59)	2 922 (+447)	2 512 (−410)	2 780 (+258)	2 638 (−142)	3 309 (−329)	3 475 (+166)
Bradford N.	1 4251 (−1065)	1 3975 (−276)	1 4312 (+377)	1 4723 (+411)	1 4969 (+246)	1 5584 (+615)	1 5274 (−310)	1 4725 (−549)	1 5082 (+357)
Bramley	2 858 (+99)	2 831 (−27)	2 737 (−94)	2 858 (+121)	2 1004 (+146)	2 982 (−22)	2 805 (−177)	3 870 (+65)	2 980 (+110)
Bridgend	2 510 (−70)	—	—	—	—	—	—	—	—
Carlisle	2 986 (+234)	2 618 (−368)	2 789 (+171)	2 763 (−26)	2 678 (−85)	2 574 (−104)	2 781 (+207)	2 800 (+19)	2 648 (−152)
Castleford	1 3217 (−1071)	1 3701 (+484)	1 4758 (+1057)	1 4520 (−238)	1 6580 (+2060)	1 6428 (−152)	1 6019 (−409)	1 6465 (+446)	1 5658 (−807)
Chorley B.	—	—	—	—	—	2 806 —	2 690 (−116)	3 394 (−296)	3 434 (+40)
Dewsbury	2 995 (+189)	1 1819 (+824)	2 669 (−1150)	2 658 (−11)	2 772 (+114)	2 1227 (+455)	2 955 (−272)	3 1140 (+185)	3 1108 (−32)
Doncaster	2 266 (+11)	2 689 (+423)	2 1543 (+854)	2 1450 (−93)	2 1906 (+456)	2 1965 (+59)	2 1458 (−507)	3 1158 (−300)	3 997 (−161)
Featherstone R.	1 2541 (−491)	1 2320 (−221)	1 2606 (+286)	2 1879 (−727)	1 4379 (+2500)	1 4269 (−110)	1 4722 (+453)	1 4001 (−721)	2 2670 (−1331)
Halifax	1 3497 (+2243)	1 4944 (+1447)	1 4891 (−53)	1 6521 (+1630)	1 8022 (+1501)	2 5921 (−2101)	2 4458 (−1463)	1 7181 (+2723)	1 6452 (−729)
Highfield	2 509 (+337)	2 363 (−146)	2 331 (−32)	2 515 (+184)	2 298 (−217)	2 453 (+155)	2 632 (+179)	3 319 (−313)	3 378 (+59)
Huddersfield	2 905 (+206)	2 678 (−227)	2 524 (−154)	2 601 (+77)	2 1114 (+513)	2 1634 (+520)	2 1306 (−328)	3 2271 (+965)	2 1985 (−286)
Hull	1 8525 (−2154)	1 6245 (−2280)	1 5538 (−707)	1 5111 (−427)	1 6804 (+1693)	1 6218 (−586)	1 6699 (+481)	1 5892 (−807)	1 4860 (−1032)
Hull K.R.	1 6715 (−251)	1 4855 (−1860)	1 4651 (−204)	1 4186 (−465)	1 5298 (+1112)	2 4851 (−447)	1 4952 (+101)	1 4752 (−200)	1 3609 (−1143)

Hunslet	1 2246 (+908)	2 722 (−1524)	1 1050 (+328)	1 2678 (+1628)	2 947 (−1731)	2 1046 (+99)	2 767 (−279)	3 770 (+3)	3 724 (−46)
Keighley C.	2 822 (+88)	2 685 (−137)	2 445 (−240)	2 958 (+513)	2 961 (+3)	2 936 (−25)	2 985 (+49)	3 1196 (+211)	3 2060 (+864)
Leeds	1 7330 (+788)	1 6928 (−402)	1 6393 (−535)	1 9911 (+3518)	1 12060 (+2149)	1 12251 (+191)	1 11102 (−1149)	1 12164 (+1062)	1 11527 (−637)
Leigh	1 3822 (−612)	2 2710 (−1112)	1 4232 (+1522)	1 4516 (+284)	2 2346 (−2170)	1 4568 (+2222)	2 1719 (−2849)	2 3014 (+1295)	1 3967 (+953)
London C.	2 949 (−1289)	2 817 (−132)	2 684 (−133)	2 615 (−69)	2 588 (−27)	2 841 (+253)	2 557 (−284)	2 724 (+167)	2 554 (−170)
Nottingham C.	2 1020 —	2 487 (−533)	2 368 (−119)	2 368 —	2 560 (+192)	2 577 (+17)	2 255 (−322)	3 270 (+15)	3 270 (−)
Oldham	1 4562 (+424)	1 4333 (−229)	1 3915 (−418)	2 3790 (−125)	1 5759 (+1969)	2 4401 (−1358)	1 5094 (+693)	2 3149 (−1945)	2 2809 (−340)
Rochdale H.	2 542 (+4)	2 1267 (+725)	2 877 (−390)	2 1106 (+229)	2 1027 (−79)	2 2510 (+1483)	1 2542 (+32)	2 1415 (−1127)	2 1308 (−107)
Ryedale-York	2 1528 (+313)	1 2828 (+1300)	2 1520 (−1308)	2 1406 (−114)	2 2021 (+615)	2 2495 (+474)	2 1857 (−638)	2 1181 (−676)	3 1701 (+520)
St. Helens	1 7336 (+2680)	1 6022 (−1314)	1 7341 (+1319)	1 8417 (+1076)	1 9514 (+1097)	1 8555 (−959)	1 7391 (−1164)	1 8456 (+1065)	1 8908 (+452)
Salford	2 1795 (−604)	1 2520 (+725)	1 2826 (+306)	1 3747 (+921)	1 5470 (+1723)	1 3720 (−1750)	2 2314 (−1406)	1 3785 (+1471)	1 4098 (+313)
Scarborough P.	—	—	—	—	—	—	—	3 777 —	
Sheffield E.	2 885 —	2 698 (−187)	2 708 (+10)	2 847 (+139)	2 838 (−9)	1 4038 (+3200)	1 4031 (−7)	2 2435 (−1596)	1 3069 (+634)
Southend Invicta	2 216 (−515)	—	—	—	—	—	—	—	—
Swinton	2 1590 (+513)	1 2706 (+1116)	2 1622 (−1084)	1 2987 (+1365)	2 1435 (−1552)	2 1678 (+243)	2 1737 (+59)	1 2702 (+965)	2 1051 (−1651)
Wakefield T.	2 1568 (−1915)	2 1714 (+146)	1 2637 (+923)	2 2416 (−221)	1 5151 (+2735)	1 5428 (+277)	1 4848 (−580)	1 5022 (+174)	1 4505 (−517)
Warrington	1 3801 (−258)	1 3618 (−183)	1 4172 (+554)	1 4974 (+802)	1 4893 (−81)	1 5412 (+519)	1 5915 (+503)	1 5204 (−711)	1 4550 (−754)
Whitehaven	2 1540 (−99)	2 1878 (+338)	2 1800 (−78)	2 1772 (−28)	2 1310 (−462)	2 961 (−349)	2 1035 (+74)	3 632 (−403)	3 1462 (+830)
Widnes	1 4266 (−421)	1 4019 (−247)	1 3840 (−179)	1 6262 (+2422)	1 8648 (+2386)	1 7858 (−790)	1 6793 (−1065)	1 6291 (−502)	1 5540 (−751)
Wigan	1 10056 (+2577)	1 12515 (+2459)	1 12732 (+217)	1 13021 (+289)	1 14543 (+1522)	1 13973 (−570)	1 14493 (+520)	1 14040 (−453)	1 14552 (+513)
Workington T.	1 920 (−14)	2 702 (−218)	2 653 (−49)	2 737 (+84)	2 774 (+37)	2 691 (−83)	2 1426 (+735)	2 1884 (+458)	3 2040 (+156)

COMPETITION ATTENDANCE REVIEW

		84-85	85-86	86-87	87-88	88-89	89-90	90-91	91-92	92-93
FIRST	Total	1,137,195	1,100,329	1,162,666	1,060,296	1,327,192	1,173,815	1,168,407	1,185,117	1,122,955
DIVISION	Av.	4,738	4,585	4,844	5,826	7,292	6,450	6,420	6,511	6,170
SECOND	Total	266,730	310,311	217,552	381,825	298,776	515,687	371,398	204,304	168,069
DIVISION	Av.	953	1,014	863	1,364	1,067	1,754	1,263	1,824	1,501
THIRD	Total	—	—	—	—	—	—	—	159,209	160,348
DIVISION	Av.								875	1,027
LEAGUE TOTALS (1st & 2nd) *plus 3rd	Total	1,403,925	1,410,640	1,380,218	1,442,121	1,625,968	1,689,502	1,539,805	1,548,630*1	1,451,372*
	Av.	2,700	2,584	2,805	3,121	3,519	3,549	3,235	3,253*	3,225*
R.L. CUP	Av.	8,497	8,280	6,965	8,764	8,666	7,339	6,748	6,899	7,771
REGAL	Av.	4,881	4,232	4,122	3,570	4,987	4,876	3,515	4,007	3,624
PREMIER	Av.	10,115	9,273	15,154	13,462	15,856	16,796	12,483	13,513	12,788
10,000+ (No. of)		27	36	43	46	59	54	43	49	38

20,000-plus crowds . . . . A 10-year review

All matches except the Rugby League Challenge Cup final at Wembley

20,077	St. Helens v. Wigan	RL Cup round 3	St. Helens	11 Mar. 1984
25,237	Hull v. Hull K.R.	Yorks Cup final	Hull C. FC	27 Oct. 1984
26,074	St. Helens v. Wigan	Lancs Cup final	Wigan	28 Oct. 1984
25,326	Hull v. Hull K.R.	John Player final	Hull C. FC	26 Jan. 1985
20,982	Hull v. Castleford	RL Cup semi-final	Leeds	6 Apr. 1985
20,968	Hull v. Castleford	RL Cup semi-final replay	Leeds	10 Apr. 1985
22,209	Britain v. New Zealand	Third Test	Elland Rd, Leeds	9 Nov. 1985
21,813	Wigan v. St. Helens	Division One	Wigan	26 Dec. 1985
23,866	Hull K.R. v. Leeds	RL Cup semi-final	Elland Rd, Leeds	29 Mar. 1986
32,485	Hull K.R. v. Leeds	RL Cup semi-final replay	Elland Rd, Leeds	3 Apr. 1986
28,252	Wigan v. St. Helens	Lancs Cup semi-final	Wigan	1 Oct. 1986
30,622	Wigan v. Australia	Tour	Wigan	12 Oct. 1986
20,180	Oldham v. Wigan	Lancs Cup final	St. Helens	19 Oct. 1986
50,583	Britain v. Australia	First Test	Manchester U. FC	25 Oct. 1986
30,808	Britain v. Australia	Second Test	Elland Rd, Leeds	8 Nov. 1986
20,169	Britain v. Australia	Third Test	Wigan	22 Nov. 1986
21,214	St. Helens v. Wigan	Division One	St. Helens	26 Dec. 1986
21,144	Warrington v. Wigan	John Player final	Bolton W. FC	10 Jan. 1987
20,355	Wigan v. St. Helens	Division One	Wigan	17 Apr. 1987
22,457	Wigan v. Halifax	Premiership semi-final	Wigan	10 May 1987
38,756	Warrington v. Wigan	Premiership final	Manchester U. FC	17 May 1987
36,895	Wigan v. Manly	World Club Challenge	Wigan	7 Oct. 1987
20,234	Wigan v. Warrington	Lancs Cup final	St. Helens	11 Oct. 1987
23,809	Wigan v. St. Helens	Division One	Wigan	27 Dec. 1987
25,110	Wigan v. Leeds	RL Cup round 2	Wigan	14 Feb. 1988
20,783	Salford v. Wigan	RL Cup semi-final	Bolton W. FC	12 Mar. 1988

(continued)

20,534	Halifax v. Hull	RL Cup semi-final	Leeds	26 Mar. 1988
25,117	Halifax v. Hull	RL Cup semi-final replay	Elland Rd, Leeds	30 Mar. 1988
21,812	St. Helens v. Wigan	Division One	St. Helens	1 Apr. 1988
35,252	St. Helens v. Widnes	Premiership final	Manchester U. FC	15 May 1988
22,968	Castleford v. Leeds	Yorks Cup final	Elland Rd, Leeds	16 Oct. 1988
20,709	Widnes v. Wigan	John Player final	Bolton W. FC	7 Jan. 1989
26,080	Leeds v. Widnes	RL Cup round 2	Leeds	26 Feb. 1989
26,529	Warrington v. Wigan	RL Cup semi-final	Manchester C. FC	25 Mar. 1989
21,076	Wigan v. St. Helens	Division One	Wigan	12 Apr. 1989
40,194	Hull v. Widnes	Premiership final	Manchester U. FC	14 May 1989
30,786	Widnes v. Canberra	World Club Challenge	Manchester U. FC	4 Oct. 1989
20,346	Britain v. New Zealand	Third Test	Wigan	11 Nov. 1989
27,075	Wigan v. St. Helens	Division One	Wigan	26 Dec. 1989
23,570	Leeds v. Wigan	Division One	Leeds	4 Mar. 1990
26,489	St. Helens v. Wigan	RL Cup semi-final	Manchester U. FC	10 Mar. 1990
24,462	Wigan v. Leeds	Division One	Wigan	10 Apr. 1990
40,796	Bradford N. v. Widnes	Premiership final	Manchester U. FC	13 May 1990
24,814	Wigan v. Australia	Tour	Wigan	14 Oct. 1990
54,569	Britain v. Australia	First Test	Wembley	27 Oct. 1990
46,615	Britain v. Australia	Second Test	Manchester U. FC	10 Nov. 1990
32,500	Britain v. Australia	Third Test	Elland Rd, Leeds	24 Nov. 1990
29,763	Wigan v. Widnes	Division One	Wigan	9 Apr. 1991
42,043	Hull v. Widnes	Premiership final	Manchester U. FC	12 May 1991
20,152	Wigan v. Penrith	World Club Challenge	Liverpool FC	2 Oct. 1991
26,307	Wigan v. St. Helens	Division One	Wigan	26 Dec. 1991
21,736	Wigan v. Warrington	RL Cup round 2	Wigan	16 Feb. 1992
20,821	Leeds v. Wigan	Division One	Leeds	15 Mar. 1992
33,157	St. Helens v. Wigan	Premiership final	Manchester U. FC	17 May 1992
20,534	St. Helens v. Wigan	Lancs Cup final	St. Helens	18 Oct. 1992
73,631	Britain v. Australia	World Cup final	Wembley	24 Oct. 1992
20,258	Leeds v. Castleford	Division One	Leeds	26 Dec. 1992
21,191	Wigan v. St. Helens	RL Cup round 2	Wigan	13 Feb. 1993
20,057	Leeds v. Wigan	Division One	Leeds	3 Mar. 1993
20,085	Bradford N. v. Wigan	RL Cup semi-final	Elland Rd, Leeds	27 Mar. 1993
29,839	Wigan v. St. Helens	Division One	Wigan	9 Apr. 1993
36,598	St. Helens v. Wigan	Premiership final	Manchester U. FC	16 May 1993

1992-93 ATTENDANCE ANALYSIS
FIRST DIVISION

Total 1,122,955

Average 6,170

Wigan maintained a 14,000-plus home gate to top the attendance chart for the ninth successive season while creating new divisional records for highest average, 14,553, and home match gate with 29,839. Six of the 14 clubs registered increases in gates from the 182 fixtures, headed by promoted Leigh who added 953 per match. First Division gates fell by 5.2% compared with

the previous seasons's average of 6,511.

SECOND DIVISION

Total 168,069

Average 1,501

The eight-club Second Division played each other home and away twice, the 112 fixtures attracting an average of 1,501, a 17.7% downward trend compared with the 1991-92 figure of 1,824. Only promoted Bramley recorded an annual increase.

THIRD DIVISION

Total	160,348
Average	1,027

The second-ever Third Division campaign registered a 17.3% increase in gates. The 156 fixtures tallied 160,348 fans through the turnstiles, an average of 1,027 compared with 875 a year earlier.

LEAGUE CHAMPIONSHIP

Aggregate	1,451,372
Average	3,225

League gates plateaued for the third successive season. The 450 fixtures in the three-tier system attracted 1,451,372 fans, an annual decrease of 0.8%, following an increase of 0.5% the previous season.

SILK CUT CHALLENGE CUP

The 1993 Wembley campaign registered a 12.6% increase in attendances, featuring the season's top gate of 77,684, a sell-out, for the Wigan-Widnes final. The 35 ties, including a replay, attracted a total of 271,992 spectators, an average of 7,771, compared with the 1992 figure of 6,899.

REGAL TROPHY

The 37 ties, including a replay, in the 1992-93 tournament attracted a total turnout of 134,092, an average gate of 3,624. Compared with the previous season's average of 4,007, this was a 9.5% downward trend.

STONES BITTER PREMIERSHIP

A total of 89,516 spectators watched the 1993 seven-tie end-of-season tourney, the average gate of 12,788 being 5.3% down on the 1992 figure of 13,513.

DIVISIONAL PREMIERSHIP

Staged for the second time, the Stones Bitter Divisional Premiership was contested by the top eight clubs in the Third Division playing off to visit the top four clubs in the Second Division. Excluding the Old Trafford final, the 10 ties attracted 24,283 fans, an average of 2,428, an annual increase of 48.3% compared with the 1992 average of 1,637.

GREENALLS LANCASHIRE CUP

Gates for the 1992 Red Rose tournament rose by 9.7%, the 15 ties pulling in a total of 78,085 fans, an average of 5,206 compared with the 1991 figure of 4,747.

JOHN SMITHS YORKSHIRE CUP

A total of 67,703 fans turned out for the 17 White Rose ties, the average gate of 3,982 being a 4.7% increase on the previous year's figure of 3,803.

FIVE-FIGURE CROWDS

There were a total of 38 five-figure crowds in 1992-93, compared with 49 in the previous campaign. The Silk Cut Challenge Cup final again topped the chart with a sell-out 77,684, followed closely by the world record crowd for an international fixture, the 73,631 at the Stones Bitter World Cup final between Great Britain and Australia at Wembley. Wigan attracted 10,000-plus crowds to all but one of their 13 home league matches. Nine matches exceeded 20,000, including three in the Stones Bitter Championship.

The 10,000-plus gates were divided into the following categories:

League	21
Challenge Cup	6
Premiership Trophy	4
Internationals	2
Regal Trophy	2
Lancashire Cup	2
World Club Challenge	1

STONES BITTER CHAMPIONSHIP	1992-93 Average	Annual Difference
Wigan	14553	(+513)
Leeds	11527	(−637)
St. Helens	8908	(+452)
Halifax	6452	(−729)
Castleford	5658	(−807)
Widnes	5540	(−751)
Bradford Northern	5082	(+357)
Hull	4860	(−1032)
Warrington	4550	(−754)
Wakefield Trinity	4505	(−517)
Salford	4098	(+313)
*Leigh	3967	(+953)
Hull K.R.	3609	(−1143)
*Sheffield Eagles	3069	(+634)

SECOND DIVISION	1992-93 Average	Annual Difference
Oldham	2809	(−340)
†Featherstone Rovers	2670	(−1331)
*Huddersfield	1985	(−286)
Rochdale Hornets	1308	(−107)
†Swinton	1051	(−1651)
*Bramley	980	(+110)
Carlisle	648	(−152)
London Crusaders	554	(−170)

THIRD DIVISION	1992-93 Average	Annual Difference
Keighley Cougars	2060	(+864)
†Workington Town	2040	(+156)
†Ryedale-York	1701	(+520)
Whitehaven	1462	(+830)
Dewsbury	1108	(−32)
Doncaster	997	(−161)
Batley	925	(−220)
Barrow	786	(−217)
Hunslet	724	(−46)
Blackpool Gladiators	475	(+166)
Chorley Borough	434	(+40)
Highfield	378	(+59)
Nottingham City	270	(−)

*Promoted 1991-92
†Relegated 1991-92

FIXTURES

PRINCIPAL DATES 1993-94

1993

29 August	Stones Bitter Championship campaign opens
3 October	WALES v. NEW ZEALAND at Swansea
16 October	GREAT BRITAIN v. NEW ZEALAND (1) at Wembley
30 October	GREAT BRITAIN v. NEW ZEALAND (2) at Wigan
31 October	Regal Trophy (Round 1)
6 November	GREAT BRITAIN v. NEW ZEALAND (3) at Headingley, Leeds
13/14 November	Regal Trophy (Round 2)
2 December	Great Britain U21 v. France U21
11/12 December	Regal Trophy (Round 3)
18/19 December	Regal Trophy (Quarter-Finals)

1994

1 January	Regal Trophy (Semi-Final 1)
8 January	Regal Trophy (Semi-Final 2)
16 January	Silk Cut Challenge Cup (Round 1)
22 January	Regal Trophy Final
29/30 January	Silk Cut Challenge Cup (Round 2)
8 February	Great Britain Academy v. France Academy
12/13 February	Silk Cut Challenge Cup (Round 3)
18 February	WALES v. FRANCE
26/27 February	Silk Cut Challenge Cup (Quarter-Finals)
12 March	Silk Cut Challenge Cup (Semi-Final 1)
20 March	FRANCE v. GREAT BRITAIN
	France Academy v. Great Britain Academy
26 March	Silk Cut Challenge Cup (Semi-Final 2)
30 April	Silk Cut Challenge Cup Final at Wembley
8 May	Stones Bitter Premiership (Round 1)
	Second Division Premiership (Round 1)
15 May	Stones Bitter Premiership (Semi-Finals)
	Second Division Premiership (Semi-Finals)
22 May	Stones Bitter Premiership Finals at Old Trafford

1993 NEW ZEALAND TOUR ITINERARY

3 October	WALES at Swansea
6 October	Bradford Northern
10 October	Wigan
12 October	Castleford
16 October	FIRST TEST at Wembley
20 October	St. Helens
24 October	Leeds
26 October	Under-21s at Workington Town
30 October	SECOND TEST at Wigan
2 November	Widnes
6 November	THIRD TEST at Leeds

STONES BITTER CHAMPIONSHIP 1993-94

FRIDAY, 27 AUGUST 1993

Castleford	v.	Leeds	7.30

SUNDAY, 29 AUGUST 1993

Bradford N.	v.	Widnes	3.00
Halifax	v.	Oldham	3.00
Hull K.R.	v.	St. Helens	3.15
Leigh	v.	Featherstone R.	3.00
Salford	v.	Sheffield E.	3.00
Warrington	v.	Wakefield T.	3.00
Wigan	v.	Hull	3.00

FRIDAY, 3 SEPTEMBER 1993

Oldham	v.	Bradford N.	7.30

SUNDAY, 5 SEPTEMBER 1993

Featherstone R.	v.	Hull K.R.	3.30
Hull	v.	Halifax	3.15
Leeds	v.	Warrington	3.00
St. Helens	v.	Salford	3.00
Sheffield E.	v.	Castleford	3.15
Wakefield T.	v.	Wigan	3.30
Widnes	v.	Leigh	3.00

FRIDAY, 10 SEPTEMBER 1993

Wigan	v.	Leeds	7.30

SUNDAY, 12 SEPTEMBER 1993

Bradford N.	v.	Sheffield E.	3.00
Castleford	v.	Hull	3.30
Halifax	v.	Featherstone R.	3.00
Hull K.R.	v.	Oldham	3.15
Leigh	v.	Wakefield T.	3.00
Salford	v.	Widnes	3.00
Warrington	v.	St. Helens	3.00

FRIDAY, 17 SEPTEMBER 1993

Widnes	v.	Castleford	7.30

SUNDAY, 19 SEPTEMBER 1993

Featherstone R.	v.	Wigan	3.30
Hull	v.	Salford	3.15
Leeds	v.	Hull K.R.	3.00
Oldham	v.	Warrington	3.00
St. Helens	v.	Leigh	3.00
Sheffield E.	v.	Halifax	3.15
Wakefield T.	v.	Bradford N.	3.30

FRIDAY, 24 SEPTEMBER 1993

Wigan	v.	Widnes	7.30

SUNDAY, 26 SEPTEMBER 1993

Bradford N.	v.	Featherstone R.	3.00
Castleford	v.	St. Helens	3.30
Halifax	v.	Leigh	3.00
Hull	v.	Warrington	3.15
Oldham	v.	Sheffield E.	3.00
Salford	v.	Leeds	3.00
Wakefield T.	v.	Hull K.R.	3.30

FRIDAY, 1 OCTOBER 1993

Featherstone R.	v.	St. Helens	7.30

SUNDAY, 3 OCTOBER 1993

Hull K.R.	v.	Bradford N.	3.15
Leeds	v.	Hull	3.00
Leigh	v.	Castleford	3.00
Salford	v.	Wigan	3.00
Sheffield E.	v.	Wakefield T.	3.15
Warrington	v.	Halifax	3.00
Widnes	v.	Oldham	3.00

FRIDAY, 8 OCTOBER 1993

Halifax	v.	Salford	7.30

SUNDAY, 10 OCTOBER 1993

Bradford N.	v.	Warrington	3.00
Castleford	v.	Hull K.R.	3.30
Hull	v.	Widnes	3.15
Oldham	v.	Leeds	3.00
St. Helens	v.	Wakefield T.	3.00
Sheffield E.	v.	Featherstone R.	3.15

TUESDAY, 19 OCTOBER 1993

Featherstone R.	v.	Leeds	7.30
Wigan	v.	Leigh	7.30

FRIDAY, 22 OCTOBER 1993

Wakefield T.	v.	Widnes	7.30

SUNDAY, 24 OCTOBER 1993

Halifax	v.	Wigan	3.00
Hull	v.	Oldham	3.15
Leigh	v.	Bradford N.	3.00
St. Helens	v.	Sheffield E.	3.00
Salford	v.	Castleford	3.00
Warrington	v.	Hull K.R.	3.00

FRIDAY, 29 OCTOBER 1993

Warrington	v.	Leigh	7.30

SUNDAY, 31 OCTOBER 1993

Bradford N.	v.	Salford	3.00
Castleford	v.	Wigan	3.30
Hull K.R.	v.	Halifax	3.15
Leeds	v.	St. Helens	3.00
Sheffield E.	v.	Hull	3.15
Wakefield T.	v.	Oldham	3.30
Widnes	v.	Featherstone R.	3.00

FRIDAY, 5 NOVEMBER 1993

Salford	v.	Warrington	7.30

SUNDAY, 7 NOVEMBER 1993

Featherstone R.	v.	Oldham	3.30
Halifax	v.	Castleford	3.00
Hull	v.	Wakefield T.	3.15
Leigh	v.	Hull K.R.	3.00
St. Helens	v.	Bradford N.	3.00
Widnes	v.	Leeds	3.00
Wigan	v.	Sheffield E.	3.00

FRIDAY, 19 NOVEMBER 1993

Bradford N.	v.	Wigan	7.30

SUNDAY, 21 NOVEMBER 1993

Featherstone R.	v.	Hull	3.30
Hull K.R.	v.	Salford	3.15
Leeds	v.	Leigh	3.00
Oldham	v.	St. Helens	3.00
Wakefield T.	v.	Halifax	3.30
Warrington	v.	Castleford	3.00
Widnes	v.	Sheffield E.	3.00

FRIDAY, 26 NOVEMBER 1993

St. Helens	v.	Halifax	7.30

SUNDAY, 28 NOVEMBER 1993

Bradford N.	v.	Leeds	3.00
Castleford	v.	Wakefield T.	3.30
Hull K.R.	v.	Widnes	3.15
Leigh	v.	Hull	3.00
Salford	v.	Featherstone R.	3.00
Sheffield E.	v.	Warrington	3.15
Wigan	v.	Oldham	3.00

FRIDAY, 3 DECEMBER 1993

Hull	v.	St. Helens	7.30

SUNDAY, 5 DECEMBER 1993

Castleford	v.	Bradford N.	3.30
Halifax	v.	Widnes	3.00
Oldham	v.	Leigh	3.00
Salford	v.	Wakefield T.	3.00
Sheffield E.	v.	Leeds	3.15
Warrington	v.	Featherstone R.	3.00
Wigan	v.	Hull K.R.	3.00

FRIDAY, 17 DECEMBER 1993

Widnes	v.	Bradford N.	7.30

SUNDAY, 19 DECEMBER 1993

Featherstone R.	v.	Leigh	3.30
Hull	v.	Wigan	3.15
Leeds	v.	Castleford	3.00
Oldham	v.	Halifax	3.00
St. Helens	v.	Hull K.R.	3.00
Sheffield E.	v.	Salford	3.15
Wakefield T.	v.	Warrington	3.30

SUNDAY, 26 DECEMBER 1993

Bradford N.	v.	Halifax	3.00
Featherstone R.	v.	Castleford	3.30
Hull K.R.	v.	Hull	3.15
Leeds	v.	Wakefield T.	11.30
Leigh	v.	Sheffield E.	3.00
Oldham	v.	Salford	3.00
Widnes	v.	Warrington	3.00
Wigan	v.	St. Helens	3.00

SUNDAY, 2 JANUARY 1994

Castleford	v.	Oldham	3.30
Halifax	v.	Leeds	3.00
Hull	v.	Bradford N.	3.15
St. Helens	v.	Widnes	3.00
Salford	v.	Leigh	3.00
Sheffield E.	v.	Hull K.R.	3.15
Wakefield T.	v.	Featherstone R.	3.30
Warrington	v.	Wigan	3.00

FRIDAY, 7 JANUARY 1994

Leigh	v.	Widnes	7.30

SUNDAY, 9 JANUARY 1994

Bradford N.	v.	Oldham	3.00
Castleford	v.	Sheffield E.	3.30
Halifax	v.	Hull	3.00
Hull K.R.	v.	Featherstone R.	3.15
Salford	v.	St. Helens	3.00
Warrington	v.	Leeds	3.00
Wigan	v.	Wakefield T.	3.00

FRIDAY, 14 JANUARY 1994

Leeds	v.	Wigan	7.30

SUNDAY, 16 JANUARY 1994

Featherstone R.	v.	Halifax	3.30
Hull	v.	Castleford	3.15
Oldham	v.	Hull K.R.	3.00
St. Helens	v.	Warrington	3.00
Sheffield E.	v.	Bradford N.	3.15
Wakefield T.	v.	Leigh	3.30
Widnes	v.	Salford	3.00

FRIDAY, 21 JANUARY 1994

Castleford	v.	Widnes	7.30

SUNDAY, 23 JANUARY 1994

Bradford N.	v.	Wakefield T.	3.00
Halifax	v.	Sheffield E.	3.00
Hull K.R.	v.	Leeds	3.15
Leigh	v.	St. Helens	3.00
Salford	v.	Hull	3.00
Warrington	v.	Oldham	3.00
Wigan	v.	Featherstone R.	3.00

FRIDAY, 4 FEBRUARY 1994

Widnes	v.	Wigan	7.30

SUNDAY, 6 FEBRUARY 1994

Featherstone R.	v.	Bradford N.	3.30
Hull K.R.	v.	Wakefield T.	3.15
Leeds	v.	Salford	3.00
Leigh	v.	Halifax	3.00
St. Helens	v.	Castleford	3.00
Sheffield E.	v.	Oldham	3.15
Warrington	v.	Hull	3.00

SUNDAY, 20 FEBRUARY 1994

Bradford N.	v.	Hull K.R.	3.00
Castleford	v.	Leigh	3.30
Halifax	v.	Warrington	3.00
Hull	v.	Leeds	3.15
Oldham	v.	Widnes	3.00
St. Helens	v.	Featherstone R.	3.00
Wakefield T.	v.	Sheffield E.	3.30
Wigan	v.	Salford	3.00

FRIDAY, 4 MARCH 1994

Salford	v.	Halifax	7.30

SUNDAY, 6 MARCH 1994

Featherstone R.	v.	Sheffield E.	3.30
Hull K.R.	v.	Castleford	3.15
Leeds	v.	Oldham	3.00
Leigh	v.	Wigan	3.00
Wakefield T.	v.	St. Helens	3.30
Warrington	v.	Bradford N.	3.00
Widnes	v.	Hull	3.00

FRIDAY, 11 MARCH 1994

Sheffield E.	v.	St. Helens	7.30

SUNDAY, 13 MARCH 1994

Bradford N.	v.	Leigh	3.00
Castleford	v.	Salford	3.30
Hull K.R.	v.	Warrington	3.15
Leeds	v.	Featherstone R.	3.00
Oldham	v.	Hull	3.00
Widnes	v.	Wakefield T.	3.00
Wigan	v.	Halifax	3.00

FRIDAY, 18 MARCH 1994

St. Helens	v.	Leeds	7.30

445

SUNDAY, 20 MARCH 1994

Featherstone R.	v.	Widnes	3.30
Halifax	v.	Hull K.R.	3.00
Hull	v.	Sheffield E.	3.15
Leigh	v.	Warrington	3.00
Oldham	v.	Wakefield T.	3.00
Salford	v.	Bradford N.	3.00
Wigan	v.	Castleford	3.00

FRIDAY, 25 MARCH 1994

Hull K.R.	v.	Leigh	7.30

SUNDAY, 27 MARCH 1994

Bradford N.	v.	St. Helens	3.00
Castleford	v.	Halifax	3.30
Leeds	v.	Widnes	3.00
Oldham	v.	Featherstone R.	3.00
Sheffield E.	v.	Wigan	3.15
Wakefield T.	v.	Hull	3.30
Warrington	v.	Salford	3.00

FRIDAY, 1 APRIL 1994

Castleford	v.	Featherstone R.	3.30
Halifax	v.	Bradford N.	3.00
Hull	v.	Hull K.R.	3.15
St. Helens	v.	Wigan	3.00
Salford	v.	Oldham	3.00
Sheffield E.	v.	Leigh	7.30
Wakefield T.	v.	Leeds	3.30
Warrington	v.	Widnes	3.00

MONDAY, 4 APRIL 1994

Bradford N.	v.	Hull	3.00
Featherstone R.	v.	Wakefield T.	3.30
Hull K.R.	v.	Sheffield E.	3.15
Leeds	v.	Halifax	3.00
Leigh	v.	Salford	3.00
Oldham	v.	Castleford	3.00
Widnes	v.	St. Helens	3.00
Wigan	v.	Warrington	3.00

SUNDAY, 10 APRIL 1994

Bradford N.	v.	Castleford	3.00
Featherstone R.	v.	Warrington	3.30
Hull K.R.	v.	Wigan	3.15
Leeds	v.	Sheffield E.	3.00
Leigh	v.	Oldham	3.00
St. Helens	v.	Hull	3.00
Wakefield T.	v.	Salford	3.30
Widnes	v.	Halifax	3.00

SUNDAY, 17 APRIL 1994

Castleford	v.	Warrington	3.30
Halifax	v.	Wakefield T.	3.00
Hull	v.	Featherstone R.	3.15
Leigh	v.	Leeds	3.00
St. Helens	v.	Oldham	3.00
Salford	v.	Hull K.R.	3.00
Sheffield E.	v.	Widnes	3.15
Wigan	v.	Bradford N.	3.00

SUNDAY, 24 APRIL 1994

Featherstone R.	v.	Salford	3.30
Halifax	v.	St. Helens	3.00
Hull	v.	Leigh	3.15
Leeds	v.	Bradford N.	3.00
Oldham	v.	Wigan	3.00
Wakefield T.	v.	Castleford	3.30
Warrington	v.	Sheffield E.	3.00
Widnes	v.	Hull K.R.	3.00

DIVISION 2

SUNDAY, 29 AUGUST 1993

Barrow	v.	Keighley C.	2.30
Bramley	v.	Whitehaven	3.30
Dewsbury	v.	Carlisle	3.30
Hunslet	v.	Doncaster	3.00
London C.	v.	Batley	3.00
Rochdale H.	v.	Highfield	3.00
Ryedale-York	v.	Swinton	3.15
Workington T.	v.	Huddersfield	3.00

SUNDAY, 5 SEPTEMBER 1993

Batley	v.	Workington T.	3.15
Carlisle	v.	Hunslet	3.00
Doncaster	v.	Bramley	3.00
Highfield	v.	Dewsbury	3.00
Huddersfield	v.	Rochdale H.	3.30
Keighley C.	v.	London C.	3.15
Swinton	v.	Barrow	3.00
Whitehaven	v.	Ryedale-York	3.30

SUNDAY, 12 SEPTEMBER 1993

Barrow	v.	Highfield	2.30
Bramley	v.	Carlisle	3.30
Dewsbury	v.	Whitehaven	3.30
Hunslet	v.	Huddersfield	3.00
London C.	v.	Doncaster	3.00
Rochdale H.	v.	Keighley C.	3.00
Ryedale-York	v.	Batley	3.15
Workington T.	v.	Swinton	3.00

SUNDAY, 19 SEPTEMBER 1993

Batley	v.	Rochdale H.	3.15
Carlisle	v.	Workington T.	3.00
Doncaster	v.	Barrow	3.00
Highfield	v.	Ryedale-York	3.00
Huddersfield	v.	London C.	3.30
Keighley C.	v.	Dewsbury	3.15
Swinton	v.	Bramley	3.00
Whitehaven	v.	Hunslet	3.00

SUNDAY, 26 SEPTEMBER 1993

Barrow	v.	Huddersfield	2.30
Batley	v.	Whitehaven	3.15
Bramley	v.	Highfield	3.30
Carlisle	v.	Swinton	3.00
Hunslet	v.	Keighley C.	3.00
London C.	v.	Dewsbury	3.00
Rochdale H.	v.	Ryedale-York	3.00
Workington T.	v.	Doncaster	3.00

SUNDAY, 3 OCTOBER 1993

Barrow	v.	London C.	2.30
Dewsbury	v.	Bramley	3.30
Doncaster	v.	Keighley C.	3.00
Highfield	v.	Carlisle	3.00
Huddersfield	v.	Batley	3.30
Rochdale H.	v.	Workington T.	3.00
Ryedale-York	v.	Hunslet	3.15
Whitehaven	v.	Swinton	3.30

SUNDAY, 10 OCTOBER 1993

Batley	v.	Highfield	3.15
Bramley	v.	Rochdale H.	3.30
Doncaster	v.	Carlisle	3.00
Hunslet	v.	Barrow	3.00
Keighley C.	v.	Whitehaven	3.15
London C.	v.	Ryedale-York	3.00
Swinton	v.	Huddersfield	3.00
Workington T.	v.	Dewsbury	3.00

UNDAY, 24 OCTOBER 1993

Barrow	v.	Bramley	2.30
Carlisle	v.	Batley	3.00
Dewsbury	v.	Rochdale H.	3.30
Highfield	v.	Huddersfield	3.00
Keighley C.	v.	Swinton	3.15
London C.	v.	Hunslet	3.00
Ryedale-York	v.	Workington T.	3.15
Whitehaven	v.	Doncaster	3.30

UNDAY, 7 NOVEMBER 1993

Bramley	v.	Ryedale-York	3.30
Carlisle	v.	Keighley C.	2.00
Dewsbury	v.	Barrow	3.30
Highfield	v.	Doncaster	3.00
Huddersfield	v.	Whitehaven	3.30
Rochdale H.	v.	Hunslet	3.00
Swinton	v.	Batley	3.00
Workington T.	v.	London C.	3.00

UNDAY, 21 NOVEMBER 1993

Barrow	v.	Rochdale H.	2.30
Batley	v.	Keighley C.	3.15
Bramley	v.	London C.	3.30
Huddersfield	v.	Carlisle	3.30
Hunslet	v.	Workington T.	3.00
Ryedale-York	v.	Dewsbury	3.15
Swinton	v.	Doncaster	3.00
Whitehaven	v.	Highfield	3.30

UNDAY, 28 NOVEMBER 1993

Dewsbury	v.	Huddersfield	3.30
Doncaster	v.	Batley	3.00
Hunslet	v.	Swinton	3.00
Keighley C.	v.	Highfield	3.15
London C.	v.	Carlisle	3.00
Rochdale H.	v.	Whitehaven	3.00
Ryedale-York	v.	Barrow	3.15
Workington T.	v.	Bramley	3.00

UNDAY, 5 DECEMBER 1993

Batley	v.	Barrow	3.15
Carlisle	v.	Ryedale-York	2.00
Doncaster	v.	Rochdale H.	3.00
Highfield	v.	Hunslet	3.00
Huddersfield	v.	Bramley	3.30
Keighley C.	v.	Workington T.	3.15
Swinton	v.	Dewsbury	3.00
Whitehaven	v.	London C.	3.30

UNDAY, 12 DECEMBER 1993

Barrow	v.	Whitehaven	2.30
Bramley	v.	Keighley C.	3.30
Dewsbury	v.	Doncaster	3.30
Hunslet	v.	Batley	3.00
London C.	v.	Swinton	3.00
Rochdale H.	v.	Carlisle	3.00
Ryedale-York	v.	Huddersfield	3.15
Workington T.	v.	Highfield	3.00

UNDAY, 19 DECEMBER 1993

Batley	v.	London C.	3.15
Carlisle	v.	Dewsbury	2.00
Doncaster	v.	Hunslet	3.00
Highfield	v.	Rochdale H.	3.00
Huddersfield	v.	Workington T.	3.30
Keighley C.	v.	Barrow	3.15
Swinton	v.	Ryedale-York	3.00
Whitehaven	v.	Bramley	3.30

SUNDAY, 26 DECEMBER 1993

Barrow	v.	Carlisle	2.30
Batley	v.	Dewsbury	3.15
Doncaster	v.	Ryedale-York	3.00
Hunslet	v.	Bramley	3.00
Keighley C.	v.	Huddersfield	3.15
London C.	v.	Highfield	3.00
Swinton	v.	Rochdale H.	3.00
Whitehaven	v.	Workington T.	3.30

SUNDAY, 2 JANUARY 1994

Bramley	v.	Batley	3.30
Carlisle	v.	Whitehaven	2.00
Dewsbury	v.	Hunslet	3.30
Highfield	v.	Swinton	3.00
Huddersfield	v.	Doncaster	3.30
Rochdale H.	v.	London C.	3.00
Ryedale-York	v.	Keighley C.	3.15
Workington T.	v.	Barrow	3.00

SUNDAY, 9 JANUARY 1994

Barrow	v.	Swinton	2.30
Bramley	v.	Doncaster	3.30
Dewsbury	v.	Highfield	3.30
Hunslet	v.	Carlisle	3.00
London C.	v.	Keighley C.	3.00
Rochdale H.	v.	Huddersfield	3.00
Ryedale-York	v.	Whitehaven	3.15
Workington T.	v.	Batley	3.00

SUNDAY, 23 JANUARY 1994

Batley	v.	Ryedale-York	3.15
Carlisle	v.	Bramley	3.00
Doncaster	v.	London C.	3.00
Highfield	v.	Barrow	3.00
Huddersfield	v.	Hunslet	3.30
Keighley C.	v.	Rochdale H.	3.15
Swinton	v.	Workington T.	3.00
Whitehaven	v.	Dewsbury	3.30

SUNDAY, 6 FEBRUARY 1994

Barrow	v.	Doncaster	2.30
Bramley	v.	Swinton	3.30
Dewsbury	v.	Keighley C.	3.30
Hunslet	v.	Whitehaven	3.00
London C.	v.	Huddersfield	3.00
Rochdale H.	v.	Batley	3.00
Ryedale-York	v.	Highfield	3.15
Workington T.	v.	Carlisle	3.00

SUNDAY, 20 FEBRUARY 1994

Dewsbury	v.	London C.	3.30
Doncaster	v.	Workington T.	3.00
Highfield	v.	Bramley	3.00
Huddersfield	v.	Barrow	3.30
Keighley C.	v.	Hunslet	3.15
Ryedale-York	v.	Rochdale H.	3.15
Swinton	v.	Carlisle	3.00
Whitehaven	v.	Batley	3.30

SUNDAY, 27 FEBRUARY 1994

Batley	v.	Huddersfield	3.15
Bramley	v.	Dewsbury	3.30
Carlisle	v.	Highfield	3.00
Hunslet	v.	Ryedale-York	3.00
Keighley C.	v.	Doncaster	3.15
London C.	v.	Barrow	3.00
Swinton	v.	Whitehaven	3.00
Workington T.	v.	Rochdale H.	3.00

FIXTURES

SUNDAY, 6 MARCH 1994

Barrow	v.	Hunslet	2.30
Carlisle	v.	Doncaster	3.00
Dewsbury	v.	Workington T.	3.30
Highfield	v.	Batley	3.00
Huddersfield	v.	Swinton	3.30
Rochdale H.	v.	Bramley	3.00
Ryedale-York	v.	London C.	3.15
Whitehaven	v.	Keighley C.	3.30

SUNDAY, 13 MARCH 1994

Batley	v.	Carlisle	3.15
Bramley	v.	Barrow	3.30
Doncaster	v.	Whitehaven	3.00
Huddersfield	v.	Highfield	3.30
Hunslet	v.	London C.	3.00
Rochdale H.	v.	Dewsbury	3.00
Swinton	v.	Keighley C.	3.00
Workington T.	v.	Ryedale-York	3.00

SUNDAY, 20 MARCH 1994

Barrow	v.	Dewsbury	2.30
Batley	v.	Swinton	3.15
Doncaster	v.	Highfield	3.00
Hunslet	v.	Rochdale H.	3.00
Keighley C.	v.	Carlisle	3.15
London C.	v.	Workington T.	3.00
Ryedale-York	v.	Bramley	3.15
Whitehaven	v.	Huddersfield	3.30

SUNDAY, 27 MARCH 1994

Carlisle	v.	Huddersfield	3.00
Dewsbury	v.	Ryedale-York	3.30
Doncaster	v.	Swinton	3.00
Highfield	v.	Whitehaven	3.00
Keighley C.	v.	Batley	3.15
London C.	v.	Bramley	3.00
Rochdale H.	v.	Barrow	3.00
Workington T.	v.	Hunslet	3.00

FRIDAY, 1 APRIL 1994

Bramley	v.	Hunslet	7.30
Carlisle	v.	Barrow	3.00
Dewsbury	v.	Batley	7.30
Highfield	v.	London C.	3.00
Huddersfield	v.	Keighley C.	3.30
Rochdale H.	v.	Swinton	3.00
Ryedale-York	v.	Doncaster	3.15
Workington T.	v.	Whitehaven	3.00

MONDAY, 4 APRIL 1994

Barrow	v.	Workington T.	2.30
Batley	v.	Bramley	7.30
Doncaster	v.	Huddersfield	3.00
Hunslet	v.	Dewsbury	7.30
Keighley C.	v.	Ryedale-York	3.15
London C.	v.	Rochdale H.	3.00
Swinton	v.	Highfield	3.00
Whitehaven	v.	Carlisle	3.30

SUNDAY, 10 APRIL 1994

Batley	v.	Hunslet	3.15
Carlisle	v.	Rochdale H.	3.00
Doncaster	v.	Dewsbury	3.00
Highfield	v.	Workington T.	3.00
Huddersfield	v.	Ryedale-York	3.30
Keighley C.	v.	Bramley	3.15
Swinton	v.	London C.	3.00
Whitehaven	v.	Barrow	3.30

SUNDAY, 17 APRIL 1994

Barrow	v.	Batley	2.30
Bramley	v.	Huddersfield	3.30
Dewsbury	v.	Swinton	3.30
Hunslet	v.	Highfield	3.00
London C.	v.	Whitehaven	3.00
Rochdale H.	v.	Doncaster	3.00
Ryedale-York	v.	Carlisle	3.15
Workington T.	v.	Keighley C.	3.00

SUNDAY, 24 APRIL 1994

Barrow	v.	Ryedale-York	2.30
Batley	v.	Doncaster	3.15
Bramley	v.	Workington T.	3.30
Carlisle	v.	London C.	3.00
Highfield	v.	Keighley C.	3.00
Huddersfield	v.	Dewsbury	3.30
Swinton	v.	Hunslet	3.00
Whitehaven	v.	Rochdale H.	3.30